The People Are Kind

"This is the first comprehensive survey of Iowa's religious history, and it is an important contribution to our knowledge of the state. *The People are Kind* will be the standard book on the subject for many years to come. This is a thoughtful, humane, readable, and deeply researched book."

—**JEFF BREMER**, author of *A New History of Iowa*

"I've long contended that Iowa is one of the most religiously diverse places on the planet, a claim amply documented by *The People Are Kind*. Bill Douglas's prodigious research and riveting narrative will introduce readers to colorful individuals like Lois Crawford, Pierre Bernard, Phineas Bresee, and Ida B. Wise Smith as well as religious groups ranging from Norwegian Quakers and the Beachy Amish to Buddhists, the Iowa Band, and the Community of True Inspiration. This is a superb book, one that will alter our perceptions of the history and culture of Iowa."

—**RANDALL BALMER**, John Phillips Professor in Religion, Dartmouth College

"With his religious history of Iowa, Bill Douglas fills a gaping hole in the historical literature on Iowa, and he does so with keen insight, generosity of spirit, inclusiveness, and wit—and with welcome attention to the public implications of religiosity. Reflecting the author's remarkably broad reading, the book is well-grounded in a wide range of secondary literature and thoroughly documented but just as thoroughly engaging."

—**MARVIN BERGMAN**, retired editor, *The Annals of Iowa*

"*The People Are Kind* offers the first comprehensive history of religion in Iowa from the land and its indigenous peoples to the present. The breadth and depth of Douglas' research will astound: the most obscure belief system is tracked. A fascinating read. In short pithy paragraphs and in twenty-four short vivid chapters—each launched with engaging epigraphs—Douglas seeks 'to amplify and qualify national generalizations' and show again and again how religious dissension led to Iowa's notable religious diversity."

—**BARBARA LOUNSBERRY**, emerita professor of English, University of Northern Iowa

The People Are Kind

A Religious History of Iowa

BILL R. DOUGLAS

RESOURCE *Publications* · Eugene, Oregon

THE PEOPLE ARE KIND
A Religious History of Iowa

Copyright © 2024 Bill R. Douglas. All rights reserved. Except for brief quotations in critical publications or reviews, no part of this book may be reproduced in any manner without prior written permission from the publisher. Write: Permissions, Wipf and Stock Publishers, 199 W. 8th Ave., Suite 3, Eugene, OR 97401.

Resource Publications
An Imprint of Wipf and Stock Publishers
199 W. 8th Ave., Suite 3
Eugene, OR 97401

www.wipfandstock.com

PAPERBACK ISBN: 979-8-3852-2445-6
HARDCOVER ISBN: 979-8-3852-2446-3
EBOOK ISBN: 979-8-3852-2447-0

VERSION NUMBER 12/30/24

Front Cover Art: Marvin Cone, Storm Clouds Over Church, 1943, oil on canvas, 24 x 30 inches, Cedar Rapids Museum of Art, gift of Peter & Wendy Turner, 88.6.

PERMISSIONS

Grateful acknowledgement for reprinting from copyrighted poetry and lyrics:

"The Sun Underfoot Among the Sundews" from THE COLLECTED POEMS OF AMY CLAMPITT by Amy Clampitt, copyright © 1997 by the Estate of Amy Clampitt. Used by permission of Alfred A. Knopf, an imprint of the Knopf Doubleday Publishing Group, a division of Penguin Random House LLC. All rights reserved.

Michael Borich, *Black Hawk Songs*, 2016

Greg Brown, "Brand New '64 Dodge," *The Poet Game*, 1994

Iris DeMent, "Let the Mystery Be," *Infamous Angel*, 1992

William Elliott Whitmore, "Civilizations," *Radium Death*, 2015.

Gratitude also for Stephen Cone Weeks granting permission to reproduce Marvin Cone's painting S*torm Clouds over Church*, on display at the Cedar Rapids Art Center, and to the Des Moines Art Center for permission to reproduce Henry Owassa Turner's *The Disciples See Christ Walking on the Water*.

Contents

Acknowledgements | ix
Abbreviations Used in the Footnotes | xi

Introduction: Defining Religion: Exploring Ways That Religion Has Defined Iowa | 1

1. Land, and the Native Americans on It | 16
2. Contact | 24
3. "To Build a House by Eating": The Flourishing of Diversity in Early White Settlement | 35
4. German Dissent and Iowa Diversity | 54
5. Outside Influences: European and New England Missionary Societies | 73
6. Reactions to Democratic Religion, Religious Competition, and the Failure to Establish Dominance | 89
7. The Civil War and the Making of a People | 120
8. The Holiness Explosion | 138
9. Quick Turnaround: From Mission Field to Missionary Zeal | 150
10. Questions of Land and Equality: James Baird Weaver, Active Methodism, and Those Left Outside | 165
11. The Kingdom Movement(s) of George Herron, George Augustus Gates, and George W. Slater, and the Social Gospel in Iowa | 178
12. Social Justice and Holiness: From Temperance to Prohibition | 193
13. The Landscape of Fin de Siècle Iowa Religion | 214

14 From Farmland as Eden to "Badly Overchurched":
    From Promise to Rural Decline | 228
15 "We Had To Create Our Own": The Creations of Jews,
    Muslims, Southern European and Orthodox Christians,
    and Edward Steiner's Applied Christianity | 242
16 "Unprogressive, Peaceful, and Religious Habits":
    The Moral Crisis of the Great War | 252
17 The New Assertiveness of Roman Catholicism | 266
18 The Counter-Narrative: Fundamentalism | 282
19 Alternative Counter-Narratives | 295
20 Leaving the Porch Light On: Chastened Rhetoric, Total War | 316
21 Protestantism at Zenith | 331
22 Complicating the Consensus: The Nineteen-Sixties | 345
23 The Counter-Narrative Strikes Back: This Dark World | 362
24 After All: The Blessings of Diversity | 375

Bibliography | 383
Index | 453

Acknowledgements

MAYBE I SHOULD JUST acknowledge everybody. But I suppose, if *Life of Brian* is right and we are all individuals, I should be more specific. Anyone who has read acknowledgements knows this is where the author apologizes for all those they missed.

Public education in the U.S. and Brazil helped instill curiosity in me. It would be a shame if future Iowans had to go to Brazil to get that.

My family history helped arc this book. My father was the son of a Baptist minister. My mother was raised a staunch Presbyterian. My father became a Presbyterian minister, and they both became Presbyterian missionaries. The subtleties of Protestant differences probably prompted an initial curiosity. And living as a minority, albeit a privileged one, in Catholic territories in Brazil and El Paso, also had an effect.

I remember two episodes from my time in Gibson, Iowa. While home on spring vacation from Sterling College in 1971, I copied the Iowa portion of a map delineating religious predominance by county that I had gotten from the college library. My Dad said, "Nineteen-fifty was a long time ago." I wasn't so sure that made the map unworthy of study.

And then there was White Oak, the church out there in the country that stubbornly held out. My recollection was that the presbytery wanted consolidation. "They have no sense of mission," my Dad lamented. But I wasn't so sure; maybe they deserved their own worship space? When my brother-in-law Dave Feltman reads this, who as a presbytery executive has had to arrange for the demise of dozens of congregations across the state, he will doubtless shake his head at my youthful romanticism. Either way, the pain remains.

Acknowledgements

I ought to focus now on gratitude rather than musings. I fear I will miss many who deserve recognition. My siblings, Sue and Andy, have been unfailingly encouraging. Jim Morrison and Shar Grant were kind enough to read parts of the manuscript. Carol Ferrell rescued a book from the Presbytery of Des Moines office closing for me. Ashley Molzen patiently if futilely pursued the track of Marcus Bach's pageants from her perch at Forest Avenue Library in Des Moines. She must stand in for the many debts I owe to many librarians.

Janet Weaver was gracious in revealing the overwhelming contents of Iowa missionaries at the Iowa Women Archives at the University of Iowa Libraries. Mary Bennett, Hang Nguyen, and Sherry Stelling of the State Historical Society libraries in Iowa City and Des Moines were always helpful.

Duncan Stewart has been an invaluable friend for his library skills. Marv Bergman has been a model editor over the years and lent sage advice to this project. Jeff Bremer, whose similarly-sized project was completed a couple of years ahead of mine, was also encouraging and helpful. Larry Hurto, a local historian par excellence, has been impossible to stump on matters pertaining to Jasper County and had plenty of local angles that improved the book. History colleagues within and outside of the academy, including Steve Rossignol, Sharon Lake, Kari Bassett, Dave Polich, Bob Neymeyer, Steve Avella, Randall Balmer, and Adam Hochschild have all been encouraging and thought-provoking. Hal Chase, Bill Silag, Barbara Lounsberry, and Jim Schaap all provided welcome help and advice.

I should acknowledge the hospitality and friendship of Dar Clausen and Joe Marron.

Frank Cordaro hired me to curate the social justice writings of Maurice Dingman, which increased my familiarity with Catholicism.

Preachers Debbie Griffin, Mark Davis, Brad Braley, Bob Brown, and Bob Cook kept my iconoclastic tendencies in tension with my communalistic ones.

Fairly early in the project, I struck up a friendship which blossomed into romance. In more ways than I can enumerate—and if I tried, Wipf and Stock would protest that it made the book too long to publish—I owe a debt of gratitude to my wife Barbara Morrison. No one will be surprised that this book is dedicated to her.

Abbreviations Used in the Footnotes

AI	Annals of Iowa (3rd Series unless otherwise specified)
BDI	Biographical Dictionary of Iowa
CH	Church History
CRG	Cedar Rapids Gazette
DMR	Des Moines Register
DMT	Des Moines Tribune
IHR	Iowa History Reader, Marvin Bergman, ed.
IJH	Iowa Journal of History and Politics, Iowa Journal of History
IWA	Iowa Women's Archives, University of Iowa Libraries
MH	Methodist History
MQR	Mennonite Quarterly Review
NYT	New York Times
OI	Outside In: African-American History of Iowa, Hal Chase et al., eds.
Pal	Palimpsest
SC-UI	Special Collections, University of Iowa Libraries
SHSI-DM	State Historical Society, Des Moines
SHSI-IC	State Historical Society, Iowa CIty
WA	Wapsipinicon Almanac

Introduction

Defining Religion

Exploring Ways That Religion Has Defined Iowa

"It is impossible not to be influenced by the natural environment in which one lives for a long time . . . The natural scenery here [in Decorah], though not on so grand a scale [as Norway's], may also exert a positive influence upon the mind—in general, a mild, peaceful influence. Vilhelm has remarked several times during sharp lightning and thunderstorms that he did not see how any person could think of doing evil at such a time—but I can understand even less how a person could do it during a restful and solemn evening hour of moonlight and starlight."

—Elisabeth Koren[1]

"Religion covers a wide field. It embraces immense subjects, high as heaven, broad as the universe. It is the union of man with God. It is the reconciliation and harmony of all things that are in heaven and of all things that are on earth."

—William Salter[2]

"By religion, I mean the instinctive, underlying attitude which everyone has to the world outside himself and especially toward the less tangible, more enduring spiritual forces . . . Religion comes first and from it springs the arts,

---

1. Nelson, *Diary of Elisabeth Koren*, 274–75. Vilhelm was Elisabeth's husband and a Norwegian Lutheran pastor in Winneshiek County.

2. Salter, *Forty Years*, 3.

the sciences, the inventions, the divisions of wealth, and the attitudes between classes and towards other nations."

—Henry A. Wallace[3]

"What geography can give all Middle Westerners, along with the fresh water and topsoil, ... is awe for an Edenic continent stretching forever in all directions. Makes you religious. Takes your breath away."

—Kurt Vonnegut[4]

In 1839, Joseph Kirkpatrick authored the first volume of theology in Iowa. The small book was only the fifth imprint to be published in the territory.[5] *Private Thoughts on Theology* seems an odd title for one who demonstrably wanted to make his views public; his theme, a discourse against supralapsarianism (though he never used that word), also does not seem aimed at the best-seller charts in Dubuque (though the local competition was not fierce).[6]

Kirkpatrick used the tried-and-true rhetorical technique of positioning himself between two self-defined extremes, between priests and infidels: "By some sectarian *Priests* [I am] called an Infidel, because [I am] not disposed to patronize Priestcraft; and by some Infidels [I am] called a Priest and fanatic because [I] say man is accountable to his God for his actions and endeavors."[7]

Kirkpatrick's religious affiliation is unclear, although clearly he wasn't Catholic or "Infidel." The two most likely candidates are Methodist and Campbellite. He seems closest theologically to Methodism, but Methodists were unlikely to write theological arguments—they were too busy founding local churches. Campbellites (Disciples of Christ is the

---

3. Speech at the World Fellowship of Faiths Conference, Chicago, Aug. 18, 1933. Quoted in Schapsmeier, *Wallace*, 187.

4. Quoted as a blurb on the back cover of *The American Midwest*.

5. Moffit, "Checklist," 7–8; WPA Historical Records Survey Project, *Check List, In Supplement*, 9.

6. Kirkpatrick, *Private*. The publisher, Russell and Reeves, also had been appointed official printer of the Iowa Territory.

7. Kirkpartick, [2]. I have transposed his third-person description of himself into the first person.

largest denomination of Campbellite descent in Iowa) were more likely to engage in theological disputations.

(For those reading this far just for a definition of supralapsarianism, it is the speculative doctrine that God planned the fall of humanity; infralapsarianism maintains that God did not. To use the rhetorical device that Kirkpatrick employed, I would suggest that the correct answer is, "God knows." Of course, that answer would not convince infidels, who were the special target of Kirkpatrick's ruminations.)

Kirkpatrick's tract was destined to remain obscure but does suggest what Iowa religion would produce: sincerity, expansiveness, a theological intensity that seems bewildering to outsiders, and a concern, however well-placed or misplaced, for the religious well-being of others, or put more negatively, a tendency to proselytize. For groups, it often meant robust competition, eager to make Iowa a Catholic, or Lutheran, or Methodist state.

While most Iowa religious conflict was not conducted in print, a myriad of different competing groups sought to dominate early Iowa. And yet, their very multiplicity confounded their ambitions and made some degree of coexistence inevitable, and cooperation often desirable and defensible. *Private Thoughts on Theology* was not so private, but instead an early example of the contested nature of Iowa religion.

The study of religion, thought Edwin Starbuck, was the extension of the laws of science to "the most complex, the most inaccessible, and, of all, the most sacred domain."[8] Starbuck was a State University of Iowa professor who pioneered teaching the psychology of religion.[9] This definition is impressive but not very helpful.

Does religion need to be defined? And relatedly, can it be? An unexamined definition might suffice for our purposes, but problems must be faced. Scholars have begun to examine definitions of religion,[10]

---

8. Starbuck, *Psychology of Religion*, 1. See also Dudiak, "Meaning of 'Quaker History,'" 1.

9. For an assessment of his importance to the new field, see Booth, *Starbuck*.

10. See, e.g., Pals, *Seven Theories of Religion*; and Peterson and Walhof, *Invention of Religion*. See also the exchange between Linker ("Why Can't the *New York Times* Religion Columnist Define Religion?") and Taves ("Is It the Job of Religion Journalists to Define 'Religion'?").

and religion turns out to be a messy category in the real world.[11] This is particularly true in the United States, where constitutional protections require constant reassessments of religion's definition and its consequent legal prerogatives.

In defining religion for the purpose of writing a religious history of Iowa, categories of problems arise. Some are rhetorical: Jehovah's Witnesses distinguish between their faith and "religion." Even Karl Barth has made a similar distinction,[12] and it has become a rhetorical device among strains of evangelicals. But all of these rhetorical or theological distinctions still fit within our chosen definition of religion. It should also be noted that the remarkably litigious Jehovah's Witnesses,[13] the (at-times) science-espousing Transcendental Meditation movement,[14] and, more recently, culture warrior evangelicals have been happy to rely on First Amendment religious protections in court cases. The evolving, peculiarly American, jurisprudence definition of religion can be helpful to historians.

While there may be a certain bias in the concept of world religions, this line of questioning would take us too far afield. And it should be noted that groups identifying as Christian are not necessarily white European; most African-Americans have been Christian, and immigrants from such places as Africa, Central America, Korea, and Burma have recently complicated Christianity in Iowa. The story of Des Moines Mennonites Ha Baccam and La Baccam, Vietnamese refugees who were of an ethnic minority in their home country, and who translated the New Testament into Tai Dam after resettling in Iowa, just begins to suggest the variegated possibilities of the Iowa religious experience.[15] (And many Tai Dam in Iowa are not Christian but have their own ancestral religion.)

If the globalization of religion in Iowa has not caused many definitional problems, other movements veering between claims to be scientific and having religious roots are problematic. The chiropractic movement, founded and centered in Davenport, is one example. So is the eccentric philosophy of Alfred Lawson, once centered in Des Moines. Both will be discussed in chapter 19, recognizing their religious elements.

---

11. See, e.g., Ostling, "Ask Any Church-State Lawyer"; Johnson, "Are Vaccine Exemptions Actually Religious?"
12. See Barth, *On Religion*, 6.
13. Peters, *Judging*.
14. See chapter 19.
15. "Tai Dam Bible."

Defining Religion

More convoluted is the case of Transcendental Meditation (TM), whose US center is in Fairfield and, judging by municipal ordinances (and its name), controls the nearby town of Maharishi Vedic City. When arguing for inclusion in public schools in the seventies, TM claimed only scientific credentials; when arguing for interning pandits from India in 2014, religious freedom defenses came into play.[16] The contradictory assertions of TM about religion also appear in internal documents.[17]

The question of secrecy inherent in dealing with claims by Lawsonomy and TM also calls into play an ancillary question of the treatment of evidence, which needs to be evaluated on a case-by-case basis: how sacrosanct are religious claims of secrecy? Questions of truth, relevance, and cultural appropriation must all be answered. Transcendental Meditation's claims to be a science were arguably undermined by its inner circle assertions of religion and its connections to Hinduism.[18] The non-Mormon obsession with Mormon temple undergarments is clearly irrelevant to truth claims and the essence of Mormonism, but whether the Hodge brothers were members of Latter-day Saints is not outside the bounds of historical inquiry (see chapter 3). But do the inner ceremonies of the Meskwaki need to be revealed for historical omniscience,[19] or should the right to privacy—in the absence of any question about truth, justice, or criminal involvement, and given the much larger issue of white expropriation of Native culture—be respected?

Evidence of denials of religious certitudes also lie within the jurisdiction of religious history. Atheists, agnostics, and the indifferent should also have a voice—although the historical evidence for the last category is seldom recoverable. Every new institution has a second-generation crisis. If the cause was anti-institutional, perpetuation seems doubly difficult. The Schleswig-Holstein and Bohemian Freethinker exiles who came to Davenport and Cedar Rapids left a legacy, but except for social groups such as the Turners, it wasn't institutional.

---

16. DMR, Mar. 17, 23, 28, 2014.

17. Persinger et al., *TM and Cult Mania*, 119–30.

18. For a discussion of Hinduism as a religion, or better a grouping of religions, see Doniger, *Hindus*.

19. On Meskwaki resistance to European-American curiosity, see Scot, *Prairie Reunion*, 181–83; McTaggart, *Wolf That I Am*; Daubenmeier, *Meskwaki and Anthropologists*; and Buffalo, "Oral History of the Meskwaki."

Martin Marty's wry observation that atheists are always disbelieving in a particular god seems apropos for many "village atheists."[20] That they opposed a particular God or god is no more evidence of truth or scandal than that their neighbors favored a particular God or god. (Whether God can be particular is a theological discussion outside the parameters of this work, but the question of particularity *vis-a-vis* universality will be relevant.)

A legal scholar has recently maintained that "to define religion is to limit religion, to set its boundaries and hence to delineate its other. But the potential shape of such definitions and oppositions are infinite in their possibilities."[21] Given that disclaimer, parameters are still needed.

So here is my working definition, not of religion, but of religious history: religious history seeks to identify and make sense of the consequences of those who espouse or contest views of God or gods or transcendent reality in ways that have a perceptible effect on a society and for which there is empirical evidence.

DEFINING IOWA RELIGION GEOGRAPHICALLY

The philosophical and ethical questions about what constitutes religion make geographical considerations look easy. But for Iowa it includes discussing denominations and a region.

The majority of Iowans have expressed their religion through Protestant denominations. The opening of settlement to whites meant immediately the start of competition among Protestant denominations, but their stiffest competitor was the Catholic Church, which also sought dominance. From the beginning, Mormons, pantheists, Freethinkers, Swedenborgians, and the religiously disinterested also provided challenges. Jews, self-repatriated Meskwakis, Inspirationists, and Muslims were not far behind. Eastern Orthodox arrived early in the twentieth century, and the Tai Dam, Hindus, Buddhists, and Sikhs in the last half of the century, although Hindu influence on Theosophists and the Iowa origins of American yoga dated earlier.

20. Schmidt, *Village Atheists*, 83, 101, 155, 209, 313. Using readers' letters to atheist periodicals, Schmidt found small-town Iowa atheists in nineteenth-century Irwin, Riceville, Oxford, and Clarksville.

21. Wenger, *Religious Freedom*, 239.

Defining Religion

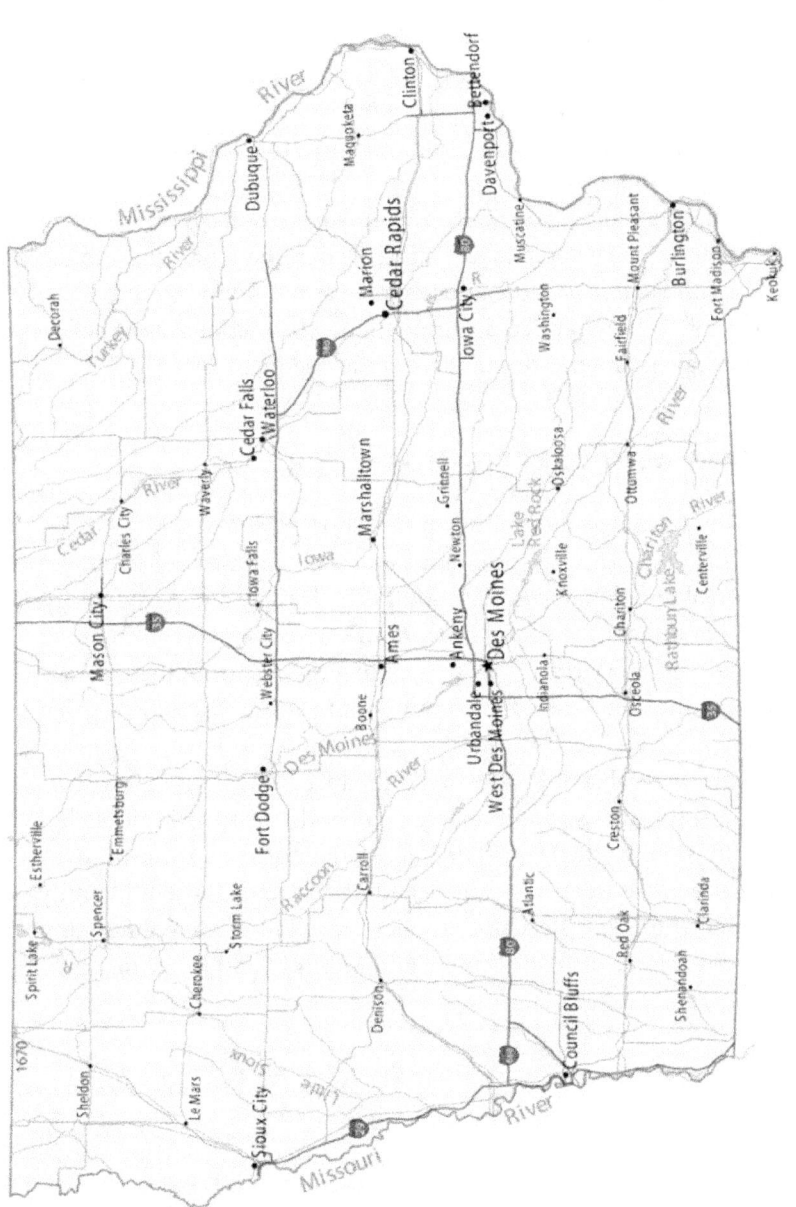

courtesy GISGeography

As was true of earlier times, some, like Disciples of Christ layperson Governor Robert Ray, welcomed and encouraged the new diversity of the last half-century; others, like Catholic Congressperson Steve King, decried it. (Since Catholics were assailed as a minority in Iowa by nativist Know-Nothings, the American Protective League, and the Ku Klux Klan, and since many of the immigrants King has assailed are also Catholic, there are multiple ironies.) Celebrating diversity and seeking dominance will both be persistent themes.

Denominationalism was and remains an identifier, but much of Iowa religious history took place across denominational lines (often modified by those lines). Themes such as mission, holiness, and social justice have often transcended denominational distinctions, even before the ecumenical and interfaith impulses of the twentieth century.

CHARTING WHO IS RELIGIOUS WHERE

Defining who Iowa is geographically means looking at maps. Maps of denominational predominance by county, especially for the mid-twentieth century, reveal broad patterns that show both diversity and particularity. Methodists dominate the southern third of the state—the continuation of a national migratory trend that spread directly west from the Delmarva Peninsula, the area around the mouth of the Susquehanna River that incubated American Methodism.

Notable by its absence is the predominance of Baptists in any Iowa county: the solid Baptist South extends up to the Missouri border but emphatically stops at the Iowa state line. In the northern third of Iowa, Lutherans predominate, part of the Scandinavian and German ubiquity in the Upper Midwest.[22] Roman Catholics prevail in urban counties, but also in rural enclaves of Irish (Emmet and Monroe) and Germans (Carroll, Jackson, and Dubuque).

---

22. More precisely, the German triangle nationally has Milwaukee, St. Louis, and Cincinnati as corners, but there is a western bulge to include much of Iowa.

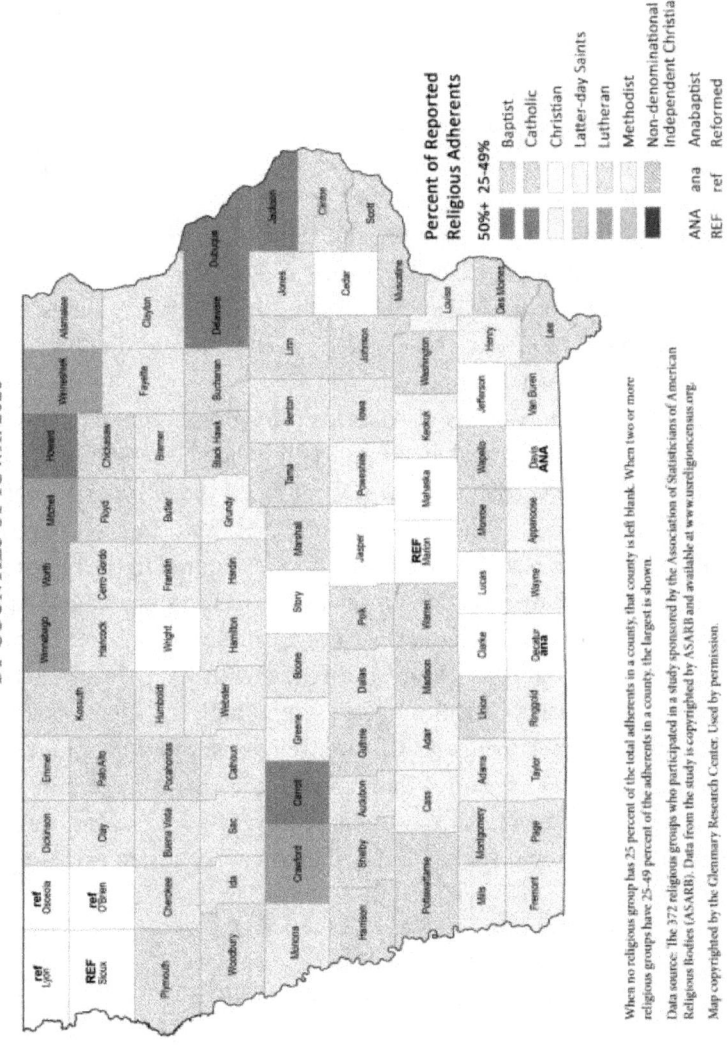

Religious Families 2020. Permission Glenmary Associates, with thanks to the Church of the Nazarene Global Ministry Center.

Smaller pockets of denominational predominance also crop up on current and past maps. There are Dutch Reformed pockets in Marion County (Pella) and its northwestern transplants. The only Reorganized Latter-day Saints (now Community of Christ) county in the country was in Decatur. (In 2020, the group declined to report a membership number.)[23] Rare occurrences of United Church of Christ (Cedar) and Presbyterian (Monona) predominance have disappeared from more recent maps. By 2020, Davis County had become majority Anabaptist, with fifteen Amish and several Mennonite congregations.[24]

Smaller denominations are also clustered; Disciples' strength paralleled Methodists', as both drew adherents from upland Southerners. There are pockets of Mennonites and Amish in Washington, Wright, Mitchell, and Davis Counties. German Dunkard Baptists (now Church of the Brethren) populate Grundy,[25] Hardin, and Dallas Counties; Quakers can be found in Cedar, Dallas, Warren, Marshall, and O'Brien.[26] All of these groups began arriving relatively early.

The PRRI 2020 Census of American Religion emphasized the particularity of Iowa religion when it looked granularly at religion by county. Among "All White Christians," Lyon County led the US with 87 percent adherents, compared to the US mean of 44 percent. In the category of White Mainline Protestants, two Iowa counties figured in the nationwide top ten, with Clayton at #4 and O'Brien at #6, with 35 percent and 34 percent adherents compared to the US average of 16 percent. And Dubuque County led the nation in White Catholics, with 45 percent (national average, 12 percent).[27] Obviously, Iowa scored high in "whiteness," too.

Of all the other measures of Iowa religions, one that is anecdotal but revealing is that of groups that have been formed in Iowa or maintain national headquarters here. The Community of True Inspiration is no longer a communal society but still exists as a church, exclusively in

23. Email correspondence with Rich Houseal, April 14, 2025.
24. 2020 USRC Families Map; Stacker.com.
25. Quick, *Vandemark's Folly*, 269. Quick's "Monterey County" is a lightly fictionalized Grundy County.
26. Jones, *Quakers of Iowa*, 53, 58, 68–70, 73, 313, 333; Tjossem, *Quaker Sloopers*, v, 9, 20, 25, 29–30, 32, 46–48.
27. Public Religion Research Institute, "American Religious Identity at the County Level." A cursory look at county denominational affiliations (see the maps in Gaustad, below) suggests that the high rate of white mainline Protestants in Clayton and O'Brien counties is due to Scandinavian Lutheran predominance (and probably German Lutheran presence also in Clayton County).

Defining Religion

the seven Iowa County towns of the Amana Colonies.[28] Several Holiness and Pentecostal denominations have roots in Iowa: the Hephzibah Missionary Association, part denomination and part missionary society, flourished and then languished in southwestern Iowa until 1949, when its assets were divided between the Wesleyan Methodists and the Church of the Nazarene (founded by an Iowan).[29]

The shocked reaction by Midwesterners to two flashily controversial preachers' sexual antics produced two Iowa-born denominations: Benjamin Harding Irwin's very public downfall led to the founding of the Fire Baptized Holiness Church in Olmitz, a long-deserted hamlet and campground now in the Lucas County portion of Stephens State Forest. The Open Bible Standard Church began in Des Moines in reaction to the mysterious disappearance of the flamboyant West Coast Pentecostal preacher Aimee Semple McPherson.[30]

One group with an influential history but no particular ties to Iowa that now has its headquarters in Dubuque is the Plymouth Brethren, whose dispensationalist interpretation of the Bible had a profound impact on fundamentalism.[31]

While denominationalism is an extremely useful tool for historians, several caveats can be added. Recently, a flood of independent, non-denominational groups have constituted an increasing proportion of the religious population. And denominational boundaries have become

---

28. The literature on the Amanas is extensive—see the bibliography. But the best place to start is Hoehnle, *Amana People*.

29. Worcester, *Master Key*.

30. Mitchell, *Heritage & Horizons*, 144–46; Blumhofer, *Aimee Semple McPherson*, 335–36.

31. Another list from 2009 draws a different set of headquarters: Evangelical Mennonites in Ft. Dodge, Augsburg Lutherans in Greenfield, the Living Word Fellowship in Iowa City, the Union of Nazarene Yisraelite Congregations in Ottumwa, the Kingsway Fellowship in Des Moines, and the Avalonian Catholic Church in Clinton. Melton, *Encyclopedia of American Religions*, 1282. A 1991 edition also lists the Gospel Assemblies (Sowders/Goodwin), a Pentecostal group based in Des Moines. Two other groups listed are questionable, for very different reasons: the Nudist Christian Church of the Blessed Virgin Jesus I have testimony to suggest is a person, not a group, who moreover is no longer in Iowa, and the Iowa Yearly Meeting of Friends has affiliations that are national and transnational. Melton, *Encyclopedia of American Religions*, Vol. 3, 342.

In addition to listing the Open Bible Standard Church and the Plymouth Brethren, the latest (14th) edition of *Handbook of Denominations of the United States* lists the headquarters of the United Reformed Churches in North America, a conservative split from the (already conservative) Christian Reformed Church in Sioux Center. For a time the Anglican Catholic Church in America was headquartered in West Des Moines. DMR, Jan. 22, 2005.

increasingly porous And, people attending the same service can come with different preconceptions, pick up on divergent messages, and go away with contradictory reactions.

IOWA AS THE QUINTESSENTIAL MIDWEST

Iowa is part of a region.[32] Despite disagreement about what constitutes the Midwest, all definitions agree that Iowa is within it, leading to the claim that Iowa is the most Midwestern of states.[33] But what that means is as nebulous as what the Midwest means. The Midwest seems the second most religious region of the country, after the South, if measured by regular attendance at houses of worship.[34] Also, the Midwest has the highest percentage of mainline Protestants of any region (with South Dakota and Iowa bringing up the percentages).[35]

"Tell me your landscape and I'll tell you who you are," claimed José Ortega y Gasset.[36] The land has always figured large in scholars' attempts to understand the Midwest—and its religions. And land has often been a theme in Iowans' religious conceptions of themselves, from the land-based theology of Early Woodland indigenous people to the prophetic defense of the ideal of the family farm by advocates as diverse as devout Methodist James B. Weaver in the late nineteenth century, militant Church of Christ preacher Milo Reno and mystic and politician Henry A. Wallace in the 1930s, and Catholic Bishop Maurice Dingman during the farm crisis of the 1980s. Land, which in Iowa is mostly now farmland, can be an awe-inducing component of religious feeling.

IOWA AS PERIPHERY

Open most books dealing with the history of American religion, and if the index even has geographical references, an increasing rarity, one is lucky to find just a couple of nods to Iowa. Iowa has been on center stage of American religion only rarely and briefly; say, President Ulysses

---

32. For an important discussion on religion and region, see Moore, at al., "Roundtable."
33. See, e.g. Cullen, "Iowa Is the Thumping Heart of the Midwest."
34. Barlow, "Demographic Profile."
35. "US States by Mainline Protestant Population."
36. Quoted in Zuba, "Sense of Place."

Grant's Des Moines speech on religion in public schools, or the Student Volunteer Movement national convention in Des Moines in 1919, which suddenly and starkly revealed the generational chasm between the sunniness of an older liberalism and the despair of those who had witnessed world war up close (see chapter 16). And when the leaders of the Roman Catholic, Anglican, and Greek Orthodox churches all visited Des Moines, independently, in the late twentieth century.[37] Of course, the pope got the most publicity, but local Christians did their best to channel that attention to the dilemma facing Iowa farmers. Farms dominate the historical discourse about Iowa, even if farmers are usually relegated to the sidelines.

Iowa has exported much of its talent, a defining feature of periphery. The most spectacular example is the case of Joseph Fort Newton, who catapulted from a small pulpit in Cedar Rapids straight to London.[38] The case of *The Christian Century*, which moved from a denominational journal in Des Moines to national prominence as an independent magazine in Chicago, is another example (see chapter 11). Annie Wittenmeyer, Billy Sunday, John Mott, Ann Landers, Robert Schuller, and Sister Corita are all examples of the talent drain from the state.

In fact, Iowa has also been a location for internal exile, as in the case of John Keane, the Americanist rector of Catholic University, reassigned as archbishop of Dubuque after the pope adjudged Americanism to be a heresy.[39] Americanism was never clearly defined, but the papal bull seemed to suggest that accepting the terms of debate of a free society was unacceptable, given the inherent superiority of Catholicism.[40] But, while the declaration of heresy affected the careers of some prominent American Catholics, most notably Keane, it did not keep Catholics away from other Christians. (See chapter 17.)

Fr. Louis Michael Colonnese, the director of the Latin American division of the United States Catholic Conference of Bishops in the seventies, subsequently a missionary expelled from El Salvador and then an activist against the US war against El Salvador, also found himself far

---

37. LemMon, *John Paul II*; DMR, Jun. 1, 2004.

38. Newton, *Sermons*. Newton is also illustrative of the permeability of twentieth-century American Protestant denominations: raised Baptist, he also served Unitarian and Lutheran pulpits.

39. Tentler, *American Catholics*, 198.

40. "Americanism." *Catholic Encyclopedia*, 34.

from the halls of power in the 1980s, administering the sacraments in Holbrook and Parnell.[41]

But in being on the periphery, often in reaction to or oblivious of the metropolis,[42] some aspects of religion may be more easily observed or uncovered. Is American religion best observed filtered or from the ground up? The lived religion tendency in US religious historiography made a brilliant case for the latter, but the nature and availability of historical evidence and the sheer impossibility of being comprehensive at a local level means that filtered versions will predominate.

Local and state studies can and should amplify or qualify national generalizations—a major justification for writing this book. The contention that individual beliefs and actions matter has to undergird all our lives, and occasionally historians can uncover evidence to validate that.

The rich legacy of social history that brought new insights is still being felt, most recently in the field of American religious history, in the turn toward connections with labor and business history.[43] In Iowa, we can point most obviously to the founding of East End Presbyterian Church in Ottumwa by meatpacking mogul John Morrell as a way of grooming workers with the purportedly Christian virtues of punctuality and loyalty.[44] The unceremonious dismissal of the Congregationalist minister in Newton for supporting the sit-down strike of Maytag workers in 1938[45] and church support for the Grain Millers of Camanche, who unsuccessfully fought union-busting in the 1980s,[46] are two examples, but much work remains to be done by historians on religion and capitalism in Iowa. The question of whether capitalism is a religion might be fruitful,[47] but I will stick to more traditional definitions.

---

41. Bridgeport, CT *Post*, Jan. 10, 2003; Green, *We Cannot Remain Silent*; Iowa City *Press-Citizen*, Apr. 2, 1981; May 21, 1982; Williamsburg *Journal-Tribune*, Jan. 3, 2018; *Free Flowing*, Apr. 1978.

42. On this Marxist view of the Midwest, which I find helpful, see Watts, *American Colony*.

43. See, e.g., Pehl, *Making of Working-Class Religion*, 3–7.

44. Warren, *Struggling with "Iowa's Pride*," 23.

45. Lane, "Labor Troubles and the Local Church."

46. Dawes, "Liberation Theology in the Bible Belt," 81–91.

47. See McCarraher, *Enchantments of Mammon*.

THE PEOPLE ARE KIND

What best defines Iowa religion? Sometimes, I will suggest, it may be outliers: religious refugees, abolitionists, Christian Socialists, pacifists. Some of those (mostly white male) subjects managed to maintain an ongoing presence in Iowa history. Another judgment upon majority Iowa religion may be the practice of the Meskwakis, and I will try out that possibility throughout the narrative.

Finally, a word on the title, and its implications. "The people are kind" is a description of settler Congregationalists in Keosauqua from an Iowa Band participant.[48] If there are hints of condescension, the notes of gratitude prevail. But the title is meant more broadly as a glimpse into the soul of the state.

Even if some chapters suggest that the phrase was chosen ironically, most who are familiar with the denizens of the state will agree that a sense of community and institutions that try to nurture the potential for human goodness have helped to shape the state, and many of us find those ideals worth preserving. Religious institutions and experiences have had a formative role in nudging the people to be kind. Many religious people may find that beside the point, but the job of a historian is not theological but analytical; revelation is beyond our purview. If people of faith can detect evidence of providence in the sifting of facts, that's fine, but that the people are kind seems an affirmation in itself.

---

48. Adams, *Iowa Band*, 39. Cf. Robinson, *Jack*, 229.

CHAPTER 1

Land, and the Native Americans on It

"When Earth-maker came to consciousness, he thought of the substance upon which he was sitting. He saw nothing. There was nothing anywhere. Therefore his tears flowed. He wept. But not long did he think of it. He took some of the substance upon which he was sitting; so he made a little piece of earth for our fathers. Then he looked at that which he made. It had become something like our earth . . . It kept turning."

—Ho Chunk creation story[1]

"Always there are antecedent events, without which any particular event cannot be explained and commemorated. This line of thought, when pursued, leads one back to a reverential explanation, 'In the beginning God,' which is a good beginning for one who wishes to make a critical examination of the centuries-old traditions that have come to fruition . . . There is something essentially hopeful in the belief that some particular venture of the spirit is in alliance with the Infinite. The Universe itself cannot be defeated. One who realizes this shouts triumphantly with Walt Whitman: 'I am partner in this universe And all mixed up in its motions.'"

—Harry Morehouse Gage, president of Coe College, 1941[2]

    1. Judson, ed., *Myths and Legends*, 1.
    2. *Sixty Years of Coe-Education*. The Neoplatonist patina of the observation is typical of much of mid-twentieth-century mainline Protestantism.

Land, and the Native Americans on It

" . . . either
a First Cause said once, 'Let there
be sundews,' and there were, or they've
made their way here unaided
other than that backhand, round-
about refusal to assume responsibility
known as Natural Selection."

—AMY CLAMPITT, "THE SUN UNDERFOOT AMONG THE SUNDEWS"[3]

OVER MILLENNIA, THE LAND that became known as Iowa was mostly a rich prairie landscape, with forests along the rivers and in some of the south, and marshlands in the north central region. The driftless region in the northeast and the Loess Hills in the west provided variety.[4] With the meandering topographical boundaries to the east and the west—the land between two rivers—and the much more recent straight political lines inscribing its north and south bounds, the boundaries' tension between nature and rationality is perhaps a metaphor for the conflict between nature-based and monotheistic religions, or framed differently, between the human attributes of gratitude and striving.[5]

Whether particular groups of Native Americans primarily engaged in hunting, fishing, farming, or mining, the land offered up bounty. Especially at night, when the wide-open vistas presented a star-lit canopy on cloudless nights, there was much to ponder. The precise geometric designs and astronomical allusions of the Moundbuilders, such as the Big Dipper configuration at what is now Effigy Mounds National Monument, provide evidence that Native ritual took the sky seriously.[6] The

---

3. Clampitt, *Collected Poems of Amy Clampitt*, 15. Clampitt was born and raised a Quaker near New Providence. In the introduction to her selected letters, William Spiegelman asks but does not answer the question, which bears on the relation between religion and culture, "Is it coincidence that she took up poetry writing for the first time since adolescence when she began to feel the attraction of the Episcopal Church in the fifties? Or that her major poetry coincides with her abandonment of the church in the late sixties and early seventies in favor of political activism?" (Of course, the answer to those questions could well be yes.) Spiegelman, *Love, Amy*, xi.

4. For a lyrical description of Iowa's ecology, see Mutel, *Emerald Horizon*.

5. Suggested: Simon, "Why Are U.S. Borders Straight Lines?"

6. *Effigy Mounds*; conversation with National Park Service ranger David Barton-Liles, Effigy Mounds National Monument, Jul. 22, 2020; DMR, Sep. 9, 2018; *Christian*

land prompted emotions of awe and gratitude, both often associated with religious feeling.[7]

Ioway scholar Lance Foster has suggested how landscape and religion were intertwined and enmeshed in Ioway culture:

> The Ioway (*Paxoge*) recognized the seven cardinal directions of the Above, the Below, the East, the South, the West, the North, and the Center, each having its own Deity Protector (*Wakanda Wawa'tin*), and all these under the Creator, *Wakanda* or *Ma'Un*. This land was an Island, resting on a Turtle, the earth on its back placed there by Muskrat, and the island floated on a great sea. The earth was our Mother, *hina mayan*. Over her was the domed arch of the Sky . . . The land itself was delineated by the rivers, especially the two great rivers, *Nyatanga* (the Mississippi) and *Nyishui* (the Missouri), the life's blood of the earth.[8]

Various Native American groups occupied what became Iowa for several millennia before contact with Europeans, but available evidence of their religious practices is scant. It is reasonable that they shared practices with those who came later, but that is speculative. It is a bit less speculative to suggest that they held a general religious system in common with most Native American groups. As in studying other groups—say Christian denominations—one can emphasize either their unity or their uniqueness.

The general characteristics of Native American religions have been summarized as:

> Four prominent features in North American Indian religions are a similar worldview, a shared notion of cosmos, harmony, emphasis on experiencing directly powers and visions, and a common view of the cycle of life and death.[9]

Another summary of the commonalities in American Indian religion is more specific:

> Most Native Americans share the following six concepts:
> 1. A belief in or knowledge of unseen powers, or what some people call The Great Mystery.

Century, Nov. 17, 2021, 8–9.

7. Nabokov, *Where the Lightning Strikes*, 6; Aveni, *People and the Sky*, 6; Miller, "Through a Glass, Brightly," 30. See also Thuesen, *Tornado God*.

8. Foster, "Ioway," 1.

9. Hultkrantz, *Native Religions of North America*, 20.

2. Knowledge that all things in the universe are dependent on one another.
3. Personal worship [that] reinforces the bond between the individual, the community, and the great powers. Worship is a personal commitment to the sources of life.
4. Sacred traditions and persons knowledgeable in sacred traditions [that] are responsible for teaching *morals and ethics.*
5. Most communities and tribes have trained practitioners who have been given names such as medicine men, priests, shamans, caciques, and other names . . .
6. A belief that humor is a necessary part of the sacred.[10]

That last point may be a gift to the larger community that is as yet unreceived.

THE MOUNDBUILDERS

The first group leaving evidence of its religious practices is the Moundbuilders along the Mississippi River. Even here, in the spectacular construction of huge mounds that often still resemble animal emblems that perhaps identified clans, archaeologists and historians must reinvoke a lost meaning.

In his history of the Mississippi River, for example, Paul Schneider has connected the Mound Builders' enthusiasm and reverence for bears with folk traditions around the world.

> In all the world of bear veneration, however, only the effigy mound people of the upper Mississippi River gathered together at sacred times of the year and constructed vast ground sculptures of bears. From archaeological excavations it appears that individual mounds were usually built in a single outpouring of effort, obviously by a fairly large group of people who had gathered at the site in a particular season of coming together and socializing. The remains of great feasts that attended the construction have been found . . .
>
> Taken together, the effigy mounds of the upper Mississippi River valley were the largest-scale collection of sculpture of any kind in the world. More than art, though, the landscape of the upper river valley was the spiritual expression of a culture that left almost nothing else behind in the way of material objects.[11]

10. Beck et al., *Sacred*, 8–9.
11. Schneider, *Old Man River*, 47–53. For another deep dive that compares the

While the religious meanings of the mounds to the Mound Builders must be partly speculative, we can be clear as to the cultural and religious significance that nineteenth-century white settlers gave them. Given that the practice had apparently been abandoned[12] and that evidently extraordinary work would have been taken to construct the mounds, European Americans conveniently theorized that the Mound Builders had only recently been annihilated by savage invaders, the current inhabitants of the land. This fantasy had the additional benefit for intruding whites of delegitimizing Native American land claims: they were only recent interlopers (too).[13] This theory had theological dimensions: an 1860 Massachusetts Sunday School curriculum included the following opinion regarding Iowa Indian graves:

> But God has allowed these savage people to be driven away as he did the Philistines before the Israelites, because of their sins. He wanted a people to inhabit these beautiful prairies, who would consecrate them to him, and who would build churches and schoolhouses over them. He wanted the voice of love and praise to come up to his ears, instead of the song of the war-dance and the yell of the battle cry.[14]

We had best pass over the irony of whites claiming the characteristic of peacefulness in 1860.

The possible connection between the Mound Builders and the lost tribes of Israel also consumed much speculative energy.[15] The theory is evident in Joseph Smith's epic newer testament, *The Book of Mormon*, in which Jesus appeared in the New World, and in which the conflict between good Indians, the Nephites or the Lost Tribes of Israel, and bad ones, called Lamanites, eventually went badly for the former, and by the time Europeans arrived, only Lamanites remained. According to

---

Mound Builders' religion to other ancient religions and assesses it in terms of Jungian psychology. See Kellison, "Symbolic World."

12. In fact, we now know that the practice continued until about 1700, or after the first European contact with Mississippi Valley indigenous people, even though the people known as Mound Builders had evolved into groups with other names.

13. Alex, *Exploring Iowa's Past*, 10–11; Lee, *Masters of the Middle Water*, 231–33, 325–26, fn. 3; Silverberg, *Mound Builders*, 40–49.

14. Quoted in Morgan, *Protestants and Pictures*, 88.

15. The topic is discussed most fully in Fenton, *Old Canaan in a New World*.

Mormon theology, though, even Lamanites could become white again if only they would convert to Mormonism.[16]

As much as whites' imaginations shaped narratives about the builders of the mounds, the archaeological evidence of their meanings remains sparse, and we ought not to repeat the interpretative mistakes of nineteenth-century whites whose agenda is clearer to us than it was to them.

THE ONEOTA CULTURE AND PROTO-HISTORICAL GROUPS

The Mound Builder culture disappeared; it was followed by the Oneota culture in northeastern Iowa, and along and near the Missouri River in the Glenwood and Blood Run villages.[17]

Archaeologists call the Oneota finds the Orr Focus. Historian of the Ioway Martha Royce Blaine has summarized what can (and cannot) be deduced from the evidence this way:

> The artifacts at ancient Ioway village sites tell us many things, but they can never tell us as much as we wish they could about the inhabitants who owned and used them. The most intriguingly human, interesting things—the thoughts, the predictions, the arguments, the humor in the day-to-day social interaction—we can only surmise. We can surmise that ceremonial events certainly took place in the villages, because most societies at this technological level utilized ritual as part of planning for survival and in considering life after death. Orr Focus sites point to some form of ceremony around death in the careful preparation of burials. Effigy figures, such as bird carvings, snakelike copper forms, ceremonial stone maces, wands, whistles, pipes, small catlinite or pipestone tablets, fossils, and small beautiful rocks appear to have had no utilitarian use and may indicate ceremonial usage. Death ritual is evident, but the ceremonial practices associated with other life events, such as birth, marriage, and status acquisition, are not hinted at in the present evidence.[18]

---

16. Bushman, *Joseph Smith*, 94–99, 161; Vogel, *Indian Origins and the Book of Mormon*, 62–69.

17. Alex, *Exploring Iowa's Past*, 145–51; Henning and Schnepf, *Blood Run*, 50–51.

18. Blaine, *Ioway Indians*, 15.

SIOUAN AND ALGONQUIN SPEAKERS

Two major linguistic groups played a role in early Iowa prehistory, protohistory, and history: the Siouan and the Algonquian. The Siouan languages descended from the earlier groups in the area and were spoken not just by the Sioux nations (Lakota, Dakota, Nakota) but by others that inhabited Iowa at some time: the Ho Chunk (Winnebago), Ioway, Otoe, Omaha, and Missouri.

The other linguistic group, the Algonquian, was represented primarily by the Meskwaki (who the French and Americans misidentified as the Fox, by confusing a clan name with the tribe's), still present in the state,[19] and their allies the Sauk (also spelled Sac), who initially moved into what became the state after being pushed west and south by other groups pressured by Europeans and European Americans. Another Algonquian-speaking group, the Illinois Confederation, was living along the upper Mississippi River when the French contacted them in the late seventeenth century.[20]

Most Native American groups associated with Iowa were originally located east of their location at the time of European contact, because other groups who had encountered Europeans earlier were forced off their land further east. Those near the Great Lakes, such as the Meskwaki and the Sauk, also felt a southerly pressure.[21] (The jostling did exist to a lesser extent before the European invasion.)

For most of these groups, political and religious history was intertwined in ways reminiscent of ancient Israel: a particular region was seen as promised by the creator to a particular people, even as those lands changed with time and conflict. (Abraham was originally from further east, too.) But the promised land shifted frequently for many Native groups.

CREATION AND CONTACT

Returning to indigenous and European views about creation can frame the events of contact and their consequences. Native Americans and

---

19. While most Meskwakis were removed to a reservation in Kansas, a remnant remained in the state semi-covertly and were reunited when the exiled Meskwakis purchased their settlement along the Iowa River in Tama County in 1857, with the blessing of the state government. See chapter 3.

20. Lee, *Masters*, 13–18, 26.

21. Lee, *Masters*, 96–97; Ostler, *Surviving Genocide*, 26–28, 220–1, 233–34, 334;

European Americans debated whether the two groups were descended from the same ancestors, as the whites would frame it,[22] or whether they were created by the same God, as indigenous peoples viewed the politico-theological question.[23] In contrast to the European concept of one universal God, indigenous thinkers posited different Gods for different groups. According to a Meskwaki leader speaking to a national religious meeting held in Iowa,

> All of us are not alike. We are different races of people. Of course your God told you what you should do. Our Man-i-to put us here and we are following the ways that he told us. I suppose that is the way you are doing . . . You should follow the way the God told you; we will follow the ways our Man-i-to told us. I will never give up my way of worship . . .
>
> You white people have so many different ways . . . to follow your religion. We have only the one way and are still following it.[24]

The natural bounty of Iowa constituted an argument for creation for both white and indigenous people. But questions about the purpose and ordering of creation can shed light on ways to view the coming conflict between the overwhelmingly Christian, European-descended settlers and the nature-attuned original inhabitants who were often bewildered by the contradictions between Christian teachings and white practice.

What became Iowa already had evidence of religious devotion before indigenous people had contact with Europeans. The purpose of the land was a religious question and would become a contested one.

---

22. Vogel, *Indian Origins and the Book of Mormon*, chapter 4.
23. Zielinksi, *Mesquakie and Proud of It*, 76.
24. Quoted in Zielinski, *Mesquakie and Proud of It*, 76.

CHAPTER 2

Contact

"[When the Congregationalists arrived,] not all Indian title to land on the sunset side of the Mississippi was [yet] settled by treaty or theft."

—Philip D. Jordan[1]

"My eyes look back
for the path we have lost. Weep no more
O my sad people. Sky shares our sorrow."

—Michael Borich, *Black Hawk Songs*[2]

"There is a great need of some of the fundamental spirituality of the old Indian religions being introduced into our modern American attitude."

—Henry A. Wallace[3]

"'Once there was an Indian who became a Christian. He became a very good Christian; he went to church, and he didn't smoke or drink, and he was good to everyone. Then he died. First he went to the Indian hereafter, but they wouldn't take him because he was a Christian. Then he went to Heaven, but they

---

1. Jordan, *To Thy Trust*, [no pagination].
2. 42.
3. Quoted in Kleinman, "Searching for the 'Inner Light,'" 207.

wouldn't admit him either because he was an Indian. Then he went to Hell, but they wouldn't take him in there either, because he was so good. So he came alive again, and he went to the Buffalo Dance and the other dances and taught his children to do the same thing."

—MESKWAKI STORY[4]

THE TENSION IN NATIVE American religions between a recognition of universal themes and an insistence on the particularity of individual nations' practices came to the fore with the prolonged crisis caused by European and European-American intrusions on Natives' land. This religious tension overlaid and complicated the political options of accommodation or resistance. (While the terms religious and political are in this context—and many others—artificial and overlapping, they remain helpful; the distinct roles that prophets and warriors played in Native societies illustrates the usefulness of the distinction.) Both the universalizing and the particularist tendencies contained admirable qualities and drew disciples from indigenous people living in what would become Iowa.

THE UNIVERSALIZING TENDENCY

The pan-Indian impulse was most notably expressed by the prophets surrounding Tecumseh. Tecumseh was a Shawnee who based his and his brother, the prophet Tenskawatawa's, movement along the Wabash River in what is now Indiana. Tecumseh and Tenskawatawa worked politically and prophetically to unify the diverse indigenous nations west of the thirteen (soon fourteen) United States.

Tecumseh managed to gather representatives and observers from as far west as the Lakota and the Sauk and Meskwaki[5] for conferences that were part religious revival and part strategy session. Several decades later, contesting the US government's occupation of Saukenauk, the Sauk chief Black Hawk reprised Tecumseh's hopes (if briefly) in the 1836 uprising now known as the Black Hawk War, the last gasp of the pan-Indian dream of an independent future for Eastern Woodland tribes.

4. Gearing, et al., *Documentary History*, 39.
5. Dowd, *Spirited Resistance*, 185; Cozzens, *Tecumseh and the Prophet*, 144, 205, 210, 222–23.

But pan-Indian sentiment persisted after military defeat and helped shape the religious response to it. After the US government's subjugation of the Plains Indians, the Ghost Dance, and soon after that the Native American Church, spiritualized pan-Indian longing.[6] (See chapter 8.) Arguably, contact with Western religions influenced such movements' messianic character;[7] undeniably, this apocalyptic character was a response to cataclysmic events that totally disrupted and threatened to destroy the land-based belief systems and societies that existed before white colonization.

THE PARTICULARIST TENDENCY AND MESKWAKI RELIGION

While contemplating these spectacular examples of a universalizing tendency in Native religion, also keep in mind the unassuming values of particularity. In looking at the relative success of the Meskwakis in fending off the coercion and blandishments of dominant culture, protecting the uniqueness of their religion seems crucial.

Whites have encountered several obstacles in describing Meskwaki religion. First, Meskwakis are, by nature and conditioning, contrarians, a trait that almost led to their extinction in 1742, when they militarily opposed not only the French but all of France's Native allies. This was pretty much everybody else in the upper Mississippi Valley.[8] Only through rescue by and confederation with the Sauks did a remnant survive. This experience only increased contrarianness, and argumentation is a Meskwaki tradition that often has stymied would-be analysts.

Second, parts of Meskwaki religion are secret. It has become a rite of passage for anthropologists and folklorists to encounter reluctance among Meskwakis to share aspects of their culture;[9] folklorist Fred McTaggart even wrote a whole book about it (in lieu of the dissertation he

---

6. Warren, *God's Red Son*, 364–75.

7. The literature on messianism in societies on the cusp of modernity is vast; see, e.g., Vittorio Lanternri, *Religions of the Oppressed*; Peter Worsley, *Trumpet Shall Sound*; Jonathan D. Spence, *God's Chinese Son*.

8. Buffalo, "Oral History of the Meskwaki," 4–6; Edmunds and Peyser, *Fox Wars*, chapter 6; Lee, *Masters*, 96–97; Johnathon Buffalo interview, *Talk of Iowa*, Iowa Public Radio, Sep. 1, 2011.

9. Daubenmier, 118. Material culture, of course, is not secret; see Phillips, "Clothed in Blessing"; Torrence and Hobbs, *Art of the Red Earth People*. On the pow-wow, see chapter 9.

had planned.)¹⁰ Anthropologist Douglas Foley, a native of Tama County, returned to the theme in his 1995 book *Heartland Chronicles*.

Third—and here *encounter* is the wrong word, *misdirection* is closer—the Native connection between religion and humor comes to the fore—Meskwakis have been known to pull the legs of anthropologists about their beliefs, jokes that got into academic circulation without having been got.¹¹

We will have more to say about twentieth century encounters between missionaries and Meskwakis, between anthropologists and atavists, and between New Age and age-old religion. Our task here is to limn the particulars of Meskwaki religion as they brought it to what became Iowa.

In 1966 Brenda Waseskuk described Meskwaki self-identity thusly:

> I am a Mesquakie—my Creator made me in his own image and he made this Country for me. He gave me my religion by which I might worship him so that I might dwell forever in the Hereafter he has prepared for me. My Creator loves me and reminds me of his love at all times by being around me. I see him in Grandmother Earth who gives me my food, both wild and from the seed . . .¹²

The Meskwaki way of life is reflected in the nation's communal approach and in its religious rituals. Meskwaki culture, like that of many other Native American groups, and unlike the larger, transactional society, places much weight on the importance of gift-giving.¹³

Meskwakis shared basic rituals with other Algonquin groups. Regarding the religious situation when anthropologist Sol Tax arrived at the settlement in 1934, Judith Daubenmier summarized that "most people continued to worship in the traditional Meskwaki fashion with a liturgy that revolved around sacred bundles held by clans within the tribe, feasts for honoring the dead, [and] adoptions to replace a deceased family member . . . A few men still fasted for visions."¹⁴

---

10. McTaggart, *Wolf That I Am*.

11. McTaggart, *Wolf That I Am*, 36–38; Daubenmier, *Meskwaki and Anthropologists*, 197; Michelsen, "White Owl Sacred Pack"; Harrington, *Sacred Bundles of the Sauk and Fox Indians*.

12. Bataille, *Worlds Between Two Rivers*, 60–61.

13. Daubenmier, *Meskwaki and Anthropologists*, 124–25.

14. Daubenmier, *Meskwaki and Anthropologists*, 31.

Clan for the Meskwaki has been as much a religious as a familial subgroup within the tribe. Many of the myths of the clan explained the origins and the purpose of the sacred bundle.[15]

One long Fox clan myth can be taken as representative of the kinds of stories the Meskwakis told. To make a long story short (and long stories were favored around the wintertime fire), a surviving twin, after fasting, is given power to deliver his people from their enemies by the wolves and power to heal by the Great Buffalo Manitou. A talking fire and stone teach him the clan songs. The Great Manitou blesses him and gives him instructions on solemn worship.[16]

The story then turns didactic, with instructions on ceremonial songs, dance, and feasting. While still in narrative form, the speeches increasingly focus on how to conduct community, sharing, and war, and even the suggestion that a warrior can will himself to a victorious outcome.[17] Meskwaki myth thus anticipated a trend in twentieth century Protestant religion, that of New Thought (see chapter 19).

This book revisits the Meskwaki settlement repeatedly, as religious trends bent to affect even the most conservative of communities. The Meskwaki ability to preserve traditions would be tested by outside forces and inner conflicts and would manifest itself in multiple ways. And Meskwaki religion can sometimes profitably and prophetically be held up as a contrast and comparison to the religions of those who sought to, but did not quite, replace their worldview.

THE CONSEQUENCES OF CONTACT

Contact with Europeans would irrevocably change Native American societies and affect its religions. For (what became) the upper Midwest, contact included French traders, Catholic and later Protestant missionaries, and finally American settlers coveting indigenous peoples' lands. While the English were not involved directly this far west, their pre-Revolutionary settlement and expansionist policies indirectly affected the

---

15. Tooker, *Native North American Spirituality*, 164–65; Foster, *Indians of Iowa*, 15.
16. Tooker, *Native North American Spirituality*, 166–86.
17. Tooker, *Native North American Spirituality*, 186, 193–94, 201–2, 213.

region by pushing eastern Native nations westward—not into an alleged wilderness but into other Native nations' ancestral lands.

The first recorded worship service of an Abrahamic religion in Iowa took place in what is now Lee County, where the Des Moines and Mississippi Rivers join. On June 15, 1673, Jesuit priest and explorer Jacques Marquette celebrated Mass while on a canoeing expedition down the Mississippi with Louis Joliet and five others. Illinois Confederation villages provided the backdrop.[18]

(The fact that the Native name for a sub-tribe of the Illinois, the Moingwenas, gave their name to the Des Moines River when the French transliterated it into "Moingona," and then called it "Des Moines," or "The Monks," somehow morphed into the legend that Trappist monks settled near Keosauqua in the late eighteenth century. No evidence exists for this, and if Trappists were involved, they are not talking.[19])

Catholic priests followed French and Metis fur traders into the upper Midwest. (Metis had both white and Native parents.) Lead mines around what is now Dubuque, first exploited by Meskwaki and Ho Chunk women, proved an additional attraction to Europeans.[20]

For about a decade beginning in the eighteen-thirties, Jesuits maintained a mission at what is now Council Bluffs, serving mostly Potawatomis displaced from Michigan. By 1843, with their "dispersal" elsewhere, the mission had been abandoned.[21] One of the legends of Catholic missions to Native Americans, famous for his explorations further west, Fr. Pierre-Jean DeSmet, served that mission.[22] He had harsh things to say about the Potawatomis, apparently clueless about the enormous social toll involved in just having been expelled from their land. DeSmit also found it disheartening, when instead of a warm welcome, the Potawatomis

---

18. Avella, *Catholic Church in Southwest Iowa*, xix, 3; Lee, *Masters*, 13–18. See also Magnuson, "Marquette's Bones."

19. Blanchard, in Harlan, *Narrative History of the People of Iowa*, 373, calls the monks' presence "tradition." Vogel, *Iowa Place Names of Indian Origin*, 16–17. Vogel also points to the Boone County town of Moingona, on the Des Moines River, and suggests that the Illinois word means "loon," probably a clan name.

20. Broihahn, "Meskwaki Mining Metamorphosis," 98–118.

21. Kempker, "Catholic Missionaries," 58, 61.

22. For glimpses of deSmet's time in Iowa, see Margaret, "Pierre Jean deSmet," 177–90; Terrell, *Black Robe*; Leveille, *Life of Father deSmet*; Avella, *Catholic Church in Southwest Iowa*, 7, 34.

rushed past the disembarking Jesuits upon their steamboat arrival to instead greet traders selling whiskey.[23]

Not surprisingly, those with less power in Native societies were sometimes most drawn to European religions.[24] Conversely, American missionary (and government) insistence that Native sex roles be reversed and that men take up agriculture hampered religious conversions.[25]

The disruption of Native nations' culture triggered by white incursion caused a crisis in Native American religions. While on the surface the French desire for trade in furs was more benign than the English and American coveting of land, and led generally (although not in the case of the Meskwakis) to military and trade alliances, even French contact resulted in overhunting and dependence both on European goods and the vagaries of European markets. When the French were defeated in the nine-year-long Seven Years' War, and a generation later the trans-Atlantic fur market collapsed after the disruptions of the French Revolution and the British naval blockade during the Napoleonic Wars, Indian economies also collapsed.[26]

Prophets rose up to call for a return to the old ways and rituals, to suggest that the greed inherent in participating in the white economic system was inconsistent with the gratitude due in practicing the old subsistence economy and simultaneously to suggest that old animosities be put aside and that all Native nations unite to repel the common enemy. The political leadership of Tecumseh and the prophetic leadership of his brother Tenskwatawa exemplified the long struggle.[27] "Sauk and Fox" members are several times listed as being at pan-Indian gatherings; more importantly for Iowa religions, Tecumseh's model of military and religious resistance set the stage for the last chapter of Eastern Woodlands resistance, the Black Hawk War.

23. Tinker, *Missionary Conquest*, 10–12, 71–72.
24. Martin and Nicholas, *Native Americans*, 159–76.
25. Lee, *Masters*, 21, 214; Dowd, *Spirited Resistance*, 7–8, 150–54; Thorne, *Many Hands of My Relations*, 83; Leavelle, *Catholic Calumet*, 166–67.
26. Lee, *Masters*, 118–21.
27. The literature on Tecumseh is extensive (and sometimes contested). Putting the episode in a longer context is Dowd, *Spirited Resistance*; describing the breadth of the pan-Indian movement and its extent among southern nations is Sugden, *Tecumseh: A Life*. Placing the movement within Native religion is Cave, *Prophets of the Great Spirit*; the religious aspects of Prophetstown are emphasized in Jortner, *Gods of Prophetstown*. Focusing in on Tecumseh and Tenskwatawa's lives is Cozzens, *Tecumseh and the Prophet*. For the larger tribal context, see Warren, *Shawnees and Their Neighbors*.

BLACK HAWK AS RESISTER AND SYMBOL

The major conflict between white settlers and Native Americans in creating the Territory of Iowa involved the Sauk. The flashpoint was the Black Hawk War, named after the leader who counseled resistance, and who after his defeat still critiqued what he knew of white religion in his autobiography:

> We can only judge what is right and wrong by our standard of right and wrong, which differs widely from the whites, if I have been correctly informed. The whites *may do bad* all their lives, and then, if they are *sorry for it* when about to die, *all is well!* But with us it is different: we must continue to do what we conceive to be as good. If we have corn and meat, and know of a family that have none, we divide with them. If we have more blankets than sufficient, and others have not enough, we must give to them that want.

Black Hawk also saw the spiritual dimension of the American occupation of Saukenauk, now known as Rock Island:

> We did not ... object to their building a fort on the island, but we were very sorry, as this was the best island on the Mississippi, and had long been the resort of our young people in the summer ... It was our garden ... I spent many happy days on it. A good spirit had care of it, who lived in a cave in the rocks immediately under where the fort now stands, and has often been seen by our people. He was white, with large wings, like a swan's, but ten times larger. We were particular not to make much noise in that part of the island that he inhabited, for fear of disturbing him. But the noise of the fort has since driven him away, and no doubt a *bad spirit* has taken his place![28]

Other Sauks, such as Keokuk, counseled accommodation. Most Meskwakis, led by Poweshiek, were not involved in the war, but their affinity with the Sauks made this irrelevant to American policymakers after Black Hawk's defeat. American authorities had already lumped the two allied tribes together in a previous treaty,[29] and this fiction made it easier to evict both groups. Both were removed to a reservation in

---

28. Black Hawk, *Autobiography*, 87–88. The fact that the island continues to be occupied by a military arsenal suggests that the bad spirit may persist.

29. The St. Louis Treaty of 1804 resulted in what one historian has called the Sauk and Fox's swindle out of a million acres of land in what is now Illinois, engineered by future president William Henry Harrison. Cozzens, *Tecumseh and the Prophet*, 144.

Kansas. According to Meskwaki history, the federal government's plan was for them "'to build brick houses and become Christians.'"[30]

The question of how to respond to the American intrusions seemed a question for which there was no answer that made cultural survival likely. But the Meskwakis managed to find a way.

While there will be ample opportunity to assess Black Hawk's claim about the deficiencies of white religion, bringing his conception of Christianity to the fore at the outset provides a chance to examine an "old religion in the new world" in a fresh way. As the amount of land controlled by Native Americans shrank, European-Americans began to be more open to such a critique by their erstwhile foes.

In fact, Black Hawk has continued to be a cultural touchstone, his appropriation by New Orleans Mardi Gras being the most exotic example.[31] In their photographic essay, Nicholas Brown and Sarah Kanouse focused on the opposite extreme, the mundane invocation of Black Hawk's name in the upper Midwest, from bowling lanes to real estate companies to country clubs.[32] The original religious significance of a name like Black Hawk is drained of meaning in such contexts and serves as an indicator of the precarity of indigenous cultural survival.

CHRISTIANIZATION AND REMOVAL: THE HO CHUNKS

Like the French, the Americans led with their missions, but the Americans' larger goal was not trade but settlement. To what extent missionaries knowingly abetted this goal is debatable and also varied.[33]

If, as Jesus maintained, no one can serve two masters, David Lowry, a Cumberland Presbyterian minister, tried to avoid the problem by serving at least three. The native Tennessean parlayed his acquaintanceship with Andrew Jackson into a contract for a Winnebago Indian School in Allamakee County[34] near Ion, to the dismay of Fr. Samuel Mazzuchelli, who had

---

30. Quoted in Gearing, *Face of the Fox*, 11.

31. Berry, *Spirit of Black Hawk*.

32. Brown and Kanouse, *Re-Collecting Black Hawk*. Mark Twain also weighed in, in *Life on the Mississippi*, 329: "Black Hawk's was once a puissant name hereabouts."

33. For the prosecution, see, e.g., Tinker, *Missionary Conquest*. For an argument that missionaries and expansionists were not always in lockstep, and that cases need to be severed and prosecuted individually, see Bowden, *American Indians and Christian Missions*.

34. Reymon, "David Lowry and the Winnebago Indian School," 108–18; Gallaher,

his own ambitions along that line.[35] The school, under pressure by illegal white settlement, later moved thirty miles west to the Turkey River, where Lowry assumed power as the federal agent as well as school principal.

However, the government caved to pressure from settlers to relocate the tribe, and in 1848 Turkey River Ho Chunks were forcibly removed to central Minnesota. Lowry accompanied them. But the desertion rate was high, both on the trek and after arrival; many Winnebagos simply drifted back eastward to rejoin their kin in Wisconsin.[36] After yet another relocation to South Dakota, most of the once-Iowa-based Winnebagos ended up on a reservation in eastern Nebraska, just across the Missouri River from Iowa.[37]

Removal of other nations was accomplished without missionary accompaniment. The federal government exiled the Oto and Ioway to Indian Territory and Kansas. The Ioway shared their reservation with the Sauk and Meskwaki, until the latter repatriated. Presbyterian missionary William Hamilton ran a school there, but low enrollment discouraged him.[38]

In the northwest, however, the continued presence of the Sioux/Lakota was seen as a threat to white settlement. The deadly Spirit Lake raid by the Lakota outlaw Inkpaduta electrified and terrorized northwest Iowa and impeded European-American settlement in that region.[39] A more consequential uprising in Minnesota while whites were preoccupied by the Civil War brought Lakota prisoners to the Quad Cities, where curiosity vied with conversion attempts.[40]

Congregationalist minister and Iowa Band member Ephraim Adams claimed that Iowa "had waited for centuries for the magic touch of

---

"Indian Agents in Iowa," 5.

35. Colton, "Father Mazzuchelli's Iowa Mission," 303–5. On Protestant-Catholic missionary rivalries in the Upper Midwest frontier, see also Pawley, *Reading on the Middle Border*, 118; and Hoffmann, *Church Founders of the Northwest*, 170, 174–75, 197–214.

36. Rigal, "No Place to Call Home," 105–11.

37. Foster, *Indians of Iowa*, 87.

38. Anderson, ed., "Letters of William Hamilton," *Journal of the Presbyterian Historical Society* 35 and 36, 157–70 and 53–65.

39. Beck, *Inkpaduta: A Dakota Leader*. MacKinley Kantor fictionalized the episode in the novel *Spirit Lake*.

40. Clemmons, "Young Folks," 121–50.

The People Are Kind

civilized life."[41] If the land had such sentience, it might not have had the patience nor the inclination; the "magic touch" might very well have seemed more like an unwelcome grab. Yet the magic touches once started were recurring and would transform Iowa not just agriculturally but also culturally, with a patchwork of belief systems.

Because of geography and chronology, the European American occupation of Iowa brought with it a myriad of new ways of looking at the world. Those unruly ideas made the particularism of the Meskwaki an unwitting model for much of religious Iowa; attempts at monopolization would also loom.

It is to those particularisms and attempts at monopolization that we turn in the next four chapters, beginning with those whose religious motivations were paramount in migration to the territory (or after 1846, the state).

But the new particularisms started from a different place than Meskwaki religion had. Most new arrivals were not overly concerned by Black Hawk's critique of white religions. The "magic touch of civilized life" that Ephraim Adams championed as the solution to prairie wilderness was about to appear, with the blessing of white religion.

---

41. Adams, *Iowa Band*, 204.

CHAPTER 3

"To Build a House by Eating"

The Flourishing of Diversity in Early White Settlement

"Mrs. Edwards was . . . a great help to [Burlington Congregational minister William] Salter . . . it was she who planned and managed a Fourth of July dinner, the proceeds of which were to be used for carpets and lamps for the church. 'Singular,' said Salter, 'to build a house by eating. Isn't this the West!'"[1]

—Philip Jordan

"This looked like squaly times for a man with no better health than mine but I have ever found as yet by the Blessing of God that I have been Able to indure the fatigues of a Mormon life which is one of trial."

—Perrigrine Session, on the prospect of crossing Iowa in a muddy springtime[2]

"This [Sioux County] was the place for centuries destined to be our home by the Creator of the universe."

—Henry Hospers[3]

---

1. Jordan, *William Salter*, 89–90. "But," Salter added, "there seems to be no other way of raising money." See also Power, *Planting Corn Belt Culture*, 119.
2. Quoted in Ulrich, *House Full of Females*, 256–57.
3. Quoted in Klumpp, "Colony before Party," 8.

The People Are Kind

ON JULY 15, 1845, a warm, sunny Tuesday morning, Burlington's religious leaders—the Methodist, Congregationalist, and Presbyterian ministers[4]—adorned a platform together. They were soon joined by the Catholic bishop, arriving by riverboat from Dubuque. In an extraordinary display of unity among rivals, on an extraordinary occasion, they witnessed the execution of two Mormons for the murder of a Mennonite minister.

Certainly, by a century and a half later, all of the denominations represented had come to oppose the death penalty, and Iowa had abolished capital punishment (once) and kept it abolished (the second time) in large part due to the denominations' insistence on the intrinsic worth of human life.[5]

While perhaps the bigger story is the convergence of Iowa's preeminent denominations (Lutherans were late to arrive), the plotline inevitably shifts to the more dramatic story of the victim and the accused. The memory of the murdered Mennonite minister, John Miller, or Johann Mueller (motive: theft), is all but obscured by the spectacle of the Hodge brothers, who faced the gallows defiantly, proclaiming (and vainly expecting a last-minute intervention from the Latter-day Saints stronghold in Nauvoo, just across the river), "We are Mormons!"[6]

Except, technically, the brothers weren't. Unbeknownst to them, and to everyone else present, and to almost everyone in Nauvoo, they had been excommunicated secretly by Brigham Young's inner circle. When their brother tried to confront Young about his unwillingness to rescue his brothers, he met the same fate as his brothers but without a judicial

---

4. Boeck, "Early Iowa Community," 41–45. A Dutch immigrant in 1847 described the denominations with buildings in Burlington as "Old (German) Reformed, Methodist, Congregational and Catholic." Dietrich Budde, in Stellingwerff, *Iowa Letters*, 71.

5. While Dick Haws, *Iowa and the Death Penalty*, has given us a thorough history of death penalty cases in the state, a study is needed of the abolition campaign and the subsequent mobilizations to keep it abolished, and its essential religious components.

6. Krehbiel, "Early Years at West Point, Iowa," 53; Gingerich, *Mennonites in Iowa*, 69; Brooks, *On the Mormon Frontier*, 38–39, 49, 53; Bonney, *Banditti of the Prairies*, 27–56; Boeck, "Early Iowa Community," 41–45; Godfrey, "Crime and Punishment in Mormon Nauvoo," 214–15, is a brief arguing against Mormon involvement; Howard and Braby, "Hodges Hanging," should be used with care. On early Iowans' suspicion of Mormons, see Winslow, "David W. Kilbourne."

Improbably, Fr. John Alleman of St. Joseph's Catholic Church in Ft. Madison forged a friendship with Joseph Smith. Hoffmann, *Church Founders of the Northwest*, 175. Perhaps the friendship was based on a shared outsidership; both Catholics and Mormons were viewed with suspicion because of their hierarchical structure. See Park, *Kingdom of Nauvoo*, 34–36.

decision: he was found with a knife in his back in Young's yard. The Mormon-controlled Nauvoo police were unable to solve the murder mystery.[7]

The jarring image of the hanged Hodges might have raised questions of whether and how different religious groups could get along—and whether they might need to. But to the dismay of would-be dominant groups, religious diversity quickly became the norm on the Iowa frontier. This chapter will examine the groups that moved here for religious reasons; three more chapters will be needed to enumerate other early arrivals. It quickly became evident that coexistence was a wiser strategy than dominance.

Religion was not a determining factor in the move to Iowa for most settlers, but it played a decisive role for some.

A STUDY IN CONTRASTING CONTRARIANISMS: HENDRICK SCHOLTE AND ABNER KNEELAND

Two very different religious dissidents both very well represent nascent Iowa's resistance to uniformity of opinion: New England pantheist Abner Kneeland[8] and Dutch ultra-Calvinist Hendrik Scholte.[9] Both were imprisoned for their beliefs before coming to Iowa and came seeking both community and tolerance.

---

7. Quinn, *Mormon Hierarchy*, 217, 427 fn. 29.

8. Commager, "Blasphemy of Abner Kneeland," 29–41; Gallaher, "Abner Kneeland—Pantheist," 209–25; Bonney, "Salubria Story," 34–45; Margaret A. Bonney Papers, IWA; Papa, *Last Man Jailed For Blasphemy*; Whitcomb, "Abner Kneeland," 340–63.

On Kneeland's connections with Garrisonian abolitionists and the Freethinkers around Fanny Wright, see Jackson, *American Radicals*, 57, 96. But while Garrison and Kneeland had neighboring offices for a time, Christopher Grasso suggests that this connection can be overdrawn (*Skepticism and Religious Faith*, 334–35). Kneeland is now claimed by both Unitarians and atheists; given the clear historical record of his opposition to Universalist theology and his pantheism, both claims seem dubious, although he did have close ties to Robert Dale Owen and Frances Wright and led the Boston chapter of their Society for Free Enquirers. Grasso, *Skepticism and Religious Faith*, 341–44.

9. Heideman, *Hendrik P. Scholte*, 226–27; tenZythoff, *Sources of Secession*; Oostendorf, *H. P. Scholte*; Lucas, *Netherlanders in America*, chapter 4; Swierenga, "Van Raalte and Scholte," 21–33; "Pella, Iowa: 150 Years: 1847–1997," *Origins* 15, 15–21; Rietveld, "Hendrik Peter Scholte and the Land of Promise," 135–44; Scholte, *Stranger in a Strange Land*.

On Scholte's widely publicized switch of political parties to Republican in 1858, and that it had no coattails among Pella Dutch, see Swierenga, *Faith and Family*, 275–79.

The decoupling of government and religion that was pioneered in this country was an uneven process, both here and in Europe. Heresy was no longer a political crime in most places as a result of the Enlightenment, and eighteenth-century thought encouraged individualistic challenges to religious as well as political hierarchies. But while cosmopolitan dissenters usually escaped punishment for divergent views, provincial dissidents were often less fortunate.

The remarkable religious careers of Abner Kneeland and Hendrik Scholte, differing in nationality, theology, political trajectory, and religio-political heritage, had two things in common: they were jailed for their religious beliefs, and they ended up in Iowa. Since their jailings were in the thirties, Iowa was a natural choice. For those seeking a new life on the American frontier in the forties, Iowa was available, a free territory, and made more attractive as other dissidents arrived.

Arguably, Kneeland and Scholte initially occupied the same theological universe of Calvinism but at opposite ends of the spectrum. Kneeland revolted from a New England Universalism that was beyond what most nineteenth century Calvinists could abide, but he pushed further; Scholte in the Netherlands repeatedly called out the state church for its inclusiveness and latitudinarianism, seeking to pull it back to the hyper-Calvinism of the Dordt Confession.

Kneeland disrupted a liberal consensus not quite yet won in Massachusetts, with an impolitic, even intemperate, attack on the "Universalist God." Scholte was even more provocative in repeatedly going to jail for conducting unauthorized house church services rather than submitting to the state church in the Netherlands that he saw as deviating from orthodoxy.

PELLA, AND POINTS NORTHWEST

Let's look at Scholte's case first. In 1619 the Dutch Reformed Church at the Synod of Dordt affirmed the doctrine of double predestination: not only were the elect selected by God to go to heaven, but God also selected the reprobate to hell. (Some had tried to blame the reprobates themselves.) The doctrine had the advantage of logic, although arguably at the expense of compassion and humility. (The Calvinist-humanist essayist and Iowan Marilynne Robinson recently put it this way: "I nominate the venerable doctrine of predestination as a classic instance of an inquiry beyond human capacity.")[10]

By the early nineteenth century, in a post-Enlightenment milieu, state church authorities saw Dordt as an archaic historical curiosity. Being the state church, church doctrine was what they said it was. But a small band of true believers led by Hendrik Scholte thought the Dordt Confession was still the final word. And final words were not to be amended.

Viewed from one angle—and this was Scholte's angle more than other Seceders'—the dispute was not over doctrine so much as authority: were church creeds or church hierarchy determinative? With the coercive power of the state available to one side, the disputation did not remain entirely theoretical. Certainly there was irony in the fact that the side purporting to favor the Enlightenment was the side capable of and willing to use the coercive power of the state.

The strategy of each side was simple and neither was effective: Scholte would hold an unauthorized service, and the state would haul him off to jail. But difficulties in maintaining the standoff on the part of the jailed party did become wearing. After multiple jail terms, the dissidents recognized the superior resources of the state and chose the alternate strategy of emigration. Departing to America also had the benefit of escaping economic depression in the Netherlands. In hindsight, Scholte said he foresaw the impending revolutions of 1848: both liberals and conservatives he equated with Babel. America was the new Eden.[11]

By the time Scholte's party arrived in the New World in 1847, many of their countrypeople had already settled in Michigan (and others had lived in New Netherlands for centuries). But Scholte's group opted for the frontier, founding the Iowa town of Pella, named after the early Christian city of refuge.[12] Scholte immediately saw the advantages of religious disestablishment and declared his intention to become a citizen. He and the other original settlers took the oath of allegiance in Dutch, because they had not yet learned English.[13]

Curiously, Scholte's later career was marked more by his business acumen and political advocacy than by his religious leadership. His

---

10. Robinson, *Givenness of Things*, 192.

11. *Iowa Letters*, 229–29.

12. On their way to what became Pella, rearguard Mormons offered to sell them Nauvoo, but they did not come to terms. *Iowa Letters*, 47; Lucas, *Netherlanders in America*, 171.

13. Lucas, *Netherlanders in America*, 191–92.

pastorate of the Reformed congregation was short-lived; he was voted out by the membership, an indication of his continuing contentiousness.[14] Moreover, in ceding land for a college in Pella, he snubbed the Dutch Reformed and instead invited in the Baptists, whom he admired for advocating separation of church and state. Only in the early twentieth century would Central College yield to demographic realities and become a (Dutch) Reformed Church institution.[15]

Scholte continued, sometimes reluctantly, preaching at the Pella Christian Church (not to be confused with the Cambellites). His preaching skills were universally acknowledged, but his increasing premillennialism disturbed some. (Whether Scholte was directly influenced by Millerites is unclear.) While most within the Reformed tradition sought to infuse society with Christian values, Scholte's theology counseled withdrawal from society, anticipating an imminent and apocalyptic end to the world.[16] This theology directly contradicted his day-to-day priorities of political involvement and wealth accumulation.[17]

As the immigrant Dutch expanded around Pella, the available land nearby proved insufficient. Henry Hospers led the transplanting of many Pella Dutch to northwestern Iowa in 1869.[18] Northwestern College was founded as an academy in Orange City in 1882.[19] In what would become the most conservative area in the state, the major conservative split from the Reformed Church in America, the Christian Reformed Church, took

---

14. By 1849, some Pella residents were calling him the "Pope of Pella." This was not meant as a compliment. His erstwhile ally in the Netherlands, Van Raalte, traveled from Michigan to organize a Reformed Church in Pella. *Iowa Letters*, 208–9, 278, 347–48, 418, 460, 461, 463, 469; Swearinga, "Van Raalte and Scholte," 21–33. But some still loved Scholte (deJong, *Iowa Letters*, 370–71), and some were mystified by him (Bosquet-Chabot, *Iowa Letters*, 376–77). Scholte actually contemplated returning to the Netherlands, but his real estate holdings entangled him. *Iowa Letters*, 434.

Part of the controversy concerned property; Scholte had retained the deed to the property the church building was on, and since it was on the town square, it seemed valuable and he wanted to sell it. Kooi, "Elusive Peace in Pella," 35–38; see also Huizenga, "Pella, Iowa," 18.

15. McMillan, "Central College."

16. *Iowa Letters*, 229.

17. For a look at Iowa Reformed theology after Scholte, see Heideman, *Practice of Piety*.

18. Klumpp, "Colony before Party," 1–34; Niewenhuis, "New Colony," 182–93.

19. Kennedy, "Northwestern College," *Origins* 19, 39–46; DeJong, *From Strength to Strength*.

root, forming the Classis Iowa in 1877. Only somewhat later, in the fifties, was Dordt College founded in Sioux Center.[20]

Novelist Frederick Manfred has portrayed the area, sometimes with a jaundiced eye about religion, in his Siouxland works.[21] But the heavily Calvinist ethos had an effect on him. In this scene from *Green Earth*, the pious mother is trying to jury rig a church service in the farmhouse parlor:

> Ma decided to hold church anyway. It would be just with their own family ...
>
> Ma went out to where Grampa sat on the cistern head. "We should be very pleased if you'd join us in worship, Pa." She gave one of those smiles that was hard to turn down ...
>
> "Now, Ada, you know I don't hold much with that autocratic institution, the church, where one man does all the ordering around and the rest of us have to just sit there and take it."
>
> "I know you don't. But this will be a family service in which all members of the family can participate." ...
>
> "Daughter, I'm a socialist. The exact opposite of what your minister believes in."
>
> "Why don't we discuss this in our service in the parlor?" ...
>
> "All right, daughter. I'll give in a little, seeing it's Sunday. Let's go into your parlor if talk religion we must."[22]

Grampa probably would have preferred discussing religion with Abner Kneeland.

SALUBRIA

Abner Kneeland was born a Baptist in Revolutionary-era New England. In early adulthood he became a Universalist, a denomination with roots in the rural North, and for three decades was a prominent minister, writing a quarter of the Universalist hymnal. In his fifties, though, he had

---

20. Schaap, *Our Family Album*, 183. A classis is the Reformed version of the Presbyterian presbytery, Methodist district, or Catholic diocese. Iowa pastor John Vander Ploeg would assume editorship of the denominational newspaper *The Banner* in the fifties. Bratt, *Dutch Calvinism in Modern America*, 154.

21. For a map showing the actual and fictionalized placenames of Siouxland, see Manfred, *Daughter Remembers*, xiv. On Manfred, see Schaap, "Frederick Manfred," 4–15.

22. Manfred, *Frederick Manfred Reader*, ed. Rezmerski, 292–93.

a crisis of faith[23] and decided that even that liberal group was too confining. He thereupon preached a pantheism that glorified all of nature as God and, as was customary, wrote pamphlets denouncing religious doctrine he disagreed with, publishing "Universalist God."

In mid-twentieth century the Universalists would merge with their more urban counterparts the Unitarians, but even in the nineteenth century they had much in common. In Massachusetts, Unitarians were working within the established Congregational Church and had taken control of many Congregationalist parishes. But Unitarians' victories were tentative and complicated when in 1833 Massachusetts disestablished religion, the last state to do so.

Orthodox Congregationalists argued that Unitarian doctrines would inevitably lead away from Christianity, to pantheism and atheism; Unitarians (at the time) were at pains to deny that such a slippery slope existed.

In this milieu, Kneeland's attack on Universalism seemed confirmation of the orthodox accusation. Using the state apparatus still available to them, Unitarians had Kneeland arrested for the crime of blasphemy. One modern biographer (who apparently had never heard of Pakistan) entitled his book *The Last Man Jailed For Blasphemy.*[24]

A complicated five-year-long legal process ensued, with the first three trials ending inconclusively. In the last trial, Kneeland defended himself. Henry Steele Commager, the scholar who looked most closely at the trials, concluded that the self-taught Kneeland "knew enough law to argue his own case but not enough to win it."[25]

No public consensus supported the conviction; Transcendentalists like Ralph Waldo Emerson and Theodore Parker condemned it. Kneeland served his two months in jail and then went west with dreams of setting up a utopian community, Salubria. Since it was 1839, he went to Iowa, settling in Van Buren County; while some followers alighted nearby, nothing remotely approaching the successful utopian communities of Icaria or the Amanas bloomed there.

---

23. In 1820 Kneeland had had an earlier bout of skepticism about the nature of revelation, but was coaxed back to Universalist beliefs by Hosea Ballou. Ballou, *Series of Letters.*

24. Papa, *Last Man Jailed For Blasphemy.* In fact, Kneeland was not the last to be arrested for blasphemy in the US, as Leigh Eric Schmidt has documented in *Village Atheist,* chapter 3.

25. Commager, "Blasphemy of Abner Kneeland," 30.

A nearby unsympathetic Congregationalist minister attributed the turning point to a skating tragedy: the sudden deaths of young people supposedly reoriented the hearts of the fledgling community back to a less frivolous and more traditional belief system. Thin ice became a metaphor for inadequate preparation for the hereafter.[26]

The parallel sagas of Scholte and Kneeland both ended with some disappointment. Scholte did not reconstitute the perfect church, nor was he close to a perfect minister himself. The secular worlds of business and politics tugged at him.

Kneeland's dream of creating a pantheistic utopian community fell short; his semi-secular vision seemed swallowed up by the religious forces at work in pioneer Iowa. What these two obstinate characters at opposite ends of a spectrum did share in common was a vision of a society where religious differences could be negotiated rather than legislated and prosecuted. Their sacrifices contributed to the fulfillment of that new concept.

ICARIA

The long-lasting (1854–98) utopian community of Icaria in Adams County is usually classified as secular, but a study of its constitution and other founding documents complicates that designation. Unlike the earlier short-lived Communia, founded by Germans openly hostile to religious practice, at Icaria attending outside religious services was a matter of personal choice. Many Icarians spent part of their Sundays communing with local Methodists.[27]

The Icarians sought to put into practice the thinking of the French utopian Etienne Cabet, who was given to write such speculations as *True Christianity*.[28] The preamble to the "Doctrine on Principles" began with a First Cause:

26. [Gaylord], *Life and Labors of Reuben Gaylord*, 105–7. For other encounters between the orthodox and the "infidels," see Adams, *Iowa Band*, 155–65. As late as 1857, Disciples of Christ Samuel Knight of Farmington complained to the *Millennial Harbinger* that "the sects and parties here are stout with Infidelity, Pantheism, Restorationism[!], and Universalism." Hargis,"History of the Disciples of Christ in Iowa," 99.

27. Smith, "Story of Icaria," 37; Snyder, *Search for Brotherhood*, 6, 18–26.

28. Sutton, *Icarians*, 116–44; Gauthier, *Quest for Utopia*, 109; Nordhoff, *Communistic Societies*, 333–39. A good listing and short description of utopian groups nationwide

NATURE—GOD.—We, Icarian Communists, do not believe that the Universe was the effect of *chance,* and we do like to admit a *first cause* absolutely intelligent and provident, that is called a *Creator, Supreme Being, God, Nature, Providence . . . .*
GOD, PERFECTION.—But we consider *God* as the *pre-eminent* and *all-powerful* One, as the *Infinite* and *Perfection* in all.
. . . We like to consider God as the *Father* of the Human Race; . . . that this better Father has only love for his children and that he loves them all equally.[29]

Before the Icarians came to Adams County, they had sojourned in Nauvoo after the Mormons abandoned the town. The Mormon stay across the Mississippi River, their internal disagreements, and their treks westward had significant repercussions for Iowa, as detailed next.

ZARAHEMLA—AND ITS SCHISMATIC DESCENDANTS

While followers of the controversial Kneeland and Scholte would both find a home in Iowa, another group would severely test the limits of toleration on the western frontier. Before Scholte and Kneeland arrived, in 1839 the followers of Joseph Smith converged just across the Mississippi River from Iowa to a town they renamed Nauvoo and also claimed the western bank as Zarahemla.[30] The resistance that early followers had encountered in Kirtland, Ohio, and Independence, Missouri, had led to a defensive culture. It is tempting to see a pattern in Mormon evictions—which can be seen as either a pattern of persecution or a pattern of backlash to Mormon attempts at domination. There are elements of truth in both generalizations, but nuance is better: Joseph Smith fleeing prosecution for bank fraud in Ohio, and Mormons attacked for not being slaveholders in Missouri, are two very different scenarios.[31]

---

may be found in Albertson, "Survey of Mutualistic Communities," 375–444.

29. Teakle, "History and Constitution," *IJH*, 15, 233, 251–53. There are also numerous references to religion in chapter 1 of the constitution.

30. On Mormons across the river from Nauvoo, see Kimball, "Nauvoo West," 132–42; on Mormon conversion there, see Mulder, "Norwegian Forerunners," 46–61.
Zarahemla was named after a Native American city in *The Book of Mormon*. A schismatic Mormon group, the Heartland Project, has been searching for the archeological remains of this large city and in 2021 thought they had found it near Montrose, Iowa, bizarrely at the same location as its Mormon namesake. Seariac, "Mormon Group Digging."

31. Park, *Kingdom of Nauvoo*, 16–18.

"To Build a House by Eating"

The founder of the Church of the Latter-day Saints, Joseph Smith, was also much given to elaborate church hierarchies, and when his erstwhile best friend John Bennett introduced him to Masonic rites, Smith was enthusiastic. Bennett may also have introduced him to alternative sexual relations, which Smith also embraced, although not publicly.[32]

In retrospect, Smith's enthusiasm for inaugurating new ecclesiastical hierarchies without ending the previous ones would splinter the movement, when questions of succession became suddenly paramount. Brigham Young's followers could argue that the splits were not numerically significant. But since the dissenters generally stayed in the Midwest, the splinter groups contributed to the religious diversity of early Iowa. The consolidation of many of them into the Reorganized Church of the Latter-day Saints (now Community of Christ) ensured a continuing presence in the state.[33]

The paranoia reinforced by hostile neighbors also led to recruiting some unsavory characters; the doctrine that stealing from non-Mormons was not a sin must have been an incentive. The Hodge brothers exemplified that tendency—and its limits.[34] The corollary to the doctrine seemed to be the caution "Don't get caught."

Brigham Young's claim to the mantle of Joseph Smith was not uncontested.[35] Sidney Rigdon, for one, had a solid case for succession. After all, Rigdon was Smith's running mate in his campaign for US president.[36] The Mormon practice of prophetic revelation invited other would-be leaders to get inspired. God seemed to be particularly active in the wake of Smith's martyrdom, and moreover seemed to be making contradictory claims. Young was ruthless and effective in playing Stalin to Joseph Smith's Lenin and consolidated power in Nauvoo, but Nauvoo seemed precarious after

---

32. After breaking up with Smith, Bennett published a tell-all anti-Mormon tract:, *The History of the Saints*. He was responsible for popularizing the tomato nationally. Smith, *Saintly Scoundrel*, 72–77; Currie, *Polk City's Early History*. Currie is particularly good at raising the issue of ambiguity surrounding Bennett.

33. Nauvoo historian Robert Flanders has estimated that about a third of Nauvoo's Mormons stayed in the Midwest, some because of religious reservations and some for economic or domestic reasons. Flanders, *Nauvoo*, 321; Bringhurst and Hamer, *Scattering*, 145.

34. Shepard, "Stealing at Mormon Nauvoo," 99–110. On Upper Mississippi frontier criminality more generally, see Lucke, *Bellevue War*, and Jordan, introduction to Bonney, *Banditti of the Prairies*.

35. Quinn, *passim*.

36. McBride, *Joseph Smith for President*, 2.

Smith's assassination, and Young's great accomplishment was to shepherd most Mormons from Nauvoo to Deseret, now Utah.

Iowans probably get too much credit for their friendliness to the Mormon Trekkers[37] compared to the Mormon reception in Ohio, Missouri, and Illinois. (The initial reception in Quincy, Illinois, had been welcoming, and Iowa territorial governor Robert Lucas also promised asylum before Mormons mostly settled east of the river.)[38] Mormons were only passing through. But the exodus was a major event in southern Iowa in 1846. As Congregational minister William Salter, on his way from Burlington to the Congregationalist state meeting in Farmington (Van Buren County), remembered in the 1880s,

> The spring of forty years ago in this immediate vicinity is also marked by the Mormon exodus from Nauvoo. We saw their camp fires on the edge of the woods by the streams, and met their long wagon-trains.[39]

The trekkers set up Winter Quarters in what is now North Omaha.[40] Southern Iowa is replete with sites that hark back to the Mormon Trail, including Mormon Creek, Garden Grove, Pisgah, and Macedonia.[41] But Nauvoo exiles were not the last Mormons traversing the state; Mormon missionaries to Europe persuaded thousands of converts to immigrate to Deseret. These immigrants usually employed handcarts to travel the vast terrain from Iowa City to the Great Salt Lake before railroads,[42] always with

37. See Morain, "Mormons and Nineteenth Century Iowa Historians." Territorial governor Robert Lucas did invite Mormons to settle in Iowa after their expulsion from Missouri. McKiernan, *Voice of One Crying in the Wilderness*, 104.

38. Park, *Kingdom of Nauvoo*, 17–19.

39. Jordan, "Notes on the Salter-Shackford Correspondence," 415. For a granular look at the local Iowa aspects, see Black and Hartley, *Iowa Mormon Trail*.

40. Bennett, *Mormons at the Missouri*.

41. Hartley, "Mormons and Early Iowa History," 239–46; Dilts, *From Ackley to Zwingle*, 88, 121, 153. Mount Pisgah was a waystation in Union County; Mormons who founded the Harrison County town of Pisgah, instead of proceeding west, appropriated the name. Iowa City also has a major street named Mormon Trek Boulevard, and there is a county park named Mormon Trail in Adair County.

42. Moulton, *Mormon Handcart Migration*; Woods and Atterberg, "1853 Mormon Migration through Keokuk," *AI* 61, 1–23; Petersen, "Mormons on the March," 142–57, 36; DMR, Jun. 22, 2003; Hafen, *Recollections*; Special Commemorative Issue: Mormon Handcart Trek, *AI* 65; Hafen and Hafen, *Handcarts to Zion*.

European Mormon converts continued to traverse Iowa even after the railroads made the journey much easier. Here is one short report: "About 700 Mormons from European countries passed through Ottumwa several days ago." Prairie City News, Jul. 20, 1877.

difficulty and with one major tragedy: at Devil's Gate, a late-starting expedition, misdirected by the Mormon leader, had over two hundred perish.[43]

Some of Joseph Smith's followers opted out of Brigham Young's brand of Mormonism and the arduous trek to Deseret. Particularly controversial was the doctrine of polygamy (Smith had practiced it but not proclaimed it. His first wife, Emma, was particularly adamant about monogamy, refusing to entertain the possibility that her husband had not practiced it.) In Iowa, the Rigdonites in Attica and the Baneemyites and Cutlerites in southwest Iowa were ephemeral but significant presences in the state; most of those who stayed presaged a more united front against the Brighamites.[44]

Sidney Rigdon had been a loyal lieutenant of Joseph Smith since Mormons headquartered in Kirtland, Ohio, in 1830. Originally a restorationist Church of Christ minister, he came to Mormonism seeking ways to live communally. Arguably, in the original hierarchy, he had the inside track to succeed Joseph Smith, but power rather than incumbency prevailed, and Rigdon found himself on the outside.

But he still had followers. While Rigdon retreated to near Pittsburgh, Rigdonites, or Children of Zion who believed that the essence of Smith's message was that they should live communally gathered in Attica, Iowa, to attempt such an experiment from 1865 to 1875. The unique feature of this arrangement was that the leader of the colony lived hundreds of miles away, and when Rigdon made no sense (e.g., "Now we are Mennonites!"), the Children of Zion could ignore him. The refusal of the world to end in 1873 as prophesied complicated things, but the order to pack up and go to Manitoba was obeyed by those continuing to be obedient, and others dispersed.[45]

An even stranger dynamic between leader and followers emerged among the Baneemyites of western Iowa. Charles Thompson was not a very exotic name for a prophet, so he borrowed from the fertile new lexicon of

---

43. Roberts, *Devil's Gate*.

44. Even more ephemeral were the Strangites, who did not settle in Iowa but were active in dissuading some who started the first trek from continuing, and a tiny split from the Hedrickites, based in Lamoni (where of course there was a much larger Josephite presence). See Bringhurst and Hamer, *Scattering*, 138–39.

45. Van Wagoner, *Sidney Rigdon*, 417–21, 443–50. Quinn, *Mormon Hierarchy*, 182–85.

Joseph Smith (also not an exotic name!), and "Baneemy" fit the bill. So did Father Ephraim. The Baneemyites also sought to live communally, founding the Monona County settlement of Preparation in 1854. This utopian experiment did not end well; while all things were to be held in common, according to Thompson's revelations—"in not very good English," the Iowa Supreme Court judged somewhat churlishly—Thompson was the "chief steward of the Lord" who held all the deeds. By 1858 doubts about the wisdom of this policy had grown to such a level that Thompson thought it expedient to leave town; the Iowa Supreme Court did not finally sort out the subsequent property dispute until 1866. The site of the town is now a state park.[46] Preparation was an anticipatory name that did not live up to its advertising.

Alpheus Cutler was a solid figure in the Mormon hierarchy all the way to Winter Quarters. Since the *Book of Mormon* was based on Jesus' appearance to Native Americans, Indian missions had a high priority among early Mormons, and Cutler received permission to remain behind in Kanesville (Council Bluffs) with his followers while the rest of the Mormon contingent continued westward. But his mission to Native Americans on reservations in northeastern Kansas was a failure, and then he and his followers became embroiled in a theological dispute with the High Council in Kanesville and were excommunicated.[47]

The Cutlerites retrenched and founded the town of Manti in Fremont County.

Their ideology was closer to Utah Mormons than other Midwestern Mormon schismatics; Cutler was actually arrested for polygamy in Iowa, and his subsequent renunciation of the practice is not entirely convincing. In the Midwest, though, a lack of distinguishing differences with the Brighamites proved a disadvantage, where those who remained preferred sharper breaks with Utah Mormons.

Underlying most sectarian Mormonism in the Midwest was not a clear vision of a future gathering of the saints but a nostalgia for a lost

---

46. Another schismatic Mormon leader, Lyman Wight, probably had a better claim to the name, but prophecy is difficult to argue with. Quinn, 198, 234, 241; Fulton, "Baneemyism," 17–20; Aumann, "Minor Prophet in Iowa," 253–60; the Iowa Supreme Court decision *Scott v. Thompson 21 Iowa 799–603*; Bringhurst and Hamer, *Scattering*, 141–60.

47. Quinn, *Mormon Hierarchy*, 203–9; Jorgensen, "Scattered Saints of Southwestern Iowa," *John Whitmer Historical Association Journal* 13, 80–97; Jorgensen, "Back to Zion," 161–76; Bringhurst and Hamer, *Scattering*, 177–89.

Nauvoo.[48] This eventually melded most Midwestern Mormons into the Reorganized Latter-day Saints, also called Josephites, made possible when the martyred leader's son, Joseph Smith III, acquiesced to lead a united front against Utah Mormons.

Somewhat oddly for a movement founded on revelation, the RLDS touted its direct descendants of Joseph Smith as RLDS leaders. But the argument for lineal descent did tamp down claims of rival revelations.

Early Reorganized history was characterized by a tension between activists eager to reestablish the communitarian side of Mormonism and its leader, Joseph Smith III, who, wary of previous failures, wanted to go slow on building utopias and spiritualize the concept. In 1870, he did allow the founding of a joint stock company to purchase real estate, the Order of Enoch. Leaders found the ideal site for affordable land in Decatur County, naming the settlement Lamoni after a king in the Book of Mormon.

Smith was pleased enough with the progress of Lamoni to move the RLDS headquarters there from Plano, Illinois in 1880. But by 1890, the restless Smith moved the church headquarters again, this time to Independence, Missouri, featured in the Latter-day Saint belief system as Eden. Lamoni remained an RLDS stronghold: the Reorganized Church founded Graceland College there in 1895, and Decatur County may still be the only county in the country with a Community of Christ plurality, although probably its claim has been supplanted by the Amish.[49]

MORE RELIGIOUS REASONS TO COME TO IOWA

A few other instances of religious motivation for the settlement of the state can be found. (We will discuss many of the German ones in the next chapter, and the German Lutheran and Roman Catholic attempts at colonization in chapter 5.)

---

48. Alma Blair locates the nostalgia even further back, to Missouri or Ohio, before temple rituals became a prominent feature of Mormonism. Blair, "Reorganized Church," in Blair, et al., *Restoration Movement*, 309–10.

49. Launius, "Mormon Quest For a Perfect Society," 325–42; Gaustad, *Atlas*, 235; "William Wallace Blair," BDI, 45–46.

St. Ansgar

Claus Laurits Clausen, a Danish-born pastor in Luther Valley, Wisconsin, combined religious and economic motives on his 1848, 1850, and 1852 expeditions to Minnesota and Iowa, seeking Norwegian Lutherans and fertile land.[50] Clausen's motives were pastoral: he saw the needy condition of his farming congregants and sought better farmland. While searching, he probably conducted the first Norwegian Lutheran service west of the Mississippi in Winneshiek County in 1852.

Along the Big Cedar River, in what is now Mitchell County, Rev. Clausen found the best prospects for a town site. He subsequently organized a wagon train of about seventy-five Norwegian Lutherans from southern Wisconsin to northern Iowa in the spring of 1853 and named the town after the Christian missionary to Scandinavia, St. Ansgar. The Saint Ansgar Chamber of Commerce boasts it is the only town in the world so named.[51] St. Ansgar subsequently hosted the founding meeting of the Norwegian-Danish Evangelical Lutheran Church (also known as "The Conference") in 1870.[52]

Like many immigrants and town founders, Clausen was a restless and multi-faceted character. We will encounter him again in chapter 7 as a Civil War chaplain and as a participant in theological battles within Norwegian-American Lutheranism around slavery. He was also a journalist, a state legislator, a commissioner of immigration, and would-be founder of a second town composed of Danish-Americans in Virginia. When that project failed, he returned to the Midwest, serving a pastorate near Iowa in Blooming Prairie, Minnesota.[53]

---

50. Prominent Swedish author Fredrika Bremer visited Wisconsin and Minnesota during Clausen's explorations and references them. Bremer, *America of the Fifties*, 225, 236. Both Bremer County and the Bremer County town of Fredericka are named in her honor, though the only Iowa towns she mentions are Guttenberg, Dubuque, and Keokuk, as she descended the Mississippi.

51. Swansen, *Founder of St. Ansgar*, 103–18; Bohach, "Settlement of St. Ansgar," 46, 296–97; Nelson and Fevold, *Lutheran Church Among Norwegian-Americans*, chapter 7; Qualey, "Claus L. Clausen," 12–29; Chamber of Commerce, St. Ansgar; Dilts, *From Ackley to Zwingle*, 166; Dykstra, *Bright Radical Star*, 181; Colton, "Coming of the Norwegians to Iowa," 381–82; Clyde and Dwelle, *History of Mitchell and Worth Counties*.

52. Swansen, *Founder of St. Ansgar*, 182; Lagerquist, *Lutherans*, 171–72; Nichol, "United Norwegian (1890)," 170.

53. Qualey, "Claus L. Clausen," 16–17.

"To Build a House by Eating"

Humboldt

While the tale of the founding of Lake Wobegon by Unitarian missionaries is fictional, Humboldt was actually founded by Unitarians. Stephen Taft founded Springvale in 1863, later changing the name to honor the German naturalist. He envisioned a community of culture and refinement, with no intoxicating beverages permitted. His goals for a college were also lofty. But Humboldt College limped along financially, succumbing in 1916. Nor did the Unitarian Church survive; by 1972, when hometown boy Harry Reasoner returned to do a television network documentary in Humboldt, there were seven churches, but the Unitarian was not among them. Taft himself, like so many early twentieth-century Iowans, moved on to Southern California.[54]

Stavanger

Norwegian prisoners of war who were taken to London during the Napoleonic Wars were befriended by Quakers, as part of their ministry to prisons, and the grateful captives transplanted Quakerism to Norway after their release. But the established Lutheran Church in Norway frowned on religious dissent. The first Norwegian Quakers sought asylum in this country in 1825, first reaching Iowa in 1840, where they settled in Lee County (and some were converted to Mormonism).[55]

In the 1850s most of the tiny Quaker community remaining in Norway resettled in Iowa, first around Stavanger in Marshall County and later to Paulina and Primghar in O'Brien County.[56] Of course, these Norwegians were not alone among their countrypeople—only Irish had a higher emigration rate to the United States, and economic hardship also factored into their emigration—but the collective decision to settle in Iowa was certainly a religious one and further complicated the story

---

54. Taft, *Empire Builder*. The seven remaining churches were Methodist, Catholic, Congregational, Baptist, two Lutheran, and Seventh-Day Adventist. See also Reasoner and Rooney, *Small Town in Iowa*, ABC News, 1972; Gregurich, "Old College Try," *The Iowan* 69:6, 50–53; Humboldt Co. Historical Museum (humboldtcohm.org).

For a twentieth century sermon preached at Unity Church in Humboldt, see Williams, "Who Is My Neighbor?"

55. Jones, *Quakers of Iowa*, 175–76.

56. Tjossem, *Quaker Sloopers*; Aarek, "Short History of the Troms Quakers," 130–31.

of a small but influential religious minority, Iowa Friends.[57] (For more on Iowa Quakers, see chapters 7 and 8.)

Matthias, Perhaps

The collapse of the messianic Kingdom of Matthias took place in New York in 1834, but rumors of Matthias's appearance in the wilds of Iowa tentatively add still another stratum to the layers of religious diversity in early Iowa. Iowa was the frontier, then a place where an ex-messiah could reinvent himself.[58]

THE NECESSITY OF COOPERATION

The circumstances of settlement fostered a culture of cooperation, often out of necessity, which in turn offered the opportunity for dialog and sometimes, mutual respect. Neighborliness was not just a biblical injunction; it might be necessary for survival. Dutch immigrant Dietrich Budde of rural Burlington described it this way, as he was awaiting the purchase of his farm:

> Most of the time Jan [his son] is out there in the country with the farmers who are ready to instruct us about all kinds of things, and who offer us a helping hand in moving our things from here . . . They are interested in having good neighbors, for farmers help each other. If your horses have gone off into the woods, you just take some of your neighbor's and ride off to the city. If someone wants to live entirely for himself, he is left to his own devices by his neighbors; and when he cannot make it, he finally has to give up his place.[59]

The 1850s brought two communal settlements to the Iowa River. The Amana colonies we will discuss in the next chapter, on dissenting Germans. The other group featured a return: in 1856, many of the Meskwakis, cash in hand and upon receiving permission from state government, returned to Iowa from their reservation in Kansas and resettled

---

57. Hamm, "Divergent Paths of Iowa Quakerism," 125–50; Marsh, *Lively Faith*, chapter 1; Jones, *Quakers of Iowa*, 175–83.

58. Johnson and Wilentz, *Kingdom of Matthias*, 177, 220.

59. Gjerde, *Minds of the West*, 107–31; *Iowa Letters*, 73; Reschly, *Amish on the Iowa Prairie*, 11.

communally. A few Meskwakis had not even left the state, living in river valleys and occasionally interacting, benignly, with white settlers. The settlement—Meskwakis correctly and vociferously dispute the characterization "reservation"—was crucial in preserving traditional Meskwaki religion, though of course not without a series of struggles.[60]

The stories and presence of religious minorities had a leavening influence in the state, helping to ensure that the competition for religious dominance in Iowa would be unsuccessful and suggesting a rationale for why that outcome might be a boon.

Religious minorities also complicate most generalizations that can be made about Iowa religion. Certainly other factors figured into the ethos of pluralism, but negotiating neighborliness among multiple religious identities played a significant part.[61]

---

60. Zimmer, "Settlement Sovereignty."
61. Douglas, "Making Iowa Safe for Differences," 2.

CHAPTER 4

German Dissent and Iowa Diversity

"When we arrived in Davenport . . . in 1852 . . . this city had a population of thirty-five hundred. It must have been a model town then because it boasted of nine ministers and only two lawyers."

—August Ficke[1]

THE AMERICAN HOME MISSIONARY Society's man in Dubuque ended a stormy pastorate at the German Congregational Church—he blamed German "rationalists and Catholics," although it's unlikely that either was in his congregation, or wanted to be—and was reassigned to take a survey of Germans in Iowa and their religious preferences. Jean Baptiste Madoulet, who despite his French-sounding name was from the Rhineland,[2] spent much of 1850 and 1851 traversing the two easternmost tiers of Iowa counties, finding pockets of Germans in every county. A description of his report to the Society evokes a dizzying array of

---

1. Ficke, *Memories of Fourscore Years*, 47. Ficke, the youngest of eight, was two when he and his family emigrated from Mecklenburg. He became a Davenport lawyer.

2. In 1852 Madoulet was called to be the first pastor of the Dutch Reformed Church in Burlington, under the auspices of the Reformed Church mission board. A layman there thought Nijmegen in the Netherlands was his hometown, but that is very close to the Rhine. At any rate, he seems to have been fluent in Dutch as well as German. (By 1854, he was asked to leave because "the family of the minister does not conduct itself in a Christian manner.") Dietrich Budde, *Iowa Letters*, 374, 393.

denominations[3] and beliefs and non-beliefs, documenting the diversity of German immigrants:

> Among those mentioned are indifferentists, radicalists, rationalists or "Freemans," "new" Mennonites,[4] Roman Catholics, "united brethren in Christ,"[5] "Albrechelents,"[6] Methodists, those who followed "Swedenborg and call themselves the new Jerusalem," the followers of "Rev. I. Weinbrenner" who are known as the Church of God,[7] Lutherans, Evangelical Lutherans,[8] and those who professed a branch of rationalism called "Christ-Platonism."[9] It made little difference to the Missionary what religion was followed, . . . if it were not . . . Congregational or Presbyterian (N.S.)[10] . . . He even had his doubts about the Old School Presbyterians having a clear road to heaven![11]

Since Germany did not exist as a nation-state before 1871, and since each principality selected its own established church (which might change with the ruler), there is a sense in which all religious groups were dissenters in one part of Germany or another. But we will deal with

---

3. Cf. the shorter but still long list of denominations in Iowa by 1846 in Kuhns, "Religion on the Iowa Frontier to 1846," 51, 52–53.

4. The first congregation of General Conference Mennonites was formed in Lee County, Iowa in 1853; later most GC Mennonites were Russian(-German) emigrants who settled in the Plains States. Perhaps this is what Madoulet is referring to. See Schlabach, *Peace, Faith, Nation,* 43, 127–28.

5. A Methodist group. On German Methodists, see Behney and Eller, *History of the Evangelical Brethren Church,* and "Merging the Streams" special issue, *MH* 57.

6. Another Methodist group; on Jacob Albrecht (also anglicized as Albright), see Draper, "Jacob Albrecht."

7. The Churches of God General Conference (Winebrenner) is a revivalistic split from the German Reformed Church. It has also been characterized as restorationist: Olson, et al., *Handbook of Denominations,* 251–52. In 2019 there were seven congregations in Iowa, the majority in the southeastern corner of the state. Churches of God General Conference (www.cggc.org).

8. Probably the (German) Evangelical Church, which drew from both Lutheran and Reformed.

9. There is a long, and some would say fruitful, dialog between Christianity and Platonism, but I was probably at least as startled as Madoulet to find it on the Iowa frontier, and I have not tracked down its meaning in the early Iowa context.

10. On the twenty-five year long split between New School and Old School Presbyterians, see Marsden, *Evangelical Mind.* While the split could be characterized as an argument between evangelical and scholastic Calvinism on how little difference it often made at the congregational level, see Ellis Parker Butler's novel about a minister in Muscatine, *Dominie Dean.*

11. Fox, *German Presbyterians in the Upper Mississippi Valley,* 26–27, chapter 5.

Catholics and established Lutherans in chapter five. Dissenters may not have been primarily motivated by religion to emigrate, but it added incentive. For example, Jews were twice as likely as gentiles to leave Bavaria for the United States.[12]

Many of German stock who moved to Iowa were already generations removed from Germany. The precedent of Pennsylvania in the eighteenth century provides a parallel for German religious development in Iowa in the nineteenth. Many groups traced their arrival in the New World to eighteenth-century Pennsylvania, when Quaker proprietor William Penn actively recruited German dissidents: Mennonites and Amish, German Dunkard Baptists (now Church of the Brethren), and Moravians. Many of them followed the frontier, with generations stopping in Ohio, Indiana, and Illinois, and some eventually pressing on to Iowa. Pennsylvania was not the only colony that practiced toleration, but it was the most pluralistic, thanks to the large-scale influx of German dissenters.[13]

German dissenters usually were influenced by Continental Pietism.[14] European Pietism can be viewed in broad brush as a reaction against the seventeenth-century politicization of religion, as Protestant and Catholic forces battled, most notoriously in the devastating Thirty Years' War. While mostly a Protestant phenomenon (it did have Catholic parallels), Pietism can also be seen as a combination of the elevation of the individual conscience in Protestantism with an older dedication to devotion from Catholicism. As Franklin Littell has pointed out, while inward-looking it was not necessarily individualistic; some radical Pietists such as the Inspirationists embraced the concept of intentional community.[15]

---

12. Rabin, *Jews on the Frontier*, 15.

13. See Schwartz, "*Mixed Multitude*"; Longenecker, *Piety and Tolerance*; Rothermund, *Layman's Progress*. For the pushback to tolerance, religious and racial, see Murphy, *Conscience and Community*, chapter 5; Kenny, *Peaceable Kingdom Lost*. Pennsylvania was not the only colony that found itself moving toward a pluralist society. See Jacobsen, *Unprov'd Experiment*. For Puritans' eventual grudging acceptance of other views, see Chu, *Neighbors, Friends, or Madmen*.

14. Stoeffler, *Continental Pietism*. For a judicious summary of pietism as it related to some Iowa groups, see Reschly, *Amish on the Iowa Prairie*, 17–21.

15. Stoeffler, *Continental Pietism*, 175–79.

INSPIRATIONISTS

No group embodied Pietism's potentially radical impulses more than the Community of True Inspiration,[16] which settled in Iowa County in 1855.[17] As a communal group, the Community of True Inspiration exists as a denomination only in Iowa.

Inspirationists began to be persecuted for not adhering to state-sanctioned religion in the 1820s and in response withdrew into safe territory and lived communally. Their leader, carpenter Christian Metz, with the authority of an inspired prophet and cognizant of the economic reality of drought beleaguering the community, had a vision of a New World. The Community immigrated *en masse* to near Buffalo, New York in 1843.

Perhaps a little too near Buffalo. Metz had problems with some members' entanglements with the large German population in the big city and sought a safer space.[18] Land along the Iowa River in Iowa County seemed the solution, and the Song of Solomon provided the name: Amana. In 1855 the Inspirationists of Ebenezer, New York, became the Inspirationists of the Amana Colonies, Iowa.

Why is the Amana Colony such a tourist attraction? Certainly the misapprehension that they are Amish and their proximity to the interstate are factors. Their material production is another. But perhaps the need for envisioning community and Amana's relative success in finding that has also been a draw. The contrast with the Amish is also a possibility: the communal willingness to accept aspects of modernity seems reassuring.

In fact, the Community of True Inspiration's eighty-year successful experiment in communal living in Iowa County is remarkable. And that the afterglow has existed even longer is also remarkable.

FREETHINKERS

The Inspirationists were not the only ones who chafed under oppressive rule in Europe. In 1848 the contradictions between Enlightenment

---

16. For the Community of True Inspiration in its European context, see Littell, 176; Schwartz, *French Prophets*; Garrett, *Origins of the Shakers*, chapter 3; and Schnieder, *German Radical Pietism*, 118–24. The Shakers would continue a dialogue with Amana in the US: Schnieder, *German Radical Pietism*, 262.

17. The best introduction to the Amanas is Hoehnle, *Amana People*.

18. On Buffalo's early unsavory reputation, see Senik, *Man of Iron*, 26–27. On the Inspirationists' struggle with worldliness, see Hagen, *Worldly Game*.

and revolutionary ideas and the authoritarian political reality in Europe collided as agitators like Marx and Engels had predicted, although the immediate outcome did not support their optimism. Every country in Europe except the most liberal (England) and the most reactionary (Russia) experienced a revolutionary upsurge of democratic demands. (Adding to the combustibility in many places, these demands were also nationalistic, sometimes unifying and sometimes secessionist.) When the revolutions failed, the most logical place for exile was a democracy; with its open borders and democratic traditions, the United States beckoned.[19] And Iowa, a free state just opening up, was an obvious choice.

The exiled 1848'ers tended to be Freethinkers in religion; for example, the Schleswig-Holstein radicals settled in Davenport,[20] many of the Bohemians and other Czechs in Cedar Rapids,[21] and Swiss Communists briefly established utopian communities in Clayton and Allamakee counties,[22] as did Hungarians in New Buda in Decatur County.[23]

According to one congregational history, Cedar Rapids Czechs in the 1860s "were led by atheists . . . Fanatic atheists roamed among the Czechs in Cedar Rapids preaching mostly concerning the denial of Christianity and claimed the expedient plan would go back to the Greek culture. For this reason the Cedar Rapids Czech community came to be known as the Czech Athens."[24]

But while European immigrant Freethinkers were generally anti-clerical and abjured organized religion, even someone as radical as the European revolutionary in exile William Weitling believed that some form of religion was necessary for the proper functioning of society. Weitling, who became the dominant figure in Communia, was also wont

---

19. Paradoxically, religious dissenters who saw the 1848 revolutions as God's judgment on Europe also saw America as deliverance. See, e.g., Dutch Reformed member Christina Bunde-Stomp, *Iowa Letters*, 305.

20. Johnson, "German Forty-Eighters in Davenport"; Passet, "Yours For Liberty"; Roba, "Einwanderung"; Noe, *Playwrights*, 36–37. German immigrants to Tama County also had an anti-clerical streak. Martin, "History of Salem Church," 11, 58.

21. Spinka, "Francis Kun," 120–21; Stelcik, *History of the Hus Memorial Presbyterian Church*, 4, 7. The most comprehensive survey of Cedar Rapids Freethinkers is in Griffith, "Czechs in Cedar Rapids (Part 2)."

22. Armstrong, "Utopians in Clayton County, Iowa."

23. Vassady, "New Buda."

24. Stelcik, *Hus Memorial*, 7.

to argue for the need for a "new Messiah." Few doubted who the prime candidate for that position would be.[25]

Another early and ephemeral group, the Fourierists of Mahaska County, drew the attention of the devout for deviating from religious norms. The Iowa Pioneer Phalanx invited Congregationalist minister Benjamin Spaulding to conduct a worship service, as would a Cumberland Presbyterian minister. But Spaulding found the turnout disappointing.[26]

Such groups, along with Abner Kneeland's homegrown pantheist commune in Salubria, presented a clear threat to orthodox religion (of whatever variety) and if contemporary accounts by the orthodox are to be believed, a loud one. However, their very anti-institutionalism made continuity a challenge; by the turn of the twentieth century, their descendants' relative reluctance to join churches was an unremarkable distinction.[27]

MISSOURI SYNOD LUTHERANS

Some German Lutherans did not come from the established church. A Saxon free church, much like Scholte in the Netherlands dissenting from the liberal drift in state churches that were influenced by theologians like Schleiermacher, emigrated to Missouri in 1839.[28] The earliest Missouri Synod foray into Iowa by Frederick Lochner in 1848 did not go so well:

> About 200 German Lutherans were then living in [Dubuque,] but Lochner found that they were steeped in rationalism . . . At Burlington he was referred to an Evangelical pastor . . . [who] took one look at his credentials and commented, "Any bum travelling through the country could forge such credentials."
>
> Lochner was distressed to see again and again how many of his fellow countrymen had joined the German Methodists . . . In his report, Lochner asked, 'How long will it be before the few remaining German Lutherans will also fall before their reaping armies?'[29]

25. Wittke, *Utopian Communist*, 69, 73–77.

26. Jordan, "Iowa Pioneer Phalanx."

27. Ficke, *Fourscore Years*, 104–6, 120. Cf. Murray and Fiske, *Bonnie Iowa Farm Folk*, 94.

28. Todd, *Authority Vested*. On their steadfast opposition to cooperation with other Protestants, see Hawley, "Communistic Swedenborgian Colony in Iowa," 7–8; Hawley, "New Church in Iowa," 195.

29. Suelflow, *Heart of Missouri*, 52–53. The Evangelical minister's concern was not without substantive evidence; a Dr. von Kropf, claiming to have been the court

The People Are Kind

The first Missouri Synod congregation in the state was in Maxfield, near Denver in Bremer County. Synod historian L. C. Wuerffel claimed it is not certain what happened to the Maxfield congregation. In the only official history of the Iowa Synod (since 1930 a part of the American Lutheran Church) the following is reported: 'The congregation at Maxfield . . . had formerly been served by a pastor of the Missouri Synod.'[30] It should be clear to everyone but Wuerffel what happened. Not until 1879 did the Lutheran Church-Missouri Synod, meeting in Ft. Dodge, organize statewide.[31] But some Lutherans managed to keep standing before Methodists' "reaping armies." Both Lochner's foray into Iowa and Wuerffel's account of the Maxfield congregation suggest that the Missouri Synod in Iowa prospered not by direct immigration of Free Church Lutherans but by locating unchurched Lutherans already in the state.

LCMS's wariness toward other denominations began early. Consider this account from Iowa City in 1849:

> [I was] directed to a widow whom I promptly looked up. This lady eyed me somewhat suspiciously and told me of her sad experiences with vagabond preachers . . . but as I continued talking with her and offered her catechisms and other literature, she learned to trust me. She complained that as a Lutheran she had been without pastoral care for a long time, since there was no hope that an orthodox pastor would ever come to Iowa City; frequently her desire for attending a service was so strong that she went to the Methodist church service because she could not have anything better . . . I advised her against attending these Methodist services and pointed her under these exigencies to the blessings of private devotions.[32]

---

preacher for the Prince of Hesse, appeared in German Creek in Keokuk County. He shifted his name and story as necessary when in Burlington. Carl Schneider, 200. Mark Twain's *Huckleberry Finn* also comes to mind, on Mississippi Valley residents' credulity of European claims. See also Hoek, *Pilgrim Colony*, 41.

The problem of fraudulent credentials continued into the 1870s, as the Des Moines Presbytery removed a minister too fond of Hostetter's Bitters who turned out also to have forged papers. Newton *Free Press and Republican*, Dec. 9, 1874.

30. Wuerffel, "Lutheran Church—Missouri Synod," 328.
31. Suelflow, *Heart of Missouri*, 55.
32. Meyer, *Moving Frontiers*, 196.

REFORMED

German Calvinists brought two denominations with them that were sometimes established in parts of Germany, Evangelical and Reformed, who merged in 1934 (and again with Congregational Christians in 1957 to form the United Church of Christ). The Evangelicals represented a truce back in Germany between Lutherans and Calvinists in the competition for establishment, granting both entities that privilege in a particular principality. The founding of the first German Evangelical Church in the state, in Burlington in 1843, has been framed as a conflict between High and Low Germans, and also between rationalism and orthodoxy. Evangelicals represented the former tendencies.[33]

Joseph Rieger presided over the first German Reformed communion in Bloomington (Muscatine) in 1843. In 1851, a Reformed Church was founded in Harmony in Dubuque County. The town later became Zwingle, after the Swiss Reformer.[34] Theodore Dresel of Burlington, sent from Basel to be a missionary to the Osage, set out to find Germans in Iowa, Wisconsin, and Illinois in 1854. Like his Missouri Synod Lutheran and German Congregational colleagues, he mostly found Freethinkers and Methodists; when he did find German Evangelicals, they resented not being contacted earlier. The name for some German Methodists, the Evangelical Association, increased the confusion. But he did succeed in eastern Keokuk County; settlers around Sigourney and along German and Dutch Creeks were receptive.[35] The German Evangelical Church in Des Moines was founded in July 1859.[36]

CONGREGATIONALISTS

Major American-based denominations also began outreach to German immigrants.

---

33. Schneider, *German Church on the American Frontier*, 189–91. For glimpses into its early congregational life, see Dietrich Budde in *Iowa Letters*, 82–83; Christina Budde-Stomp, 358.

34. DMR, Nov. 27, 2016.

35. Schneider, 426–27; Kuhns, "Evangelical and Reformed Church in Iowa," 174. See also Fridli, "Winning of the West," in *History of the Evangelical and Reformed Church*, 120, for a good short account of the founding of the church in Storm Lake in 1869.

36. Des Moines *Leader*, Jul. 2, 1899.

"The state of Iowa is the cradle of German Congregationalism in the United States," adjudged one historian.[37] The earliest German Congregationalist church still in existence in the country was founded in Sherrill, northeastern Dubuque County, in 1849[38]—or more precisely, the earliest German Congregational church in existence that is still Congregational. Peter Fleury of the American Home Missionary Society organized the church; earlier he had organized congregations in Garnavillo, no longer in existence, and in Dubuque, which soon became Presbyterian.[39]

Iowa also had the first state association of German Congregationalists, in 1862.[40] In 1864, this association became a "minor association" within the Iowa General Association of Congregationalists (along with a Welsh association) but not without debate centering on jurisdictional concerns. The resolution as passed clarified that yearly statistics would not count Germans twice.[41]

In 1894 German Congregationalists moved their college from Nebraska to Wilton, Iowa; a decade later it merged and moved again to South Dakota.[42] While the American Home Missionary Society was able to recruit some German-speaking pastors from Pietist strongholds in Germany and Switzerland, Congregationalism remained alien to most German-Iowan Protestants. The American evangelical insistence on personal conversion seemed strange to Germans raised in state churches that stressed Word and sacraments as the means of grace.[43]

PRESBYTERIANS

Adrien Van Vliet was the third to pastor the German Congregational Church in Dubuque, after founder Peter Fleury and contentious brawler Jean Baptiste Madoulet. Van Vliet brought a needed maturity and calm to the congregation. A Hollander, he had been a Seceder—but did not succeed as a sectarian. Perhaps what he learned from that experience was

37. Eisenach, *History of the German Congregational Churches*, 1.

38. Zikmund, *Hidden Histories*, 179.

39. Fox, *German Presbyterianism in the Upper Mississippi Valley*, chapter 4. I am using Chrystal's spelling, "Fleury," rather than Fox's "Flury" or Eisenach's "Fluery."

40. Zikmund, *Hidden Histories*, 74.

41. *Minutes . . . Grinnell*, 3, 5; *Minutes, 1863*, 6; Eisenach, *History of the German Congregational Churches*, 19; Christensen, "Denmark," 132–33.

42. Zikmund, *Hidden Histories*, 76.

43. Zikmund, *Hidden Histories*, 65–66.

that determining a congregation's identity was a sensitive project, better achieved by consensus than unilateral proclamation.

Van Vliet emigrated to America and joined a Dutch Reformed Church in New York City, the Second Presbyterian Church in St. Louis, and then the Congregational Church in Platteville, Wisconsin, where they encouraged him to become a minister. Taking over the congregation in Dubuque, he defused the situation Madoulet left him but still faced a doctrinal crisis. He convinced the mostly Swiss congregation, after a struggle, that they were really Presbyterian, writing an apologetic letter to the mostly Congregationalist AHMS to that effect.[44]

Van Vliet began training German-speaking students to become Presbyterian ministers; eventually the school run out of his house became the University of Dubuque Theological Seminary. Most of his students had to gather German immigrants into new congregations. These German-speaking Presbyterians coalesced into an unofficial convention in 1862, but not until 1906 were they denominationally recognized as a non-geographical entity, the Synod of the West. In 1912 the seven-state synod met for the first time in Nora Springs in Floyd County. Lyon and Grundy Counties were strongholds, and the University of Dubuque anchored the synod.[45]

Much of the German Presbyterian strength in Iowa was Frisian. Friesland was a nation split between Netherlands and Germany but united by a language, Frisian, and an early avowal of Calvinism.[46] While the Dutch Reformed and German Reformed Churches in America seemed natural homes for Dutch and German Frisians, the Presbyterians offered them a relative autonomy. The Presbyterian emphasis on doctrine was a good fit, but Frisians additionally sternly monitored their ministers to ensure that their sermons were biblically based. East Frisians navigated three languages: Frisian at home, English in the outside world, and German in church.[47]

---

44. Fox, chapter 6

45. Straatmeyer, *Child of the Church*, 1–17, 57–60; Fox, 170–79; Rohrer, "German Presbyterians or Christian Americans," 183–94; Wilkie, *Dubuque on the Mississippi*, 189; *North Central Iowa Presbytery Bicentennial History*, 4–5, 52, 61, 94, 102.

46. For Frisian nationalism (at its most romantic), see the Siouxland novels of Iowan Frederick Mannfred. On Emden as the first Calvinist outpost outside of Geneva, see Benedict, *Christ's Churches Purely Reformed*, 68–73.

47. Saathoff, "Eastfriesen in the United States," 89–93, 100.

CHRISTIAN REFORMED

Some East Frisians in Iowa gravitated to the Christian Reformed Church, the more conservative of the two major Dutch Reformed churches in the US. The Classis Ackley was formed in 1896, on an ethnic rather than a geographical basis, and renamed Classis Ostfriesland in 1898. Language difficulties ensued, as most Christian Reformed pastors were fluent in Dutch, but their East Frisian congregants spoke German as their liturgical language. The German language-oriented college in Grundy Center in 1916 was short-lived, lasting a decade. The generational decline of a language barrier, rivalry with the Western Academy in Hull, and the Depression all contributed to the school's demise.[48] The ethnically organized Classis Ostfriesland has become the geographical classis of North-Central Iowa.[49]

Herbert Quick had several stories to tell about his East Frisian neighbors in Grundy County (whom he simply calls Germans). His mother was able to persuade a neighbor to come to a religious service after she assured him that the preacher did not kneel when he prayed. Frisians were leery of emotion in worship.[50]

BAPTISTS

Like the German Presbyterians, German Baptists also tended to be East Frisian. The first Iowa congregation of what became the small denomination the North American Baptist Conference was in Aplington, settled by members of the Ostfriesen Baptist Church from Silver Lake, Illinois (now Baileyville), just south of Freeport. In 1872, they formed a congregation called the Baptized Christians of Pleasant Valley (Township), Iowa. Thirteen Iowa congregations were affiliated with the North American Baptist Conference in 2019, with a concentration in the Frisian areas of Grundy and Lyon Counties.[51]

---

48. Waddilove, "Grundy College," 54–60.
49. Schaap, *Our Family Album*, 199.
50. Quick, *One Man's Life*, 210–12.
51. "History" (Aplington Baptist Church); "Directory" (NAB Conference); conversation with Robert Neymeyer, Waterloo, Nov. 14, 2019; Olson, *Handbook of Denominations*, 177–78. The congregations are located in Aplington, Parkersburg, Steamboat Rock, Elgin, Cedar Falls, Ft. Dodge, Victor, Coralville, Burlington, Buffalo Center, Rock Rapids, and two in George.

The porousness of the concept of "German" in nineteenth-century Iowa is illustrated by the Budde-Stomp family, non-Frisian Dutch who crossed the Atlantic with Hendrik Scholte but who settled in Burlington instead of Pella. They eventually joined the German Presbyterian church in Mount Pleasant.[52]

GERMANS IN THE DUTCH REFORMED CHURCH

East Frisians also congregated in the Reformed Church of America, also known as Dutch Reformed. From German Valley in northern Illinois, beginning in 1854,

> An ever-increasing movement into Iowa set in until in the counties of Grundy and Butler an Eastfrisian colony arose which soon surpassed that in Illinois and is at present regarded as the strongest settlement of these people. It includes the towns of Parkersburg, Aplington, Stout, Holland, Wellsburg, Ackley, Austinville, Kesley, Bristow, and Dumont. A little later . . . more adventurous spirits . . . established settlements in northern Iowa (Belmond, Meservey, Alexander, Titonka, Buffalo Center), [and] in northwestern Iowa (George, Little Rock, Rock Rapids, Sibley, Ashton).[53]

It took two decades, though, before the Dutch Reformed presence in Frisian Illinois was transplanted to Iowa.

METHODISTS

German Methodists were also attracted to the state—to the dismay of Lutherans, Reformed, and Congregationalists, as we have seen. They came in three varieties: the Pennsylvania-born denominations of the United Brethren and the Evangelical Association, and an outreach by the Methodist Episcopal Church to German immigrants. (By 1968, after several late nineteenth-century schisms and several twentieth-century mergers,

---

52. *Iowa Letters*, 561–62.

53. Schnucker, *German Element*, 14, 20. Schnucker also compiled the German language hymnbook used by Frisians in the Dutch Reformed Church. Schnucker, *German Element*, 23.

almost all German Methodists would be incorporated into the United Methodist Church.)[54]

United Brethren circuit riders were active in Lee County as early as 1836; by 1844 an Iowa branch had been formed. At least two streams of United Brethren poured into Iowa: in 1847, they moved from Pennsylvania to Lisbon in Linn County, and subsequently to "Cedar Rapids, Tama, Toledo, Marshalltown, Garwin, Badger Hill (Gladbrook), Ames, Webster City, Ventura, Moville, [and] Adaville." A more northerly stream began from Indiana in 1851, settling first around Castalia in Winneshiek County, with many others travel[ing] the same route and establish[ing] churches in . . . Postville, McGregor, Lansing, and Goshen . . . and eventually Fayette, West Union, Sumner, Murphy, and Finnell, which is near Sumner. Some went on west to Dumont, Mason City, Washington Chapel near Cedar Falls, Waterloo, Strilson, Bristow, Hudson, Webster City, Lundgren, and other places.[55]

While the United Brethren spread over the state, their name belied their culture; they didn't always get along. Bishop Milton Wright of Cedar Rapids was prominent in a denominational split over whether to allow membership in secret societies. He is better known today as the father of Orville and Wilbur.[56]

In 1856 the United Brethren in Christ founded Western College in Shueyville in Johnson County. It later moved to Toledo in Tama County, renamed Leander Clark after a major local donor.[57] (It folded into the Cedar Rapids-based Presbyterian college Coe in 1917—over the objections of the denomination, who litigated the matter.)[58] A United Brethren college also existed briefly in Lisbon, Linn County.[59]

---

54. Nye, *Between the Rivers*, 135–40. According to the UB.org website, there was one Old Constitution United Brethren in Christ congregation remaining in Iowa in 2019, McGuire Bend United Brethren Church, near Dayton in Webster County.

55. Nye, *Between the Rivers*, 98, 100. Nye sources a paper by MacCanon, "A Short History of the United Brethren in Christ," presented at LeMars, 1975, copy at SHSI-DM.

56. Kisker, "Unpopular Religion," 45–63. MacCanon (p. 22) rightly labels as apocryphal a story that a Cedar Rapids sermon by the bishop declaimed, "If God had meant for man to fly, He would have given him wings." Likely the tale began as a retrospective dig at Wright for not being progressive enough.

57. Ward, *Western-Leander-Clark College*; Nye, *Between the Rivers*, 100. See also Higginbottom, *Foundation*, 139 fn 87. Coe College maintained a nominal connection with German Methodists until 1969. MacCanon, *Short History*, 10.

58. Behney and Eller, 266–67; Nye, *Between the Rivers*, chapter 6.

59. Nye, *Between the Rivers*, 100.

The Evangelical Association also arrived early; by 1843, it had preachers in Iowa. In 1844 its first congregation was organized, in that hotbed of firsts for German Iowa churches, Sherrill Mounds. (We can speculate that German-seeking missionaries were attracted to Dubuque, and if they weren't seeking German Catholics, Sherrill was the next stop.)

In 1894 the Evangelical Association in Iowa experienced a schism. Perhaps tipping his hand about which side to take, Deaver observes that "in the middle of the nineteenth century a rather pronounced emphasis on the doctrine of total sanctification proved to be an ominous indication of serious difficulty." We will leave ominous indications to a future chapter; "the disturbances" also resulted from "what some regarded as an undue centralization of authority in the episcopacy." Without apparent irony, the dissidents called their new organization the United Evangelical Church.[60]

In 1900 the Association founded Western Union College in LeMars. Its name sometimes telegraphed the wrong message, and it was changed to Westmar.[61] The Evangelical Association was also prominent in Cedar Falls, especially after it won the bidding for the denomination's retirement home, Western Homes, which still exists.[62]

The Methodist Episcopal Church also aggressively recruited German immigrant members. German-speaking Iowans fell within the jurisdiction of the Northwest German or the St. Louis German conferences. The Fallgetters of Howard County were typical German Methodists who homesteaded, prospered, and became temperance advocates.[63]

Two German Methodist Episcopal colleges were active for a time in the state. Mount Pleasant College shared a campus with Iowa Wesleyan, which made for a smooth transition when a merger became necessary. Charles City College began in Galena, Illinois; it advertised in Iowa for who would give it the best deal to relocate. In 1891, Charles City won, including the naming rights. The college merged in 1914 with a more viable Methodist college, Morningside of Sioux City.[64]

---

60. Deaver, *One Hundred Years*, 28–31.
61. Nye, *Between the Rivers*, 104–15.
62. "Our History" (Western Home Communities); Nuhn, *William C. Nuhn*, 7–8.
63. Douglass, *Story of German Methodism*, 80–81, 53–57.
64. Douglass, *Story of German Methodism*, 164–68. (The author should not be confused with religious sociologist and Iowa College graduate Paul Douglass, the son of Truman Douglass, an Iowa Congregationalist leader and historian.)

ANABAPTISTS

Anabaptists were the quintessential European dissenters. Most of the early Iowa Anabaptists were born in this country, although, especially in the case of the Amish, that did not make them acculturated. Amish Mennonites, those who became Old Order Amish, and German Dunkard Baptists (who rebranded as the Church of the Brethren, meeting in convention in Des Moines in 1908)[65] mostly took a due westerly route to Iowa from Pennsylvania or intermediary points. Mennonites first moved to Lee County in 1839 from Ohio; Amish followed shortly, in 1843.[66] But some Mennonites emigrated from Europe. Sebastian Gerig, an Alsatian (then Alsace was French—it was regularly traded back and forth to Germany depending on the latest war), managed to save enough money from New Year's tips from his bread delivery customers, along with money from his older sister, to leave France before the compulsory military draft at age 18, which would have made no exemption for his nonresistant beliefs. Gerig soon brought over his soon-to-be-of-draft-age younger brother and eventually other family members.[67]

Mennonites and Amish settled in southeastern Iowa. In 1860, Mennonites gathered at West Point, Iowa, to found the General Conference Mennonite Church, a denomination that became more prominent when Russian Mennonites settling in the Plains States joined.[68] Given the tangled property history of the so-called "Half-Breed Tract,"[69] land titles in Lee County proved problematic; rather than deal with the court system, they moved on into Henry, Washington, and Johnson Counties, with Kalona the hub.[70] Several generations later, population pressures pushed Mennonites to Wright and Calhoun Counties in central Iowa.[71]

---

65. Ronk, *History of the Brethren Church*, 147; *DMT*, Jun. 2, 5, 6, 1908.

66. Schlabach, *Peace, Faith, Nation*, 41; Gingerich, *Mennonites in Iowa*.

67. Yoder, *Same Spirit*, 1–3.

68. Pannabecker, *Open Doors*, 40–50; Krehbiel, "Early Years at West Point, Iowa," 55–56; Gingerich, "Mennonites in Lee and Davis Counties," 51; Neufeld, "Mennonites Settle in Lee County," 170–73.

69. Assigning separate land to Metis was a common feature of land treaties entered into by the US government in the first half of the nineteenth century. Hyde, *Born of Lakes and Prairies*, 143–45.

70. Schwieder, *Peculiar People*, chapter 2. For property issues on the Iowa frontier, see Swierenga, *Pioneers and Profits*.

71. Yoder, "Amish in Wright County"; Schwieder, *Peculiar People*, 19–20.

Similarly, the high birthrates of the Amish led to Beachy Amish settlement in Davis County and Old Order presence in Buchanan, Fayette, and most recently in Tama County.[72] In 2023, the Young Center for Anabaptist and Pietist Studies counted an Amish presence in twenty-three Iowa counties.[73]

Disagreements about technology are theoretically infinite and sometimes seem factually so. The Old Order settlement in Kalona has seemed less prone to shunning than most:

> Some Old Order Amish groups . . . excommunicate and shun members even for transferring to other districts, while others excommunicate only for going with car churches. A few, including the large Old Order settlement at Kalona, Iowa, do not excommunicate or shun at all so long as the former member joins *some* relatively plain church of Anabaptist origin. Among the New Orders, there seems to be tacit agreement that the Kalona understanding is correct.[74]

The Old Order challenge to modernity and the Mennonite questioning of the totalism of the modern state have provided important leavens and contrasts to the assumptions of modern society. Another offshoot of the Mennonites, the Old Order River Brethren, has a small presence in Dallas County.[75]

The Church of the Brethren gave a Pietist tinge to Anabaptism; a Brethren historian has stressed its historical link to Inspirationists and Moravians.[76] The first Iowa Dunkard, or German Baptist Brethren, congregation was formed in Jefferson County outside of Libertyville in 1844.[77] Herbert

---

72. Schwieder, *Peculiar People*, 140; Schwieder and Schwieder, "Beachy Amish"; Phipps, *Between Gravity and What Cheer*, 73; personal observation of Tama County roadsigns, Apr. 25, 2021.

73. "Young Center for Anabaptist and Pietist Studies."

74. Waldrep, "New Order Amish and Para-Amish Groups," 412.

75. "Old Order River Brethren Counties (2010)"; Breckbill, *History Old Order River Brethren*, 193. According to the Table of Contents, the section on Iowa District is on p. 196, but despite the heading it contains only a genealogy. See also Schwieder and Schwieder, "Beachy Amish," 49.

76. Ronk, *History of the Brethren Church*, 29–33, 53.

77. Mohler, "Dunkers in Iowa," 274; Durnbaugh, *Church of the Brethren*, 13. For fourteen short congregational histories, see Rodabaugh and Brower, *History of the Church of the Brethren in Southern Iowa*.

Quick's novels provide valuable glimpses into the world of nineteenth-century Brethren in Grundy County. Brethren have also been prominent in Dallas and Keokuk counties and have had a smaller presence throughout the southeastern half of the state.[78] A fundamentalist split, the Grace Brethren Church, has also been present in the state.[79]

The German Baptist Brethren was well-established enough in the state by the 1870s that a rural congregation, now the South Waterloo Church of the Brethren, hosted the national annual conference of the denomination in 1870, a prodigious undertaking for a relatively new congregation.[80]

OTHERS

The list of just German-originated religious groups in early Iowa is already overwhelming but not yet complete. Swedenborgians and Moravians also settled in the state.

The Church of the New Jerusalem, whose doctrines were sown in this country most notably by John Chapman, a.k.a. Johnny Appleseed, followed the teachings of eighteenth-century Swedish scientist and mystic Emanuel Swedenborg. Swedenborg espoused a spiritualized, Enlightenment-friendly Christianity. Westphalian cobbler Hermann Diekhonner led a group of German Swedenborgians to St. Louis in 1844, and this group—reinforced by Forty-eighters but depleted by cholera—moved to Iowa to form Jasper Colony in 1851. Autodidact Diekhonner infused Swedenborg's spirituality with the utopian socialism that occupied much oxygen in nineteenth century Europe, a brew that many Forty-eighter exiles found attractive.[81]

---

78. Hamer, et al., *History of the Great Plains District*; Kirkpatrick, *English River Congregation*.

79. No issue, mostly relating to lifestyle, was too small for some nineteenth-century Brethren to split over. Installing a pulpit or a carpet in the sanctuary might lead to a member's withdrawal. Enforcing the Annual Conference's strict dress code led to a schism in the South Waterloo German Baptist Brethren Church in 1885, and the founding of a rival congregation, Enon Church, with a more liberal attitude towards church discipline. Snavely, *Orange Township Lore*, 10–11.

On the closure of the Grace Brethren congregation in Des Moines, see the DMR, Sep. 27, 1999. The space is now parking for the Capitol complex.

80. Snavely, *Orange Township Lore*, 35–36.

81. Hawley, "Communistic Swedenborgian Colony in Iowa."

Jasper Colony, referencing the New Jerusalem lavishly described in Revelation 21:19, formed as a communistic settlement in Iowa County, about four miles south of what is now Norway (and several miles north of what became a much more successful communal experiment, the Amana Colonies). It turned out, though, that while the colonists were committed Swedenborgians, they weren't sold on the abolition of private property; that Swedenborg had not advocated it seemed persuasive to most colonists, and by 1853 a redistribution of land back to private hands began. A disheartened Diekhonner returned to St. Louis, but the congregation he had started remained active and the center for Iowa New Church outreach, surviving into the twentieth century.[82]

The Moravian Church had several outposts in Iowa. Moravians from North Carolina settled the Appanoose County town of Moravia around 1850; other congregations formed in Blairstown, Harmony, and Gracehill, who left records for the Moravian Church archives, and Richland, Florenceville, North English, Independence (identified as being in Van Buren County), and Victor, who did not. By 1908 only Gracehill in Washington County remained. The Moravian historian blamed increasing concentration of farmland ownership for the decline. Whether or not this was the case for the Moravians, we will return to that lament (see chapter 14).[83]

Even though German Iowans, like their neighbors, spent much time distinguishing their theological position from others', sometimes a common language was stronger than religious differences. Gustav Regier, who entered the historical record as an anti-Prohibitionist, served as pastor of both Mennonite and German Evangelical congregations.[84] More bizarrely, Joseph Schroeder, a former seminarian who served as Mennonite pastor in Polk City for several years, was really a secret Catholic.[85]

82. Hawley. See also Hawley, "Historical Background of the Jasper Colony." Not all Iowa Swedenborgians were of German background; see Folmar, *"This State of Wonders,"* 6. The church building still stands, the only Swedenborgian church in Iowa: Jacobsen, National Register of Historic Places application, 1983.

83. Buxbaum, *Iowa Outpost*; Hamilton, *History of the Church Known as the Moravian Church*, 402–4, 482–86, 522–23. On molasses-making at Gracehill, see Buxbaum, "Pommey Piling," *AI* 8, 309–12. The National Register of Historic Places application for Gracehill lists Newton as a location, but this is not in Hamilton, and local historian Larry Hurto also doubts it. E-mail correspondence, Apr. 29, 2019. Engel parses the number of congregations in Iowa at "as many as ten." Engel, *Gracehill's One Hundred Years*.

84. Ehrstine and Gibbs, "Iowa's Prohibition Plague," 36.

85. Currie, *Polk City's Early History*, 57–59; Gingerich, *Mennonites in Iowa*, 146–48.

Early Jewish immigration into Iowa was heavily German. But the first Jewish immigrant was French: Alexander Levi came to Dubuque in 1833 and became the first naturalized citizen in the territory in 1837. The first synagogue was organized in Keokuk in 1855. In a foretaste of future divisions, by 1858 it disbanded as the prosperous Germans and the less prosperous Eastern Europeans could not agree on a common form of worship service. Early Jews in Iowa tended to be sole entrepreneurs, but there was a countervailing desire to establish a minyan (which required ten adult Jewish males) of like-minded souls.[86]

The variegated threads of Pietism, rationalism, communalism, and competing orthodoxies provided a rich context for an emerging religious landscape. This would have been true if it had only included Germans; obviously, the complications did not end there. Evident in the stories is the jostling for position: well-positioned groups like the Methodists drew resentment by more precariously positioned groups for raiding their natural constituencies, and late arrivals scrambled to catch up to earlier-arriving rivals. But the consequence of diversity was the improbability that any single religious group could dominate the state. Nonetheless, some groups were sufficiently well-situated or well-connected to make the attempt. We turn next to groups who could get backing for their projects, whether from back east or from Europe, and plausibly lay claim to the state.

---

86. Bell, "'True Israelites of America.'" Other general accounts include Glazer, *Jews of Iowa*; Rabin, "'Nest to the Wandering Bird'"; Bell, "To Light Out for the Territories"; Wolfe, *Century of Iowa Jewry*; Jones, "Brief History of Judaism in Iowa."

CHAPTER 5

Outside Influences

European and New England Missionary Societies

"Of all the agencies utilized by man in maintaining traditional civilization on the successive frontiers in America, it should be abundantly clear that none was more successful than organized religion."
—Louis B. Wright[1]

"The Iowa Band has supplied for the country the romance of home missions . . . What contagious warmth of feeling used to pervade the meeting of the General Association of Iowa at the moment when the members of the Iowa Band, Fathers in Israel, doughty pioneers, stood together at the pulpit and sang, 'My days are gliding swiftly by!'"
—James J. Hill[2]

"[With the settlement of Iowa,] the base-line of the army of occupation for Christ is moved so much further towards the prophesied boundary [the Pacific]."
—Ephraim Adams, *The Iowa Band*[3]

---

1. Wright, *Culture on the Moving Frontier*, 168.
2. Adams, *Iowa Band*, xiii.
3. Adams, *Iowa Band*, 12.

The People Are Kind

FOR RELIGIOUS BUREAUCRATS IN Europe and New England, frontier Iowa represented a signal opportunity to conquer a new territory.[4] In very different ways, the Catholic, German Lutheran, and Congregational projects all represented attempts to implant religion from the top down.

Of course, once on the ground, a top-down strategy became infeasible; emissaries of far-off religious bureaucracies had to deal with local conditions just as everyone else did. As Bishop Matthias Loras memorably put it, "The diocese will be formed in the course of time. In the meantime, we are going to try not to die of hunger this winter."[5] Congregationalist missionary pastor William Salter concurred that material conditions, and specifically Iowa winters, affected institutional and spiritual realities, complaining that "the constant necessity . . . to keep warm prevents any steady devotion of the mind to Divine things."[6]

In the long run, competition from grassroots groups rather than living conditions prevented Catholics, Congregationalists, and German Lutherans from dominating Iowa. The subject of missionary influence and missionaries being influenced is a rich one, which we examine in chapter 9; for early Iowa, the best that can be said of missionary efforts is that they may have kept groups competitive. Outside influences certainly affected the contours of Iowa religion but not emphatically.

CATHOLICS

Catholics had a head start in trying to make Iowa after their own image: Fr. Jacques Marquette had metaphorically planted the flag with the first Christian worship service, in a Peoria nation village on the Des Moines River in 1673.[7] Other Jesuit missionaries followed. French, French Canadian, and Metis fur traders and lead miners—and occasionally Native American converts—provided congregants in a far-flung territory that was successively claimed by French, Spanish, and American governments.[8]

Sporadic visits to what would become Iowa became more commonplace in the 1820s, with priests stationed in nearby Prairie du Chien and

---

4. Klein, *Foundations*, 409.
5. Quoted in Walch, "Man of Deeds," 174.
6. Jordan, "William Salter's 'My Ministry in Iowa,'" 549.
7. A view of the episode from the Native American angle is in Lee, *Masters*, 13–18.
8. Thorne, *Many Hands of My Relations*, chapter 6.

Outside Influences

Galena and visits from faraway episcopal sees in Detroit and St. Louis.[9] The Diocese of Detroit was technically in charge of what was then the Wisconsin Territory, but access was far easier from St. Louis. The Vatican resolved the problem by creating a new diocese. Or, from the new bishop's point of view, the Vatican had simply decentralized the problem.

On April 19, 1839, the newly ordained Bishop Mathias Loras arrived in Dubuque by steamboat, charged with founding the diocese of Dubuque.[10] His jurisdiction was vast in area, encompassing all of what is now Iowa, Minnesota west of the Mississippi, and the Dakotas east of the Missouri River.[11]

The designated area was as sparse in Catholic churches as it was vast in territory—and even sparser in priests; before the new bishop arrived with two reinforcements, only the Italian-born Dominican priest Samuel Mazzuchelli was on the scene.[12] (He had replaced the first priest stationed at Dubuque, Fr. Charles Fitzmaurice, who had died of cholera shortly after arriving.)[13] With thirty thousand Native Americans still within its expansive boundaries, "it was chiefly for the conversion of the native [Americans] . . . that this outpost of Christendom had been established."[14]

This missionary diocese was backed financially by three European groups: the Society for the Propagation of the Faith,[15] based in Lyons; the

---

9. Kempker, "Catholic Missionaries," 54–58.

10. For a grandiloquent retelling of Loras's arrival by St. Paul Archbishop John Ireland at a 1901 investiture ceremony, see Ireland, "Coming of Bishop Loras." Ireland of course highlighted the contrasts between the church's situation in 1839 and 1901.

11. In practical terms, Catholics were concentrated along the Mississippi, but practicalities also meant that Loras was dealing with the lead-mining areas of Wisconsin and Illinois that were technically not in his diocese but were only accessible by him. Auge, *Man of Deeds*, 47–49. Like the missionaries of some other churches, most notably the Presbyterian Sheldon Jackson, Loras sometimes had an expansive view of the western boundary of his jurisdiction, suggesting it might extend to Oregon. Auge, *Man of Deeds*, 108. Methodist Protestants aimed northward in 1847, deeding all territory north to the Arctic Ocean to the Fort Des Moines Mission. Harvey, "Hail and Farewell," 72.

12. On Mazzuchelli, see Mazzuchelli, *Memoirs of Father Samuel Mazzuchelli*; Tentler, *American Catholics*, 69–72; O'Greal, *Samuel Mazzuchelli*. For his life as an adventure story, see the popular biography, Evans, *Seed and the Glory*.

13. Barnhart, "Church Foundations in Iowa," 98. For Catholic priests occasionally active in Iowa in the 1820s, see Kempker, "Catholic Missionaries," 54.

14. Hoffmann, "Missionary Enterprise," 184.

15. Klein, *Foundations*, 214, 285, 338, 352, 386, 409–10, 426, 448, 483, 536–38, 588–95, 616, 619–23, 633, 657, 662, 674–75, 680, 702, 710–11, 744–45, 755, 807, 810, 876, 885, 903, 932.

The People Are Kind

Leopoldine Society of Vienna;[16] and the Missionverein of Munich.[17] The bishop's correspondence bulged with thank you notes and fundraising letters, starting in 1838 before even arriving in Dubuque, with the plaintive statement "this infant diocese [is] absolutely destitute."[18]

The continuous appeals included a heartfelt description of a new parish on the prairie made possible by Austrian backing:

> Allow me, Monsignor, to tell you what Divine Providence has just accomplished through my ministry in order to give birth to a new Catholic parish in Iowa. It was yesterday that the arrangement was concluded . . . Thirteen Catholic families, for the most part German, are established 15 miles [south] from Iowa City, where the general assembly of representatives of the Territory takes place each year. These good Catholics have found some fertile lands . . .
>
> This charming area is not far from the celebrated Mississippi River which is nearly all year covered with steamboats . . . But a church was lacking for these 13 families to unite them by the sacred bonds of religion and to draw nearer to them, from five or six miles in the vicinity, new Catholics from older states of the Union and from Europe . . . I have marked the place which is to be sanctified as a church at the top of a charming hill which overlooks a large plain on one side, and on the other a beautiful river [the English River] whose banks are covered with tall trees. Nearby is a very pure spring. I have named the church after St. Vincent, the name that the Germans here often give to their children.[19]

At $1.25 an acre for government land, the bishop recognized a good investment. He spent $20,000 *in his first four years* buying up land for the diocese, far more than needed to erect church buildings.[20] While Loras himself was careful to warn prospective immigrants that settling in frontier Iowa would be no picnic, sometimes his associates were more exuberant: "The garden of America, the El Dorado of the West" was how

---

16. Klein, *Foundations*, 172, 221–22, 247, 372–75, 420–22, 515–17, 550–52, 561–62, 929.

17. Klein, *Foundations*, 816–17, 889; Hoffmann, "Europe's Pennies," 39–48; Auge, *Man of Deeds*, 93–94.

18. Klein, *Foundations*, 172. See also Court Chaplain of Munich to Loras, Sep. 7, 1850, quoted in M. M. H., "Letters and Documents," 45–46.

19. Klein, *Foundations*, 550–51. Fairly early on, St. Vincent folded into St. Mary in Riverside. Schmidt, *Seasons of Growth*, 58, 78.

20. Auge, "Dream of Bishop Loras," 172.

one of his parishioners pitched Iowa to the New York-based Irish Emigrant Society.[21]

Loras's dogged work, shrewd investing, and skillful begging enabled the diocese to almost keep pace with the burgeoning number of Catholics flowing into the state in the years between statehood and the Civil War, but his soaring dreams for a Catholic-dominated Iowa fell far short of reality. Three frontier parishes are illustrative of the attempts at colonization and the limitations of such a strategy.

Just south of the Dubuque County line in Jackson County, halfway between what are now the towns of Cascade and Zwingle, Loras was instrumental in planting an Irish settlement in 1838. The bishop dispensed $600 from European missionary societies to help defray the cost of a church building.

Originally called Makokiti, a corruption of the Indian-named Maquoketa River, the major point of contention between natives of Cork and Limerick was how to rename the settlement appropriately. Eventually, Limerick native, orator, and future Dubuque politician Dennis Mahony won the day for Garryowen.[22] But Mahony moved to Dubuque, and most of his countrypeople moved on as well; the rural parish of St. Patrick's remains, without an accompanying town.

In the wake of the crushing famine of the eighteen-forties, much of Catholic immigration to Iowa was Irish. Fr. Thomas Hoar, a parish priest in Wexford, Ireland, who had spent time in the United States, encouraged his parishioners to replicate their community in America. Close to a thousand of them relocated to Arkansas, where a welcoming bishop shepherded them to land near Ft. Smith. But this arrangement proved unsatisfactory for most of them.

At that point Hoar intervened, coming to the US in person in 1851 to see if the colony could be salvaged. With several hundred families waiting in St. Louis, he determined a location in Allamakee County, which he

---

21. Auge, "Dream of Bishop Loras," 173–74. Cf. Auge, *Man of Deeds*, 96–97, which includes the costs of building and puts the tally at $35,000. Sometimes the Dubuque diocese's exuberance brought them the hostility of eastern prelates who preferred that immigrant Catholics stay in the cities. Kelly, *Catholic Immigrant Colonization Projects*, 268–69.

22. Kelly, *Catholic Immigrant Colonization Projects*, 147–50; Hoffmann, *Centennial History of the Archdiocese of Dubuque*, 10–15; Bovee, *Church and the Lan Conference*, 9–11.

Traveling between Maquoketa and Cascade in 1845, Congregationalist William Salter made note of the town and the European Catholic financial backing it had. "William Salter's Letters to Mary Ann Mackenzie," 124.

christened Wexford. Whether because they were out of money or found St. Louis congenial or both, most did not venture north.²³ Once again, the town has not survived, although a rural parish, Immaculate Conception, has. An attempt to establish a Trappist monastery there failed.²⁴

A group of German immigrants who had settled in western Ohio wanted to bring over extended family but realized that such chain migration was made difficult by the density of settlement in the state. They trekked to Iowa and, after Johnson County seemed infeasible, sought the advice of the bishop. He recommended western Dubuque County. They were not Austrian but named their town New Vienna in tribute to the Vienna-based Leopoldine Society, one of Bishop Loras's most faithful patrons.²⁵ The community later spilled southward to Dyersville, which would become the site of one of two of Iowa's basilicas. (There are only eighty-five basilicas in the country.)²⁶

Loras's appetite for land acquisition often paid off (although some of his priests believed at the price of their impoverishment). In 1849 he was able to transplant many of the impoverished Trappist monks of Mount Melleray, Ireland, onto land west of Dubuque at what became New Melleray Abbey. Arguably, contemplative monks should not have been a priority in a diocese perpetually short of parish priests, but New Melleray took root.²⁷ Loras's successor as bishop would be the abbot of the monastery, Clement Smyth.²⁸

---

23. Kelly, *Catholic Immigrant Colonization Projects*, 177–81; Hoffmann, *Centennial*, 50.

24. "Welcome to Immaculate Conception Parish."

25. Auge, *Man of Deeds*, 121; Kelly, *Catholic Immigrant Colonization Projects*, 150–52; Hoffmann, *Centennial*, 30–33.

26. The other Iowa basilica is St. John's in Des Moines.

27. The literature on New Melleray is extensive, though much of it is dated. See, e.g., Perkins, *History of the Trappist Abbey of New Melleray*; McDermott, *Trappist Monk Reformed Cistercians*; Mahan, "New Melleray Abbey"; *Cistercians of the Strict Observance*; Whalen, *Trappist Way*; Hoffman, *Arms and the Monk*; Hussmann, "Voices from the Cloister."

28. On Smyth, see Gallagher, *Seed/Harvest*, 1–24 (Thomas E. Auge, "This Savage Land"); Colman Heffern, "Clement Smyth," 351–79; [Henry], *Life of the Most Reverend Clement Smyth*.

CATHOLIC-PROTESTANT COMPETITION

Early Catholic ambitions in Iowa were sweeping. Loras and Mazzuchelli launched protracted meetings with the goal of converting Protestants.[29] Loras engaged in a long argument with a Baptist minister.[30]

But such bravado could have countervailing effects. Lutherans and Congregationalists seized upon ambitious Catholic declarations such as "we have got the West." In an 1843 *Home Missionary* article entitled "Romanism in Iowa," the report sounded dire: "At every important point on the Mississippi, the Romanists have commenced their work, and stationed their men."[31] In his report to the American Home Missionary Society, agent Ephraim Adams would be even more alarmist: "Errorists are as busy as ever, while there's scarcely a town of any importance along *the banks of our noble* river where the man of Sin has not secured a permanent foothold . . . That [Rome] . . . makes large calculations upon this region is all too evident."[32]

Congregationalists used such quotes to spur on their own efforts and fundraising.[33] In addition to theological Reformation-era hostilities, American Protestants raised political objections to the Roman church: its hierarchical structure was compatible with monarchy but seemed antithetical to democracy.

Bishop Loras's anti-revolutionary personal history, stemming from his father's execution during the French Revolution when Loras was an infant, did nothing to alleviate these concerns.[34] If Congregationalists had known that Loras owned a slave until 1852, that would certainly have been added to their rhetorical arsenal against Catholicism.[35]

---

29. Auge, *Man of Deeds*, 87, 111–13; Klein, *Foundations*, 247, 409, 443.

30. Billington, *Protestant Crusade*, 255.

31. Quoted in Gjerde, *Catholicism and the Shaping of Nineteenth-Century America*, 122.

32. Houf, "American Home Missionary Letters from Iowa," 112.

33. See, e.g., *Home Missionary*, Jul. 1842; Mar. 1843; Auge, *Man of Deeds*, 111–13.

34. On the importance of the French Revolution to early nineteenth-century American Catholics, see Cakje, "French Revolution and American Catholicism."

35. Auge, *Man of Deeds*, 37–40, 108. Loras kept his slave in Alabama when he was assigned north, although he later considered bringing her to Iowa. Such an action would have been illegal under Iowa case law, until the US Supreme Court's 1857 *Dred Scott* decision basically made slavery legal nationwide. See, e.g., Acton and Acton, *To Go Free*, chapter 1; VanderVelde, *Mrs. Dred Scott*; Fehrenbacher, *Dred Scott Case*.

LUTHERANS

The German Lutherans who formed the Iowa Synod gratefully sought help from Europe. Like the initial boundaries of the Diocese of Dubuque, the Iowa Synod would encompass a much wider area than the state of Iowa and would become a constituent member of the American Lutheran Church, as various strands of Lutheranism coalesced in the twentieth century. (Now those strands are wound around the Evangelical Lutheran Church of America.) But while Mathias Loras spent most of his career across the Atlantic from his native France, the German Wilhelm Loehe was instrumental in the founding of the Iowa Synod without ever venturing onto the ocean.

Loehe's Pietism was unfashionable with leaders of the state church, who preferred a religion steeped in rationalism and ethical teaching. He consequently spent almost four decades as pastor of the Bavarian village of Neuendettelsau. From this unprepossessing vantage point, Loehe not only built a national network of social service agencies that survives today in Germany, but also enabled the growth of Lutheranism in the American Midwest through incessant fundraising and recruitment of "emergency helpers," or *nothelfers,* his word for German missionaries to the Michigan and Mississippi Valley frontiers.[36]

While his colonization projects were focused elsewhere, principally around Saginaw, where it included temporarily successful outreach to the Ojibwe; as so often happens in American religion, dissension sowed diversity.

Loehe initially worked with Missouri Synod Lutherans.[37] Their shared pietism at first obscured a disagreement about the nature of the Church that only Lutherans could appreciate. In fact, Loehe and the Missouri Synod could not even agree whether the difference was a question of polity or of doctrine.

The Saxon immigrants of what became the Missouri Synod, fresh from a bitter experience with a charismatic leader, built lay democratic control of the congregation into their structure: a pastor could only be called by a congregation, not assigned by a hierarchical entity. Loehe,

---

36. Geiger, "Biography of Wilhelm Loehe."

37. My summary relies primarily on Hoek, *Pilgrim Colony.* See also Ratke, *Confession and Mission*; "Wilhelm Loehe and His Legacy," *Currents in Theology and Mission* 33 (April 2006)—especially the Nessan article, "Missionary Theology"; Zeilinger, *Missionary Synod With a Mission*; Heintzen, *Love Leaves Home*; Main, "Fraulein Chooses Backwoods Iowa."

by the very nature of his work as a mission coordinator, needed a more top-down approach, one that was also more consistent with historical Lutheran polity.[38] The Missouri Synod was more democratic but also much more dogmatic; while Loehe supporters argued for flexibility in polity, for the Synod advocates it became an uncompromisable question of doctrine. Put theologically, Loehe had a developed doctrine of the invisible church, but the Missouri Synod could not see it.

The flashpoint came in Frankenhild, the newest colony outside of Saginaw, where Loehe loyalists clashed with others worried about Loehe holding the deed to the church building. Since Loehe's organization had paid for it, ownership ought not to have been a surprise, but Missouri Synod distrust of hierarchy had seeped into the settlements. Loehe loyalists decided to relocate to Iowa, and Loehe subsequently refocused his prodigious fundraising and missionary-sending skills to supporting the Iowa Synod, which would have a more traditionally Lutheran view of the Church and a less dogmatic approach to church conflict than the Missouri Synod.

The rudimentary elements of what became Wartburg College in Waverly and Wartburg Seminary in Dubuque were present in Michigan. Pastor Johannes Deindoerfer, seminary professor Georg Grossmann, and lay Frankenhilf colony leader Carl Amman led the repositioning of Loehe's missionary activity to Iowa; Deindoerfer and Amman sought out and obtained land in Clayton County. St. Siebald Church near Strawberry Point became the "pilgrim colony" that established the Iowa Synod. The Iowa Synod geographically encompassed a wider region than the state but was centered in Northeast Iowa.

Through Loehe, the Iowa Synod developed connections to German aristocrats in the Baltic region who were generous in their support of the mission synod. One of them, Auguste von Schwartz, even left her native Latvia to volunteer her services for the fledgling Wartburg Seminary.[39]

While significant numerically, Lutherans were too divided by nationality, theology, and conflicting church structures to contend seriously for religious domination in Iowa. In addition, their mostly immigrant status kept them somewhat on the margins of prestige and preoccupied by questions of identity and heritage that did not lend themselves to an assertive relationship with the larger society for quite

---

38. See Nichol, "Wilhelm Lohe."
39. Lohrmann, "Prairie Royalty," 78–87.

a while. Congregationalists, though, while smaller in numbers, had the advantage of writing the narrative.

CONGREGATIONALISTS

Another group fond of invoking the image of a pilgrim colony had designs on frontier Iowa. Many of the innumerable obstacles that New England-based Congregational churches had faced in gaining any traction in the fiercely competitive religious marketplace of the Midwestern frontier had finally been mitigated by the time Iowa opened for white settlement.[40]

The Plan of Union of 1801 recognized that while they had differences in polity, Presbyterians and Congregationalists shared the same basic evangelical Calvinist theology and sensibility. The plan was basically a non-competition agreement: if one denomination had established a church in a frontier community, the other would not set up a rival congregation. The backstory was an environment in which religious competitors like Methodists and Baptists, willing to dispense with an educated clergy, seemed to have a decided advantage in an environment that valued initiative over tradition and pragmatism over erudition.[41]

The American Home Missionary Society, formed in 1826, institutionalized this pact.[42] For the first several decades of the agreement, the fact that only Presbyterians had a national organization made them better equipped to undertake outreach to the frontier. Moreover, New England Congregationalists were mired in a theological dispute between evangelical trinitarians and deist-leaning unitarians. (The unitarians would soon in turn be outflanked in heterodoxy by Transcendentalists and, as we have seen, upstarts like Abner Kneeland.) In the late thirties, though, the scales tipped in favor of the orthodox Congregationalists, at least in terms of organizing on the frontier.

While the rift between New School and Old School Presbyterians seems much less severe theologically than the unitarian-trinitarian divide in Congregationalism, it coincided with Iowa settlement. The 1837 split also foreshadowed the growing sectional divide in the nation over the institution of slavery. On the surface a conflict between New School

---

40. Rohrer, *Keepers of the Covenant*, especially chapters 2 and 7.

41. Rohrer, *Keepers of the Covenant*, 13, 118–26. Rohrer is much more careful about generalizing regarding evangelical Congregationalists than earlier historians.

42. Christensen, "Denmark," 109.

evangelicals' insistence on repentance and Old School confessionalists' reliance on the creeds, in fact the evangelicals' call for social as well as personal repentance seemed to Southerners too much like an attack on the institution of slavery. It was.[43] Congregationalists had no base in the South and thus were immune from that particular internal division, and they would carry an anti-slavery stance with them to Iowa that would blossom into full-blown abolitionism.

New School Presbyterians continued their alliance with Congregationalists, but in new frontiers like Iowa they were also now in competition with their erstwhile co-religionists of the Old School. This put New Schoolers at a double disadvantage; the Old School was no longer obliged to observe the non-competition agreement, and orthodox Congregationalists had become missionary-oriented.[44]

While Unitarians came to power in Massachusetts Congregationalism and at Harvard, their ascendancy in New England was by no means complete. Evangelical seminary students at Yale formed a pact to become home missionaries to Illinois; this inspired fellow evangelical seminarians at Andover to make a similar pact to minister to the frontier. Since the year was 1843, they became the Iowa Band.

The inspiration was both by Yale Band example and through personal exhortation. Yale Band member Asa Turner[45] had crossed the Mississippi in 1838 to minister to the first Congregational church in Iowa, established two years earlier in the Lee County village of Denmark. The next year the American Home Missionary Association appointed him missionary agent for Iowa, charged with scouting missionary opportunities in the state,[46] and he began beseeching everyone he could back east for reinforcements. Meanwhile, fellow Yale Band member John Holbrook[47] established a Congregational beachhead in Dubuque, Reuben

43. On the schism, see Marsden, *Evangelical Mind*.

44. Shifts in denomination between New School Presbyterians and Congregationalists were not uncommon among early Iowa congregations. See, e.g., *First Congregational Church, Cedar Rapids*, 1. In this telling, the first attempt at a Congregational church in Cedar Rapids ended when the congregation became the First Presbyterian Church; in the Presbyterian version, "Congregationalists often worshiped at First Presbyterian before they organized their own church." Fisher and Hay, *In the Heart of the City*, 5.

45. Christensen, "Denmark," 108–43; Magoun, *Asa Turner*.

46. Hawley, "Asa Turner and the Welsh."

47. Holbrook, *Prairie Breaking* and *Recollections of a Nonagenarian*. He also wrote the first religious narrative published in Iowa, *Sketch of the Religious History of Dubuque*, in 1846, and the first published sermon in 1853. Moffitt, "Checklist of Iowa

Gaylord[48] began labors in Mount Pleasant (later retrenching to Danville), Julius Reed had just moved to Fairfield, and several others without books published by or about them also began pastorates in Iowa.[49]

Truman Douglass has given us the sprightliest account of the Iowa Band, even if his prose is sometimes as overblown as this clause: "And as they prayed, behold, a star appeared, which at length settled low over the unbroken prairies of Iowa!"[50] (Somebody must not have had their eyes closed.) He captures Asa Turner's mood swings as Turner hears about a positive response after years of fruitless begging, from joy to incredulity. Eventually, Turner settled into gruff advice-giving mode:

> Come prepared to expect small things, rough things. Lay aside all your dandy whims boys learn in college, and take a few lessons of your grandmothers, before you come. Get clothes, firm, durable, something that will go through the hazel brush without tearing. Don't be afraid of a good, hard hand, or of a tanned face. If you keep free of a hard heart, you will do well. Get wives of the old Puritan stamp, such as honored the distaff and the loom, those who can pail a cow, and churn the butter, and be proud of a jean dress or a checked apron.[51]

The evidence suggests that Asa Turner relished his opportunity to be a frontier mentor.

The American Home Missionary Society sent off the eleven members of the Iowa Band with a ceremony at Andover Seminary. Nine of them, along with two wives, traveled together through Albany, Buffalo, and Chicago, canoeing across the Mississippi to an enthusiastic reception in Burlington on October 23. Following Congregational protocol, Turner declined to assign them to parishes; he put them in a room with a map and let them sort it out. It wasn't exactly a congregational call, but the process seemed to run smoothly. Since all were graduates of a

---

Imprints, 1837–1860," 11.

48. Gaylord, *Life and Labors of Reuben Gaylord*.

49. Reed, *Reminiscences of Early Congregationalism*.

50. Douglass, *Pilgrims of Iowa*, 52.

51. Douglass, *Pilgrims of Iowa*, 52–56. A later denominational history, Johnson, *First Century of Congregationalism in Iowa*, covers the same ground as Douglass but more stolidly. A good short summary is in Goodykoontz, *Home Missions*, 248–53. Other sources on the Iowa Band include reminiscences such as Salter, *Sixty Years*; Adams, *Iowa Band*. Jordan's purplish prose and obvious identification with his subject should not distract from the solid scholarly work he did in *William Salter*.

Congregational seminary, Douglass's surprise at their congregations' choice of Congregationalism over Presbyterianism seems surprising.[52]

It would be wrong to portray the Iowa Band—or just about any frontier religious project in Iowa—as an unmitigated success. Even eventually successful ministers had difficulties in places like Maquoketa and Mount Pleasant. Historian Philip Jordan complicates the picture by examining Ebenezer Alden. After enlisting only five members in Solon and itinerating to an indifferent group of Presbyterians and Congregationalists in Iowa City, he moved to Tipton. His work in Cedar County was also discouraging; after four years, he had recruited only twenty-nine members, and the American Home Missionary Society cut off its subsidies. He returned to New England permanently in 1848.[53]

The Iowa Band was nearly as important as it thought it was. Longevity and education made several of the band prime shapers of the historical narrative of Iowa, most prominently the longest-lasting of the band, William Salter, who spent six decades as senior pastor of the First Congregational Church in Burlington. He also wrote an early history of the state and a biography of Republican governor and senator James Grimes. Even discounting the personal biases and nostalgias, undeniably the Iowa Band made its contributions to the religious, educational, political, and cultural legacy of the state. Historian John Von Rohr has made the case that "Iowa in the 1840s and 1850s led the Midwest in what has been termed a 'Congregational Renaissance,'"[54] which Iowa novelist and essayist Marilynne Robinson has celebrated.[55]

The Iowa Band made coeducational higher education a priority and founded Iowa College in Davenport. Iowa College found the city government of Davenport hostile to its aims (and vice versa) and accepted the invitation of town founder Josiah Grinnell to merge with the embryonic "Grinnell University" and relocate in his eponymous town in 1859.[56] (Grinnell became the college name only early in the twentieth century.)

---

52. Douglass, *Pilgrims of Iowa*, 59.

53. Jordan, "Missionary Who Fled Iowa." Alden preached the funeral service for Daniel Webster in 1852. Speaking of Bellevue, Willam Salter claimed, "The only evidence I have that I have preached here is that they hate me." "Salter Letters," 119.

54. Von Rohr, *Shaping of American Congregationalism*, 270.

55. E.g. in "Who Was Oberlin," in *When I Was a Child I Read Books*, 165–82; "McGuffey and the Abolitionists," in *Death of Adam*, 126–49.

56. Nollen, *Grinnell College*, 50–61.

The People Are Kind

Iowa Band narratives usually avoided the obvious: Congregationalism did not become dominant in Iowa, despite the heroic efforts of the protagonists. Catholicism, it turned out, was not the chief obstacle; the proliferation of religious pluralism was.

In comparing the three projects, four points on ecclesiastical structure, geography, social status, and theology can help frame the outside attempts at sluicing the flow of Iowa religion.

Depending on outside help clearly had drawbacks. The disadvantages of requiring that clergy have higher education in a frontier environment were mitigated somewhat by the Herculean efforts of Catholic, Lutheran, and Congregationalist pioneers, but sometimes the gap between classes chafed, both for clergy and laity. Bishop Loras was in desperate need of priests with Irish and German background, but sometimes that led to hiring those ill-suited to frontier ministry, or even ministry at all. Wilhelm Loehe was blind-sided when his colonists began considering the possibility that congregations could act independently of the larger church. Asa Turner spent years crying in the wilderness before his pleas for more frontier ministers were answered. And again and again, from all three groups and more besides, we hear the astonishment and frustration that the Methodists got there first.

Dubuque was an early center of religion in Iowa. Arguably, the roots that religion planted made it a more vibrant city than its early river city rival Burlington. Catholics would bring the prestige of an archdiocese, the colleges of Columbia (later Loras) and Clarke, and a vibrant motherhouse of Franciscan nuns (BVM.) Lutherans would bring Wartburg Seminary. Congregationalists did not prosper in Dubuque despite John Holbrook's early efforts, but their erstwhile allies the Presbyterians, having won over some German Reformed adherents, went on to establish the University of Dubuque and its Seminary.

Catholics are perhaps indirectly responsible for Congregationalism's faltering in Dubuque, as Holbrook felt the need to keep up when the bishop built St. Raphael's Cathedral and consequently plunged the congregation into severe debt with his counter-programming building project. The relatively sparse members of the congregation were left with a steeple that rivaled the Catholic spire but with no clear way to pay for it.[57]

---

57. Gutjahr, "'Hundreds of Souls Lie in the Balance,'" 59.

All three religious entities, whether established in Europe or recently disestablished in New England, had to negotiate with the somewhat alien concept of democracy. Bishop Loras was by heritage and upbringing anti-revolutionary; his father and many of his family had been executed for being royalists. While he dealt more naturally with the hierarchical society of the American South, he was flexible enough to learn how to deal with the more democratic frontier Midwest and had the theological sophistication and political savvy to advocate for supporting the established state institutions. This was crucial in a Protestant-heavy environment naturally skeptical of ecclesiastical hierarchy.

For pro-Loehe Lutherans, the question of democracy was ecclesiastical, and they rejected injecting lay input into church decision-making. In the insular world of nineteenth-century immigrant denominations, this would not become a major liability.

For Iowa Band-era Congregationalists, the question of democracy had a complicated recent history both ecclesiastical and political. The democratic roots of Congregational polity were a constituent ingredient in the Revolutionary explosion, but after the Revolution's success, New England Congregationalists often struggled to make sense of the new social egalitarianism and religious populism that the new era enabled. They were more likely, for example, to side with anti-revolutionary Britain than revolutionary France.[58] In Iowa, this contradiction played out in two disparate ways: an accommodation to the egalitarian ethos and an ethical challenge to the political consensus that democratic values only extended to white people.

What united the three rivals for dominance was the missionary impulse at the core of the careers of Loras, Loehe, and the Iowa Band. The theological underpinning, which managed in some ways to transcend the perceived ecclesiastical divide between Protestantism and Catholicism, was Pietism: the stress on the necessity of personal conversion that made urgent the great missionary project of the nineteenth century. This would produce in Iowa religion a turn to Holiness, a commitment to the larger missionary project, and obsessions about alcohol.

---

58. Rohrer, *Keepers of the Covenant*, chapter 1; Hatch, *Democratization of American Christianity*. See also Wood, *Radicalism of the American Revolution*.

The outside influences on religion in early Iowa were significant but not determinative. The next chapter will address the much more complicated situations on the ground. Catholics, Lutherans, and Congregationalists dealt not only with internal divisions but also, and more strikingly, with the overwhelming presence of competing groups. The groups were overwhelming in their variety, but also in some cases in their prevalence, a fact most notable in the Methodists, who would keep any other religious group from even approximating their pipe dreams of dominance in the state.

CHAPTER 6

Reactions to Democratic Religion, Religious Competition, and the Failure to Establish Dominance

"We must live in hopes."
—Elisabeth Koren[1]

"Iowa emigration of the early fifties . . . often took whole colonies out of a neighborhood from the lakes to the Ohio and transferred them to some choice locality in Iowa, where former friends still found themselves neighbors and in force large enough to plant the church they loved amidst their new houses . . . So it was that the first time I looked an Iowa congregation in the face I could count fifty-one persons, old and young, who had come from the same old church back on a Pennsylvania hillside."
—Rev. J. C. McClintock[2]

"In the beginning God created the Land and the Scotch Grove Presbyterian Church. And the Land was our grandfather's. As far as I could see all the way to the east as far as the Church. The Church was at the end of our grandfather's land and that was where he lived now, for he had died on Christmas Day when

---

1. Nelson, *Diary of Elisabeth Koren*, 41.
2. *Interior*, Jun. 23, 1892, quoted in Morrill, "Launcelot Graham Bell," 234.

The People Are Kind

Jesus was born. That was the Resurrection."

—Barbara J. Scot[3]

When the territorial legislature in Iowa City passed a bill on July 31, 1840, granting free lots to all qualifying churches in town, the Methodist Protestants, Methodists Episcopal, Presbyterians, Unitarians, and Roman Catholics all lined up to get their plots.[4]

This grouping is not necessarily representative of the whole state but is suggestive: Methodists were so far ahead of others that two groups signed up, Old School Presbyterians had established a foothold[5] before the Congregationalists[6] and New School Presbyterians, who were still cooperating; Unitarians, by this time, considered themselves separate from Congregationalists, and Catholics had early political influence.[7] This (possibly unconstitutional) grant does suggest an early alliance between the state and prevailing denominations.

THE CHALLENGES OF RELIGIOUS COMPETITION

One of William Salter's strengths was his ability to grasp and articulate the nuances of a local situation. In traveling through eastern Iowa on his way to Congregational Association meetings, he had a shrewd eye for competition and opportunity; for example, in this 1845 assessment of Davenport, writing to his fiancée:

> No town on the Mississippi is more handsomely situated than Davenport. It has a population of 900, but they are divided into all of the different sects. The Congregational Church is small . . . It [has] but little character in the community. It would seem

---

3. Scot, *Prairie Reunion*, 20.

4. Colton, "Father Mazzuchelli's Iowa Mission," 300. Colton erroneously called the Methodist Protestants the Primitive Methodists. Morris, "Beginnings of the Methodist Protestant Church in Iowa," 46–47; "History of Johnson County," 302–3.

5. According to the congregational website (see "Brief History of First Presbyterian Church, Iowa City"), Presbyterians did not begin formally organizing until later in the summer.

6. Congregationalists would not enter the scene in Iowa City until 1856. See also Skjelver, "Randall's Congregational Church in Iowa City," 361–70.

7. Auge, *Man of Deeds*, 57, 79, 92, 95, 141, 190.

strange to you to be in a place where Methodists and Campbellites, [and] Romanists, were the leading sects.[8]

Iowa, then, might have seemed strange for New England Congregationalists, sheltered as they were (at the time) from the growing reality of a pluralistic America. Hence the missionary urgency.

Other traditions reacted in similar ways—sometimes defensively, sometimes exclusively—but more often as junior partners in the American Protestant equivalent of an establishment. The quest to exert hegemony proved ephemeral, even for the omnipresent Methodists.

Complicating and roiling the religious landscape just before statehood was "the Millerite excitement [which] created havoc in some of the communities and churches of Iowa in the early Forties."[9] The apocalyptic prediction that the endtimes were imminent produced shock waves across denominational lines that startled the more orthodox.[10]

This chapter will deal with eight groups; not all would contend for dominance but were all part of the mainstream of Iowa religion. Very broadly, they can be classified as populist, confessional,[11] and Catholic. Populist groups included Methodists, Christians/Disciples of Christ,[12] and Baptists. The Methodists would claim ascendancy in numbers. Confessionalists included Congregationalists, Presbyterians, Scandinavian and German Lutherans, and Episcopalians.[13]

This chapter also looks more at denominations from the bottom up; in the case of the Catholics, for example, such a view reveals divisions beneath the banner of unity. (Protestant disagreements usually meant denominational splits or individuals leaving.[14])

8. "William Salter's Letters to Mary Ann Mackenzie," 166.

9. Blanchard, "'Pioneers' of a Great Cause," 61.

10. The Adventist belief in soul sleep after death was one theological aberration. Blanchard, "'Pioneers' of a Great Cause," 61.

11. The terms "populist" and "confessional" seem more helpful and easier to delineate along denominational lines than Richard Jensen's categories of "pietist" and "liturgical." Jensen, *Winning of the Midwest*, chapter 3.

12. Or "Campbellites." The term is not without baggage, as early followers of the restorationist movement found it derogatory; some scholars prefer the term "Stone-Campbell movement." I use the term as a shorthand for that particular movement because "Christian" can be construed too broadly and "Disciples" is more modern and describes only part of the nineteenth-century movement.

13. These correspond to the "Seven Sisters" of mainline Protestantism. For a short discussion, see Coffman, *Christian Century*, 4–5, 226–27, fn 5.

14. For a list of Protestant groups active in the state before statehood, see Kuhns,

While outlining the origin stories of the groups not yet described, this chapter will touch on variety within denominations, attitudes towards other groups, general influence on Iowa society, and reactions to the consuming moral, spiritual, and political question hovering over the country in the early years of Iowa statehood: the issue of slavery. (An often twinned issue, temperance, will be discussed in chapter 12.)

The relative attitudes of different religious groups on the issue of slavery can be examined by subjecting election returns to regression analysis. Robert Dykstra has broken down the 1856 presidential vote and the 1857 referendum vote on equal rights for blacks by denomination. The referendum failed badly, with many abstentions. The 1856 presidential vote for Republican John Fremont seems a better gauge for measuring anti-slavery sentiment.[15] Dykstra also compared votes in the 1854–1855 legislature to legislators' religious affiliation, an analysis cited in the footnotes. The Civil War would change attitudes toward racial equality—see chapter 7.

THE CONFESSIONALISTS

The confessionalists include Dutch and German Reformed churches discussed in previous chapters, and also Congregationalists and German Lutherans, viewed from a top-down perspective in previous chapters but discussed more horizontally here. Confessionalists thought the church more important in religion than Pietists did and usually had been associated with established state churches.

PRESBYTERIANS

While Methodists claimed greater numbers and Congregationalists a more compelling origin story, a case can be made for Presbyterians as the quintessential Iowa denomination. The middle-class rectitude instilled by the Scottish Reformation could seamlessly sync with the twinned small-town values of community and self-reliance that undergirded the Iowa ethos. In a 1995 memoir that explores her Calvinist roots in Scottish-tinged Jones County, where settlers as early as 1839 took the unusual

---

"Religion on the Iowa Frontier," 51–53.

15. Dyskstra, *Bright Radical Star*, 253, table 5–9. Also listed are the Quakers, who had the highest Fremont percentage, at 80 percent. See also 186, 255, 290.

route of emigrating south from Winnipeg, Barbara Scot excavates the gender and generational factors that led to an obsession with farmland, for good and ill.[16]

Iowa's religious diversity was also represented internally by Presbyterians, with considerable variety in early Iowa: Cumberland, Old School, New School, Reformed (Covenanter), United, and Free Presbyterians, and (despite the name) Welsh Calvinist Methodists all found niches in Iowa.[17]

Cumberland Presbyterians, as noted in chapter 2, had an important if ephemeral role in Iowa, with Rev. David Lowry's role as agent to the Ho-Chunks. As much populist as confessional, the group had split from the larger denomination over revivalism and an educated ministry.[18] The majority of Cumberland Presbyterians rejoined the larger body in 1906, but a minority remains independent. According to their historical foundation, at least nineteen congregations have been active in Iowa, but according to the North Central Presbytery roster only Shinar in New London was still functioning in 2019.[19] In addition, one Colored Cumberland Presbyterian congregation was active in Marshalltown in the twentieth century, one of four African-American congregations formed there during the Great Migration, transplanted from Greene County, Alabama.[20]

Dissenters from the established Church of Scotland formed two groups, Seceders and Covenanters. In 1858, the majorities of those groups in the US merged to form the United Presbyterian Church. It lasted precisely a century before merging with the larger (Northern) Presbyterian Church.[21] Henry Wallace, before he founded the agricultural newspaper *Wallace's Farmer*, was a United Presbyterian minister in Iowa, and the

---

16. Scot, *Prairie Reunion*, e.g., 59–60. The Scotch Grove Presbyterian Church is also described in the special issue on congregational history of *The Journal of Presbyterian History* 91, 94. Unfortunately for the issue's premise that sources outside church minutes should be explored, there is no mention of Scot's book in the article. (The article also mischaracterizes the Hummer Bell episode—which really has nothing to do with Scotch Grove other than that Hummer happened to preach there.)

17. On the latter, see *North Central Iowa Presbytery Bicentennial History*, 3, 71, and Tyler, "Migrant Culture Maintenance," 57.

18. McDonnold, *History of the Cumberland Presbyterian Church*, 324, 326, 336–37. Several glimpses of antebellum Cumberland Presbyterians occur in Hargis, "History of the Disciples of Christ," 62, 103.

19. "Iowa Cumerland [sic] Presbyterian Churches"; "North Central Presbytery's Congregations."

20. Kuhns, "Presbyterians in Iowa," 114; Marshalltown *Times-Republican*, Jan. 21 2013.

21. Jamison, *United Presbyterian Story*. Jamison's first pastorate was in Indianola.

journal's most popular column was his weekly irenic Sabbath School guide, still being republished decades after his death.[22]

Tama County native Margaret Wilson, who won the 1924 Pulitzer Prize in fiction, has given a charming portrait of the devout psalm-singing United Presbyterians of northern Tama County in *The Able McLaughlins* (and a more cloying picture in the sequel).[23] Early in the book, a stranger spending the night with the family is startled that after supper they sing a psalm, read Scriptures, and have an extensive prayer:

> "Nothing lacking but the collection," he thought, somewhat resentfully. Not having heard a sermon in some time, he had forgotten that. The next morning after breakfast, "By golly!" said the stranger to himself. "They're going to do it again!" And they did. The mother lifted the Psalm from memory, and then they repeated some part of the Bible. The stranger was the more ill at ease because young Hughie's eyes were fixed accusingly on him. Again the father prayed for all the inhabitants of the world, by name or class.
>
> ... [After the stranger left,] presently Hughie said: "Mother, why did that strange man not say the Psalm?" ...
>
> "Maybe he didna ken it." ...
>
> "Didna ken the fifteenth Psalm, and him a grown man!" Hughie had never seen anyone before who couldn't say the fifteenth Psalm.
>
> "Aw, mother," he said remonstratingly. "Even Davie [his younger brother] knows that!"[24]

Scotland-raised "Tama Jim" Wilson, the first Iowan to become US Secretary of Agriculture, asserted that he was reared on "thrift, Psalms, and oatmeal."[25]

---

22. Wallace, *Uncle Henry's Own Story*; Lord, *Wallaces of Iowa*, 51–54, 72–75; Stoker and Arrington, "Weekly Sabbath School."

23. For literary criticism of Wilson, see Burns, *Kinship With the Land*, 60–61, 66, 76; Andrews, *Literary History of Iowa*, 35–38. The sequel, with a convoluted plot, has sympathy for those of Southern origin who were "cultured" (but not the cruder Southern Uplanders) and seems to reflect the attitudes of the 1920s more than the 1860s.

24. Wilson, *Able McLaughlins*, 11–18. See also the reminiscences by Murray, "Sabbath at the Kirk" and "A Beloved Dominie."

25. Wilcox, *Tama Jim*, 16, 184. James Wilson was one of the founding members of Tranquillity Presbyterian Church in Traer and engineered its move from United Presbyterian to Presbyterian when the U.P. Synod threatened to close the rural congregation. Murray, "Beloved Dominie," 410.

A few Reformed Presbyterians refused to become United Presbyterians, and several congregations in southeast Iowa have persisted. E. Raymond Wilson, who grew up in Morning Sun in the early twentieth century and in adulthood became a prominent Quaker, drolly explained that he was the product of a mixed marriage, with a Reformed Presbyterian mother and a United Presbyterian father.[26] As of 2019, there were three Reformed Presbyterian congregations in the state.[27] When Henry Wallace served as a United Presbyterian minister in Morning Sun, he was irked by Covenanters' pledge to abstain from politics until the government passed a constitutional amendment acknowledging that it was "under God."[28]

In 1837 Presbyterian disagreement over revivalism in the main denomination boiled over into schism, a split overlaid by divisions over slavery. Of course, the southern churches went with the Old School's refusal to condemn slavery as a sin, but the center would not hold, and even the New School would get defections to a tiny, pro-abolitionist Free Presbyterian Church, while the Old School split into Northern and Southern denominations when the Southern states seceded. Northern Old and New School churches reunited in 1870;[29] the Civil War would not end for Presbyterians until 1983.

Old School Presbyterians predominated in antebellum Iowa. The Calvinist view of the depravity of humanity could sometimes surface even in the precincts of the elect. An estrangement between minister Michael Hummer and his Iowa City congregation led to a dispute over the ownership of the church's bell. A local poet found the confrontation, with Hummer having lowered the bell but not himself, noteworthy:

> Hummer's bell! Ah, Hummer's bell!
> How many a tale of woe would tell
> Of Hummer driving into town
> To take the brazen jewel down.
> And when high up in his belfre-e
> They moved the ladder, yes sir-e-e;
> Thus, while he towered aloft, they say,
> The bell took wings, and flew away.[30]

---

26. Wilson, *Thus Far on My Journey*, 10.
27. Clarinda, Morning Sun, and Washington. "Congregations" (RPCNA).
28. *Wallaces of Iowa*, 74–75.
29. Fitzmeier, "Old School Presbyterians," 180–82.
30. Florman, *Moments in Iowa History*, 11; Huff, "Hummer's Bell," 69–75; Magill,

Hummer's difficulties with congregations and with presbytery continued. His new "New Light" congregation in Keokuk featured Spiritualism with dashes of Swedenborgianism and Mormonism. His bell would convert to Mormonism, too.[31] Presbyterianism on the frontier was not for the weak of doctrine; there were too many competing notions.

The New School Presbyterians continued their partnership with Congregationalists in the American Home Missionary Society and the Plan of Union until 1852[32] but at a disadvantage: Old School Presbyterians and Congregationalists outnumbered them.[33] The first Presbyterian church in Iowa, formed just before the split, became Old School. In 1838 two New School congregations formed in Ft. Madison and Burlington, but by 1843 the Burlington church had become Congregationalist.[34]

The abolitionist agitation of the 1840s and 1850s triggered a radical "come-outer" movement in some Protestant denominations, seeking "no communion with slaveholders." The Presbyterian version was the Free Presbyterian Church. Two such churches formed in the state, in Jasper and Lee counties.[35] The church at Wittenberg in Jasper County was also the site of an erstwhile manual labor college. After the Civil War and dissolution of the Free Presbyterian Church, Wittenberg opted to become Congregationalist rather than return to the Presbyterian fold.[36]

"Hummer's Bell," 26–28; Gallaher, "Hummer's Bell," 155–64; Van der Zee, "History of Presbyterianism in Iowa City," 536–49. Later discoveries make clear that Andrews, *History of the First Presbyterian Church*, 2, is overly skeptical of the story.

On the whereabouts of the bell, which was smuggled to Salt Lake City in 1850, see Watt, "Tale of Two Bells"; Tracy, Leonard, and Watt, "Nauvoo Temple Bells." The latter article finally solved the mystery, showing that the bell is now the Temple Bell, at some point mistaken for or misrepresented as the original Nauvoo bell.

31. On Hummer's colorful, controversial, and religiously confounding career, see "Hummer, Rev. Michael J."

32. Longfield, *Presbyterians and American Culture*, 110. Longfield suggests that there was a gradual drift apart between New School Presbyterians and Congregationalists during the 1840s. But in Iowa, often the affinity continued. See Andrews, *History of the First Presbyterian Church*, 4, on the roots of the Iowa City Congregational Church in New School Presbyterianism.

33. At the thirtieth anniversary celebration of Iowa Presbyterianism in 1870, eighty-three Old School, thirty-five New School, and four Free Presbyterian ministers showed up. McElroy, *Men of the Past*, 5.

34. Blanchard, "Religion in Iowa," 402–5.

35. Petersen, *Story of Iowa*, vol. 2, 699. Joining the Free Presbyterians was not the only option; Peter Melendy, who would later become a stalwart "public-spirited citizen" of Cedar Falls, was a member of the Sixth Presbyterian Church of Cincinnati when it became Vine Street Congregational Church. Wright, *Peter Melendy*, 39–41.

36. Kerr, "Wittenberg Manual Labor College"; *History of Jasper County*,

In addition to the German Presbyterians discussed in chapter 4, Iowa Presbyterians found common cause with Czech Reformed immigrants. The Czech Jan Hus had preceded Luther in his break from Roman Catholicism; his theological descendants in Iowa eventually found Presbyterianism congenial. Frantisek Kun, a Czech minister homesteading in Tama County, walked forty miles (one way) to pastor a Czech Reformed church in Ely, conducting services "in Czech, German, or English as circumstances dictated."[37] In 1889 Hus Memorial Presbyterian Church was organized in Cedar Rapids; in 1910, meeting in Cedar Rapids, the Central West Presbytery consolidated all Czech-speaking Presbyterian congregations in the country, an arrangement lasting until the final meeting of the presbytery, again in Cedar Rapids, in 1948.[38] Some Czech Reformed congregations remained independent of American denominational "entanglements" well into the twentieth century;[39] Presbyterian pastors served the Ely congregation, but it did not become Presbyterian until 1958.

Except for Reformed Presbyterians, Presbyterians were firmly within the evangelical Protestant consensus ascendant in nineteenth century Iowa and often equated biblical values with democratic values. Representative of that civic spirit was Rev. Thompson Bird, pastor of the first Presbyterian Church in Des Moines[40] (now Central) and the city's first mayor.[41] When he became the westernmost Presbyterian (New School)

448–50; McElroy, "Wittenberg Manual Labor College," and "Wittenberg Congregational Church," 129–35 and 177–78; Hurto, *History of Newton*, 84–86.

37. Vavra, *Our First 50 Years*, 274–82; Stelcik, *History of Hus Memorial Presbyterian Church*, 7; Spinka, "Francis Kun"; "First Presbyterian Church Near Ely, Iowa." The distance Kun walked has often been called sixty miles; according to the updated 2015 edition of *Our First 100 Years*, i, "Rev. Kun lived near the now-vanished town of Redman in . . . eastern Tama County . . . It is believed that the 'sixty miles' was calculated from the city of Tama."

38. Stelcik, *History of Hus Memorial Presbyterian Church*, 6; *North Central Iowa Presbytery*, 97.

39. The Czech Reformed Church of Cedar Rapids joined the Evangelical Synod in 1935, which is now part of the United Church of Christ. Griffith, *History of Czechs*, 282.

40. Led by Rev. Samuel Cowles, Old School Presbyterians founded First Presbyterian Church on the same day, but it did not survive; the First Presbyterian that did was an offshoot of Central Presbyterian. The early Presbyterian historian William Harsha described it as "doubleheading." Harsha, *Story of Iowa*, 277.

41. The lack of detail in early historical accounts suggests that his tenure as mayor was uneventful. Brigham, *Des Moines*, 446–50; Adams, *Pioneers of Polk County, Iowa*, 16–20; Dahl, *Des Moines*, 3; Pratt, *From Cabin to Capital City*. Harlan, *History of Des Moines*, 3, puts the election of Bird in 1846; since this is two years before his move to

minister in the state in 1848, the American Home Missionary Society agent "thought it almost a waste of money to sustain him." Indeed, his first congregation consisted almost entirely of women, lacking a quorum of men to form a session of elders.[42] But not atypically for Iowa pioneers, he persevered. His wife opened Des Moines' first school, a private "female seminary," in 1851.[43]

As much as Presbyterians were involved in the doings of the state, they were surprisingly self-absorbed when writing their own history: the titles *The Iowa Story* and *Men of the Past* imply sweeping subjects. Both deal with the somewhat smaller universe of Iowa Presbyterianism.[44]

Slavery concerned Iowa Presbyterians but less so than Congregationalists. A spectrum of opinion existed, ranging from the two Free Presbyterian congregations who wholeheartedly embraced abolitionism and rejected fellowship with slaveholders through the generally anti-slavery allies of the Congregationalists, the New School Presbyterians, to the Old School less willing to discuss such a divisive and political issue. In 1856, Presbyterians did vote 54 percent for the anti-slavery presidential candidate John Fremont.[45]

CONGREGATIONALISTS

Congregationalists were leaders along with Quakers in the anti-slavery and abolitionist movements in Iowa. This had early roots: Iowa pioneer Asa Turner had worked closely with Presbyterian minister and abolitionist martyr Elijah Lovejoy while Turner was in Quincy, Illinois, and Lovejoy in Alton.[46] Turner's pastorate in Denmark (Lee County) helped make

---

Des Moines, this is unlikely. Pratt's dating of the election as occurring in 1851 seems more reliable.

42. Howe, "Dispensation of the Holy Spirit," 12. Hubbard, *History of the Presbyterian Church in Iowa*, 169, gives the earlier date for Bird's arrival in Des Moines. See also Kuhns, "Presbyterians in Iowa"; Harsha, *Story of Iowa*, 277.

43. Hammer, *Book of Des Moines*, 279.

44. Harsha, *Story of Iowa*; McElroy, *Men of the Past*.

45. Dykstra, *Bright Radical Star*, 253. There were ten Presbyterians in the 1855 legislature. Six were progressives (forerunners of the Republican Party), along with an evenly split Whig delegation of two, and two conservative Democrats: "Presbyterians tended to be . . . progressives, except for the three Old School Presbyterians who were white supremacists." Dykstra, *Bright Radical Star*, 123, 125.

46. Magoun, *Asa Turner*, 163–65, Soike, *Necessary Courage*, 25–26. Soike also notes Turner's protection of Presbyterian minister David Nelson, who had to flee Hannibal,

the town an early stop on the Underground Railroad.⁴⁷ The first state Congregational Association passed a resolution calling for no fellowship with slaveholders. This early come-outer tendency was later moderated.⁴⁸

The fictional Congregational abolitionists in Marilynne Robinson's novel *Gilead* were based on the Rev. John Todd and the people of Tabor, whose proximity to Bleeding Kansas and slaveholding Missouri put them on front lines of defense of the Lawrence government and the Underground Railroad's first stop.⁴⁹ For Robinson, as she makes clear in essays, Midwestern Congregationalists represented a new possibility for American civilization.⁵⁰

Only Quakers had a higher percentage of support for the antislavery presidential candidate in 1856; Congregationalists gave him 68 percent support.⁵¹

LUTHERANS

Lutheranism was mostly an immigrant religion in Iowa. Previous chapters discussed the German Lutheran Missouri Synod and Iowa Synod. Scandinavian Lutherans in the nineteenth century divided and subdivided along lines first of nationality and then theology. Once unmoored from state churches, they formed a bewildering array of denominations. Twentieth-century American Lutheranism featured the countervailing tendency of mergers, culminating in the Evangelical Lutheran Church in America in 1988.

Missouri, and who brought Lovejoy into the abolitionist fold.

47. Soike, *Necessary Courage*, 25–29; Christensen, "Denmark"; Quinton, "Early Denmark"; McFarland, "Congregationalism and Its Contribution," 28–39.

48. Jordan, *William Salter, Western Torchbearer*, 58–59. Local actions sometimes fell short of the ideal. While Muscatine Congregationalists resoundingly supported their pastor's anti-slavery views against an accusation that he was lying about the South, several months later they rejected an attempt by an African-American woman to integrate the church. Richman, "Congregational Life in Muscatine, " 355–56. See also Kuhns, *American Home Missionary Society*, 25, 36, 52.

49. Morgans, *John Todd*.

50. Robinson, *When I Was a Child I Read Books*, 170–72.

51. Dykstra, *Bright Radical Star*, 253. Dykstra found no Congregationalists in the 1855 legislature, 124.

Norwegians

The beginnings of Norwegian and Danish Lutheranism in Iowa were intertwined,[52] exemplified by Danish-born Claus Clausen leading his Norwegian congregation to St. Ansgar (see chapter 3). In 1853 Ulrik Vilhelm Koren, a recent seminary graduate from the University of Norway, became the first Norwegian Lutheran pastor in Iowa, settling and remaining at the Washington Prairie Church near Decorah. His wife Elisabeth Koren left a remarkable diary of their first three years in Iowa.[53]

The founding of Luther College in 1862 sealed Decorah as a center for Norwegian-American culture and religion.[54] Norwegians also congregated around Story County. Sheldahl, for example, was named after its first Lutheran pastor.[55]

Theological differences emerged, reflecting the strains between Pietism and confessionalism that the lack of a state church apparatus exacerbated. To oversimplify, three rival groups vied for Norwegian Lutherans: the Pietist low-church Hauge Synod, the high-church Evangelical Lutheran Synod, and a moderate body between the two, the United Lutheran Synod. Northern Story County, with nine Norwegian Lutheran churches in four towns, reflected the complexity.[56] The first split named itself "The Evangelical Lutheran Congregation of the Unaltered Augsburg Confession of Story and Hamilton County," certainly a competitor for longest church name. Long after national mergers, local congregations in Story County clung to their particular identities.[57]

A small split in Norwegian Lutherans led to what is now the Evangelical Lutheran Synod, founded in Lake Mills in 1918.[58] But Norwegians were more apt to lament their disunity than the Danes. In practice,

---

52. Oppedal, "Scandinavian Heritage in Our Country Churches," 20, 25–27. Oppedal erroneously attributes the closeness to fear of Native American raids following the Spirit Lake Massacre in 1857, but the cooperation preceded that event.

53. O. N. Nelson, *History of the Scandinavians*, vol. 2, 176–78; Nelson, *Diary of Elisabeth Koren*. See also chapter 21 for the later history of the Washington Prairie Church and also Christianson, "Ulrik Vilhelm Koren," for more on the Korens.

54. David T. Nelson, "Luther College"; Jordahl and Kaasa, *Stability and Change*; Jordahl, "Stability and Change"; Veblen, "At Luther College"; Nelson, *History of the Scandinavians*, 178–84.

55. Twedt, *Central Iowa Norwegians*, vol. 1, 115–21.

56. Twedt, *Central Iowa Norwegians*, vol. 3, 91, extends the list northward into Hamilton County, but the complexity remains similar.

57. Paul C. Nelson, "Norwegian Lutheran Churches of Story County."

58. Melton, *Encyclopedia of American Religions*, vol. 1, item #168.

compromises were sometimes worked out. When in the spring of 1897, bad weather prevented a funeral procession from reaching the church of the Norwegian Synod at Thor, Iowa, mourners were permitted to use the nearby edifice of the United Lutheran Church instead.[59]

The Danes might have been less forbearing.

Danes

Danes suffered the most severe theological split in Scandinavian-American Lutheranism. While the schism was not finalized until 1894,[60] fractures over confessionalism and Pietism were evident from the beginning. Characterized as "gloomy Danes" and "happy Danes," the split can be illustrated by differences between the two most prominent Danish theologians of the nineteenth century, Soren Kierkegaard and N. F. S. Grundtvig—although Kierkegaard is really too idiosyncratic to represent most Pietists. But his insistence on the importance of the individual did mesh with the wider Pietist insistence on personal conversion. Grundtvig's church confessionalism was enlivened by a polymath's cheerful take on folk nationalism, a concept that did not travel well through the next century.[61] (While neither made it to Iowa, Grundtvig's son Frederik pastored in Clinton for two decades.)[62]

The disagreement became so bitter that when Scandinavian Lutherans, including the Happy Danes, coalesced into the Lutheran Church in America, the Gloomy Danes joined the predominantly German American Lutheran Church.[63] The Happy Danes founded Grand View College on the east side of Des Moines.[64] Danes in Cedar Falls and Elkhorn were also troubled by the conflict.

59. Brondahl, *Ethnic Leadership and Midwestern Politics*, 42.

60. Hansen, *Church Divided*; Hansen, "Principles and Polemics," *The Bridge* 4, 39–56.

61. On Grundtvig, see, e.g., Knudsen, ed., *N. F. S. Grundtvig: Selected Writings*; Nielsen, *N. F. S. Grundtvig*; Knudsen, *Danish Rebel*; Allchin et al., *Heritage and Prophecy*. The North American Center for Grundtvig Studies is housed at Grand View College in Des Moines.

62. Christensen, "Fredrik Lange Grundtvig." The younger Grundtvig and his Swedish bride were en route to honeymoon in Tahiti but made it only to Wisconsin. The misadventure is considerably less tragic than that related about Scandinavian immigrants in Ole Rolvaag's *Giants in the Earth*.

63. Jensen, "United Danish," 143–63.

64. Hansen, *We Laid a Foundation Here*; Hansen, *That All Good Seed Take Root*.

Swedes

Swedes were more likely to prefer urban settings than other Scandinavians, but some made their way to Iowa, to places like Swedesburg and Stanton. The first Iowa settlement, and what would become the oldest Evangelical Augustana Lutheran Church congregation in the country, was in New Sweden in Jefferson County. An attempt by other Swedes to join New Sweden led to the founding of Swede Point (now Madrid) and Swede Bend (near Stratford), when the intrepid but lost pioneers turned left at the Des Moines River instead of the Skunk and overshot Jefferson County by the considerable distance of 175 miles.[65]

Swedes were somewhat less committed than other Scandinavians to Lutheranism.[66] Magnus Hakansson,[67] the first pastor of the New Sweden congregation, invited a Methodist minister friend from Illinois to speak, which he soon regretted. Jonas Hedstrom's preaching split the congregation in two, and New Sweden became the site of the first Swedish Methodist Church west of the Mississippi. In 1854 it became home to an early Swedish Baptist Church in Iowa, which even the wavering Lutheran Hakansson temporarily joined.[68]

The Pietist strain in Swedish Lutherans was also more apt to result in post-Lutheran denominations such as Evangelical Free and Evangelical Covenant. Des Moines Swedes, for example, were drawn to such pietist groups as well as Augustana Synod Lutheranism. Swedish Iowa Pietists in Swede Point and Des Moines were particularly important in establishing the Evangelical Covenant Church.[69]

In 1868, the Burlington Lutheran pastor and land agent for the Burlington Railroad—Bengt Magnus Halland—inspected the railroad's land

---

65. Olson, *Augustana Lutheran Church in America*, 66–69, 92–106; Proescholdt, "New Sweden, Iowa"; Melloh, "New Sweden, Iowa"; Barton, *Peter Cassel*; Norelius, *Pioneer Swedish Settlements*, 45–64.

66. Stephenson, *Religious Aspects of Swedish Immigration*, 208–9: "With Eric-Jansonists, Episcopalians, Methodists, Baptists, Mormons, and Lutherans contending for the faith, the first two decades of Swedish America were rich in controversy." (The Eric-Janssonists were a utopian community based in Bishop Hill, Illinois.) See Elmen, *Wheat Flour Messiah*.

67. Hakannsson is also spelled Hokanson. I have followed Stephenson's usage.

68. Proescholdt, "New Sweden, Iowa," 32–33, 35–36; Melloh, "New Sweden, Iowa," 2; Soderstrom, *Confession and Cooperation*, 39–42.

69. Henning and Beam, *Des Moines and Polk County*, 64; Westchester Evangelical Free Church, 1–15, 70–71; Gustafson et al., *Century of Grace*, 4, 8–9; Olsson, *By One Spirit*, 201–4, 208, 226–27.

parcels in Page and Montgomery counties, leading to the founding of Stanton. Halland sought only "non-drinking, God-fearing Swedes." The Augustana Synod aided the promotion of the new settlement. Halland moved to Stanton to pastor the Mamrelund Church, built on lots donated by the railroad, which became the largest church in the Iowa Conference.[70]

The Augustana Synod originally formed as pan-Scandinavian but soon split into Norwegian-Danish and Swedish synods. Even Norwegian congregations wanting to remain in the Augustana Synod were refused by the Swedish.[71]

To further complicate the Lutheran picture, even Frankean Lutherans were present in Iowa. Alone among Lutheran groups, they adopted the abolitionist principle of no communion with slaveholders. The congregational gossip that Elisabeth Koren reported in her diary was often about "sectarians," Frankean Lutherans and Methodists who tried to lure Norwegian immigrants away from the all-but-established Church. Despite equivocations, Lutherans were the third most likely denomination to support Fremont in 1856, with solid 61 percent support.[72]

EPISCOPALIANS

As the Protestant Episcopal Church appointed Jackson Kemper in 1835 as its first missionary bishop to Indiana and Wisconsin Territory (which included Iowa), it quarreled over jurisdiction more than it organized parishes.[73]

Episcopalianism included a range of theological positions, from evangelical to Anglo-Catholic. While jurisdictional bickering had

---

70. Legreid, "'By the Oaks of Mamre'"; Stephenson, *Religious Aspects of Swedish Immigration*, 302–3; McIntosh, "Biography of a Church," *Pal* 29, 129–44. Webster County had the most Swedish Lutherans in the state in 1915, with 2100. Anderson, "Swedish Lutheran Church in Iowa," 592.

71. Brondahl, *Ethnic Leadership and Midwestern Politics*, 42.

72. Dykstra, *Bright Radical Star*, 253. Lutherans did not have members in the legislature in 1855; later in the decade Claus Clausen would break that barrier. Koren, *Diary of Elisabeth Koren*, 103, 118, 119, 122, 150, 219. Locating Frankean Lutherans within the American religious context is Strong, *Perfectionist Politics*, 92–98.

73. Horton, *Beautiful Heritage*; Carpenter, "Episcopal Church in Iowa."

slowed progress in Iowa, the High Church[74]/Evangelical[75] divide actually spurred parish organizing. The evangelical-minded Episcopal Western Missionary Society sought to outflank the High Church Bishop Kemper by planting enough churches for a separate diocese.

This strategy succeeded, and in 1853 the Diocese of Iowa called its first bishop, Henry Washington Lee.[76] Historian Loren Horton is undoubtedly right to debunk the story that the bishop accepted the position because three of the counties on the Iowa map bore his names.[77]

Iowa Episcopalians began (and ended) their higher education project early. Griswold College in Davenport was founded in 1859, on the site of Iowa College, which had relocated to Grinnell. (Congregationalists were motivated sellers because the city government was hostile to their anti-liquor stance and twice built a street through their campus.) Except for St. Katherine's, the girl's preparatory school, Griswold College did not outlast the century.[78]

Wealthy immigrants from England reinforced the denomination, as Curtis Harnack observed:

> Membership in the Episcopal Church helped knit the Closes into the community. William served as superintendent of the Sunday School and Fred was a mainstay in the choir. Their religious upbringing had been conventional, without fervent overtones; their father, according to their mother's Commonplace Book of 1855, was a man whose religion consisted of charity and good works rather than faith . . . William found belonging to the Episcopal church [of Denison] an expensive proposition.[79]

Episcopalians had a certain social cache that attracted prominent members of a community. Wealth has a way of influencing one's opinion on the *status quo*, and Episcopalians did not have anti-slavery sentiments. In fact, only 17 percent voted for anti-slavery candidate Fremont in 1856, the second-lowest rate of Iowa denominations.[80] But post-Civil War,

---

74. Mullin, *Episcopal Vision/American Reality*.
75. Butler, *Standing against the Whirlwind*.
76. Carpenter, "Episcopal Church in Iowa," 446–53.
77. Horton, *Beautiful Heritage*, 31.
78. Horton, *Beautiful Heritage*, 41–42; Chitty, "Griswold College"; Szasz, "Episcopal Bishops in the Trans-Mississippi West"; Vail, *Sermon Preached*, 6.
79. Harnack, *Gentlemen on the Prairie*, 23.
80. Dykstra, *Bright Radical Star*, 253.

Episcopalians would establish African-American missions in Keokuk, Des Moines, and Mooar.[81]

Iowa has a relatively low proportion of Episcopalians. In 1980, the diocese of Iowa was eighty-fifth out of ninety-five dioceses in its membership density.[82]

THE POPULISTS

The democratic roots of the populist groups have been well-described by James Rohrer:

> Nathan Hatch has demonstrated that the Methodists, Baptists, and a host of other early republican sects blatantly integrated ascendant Jeffersonian political values into their presentation of the gospel. A great deal of their popular appeal lay precisely in their ability to assure people that God heartily endorsed the dominant values of the new nation, and was, in fact, a most democratic deity. They also gained popular appeal by proclaiming the absolute right of all people to interpret the Scriptures for themselves, and by denouncing creeds, confessions, and ancient expressions of doctrinal orthodoxy as man-made religious cant. Finally, they tended to elevate the authority of subjective religious experience over propositional truth.[83]

Populist religion dominated the Upland South, and that region provided the majority of early settlers to Iowa. The culture clash between Upland Southerners and Yankees was significant.[84]

CAMPBELLITES

Followers of Alexander Campbell and Barton Stone sought to restore the original New Testament church and unite all Christians in a simple creedless group.[85] While they sought to overcome denominational-

---

81. Horton, *Beautiful Heritage*, 85; Britton, "Negro in Iowa."
82. Prichard, *History of the Episcopal Church*, 283.
83. Rohrer, *Keepers of the Covenant*, 149.
84. Power, *Planting Corn Belt Culture*; Etcheson, *Emerging Midwest*.
85. Conkin, *American Originals*, chapter 1. The restorationist tendency has been traced back to the early American Puritans by University of Iowa professor Theodore Bozeman in *To Live Ancient Lives*. Early restorationists had roots in Presbyterian, Baptist, and Methodist dissenters, and in the Sandemanians.

ism, an Iowa historian has called "the irony of inconsistency"[86] that by the early twentieth century they clustered into three groups: Churches of Christ, the Christian Church, and Disciples of Christ. In Iowa, the Disciples predominated.[87]

Just as Cambellites and Stoneites were joining forces in 1832, restorationists crossed the Mississippi in the first wave of white intrusion. Ten Campellites formed a congregation in Dubuque in 1835, but it soon withered. More permanent was the congregation at Lost Creek, five miles north of Ft. Madison, in 1836.[88]

Similar in theology to Presbyterians and in polity to Baptists, in the nineteenth century Campellites lacked the structure of other denominations and compensated by publishing polemical newspapers and engaging in debates. Topics for debate included "creeds, the authority of the Scriptures, the authority of bishops, baptism, Sabbath or Lord's day, the Holy Spirit, and other controversial subjects."[89]

Some debates were published; one surviving pits Elder George Thomas Carpenter of the Church of Christ and Rev. John Hughes of the Universalist Church, at the Universalist Chapel in Bloomfield from February 2 to 5, 1875. Moderated by the town's most prominent citizen, General James B. Weaver (a devout Methodist), the printed transcript extends to 475 pages![90]

Disciples founded a newspaper in Mount Pleasant in 1850, the *Western Evangelist*, which moved to Fort Madison in 1852.[91] The religious journalism tradition of Iowa Disciples was consequential, most notably with *The Christian Century*, which began in Des Moines as

---

Alexander Campbell visited Iowa in 1857. Hargis, "History of the Disciples," 41, 177. The January 1858 *Millenial Harbinger* listed stops in Keokuk, Montrose, Fort Madison, Burlington, Mount Pleasant, and Davenport, missing a connection to Iowa City.

86. Blanchard, "'Pioneers,'" 55.

87. See Gaustad, Fig. 2.110.

88. Hargis, "History of the Disciples," 27–29, 33–34; Lair, *From Restoration to Reformation*, 10–17.

89. Blanchard, "'Pioneers,'" 62, 132.

90. Carpenter, *Debate on the Destiny of the Wicked*. See also McCreery, *Theological Discussion*; recording of the Thompson v. Hancock debate in West Grove (near Moulton) in 1891 ("West Grove Debate"); Daily v. Hutson debate in Toddville in 1908, ("Listing of Debates"); Quinter v. McConnell 1867 debate in Dry Creek, Linn County, Quinter, *Life and Sermons of Elder James Quinter*, 45–44. Hargis, "History of the Disciples," 37, 38, found two debates with Methodists, in Oskaloosa in 1838 and in Drakesville in 1853.

91. Hargis, "History of the Disciples," 35, 48; Blanchard, "'Pioneers,'" 65, 73.

The Christian Oracle in 1884. With Drake University graduate Charles Clayton Morrison as editor, it became the country's preeminent liberal Protestant journal of the twentieth century, dropping its denominational ties only in 1917.[92]

With such a decentralized structure, fault lines between the Disciples of Christ and the Churches of Christ lack evidence. The US Census declared them separate denominations while conducting its religious census in 1904.[93]

Disciples focused on supporting one institution of higher learning, founding Oskaloosa College in 1861 and moving the struggling school to the Des Moines suburb of University Place in 1881. The college name changed to recognize its largest financial backer, General Francis Marion Drake of Centerville. University president George Carpenter's fundraising pitches were not cold calls; Drake was his brother-in-law.[94]

Disciples in Iowa were almost universally skeptical about supporting anti-slavery causes before the Civil War; only 6 percent voted for Fremont in 1856.[95] Aaron Chatterton, editor of the Davenport-based *Evangelist*, kept neutral on slavery during the fifties, a position that would become untenable.[96]

BAPTISTS

As early as 1834, Baptists had organized Long Creek Baptist Church in Danville. Next was the charmingly named "Baptist Church of Christ, Friends of Humanity" in rural Burlington. The first Baptist association met in a grove near Burlington in 1839, and in 1842 the first state

---

92. Lair, 39–41; Coffman, *Christian Century*, 9, 12; Delloff et al., *Century of* The Century.

93. Hudson, *Diverse Community of Believers*, 22–25; Turner, "Christian Women's Board of Missions"; Hargis, "History of the Disciples," 41.

94. Lair, 26–38; Blanchard, *History of Drake University*, 11–23; Ritchey, *Drake University*, 17–52; Finney, "Reaching For the Peak." Francis Drake later became a governor of Iowa. Harrell, *Social Sources of Division*, 31.
For a short summary of the history of Drake's Divinity School, which closed in 1968, see DMR, Sep. 12, 2001.

95. Dykstra, *Bright Radical Star*, 253. Three Disciples legislators were ultra-conservatives, but Thomas Turner, an ex-Disciple, listed his religion as "Anti-Slavery." Dykstra, 125.

96. Harrell, *Quest for a Christian America*, vol. 1, 126.

convention convened in Iowa City.[97] Baptists can also claim the first institutional religious imprint in the state, the fifth overall, with the Minutes of the Des Moines River Baptist Association, printed in 1840,[98] preceding the Congregationalists' first published minutes by five years.[99]

Ruby Bixby, Free Baptist minister, arrived in Clayton County in 1846.[100] She can be credited as the first woman pastor in the state. *Free Baptists* were less Calvinistic than other Baptists; according to Frederick Kuhns, a careful historian who reveled in tracing the trajectories of small religious groups in the state, the 27 Free Baptist congregations in Iowa merged with the larger Iowa Baptist Convention in 1910.[101]

German Baptist settlement patterns closely resembled those of German Presbyterian and Congregational, often occupying the same communities.[102] (See chapter 4.) Swedish Baptists arrived in Iowa early, as the first Swedish Lutherans found out (see above). The first Swedish Baptist church in North America was across the river in Rock Island, and Village Creek in Allamakee County was not far behind, in 1852.[103] A conference of Danish Baptists also existed in the state.[104]

The first African American Baptist church in Iowa was in Keokuk.[105] The Second Baptist Church of Mt. Pleasant, still in existence as a congregation, is likely the oldest continually operating African American church in the state, dating back to 1863.[106] African-American Baptist congregations who maintained a nominal connection with the Northern Baptist Convention were often designated as Missionary Baptist churches, but most African American Baptists were members of the National

97. Kuhns, "Baptists in Iowa," 339, 340-42; Mitchell, *Century of Iowa Baptist History*, 17-33; Stanford, *Sketches*, 7; Moffitt, "Checklist of Iowa Imprints," 8.

98. WPA Historical Records Survey Project, *American Imprints Inventory: No. 15 A*, 9. This is a supplement to Moffitt, "Checklist of Iowa Imprints."

99. Moffitt, "Checklist of Iowa Imprints," 10.

100. Meyn, *History of Clayton County*, vol. 2, 14.

101. Kuhns, "Baptists in Iowa," 361-62; Blanchard, in Harlan, *Narrative History*, vol. 2, 412.

102. Kuhns, "Baptists in Iowa," 362-66.

103. Ahlstrom, *Eighty Years*.

104. *Minutes of the Ninety-Ninth Annual Meeting of the Iowa Baptist Convention*, 3. I am indebted to Hang Nguyen of the State Historical Library, Iowa City, for bringing this fact to my attention. The 1940 minutes list eleven congregations.

105. Hawthorne, "Church."

106. Smith, *Negro Churches in Iowa*, 36, 37; Munson, "Which Black Church Is Iowa's Oldest," DMR, Jan. 21, 2016.

Convention.¹⁰⁷ A rare look at the workings of an Iowa antebellum African American congregation is provided by the speaking tour of Dr. J. Prescott of Tama County, who visited the Baptist Church in Oskaloosa in 1859 promoting his plan to resettle free blacks in northwestern Iowa. The plan was enthusiastically received, although white outrage in Oskaloosa and elsewhere in the state effectively killed the idea.¹⁰⁸

After detailing the varieties of Presbyterianism and Lutheranism, the assertion that Baptists were even more prone to sectarian division may seem impossible. But while the former two groups (along with the Methodists) experienced a period of mergers in the twentieth century, Baptist history continued to be marked by schisms.¹⁰⁹

This description of "Hardshell" Primitive Baptists in rural Monroe County can stand for a multitude of small independent or very loosely affiliated Baptist congregations:

> When they called their church the True Church they meant that it was an honest daughter of the churches of the Corinthians and Thessalonians and others founded by the Apostles. They strove to maintain the practices of primitive Christianity. Their only ceremonies were communion and feet washing. Their elders took only thank offerings of food and shelter. No music profaned the church. The Hardshells chanted hymns exactly as Negroes chant spirituals.
>
> Epistles were exchanged between churches. They had no Sunday-schools, no Christian Endeavor societies, or missionaries. They regarded themselves as a little band of saints selected and maintained by the will of God through the centuries . . .¹¹⁰

---

107. Smith, *Negro Churches in Iowa*, 43. In her 1926 survey, the ratio was 33 to 1 for affiliation with the National Convention. There were several methodological problems with a self-reporting survey, however. And the possibility of dual affiliation exists. On African Methodist Episcopal ministers' criticism of what they saw as black Baptist dependence on white Baptist largesse, see Schwalm, *Emancipation's Diaspora*, 145.

108. Schwalm, *Emancipation's Diaspora*, 34.

109. On the relatively small Southern Baptist Convention presence in Iowa, which began in 1954 in Anamosa, see "Timeline of History of Baptist Work in Iowa." According to the website, "Prior to the Civil War two Baptist churches in Iowa sent messengers to the Wakonda Baptist Association in Missouri. They discontinued sending messengers during the war and we have no record of what happened to these churches."

110. Stevens, "Downfall of Elder Barton," *American Mercury* (Dec. 1931), 464. By no music, Stevens clearly meant no musical instruments. One Primitive Baptist church, founded in 1841, remains in the state today, in rural Eldon. "Ready to Harvest" (YouTube channel); "March to Zion"; "Des Moines River Primitive Baptist Church."

Most Iowa Baptists were Northern Baptists, and if they hailed from the Southern Uplands they tended not to bring with them a strong attachment to slavery but rather an expansive view of the Union. But in no denomination in Iowa were the differences over slavery more extreme, as the next chapter makes clear. Baptists were evenly divided about Fremont in 1856; the one Baptist legislator in 1855 was a progressive.[111]

METHODISTS

As Chapter 3 indicated, drawing on reports from other denominations, Methodists seemed ubiquitous in Iowa—"as ubiquitous as they were earnest," to use Dubuque historian William Wilkie's phrase.[112] Sometimes they were accused of raiding other churches, as with the German Evangelical Church in Burlington in 1848.[113] More important to their success was the demographic composition of early Iowa of Upland Southerners and the efficient circuit-rider system that was well-honed by the time it arrived in Iowa.

As early as 1833 there is evidence of Methodist activity in what became Iowa.[114] The General Conference in 1836 resolved a jurisdictional dispute between Missouri and Illinois in favor of Illinois and its legendary frontier bishop, Peter Cartright. By that time, circuit riders had established "classes" (jurisdictional units) both in Dubuque and Flint Hills (Burlington) and had made inroads in Ft. Madison and Mt. Pleasant, even venturing up the Des Moines and Skunk Rivers.[115] The first Methodist church building, Old Zion in Burlington, doubled on weekdays as territorial capitol and courthouse.[116]

---

111. Dykstra, *Bright Radical Star*, 125, 253.

112. Wilkie, *Dubuque on the Mississippi*, 153.

113. Stellingwerff, *Iowa Letters*, 90–91.

114. The standard work on Iowa Methodism is Nye, *Between the Rivers*, which does a good job of incorporating older works into the narrative. Still useful are Haines, *Makers of Iowa Methodism*; Gallaher, *Century of Methodism in Iowa*, and "Methodists in Iowa"; Fellows, *History of the Upper Iowa Conference*; Waring, *History of the Annual Conference of the Methodist Episcopal Church*. For a useful institutional study, see Feinmen, "Methodist Upper Iowa Conference," 226–41.

115. Nye, *Between the Rivers*, 7–13. Nye rightly points out that the claim to "first church" depends on what criteria is provided. On the case for Burlington, see Gallaher, "First Church in Iowa."

116. Swisher, "Old Zion Church."

Methodist Protestants (MPs), who split away from the Methodists Episcopal over the issue of lay control of the church, were in Iowa by 1837, with a church established in Winchester in Van Buren County in 1840. John Libby, an MP minister who doubled as territorial representative for the federal Bureau of Indian Affairs, was influential in persuading the legislature to grant lots to churches in Iowa City and in overseeing the first brick building and the first church building in town, at Iowa Avenue and Linn Street. An even more ambitious project followed, the first academy in the territory. Underfinancing and competition from five similarly underfunded institutions brought its demise after one year, but the schools' merger into Iowa City University arguably presaged the State University of Iowa. The MP school planned a theological seminary presided over by the venerable Nicholas Snethen, an associate of Francis Asbury. He visited Iowa City but died on his way to a return visit there. Iowa City MPs also published Iowa's first religious periodical, the short-lived *Colporteur*. In 1846, the MP Iowa Conference was formed.[117]

The conference actually divided into two for a decade, as a matter of expediency; the Des Moines River was often flooded in the spring and impossible to cross; rather than change the conference time, they met on both sides of the river. But differences over slavery also factored in.[118] Another experiment in higher education, Ashland Seminary in Wapello County, lasted for two years before the principal absconded with the endowment. In 1939, as Southern and Northern Methodist Episcopal churches reunited, the Methodist Protestant Church joined in, forming the Methodist Church.[119]

Primitive Methodists had been excluded from the larger Wesleyan movement in Britain for "unauthorized" lay-led revivals; Welsh miners brought Primitive Methodism to Dubuque's lead region. But according to its Midwestern historian, not until the 1870s did Primitive Methodists establish a church in Dubuque, and it entered the coalfields of Angus,

---

117. Morris, *Beginnings of the Methodist Protestant Church*, 45–51; Nye, *Between the Rivers*, 15, 81–94; Harvey, "Hail and Farewell." The most thorough examination of Iowa MPs is Morris, "History of the Methodist Protestant Church in Iowa." He suggests (p. 79) a correlation between areas of historic MP concentration and areas where Methodism continues strongest "today."

118. In 1851, J. M. Dawson, president of the annual conference, introduced a resolution to forestall a ban on membership by slaveholders. The motion was defeated, and some pastors continued an anti-slavery criterion for membership. Morris, "History of the Methodist Protestant Church in Iowa," 37–40.

119. Nye, *Between the Rivers*, 87, 88, 94; Harvey, "Hail and Farewell," 75, 78, 79.

Frazer, and Boone even later.[120] A local website suggests that the Boone congregation may have survived into this century.[121]

The come-outer abolitionist Wesleyan Methodists were also active early; a regional meeting took place near Burlington in 1845.[122] The Wesleyan Church had nineteen Iowa churches in 2019, including several Spanish-speaking congregations.[123]

The statistical report offered at the organizing meeting of the Iowa Conference of the Methodist Episcopal Church, held in Iowa City in 1844, felt it necessary to count members by race: 5431 white and 12 "colored" members.[124] African Americans were present from the beginning, pledging to help construct the first Methodist church building, in Dubuque.[125] But African American Methodists also gathered in denominations controlled by African Americans. An African Methodist Episcopal church was established in Muscatine around 1849; the 1850 census lists African American Muscatine County resident Dan Anderson's occupation as preacher. By 1856, Rev. Richard Harvey Cain was the pastor; he would become a bishop and a South Carolinian congressperson.[126]

African-Americans in Keokuk founded the second AME church in Iowa in 1857, followed by Burlington in 1867. The Des Moines *Christian*

120. Tyrell, "Primitive Methodism," 23–27, 35–36; Nye, *Between the Rivers*, 153, has English Primitive Methodist preacher Elizabeth Atkinson "preach[ing] often at the Methodist Episcopal mission in Dubuque, as early as 1836." For an autobiography of a Methodist Protestant minister in Iowa, see Newell, *Biography of Rev. A. Newell*. At least one pre-Civil War English emigre minister joined the MPs. Harvey, "Hail and Farewell," 72.

121. "Churches" (Boone County).

122. McLeister and Nicholson, *Conscience and Commitment*, 48.

123. Email correspondence with Wesleyan Church Communication Assistant Melissa Zuber, Oct. 14, 2024.

124. Nye, *Between the Rivers*, 12.

125. Dykstra, *Bright Radical Star*, 7. The practice of counting African Americans separately continued for another decade: "The Iowa Annual Conference, organized in 1844, had twelve black lay members out of 5,403." Shockley, *Heritage and Hope*, 46. "In 1854 . . . the distinction between white and colored disappeared, a significant fact." Harlan, *Narrative History*, vol. 2, 387.

126. Munson, "Which Black Church Is Iowa's Oldest?"; African American Museum of Iowa, permanent exhibit, Cedar Rapids, and email correspondence with curator Felicite Wolfe, Nov. 1, 2019. On Cain, see Dykstra, 16–17, 238; and Schwalm, *Emancipation's Diaspora*, 35–37. It is possible that Anderson was minister of another denomination, most likely Baptist. If so, it is possible that it may have been established even earlier than the Muscatine AME congregation.

Cain had an extraordinary career as a Reconstruction-era congressperson; the best source on this is "Cain, Richard Harvey."

Methodist Episcopal was organized in 1909, and Des Moines's Kyle's *AME Zion* in 1919; they are the only congregations of their denominations in Iowa.[127] What is generally true of religious Iowans is even more true of religious African-Americans:

> The black church offered much more than just a place to worship. It was the center of the black public sphere. When men and women dedicated themselves to their churches, they were building and sustaining community centers as well as houses of worship.[128]

Henry Clay Dean may be seen as representative of the early political sensibilities of many Methodists, although his difficulty in navigating changing landscapes put him increasingly outside Iowa Methodism's mainstream. Dean was a Mount Pleasant resident, minister, prominent criminal defense attorney, anti-Know Nothing and Democratic Party politician, and, in 1857, chaplain of the US Senate. He opposed the 1844 schism of the Methodist Episcopal Church into Northern and Southern branches, seeing it as a harbinger of civil war. As fellow Methodist ministers joined the secret anti-Catholic group the Know-Nothings, Dean solidified his friendship with fellow Democrat and prominent Catholic US Senator George Jones.

Mark Twain testified to Dean's skills as an orator: "He used no notes, for a volcano does not need notes."[129] Dean's "caustic and unwise remarks" during the Civil War resulted in a two-week jailing at a Keokuk military prison.[130] By then, most of his Iowa co-religionists solidly favored the Union.

Contrapuntal to Dean was Methodist layman James Jordan. His family had left the Upland South for Michigan partially because they disliked slavery, and his resettlement from Missouri in 1845 to what became West

---

127. Schwalm, *Emancipation's Diaspora*, 39; Smith, "Negro Churches in Iowa," 37–39, 41, 58–59. Schwalm also documents early AME activity in Oskaloosa, Ottumwa, and Mt. Pleasant: 147, 195, 191. For a short description of a CME congregation in Newton, see Hurto, *History of Newton*, 135.

128. Schwalm, *Emancipation's Diaspora*, 147.

129. Twain, *Life on the Mississippi*, 323; Grey, *Hidden Civil War*, 320. For a more sympathetic (but unsourced) view of Dean, see Beisel, "Henry Clay 'Dirty' Dean." Beisel grounds her narrative on Dean's massive post-war diatribe, *Crimes of the Civil War and Curse of the Funding System*.

130. Robeson, "Henry Clay Dean"; Gray, 88; Clark, "History of Liquor Legislation in Iowa," 69.

Des Moines reflected that. But Jordan would go further than sentiment, opening his home as a waystation on the Underground Railroad.[131]

Dean and Jordan represented the extremes in the broad spectrum of opinion within Iowa Methodism. Methodist Protestants did not remove a racial restriction from membership requirements until 1857.[132] Like Methodist Protestants, early on Methodists Episcopal divided jurisdictionally into northern and southern Iowa conferences. Dykstra has traced that divide regarding slavery. Upper Iowa Methodists gave the anti-slavery Fremont 52 percent; southern Iowa Methodists gave him only 28 percent.[133]

CATHOLICS

Obviously, Catholics lived outside the Protestant consensus. The Catholic challenge was partly demographic; their population became too large to ignore. But the church's size and professed "catholicity" hid disunity; early Iowa Catholics were beset by ethnic differences. Germans, Irish, and Bohemians were the major players. Often the laity wanted a parish catering to a particular nationality, distinct in language or religious custom.

The Irish, wont to strike with their pocketbooks if they didn't get their way, particularly frustrated Bishop Loras. He even went into internal exile and threatened to move the see from Dubuque to Burlington to quell the rebellion. Finding priests with particular language skills and cultural sensitivity complicated the bishop's job.[134]

A recent study of nineteenth-century Iowa City Catholics[135] reinforces the picture of competition among ethnic groups for parishes and priests. The center aisle in the sanctuary of many denominations has sometimes served as a boundary.[136] St. Mary's, the first Catholic church

131. Gately and Davison, *Pursuit of a Dream*, 98–100, 127, 128, 133–44, 150–51.

132. Harvey, "Hail and Farewell," 78.

133. Dykstra, *Bright Radical Star*, 253. Methodists predominated in the 1855 legislature, and they were evenly split between nine conservatives and nine progressives. Dykstra, *Bright Radical Star*, 124–25.

134. Auge, 143–52, 205–25.

135. Pfeifer, "Making of Midwestern Catholicism." See also Walch, *Irish Iowa*. Chapter 3 has an overview of Irish Iowa Catholicism. Among the Irish Catholic churches founded during the Hennessy archbishopric were at "Emmetsburg, Ida Grove, Marcus, Duncombe, Shaller, Ellendale, Estherville, Lohrville, Sioux Rapids, Churdan, Clare, Moville, [and] Akron." 38.

136. E.g., when in 1967 the Methodist Church and the Evangelical United Brethren

in town, has local lore that Irish occupied the east side and Germans the west. The statues of St. Patrick and St. Boniface on those respective sides lend credence to the tale. The Czechs' arrival[137] further complicated the landscape, with all three groups desiring their own parish, often unsuccessfully. In Spillville, Antonin Dvorak spent a summer playing organ at St. Wenceslaus Catholic Church to the delight of local Czech Catholics.[138]

The continuing rivalry and jealousy between Irish and German Catholics was also a factor in splitting off the Sioux City Diocese from the Archdiocese of Dubuque, at a time when Irish dominated the hierarchy.[139]

Beginning in 1868, thanks to the initiative of a German Catholic real estate agent, an internal migration of German Catholics from Dubuque County to Carroll County began.[140]

One other early Catholic micro-group deserves mention. Immigrants from Luxembourg settled southeastern Dubuque and northeastern Jackson Counties in the mid-1850s. Much like the Dutch, some of them hopscotched the state later in the century, landing in Plymouth and Sioux Counties.[141]

Women religious orders carved out a unique position for women in nineteenth century American religion. Orders provided a degree of autonomy and professionalism hard for women to attain elsewhere.[142] Schools, hospitals, and colleges run by communities of women provided unspoken counterexamples to the prevailing culture, even if conclusions were not usually drawn from such examples.

---

merged nationally and the Charles City Methodist Church was destroyed by a tornado locally, the new building was intended to serve all Charles City Methodists. When asked about the merger, one congregant said of the new sanctuary, "Fortunately there is a wide center aisle." Anecdote told by Charles City native David McCartney to author, Iowa City, Sep. 6, 2019. On the Charles City UMC's other architectural merits, see Richey et al., *Methodist Experience in America*, 416–17. Aisles sometimes also served as a gender divide.

137. For a short history of Czech Catholicism in Cedar Rapids, see Griffith, *History of Czechs*, 270–74. See also Cada, "Pioneers, Czech-American," 17, 18, 22–23, 30–31, 45. A detailed description of where Czech Catholics settled can be found in Dostal, "Bohemian (Czech) Catholics," 3–10. See also North Tama *Telegraph*, Jun. 16, 2023.

138. Noll, *Old Religion in the New World*, 2.

139. Gallagher, *Seed/Harvest*, 60–66.

140. Morrison, *Taste of the Country*, 29.

141. Bunkers, *In Search of Susanna*; "Luxembourg Heritage Society of Northwest Iowa"; Hoffman, *Centennial History of the Archdiocese of Dubuque*, 36, 61, 126–28, 337, 484. The Bunkers memoir has a rich description of growing up Catholic in Iowa.

142. Riley, "BVM Catholic Schools."

Increased power increased opportunities for conflict: a row developed between Archbishop Hennessy and the Sisters of Charity of the Blessed Virgin Mary (BVM), as Hennessy tried to assume title to the order's property in Dubuque. The mild-mannered but strong-willed superior Mary Frances Clarke thwarted this power grab.[143] Turf battles between the archbishop and the Mother Superior were continual in Dubuque.[144]

To be sure, dealing with nuns was not the only sketchy aspect of the archbishop's behavior; many of his priests resented him, too. Hennessy left a legacy of financial mismanagement, a hefty inheritance for members of his family, no financial records (apparently burned), and contradictory pledges for funding. His successor had to untangle it all.[145]

Catholics in Iowa for the most part bore no strong opinions on slavery; Bishop Loras, as we have seen (chapter 5), actually owned a slave, although remotely. His connections to the early political power structure built ties with the ruling Democratic Party, which during the eighteen-fifies, perceived as the pro-slavery party, would lose power in the state. That nativism was an element of the emerging Republican Party kept the Democratic Party attractive to Catholics, especially to the Irish who bore the brunt of nativist hostility.[146]

Religious competition sometimes manifested itself as nativism. The anti-Catholic Know-Nothing Party was prominent in Iowa for a brief time in the fifties[147] as the Whig Party imploded. Know-Nothings coalesced with the new anti-slavery party dominating Iowa by 1860, the Republican Party.[148] For many Catholics, Democratic Party support became a badge of their minority status. Just 18 percent of Catholics supported Fremont in 1856; only Episcopalians and Disciples had a lower percentage.[149]

143. Harrington, *Creating Community*.

144. Coogan, *Price of Our Heritage*, vol. 2, 41–46, 118–20, 151–55, 177–79.

145. Coogan, "Redoubtable John Hennessy," 21–34; Gallagher, *Seed/Harvest*, 25–50. On the subsequent official history's diluting of Coogan's work, see Douglas, "Seed/Harvest," 388–89. For an in-depth look at one priest's legal battle with the archbishop, see Eckelberg, *Journey*, 27–37.

146. For a sarcastic anti-Irish jibe in the guise of a history article, see Tuthill, "Garry Owen Vote."

147. Dykstra, "Know-Nothings Nobody Knows," 9, 14, 17.

148. Rosenberg, *Iowa on the Eve of the Civil War*, 158.

149. Dykstra, *Bright Radical Star*, 253. There were no legislators who identified as Catholic in 1855.

Bishop Loras had been a strong supporter of individual temperance,[150] but as the temperance movement rolled toward state-sponsored prohibition (see chapter 12), the political lines dividing Protestants and Catholics became more starkly drawn.

OTHERS, INTERGROUP INTERACTIONS, AND THE STATE OF ANTEBELLUM RELIGION

Even after dealing with the eight major religious groups, German dissenters, and religious refugees, we haven't quite encompassed all of the ferment that was frontier Iowa religion. Pacifist groups as diverse as Quakers and Seventh-Day Adventists we will cover in the next chapter, but mention should be made of groups such as the Spiritualists. Not always an organized religion, Spiritualism did have a congregation in Keokuk. Evidence elsewhere in the state is usually by detractors; in her diary, Bloomington (now Muscatine) schoolteacher Mary Elizabeth Barrett (Walton) recorded talking to someone who said he had been a medium "for about a month . . . He asked me if I would allow him to have a performance of spirit rappings after the spelling school Thursday eve, but I would not consent to it . . . I do not see how he can believe such delusion."[151]

In addition to all the demarcation of differences by the divergent denominations, there were counter, unifying, centrifugal tendencies. William Salter recalls meeting a fervent Methodist who told him he felt warmly about all Christians, regardless of their "tenements."[152] Salter could be deft at simultaneously welcoming ecumenical feelings and poking fun at groups exhibiting less sophistication.

---

150. Auge, *Man of Deeds*, 144–46.

151. "Launching Spiritualism in Keokuk." Keokuk *Gate City*, Aug. 28, 1914; Mary Elizabeth Walton Journal, Ms. 115, SHSI-DM. Evidence of the popular disapprobation of Spiritualism is indicated when accusations of Spiritualism were raised in the 1857 gubernatorial campaign by Democratic newspapers; Republicans countered that their candidate was in good standing in the Presbyterian church. Rosenberg, *Iowa on the Eve of the Civil War*, 159–60.

For another example of spiritualism's potential to divide, see Baker, *Sacred Cause of Union*, 20–21.

152. Salter, *Sixty Years*, 263.

The People Are Kind

While the Civil War engendered some divisiveness in the state, it would primarily bring denominations together. For the first time we see evidence of interdenominational union services on fast days and days of thanksgiving.[153]

As Protestant denominations grew closer together and found a consensus on social matters, it came at the expense of Catholics, for whom a Protestant consensus often meant shutting out Catholic voices on matters ranging from temperance to Bible reading in public schools.

In a frank diary, Kentucky-born Ft. Dodge attorney John Duncombe wrestled with his personal moral progress or lack of it. He sometimes attended Presbyterian services, but as a Democratic Party activist he resented Protestant ministers taking political stances on such issues as slavery (especially since their stands were contrary to his). He perfectly captures a mixture of personal angst and social uneasiness that preoccupied many in frontier Iowa as the nation slid ever closer to an unthinkable precipice:

> Morally—I think I may not have improved any. I am Sorry for it. I wish I might. But I have very little restraint thrown around me. The truth is I have for a long time felt as if ministers of the gospel preached more politicks than Religion—This has to a very great extent destroyed their influence over me. They pray now for negroes more than white men . . . The result of all of this is, vital religion is becoming very Scarce—Real honest piety is read about I fear more than felt . . . Men in this Country and particularly in the Great West are giving their attention almost exclusively to gain—hoarding wealth . . . I wonder if I am as good a man as I was a year ago?[154]

The questions of whether personal piety was declining, of whether slaves deserved more prayers than well-off lawyers, and of whether and

---

153. Windsor, *Justice and Mercy*; *Des Moines Leader*, June 28 and 29, 1899; Henry Wallace, *Fast That God Has Chosen*. The title page lists the denominations participating: "Baptist, Congregational, Disciples, Dutch Reformed, Methodist, and United Presbyterian."

154. Natte, "'Reckless Life,'" 61, 64, 66, 84. 85, 90, 92, 107 ("Elder Dodder preached very well. But I must confess that I lost the string of his discourse on account of the short nap I took . . . "), 120; Dodder is listed as Presbyterian on the congregational website of the First Presbyterian Church of Ft. Dodge: see "Our Story." The diary entry is March 26, 1856.

how those two questions were interrelated, haunted the nation and the state in the 1850s. Failing to resolve these questions had explosive results.

Duncombe's other question, about whether humans can serve both God and Mammon, would also preoccupy upcoming decades.

CHAPTER 7

The Civil War and the Making of a People

"That was an incalculably sad day in Israel, when word came of the transgression of Benjamin and its armed revolt against the nation."

—A. A. E. Taylor, sermon in the [Old School] First Presbyterian Church, Dubuque, April 28, 1861[1]

"The past year has been one of trouble and rebuke to our country. God has been visiting the nation for its iniquities."

—Isaac E. Carey, discourse for thanksgiving in the [New School] Presbyterian Church, Keokuk, November 28, 1861[2]

"It is now two years since we submitted our national difficulties to the arbitration of the sword. During these eventful years, we have alternated between hope and despair."

—Henry Wallace, United Presbyterian minister at a union service sermon in the Second Baptist Church, Davenport, on the National Fast Day, April 30, 1863[3]

    1. Taylor, *Israel Against Benjamin*, 3. See also Johnson, *Warriors into Workers*, 67.
    2. Carey, *War an Occasion for Thanksgiving*, 4.
    3. Wallace, "Fast That God Has Chosen," 3, original in SC-UI. The title page suggests that it was copied from a published sermon, Davenport, 1863.

"Let . . . memory [of the Lincoln assassination] be perpetual: that the abominations of secession, and all the foul and hellish spirit of the slave system condensed into one act, may be forever seen, and be heralded at once, of its own unequalled shame, and its most merited and accursed doom."

—WILLIAM WINDSOR, UNITED SERVICE SERMON IN THE METHODIST EPISCOPAL CHURCH, DAVENPORT, ON THE NATIONAL FAST DAY, JUNE 1, 1865[4]

BY 1860 THE ISSUE of slavery preoccupied Iowans, and in 1861 a civil war consumed the focus of the state and the now divided nation. The war reshaped the contours of Iowa religion in predictable and unforeseen ways. The pressure for consensus begat new categories of religious outsiders. The moral question of white supremacy was not resolved by the carnage. All of these forces had a sobering effect on a recently settled state that had been drawn to ebullience in religious practices.

SLAVERY AS PRELUDE

In 1841 Quakers from the first Society of Friends meeting (the Quaker equivalent of a congregation) west of the Mississippi,[5] residents of Salem in Henry County, visited the territorial governor, John Chambers, in nearby Burlington. They forthrightly chastised him for bringing slaves into the state. They left him anti-slavery literature. They apparently were not persuasive.[6]

Many early Iowa Quakers could be seen as religious refugees who had left the upper South because they objected to slavery. For example, Samuel Kellum's North Carolinian neighbors ostracized him for eating at the same table as African Americans. That his brother-in-law Levi Coffin became a leader of the Underground Railroad would have increased the disapproval.[7]

---

4. Windsor, *Justice and Mercy*, 1.
5. Elliott, *Quakers on the American Frontier*, 116–19.
6. Schwalm, *Emancipation's Diaspora*, 32.
7. Hawley, "Salem," 340–41; Hawley, "Correspondence," 115; Swisher. "Beginnings of Salem," 140–43.

Another early Salem Friend, Thomas Clarkson Frazier, had been expelled from the Indiana Yearly Meeting of Orthodox Friends (along with Coffin and others) because his abolitionism was deemed divisive. The Salem meeting then joined the Indiana Anti-Slavery Yearly Meeting, signaling that, like early Iowa Congregationalists and a few Free Presbyterians and Frankean Lutherans, they were on the far left regarding slavery.

The 1848 incident that would define Salem unfolded in a way that made other Iowans side with fugitive slaves rather than slaveholders. Nineteen freedom seekers from Missouri sought refuge in Salem. With prices on their heads, a price driven by the economic value of humans considered chattel, bounty hunting had become a profitable profession for Missourians and a money-making hobby for Iowans unfettered by an excess of scruples. But juxtaposed against those financial incentives, what became clear to many Iowans was the stark reality that desperate people were fleeing for their lives. A group of slave-catchers descended on the town.[8]

The bounty hunters were generally unsuccessful in their quest and began taking out their frustrations on Quakers. But the Quakers' neighbors, outraged by this invasion of their territory and uncommitted to nonviolence as the Quakers were, prepared a counterattack. It led to a new resolve among many in a previously neutral and often racist state to resist slave state incursions.[9]

Although documentation is scarce, we can reasonably expect that African Americans were heavily involved in sheltering freedom seekers. Documenting a secret operation is most difficult when it is successful, with success defined as not leaving evidence leading to recapturing fugitives or incriminating abettors. And hiding black asylum seekers among others of their color was an effective strategy in a mostly white state.

Post-Civil War Iowans claimed many more Underground Railroad stations than actually existed; this fact is a caution to historians and amusing to modern Americans, but the exaggeration has historical importance: in retrospect, these radicals were on the right side of history, even if it was safer to join them retrospectively. War wound together many (though not all) of the disparate elements of the frontier. The victory of the North also privileged those elements who were anti-slavery before it was fashionable.

8. Soike, *Necessary Courage*, 25–32.

9. Soike, *Necessary Courage*, 33–46; Dykstra, *Bright Radical Star*, 88–105; Delbanco, *War Before the War*, 213.

The Civil War and the Making of a People

The intensity of abolitionist fervor against the sin of slavery began to break apart national denominations.[10] In addition to the North-South split, radical "come-outers" advocated a complete break with slaveholders, a step too far for most Northern churches. But Iowa had two congregations of the Free Presbyterian Church. Round Prairie Presbyterian Church, in rural Kossuth in Des Moines County, was the home church of Jeremiah Anderson, who participated in John Brown's Harpers Ferry raid.[11] Wittemberg, in Jasper County, had an ambitious manual labor college experiment.[12]

The Frankean Lutherans around Decorah who disturbed other Norwegian Lutherans with their low-church, Pietist approach to ecclesiology, also ruffled convention with their abolitionist social ethics.[13] There are hints that the abolitionist Wesleyan Methodists were afoot in the state.[14] The pockets of Freethinkers in the state overlapped with abolitionist strongholds; they cooperated easily with their more religious neighbors.[15]

The apocalyptic abolitionist John Brown has been blamed for or credited with sparking the Civil War. After relocating to Kansas, he had a close if complicated relationship with the (mostly) religiously-based activists of the Underground Railroad in Iowa. His fraught relationship with John Todd and the Congregationalists of Civil Bend and Tabor is illustrative: they supported his efforts to bring slaves to freedom but were appalled by his violent methods.[16] But violence soon came to the fore.

---

10. Goen, *Broken Churches, Broken Nation*.

11. Soike, *Necessary Courage*, 29. Anderson also rode with John Brown in Kansas. Sinha, *Slave's Cause*, 354.

12. Petersen, *Story of Iowa*, 699; *History of Jasper County*, 448–50; McElroy, "Wittemberg Manual Labor College," 129–35, 177–78. Rather than revert to New School Presbyterian, Wittemberg became Congregationalist after the war.

13. Nelson, "Diary of Elisabeth Koren," 118; Strong, *Perfectionist Politics*, 92–98.

14. Schwalm, *Emancipation's Diaspora*, 38.

15. Holmgren, *Abolitionists and Freethinkers*, 22–46.

16. Morgans, *John Todd and the Underground Railroad*, 85–88, 120; "John Brown among the Quakers"; Soike, *Necessary Courage*, 137–39, 144. For a glimpse of Tabor as a safe haven for abolitionists heading for Kansas, see Keith, *When It Was Grand*, 28–29. Marilynne Robinson has fictionalized the Tabor Congregationalists in her novel *Gilead*.

THE THEOLOGICAL, SPIRITUAL, AND PHYSICAL TRAUMA OF THE WAR

After military forces from the seceding Southern states attacked the Union base at Ft. Sumter, Iowans had less inclination to debate slavery. A remarkable exception was the Norwegian Lutheran debate about whether slavery was a sin, and if so, how severe a sin. Quoting historian Magnus Rohme's summary of their defense of slavery suggests both the tortured biblical reasoning and the disconnect from American political realities and its Enlightenment heritage:

> Freedom was the highest temporal good, but one can and must do without it if God decrees. We have no rights by nature; "we brought nothing into this world . . . and having food and raiment, let us . . . be content." (I Tim. vi. 7, 8). By nature we are slaves to sin, and as punishment we deserve every distress and misery in time and eternity. Consequently we can demand nothing as a *right* . . . Not even the Golden Rule requires [that a Christian must free his slaves]; else must the employer divide his substance with the employee, the rich with the poor. This rule does not make our neighbor our equal . . .
>
> Even though slavery is not a sin in itself, nevertheless it is conceded that it is an evil in itself, from which many fearful sins and abominations easily spring, and actually do spring . . . Slavery is a result of sin, but not a sin in itself.[17]

Perhaps sensing the logical gyrations in this argument, the Norwegian Synod sought confirmation from the old country. University of Christiana theologians, stunned by the premise of the Americans' question, did not answer in detail but dismissed the argument minimizing the sinfulness of slavery.

Ironically, the debate's origin derived from Norwegian clergy's seminary associations with Missouri Synod Lutherans, but the lay revolt it caused, while in theory sympathetic to Missouri Synod lay-friendly polity, did not share the same ethical goals. Leading anti-slavery forces was Erik Ellefsen, a lay delegate from Big Canoe (Winneshiek County). Ellefsen outraged the clergy by daring to disagree with their biblical interpretations. An influential, and eventually anti-slavery, figure in the dispute was Claus Clausen, who ultimately sided with lay dissenters in the split. For both Ellefsen and Clausen, this was also an anti-elitist

---

17. Rohne, *Norwegian-American Lutheranism*, 205.

challenge to the aristocratic assumptions of Norwegian Synod clergy.[18] Clausen continued his argument with the Synod intermittently, vacillating between democratic instincts and wanting reinstatement.[19]

Episcopalians, who never formally split during the war, were reluctant to commit on the political and ethical issues. Bishop Henry Washington Lee assiduously avoided such topics, claiming to adhere strictly to preaching the Gospel.[20]

And suddenly the country was at war with itself. And that war turned out to be devastatingly, unimaginably destructive. And the providential language used to explain it proved woefully inadequate. And Iowa, as well as the nation, emerged from the war chastened and different and sobered, for a while. And religious Iowans tried to make sense of the war and to respond to the variety of suffering it caused. The evidence we have for Civil War spirituality, primarily in letters and sermons, provides a deep if random dive into lived religion at a time of personal as well as national crisis.

The magnitude of the carnage had to lead to a reexamination of theodicy. "An Iowan chaplain sadly asked what had happened to the souls of the dead and how soon the grieving might be comforted."[21] In a similar vein, one Iowa soldier wrote in his diary, "May God hasten the day when this cruel war will be brought to a close."[22] "I am not the same man, Spiritually, that I was," thought one corporal in the 2nd Iowa.[23] Experiencing the horrors of combat would stay with many who survived the war. William Salter's relatively short stint providing material aid left a lasting impression; his biographer noted that "visions of the dead and of the mutilated returned to haunt him" for the rest of his life.[24]

---

18. Rohne, *Norwegian-American Lutheranism*, chapter 10; Hamre, "J. A. Bergh"; Jordahl, "Norwegian (1853): The Gentry Tradition," in *Church Roots*, 102–6, 211; Swansen, *Founder*, 147–53.

19. Jacobson, "Introduction," 56–77.

20. Horton, *Beautiful Heritage*, 36–38.

21. Rable, *God's Almost Chosen Peoples*, 183.

22. Rable, *God's Almost Chosen Peoples*, 338.

23. Miller, *Both Prayed to the Same God*, 13, 182.

24. Jordan, *To Thy Trust*, [no pagination].

The People Are Kind

Lieutenant John Quincy Adams Campbell—a properly Yankee given name![25]—of the Iowa Fifth Infantry reinforced Grant's troops at Chattanooga in late 1863. Using Old Testament imagery, Campbell wrote that the war's meaning would be clear to posterity, if not to the present generation: "The difficulties of this war have proved knotty questions to our Belshazzars and 'wise men' but in a generation from now, every child will be a Daniel—able to interpret the handwriting of God, telling us that we have not been faithful to the charge he committed to our trust. My earnest prayer to God is that we may have mercy and not judgment. I believe that the Nation will yet emerge from the conflict, entire and triumphant but it will only be after she has been purged by fire."[26]

Channeling the prophets Micah and Isaiah, United Presbyterian Henry Wallace preached at a union service that "our fasts will never avert the judgments of the Almighty, or receive his blessings, until it be the result of a deep and abiding conviction of national guilt."[27]

Nor was Wallace alone in his judgment. Home on leave in Keokuk in 1862, Cyrus Boyd heard in a sermon that "human slavery was the Cause [of the war] and we should have no lasting peace until the Curse was wiped out." Boyd agreed.[28]

Whether the nation could recover its moral compass was up for debate. From Vicksburg in 1863, William Nugen wrote back to New London to say he "was glad to heare [sic] they are having such a revival."[29] Prayer meetings in the First Iowa in 1861 helped establish unity in the regiment.[30] But "the war does not seem to have improved public morals in the slightest degree," wrote a civilian disgusted by speculators suspected of prolonging the war.[31] Some soldiers also struggled to maintain

---

25. On John Quincy Adams's post-presidential career as an anti-slavery Congressperson, see Miller, *Arguing about Slavery*.

26. Rable, *God's Almost Chosen Peoples*, 299.

27. Wallace, *Fast That God Has Chosen*; cf. Rable, *God's Almost Chosen Peoples*, 236. In the sermon, Wallace also attacked the graft that he saw taking place at the local military camp, McClellan Heights, which was controversial locally. Lord, *Wallaces of Iowa*, 52–53. See also Byrd, *Holy Baptism*, 187–88.

28. Woodworth, *While God Is Marching On*, 112–13. Mildred Throne initially serialized Boyd's diary in 1953 in the *IJH*. It was republished in book form in 1977 with a new introduction by E. B. Long, and again in 1998 with an introduction by Earl J. Hess.

29. Woodworth, *While God Is Marching On*, 220.

30. Woodworth, *While God Is Marching On*, 180.

31. Rable, *God's Almost Chosen Peoples*, 189.

their religious and moral equilibrium.[32] Even a chaplain got caught up in the looting.[33]

But most chaplains were hard-working and compassionate, like Dennis Murphy of the Nineteenth Iowa, who helped carry the loads of battle-weary soldiers back to Benton Barracks, Missouri, in September 1862.[34] Also in 1862, Henry Ankeny of the Fourth Iowa wrote his wife approvingly of the chaplain, "He was very much rejoiced that the Lord was on our side and knew he always would be, but he was inclined to think we could fight better on full rations. It is supposed that the Lord will take the hint—I hope so."[35]

Cyrus Boyd complained of the absence of a chaplain: "The Chaplain is not here now, and we have no preaching and Sunday goes like every other day. Men are playing cards all through camp."[36] Ankeny reported from Rolla, Missouri, in November 1861 that it was "too cold for our chaplain to preach, so we have nothing to do but to sit in our tents and write and freeze."[37]

St. Ansgar founder and Lutheran pastor Claus Clausen was recruited as chaplain for the Scandinavian regiment, the Wisconsin Fifteenth. Although he resigned shortly due to ill health, he was perceptive on the duties of a chaplain:

> I encountered many, both officers and men, who didn't seem to care in the least about God's word and those things associated with it, and they not only showed indifference toward religion but even open contempt. I almost despaired about being able to do anything in such a group of men, but, as I became better acquainted with them, I rejoiced to discover an undercurrent of religious feeling which I had not detected from the beginning . . .
>
> A chaplain soon finds that his position is surrounded with many difficulties.
>
> The order and regularity in the performance of his professional duties, to which he is accustomed in his congregations, naturally cannot be carried out here, and he is obliged to take

---

32. Lyon, "Christian Soldier," *Pal* 24, 50–64.
33. Lyftogt, *Iowa and the Civil War*, vol 1, 196.
34. Woodworth, *While God Is Marching On*, 155.
35. Woodworth, *While God Is Marching On*, 100–101. Cf. Silas Haven in Miller, *Punishment*, 164, 169.
36. Woodworth, *While God Is Marching On*, 181.
37. Woodworth, *While God Is Marching On*, 182.

advantage from time to time of such opportunities as arise to preach the word of God to his flock . . .

If attendance had been compulsory we could not, from the number present, have drawn any conclusion in regard to the moral and spiritual condition of the unit, but as it was, each could, in that respect, follow his own inclination, and still it was apparent that the majority of the regiment attended the services, and followed the proceedings with intense interest, which tempts one to conclude that the results were favorable . . .

As chaplain I naturally have had opportunities to converse with the soldiers about their spiritual welfare and I always found men who, with joy, grasped these opportunities to open their hearts.[38]

As Clausen noted, chaplains were not always well received. Cyrus Boyd reported with shock that some men in Company K of the Fifteenth Iowa had held a "blasphemous" mock prayer meeting.[39]

Later in the war, Burlington Congregationalist William Salter served a forty-day stint with the US Christian Commission, assisting Union army chaplains in Tennessee, Alabama, and Georgia. He summarized his work in a diary:

> conducting 17 meetings and attending 5 more; giving 18 sermons and addresses; offering spiritual counsel to about 100 soldiers; writing 100 letters home for wounded soldiers; providing supplies to about 50; and distributing 150 Bibles, 100 hymnals, 1500 tracts, 3000 papers, and 100 pamphlets.[40]

The most prominent Iowan aiding the cause directly on the battlefield was not a chaplain but a Methodist layperson. Annie Wittenmyer of Keokuk first rose to prominence with the Iowa Sanitary Commission; her signal wartime accomplishment, working with the US Christian Commission, was reforming diets in military hospitals, which probably saved more lives than the primitive efforts of medical doctors.[41]

Sergeant Harold White of West Liberty, in complaining that looting Confederate soldiers had stolen his Bible, was conscious of the irony:

38. Quoted in Swanson, "'Country Life Movement,'" 141–43.

39. Swanson, "'Country Life Movement,'" 208.

40. Salter, "Early Days," 154. Salter also retrospectively summarized his experiences in his *Sixty Years*, 302–10, and in *Memoirs of Joseph W. Pickett*, 24–33. See also Miller, *In God's Presence*, 91.

41. Guinn, "Annie Wittenmyer"; Martin, "Wittenmyer, Sarah Ann ('Annie') Turner"; Salter, "Early Days," 126, 138; Salter, *Sixty Years*, 304–5.

The Civil War and the Making of a People

"The marauding vagabonds had carried off my Bible also; for what purpose I can't conceive, unless to have the ten commandments and more especially the one that says, 'Thou shalt not steal,' hard by to refer to in case of need."[42]

An indication of the religiosity of at least some Iowa officers is that ordering wayward soldiers to memorize Bible verses was used as a disciplinary measure.[43]

As the war dragged on, the religious composition of the troops seemed to change:

"As a whole, Iowa's recruiting class of 1862 differed in several respects from the men who enlisted in 1861. In addition to being older on average, the second year recruits were typically wealthier and more likely to vote Republican. They also tended to come from evangelical Protestant denominations. Although religion alone cannot explain the motivations of Iowa's latest recruits, the denominational profile reflected strong evangelical roots. Few German atheists enrolled in 1862, but thousands of Calvinists and Methodists did. The appeal for temperance men attracted enough recruits to fill an entire regiment. Led by a Wesleyan minister appointed by its colonel, the 24th Infantry came to be known as the Methodist Regiment."[44]

Regardless of the religious background of the soldier, the war challenged received beliefs. The agonizing mystery of what God's providential plan was in allowing the war to continue haunted Iowans. Caroline Kasson, wife of Iowa Congressman John Kasson, also served as Washington correspondent to the Des Moines *Register*. She witnessed an early Union loss, at Bull Run, which did more than ruin the picnics of Washington elites: "We walk in a fevered dream and bow to God's mysterious decree."[45]

Similarly, Marquis Townsend of the Thirteenth Iowa wrote his sister that "I fell[?] to trust all to God for he doeth all things well."[46] Silas Haven of Rockford went to war with a very personal sense of providence, believing that "I am under the protection of providence and I feel to thank God

---

42. Throne, "Letters From Shiloh," 257, quoted in Lyftogt, vol. 1, 372.
43. Lyftogt, *Iowa and the Civil War*, vol. 1, 186.
44. Baker, *Sacred Cause of Union*, 156–57.
45. Lyftogt, *Iowa and the Civil War*, vol. 1, 163.
46. Woodworth, *While God Is Marching On*, 33.

for his mercies and blessings."[47] Haven maintained this belief throughout the war[48] and managed to survive it, but it is no wonder that some Iowans came to doubt the cost of the sacrifices being made.

Haven, though, hewed to a religious view of the war that was severe but gave him comfort:

> War is a terrible thing and is inflicted upon a nation for the punishment of sins. The sins of this nation has been great, both North and South, and God in his mercy has born[e] long with us. We are now . . . under chastisement and it is time that we as a nation repent of our sins . . .[49]

The exigencies of martial law brought the potential for conflict between religion and the state. Iowa General Tuttle, responsible for the occupation of Natchez, Mississippi, alienated the town's entire religious establishment by ordering that pastors cease praying for Jefferson Davis and redirect God's attention to President Lincoln. The Catholic bishop was the first to defy this order, but the Protestant clergy backed him up.[50]

VARIETIES OF DISSENT

Not all Iowans approved of the war. Dissent took various forms. Baptists, some with roots in the abolitionist-minded Burned-Over District in central New York and some hailing from the slaveholding South, had the widest spectrum of opinion of any denomination. It is no accident that the most notorious Copperhead martyr was a Baptist minister, Si Talley, from Ioka in Keokuk County.

The settlement of southern Iowa by upland Southerners predisposed some Iowans to nostalgic sympathy for the Confederate cause.[51] Talley found his oratorical skills resonated more in political rabble-rousing than in preaching. Following an anti-draft rally in Hobbs Grove, Talley led an armed parade through abolitionist-leaning South English,

---

47. Miller, *Punishment on the Nation*, 15, 18.
48. Miller, *Punishment on the Nation*, 96, 110, 122.
49. Miller, *Punishment on the Nation*, 60.
50. Lyftogt, *Iowa and the Civil War*, vol. 2, 302–4.
51. Cf. Pitcher, *My Heritage*, 54: "Granny was my grandmother on my mother's side. She was born . . . at Tallyrand, Iowa in 1859, Keokuk County Her parents came from the Carolinas which might explain her sympathy for the South."

home of Methodist, Baptist, and Christian churches.[52] John Brown had stopped there at Cora Glandon's house in 1856. The resident populace was also armed and someone fired. According to some accounts, only Talley was killed. His supporters from Wapello, Poweshiek, and maybe Mahaska counties vowed revenge and gathered along the Skunk River in western Keokuk County. Governor Grimes appeared personally to quell the threat of armed revolt.[53]

With some roots in Kentucky, Iowa Disciples were also particularly conflicted on the war. In her fine microhistory of early Iowa Disciples, Mina Davis Hargis uncovered several local examples. "Unwise notions and utterances on war issues caused intense friction" at the Pleasant Hill Church in Washington County. In Knoxville, a prominent local leader, Claybourne Hall, was a Southern sympathizer. The congregation told him to go South. He did, permanently. And in Davenport, the congregation's numbers were augmented by Kentucky refugees from the war. Rev. Amos Buchanan, who preached in Albia, was a pro-Northern refugee from Missouri.[54]

The affiliation of Catholics with the Democratic Party, so beneficial during Bishop Loras's time, ceased being advantageous. Dubuque Copperhead and Catholic Dennis Mahony tested the limits of free speech in wartime as a newspaper editor. The Lincoln administration did not pass the test.[55] Fortunately for Mahony, he had friends in high (ecclesiastical) places; Archbishop John Hughes of New York intervened with Secretary of State Seward to arrange Mahony's release from prison.[56]

Peace churches also dissented, in a very different way. Quakers were the most conflicted, as their peace testimony and abolitionist witness

---

52. "Excerpts from the 1976 Bicentennial Edition of the South English Herald"; Hargis, "History of the Disciples of Christ," 80. In the twenty-first century, South English had an American (formerly Northern) Baptist Church and a Church of the Brethren several miles east of town.

53. Jackson, *Iowa's Talley War*; Stiles, "Skunk River War (Or Tally War)"; Soike, *Necessary Courage*, 268; Gray, *Hidden*, 164–65; Lyftogt, *Iowa and the Civil War*, vol. 2, 282–300.

Lyftogt, following Stiles, confuses two different Keokuk County groves: Noffsinger Grove was on the banks of the English River, not the Skunk.

54. Hargis, "History of the Disciples of Christ," 36, 41, 89; Blanchard, "Pioneers of a Great Cause."

55. Kellison, "Prisoner of State," 113–18; Neely, *Fate of Liberty*, 58, 61; Wubben, *Civil War Iowa*, 51–92; Wubben, "Dennis Mahony."

56. Neely, *Fate of Liberty*, 58.

clashed.[57] Quakers like the Coppoc brothers of Springdale had already abandoned nonresistance principles before the war's outbreak, riding with John Brown on his ill-fated raid on the federal arsenal in Harpers Ferry, Virginia. Edwin Coppoc was among those hanged; Barclay escaped, and escaped extradition to Virginia with the connivance of Iowa authorities but died early during the Civil War.[58]

Iowa's new 1857 constitution recognized the right of conscientious objection—with the glaring loophole of it being in effect "in times of peace."[59] Iowa already had most of the historic peace churches represented in the state; the Quakers, Mennonites, Dunkards (now Brethren), and the Community of True Inspiration (the Amana colonies) jointly petitioned the legislature for the ability to exercise that right. The legislature ignored their petition. Draftees had to buy their way out of the military.[60]

The newly established Seventh-day Adventists separately petitioned the legislature. Iowa Adventists were more assertive in their pacifism than the founder, Ellen White.[61] White wrote, "In Iowa, they carried things to quite a length, and ran into fanaticism. They mistook zeal and fanaticism for conscientiousness. Instead of being guided by reason and sound judgment, they allowed their feelings to take the lead . . . Instead of making their petitions to the God of heaven . . . they petitioned the legislature and were refused."[62] But circumstances forced White to come around to the Iowa Adventists' point of view.

Perhaps no one personified the ambivalence some Iowans felt about the war better than Fr. Jeremiah Trecy, who had pastored churches in Iowa and managed to get credentialed as a chaplain by *both sides*.[63] Arguably the role of chaplain could encompass the needs of both Union and Confederate soldiers in proffering solace and perhaps an attempt at explanation. But the difficulties the nation would experience during

57. Jordan, "Dilemma of Quaker Pacifism"; "John Brown Among the Quakers."

58. Reynolds, *John Brown*, 261, 328, 370–78; Carton, *Patriotic Treason*, 6, 12, 259, 284, 294–312.

59. Pettys, *Iowa State Constitution*, 241; Stark, *Iowa State Constitution*, 133.

60. Shambaugh, *Constitution of Iowa*, 325–26; Ross, "Development of the Iowa Constitution of 1857"; Jones, *Quakers of Iowa*, 256, 333; Lehman and Nolt, *Mennonites, Amish, and the American Civil War*, 71; Gingerich, *Mennonites in Iowa*, 59, 101; Wright, *Conscientious*, 28–29, 51–52, 73; Hoehnle, "With Malice Toward None."

61. Morgan, *Adventism*, 32–33; Bull and Lockhart, *Seeking*, 143. See also Brock, *Against the Draft*, chapter 8.

62. White, *Testimonies for the Church*, vol. 1, 356–57.

63. Miller, *Both Prayed*, 115–16.

Reconstruction were anticipated by the elemental problem of occupying troops and the occupied attempting worship together;[64] one Iowa soldier loudly prayed for the destruction of the rebellion even as he was a prisoner of war.[65] The contrasting pulls of holding a common faith and being aggrieved by suffering for fighting in a righteous cause dominated the postwar era.

NEW REALITIES

While the Confederacy was clear that it seceded to establish a government based on white supremacy,[66] in the north war aims evolved, from simply protecting the Union to realizing the solution to slavery was abolition.

The four sermons that provide the epigraphs to this chapter also illustrate the chronological and ideological progression of a people's understanding of the reasons for the war. At its beginning, Old School Presbyterian A. A. E. Taylor saw the war as a fight for the union, much as Israel fought the tribe of Benjamin's secession. He never explicitly mentioned slavery, although those congregants inclined to do so could hear hints.

By late 1861, New School Presbyterian Isaac Carey was clear that the war was about slavery and its abolition. Probably, Carey was the preacher Cyrus Boyd heard while home on leave in 1862. Later in the war, and afterwards, united service preachers in Davenport went even further: the war must lead to racial equality. Henry Wallace and William Windsor prepared Iowa for its postwar turnaround on the question of black male suffrage. After Windsor's particularly bitter denunciation of the south and its treatment of Union prisoners of war, he contrasted the loyalty and bravery of freed slaves in the conflict with the treachery of Southern whites as an argument for political equality.

Iowans came to realize the consequences of such a stand: in the 1868 vote for black male suffrage, the "bright radical star" of Iowa shone, in choosing racial equality and reversing the previous decade's resounding vote for white supremacy. In the referendum, "the members of all church groups dramatically elevated their support for black suffrage between 1857 and 1868." Only Catholics, Baptists, and Disciples did not

---

64. Rable, *God's Almost Chosen Peoples*, 330.
65. Rable, *God's Almost Chosen Peoples*, 367.
66. Williams, *People's History of the Civil War*, 330.

provide majority support for the constitutional amendment.[67] Iowa Congregationalists were particularly active in the Reconstruction project of providing education to freed slaves.[68]

Catholics' skepticism about Republican war aims to keep the union and to abolish slavery had the unintended consequence of cementing their minority status, and furthered the consolidation of a Protestant hegemony in the state. President Grant's noteworthy 1875 Des Moines speech to veterans of the Army of the Tennessee[69] drew the lines: there could be no government support for religious educational institutions. But Catholics objected to no effect; public school systems privileged Protestant versions of the Bible and prayer.[70]

The problems with Protestant hegemony would only be addressed in the next century, while a new civil order was being constructed.

REVISIONIST VIEWS OF THE STRUGGLE

Cyrus Boyd's insistence that he was fighting to remove the scourge of slavery and the radical postwar victory for black suffrage marked a high point for racial equality; by the early twentieth century much of those gains had been eroded. A glimpse at a few early twentieth-century Iowa novels with religious themes shows a rewriting of events to privilege sectional rather than racial reconciliation.

Dominie Dean, the earliest and best of the novels, was primarily a 1917 plea for establishing a pension system for Protestant ministers and provided the mildest critique of Northern war aims. The hero, an Old School Presbyterian minister in Muscatine, at one point befriended an outcast who made bitter comments about the ongoing war. It turned out that he was not a Copperhead but a father grieving sons lost in the war. This mild anti-war take was ill-timed to be popular as the country entered World War I.[71]

The Law and the McLaughlins, a weak sequel to Margaret Wilson's Pulitzer Prize-winning *The Able McLaughlins,* distinguished between the

67. Dykstra, *Bright Radical Star,* 254–56.
68. Kaiser, *Grinnell Stories,* 9–28; Butchert and Rolleri, "Iowa Teachers."
69. Green, *Bible, the School, and the Constitution,* 187–88, 190; Green, *Second Disestablishment,* 193–95.
70. Green, *Bible, the School, and the Constitution,* 226.
71. Butler, *Dominie Dean,* 7. See also Frederick, "Town and Country in Iowa Fiction," 58.

rough-and-tumble Upper Midlands settlers of southern Iowa, who the more educated Scottish settlers disapproved of, and the refined plantation owners, who could be forgiven their errors because of their superior manners. Lost was any sense of the war being about slavery.[72]

Probably the most egregious example of an Iowa novel twisting the state's involvement in the Civil War[73] was written by Mathias Hoffmann. In the historical romance *Young and Fair Is Iowa*, where all the women are pure, all the men are strong, and the hero becomes a Catholic in the end, Hoffmann, unable to speak ill of any Catholic, whitewashed the problematic racism of Dennis Mahony.[74]

Iowans did not completely lose their sense of moral superiority about the Civil War; they gloried in the Underground Railroad and exaggerated their involvement. But increasingly in the early twentieth century, a consensus that valued sectional reconciliation over racial justice obscured the meaning of the war for Iowans who had fought it.

Only in the late 1950s, with the incipient civil rights movement as a backdrop, did Iowa novelists reexamine the purposes and sacrifices of the Civil War, notably in MacKinlay Kantor's Pulitzer Prize-winning *Andersonville*. He also wrote a sympathetic portrait of a disabled Civil War veteran in *Long Remember*.[75]

THE ASSASSINATION

Writing back to her family in the Netherlands just after the end of the war, Christine Budde-Stump poignantly described the relief, the horror, and the sadness that so many Iowans must have felt:

> Although we were graciously spared from being in the fighting zone, it still drips down, affecting us all. Constantly we live in fear that Johan will be drafted, that is, his [lottery] number drawn . . . At the beginning of the year things still looked somber . . . Pr. Lincoln was re-elected by a majority. He was a man of sterling character who had the welfare of the country at heart. Four long years the North had fought in vain, [but] now the

---

72. Wilson, *Law and the McLaughlins*; Andrews, *Literary History of Iowa*, 38.

73. I'm speaking of novels with religious themes; Josephine Herbst's takedown of "carpetbaggers" is also in contention.

74. See e.g., Lendt, "Copperhead Movement in Iowa," 414.

75. For an affectionate but critical portrait of Kantor, see Shroder *Greatest Novelist Who Ever Lived*.

> Lord gave the victory... Richmond was... taken. The Negroes were the first to march in; the slaves are free, the president [Jefferson Davis] fled and was captured in women's clothing. The South has been ravaged something awful...
>
> [After relating Lincoln's assassination], This all happened on Friday in April, and by Saturday the news was already known in our city [Burlington] via telegraph... We were also deeply touched by it all, and especially because the murderer's bullet struck him in a theater. I do not want to pass judgment, but let us walk circumspectly so that we are not conformed to the world.[76]

Budde-Stump did not want to judge, but she couldn't help herself; getting shot in the theater seemed among the most painful of wounds. But she also encapsulated the majority feeling of Iowans about the assassination and its emotional and religious repercussions.

Iowans came out of the war more united. As Congregationalist minister George Magoun of Lyons (now Clinton), addressing the American Home Missionary Society in 1862, put it,

> Certainly unity of principle is worth more to a nation than homogeneousness of race. A people heterogeneous in origin only, is like timber that is season-cracked. A people divided on any radical and common idea is like timber with a huge split running clean through... The Great [Mississippi] Valley already disproves the theory that the descendants of the Puritan and the Cavalier, Old World men and New, can not mingle and make one. A birth census of our troops before Island Ten or Corinth would be instructive.[77]

While Magoun's timber analogy may not translate well to twenty-first century audiences, his message was clear: whether it was due to war or living alongside each other, or both, a new sense of solidarity about what it meant to be an Iowan was being born.

The traumas of the war had created a certain solidarity that could be summoned up for varied (and increasingly fractious) reasons in the generation to come. The dissenters from the war more clearly felt themselves to be outsiders. Preachers like Henry Wallace and William Windsor were

---

76. Stellingwerff, *Iowa Letters*, 538–39.
77. Quoted in Stephenson, "Nativism in the Forties and Fifties," 202.

at least partially responsible for Iowa voters forthrightly rejecting the racist referendum of the previous decade barring black male suffrage.

The confrontation of the sin of slavery, theologically and physically, could—and did—lead to a recognition of other social ills. Confronting growing economic inequality, recovering personal piety, stoking missionary zeal that was often molded by American nationalism, and blending the individualism of Pietism and the social conscience of abolitionism into the temperance movement—such issues would preoccupy religious Iowa for the rest of the century.

The spiritual context for most denominations in the postwar era was the challenge of Holiness: how much should personal experience count in proportion to received tradition? Lincoln had died a martyr, but he died attending the theater; what was the proper balance of social justice and personal morality? And how was experiential religion to be policed? The Civil War was decisive on the issue of slavery but opened up entirely new sets of questions that could seem intractable. Vindication did not stop history, and the consequences would lead religious Iowans in both inward and outward directions.

CHAPTER 8

The Holiness Explosion

"The Society of Friends is dead. This [a Holiness revival] has killed it."
—Anonymous Bear Creek Friends Meeting member, standing on a chair and speaking in meeting for the only time in her life, 1877[1]

"When I arrived [Noah] Troyer was already in a trance . . . He lay there a little while longer, when suddenly he began to beat wildly about him with his hands, as if his nerves had received a sudden shock . . . he began to utter sounds, and finally lifted up his hands and commenced to pray in the English language . . . a very powerful and earnest prayer . . . for strength and assistance. Saying Amen, he fell upon his knees, and began to pray in the German language for help in his undertaking, in a more earnest manner than I ever before heard a minister pray."
—Jacob Naffziger, 1879[2]

"As I waited and waited, and continued in prayer, looking up, it seemed to me there came from the azure a meteor, an indescribable ball of condensed light . . .

---

1. Hamm, *Transformation of American Quakerism*, 141. Bear Creek is in Dallas County, near the Quaker-named Earlham, where both a Conservative (that is, harkening back to original seventeenth-century Quakerism) meeting and a Friends Church (accepting a programmed worship and evangelicalism) coexist.
2. Nofziger, "Further Account," 110.

The Holiness Explosion

I distinctly seemed to hear a voice saying, 'Swallow it, swallow it,' and in an instance it fell upon my lips and face . . . There came with it into my heart and being a transformed condition of life and being, a transformed condition of life and blessing and unction and glory, which I had never known before."

—PHINEAS F. BRESEE[3]

THE HOLINESS MOVEMENT THAT dominated much of the religious landscape of Iowa in the last half of the nineteenth century had deep roots and wide effects.

Holiness was sprawling, epitomized by the Keswick Movement but not confined to it, with every denomination affected by it giving it a new wrinkle, and with successive generations becoming ever more anxious for newer manifestations of the Spirit. Certainly the role of Methodism was pivotal in launching the movement, beginning with Methodist founder John Wesley's assertion of the possibility of perfection. European Pietism and American revivalism paralleled and fostered the movement. Pietism we discussed in connection with Scandinavian Lutheranism, the Church of the Brethren, and other German groups, in chapters 4 and 6. Pietism emphasized the individual's direct relationship with God.

Within Holiness, and seeking to perfect it, the Keswick movement formulated a specific set of steps that, it claimed, would lead to the Holiness goal of sanctification.[4]

THE REVIVALIST CONTEXT

Revivalism had a long history in the US, exemplified by the First and Second Great Awakenings. It evolved after the Civil War; the differences between Finney and Moody were significant. For New School Presbyterian Charles Finney, the road to sanctification was as much social as individual; he was active in the abolitionist movement. For postwar revivalists like Dwight Moody, and a generation later, the Iowan Billy Sunday, individual conversion became paramount. The crucial social issue for postwar revivalists shifted from slavery to alcohol abuse, and this

---

3. Quoted in Girvin, *Phineas F. Bresee*, 82.

4. Long, "Consecrated Respectability," chapter 8. The movement did not inspire the naming of Keswick, Iowa. Dilts, *From Ackley*, 109.

shift meant a new emphasis on personal responsibility. (We will discuss the complicated issue of temperance in chapter 12 and Billy Sunday's complicated relationship to Iowa in chapter 19.)

Moreover, in an increasingly urbanized society dominated by industrial capitalism, religion could be seen as a refuge from the chaotic nature of modernity. While this tendency became even more pronounced in the early twentieth century with the advent of fundamentalism, the Holiness movement anticipated it. Paradoxically, Holiness also had a modernizing effect on relatively insular groups like the Quakers and the Amish Mennonites, with religious techniques and a common religious language that spanned denominations and an emphasis on individualism that challenged groups that depended on communal consensus.

Methodist minister Mahlon Day Collins's son well describes a representative revival meeting that his father presided over:

> During the sermon, one heard frequent, fervent "Amens," "Hallelujahs," "Praise Gods," and other words of approbation and signs of exaltation. With the opening of the after meeting, came more frequent shouts mingled with vociferous rendition of gospel songs. When a sinner stood up, signifying conversion, the welkin rang with mingled shouts of brothers and sisters. Many other sounds of religious fervor joined the volume.[5]

Typical was the revival in one community: centering in Elm Grove Church, Madison County, in the decade of the 1860s. It affected Methodists, Evangelicals, and Christian Union members.[6]

QUAKER DISRUPTION

No group was affected more profoundly by Holiness teaching in Iowa than the Quakers, who were split asunder. The Society of Friends did have a tradition of emphasizing religious experience, and the first Quakers were disruptive of what they saw as lifeless worship services in the established

---

5. Collins, "Story of a Collins," 78, in Mahlon Day Collins Papers, SHSI-DM.

6. Ogburn, "Pioneer Religious Revival." Probably the Evangelicals were German Methodists, not German Reformed; the Christian Union was an anti-abolitionist split from the (Northern) Methodist Episcopal Church in 1864, if my reading of its not entirely coherent website is correct (see "Christian Union"). See also Richey et al., *Methodist Experience in America*, 203–4. There were still two Christian Union churches in Warren County, in Indianola and Milo, in 2021. The name "Churches of Christ in Christian Union" deceptively suggests an affiliation with Restorationist Disciples/Christian/Churches of Christ.

church and other sects. On the other hand, their worship practice of waiting on the calling of the Spirit had sometimes led to quietism, and their rigorous moral formation was usually manifested by an aura of personal dignity antithetical to the wilder, emotional expressions of revivalism. These contradictions would come into explosive and divisive conflict in Iowa Friends' meetinghouses, beginning in the 1870s.[7]

The revivals that seeped in from Ohio and Indiana began in central Iowa at meetings at Honey Creek (New Providence, Hardin County) and Bangor (in nearby Marshall County.) (Quaker meetings are the equivalent of congregations, except that monthly and yearly meetings have a wider jurisdiction.)

In actions that might be seen as contradicting assertions of seeking perfection, Holiness advocates began to consolidate power within the Iowa Yearly Meeting. This was, as consolidations of power usually are, messy.

One of the most prominent Quakers in the state, Joel Bean, was in accord with most of the Holiness program—but he dared dissent on details. Specifically, Quaker revivalists, in order to conform to the standard Protestant doctrine of original sin, which seemed necessary if converting sinners was the goal, had begun denouncing the distinctive Quaker doctrine of the inner light, that there is "that of God in everyone." Denying this doctrine was a bridge too far for Bean. Also, the Holiness doctrine of instant sanctification seemed contrary to experience and to the Quaker methodology of careful self-examination over a lifetime.[8]

When Joel and Hannah Bean found themselves stymied in their own West Branch meeting by revival enthusiasts, they moved on to California in 1883. Holiness connections between Iowa and California, both Quaker and non-Quaker, would be multitudinous.

The bitterness of the divisions wrought by Holiness among Quakers continued throughout the twentieth century. Cecil Hinshaw, the visionary president of William Penn College, was viewed suspiciously by some outside the Conservative Iowa Yearly Meeting, despite his Kansas Holiness background, as he sometimes accepted unprogrammed worship.[9] (In the peculiar language of Quakerism, Conservative Friends were those who kept the original orientation of the group, opposed the "hireling

---

7. Hamm, "Divergent Paths of Iowa Quakers"; Marsh, *Lively Faith*; Holden, *Friends Divided*, chapter 13, "Iowa's Quaker Multiplicity." See also Wood, "Evangelical Quaker Acculturation"; Brinton, "Revival Movement in Iowa."

8. Hamm, "Joel Bean and the Revival in Iowa."

9. Douglas, "Penn in Technicolor," 61–62.

ministry" and the revivalistic tendencies of American evangelical Protestantism, and were more likely to uphold traditional Quaker pacifism—which usually meant that they were not political conservatives.)

Poet Amy Clampitt, who was born in 1920 and raised in the Quaker community of New Providence, felt she had grown up in "a 'benighted' hybrid of church and meetinghouse."[10] More than a century after the fact, an Iowa Quaker could begin her family stories with the following lament:

> Thomas was born to Quaker parents in the year of the Great Separation in 1877, on a farm in Keokuk County, Iowa . . . Thomas was several years old before he knew there were other kinds of Quakers in the world, people who worshipped differently with organs and hymns and had just one person who was allowed to speak, who stood before you in a pulpit and told you what to believe and when to stand up and sit down. He came to know that in the year of his birth his parents and grandparents and a few others left a Meeting House across the County and stood in the yard and cried, and had never gone back because they weren't welcome."[11]

The contention that the Holiness movement was more divisive among the Quakers than any other group seems sound.

THE AMISH SLEEPING PREACHER

Surely one of the most peculiar manifestations of a kind of Holiness occurred among the Johnson County Amish. People came from miles around to see the spectacle of Noah Troyer, the sleeping preacher. He may have engaged in glossolalia; that evidence isn't clear. What is clear is that in his sleeping trance, he challenged the authority of Amish ministers chosen by lot and suggested a more direct form of revelation and authority. While Troyer's trance state seemed genuine, attested to by numerous spectators and medical doctors, his more inclusive message did presage and coincide with the impending division between tradition-upholding Old Order Amish and more flexible Amish Mennonites. Unconscious

---

10. Salter, "Foreword," xiii-xiv. Clampitt, who settled in New York City, for a time became an Episcopalian, but stopped when she viewed its leaders as insufficiently opposed to the US war in Indochina. For where Amy's father finally came down on the subject of Holiness, see Roy Clampitt, *Life I Did Not Plan*. Her grandfather Frank Clampitt also wrote an autobiography.

11. Lacey, *Silent Friends*, 3, 10.

preaching turned out to be one of the few safe ways to challenge Amish religious authority; several other Amish sleeping preachers took up Troyer's mission after him.[12]

METHODISM AS INCUBATOR AND INOCULATOR

The perfectionist strain in Methodism was present from the beginning, but by the time of the Gilded Age, or the second generation of Iowa Methodists, it became muted in many increasingly middle-class, respectable congregations.

Doubtless there was also a developing regional divide in American Methodism between the heartland and the coasts: Phineas Bresee was esteemed among Iowa Methodist clergy, serving parishes in Koszta (Iowa County), Marengo, Pella, Grinnell, Galesburg (Jasper County), Chariton, Red Oak, Clarinda, Council Bluffs, Creston, and Des Moines.[13] Then as now, bishops moved Methodist pastors around frequently. Almost simultaneously with Joel Bean, but on an opposite trajectory, in 1883, at age 44, Bresee moved to Southern California. There he felt increasingly estranged from his fellow Methodists, whom he thought were ignoring Wesley's doctrine of sanctification.

Seeking to "Christianize Christianity,"[14] Phineas Bresee was arguably the most important Iowan in the Holiness movement. After being a Methodist pastor in Iowa for decades, his response to the different religious environment in southern California was to found a new denomination, the Church of the Nazarene, the first and largest Holiness breakoff from mainline Protestantism.[15] Were Iowa Methodists more congenial to Holiness or simply more accepting of differences in theology and practice? Later evidence suggests the latter,[16] but probably both were true.

---

12. Troyer, *Sermons*; Reschly, *Amish on the Iowa Prairie*, 132–57; Nolt, *History of the Amish*, 161.

13. Girvin, *Bresee*, 33–40, 45, 50–55, 59, 67, 69, 70; Jones, "Holiness Complaint with Late-Victorian Methodism," 59–63.

14. Redford, *Rise of the Church of the Nazarene*, 46.

15. Smith, *Called unto Holiness*, chapters 2 and 5.

16. In 1944, the pacifist pastor of Collegiate Methodist in Ames, Sam Nichols, received an honorary degree from Iowa Wesleyan College. The commencement speaker then gave a jingoistic speech. Nichols was unfazed by the contradictions: "That's the Iowa Conference" was all he would say.

Paralleling the career trajectory of Bresee was that of Edgar Ellyson, who was headmaster of the Friends Church school in Marshalltown, moved to Texas, and became prominent in Nazarene education endeavors.[17]

The Methodist Deaconess movement was also contested territory. Iva Dunham Vennard, founder of Vennard College in University Park near Oskaloosa, stressed that evangelism should be paramount.[18]

It was likely breathtaking for the Presbyterian Isaiah Reid of Nevada to be elected to lead the Iowa Holiness Association. But he soon found himself a gatekeeper, trying to protect the association from radicals like Benjamin Irwin who wanted to burn down ecclesiastical structures and start over.[19]

HOLINESS HEATS UP

In the 1890s, Holiness craving for intensity grew, and parts of it came ever closer to what would become the Pentecostal movement of the next decade. No one pushed the limits of Holiness intensity more than Benjamin Hardin Irwin.[20]

This Lincoln, Nebraska, firebrand was not satisfied with mere sanctification after salvation; he wanted even more religious breakthroughs, starting with "baptism by fire" and going on to baptism by dynamite and even more explosive experiences with "lyddite" and "oxidite." Intensity of religious experience replaced the comforts of assurance in Irwin's schema.[21]

Irwin was invited by Wesleyan Methodists to hold protracted meetings in Des Moines, Coon Rapids, Guthrie Center, and Woodward and organized his first religious group as the Fire-Baptized Holiness Association of Southern Iowa during a revival at Olmitz in Lucas County. Olmitz was more of a campsite than a town, one frequented by Holiness gatherings in the nineties. It was also in Iowa's coal belt, which became fertile ground for Irwin and associates to spread their message of direct experiences of God without the mediation of middle-class churches.[22]

17. Marshalltown *Times-Republican*, Sep. 26, 1904; Smith, *Called unto Holiness*, 146, 166, 217–18, 258, 261, 331; Watson, *William Penn College*, 45.

18. Pope-Levison, "'Thirty Year War' and More."

19. Dieter, *Holiness Revival*, 262; Stephens, *Fire Spreads*, 180, 174; Synan, *Holiness-Pentecostal Movement*, 47, 63; Kostlevy, *Holy Jumpers*, 26, 33–34, 72.

20. Fankhauser, "Heritage of Faith," chapter 6.

21. Stephens, *Fire Spreads*, 180–83.

22. Synan, *Holiness-Pentecostal Movement*, 63, 67.

The Holiness Explosion

The Fire-Baptized Holiness Association was a challenge not just to mainline Protestant churches but also to the Iowa Holiness Association, who saw Irwin's teachings as a devaluation of sanctification and his come-outerism as an ecclesiastical challenge to those working within existing denominations. His Iowa associate was Rev. Dull, who came to Holiness from the Iowa Yearly Meeting of Friends.

Irwin also shared with some late twentieth-century Pentecostal leaders a kind of antinomianism that reasoned that being beyond sin, any behavior was acceptable to the Lord. This reasoning, accompanied by a blatant disregard for discretion, usually leads to disgrace—especially if one is to solicit a prostitute in downtown Kansas City while carrying a suitcase emblazoned with the logo of the "Fire-Baptized Holiness Association!" Upon his arrest, journalists were quick to recognize a juicy story. Such headlines are not conducive to the image of piety that most persons of the cloth find helpful to project.

Fire-Baptized Holiness folks regrouped in Olmitz, eventually becoming the Pentecostal Holiness Church.[23]

Another radical Holiness group that made inroads into Iowa was the Metropolitan Church Association, From its communal headquarters in Waukesha, it founded outposts in Fort Dodge and Waterloo during the 1920s.[24]

For the increasingly edgy extremes of Holiness, what would be the next test of religious experience? Only in retrospect was the answer obvious: glossolalia. Early Pentecostalism's Iowa connections are incidental: Charles F. Parham, one of the leaders of the Azusa Street Revival of Los Angeles that would found Pentecostalism, was born in Muscatine on June 4, 1873. But Parham grew up in Topeka.[25]

More crucial are Parham's connections with Benjamin Irwin; the bubbling pot of extreme Holiness boiled over early in the twentieth century into Pentecostalism, as speaking in tongues became the new distinguishing mark of sanctification. The respectability of Phoebe Palmer's holiness concepts was rejected in favor of Irwin's exuberance. But taming tendencies played the long game.

23. Synan, *Holiness-Pentecostal Movement*, 67.
24. Kostlevy, *Holy Jumpers*, 136, 147, 152.
25. Goff, *Fields White unto Harvest*, 17–20.

INSTITUTIONAL MANIFESTATIONS

Tensions also cropped up between Holiness churches and the newer Fundamentalist movement. Writing to a Holiness newspaper, C. G. Curry of Farmington warned that the interdenominational tendencies of Fundamentalists might water down distinctive Holiness doctrine.[26] Nonetheless, in the long run the individualism that characterized Fundamentalism would draw most Holiness advocates into its orbit. (And there would be negotiations, as orthodox Protestant Fundamentalists wondered at the new departures of Holiness—and then Pentecostal—denominations, heedless of their own innovations.)[27]

Of course, the Holiness movement would establish its own institutions. And modernity also caught up with the Holiness movement: the last of the national Holiness camp meetings took place in University Park, just outside of Oskaloosa, in June of 1942.[28] The too-ambitiously named University Park, not coincidentally, was the home of Vennard College.[29]

The same ethos that infused Vennard propelled the Hephzibah Faith Missionary Association, a Tabor, Iowa-based group. As its name implied, it was part denomination and part missionary society. When it folded in 1949, it divided its assets between the Church of the Nazarene and the Wesleyan Methodist Church,[30] signaling its affinity with both Holiness and Methodism.[31]

The vigorous Salvation Army march into Iowa, combining Holiness with outreach to the impoverished, began with a church in Maquoketa.[32]

---

26. George, "Selfhood and the Search for Identity," 158.

27. The most cogent critique of Fundamentalism remains Douglas Frank, *Less Than Conquerors*. This attack at short range seems more effective than more broadside efforts by Balmer and Fitzgerald, among others.

28. George, "Selfhood and the Search for Identity," 100.

29. DMR, Nov. 13, 2008; March 6, 2007; Harris, *Torch Goeth Onward*. Previous incarnations of the Iowa campus were Central Holiness University, John Fletcher College, and Kletzing College. Jones, *Guide to the Study of the Holiness Movement*, 554, 563–64; "Heritage" (Vennard College Alumni Association); Kostlevy, *Historical Dictionary of the Holiness Movement*, 303.

30. McLeister and Nicholson, *Conscience and Commitment*, 224–25, 361, 438; *Iowa Redbook*, 1986, 196.

31. Worcester, *Master Key*. Hephzibah was the name of the people of Beulah land, in Isaiah 62:4. For references to the association's newspaper, *Sent of God*, see Synan, *Holiness-Pentecostal Movement*, 41, 47, 67, 230.

32. CRG, Jan. 14, 2000; "Salvation Army" (Historical Marker Project).

The Holiness Explosion

Benjamin Irwin was by no means the last of Holiness-Pentecostal pastors to be flamboyantly caught in an inappropriate situation. In reaction to the well-publicized escapades of Aimee Semple McPherson, some Midwestern churches, led by a congregation in Des Moines, withdrew from her orbit and founded the Open Bible denomination (later merging with a Pacific Northwest group to form the Des Moines-based Open Bible Standard Churches).[33]

From 1927 to 1933, Ottumwa served as national headquarters of the Pentecostal Church of God.[34]

Permission Messenger Publishing House

The Church of the Nazarene also found beachheads in Iowa, perhaps challenging Phineas Bresee's acceptance of Iowa Methodism while he was a Methodist in good standing in the state.[35]

In 1918, what would become the largest black Pentecostal denomination, the Church of God in Christ, entered the state with a revival in

---

33. Mitchell, *Heritage and Horizons*, 130–49; Blumhofer, *McPherson*, 334–36. It should be noted that Foursquare Gospel churches continued in the state. DMR, Feb. 19, 1997.

34. "Our Story" (Pentecostal Church of God).

35. Whitlatch, *On Good Soil*.

Des Moines. By 1930, there were also churches in Sioux City, Waterloo, Cedar Rapids, Davenport, and Ottumwa.[36]

Jane Smiley, in her trilogy of a twentieth century central Iowa family, wrote in the first book *Some Luck* about the farm family abandoning mainstream Protestantism and finding consolation in Pentecostalism in the thirties. But their sojourn there was only temporary. (Perhaps tellingly, religion is absent from the trilogy in the middle years of the twentieth century but reemerges in the third volume.)[37]

Ensconced in a more traditional reality and yet open to the benefits of the Holiness movement, Joel Bean can serve as critic for the Holiness movement. Its individualism and intensity could have negative as well as positive outcomes.

Bean's attempt to balance the intensity of Holiness with a Quaker sense of propriety was not one that he could sustain.

A NATIVE AMERICAN TAKE ON HOLINESS

And yet the yearning of the human spirit for a Holy Spirit cannot easily be contained, especially when human circumstances are dire. By the turn of the century, an expanding technocracy, the mechanization of work, the loss of individual control over production, and a new economy of consumption all played roles in the rise of the Holiness movement.

Revivals of "holy rollers" and holiness believers, replete with unorthodox behaviors, were contemporaneous with the Ghost Dance.[38]

The link between the Ghost Dance and Holiness, despite the cultural differences, seems clear. While the Ghost Dance did not appear on the Meskwaki settlement, soon after a similar movement linking messianic

---

36. Consecration and Installation Service for Bishop Hurley Bassett, Oct. 8, 1976 bulletin, scanned copy in possession of the author. Thanks to Kari Bassett of the Black History Research Collective for sharing this. Cf. Gaustad, Fig. 2.125, which showed COGIC strength in Polk, Black Hawk, Marshall, and Scott counties in 1990.

37. Smiley, *Some Luck*, 172–74. The other titles in the trilogy are *Early Warning* and *Golden Age*. Suggestively, the middle volume doesn't deal with religion, but it returns as a topic in the concluding volume.

38. Warren, *God's Red Son*, 39. For another glimpse at the intersection of white working class and Native religion, see the Iowa-born poet Meridel LeSueur, "Ancient People and the Newly Come," in *Growing Up in Minnesota*, 25–29. Also note Nolt, *History of the Amish*, 161.

prophecy and Native identity did gain a foothold. The Native American Church, best known for its use of peyote as a sacrament, was more insistent on its links to Christianity than the Ghost Dance and received more pushback for that, both from Christians and from native traditionalists. In the Native American Church, pan-Indian religion once again became an option available to the Meskwaki settlement.[39] But most Meskwakis preferred particularism.

The Holiness stress on personal conversion dovetailed with a new, wider emphasis among American Protestants on the crucial importance of missionary activity. Iowa quickly moved from a mission outpost to an exporter of missionaries, as the next chapter describes.

---

39. Baker, *Study of the Presbyterian Mission*, 24–25; Niezen, *Spirit Wars*, 171. It is also suggestive that one of the congregations catering to the Meskwaki in the twenty-first century, if not quite on the settlement, is a Friends Church, and the other is Pentecostal, an Assembly of God congregation.

CHAPTER 9

Quick Turnaround

From Mission Field to Missionary Zeal

"We are no longer the recipient of the lavish bounty of the East."
—Episcopal Bishop William Stevens Perry, 1878[1]

"No one thing in Africa produced a more profound impression on me than the psychological accuracy with which the Africans had given drum-names to the missionaries. The drum-name of the late Charles W. McCleary, the name he was known from Batanga to Elat, was "The Beloved.""
—A. W. Halsey[2]

"To the Chinese girls
Students in
The Mary Porter Gamewell School
In Peking
Who Learn There the Ideal
Of Christian Womanhood
And Who Purpose to Work it out
In Daily Living
This Book is Dedicated."
—Ethel Daniels Hubbard[3]

   1. Quoted in Horton, *Beautiful Heritage*, 68.
   2. Hinkhouse, *"Beloved,"* 3.
   3. Hubbard, *Under Marching Orders*, 1909, iii.

Quick Turnaround

"This story . . . is about a farmboy of Irish-Swiss descent, Ronald William Hennessey, born and bred in the corn and oat fields of eastern Iowa during the Depression. He was drafted into military service some years after high school and sent to war in Korea, where the reality of war made him feel a call to become a missionary. He returned home, farmed a bit more, entered a Roman Catholic seminary, and was ordained a priest in 1964. That same year, he was missioned to Guatemala."

—THOMAS MELVILLE[4]

IN THE BASEMENT OF Frischel Hall at Wartburg Seminary in Dubuque are exhibits of artifacts that at first seem out of place at a North American Lutheran theological school: Papua New Guinea tribal drums, bowls, and weapons.[5] A legacy of World War I's disruption of German missions and the Australian Lutheran Church's efforts to seek American help, this strand of memorabilia begins to suggest the breadth of the missionary movement in Iowa. The pieces are one small material indication that links Iowans to people all over the world.

In just a generation, Iowa went from mission field to missionary exporter. From American westward expansion and the collateral consequences of engaging Native Americans now mostly confined to reservations, American Christians increasingly pivoted toward global concerns. The closing of the frontier and the turn toward an international presence were intertwined; as Iowa Congressperson John Kasson put it in 1881, "We are rapidly utilizing the whole of our continental territory. We must turn our eyes abroad, or they will soon look inward upon discontent."[6]

That discontent happened, and was evident in Iowa as Kasson pontificated, but issues raised in the mission fields also circled back to haunt, confronting Americans with questions of gender, race, class, and imperialism they had sought to avoid by pushing onward.[7] But onward meant confronting the exotic nature of the non-Western world.

4. Melville, *Through a Glass Darkly*, 12.
5. "Papua New Guinea Museum."
6. Quoted in Williams, *Tragedy of American Diplomacy*, 20.
7. See, e.g., Hollinger, *Protestants Abroad*; Cox, *Imperial Fault Lines India*; Walls,

The People Are Kind

Sometimes the link between Iowa as missionary field and Iowa as sender of missionaries was explicit. Faced with an unprecedented number of conversions in southern India, Iowa Baptist John Clough confronted the question of how dependent the new churches should be on Western support. Clough recalled the aid of East Coast and European groups in church-planting in Iowa to justify support for indigenous churches in Asia.[8]

This chapter will attempt an overview of Iowa missionary activity through the twentieth century. This will be impressionistic; comprehensiveness would require volumes,[9] but ignoring mission would skew the picture of Iowa religion too much toward inward-looking. The prominence of women as missionaries will also be noted.[10]

MISSION TO THE US WEST

A monument stands atop Prospect Hill on Sioux City's southern edge, erected by Iowa Presbyterians in 1913. There, in April 1869, with Columbus-like audacity, Presbyterian missionary Sheldon Jackson and associates looked across the Missouri River and proclaimed all the land westward to the Pacific to be under the jurisdiction of the Western Iowa Presbytery. That this end-arounded national authorities of the Presbyterian Church does not detract from its boldness.[11] Jackson's legacy lives on in the name of the northwest Iowa presbytery, Prospect Hill.[12]

Missionary Movement in Christian History.

8. Harris, "Social Dimensions of Foreign Missions," 93.

9. A glance at state denominational histories hints at the breadth of the movement. Iowa Baptists already had sent out fifty-eight missionaries by the time of their centenary in 1937. The Iowa Yearly Meeting of Friends had sent fifty-one missionaries to Jamaica by 1963 and a handful elsewhere.

10. On the outsize role of women in the American mission project, see, e.g., Robert, *American Women in Mission*; Huber and Nancy C. Lutkenhaus, *Gendered Missions*; Hill, *World Their Household*; Hunter, *Gospel of Gentility*.

11. Bishop Loras once made a similar claim, suggesting that the territory of Oregon was within the jurisdiction of the Diocese of Dubuque. Auge, *Man of Deeds*, 108.

12. Bender, "Sheldon Jackson's Crusade"; Lazell, *Alaskan Apostle*; Szasz, *Protestant Clergy*, 20–21.

A decade and a half earlier, the newly constituted Synod of Iowa had been given smaller parameters, " . . . North of the State of Missouri and East of the Rocky

Jackson's maneuver was temporary and symbolic; the religious demographics of the West trended more unchurched than other regions.[13] He later achieved fame in Alaska, where a junior college bears his name.[14]

Iowa Protestant outreach was not restricted to Western settlers. Increasingly in the late nineteenth century, unease about European-Americans' treatment of Native Americans surfaced. Iowa Quaker leaders Enoch Hoag, Brinton Darlington, and Lawrie Tatum, horrified at the news that Indian policy might be moved from the troubled Interior Department back to the War Department, dissuaded the Grant administration of that course. Quakers and other religious groups were invited to administer the reservations.[15]

Quaker national leadership scrambled, nominating several Iowans to posts. Enoch Hoag of Muscatine was appointed superintendent of the Central region (now Oklahoma). Two Indian Territory agents left memoirs: Thomas Battey of Viola and Lawrie Tatum of Springdale. While mitigating some rough edges of Indian policy, the underlying injustice of the theft of indigenous land was not resolved by adding kindness to the system.[16]

MISSION TO THE SOUTH

Simultaneous with Sheldon Jackson's Presbyterian landgrab, other denominations engaged in more concrete interior mission projects. Iowa Congregationalists and Campbellites worked on Reconstruction efforts to aid the Freedmens' Bureau and pioneered in educational missions to the South.[17]

Harlan Paul Douglass was a native of Osage, Iowa, and graduate of Iowa College during the Gates-Herron era (see chapter 11). He followed his father Truman Douglas into the Congregational ministry but had a career course correction in 1906 when his pastorate in Springfield,

---

Mountains." "Records of the Synod of Iowa," 39, 110.

13. Szasz, *Protestant Clergy*. Jackson's method of organizing churches in the mountain West was frenetic but hit-and-miss, with no time for follow-up. Cf. the use of "Presbyterian Church" as a location in the anti-Western movie *McCabe and Mrs. Miller*.

14. Lazell, *Alaskan Apostle*.

15. Milner, *With Good Intentions*, 1, 20, 88; Jones, *Quakers of Iowa*, 203–14.

16. Battey, *Life and Adventures of a Quaker*; Tatum, *Our Red Brothers*; McLean, *Hulda's World*, 86.

17. Butchart and Rolleri, "Iowa Teachers among the Freedpeople of the South."

Missouri, was shaken by a triple lynching there. The victims of the lynching were posthumously adjudged innocent, but no lynchers were convicted. Douglass became leader of the American Missionary Association, reorienting it toward promoting racial equality.[18]

As Douglass moved from local ministry to a national focus, another Iowan began a local project in the South. In 1909, African-American Iowan Laurence C. Jones launched the Piney Woods School in Mississippi, depending on religious support for viability (at least until 1954, when he appeared on the television show *This Is Your Life*, which enhanced publicity and fundraising considerably). Methodists at Upper Iowa University in Fayette consistently supported Jones's enterprise.[19]

THE LURE OF FOREIGN MISSIONS[20]

After the Civil War, Iowa Protestants embraced the concept that the kingdom of God would bloom when the gospel was taken to every land. This essentially postmillennialist notion was capable of variations, as premillennialists came to dominate the mission scene by the late twentieth century.

Supporting such a movement presented challenges. For Iowa City women Disciples, there were at least three: in a denomination of very diffuse power, could Women's Missionary Societies be effective? Could women act independently within the congregation? And also, specific to Iowa City, it was a time of congregational turmoil—was that an opportune time to launch an ambitious endeavor?[21] Minister's wife Caroline Neville Pearre calculated that the answers ought to be yes, and in April 1874 started the Iowa City Women's Missionary Society, the first local Disciples society in the country. Later that year, Pearre was active in forming the national society, becoming its first secretary.[22]

---

18. Luker, *Social Gospel in Black and White*.

19. Day, *Little Professor*, 9, 171–73, 184–85; Jones, *Piney Woods*; DMR, Aug. 8, 2008; DMR, Aug. 24, 2008; Campbell, *Providence*, 240.

20. In the precise vocabulary of mid-twentieth century missiology, "mission" became the preferred word, but the plural was ubiquitous in the nineteenth century.

21. Hudson, *Community of Believers and Seekers*, 23–25; Turner, "Christian Women's Board of Missions," 54; Harrison, *Forty Years of Service*, 4, 26–36.

22. Hudson, *Community of Believers and Seekers*, 25; Moseley, "Christian Church," 240–41. Moseley lists the Des Moines fellowship as also starting in 1874. For another mention of an early local women's Disciples missionary fellowship, in Davenport starting in 1874, see Ozieblo, *Susan Glaspell*, 14.

Quick Turnaround

It was an idea whose time had come:

> The organizing ability and untiring energy that went into the [Christian Women's Board of Missions] would have made almost any enterprise a success. The regular meetings of the local auxiliaries . . . and the publication of the monthly *Missionary Tidings* and other literature constituted a vast program of missionary education. A system of regular dues produced a trickle of dimes which aggregated a torrent of dollars. By 1909 there were 60,000 adult members.
>
> Offerings up to that time had totaled nearly $2,500,000. Missions were conducted in Jamaica, India, Mexico, Puerto Rico, Argentina, and Liberia . . .[23]

The women's missionary societies of other mainline Protestant denominations replicated that zeal and energy.[24]

The attempt to cover the globe meant that Iowa missionaries might land in the middle of chaotic events. Iowa College Congregationalists in Turkey became protectors of Armenians. Mary E. Brewer, class of 1885, "went out"—to use the missionary term—in 1888, assigned to her father's childhood missionary home in Turkey (the same year her sister went out to the Sandwich Islands, where their mother was a child of missionaries). In Sivas, Brewer was principal of the Girls' Boarding School. Legally prohibited from converting Muslims, Congregationalists focused attention on their fellow Christians, the Armenians.[25]

23. Ozieblo, *Susan Glaspell*, 128. One Iowa Disciple who became a missionary was Myrle Olive Ward, a native of Hamburg, Iowa, who served both in Jamaica and, for decades (1925–1959), as a teacher in the Belgian Congo. Myrle Olive Ward Papers, IWA.

24. E.g., see Klumpp, "From Prairie to Parsonage," 63–64.

25. *Iowa College Quinquennial 1897*, 77; "Gift of Iowa College to Foreign Missions," in Grinnell College Special Collections, "Foreign Missions" folder, 55 Pl-5; "Letters by and Information about Miss Mary E. Brewer, 1889–1899," F5 S1; *Grinnell Herald*, Dec. 19, 1895; *86th Annual Report*, 127, 48–49; *American Board of Missions Almanac*, 1897, 24–25, 1896, 38–39.

Another Iowa College alumna was also a missionary to Turkey who witnessed the 1895 massacres. Idaline Mellinger, stationed in Oorfa, went on an extensive speaking tour in England and Scotland on behalf of Armenian relief. See Boyd-Bayly, *Brief Memoir of Ida Mellinger*. Mellinger herself collaborated with Deborah Alcock (Boyd-Bayly's mother) on *By Far Euphrates*, which for reasons I can't fathom was written as a work of fiction. Like Iowa public schoolteachers well into the 1940s, for single female Congregationalist missionaries, getting married was a breach of contract. Mellinger married an Armenian physician in 1899.

The People Are Kind

On November 12, 1895, a weeklong attack on the Armenian community in Sivas began. About 1200 Armenians were killed.[26] "Miss Brewer has been in the very midst of the Armenian Massacres," reported her *alma mater*. "She has often imperiled her own life to save others, showing heroism that has received wide recognition."[27]

A shaken Missions Board reported of the whole region,

> The marked event of the year . . . has been the wave of massacre and robbery and outrage which swept the whole field of this mission [Western Turkey] during the months of October, November, and December . . . The whole weight of this calamity fell upon the Armenian people . . . This experience has no parallel in the history of the missions of the Board.
>
> . . . We take note of the steadfastness and heroism of the missionaries, not a man or a woman leaving his post or quailing before the terror or declining to share the fortunes of the people so fearfully assailed . . .[28]

Iowa College president George Gates lauded the missionaries for their nonviolence. But not all Congregationalists drew the same conclusion from the Armenian persecution; Josiah Strong wanted the US to intervene militarily, and the outrage about Ottoman attacks on mission compounds anticipated calls for military intervention in Cuba in 1898.[29] The attack on Armenians presaged many twentieth century American missionary quandaries.

By 1890, many Iowans heard calls to the mission fields. Here is a representative sampling:

For an overview of ABFM's educational missions in Turkey, see Keller and Keller, "American Board Missions in Turkey," 49–74.

26. Balakian, *Burning Tigris*, 59; A two-page eyewitness report can be found in Bliss, *Turkey and the Armenian Atrocities*, 462–64. Bliss identifies the eyewitness only as "a perfectly reliable source;" we can speculate that it came from one of the five Congregational missionaries in Sivas, or perhaps from the American consul.

27. *Iowa College Quinquennial 1897*, 77.

28. *86th Annual Report*, 48–49.

29. Reed, *Reminiscences*, 236–39.

Quick Turnaround

Loduska Wyrick served with distinction as a missionary to Japan, starting in 1890. She was the first graduate of Drake University's College of the Bible to become a missionary.[30]

"*The Gospel Missionary* reported . . . on a group of medical missionaries, led by a woman, who departed from Iowa for the Congo."[31]

Charles Warner McCleary, a Presbyterian from Crawfordsville, died "a martyr" in Elat, Cameroon, succumbing to an unidentified tropical fever. The frontispiece in his memorial biography has a photograph of him with pith helmet, looking a bit perplexed at his new world.[32] He was one of several missionaries educated at Parsons College in Fairfield.[33] Parallel tinges of guilt and pride appear in retelling his life, with death seen as martyrdom.

Frontispiece, *The Beloved*

30. DMR, Sep. 12, 2001. By 1905 "about 23 missionaries had gone out from Drake." Drake *Delphic,* Sep. 21, 1905.

31. Quoted in Robert, *American Women in Mission,* 207.

32. Hinkhouse, "*Beloved,*" 9.

33. Hubbard, "Our Picture Gallery," in *Presbyterian Church in Iowa,* 78–79 (separate pagination).

One of the few African American Iowa missionaries was Susan Angeline Collins. Collins moved as a youth with her family to a tiny African American farming enclave near Fayette after the Civil War and graduated from Upper Iowa University. She spent her adulthood as a Methodist missionary in Angola, returning to Fayette upon retirement to bask in the admiration of her fellow congregants.[34]

Even a relatively small denomination such as the United Brethren in Christ could list fifteen foreign missionaries and three martyrs from Iowa.[35]

Iowa Catholics would also develop a missionary presence. Divine Word College in Epworth bills itself as "the smallest college in Iowa, [but part] of the largest international order of men in the Catholic Church."[36] (That it is in the Methodist-sounding town of Epworth is due to an earlier incarnation of the college.[37])

The largest missionary presence was in Asia, in the two most populous regions, China and India.

CHINA

While Africa and New Guinea may have felt more exotic, populous China seemed key to the goal of the evangelization of the world.

Mary Porter Gamewell, a Methodist from Davenport, had a "missionary career (1871–1906) cover[ing] the heroic age of the Women's Foreign Missionary Society of the Methodist Episcopal Church." She was martyred during the Boxer Rebellion, an anti-Western movement that targeted Christian missionaries. The school she founded in Beijing was renamed for her.[38]

A book memorializing Gamewell, Ethel Daniels Hubbard's *Under Marching Orders,* inspired another Iowa woman to go to China. Ortha May Lane entitled her own book *Under Marching Orders in North China* as a nod to her heroine. Lane also became a mission scholar; she was the

---

34. Van Buren, *Susan Angeline Collins.* For a few glimpses of Iowa African Methodist Episcopal views on international relations and support for African missions, see Little, *Disciples of Liberty,* 190; Williams, *Black Americans and the Evangelization of Africa,* 182–83.

35. MacCanon, *Short History of the United Brethren in Christ,* 23.

36. "History" (Divine Word College).

37. Epworth is the birthplace of John Wesley. Dilts, *From Ackley to Zwingle,* 80.

38. Hubbard, *Under Marching Orders;* Tuttle, *Mary Porter Gamewell,* v.

first woman in the United States to get a doctorate in religion at a state university.³⁹ In her dissertation she diligently cataloged references to missions in American periodicals, then she went back to missionarying.⁴⁰

Another Iowan who combined mission work with academic studies—and diplomacy!—was Margaret Moninger. The Presbyterian Moninger was born and raised on a Marshall County farm, graduated from Grinnell, and taught school in New Providence before her missionary career.⁴¹

Iowa Catholics were also in China. Illustrative is the career of Sister Mary Dominica Urbany of the Franciscan Sisters of Perpetual Adoration. A native of Luxembourg, orphaned as a child, she grew up in Festina. After serving as superior to the nuns at Carroll Kuemper High School, for the last eight years of her life she served in China, dying in 1936.⁴²

INDIA

Much of Western mission is a story of unintended consequences.⁴³ In India and Pakistan, British and American missionaries followed the traditional strategy of appealing to local elites, stressing the quality and importance of Western education. But United Presbyterians were late arrivals, which meant laboring among the low castes and outcasts. Not surprisingly in retrospect, these classes proved exceptionally receptive to a religion that frowned on caste and preached social equality. The late University of Iowa professor Jeff Cox wrote about the United Presbyterians' spectacular success and subsequent embarrassing ceding of the converts to the Anglican Church, which claimed a territorial monopoly.⁴⁴

Novelist Margaret Wilson turned her attention from the settling of Iowa to contemporary India. She was a United Presbyterian missionary

---

39. Ortha May Lane, *Under Marching Orders in North China*; Ortha Lane Papers, IWA.

40. Lane, *Missions in Magazines*. For a glimpse of her continuing mission work, in the Philippines after work in China was no longer possible, see Spencer *Daily Reporter,* March 25, 1956.

41. Lodwick, *Educating the Women of Hainan.*

42. Sr. Mary Dominica Urbany Papers, Iowa Women's Archives, University of Iowa Libraries.

43. The literature detailing the ironies of missionary encounters is voluminous. See, e.g., Hollinger, *Protestants Abroad*; Walls, *Missionary Movement in Christian History*; Case, *Unpredictable Gospel.*

44. Cox, *Imperial Fault Lines.*

to the Punjab in the first decade of the twentieth century, and her novel *Daughters of India* features a no-nonsense Iowa-born woman missionary. She also wrote a sequel, *Trousers of Taffeta*. Wilson saw in the India mission field glimmers of a global feminist solidarity.

Fellow United Presbyterian Kate Alexander Hill grew up not far from Wilson's Tama County, near Newton. She served the mission field that Wilson fictionalized.[45] A graduate of the short-lived Presbyterian college in College Springs, her career epitomized both the allure and limitations of being a woman missionary. The vocation provided adventure and independence, but unmarried women were still at the bottom of a hierarchy. Her letters home to aunts and sisters remember Pakistan's villages fondly, but her conscription to provide childcare for ailing married missionaries she found less rewarding.[46]

Illustrative of the strategic value of working with the lower classes was the career of John E. Clough, an Iowa Baptist and Upper Iowa University graduate who embarked from Strawberry Point to India with his first wife Harriet in 1864. He achieved considerable success in the mass conversion of Dalits in South India's Andhra Pradesh. But Clough anticipated twentieth-century missiology in refusing to equate Christianizing with Westernizing; he advocated waiting to baptize converts until their neighbors were ready and worked to ensure harmony with those unconverted.[47]

Clough undoubtedly had help in his missiological theorizing from his second wife Emma Rauschenbusch, who held a doctorate from Berne. She also kept him in contact with theological trends through her brother, Social Gospel advocate Walter Rauschenbusch.

But the political sympathies of missionary Iowans were mixed. In chatty letters to the "Home Folks" back in Webster City, Methodist Leona Ruppel viewed the civil disobedience campaigns gripping India in the 1930s with annoyance, seeing them as disruptive.[48]

---

45. Cox, *Imperial Fault Lines*, 168–69; Hurto, *History of Newton, Iowa*, 487–88.

46. Cox, *Imperial Fault Lines*, 168; Newton *Journal*, Sep. 7, 1904. Cf. "Any time when her brother is on furlough [Mary Parish] has full charge of the station . . . in Pegu, Burma." Mitchell, *Century of Iowa Baptist History*, 87.

47. Harris, "Emma Rauschenbusch Clough," 87–100; Evans, *Kingdom Is Always but Coming*, 43, 91, 130, 249; Blanchard, "Introduction and Acknowledgement," 406.

48. Leona Ruppel Papers, IWA.

THE MISSION BOOMERANG

Not all who set out to be foreign missionaries got to the field. Mahlon Day Collins, an experienced and successful Methodist minister who had pastored churches in Denison, Corning, Council Bluffs, Chariton, and Des Moines, left his pulpit in Clarinda in 1890 with the goal of becoming a medical missionary to Africa. At his own expense, he attended Boston College medical school, graduating at age 56. In his valedictory speech, he facetiously claimed his parents had anticipated the moment, since his initials were M.D. But upon presenting himself to the Methodist Mission Board in New York City, he was informed that there were no available funds to send him abroad. He managed to cobble together an interrupted ministerial career stateside.[49]

Collins's return from mission aspiration was much quicker and more sudden than most individual experiences, yet it could stand in for the mission experience as a whole. Foreign mission affected the sender as well as the sent. Unintended consequences seemed to increase as the twentieth century proceeded.

One example was that of the Karens in Burma, who as a disadvantaged minority in the nineteenth century were much more receptive to Christianity than the elites whom Western missionaries were keener to convert.[50] By the twenty-first century, both the ethnic and religious minority status of the Karen led to their persecution, and the US recognized them as refugees. Karen Baptist churches in Des Moines and Marshalltown are monuments to that complicated legacy.[51]

Illustrative of how increased globalization could deepen missionary connections is the case of Marion Farquhar, a Page County native who served as Presbyterian missionary to Sudan from the 1940s to the 1980s. At a Presbyterian missionary retirement home in Washington, Iowa, she was able to aid Nuer refugees fleeing conflict in Sudan who wound up in Iowa in the 1990s.[52]

The Student Volunteer Movement conference in Des Moines over the 1920 New Year's weekend would unveil the crisis in Christianization that

49. Mahlon Day Collins Papers, IWA, 103–9.
50. Case, *Unpredictable*, 19–75.
51. Iowa Public Radio, "River to River"; mwnkbcusa.org.
52. Marion Farquhar Papers, IWA.

World War I wrought (see chapter 16). A long period of re-envisioning missions ensued. Iowa State University graduate and Harvard philosophy professor William Hocking was principal author of the groundbreaking 1932 *Re-thinking Missions* report, raising questions about the missionary project and its ties to Western culture and imperialism.

But missionary tales continued.

Samuel Zwemer, a Reformed pastor ordained in Iowa, became a missionary for the Syrian Mission of the Presbyterian Church and an expert on Islam who later taught at Princeton Seminary.[53]

Dr. Virginia Voorhies Milner was in the early 1940s a Presbyterian medical missionary to rural northern New Mexico.[54]

Marianne Michael, a native of Guthrie County, served as Church of the Brethren missionary to Nigeria from 1948 to 1961. Upon her return she settled in Iowa City, becoming a professor of social work.[55]

Anna Marie Mitchell of Fenton taught Christianity and English in Japan from 1950 to 1987. Upon retiring, she ruefully admitted that many Japanese were keener to learn the latter than the former. But the post-war Lutheran mission could claim some success; one indication was the 1974 goodwill visit of 179 Japanese Lutherans to dozens of Iowa churches, including Mitchell's home church near Cylinder.[56]

Even in the late twentieth century it was still possible—perhaps necessary—to re-envision mission work as solidarity: Fr. Ron Hennessey, from rural Dubuque County, began his career in Guatemala and El Salvador suspicious of change. He came to realize that the social justice message of the Church had a special relevance for the poor of Central America.[57]

The Presbyterians Jean and Bill Basinger from Wright County supported the democracy movement in South Korea, which they continued after their return to Iowa.[58] Methodist Gil Dawes brought back liberation theology from his mission work in Argentina, applying it to working class congregations in Camanche, Cedar Rapids, and Des Moines.[59]

53. Balmer, *Encyclopedia of Evangelicalism*, 654.

54. *La Doctorcita* 232hillside.us/SantaFe/doctocita; embudovalleylibrary/collections/embudopresbyterianhospital

55. Marianne Michael Papers, IWA.

56. Anna Marie Mitchell Papers, IWA.

57. Melville, *Through a Glass Darkly*; DMR, Sep. 12, 1982.

58. Stentzel, *More Than Witnesses*.

59. Dawes, "Working People and the Church"; DMR, Feb. 22, 1997; DMR, Apr. 21, 2001.

Quick Turnaround

Gene Matthews, influenced by his Methodist pacifist pastor in Wapello, Leonard Tinker,[60] was another missionary who defied the dictatorship in South Korea.[61]

Late twentieth-century mission often meant shorter terms of service and redefining missionaries as "coworkers" who were expected to take the same salary and adopt the same standard of living as religious workers native to the country.[62]

As mainline Protestants retrenched and turned over authority to indigenous churches and American Catholics increasingly distanced themselves from US government interventions, fundamentalist and evangelical groups marched in the opposite direction.

One University of Iowa Writers Workshop graduate is Tim Bascom, whose memoir describes growing up as the child of missionary parents in Ethiopia.[63]

An indication of ongoing interest in mission was the Global Mission Event held at Luther College in 2000, attended by a national crowd of 1400 and keynoted by ELCA bishop George Anderson.[64]

Christianity was not the only religion in Iowa that wanted to publicize its views and display its rites to the larger world. In 1915 the Meskwakis began an annual powwow, with the explicit purpose of showcasing the nation's unique history and intriguing religion.[65]

---

60. Stentzel, *More Than Witnesses*, 200. Tinker later became a staff member of the American Friends Service Committee in Des Moines and elsewhere but is best known as the father of Mary Beth and John Tinker, plaintiffs in the landmark Supreme Court case Tinker v. Des Moines Board of Education, which extended First Amendment rights to public high school students.

61. Stentzel, *More Than Witnesses*, 196–242.

62. Fate, "Rain Makes the Roof Sing."

63. Bascom, *Chameleon Days*. Bascom has spent most of his adult life as the husband of an Episcopal priest in Iowa.

64. Waterloo/Cedar Falls *Courier*, Jul. 23, 2000.

65. Spencer, "Powwow Time"; Warren, "To Show the Public." Other descriptions have not stressed the outreach aspect.

The people are kind. Iowans are apt to share, and there are probably ways to quantify Iowans' generosity, but kindness is probably best left unmeasured. Human motivations are almost always mixed, and sharing ideology is complicated. Race, class, and imperialism all complicated missionary activity, even when missionaries wished it wouldn't.

The cultural shocks inherent in the missionary enterprise meant that mission fields could be places for testing women's equality, for challenging racist assumptions, and for questioning economic inequality. But religious Iowans were discovering that Iowa could be such a place, too. The next two chapters will explore some of the responses to such challenges.

CHAPTER 10

Questions of Land and Equality

James Baird Weaver, Active Methodism, and Those Left Outside

"God created [woman] a conscious, sentient, responsible, intellectual personality, as much as man."

—Rev. Martha Janes, Spencer, 1884[1]

"Thy wife, thy handmaid not, yet thou dost say,
'I first in Eden rule.' Thou, then, hast sway.
Must I, my Adam, mutely follow thee?
Run at thy bidding, crouch beside thy knee?
Lift up (when thou dost bid me) timid eyes?
Not so will Lilith live in Paradise."

—Ada Langworthy Collier[2]

"Political rights are not natural rights. To say so is so much BALDERDASH!"

—Editor, Council Bluffs *Bugle*[3]

---

1. Quoted in Egge, *Woman Suffrage and Citizenship in the Midwest*, 88.
2. *Lilith: The Legend of the First Woman.*
3. Dec. 15, 1855, quoted in Noun, "Amelia Bloomer," 586.

The People Are Kind

"Resolved, . . . that the Bible is the Palladium of our liberties."
—NETTIE SANFORD[4]

"[Some say] what defeated Weaver . . . was the same thing that defeated Harlan, [his association with] the Methodist Church."
—BLOOMFIELD *DEMOCRAT*, JUL. 23, 1874[5]

"We [African Americans] have had a great injustice done to us."
—REV. WILLIAM DOVE, KEOKUK, 1874[6]

FOR JAMES BAIRD WEAVER, Civil War hero from Bloomfield who many believed had been unfairly maneuvered out of the Republican nomination for Congress in 1874 and for governor in 1875 because of his Prohibitionism,[7] Methodist principles were clear: no compromise with evil, and in the late seventies, with racism apparently defeated, and alcohol also apparently being successfully challenged, issues of economic equality loomed large.

Racism had not been defeated, and there would be a long-playing interplay between liquor and religion. But the small farmers constituting a majority of the state's population felt real grievances, often expressed in religious terms. James B. Weaver sought to amplify those laments and

---

4. Resolution against free love as advocated by Victoria Woodhull, tabled as not germane by the Iowa Woman Suffrage Association convention in Des Moines, 1871. Noun, "Bloomer," 610–11.

5. Quoted in Haynes, *James Baird Weaver*, 72–73. To be clear, the accusation was that Weaver's staunch support for Methodist positions had made him unpalatable to the Republican Party, which at the time was running away from endorsing Prohibition while simultaneously courting its supporters.

Former senator James Harlan (also president of the Iowa Methodists' flagship college, Iowa Wesleyan) had lost the power struggle for control of the Republican Party to future senator Willam Boyd Allison. "Weaver, James Baird," BDI, 544.

6. Quoted in Schwalm, *Emancipation's Diaspora*, 200. The occasion was the segregating of Keokuk's public schools.

7. Mitchell, *Skirmisher*, 55–57; Haynes, *Weaver*, 70–80, 431; DMT, Mar. 25, 1909. See also Russell, *Bare Hands and Stone Walls*, chapter 5. As a young journalist from Davenport, Russell was mentored on what to look for at a political convention (lobbyists!) by Weaver. For the Russelll-Weaver connection, I am indebted to Smith, *Rise of Industrial America*, 443–46, 456.

became a prominent voice questioning the Gilded Age consensus that rapacious industrialization was good for the country. If his rhetoric borrowed from apocalyptic passages, the dire conditions seemed to justify it.[8]

With Iowa farmers increasingly suffering because of their entanglement in the larger economic system and market dependence on monopolistic transportation systems, any national economic downturn could spell economic ruin for farmers (as could poor crop yields.) And nineteenth-century America had more than its share of panics, depressions, droughts, and blights. Rural Iowans searched for religious explanations for such suffering.

The economic populism nurtured by Hebrew Testament prophetic calls for justice for the landless and the oppressed was premised on notions of equality that often had religious roots. The debate on economic equality intertwined with, and sometimes complicated, a parallel debate on gender equality that became mostly focused on the question of suffrage. And the question of racial equality, raised but not solved by the Civil War, lingered. That the focus on class and gender often obscured and sometimes exacerbated racial inequality must be acknowledged.

In grappling with these issues of fundamental political and religious importance, religious Iowans struggled for the proper response. Sometimes issues of equality would be raised within religious institutions; the question of women's ordination to the clergy, for example, while still an outlier, began to be addressed, and the Women's Christian Temperance Union and women's missionary societies carved out autonomous spaces for women locally.

GROWTH IN ECONOMIC INEQUALITY AND THE LEFT POPULIST RESPONSE

The existence and persistence of prairie radicalism had religious roots.[9] The political career of James Baird Weaver was inseparable from his Methodism. Born in Ohio in 1833, he grew up in Bloomfield, Iowa, distinguished himself during the Civil War, breveted out as a general, and settled back into small-town life as a lawyer and local Republican officeholder.

---

8. Jaher, *Doubters and Dissenters*, 45, 55, 134–38.
9. Bicha, "Prairie Radicals," 79–94.

Weaver fought the Civil War as a true believer. Reporting as regimental commanding officer at the battle at Corinth, with Union losses heavy but the North victorious, he valorized the fallen as dying "for the cause of Christianity and constitutional liberty."[10] After the war, his oratorical skills and Civil War background—the term "waving the bloody shirt" was supposedly first used to describe Weaver's speeches[11]—made him an up-and-comer in the now dominant Republican party.

But success as a politician in the post-war Republican party depended on more than rhetorical skills and a war record; it required skill at compromise and accommodation to business and finance. This patience Weaver lacked. In rejecting his bids for Congress and governor, however, the Republican machine unwittingly uncovered Weaver's real calling: stumping for economic justice on a third-party ticket.

Weaver won election to Congress in 1878 on the Greenback Party slate, becoming a three-term third party Congressman, running for president as a Greenbacker in 1880 and for the People's Party in 1892. He advocated for an agrarian ideal that echoed strains of the Hebrew concept of the Jubilee.

Although the record is scant, remarkably Weaver seems to have anticipated the personalist theology which trended in American Methodism and beyond in the 1930s and which also influenced Martin Luther King, Jr.[12] Consider this eulogy he gave in 1911:

> The most wonderful and fascinating phenomenon in the whole sphere of human association is human personality. The thing we cherish most in history is not so much the record of events as the revelation of men and women . . .
>
> It is the crowning charm of revelation that God has revealed himself to man in the personality of Jesus—a being of real flesh and blood, a hero of heroes, who could be seen and who walked, talked, ate, slept, and wept. It is a constant source

---

10. Mitchell, *Skirmisher*, 43–44.

11. In Weaver's telling, the term actually originated before the Civil War: a minister named McKinney from Davis County migrated to Texas, where a mob whipped him for preaching to an interracial gathering in Ft. Worth. After returning to Iowa, Weaver displayed McKinney's bloodied shirt in speeches that showed the cruelty of pro-slavery advocates. Haynes, *Weaver*, 24–25, 448 fn 19; Mitchell, *Skirmisher*, 29.

Weaver, campaigning for president on the Greenback ticket in 1880, sometimes faced hostility in the South. Mitchell, *Skirmisher*, 104–5.

12. See, e.g., Baldwin, *There Is a Balm in Gilead*, 2–3, 29, 118. On a parallel Catholic personalism, exemplified by such thinkers as Jacques Maritain and Dorothy Day, see Wolfe, *Year of Our Lord 1943*.

Questions of Land and Equality

of thankfulness that he is not mere cold abstraction or principle, but a real person whom we can touch with our consciousness and embrace with our arms of faith and love.[13]

Perhaps Weaver had missed his calling after all and should have become a theologian. Certainly in the above statement an individualistic Pietism that dominated nineteenth-century Methodism vies with his more socially-oriented, Old Testament, prophet-based commitment to economic justice.

Weaver died in 1912, at the height of the Progressive movement, living to see many of the reforms that he struggled for be enacted, often by Republicans who embraced the progressive label. He was generally, in his later years, an advocate for fusion of third parties with the Democrats. This granted him an entree back into acceptability. He spent his last years as mayor of Colfax, and Rev. Edward Pruitt, minister of the Colfax Methodist Church, presided at his funeral at First Methodist in Des Moines. Rev. Orien Fifer[14] of Grace Methodist Church of Des Moines also spoke, and somewhat remarkably for the time, so did Fr. Joseph F. Nugent from Visitation Catholic Church on the working-class east side of Des Moines.[15]

In addition to the Methodist influence on and of Weaver, a strain of agrarian populism among Disciples in southern Iowa emerged and dovetailed with insurgent Methodism. The Greenbacker plurality in the election of 1880 owed much to Disciples' backing.[16] A decade later, Disciples minister Edward Amherst Ott was a People's Party candidate for Congress in the Seventh District, which included Des Moines.[17]

---

13. Haynes, *James Baird Weaver*, 442.

14. Andrews, *Tradition of Grace*, 17–19.

15. Haynes, *James Baird Weaver*, 412, 415, 424–29; Avella, *Catholic Church in Southwest Iowa*, 93–94. Avella also suggested to me that such Catholic-Protestant intersections were not rare, especially in places like the Diocese of Des Moines where Catholics were in the minority. Email, Nov. 7, 2020.

16. Dykstra, *Bright Radical Star*, 254.

17. Harrell, *Social Sources of Division*, 139; Haynes, *Third Party Movements*, 326. Ott was also a professor of oratory at Drake University. Ritchey, *Drake University*, 85.

UTOPIAN SCHEMES

Some Disciples also voiced support for the Single Tax proposal of Henry George.[18]

Weaver lieutenant E. B. Gaston prominently supported George's ideas within the Iowa People's Party. While Gaston's religious affiliation isn't clear, his father served as an early minister of Central Christian Church in Des Moines. In 1894, Gaston moved from electoral activism to communalism, or what he called "cooperative individualism." He organized a utopian community while living in University Place (now part of Des Moines), setting it up in Fairhope, Alabama, where a considerable part of the town is still owned collectively as of 2021.[19]

Some Iowa Quakers were also attracted to Fairhope early in the twentieth century, and Friends bearing Iowa Quaker names like Rockwell and Mendenhall were instrumental in setting up the Friends meeting there.[20]

In launching a utopian community, Gaston and his Iowa colleagues did not have to look out of state for models. Not only the religiously-based Amana colonies in Iowa County but the more secular Icaria in Adams County provided long-lasting examples of cooperative success.

James B. Weaver was a staunch supporter of women's suffrage, as well as of its companion in Iowa and elsewhere in the Midwest, Prohibition. Weaver also supported racial equality, but it was less frequently on the agenda.

STRUGGLES FOR WOMEN'S EQUALITY

Economic inequality was not the only social injustice that late nineteenth-century Iowans perceived. Mary Newbury Adams, a Dubuque intellectual in touch with the Transcendentalists,[21] was invited to speak at Congregationalist Iowa College as part of graduation ceremonies in 1869, by the women's literary society. Her invitation became controversial and was contravened by the faculty, apparently fearing that a female

---

18. Harrell, *Social Sources of Division*, 148.

19. Gaston, *Man and Mission*, 13–31; deGroot, *Central of Des Moines*, 50–52; Gaston, *Coming of Age in Utopia*, 32–37, 42–44; Jones, *Quakers of Iowa*, 43.

20. "Friends Historical Association Past Events."

21. Stein, "Mrs. Alcott of Concord"; Noun, *Strong-Minded Women*, 113–15, 263–64.

Questions of Land and Equality

speaker at an event where men were present might be seen as risque.[22] Adams would maintain her interest in liberal religion through contact with Transcendentalists and as an early devotee of Theosophy, but her commitment to Congregationalism understandably cooled. She also became an advocate for women's suffrage.

Adams was joined in her early feminism by fellow Dubuquer Ada Langworthy Collier, whose 1885 poem "Lilith"[23] explored alternatives to a supposed God-given patriarchy. Lilith was, in Hebrew mythology, Adam's first wife, who had a mind of her own. In Collier's poem, her heroine Lilith figures out a life of her own.[24]

But Dubuque intellectuals were not the only ones working for women's rights. Much closer to average Iowans was the Rev. Martha Janes of the Free-Will Baptist Church, leader of Spencer's suffrage movement. By the time she arrived in Spencer in 1880, she was already experienced at leading evangelistic efforts throughout the state. Working within the local Women's Christian Temperance Union, she used a weekly front-page column in the *Clay County News* to argue provocatively for equal rights. While the relationship between the temperance and suffrage movements was sometimes fraught, it was also symbiotic.[25]

Amelia Jenks Bloomer was among the first Iowans to advocate for women's equality. While popular culture fixated on her fashion innovation—and a cursory glance at twenty-first century dress suggests that she has won that argument—the Council Bluffs transplant and Episcopalian came to concentrate on less flamboyant reforms during most of her time in Iowa.[26] She is the only Iowan that the Episcopal Church has declared a saint.[27]

As the suffrage movement progressed in Iowa, suffragists recruited male clergy allies willing to extend the franchise to some of their most loyal and fervent constituents.[28] "Think of all our churches as being practically

---

22. "Adams, Mary Newbury (or Newberry)," *BDI*, 3.

23. "Collier, Ada Langworthy."

24. The myth of Lilith was occasioned by the rabbinical necessity to explain the two creation stories in Genesis, although the explanation that Lilith left Adam because of her independence suggests a trouble in paradise before the fall that seems to require additional adjustments.

25. Egge, *Woman Suffrage and Citizenship in the Midwest*, 85–89, 105–7.

26. Kujawa-Holbrook, *Freedom Is a Dream*, 66–73; Noun, "Amelia Bloomer"; "Bloomer, Amelia," *BDI*, 47–49.

27. "Stanton, Bloomer, Truth, and Tubman."

28. Breeden et al., *Iowa Clergymen for Woman Suffrage*, Special Collections, Drake

disfranchised," one woman activist argued in Norwalk in 1905. "Two thirds of the church membership are helpless at the polls. The churches are seriously charged with not voting as they pray. Surely two thirds of the churches do not vote as they pray—as devout as they may be."[29]

This line of argument would spark a backlash in the form of the Men and Religion Forward movement, which alleged a weakening of males' position within churches, due to their relative lack of attendance.[30] This issue dominated most Des Moines pulpits in June 1911,[31] and would draw a wickedly satirical portrait of the movement as adolescent boys in Ruth Suckow's novel *The Bonney Family*.[32]

Mary Jane Whiteley Coggeshall was a Des Moines Quaker whose organizing and oratorical skills brought her onto the national suffrage stage and won her the esteem of the preeminent suffrage organizer[33] Iowan Carrie Chapman Catt.[34] Coggeshall's rhetoric had rootedness but also limitations. Coggeshall was not above arguing that middle-class white (Protestant) women were more deserving of the vote than new immigrants.[35]

There was also African American support for suffrage: Rev. Henry McCraven of Des Moines, citing Lucretia Mott's support for African Americans, wanted to return the favor.[36]

Women's suffrage was both infused and complicated by the parallel issue of alcohol prohibition. For almost two decades, the foremost

---

University, originally in *Woman's Standard* in 1890 or 1891. The ten statements were by Breeden, Central Church of Christ, Des Moines; C. C. Harrah, First Congregational, Newton; Mary Safford, Unitarian, Sioux City; George Henry, Lutheran, Des Moines; E. P. Bartlett, Baptist, East Des Moines; A. L. Frisbee, First Congregational, Des Moines; Wm. Watson, First Friends, Des Moines; B. F. W. Cozier, Grace M. E., Des Moines; Jno. Geiger, Congregational, Oskaloosa; and B. St.John, North Park [Congregational], Des Moines. See also DMT, Mar. 15, 1909.

29. Coggeshall, quoted in Ferris, *Mary Jane Whiteley Coggeshall*, 58.
30. Bederman, "'Women Have Had Charge of the Church Work.'"
31. Douglas, "Iowa Protestantism of 1911."
32. Suckow, *Bonney Family*, 91–92.
33. DMR, Nov. 12, 2017; Ferris, *Mary Jane Whiteley Coggeshall*.
34. On Catt, see "Catt, Carrie Chapman," *BDI*, 79–81.
35. Speech at Iowa Equal Suffrage Association Convention, Boone, Oct. 6, 1903, quoted in Ferris *Coggeshall*, 48.
36. Schwalm, *Emancipation's Diaspora*, 212. That Mott originally opposed women's suffrage, seeing it as a distraction from the abolition of slavery, had long since been forgotten.

proponents of prohibition were women, and the Women's Christian Temperance Union gave pro-woman arguments for prohibition and how women's suffrage might be necessary to achieve it. But, as we will see in chapter 12, such arguments alienated much of the (male) electorate, who did not want to dilute their own power.

The quest for gender equality transcended the issue of suffrage; it also penetrated religious institutions. Some Protestant churches began grappling with the issue of ordination. In 1846 Ruby Bixby became the first woman to be ordained by Free-Will Baptists and the first woman in Iowa to be ordained. She co-pastored with her husband some fourteen Iowa churches.[37]

An Iowa sisterhood of Unitarian ministers sprang up, representing both an acceptance of women's ordination by the denomination and the reality that women ministers were apt to serve the smallest, least prestigious, and least urban congregations.[38] That trend has continued as women ministers have become more ubiquitous.

In addition to Free-Will Baptist and temperance activist Martha Janes, the Methodist Protestant Church in Iowa also accepted a woman into the ministry, despite the national denomination's reluctance. Pauline Williams Martindale was apparently not ordained until 1875, when she was in Kansas, but in 1872 Martindale was received into the Iowa conference and ministered at Union, Iowa, and then in Montezuma. In both places she co-pastored with her husband. But the 1870 federal census for Taylor County listed her as a minister even earlier.

Pauline Martindale was the more dynamic preacher of the couple; a reporter for the Pittsburgh-based *Methodist Reporter* gushed that "never in our finest churches in the east, under the sound of any human voice, however masculine and doctorly, have we witnessed such a melting of souls, such a deep interblending of emotions . . . as when a woman preached—far out upon the prairie." She went on to have a noted career as an evangelist in Kansas.[39]

The technicalities of ordination within particular denominations can obscure the slow but building pressure for gender equality in religious institutions. There were stirrings in other denominations about

37. Merry, *History of Delaware County*, 16.

38. Grant, *Prophetic Sisterhood* and *Woman's Ministry*; Zink-Sawyer, *From Preachers to Suffragists*, 98.

39. Thompson, "'Against the Odds, They Did Preach'"; Nye, *Between the Rivers*, 92, 153; Morris, "History of the Methodist Protestant Church in Iowa," 71–72.

women's ordination. For example, David Dungan supported women's ordination among Disciples.[40]

The trend towards women's ordination did not end in the nineteenth century; mainline Protestant denominations opened their clergy ranks by the latter half of the twentieth century,[41] and women increasingly came to dominate the profession in small towns.

As we have seen in chapter 9, women's mission societies offered another avenue for independent organizing. Such independence, of course, was not uncontested; in many denominations, it continued into the 1920s.[42]

Another avenue for autonomous organizing began at Iowa Wesleyan University in 1869. Like most Iowa colleges, it was coeducational. On January 24, students in the women's dormitory inaugurated the second oldest still-existing secret society for women in the country, the P. E. O. (The meaning is still technically secret.) The society is still headquartered in Iowa, now in Des Moines.[43]

In studying memorials to Methodist pastors' wives in the Northwest conference, Andrew Klumpp has suggested a declension from frontier equality to circumscribed domesticity in the late nineteenth century.[44]

While Iowa women could point to signs of progress towards equality in the last third of the nineteenth century, for Iowa African Americans the goal of equality slipped further away.

FRAYING OF RACIAL EQUALITY

While for embattled farmers and unfranchised women, religious organizations and beliefs were one of several institutions and ideologies that they could invoke, for African Americans, the church was usually the only intercessor in navigating routes towards racial equality and social acceptance. While poor people and women fought to expand their rights, in post-Reconstruction Iowa African Americans sought to cling onto their hard-won gains in increasingly threatening times. Of course, the three issues were intertwined; most African-Americans were poor, and

40. Harrell, *Social Sources of Division*, 9, 265–66.
41. Zikmund et al., *Clergy Women*, 70–89. See also Chaves, *Ordaining Women*.
42. See, e.g., Hill, *World Their Household*.
43. Moudry, "Society of Our Own."
44. Klumpp, "From Prairie to Parsonage," 61–72.

half of them were women, but race often pitted black and white workers against each other, as in the Iowa coalfields,[45] and relations on a national level between white suffragists and Black activists were often fraught.[46]

Nonetheless, African Americans had to defend their hard-won if inadequate gains, and their churches were the vehicles used to protect, and if possible expand, their limited rights.

Records are best for the African Methodist Episcopal Church. The local church was the center for celebrating Emancipation and for launching campaigns against exclusion from society. It also could become a place where rivalries between an entrenched patriarchy and a vigilant women's network could play out.[47]

Records of Black Baptist churches in Iowa are scarcer.[48] One exception is the short memoir *The Life Story of (Rev.) Wm Brown 1930*. Brown felt continuing anger at the cruelties and injustices of slavery as well as gratitude toward the church for his literacy and opportunity to advance in society after abolition.[49]

Born into slavery in Kentucky, Brown was raised a slave in northeastern Missouri, hired out at age ten, for ten dollars a year and taxes—Brown emphasized that slaves were taxable property. "Mean as some of

---

45. Blowing up the entrance to the Consolidation Coal Company mine at Muchakinock, where African Americans were employed, to enforce adherence to the United Mine Workers state-wide strike of 1891, is likely an example, although the cause of the explosion was never proven. See my unpublished paper, "Hoping Against Hope," copy at SHSI-IC. But black and white miners could also live in relative harmony, as was the case in the successor to Muchakinock, Buxton. A railroad strike and importing black strikebreakers in 1911 was the initial impetus for black migration from Mississippi to Waterloo. Scharnau, "African-American Wage Earners," in *OI*, 226–27.

While the evidence about the religious life of Buxton is scant, its more general story has been told in Schwieder, *Buxton*; Chase, *Creating the Black Utopia*; Gradwohl and Osborn, *Exploring Buried Buxton*.

46. The evidence for the strategic racism of Iowa master strategist of the suffragist movement, Carrie Chapman Catt, went on agonizingly full display when the Iowa State University YWCA renamed its building after Catt in the 1990s, and campus anti-racist activists challenged that choice. DMR, Mar. 31, 1996; CRG, Nov. 10, 2023; *Ames Tribune*, August 22, 2021.

47. Schwalm, *Emancipation's Diaspora*, 142–56; Brigham, "Transforming Places," 107.

48. There are glimpses. For example, nationally known education speaker Frances Harris spoke at a black Baptist church in Keokuk in February of 1874. Schwalm, *Emancipation's Diaspora*, 202. A. M. E. pastors were also sometimes critical of black "Missionary" Baptist churches' financial dependence on the white Northern Baptist Convention. Schwalm, *Emancipation's Diaspora*, 145.

49. Box 3, F. [2] "1830–867," Frances Hawthorne Papers, IWA.

them were, they would let us join their churches, but we had no voice." He is especially bitter his master failed to inform him of the Emancipation Proclamation, and he worked without pay for two more years.[50] (Technically, his master was correct; as a war measure, the Proclamation applied only to states in rebellion, not to border states like Missouri.)

Henry Owassa Turner, The Disciples See Christ Walking on the Water, 1902–1912, Oil on canvas, 49 3/4 × 39 7/8 inches, Des Moines Art Center Permanent Collections; Gift of the Des Moines Association of Fine Arts, 1921. Photo Credit: Rich Sanders, Des Moines

50. Brown, 3, 4. 11, 16–21.

Brown credited his election as church clerk with improving his literacy skills. Probably in 1871, he was called to a church in Keokuk by schismatics from the First African Baptist Church.[51] He accepted the call, wanting to keep them Baptist. This began a decades-long career as Baptist minister in Iowa. His longest patorate was at Albia and Hiteman in the coal fields, where he spent eighteen years.[52] Brown's memoir concludes with a call for future generations of African Americans not to forget the evils of slavery and what it took to overcome the obstacles placed in former slaves' paths.

Summing up the post-Reconstruction quagmire for Iowa blacks, Rev. William Hilary Coston of the Mt. Pleasant African Methodist Episcopal Church saw the issue bleakly in 1888, when he contended that "we suffer in consequence of Republican perfidy on one hand and Democratic ku-kluxism on the other."[53]

Iowans after the Civil War were either occupied with spelling out what the equality championed by the winning side meant, usually relying on religious arguments, or were preoccupied by quests for personal gain that countermanded those demands. As James B. Weaver discovered the hard way, the new capitalist ethos also usually relied on religious justifications. That rationale would be challenged theologically and biblically by the Kingdom Movement, based in Iowa.

---

51. According to Essie F. Britton, the First African Baptist Church was founded in Keokuk in 1864, and Pilgrim's Rest Baptist in 1871. Britton, "Negro in Iowa," typescript, copy in Hawthorne Papers, Box 3, F. [2.], IWA.

52. *Brown*, 14–16.

53. Davenport *Daily Gazette*, quoted in Schwalm, *Emancipation's Diaspora*, 191.

CHAPTER 11

The Kingdom Movement(s) of George Herron, George Augustus Gates, and George W. Slater, and the Social Gospel in Iowa

"What are we shooting Filipinos for?"
—George Augustus Gates[1]

"The conception of Christ as the Saviour of individuals only is insufficient for fulfilling of prophecy or the solution of historic problems. The institutions of men must be saved from sin and paganism as truly as individual souls."
—George D. Herron, *The Larger Christ*[2]

"The Socialist's position is that economic justice must be maintained first before any large measure of the Kingdom of God on earth exists. Hence, the Christian Socialist."
—George W. Slater[3]

1. *The Kingdom*, Mar. 30, 1899.
2. Herron, *Larger Christ*, 30–31.
3. Foner, *Black Socialist Preacher*, 353.

The Kingdom Movement(s) of George

IOWA HAS PLAYED A part in many theological movements, but of only one can it be said to have played a crucial role: the Christian Socialism of the late nineteenth and early twentieth centuries. The originality and boldness of George Herron, the protectiveness of Herron's position and the extension of the Social Gospel to issues of militarism and racism by George Augustus Gates and the linking of Christian Socialism to the struggles for racial equality by George W. Slater stand out.

The Social Gospel movement that the three Georges precipitated in Iowa was often less radical but incorporated their analysis and that of the populist revolt, continuing to probe the question, "Who is my neighbor?"

GEORGE HERRON

On September 22, 1890, a small-town Congregationalist pastor in Minnesota electrified a prominent Minneapolis audience with a jeremiad entitled "The Message of Jesus to Men of Wealth,"[4] and his speech went the nineteenth-century equivalent of viral.[5] Even though Herron had correctly divined Jesus' critique of capital, the response was positive.

Overnight, George Davis Herron could write his own ticket for his next pulpit. He accepted the associate pastorate of the First Congregational Church in Burlington, Iowa, Iowa Congregationalism's flagship at the time. William Salter, the longest-lasting of the Iowa Band, was still its senior pastor, fifty years on.

The arrangement, intended to ease an aging Salter's burden, did not; this combination of outsized egos soon proved explosive. In defense of Herron, none of the succeeding associate pastors lasted long either. In defense of Salter, Herron had a knack of making enemies, too. Factoring out the very real personal animosity, the short Salter-Herron co-pastorate can better be seen as a generational divide than a theological one. But the divides overlapped. History is not only written by victors, but also by long-lived survivors. William Salter not only experienced the Iowa Band's founding of Congregationalism on the frontier and the purifying fire of the Civil War; he lived to write about it and thus define it. But history for Salter stopped triumphantly in 1865; for Herron, the following tumultuous quarter century was foundational.

---

4. The talk was reprinted as chapter 4 of his 1894 book, *The Christian Society*.
5. "Herron, George Davis," *BDI*, 234–35.

The People Are Kind

Growing up poor in Indiana, Herron had lived the farm protest movements led electorally by Weaver in a way that the more comfortably located Salter had not. Herron's rhetorical genius injected the insights of Old Testament prophets into the economic conversation, an insight now commonplace but jarring to American Christians who had begun taking God's favor for granted.

Theologically, politically, generationally, and personally, Salter and Herron were spectacularly unfit for partnership. There was congregational dissension as well, with some restive with Salter's seemingly interminable tenure. The contest of egos was neatly resolved when a wealthy member and admirer of Herron, lumber heiress Caroline Rand, endowed a chair of Applied Christianity at Iowa College and installed Herron as professor. To foreshadow Herron's downfall, in addition to Herron's wife and family, his benefactor and her daughter Carrie moved to Grinnell.[6]

The Herron-Salter clash signaled a changing of the guard in Iowa Congregationalism, presaging the evolution of Iowa Protestantism. "From Salvation to Service" is how a historian of nineteenth-century Iowa College described the transition.[7] The Herron-Gates alliance at the college enabled a radical tendency within the Social Gospel movement that would come to question not just capitalism but also militarism and racism.

Herron's popularity, though fleeting, was due to his adeptness at translating the message of the Jewish prophets: that God was unhappy with God's people when they ignored their historic sense of community, a history rooted in their liberation from slavery, and began practicing their

---

6. Jordan, *William Salter*, 188. While Jordan does not document that Herron and Salter did not get along, he does suggest disagreement between the pastors and dissension within the church. The dynamics of why Herron was called there and why some remained supportive of him is a congregational conflict that I have not been able to document. Political differences and a clash of egos undoubtedly contributed; none of Salter's other assistants lasted long either. Pryor, *History of the First Congregational Church*, 10; Burlington *Saturday Evening Post*, Jan. 28, 1893.

For evidence of continuing pro-Herron sentiment in the Burlington church, see articles by Burlington members in *The Kingdom*: Jan. 13, 1898; Apr. 20, 1894. On Salter's economic conservatism, see his review of Shailer Mathews's *Social Teaching of Jesus* in *Congregational Iowa*, Jan. 1898.

Interestingly, Salter's son William Mackenzie Salter authored several pamphlets for the Anti-Imperialist League. McCartney. *Power and Progress*, 354. The younger Salter left Congregationalism for the Society of Ethical Culture.

7. Wall, *Grinnell College*.

own oppression. Herron also recaptured the prophets' anger at such a betrayal of God. But if Herron had correctly refracted the message, the messenger could still be attacked, which happened. While some disliked his arrogance, another line of attack proved more fruitful.

The revelation of Herron's adulterous affair with his benefactor's daughter, Carrie Rand, led to his ouster from Iowa College. The college president, George Augustus Gates, had shielded Herron from theological and political attacks, but for nineties Protestantism, this was beyond the pale, and even in retrospect, Herron's treatment of his wife and children seems indefensible.

Herron would shine prominently but briefly in early Socialist Party organizing and end up two decades later in Europe, ensconced in an Italian villa, all but deifying Woodrow Wilson for his Fourteen Points that would put a permanent end to war.[8] The urgency of the message of Jesus to men of wealth had faded for Herron.

GEORGE AUGUSTUS GATES

The president of Iowa College, George Augustus Gates, and Herron had much in common, explaining Gates' protective attitude towards Herron. Gates had been challenged about his theology when he unsuccessfully sought ordination in New Hampshire after graduating from Andover Seminary in 1880.[9] Moving to New Jersey enabled his ordination, but the episode inoculated him against accusations of heresy hurled at Herron. Both were second-generation Iowa Congregationalists, impatient at the Iowa Band's wallowing in nostalgia.[10] Herron's initial contribution to the Christian Socialist aspects of the Social Gospel were spectacular, but might easily have flamed out (earlier) without institutional support from Iowa College and Gates.

---

8. Herron, *Menace of Peace*, 7; Dorn, BDI, 235.

9. Gates, *Life of George Augustus Gates*, 6–8; Williams, *Andover Liberals*. While Williams cites 1881 as the final turning point at Andover from Calvinist orthodoxy to evangelical liberalism, the change had been in the making for some time.

10. The pages of *Congregational Iowa* in the nineties were dominated by Iowa Band-era reminiscences.

Frontispiece, *Life of George Augustus Gates*

The ideological alliance between Herron and Gates should not obscure their differences. Gates was a much more precise thinker. Herron's combination of stridency and vagueness[11] has made him a favorite with historians who can mine his books for critiques of whatever they are looking for.[12] Instead of making him more moderate than Herron,

---

11. Ferenc Morton Szasz has argued that lack of specificity was deliberate among Social Gospel preachers, and he quotes Rev. Samuel Zane Batten, who taught social science at Des Moines College: "The preacher is not here to preach ethics or sociology, he is not here to preach the rights of labor or the rights of capital. He has nothing to do with platforms of parties or the programs of reformers. But he is here to bear witness to righteousness and love in all the relations of life." Szasz, *Divided Mind*, 66.

12. See, e.g., Curtis, *Consuming Faith;* Dieterich, "Radical on Campus"; Crumden,

perhaps specificity made Gates more visionary, specifically on two issues crucial to the twentieth century: war and racism.

Gates was almost alone among Social Gospel leaders in opposing the war against Spain in 1898. Even Herron was silent until it morphed into war against Philippine independence. Even then, Gates's protests were more memorable: "What are we shooting Filipinos for?" was among the most plaintive calls for peace.[13]

Gates called attention to how wasteful war was:

> With reference to the war with Spain I have some very decided convictions. These convictions are not popular, but they are nonetheless firmly held. I find myself in entire agreement with Charles Sumner's great oration in 1845, "The True Grandeur of Nations," which began his public career.[14] It is good reading these days. It ought to be true at this age of the world that 'there is no dishonorable peace; there is no honorable war.' Yet I have to pinch myself 'to see whether I am alive' at the end of the nineteenth century or whether I am still 'dead in trespasses and sins' in the old days when Jehovah went forth to war.[15] It is a night-

---

"George D. Herron." The closest reading of Herron has been by C. Howard Hopkins, who credits him with a theology based on sacrifice. Hopkins, *Rise of the Social Gospel*, 188–94.

Dombrowski was among the first to romanticize Herron, saying he "would provide rich material for a romantic novel." Dombrowski, *Early Days of Christian Socialism*, 171. Dombrowski apparently did not know that Herron had provided a model for Thomas J. Dixon, Jr., of *The Klansman/Birth of a Nation* infamy, for his novel *The One Woman*. Or perhaps it would be more accurate to say that the romanticization began with Herron himself; two portraits apparently based on interviews with Herron have strikingly similar phrases portraying his suffering nature: fellow Iowa College professor Walter Dennison and Christian Socialist J. Stitt Wilson, who was among those who filled in at Iowa College while Herron was absent lecturing around the country, both portray Herron as martyr to the cause: *Social Gospel*, 14: *Social Crusader*, 3, 1–3.

On Herron's lack of specifics, see Nelson, 11, 24, 30, 57, 67; Handy, 110; Frederick, *Knights of the Golden Rule*, 164.

13. *The Kingdom*, Mar. 30, 1899. For Herron on the war in the Philippines, see his Chicago address introduced by Frances E. Willard: "American Imperialism," *Social Forum* 1, 1–18.

14. The similarities of the Mexican-American to the Spanish-American War are intriguing. On dissent during the former, see Greenberg, *Wicked War*, 268. For those looking for a Congregationalist pedigree for anti-war activism, see the pamphlet by Thompson, *Congregational Dissent Against the War of 1812*.

The Iowa Congregational Association went on record opposing the Mexican War.

15. Here, and in the Suckow quote above, a certain Marcionite tendency may be detected. For a theological critique of the Social Gospel movement, see Visser T'Hooft, *Background of the Social Gospel in America*, especially 182–86.

mare to think what is going on,—great warships blowing each other to pieces and killing off men by the hundred, squandering money as if there was nothing else to do with money (one discharge of a great gun costs as much as a college professor's salary for a year), and then, after we have got all done cutting each other's throats and blowing each other's heads off, the situation is just as it was before. We must get together and get to some kind of agreement even then. Why not get together and come to an agreement without the ghastly preliminaries?[16]

He also anticipated Gandhi's insight into nonviolent alternatives:

> Suppose, instead of an army of soldiers, we had sent one of teachers—perhaps half as many, for their pay must be a bit more. There would be then only 14,000 teachers! "But some of them might be killed." In God's name, how many Americans are laying down their lives now, and that too, taking ten or a hundred Filipinos to every one? Does some one say that this is asking too much of a teacher? Then the question is pertinent: Since when has it become an admitted fact that only the soldier in all Christendom is ready to lay down his life? The writer of this article belongs to the teaching and not the fighting class, and will not admit the slander upon his profession which any such theory implies.

Finally, Gates proposed a Christian alternative to the war:

> Send missionaries then. Since a graduate of Iowa College, a young woman who the students support in Sivas, went into a mob of murdering Turkish soldiers and dragged an Armenian woman out from knives, bayonets and bullets to safety in her own house, it may not be said that American young women and men cannot be as brave in the service of school and church under Him they call Master (General) as any soldier in any army.[17]

This last piece of advocacy for nonviolent activism would, in another half century in ways no one could anticipate, coincide with his other great cause, opposing racism.

After leaving Iowa College, Gates became president of Fisk College, an African American institution in Nashville. This was swimming against the tide not just of the larger US society but even the Social Gospel movement. With the prodding of African American activist George

---

16. "War Spirit." *The Kingdom*, Mar. 26, 1898.
17. *The Kingdom*, Mar. 30, 1899.

Haynes and encouragement from his former Iowa College student, now American Missionary Association official H. Paul Douglass, Gates at Fisk set up the first program for African-American social workers.[18] His "neo-Abolitionism," to use Ralph Luker's phrase, challenged the pseudo-scientific consensus about racial superiority.

Jesse Macy clearly exaggerated when he claimed that Gates "led the Governor of the state [of Tennessee] . . . to an entire change of attitude toward our negro citizens"—the political scientist apparently mistook the words of a politician speaking before a receptive audience for repentance.[19] But Gates did model equality during his time in the South. As Gates put it, addressing the Congregationalist Home Missionary Society in 1894, his conception of mission was "to preach the gospel of the solidarity of the human race."[20]

This clear vision, in spite of a scientific consensus that favored racism and a political system jury rigged to uphold it, did not stop a war or overturn racism but did expose justifications for them and point toward alternatives.

GEORGE W. SLATER

While concepts of class dominated early twentieth century socialism, often downplaying race, some African Americans found hope in the message of Christian Socialism.[21] Prominent among them was George W. Slater, pastor of the African Methodist Episcopal Church in Clinton during much of his time in the Christian Socialist movement.[22] His ser-

---

18. White, *Liberty and Justice For All*, 253. Ironically, those at the opposite end of the spectrum on the issue of racial equality could also be anti-imperialist, for the opposite reason of not wanting to associate with "lesser" races. See Lasch, "Anti-Imperialists," *Journal of Southern History*, 24, 319–31. Luker, *Social Gospel in Black and White*, 1, 14, 83, 182–83, 302–3.

19. Macy, preface to Gates, *Life of George Augustus Gates*, xii; Gates, *Life of George Augustus Gates*, 52–53.

20. Quoted in Luker, *Social Gospel in Black and White*, 14.

21. For another glimpse at an encounter between African American churches and socialism, see Noe, *Three Midwestern Playwrights*, 42–43.

22. Foner, *Black Socialist Preacher*; Gary Dorrien misidentifies Slater as Baptist in *New Abolition*, 7. See also Angell and Pinn, *Social Protest in the African Episcopal Church*, 346–47, 311; *Christian Socialist*, Mar. 1, 1913; Jun. 15, 1913.

mon at Second Baptist Church in Ottumwa made him noticed in Iowa and led to his hiring at Clinton.[23]

He is remembered today (if at all) as the father of Duke Slater, football star at the State University of Iowa during the 1920s and later a judge in Chicago. Slater Hall is named after him at his alma mater.[24]

The elder Slater moved to Des Moines in the 1920s and initiated a successful and groundbreaking civil rights case when he was refused service at a downtown cafe,[25] a couple of decades before Edna Griffin and the Progressive Party challenged Katz Drug Store's discriminatory serving policies in 1948.[26]

After moving to Canada, Slater returned to Des Moines and then moved on to Council Bluffs in the thirties, where in 1932 he organized a successful campaign to remove "No Colored Trade Solicited" signs from the windows of local restaurants.[27]

In moving to Council Bluffs, Slater could access educational opportunities across the river at the Presbyterian Theological Seminary at Omaha. While he had attended the University of Chicago and Illinois Wesleyan University, as he had had to pursue his education one semester at a time, he was not eligible for his bachelor's in theology at Omaha until he completed undergraduate work at the University of Nebraska-Omaha, which he did, in his sixties.[28] Slater's pastoral and Social Gospel career, from Christian Socialist to civil rights activist to theological enthusiast, is a striking example of what a grassroots African American minister's life might embody in the early twentieth century.

23. Rozendaal, *Duke Slater*, 11.

24. McMahon, "'Pride to All,'" *OI*, 484–86; Patterson, *Slater of Iowa*; *Daily Iowan*, Aug 16, 1966; DMR, Aug. 16, 1966; Schrader, "Duke Slater," in *Greatest Moments in Iowa Hawkeyes Football History*, ed. Mark Dukes and Schrader, 8, 18. Rozendaal, *Duke Slater*, has done the most research on Duke's father and best situates the elder Slater's politics into the context of his son's career.

25. McDaniel, "Catholic Action in Davenport"; S. Joe Brown, "African Methodism in East Des Moines," Nov. 21, 1948, 4; DMR, Apr. 7, 1931; *Iowa Bystander*, Apr. 17, 1931. *The African-American Bystander* was critical of Slater and the NAACP for asking for only a nominal fine of one dollar.

26. Lawrence, "'Since It Is My Right.'"

27. Rozendaal, *Duke Slater*, 148–49.

28. Rozendaal, *Duke Slater*, 9, 149; Council Bluffs *Nonpareil*, Oct. 4, 1940; Oct. 6, 1940.

The Kingdom Movement(s) of George

OTHER CHRISTIAN SOCIALISTS

Christian Socialists before Herron and Slater were reluctant to commit politically, but with the new century and a potentially viable political party, some committed. Some more Marxian Socialists thought atheism was obvious, but the Socialist Party built a big tent; prominent Iowa Socialist John M. Work, born in Washington, Iowa, summarized the predominant Socialist attitude toward religion thusly—and, aware of its importance, put the chapter on religion toward the beginning of his book:

> No, Socialism is not antagonistic to religion.
> Capitalism is antagonistic to religion.
> Capitalism compels the masses to scramble for a bare existence. It compels most of them to break the Golden Rule every day. It deprives them of the time to develop their spiritual natures . . .
> Of course religion and the church are two separate and distinct things.[29]

Several other Christian Socialists not named George were active in Iowa in the early twentieth century. Oscar F. Donaldson was a real estate and insurance agent and lay Congregationalist in Webster City and founder of the national newspaper *The Christian Socialist*. While the periodical soon moved to Danville, Illinois, and then Chicago, Donaldson loyally kept supporting it financially.[30]

Donaldson had a startlingly brilliant vision of religion that supported his democratic argument for the ordinary person, even if it was one destined for obscurity. Here is his blending of creation and eucharistic theology to argue for solidarity:

> God spreads the bounty of every land and clime, providing by the recreative powers of nature for the sustainance of man . . . Commerce gathers and brings to each and all these bounties, preparing and serving—THE LORD'S SUPPER. Christians ask that commerce (the observance of the Lord's Supper) be so arranged so that we can say to our fellow man, "Take, eat." . . .
> The Lord's Supper is not separate from our everyday life . . . Your religion is what you do every day, including Sunday,

---

29. Work, *What Is and What Isn't*, 24. On Work, a Christian Socialist, see Cumberland, "Red Flag," 447–48, 450; Kipnis, *American Socialist Movement*, 268–72.

30. *Christian Socialist*, Dec. 1903; Lee, *History of Hamilton County*, 456–57. According to Lee, Donaldson wrote a book, *Workingman's View of the Bible*, but it doesn't seem to be extant; in 1944 he wrote *The Soul and Its Life, or Thinking of Life Clearly*.

The People Are Kind

not what your idea of the Creator is or the formal worship you participate in.[31]

Noah Garwick, pastor of Central Church of Christ in Waterloo, was even more closely identified with Socialist electoral work. In 1908 he ran for mayor and in 1910 for Congress as a Socialist.[32] One supporter provided content for the local newspaper by offering this ultra-gendered portrait of Garwick:

> Noah Garwick is a living illustration of virile Christian manhood . . . He contrasts strikingly with the vast array of kindly disposed old ladies of the male persuasion who occupy so large a number of our pulpits and bring the Christ message into ridicule in their eagerness to twist its words into conformity with the wishes of the money bags salary payers.[33]

For at least one supporter, there was no daylight between Christian Socialism and the Men and Religion Forward Movement.

One other piece of evidence suggesting the extent to which the message of Christian Socialism had soaked into small-town Iowa in the early twentieth century is the report of Ella Carr on her campaign trip to southern Iowa on behalf of Socialist presidential candidate Eugene Debs. She stumped North English, Ottumwa, Bussey, Bloomfield, Corydon, Kellerton, Mt. Ayr, Redding, Clarinda, Shambaugh, Villisca, Hastings, and Sidney; Carr referenced Brethren in North English, Rev. Rodein of the Christian Church and Rev. Harvey of the Methodist Church in Kellerton (Harvey was a Socialist candidate for state senate); Rev. Hardaway in Mt. Ayr; the Presbyterian Church in Clarinda; and William Scott, a "loyal supporter of the *Christian Socialist*" in Villisca.[34] Carr knew how name-dropping could extend down as well as up, a trait that future historians appreciated.

THE BROADER SOCIAL GOSPEL MOVEMENT

Other electorally based reform efforts included the United Christian Party, which convened its first convention in Des Moines over the Fourth

---

31. *Christian Socialist*, Dec. 1903.

32. Waterloo *Courier,* Mar. 6, 7, 11, 13, 14, 16, 18, 19, 21, 24, 25, 26, 27, 28, 30, and 31, 1908; *Christian Socialist,* Feb. 15, 1908; Brooklyn, NY *Daily Eagle, May* 3, 1908.

33. Waterloo *Courier,* Mar. 25, 1908.

34. *Christian Socialist,* Oct. 1, 1912.

The Kingdom Movement(s) of George

of July weekend in 1899, with a vaguely Socialist, quasi-Prohibitionist platform. The party fielded national tickets between 1900 and 1912, with paltry electoral results. The founder and perennial chair of the party was Rev. William Benkert of the Davenport Church of God.[35] In 1908 the vice-presidential candidate was Lorenzo Coffin of Ft. Dodge, best known for railroad safety reforms, who also founded houses of hospitality for ex-prisoners and unwed mothers.[36]

Most religious Iowans did not join the Socialist movement. But Christian Socialists had the effect of drawing the connections between social structures and religious beliefs. A wider lens suggests that much of Iowa Protestantism was influenced by the Social Gospel.

Not a Socialist but a contributor to Gates's and Herron's Kingdom Movement centered in Grinnell was Jesse Macy. The political scientist Macy was perhaps the most accomplished Iowa College faculty member—he has been credited with teaching the first political science course in an American college.[37] Having moved beyond his childhood Quakerism, he cheerfully wrote articles for his colleagues' Kingdom Movement and presented at their roundtables.[38] But influenced by the racialized science of the time, he counseled caution in challenging the institutions of Jim Crow.[39]

Iowa Methodists also drifted toward social service.[40] Notable was the Iowa Bible Training School at 921 Pleasant in Des Moines, also known as Hawthorn Hill, part of the deaconess movement that emphasized social work.[41]

Typical of denominational change was the case of the Episcopalians. In 1903, the Iowa Convention passed a resolution condemning the Russian persecution of Jews. "This was," the most recent denominational historian has maintained, "the precursor to hundreds of such resolutions

---

35. *Des Moines Leader*, Jul. 2, 1899; Jul. 5, 1899; Miller, *Following in His Steps*, 94; *Iowa Official Register*, 1900, 227–29, 310–11.

36. "Coffin, Lorenzo Stephen," *BDI*, 91–93.

37. Sherwood, *Roosevelt and Hopkins*, 17–18.

38. On Macy, see Noyes, *Jesse Macy*; Nollen, *Grinnell College*, chapter 10; Wall, *Grinnell College*, 196–97, 249, 251; Colman, "In Pursuit of Harmony,"; Luker, *The Social Gospel in Black and White*, 227–30, 239–40.

39. Luker, 227–28, 230, 239–40.

40. Freer, *Laity and Education*.

41. Toulouse, "Origins of the *Christian Century*"; Nye, *Between the Rivers*, 233–36.

presented to Conventions during the 20th century, about most of the political, social, and moral issues of any particular era."[42]

SOCIAL PROTESTANTISM: THE CASE OF DES MOINES

Illustrative of the tension between the Social Gospel and an economically conservative religious establishment is what happened when Kelley's Army arrived in Des Moines. The economic depression of 1893 was among the worst in the nation's history and left many homeless, including Civil War veterans. Like Jacob Coxey's similar "army," Kelley organized homeless veterans to march on Washington to demand early payment of Civil War pensions, citing the economic emergency. When the Army encamped in Des Moines, they were met by the young president of Drake University, Barton Aylesworth, who deployed students to survey and record the deprivations that marchers were eager to relate.

News of Aylesworth's hearty welcome of the "tramps" was met with shock by many of the university's donors, notably the eponymous Francis Drake. A board resolution essentially rebuked Aylesworth's friendliness to the impoverished.[43]

The Central Church of Christ, on Piety Hill in downtown Des Moines, especially under the leadership of Harvey O. Breeden, was prominent in promoting progressive thought in the capital city.[44] He was also prominent in denominational circles, being elected president of the International Convention of the Disciples of Christ in 1904.[45]

Theology in the urban pulpit no longer required equating acts of God, as an insurance term, with divine providence. A case in point were reactions to the 1913 tornado that killed 94 people in Omaha. While Howland

---

42. Horton, *Beautiful Heritage*, 67.

43. Harrell, *Social Sources of Division*, 151–52; Ritchey, *Drake University*, 70–73.

44. Putz, "Building a City on a Hill"; Coffman, *Christian Century*, 16–17; deGroot, *Central of Des Moines*, 63–83; Harrell, *Social Sources of Division*, 81; Burke, *Swami Vivekananda in the West*, 198–215; Stavig, *Western Admirers*, 300–303. Central Church of Christ merged with the University Place Christian Church in 1970 to form First Christian Church, until 2019 located across the street from Drake University. In 2019 First Christian moved to the suburb of Urbandale, changing its name to New Beginnings Christian Church.

45. Blanchard, "Pioneers of a Great Cause," 195–96, typescript in Divinity Special Collections, Cowles Library, Drake University.

The Kingdom Movement(s) of George

Hanson of First Baptist in Des Moines suggested, "There is still a God of Tornado!," William Gage of Highland Park Presbyterian on the northside called it "a freakish wind."[46]

The evolution of *The Christian Century* is also part of the Iowa Social Gospel story. What began in Des Moines as a regional Disciples newspaper called *The Christian Oracle* in 1884 was transformed by Drake Divinity School graduate Charles Clayton Morrison into the premiere national liberal Protestant journal in the twentieth century. In 1891, it moved from Des Moines to Chicago and was subsequently renamed *The Christian Century*. Morrison bought the magazine at auction for $1500 in 1908 and gradually cut denominational ties, ending the affiliation in 1917.[47]

Wallace Short was in some ways a representative Social Gospeler. Chapter 12 elaborates his improbable career as Congregationalist minister, member of the Bartenders Union, and Labor Party mayor of Sioux City. Short was prominent in left-of-major-party politics in the state for decades, and after parting ways with the Congregational Church over Prohibition, served an independent People's Church pulpit. His career as mayor was marked by his defending civil liberties during World War I. This was a departure from previous city administrations, who had sparked a free speech fight with the Industrial Workers of the World in 1915, with Wobblies overfilling the jails until the city gave in.[48]

Samuel Zane Batten, a prominent Baptist Social Gospel advocate, taught at Des Moines University early in the twentieth century. (He left before its takeover by the fundamentalist Baptist Bible Union in 1927—see chapter 18.) His book *The Social Task of Christianity*, written in 1911 while he was professor of Social Science at Des Moines College and national chair of the Social Service Commission of the Northern Baptist Convention,[49] called for an understanding of the social nature

---

46. Thuesen, *Tornado God*, 112–13.

47. Coffman, Christian Century *and the Rise of the Protestant Mainline*.

48. Cumberland, *Wallace Short*; Short, *Just One American*.

49. Curtis, *Consuming Faith*, 141–42; White and Hopkins, *Social Gospel*, 78, 85, 93; Dombrowski, *Early Days of Christian Socialism*, 10, 18, 107; Putz, "Building a City," 32.

Batten's book *A New World Order* turned out to be unfortunately named, as decades later it drew the attention of conspiracy theorists who equated Batten's garden-variety Wilsonian internationalism with a supposed Rockefeller-backed globalist domination. After all, weren't Batten and Rockefeller both liberal Baptists? What are the odds? To which the rejoinder might be, if you own much of the world, what's the need to take it over?

of Christianity: salvation was not from a sinful world but through the world's transformation.[50]

THE SETTLEMENT MOVEMENT

The Settlement Movement inaugurated by Jane Addams at Hull House in Chicago also influenced Iowa. Flora Dunlap worked with Addams before starting the Roadside Settlement in Des Moines.[51] Jane Boyd, born into a devout home in Tipton, provided similar succor for the poor in Cedar Rapids.[52]

Sometimes progressive causes coexisted with more traditional pieties. The earnestness with which "Mother" Eliza Ryder Wheaton of Tabor, Iowa, sought the rehabilitation of prisoners was chronicled in her book *Prisons and Prayer, or A Labor of Love*,[53] being "An account of nearly Twenty-two years of Gospel Work, seeking the lost, in Prisons, Reformatories, Stockades, Rescue Homes, Saloons, and Dives, on the Streets, Railway Trains, etc."

In 1920, Unitarian and town founder of Humboldt Stephen Taft, by then in retirement in Los Angeles, debated a socialist on the key to social reform. Taft maintained that personal change had to precede social transformation. He was representing the Prohibition Party's viewpoint.[54] Or could social engineering change individuals? Could the abolition of alcohol be transformational? Many Iowans thought so, for a variety of reasons, and this experiment dominated much of the political discourse of the state for decades, contradicting, confirming, and complicating Christian socialist narrative.

---

50. Batten, *Social Task of Christianity*, 80–81.
51. Dunlap, "Roadside Settlement of Des Moines"; Putz, "Building a City."
52. Fisher and Hay, *In the Heart of the City*, 28.
53. Wheaton, *Prisons and Prayer*.
54. Taft, *Empire Builder of the Middle West*.

CHAPTER 12

Social Justice and Holiness

From Temperance to Prohibition

"We, many of us, feel keenly the slurs, and the many unkind things said and done, but we must remember that all who first advocate a reform are looked on with contempt. Many of us can remember a time when an anti-slavery man was looked on with contempt . . . but they persevered, their numbers increased, and finally in a terrible struggle, the shackles were lifted for millions for whom they had plead, toiled, and suffered."

—Mrs. S. L. Smith, Marshalltown[1]

"Iowa will go Democratic when hell goes Methodist."

—Jonathan Dolliver[2]

" . . . [T]he religious focus of the grassroots formed the foundation for the [Women's Christian Temperance Union] organization's politicized national agenda."

—Sarah Boyle[3]

---

1. *Proceedings of the Women's Christian Temperance Union of Iowa, 1876*, 2, copy in IWA.
2. Quoted in Pegram, *Battling Demon Rum*, 80.
3. Boyle, "Creating a Union of the Union," v.

The People Are Kind

"Prohibition, local option, prohibition again, nonenforcement, cowardice under the name of 'Mulct Law'—these are the successive steps in the effort to solve the liquor question in Iowa . . . 'Iowa canted, decanted, and recanted,' said a cynic at Des Moines a few weeks ago."

—TRUMBULL WHITE, 1908[4]

ON THE NIGHT OF August 3, 1886, crusading minister George C. Haddock[5] of the First Methodist Episcopal Church of Sioux City confronted a group of men he suspected of illegally transporting liquor into downtown. Haddock was armed with a confidence in the justice of his cause of upholding Iowa's new prohibition law. Unfortunately, those he faced were armed with pistols.

Rev. Haddock's murder that night made him a prohibitionist martyr. The murder trials prolonged the controversy. The prosecution was made more difficult by the defendants' strategy of pointing the finger at different trigger men, depending on who was currently on trial. When a brewery foreman was convicted, the dry forces thought the sentence far too light, while the wets campaigned for his release.[6]

Until 2013, a plaque on the sidewalk in downtown Sioux City commemorated the site of Haddock's death; the construction of a casino forced its removal to the Sioux City Public Museum. Haddock also had streets named after him in temperance towns in southern California. The assassination convinced Governor William Larrabee, himself a Methodist lay preacher, that the prohibition law on the books ought to be enforced, and saloons were closed in thirty-seven more counties in 1885.[7]

That prohibition was flaunted so openly might have given some drys pause about their strategy. But the fraught question of alcohol consumption was complicated, wrapped as it was around both principles of social justice and holiness, and intermixed as well with triggering issues related to feminism, nativism and ethnic pride, social class, and raw politics.

---

4. "Does Prohibition Pay? [Part] III," *Appleton's Magazine* 12, 343.

5. Smith, "Martyr for Prohibition"; siouxcityhirynotablepeople/29-reverend-george-haddock; www.siouxcityfirst.com/PicturesanditemsfromRevGeorgeHaddockschurch; Haddock, *Life of Rev. George C. Haddock*.

6. NYT, Jan. 7, 1887; March 31, 1887.

7. Ostler, *Prairie Populism*, 55; Andersen, *Politics of Prohibition*, 160; *Des Moines Leader*, Jun. 29, 1889.

For those inclined to imbibe, or more precisely willing to imbibe openly, questions of personal freedom and often cultural and ethnic identity were at stake.

For those opposed to drinking alcohol, an oppositional culture founded on propriety and religious devotion could provide identity as well. For some religious Iowans, the strong moral tendency and the urgency to use politics to address social injustices, which had found a home in the abolitionist movement, coupled with the urge for personal purity nourished by the Holiness movement,[8] combined to set the stage for the Prohibition crusade. The considerable overlap between the streams of social justice and Holiness meant the temperance-turned-prohibitionist movement was already a political force by the 1850s.

All of this tangled web of morality, addiction, and liberty played out, as it turned out, over a checkerboard of Iowa counties, in the legislature, and in repeated statewide referenda, for over a century, but particularly *before* the ratification of the Eighteenth Amendment to the federal constitution in 1919. Iowa, like Maine, was considered a flagship state for Prohibition, even if reality often did not conform to that ideal. And for many, abstinence from alcohol became a central tenet of the Christian faith, despite scant support for such a position in Christian Scriptures or history.

The long fight can be divided chronologically into four distinct eras: antebellum anti-alcohol campaigns, which shift from personal temperance to state prohibition; the era where women reformers dominated, from about 1874–89; the Progressive era, where men take over and botch things up, 1890–1919; and the era of national prohibition and its aftermath, arguably 1920–63. (I will include later anti-prohibition temperance efforts with the first section.)

ANTEBELLUM TEMPERANCE AND PROHIBITION

Our first step is to acknowledge the problem: alcohol consumption at the beginning of the temperance movement had reached staggering proportions in the early decades of the nation. According to historian William Rorabaugh, per capita alcohol consumption of distilled spirits peaked around 1830 at five gallons per person per year, or triple what the consumption rate was when Rorabaugh published in 1979. That

---

8. For a short but cogent discussion about how the doctrine of perfectionism played out in Prohibitionism, see Parsons, "Slaves to the Bottle."

consumption might have approached those levels at other times in human history does not detract from the social toll, economic costs, and domestic misery such a figure suggests.[9]

Feminist and temperance advocate Amelia Bloomer, for example, who later settled in Council Bluffs, found it difficult to make her wedding alcohol-free, even though she lived in the religiously fervent "Burned-Over District" of upstate New York. Nor did she find it possible to separate temperance and suffrage as issues, sometimes to the dismay of suffragists like Elizabeth Cady Stanton and Susan B. Anthony.[10] The uneasy alliance would be a recurring theme.

The situation as Iowa opened for white occupation suggests the trope of the drunken Indian might be projection, along with more of a tolerance to the outer effects of alcohol.[11] The low cost of whiskey certainly contributed to its availability; an early settler recalled that a Davenport store provided all the whiskey you could drink for a nickel.[12]

German-American Joseph Eiboeck, editor of the Des Moines *Iowa Staats-Anzeiger* and a leader of the anti-Prohibitionist movement, claimed that prior to 1855, when the first Prohibition law went into effect, "every corner store kept a barrel of whiskey available from which any patron could avail himself free of charge as much as he liked."[13] For Eiboeck, this seemed a drinker's Eden; for his opponents, it was a rude frontier in need of civilizing.

On the other hand, Daniel Clark, the scholar who has taken the closest look at Iowa's nineteenth century legislative history on liquor, claimed that the territorial period, 1836 to 1846, had a "more active temperance feeling than any other period of equal length during the history of Iowa,"[14] with sympathetic governors approving legislative restrictions on alcohol sales. One innovation of the territorial era began in Farmington, pioneering the local option.[15] The territorial period also saw the first local temperance societies. While Clark listed the first in Ft. Madison in 1838, Burlington and Bloomington [now Muscatine] in 1839, and

9. Rohrabaugh, *Alcoholic Republic*, 8.
10. Noun, "Amelia Bloomer," 579–84, 593, 601–7, 616.
11. Rohrabaugh, *Alcoholic Republic*, 7.
12. Ficke, *Memories of Fourscore Years*, 74.
13. Ehrstine and Gibbs, "Iowa's Prohibition Plague," 23.
14. Clark, "Beginning of Liquor Legislation," 196. Some of Clark's own articles make this claim suspect.
15. "Beginning of Liquor Legislation," 197, 206, 211.

Davenport and Iowa City in 1842,[16] Dubuque historian William Wilkie documented a temperance society there as early as March 1834, led by Joseph Plumbe, Jr.[17]

Abolitionism exemplified the reform enthusiasm in early nineteenth-century America but did not confine it. In 1844, Maine became the first state to prohibit the sale of alcoholic beverages. Shortly after Iowa's statehood, a local option law passed the legislature. An indication of the contemporary enthusiasm for temperance is that in local elections held April 5, 1847, only Keokuk County voted in favor of granting liquor licenses. The agitation for total Prohibition increased, with petitions to the legislature and the founding of a temperance newspaper, *The Sunbeam*. In 1855, Iowa followed Maine's lead and passed total Prohibition.[18]

Typical of Iowa prohibitionists was Hiram Price, who moved to Davenport from western Pennsylvania in 1844. He soon joined the fraternal organization the Sons of Temperance. Like most prominent Iowa prohibitionists, Price was a devout Methodist. The storekeeper was active in the agitation for a Maine-style prohibition law[19] and kept up his activism throughout the century.

While Democratic Governor Stephen Hempstead had staved off the growing clamor of temperance advocates by moving to increased regulation, the increasingly politically unstable early fifties made such fence-straddling tenuous. In the last successful gasp of the Iowa Whigs, they capitalized on temperance discontent and Democratic defections to take the governor's office in 1854.[20]

But the prohibitionist majority in the legislature proved as ephemeral as the Whig party. Its successor, the brand-new Republican party, adopted the opposite and also successful strategy, subsuming all other issues into organizing around free soil.[21]

16. "Beginning of Liquor Legislation," 196, 200, 208, 209.

17. Wilkie, *Dubuque on the Mississippi*, 156.

18. Tyrrell, *Sobering Up*, 12, 243; Blocker, *Retreat From Reform*, 57; Clark, "History of Liquor Legislation," 56–64.

19. Lender, *Dictionary of American Temperance Biography*, 407–8; Clark, "History of Liquor Legislation," 57.

20. Tyrrell, *Sobering Up*, 260; "Hempstead, Stephen P.," BDI, 226–27; Cook, "Political Culture of Antebellum Iowa," IHR, 95n22.

21. Cook, "Political Culture of Antebellum Iowa," 101–4; Tyrrell, 268–69.

As the movement shifted from temperance to abstinence, it also moved from stressing personal responsibility to political solutions:[22] the push for enacting and enforcing laws against the production, sale, possession, and consumption of alcoholic beverages. Ian Tyrrell argues that the move from temperance to prohibition was a shift from working-class solidarity to middle-class respectability, exemplified by the Sons of Temperance's acquiescence to prohibition:

> The prohibitionist movement of the late 1840's and 1850's involved above all else an alliance of property and middle-class respectability against the spectre of pauperism and urban crime . . . The division of prohibition was never simply between native born and foreign born, nor was the prohibitionist issue articulated in those terms. The division was preeminently one of class rather than ethnicity . . . The Sons of Temperance bowed to evangelical pressure . . . [and also] became more closely identified with the interests of employers.[23]

The fullest articulation in Iowa of the principle of temperance as personal morality rather than state control was by another Sioux City minister: maverick pastor and Labor Party mayor Rev. Wallace M. Short. Like Haddock, Short also had a flair for the dramatic, but his actions only cost him his religious affiliation, not his life. He was a Social Gospel minister who became a skilled radical politician.[24] For his questioning of prohibition orthodoxy, he lost his standing as a Congregationalist minister in 1914 but continued pastoring the People's Church.[25] An honorary member of the Bartenders Union, he fused support for personal liberty with sympathy for workers, some of whom depended on the liquor trade for a living and many more who relied on it as a coping mechanism and social lubricant.

Short summarized his version of temperance in a 1915 sermon, "The Deeper Meaning of the 'Temperance' Question." He drew a clear distinction between personal temperance and governmental prohibition:

---

22. For a recent view distinguishing temperance and prohibition, see Thompson, "Myth 1," in *Prohibition's Greatest Myths*, ed. Lewis and Hamm, 1–19.

23. Tyrrell, 216–17. Cf. Fletcher, *Gender and the American Temperance Movement*, 12–13.

24. Cumberland, *Wallace Short*.

25. Short chronicles his unsuccessful attempt at retaining his credentials within the Iowa Congregational Association in his *Let There Be Light*.

> Some of us are profoundly concerned over this prohibition question, not mainly for the sake of the liquor question itself, but because it is the storm center of the great intellectual and moral battle of our nation over a problem that is vastly larger. This vaster problem has to do with the whole question as to the use of physical force, or the use of moral inspiration and instruction, in the creation of character and in the building of a state or nation of noble and happy men and women.[26]

While Short's position aimed to be forward-looking, applying a Social Gospel analysis to empathize with working people, it also harkened back to a time before the concept of temperance had hardened into the prerequisite of advocating prohibition.

The linkage between the movement to abolish slavery and temperance was strong, but the reasons are not readily apparent.[27] In early temperance advocacy, all of the lines were not yet drawn—between native-born and ethnic, or in some analyses, between Pietist and Confessional perspectives: for example, the French-born Bishop Mathias Loras advocated temperance, a position that later Roman Catholics found inconsistent with European practices.[28] Later, one of Loras's successors, Archbishop John J. Keane, led the Iowa and national Catholic Total Abstinence Unions.[29]

For another example, before the Civil War, the Drakesville Church of Christ was torn by the temperance question. This is not as surprising as it might seem at first glance, since the restorationist tradition vowed to speak only where the Scriptures speak, and the Bible has little to say on

---

26. Short, *Deeper Meaning of the "Temperance Question,"* 20.

27. Rohrabaugh, *Alcoholic Republic*, 219.

28. Auge, *Man of Deeds*, 86; Mark Wyman, *Immigrants in the Valley*, 173, 185. But Loras was not the last Dubuque prelate to advocate temperance. Catholics during the tenure of Archbishop John Keane often found themselves tiptoeing around the subject in his presence. Gallagher, *Seed/Harvest*, 68. For another instance of Catholic teetotalism, see Avella, *Catholic Church in Southwest Iowa*, 130–31.

29. Benson, *Century of Service to God and Community*, 60; Ahern, *Life of John J. Keane*, 20–21, 328, 333; Gallagher, *Seed/Harvest*, 56.

the subject.[30] But later, Disciples would be in the forefront of the struggle against alcohol consumption.[31]

The 1857 exemption of beer, wine, and cider from the prohibition law, and the gradual drift to local control of the liquor question, culminating in 1868, along with the perennial issue of enforcement, characterized Iowa attitudes for the next couple of decades (and all other issues were subsumed while the Civil War raged). An advantage of local control was that it might lead to innovation: in 1853, Mount Pleasant recognized alcoholism as a medical problem by putting liquor sales under physicians' control. But the popular concern about alcohol consumption prevalent in early statehood reemerged in the seventies.[32]

WOMEN'S LEADERSHIP AND THE 1885 PROHIBITION ACT[33]

After the Civil War, there was a marked shift in the anti-alcohol movement from temperance to abstinence to prohibition, from an emphasis on personal responsibility to calls for a public crusade. Women became the early de facto leaders in that transition.[34] The advocacy that had first been possible for women in the abolitionist movement was readily transferable to a movement that could combine social reform and advocacy for women caught in marriages damaged by alcohol abuse. And as women increasingly addressed the public sphere, the question of women's disenfranchisement became obvious.

Annie Wittenmyer,[35] an Iowan who had become prominent for her relief work during the Civil War (see chapter 7), was elected the first

---

30. Hargis, "History of the Disciples of Christ," 65. Ian Tyrell suggests that Midwesterners originally from the southern uplands were much less receptive to temperance than others, at least in the 1850s. *Sobering Up*, 244.

31. Harrell, *Social Sources of Division*, 230.

32. Clark, "History of Liquor Legislation in Iowa," 64, 66–67, 77, 80–81, 85–86, 339, 348.

33. A lucid reconstruction of this era can be found in Campbell, "Did Democracy Work," 87–116.

34. Clark also points to an 1871 Methodist convention in Iowa City and the establishment of the People's Temperance Association in Des Moines the same year. 354–55.

35. Gallaher, "Wittenmyer," *IJH* 29 (1932) 563–69. Probably because she was an abrasive if effective figure in the Civil War, and was on the losing side of Women's Christian Temperance Union battles, most notoriously in opposing women's suffrage, the degree to which she was a polymath, especially on religious matters, has been lost.

national president of the Women's Christian Temperance Union. In her inaugural address she had no doubt of the issue's urgency:

> We have been called by the Spirit of the Lord to lead the women of the world in a great and difficult reform movement, and thousands in our own and other lands are looking to us with hope and expectation. The drink system is the common enemy of women the world over, . . . and as the success of all moral reforms depends largely upon women, the world will halt, or move in its onward march towards millennial glory, as *we* halt or march.[36]

If all moral reforms depended upon women, as Wittenmyer posited, it followed for most temperance followers that women should have the right to vote. Wittenmyer demurred, distinguishing between moral and political reform. "We do not prepare to trail our skirts in the mire of politics," she sniffed.[37] But soon pro-suffrage Frances Willard deposed Wittenmyer as leader, and the Iowa WCTU was campaigning for women's suffrage.[38]

Temperance support for the suffrage cause would become both indispensable and problematic for the cause of suffrage. The suffrage movement in many places depended on the energy of WCTU local activists who supported Frances Willard's "Do Everything" strategy, and saw the vote as the probable means to electoral victory on prohibition. On the other hand, such support almost automatically soured pro-wet voters, who by law were only male, and hence necessary in gaining a male majority to approve expanding the franchise.[39]

In the introduction to his satirical anti-Prohibition novel *Iowa Cranks*, Edwin Chapin was clear in assigning blame for a dry Iowa to women: "It

---

Reformation scholar Hans Hillebrand credits her book *Women and the Reformation* as first to address the subject. Hillebrand, "Was There a Reformation in the Sixteenth Century?" *CH* 72, 547n48.

36. Quoted in Mattingly, *Well-Tempered Women*, 46.

37. Sillanpa, *Annie Wittenmyer*, 33.

38. Bordin, *Women and Temperance*, 120, 134. For mid-1877 local reports on the WCTU in Iowa, see Annie Wittenmyer, *History of the Women's Temperance Crusade*, Philadelphia, 1878, 668–83; included are Manchester, Wilton Junction, "Vallisca" [Villisca], Vinton, and Clinton.

39. Egge, *Woman Suffrage*, 86–93.

was a novelty [in 1871] to have woman declaim from the platform[40] ... Politics, the sciences and philosophy were hardly understood by them, but a temperance lecturer was in the realm of feeling and home life." Later in the introduction, he maintained that the ability of women to make the Republican Party "their slaves ... may or may *not* be an argument for woman suffrage."[41] But Chapin left little doubt as to his opinion.

Chapin was right about one thing: women's temperance advocates would use "the realm of feeling and home life" to their advantage in entering the public sphere. The national Women's Crusade of 1873 and 1874 was a spontaneous nonviolent direct action campaign against saloon owners that began in Ohio. At least temporarily, it was successful in getting many saloon owners to close, especially in small towns. In Iowa, however, it focused on city councils and their prerogative to grant liquor licenses. In Manchester, Corydon, Atlantic, Ottumwa, Des Moines, and elsewhere,[42] women marched on city council meetings and raised objections to business as usual. When one Des Moines city councilor questioned the detrimental effects of alcohol, the protestors were ready with a witness, a Mrs. Kenworthy, who testified that her husband's excessive drinking "had made him a pauper, had driven his children from home, ... [and who] was soon to fill a drunkard's grave." Saloonkeepers' attempts at taking the moral high ground were unpersuasive; when they went on the offensive in Dubuque, they unsuccessfully urged the city council to license ministers and charge them a $300 fee.[43]

Despite Dubuque saloonkeepers' assumptions and the religious motivations of most of the Women Crusade's participants, a direct action

40. This was an understatement; while some abolitionist women were able to declaim publicly, it often was considered a scandal. As late as 1868 the good abolitionist faculty members of Iowa College in Grinnell were so uncomfortable with the prospect of a woman speaking at graduation ceremonies that they rescinded an invitation that had been extended by the Grinnell Ladies Literary Society to Mary Newbury Adams of Dubuque to speak. Lex, "Mary Newbury Adams"; "Adams, Mary Newbury (or Newberry)," BDI, 3.

41. Chapin, *Iowa Cranks*, 3–5. The plot revolves around unscrupulous mercenary special constables taking advantage of the political situation to accumulate bribes for not prosecuting those caught by their warrantless home searches for liquor. In his anti-Prohibition history, Joseph Eiboeck made a similar claim about attorneys. Ehrstine, "Iowa's Prohibition Plague," 26, 74.

42. Clark, "History of Liquor Legislation in Iowa," 358–59; Blocker, "'Give to the Winds Thy Fears,'" 25, 76, 93. Blocker, using Wittenmyer's 1878 history and newspaper accounts, counts thirty-nine crusades in Iowa.

43. Clark, "History of Liquor Legislation in Iowa," 358–59; Blocker, "'Give to the Winds Thy Fears,'" 59.

campaign led by women was not universally embraced by the (male) Iowa religious establishment. In Keokuk, a clear majority of ministers tried to dissuade crusaders.[44]

The disruptive quality of the prohibition campaign, and the impressive rapidity with which it was institutionalized, is summed up in this early inside account of the Iowa Women's Temperance Union:

> December 23d, 1873 marks an era in the history of Temperance Reform. "In the fullness of time," as the long preparatory work of the preceding years had made the people ready for action, when the increased drunkenness consequent upon the war, made the people cry out, as never before, on account of drink, suddenly as lightning from out [of] a clear sky, God gave us the Women's Crusade . . . In the summer of 1874 the Women's Christian Temperance Union of Marshalltown sent out a circular letter concerning the advisability of a state convention to organize an Iowa Women's Temperance Union. The society at Cedar Rapids replied favoring it, and asking that it be held in Cedar Rapids.[45]

In the wake of the Women's Crusade, activists founded the Iowa Women's Christian Temperance Union late in 1874.[46] The WCTU's social reform agenda would become larger than Prohibition; addressing the double standard in prostitution laws and sheltering unwed pregnant women would become priorities,[47] as would women's suffrage.

One of the leaders of the Iowa WCTU and superintendent of its national bureau on legislation was J. Ellen Foster of Clinton. Like Willard, with whom she was at first allied, Foster was a devout Methodist. She had nominated Willard for president of the union on Willard's first foray in wresting leadership from Wittenmyer.[48] She had impressed the press early with her speaking abilities; the DeWitt *Observer* proclaimed, "We have an Elizabeth Cady Stanton in our midst." She also brought her expertise as a

---

44. Blocker, "'Give to the Winds Thy Fears,'" 160.
45. *Proceedings of the Women's Temperance Union, 1874*, 1, IWA.
46. Clark, "History of Liquor Legislation in Iowa," 359; *Proceedings of the Christian Temperance Union, 1874*.
47. Benedict, *Woman's Work for Woman*.
48. Bordin, *Frances Willard*, 105.

lawyer.⁴⁹ At a meeting in Burlington in 1878, Foster was the one to propose that Iowa should enact prohibition by constitutional amendment. In the 1882 referendum, Methodist and Swedish Lutheran churches were among the denominations prodding their members to vote yes.⁵⁰

Judith Ellen Foster. Library of Congress.

After the successful referendum campaign led by Foster, the Iowa Supreme Court voided the vote on a technicality. But Foster and other

---

49. While Foster was not the first woman lawyer to practice in Iowa, she did later have the distinction of being the first woman to argue a case in Indiana. Letter from James R. Farmer to Clinton Public Library, Dec. 10, 1993, copy in Clinton Public Library; *Indianapolis Journal*, Jan. 5, 1881; Oct. 31, 1907.

50. Ehrstine, "Iowa's Prohibition Plague," 46.

drys persuaded Republicans to live up to their state platform and enact prohibition through legislation in 1884.[51] At a state Temperance Alliance convention held in Des Moines on January 23 and 24, 1884, speakers included former Congressman H. O. Pratt, currently a Methodist preacher; the attorney general; United Presbyterian Henry Wallace; Methodist Episcopal Bishop John Hurst, and George Magoun, Congregationalist president of Iowa College. But "none [was] more in favor than Mrs. Foster."[52]

Republican legislators lived up to their campaign promise, and Governor Larrabee began enforcing the ban on alcohol. Foster was grateful. She became a loyal Republican. This put her on a collision course with national WCTU leader Frances Willard, who in 1888 urged support for the Prohibition party.[53] (In fact, in 1892 Methodists Frances Willard and James B. Weaver came close to brokering an agreement fusing the Prohibition and Populist parties, agreeing on most of the issues, but differences in emphasis proved insurmountable.)[54]

But the reality in Iowa was not as simple as Foster maintained; in fact, the Prohibition party's success in 1877 had denied the Republicans a majority in the legislature for the first time in two decades, and arguably that defeat rather than the referendum's success provided the incentive to add prohibition to the Republican platform and ensure party support of legislative prohibition measures.[55]

In the dispute over supporting a third party, the Iowa WCTU, a significant portion of Pennsylvania's union, and other scattered locals seceded from the national WCTU. While Foster led the revolt, she did not take a leadership role in the breakaway Non-Partisan Women's Christian Temperance Union; from 1896 to 1898, Annie Wittenmyer

---

51. Mott, "Judith Ellen Foster"; Ehrstine, "Iowa's Prohibition Plague," 44; Clark, "History of Liquor Legislation in Iowa," 366; Kerr, *Organized for Prohibition*, 5, 47–48, 57–58, 69. The *DeWitt Observer* quote is from Jun. 8, 1874. For a summary of her later career as a bureaucrat in Washington during Republican administrations, see the *Clinton Herald*, Jun. 8, 2016.

52. Mott, "Judith Ellen Foster," 135.

53. Mott, "Judith Ellen Foster," 135; Pegram, *Battling Demon Rum*, 72; Bordin, *Woman and Temperance*, 125–27. Sarah Boyle has a blow-by-blow account of the disagreement in chapters 2 and 4 of her dissertation, "Creating a Union of the Union."

54. Blocker, *Retreat from Reform*, 54–55. Cf. Meyer, *We Are What We Drink*, 97. Like most Iowa politicians, Weaver was not always straightforward in maintaining his position on prohibition; in 1885, seeking an alliance with the Democrats, he tried to finesse the Greenback Party's position but was called out by Joseph Eiboeck, the state's foremost wet advocate. Ehrstine, 14.

55. Blocker, *Temperance*, 89; Boyle, "Creating a Union of the Union," 102.

was president. The word "non-partisan" needs parsing; while opposing the Prohibition party, the organization in effect was aiding the Republicans. The breach was healed after Willard's untimely death in 1898, as the small Nonpartisan group reunited with the larger union.[56] By that time, though, the WCTU's preeminence in the prohibitionist movement was being supplanted.

On February 26, 1889, Governor (and Methodist lay preacher) William Larrabee, who in response to the Haddock martyrdom had cast his lot with prohibitionists, wrote Rev. Charles Cardwell McCabe of the National Temperance Society on the effects of prohibition in Iowa. McCabe had the letter printed as a pamphlet. Larrabee reported that the number of banks in the state was up, and the number of tramps was down. He apparently saw a causal connection between those statistics and the prohibition of alcohol.[57] Larrabee approved of both trends but did not consider whether economic conditions might have factored into the results.

Ellen Foster's pro-Republican strategy had its dissenters in Iowa. Prominent among them was Disciples minister D. R. Dungan. Dungan authored the heartfelt book *Rum and Its Remedy* and worked to make the Prohibition Party viable—which it was, briefly.[58]

The Iowa Women's Christian Temperance Union had an agenda beyond prohibition; beyond suffrage, it also advocated on issues controversial to middle-class Victorian Protestant congregations, such as supporting sex workers who wished to retire, and sheltering unmarried pregnant women. Lovina Benedict, who scoured the state seeking donations for such projects, was frequently denied access to local congregations, and only after raising the money did the WCTU endorse her efforts. The issues she raised, although often taboo for Iowa Protestant gatekeepers, seem common decency today.[59]

56. Andersen, *Politics of Prohibition*, 116, 123. In a Methodist newspaper, Foster critiqued third parties as "political monasticism." Andersen, *Politics of Prohibition*, 135–36; Meyer, 120.

57. *Prohibition in Iowa*.

58. Harrell, *Social Sources of Division*, 212, 216, 232, 240; D. R. Dungan, *Rum and Ruin*. Foster also faced some opposition within the Iowa Union. In 1885, a motion that she be reelected state president by acclamation faced an objection; she did prevail on a vote of 91–53. Boyle, 127–28.

59. Ward, *White Ribbon Story*, 130–31; Benedict, *Woman's Work for Woman*; Epstein, *Politics of Domesticity*, 126; Boyle, "Creating a Union of the Union," 118–19, 225.

Social Justice and Holiness

Iowa State Leader, June 29, 1899. Marshalltown area ministers were dissatisfied with their pay for conducting services at the Iowa Veterans Home. Ex-governor Larrabee, now on the Board of Control, threatened to take over their jobs. (He was a lay Methodist minister.) He also accused the ministers of acting as a monopoly. The questions about organized religion as a monopoly and to what extent the state can interfere in the free exercise of religion are not considered in the editorial cartoonist's glee in treating the matter as a labor dispute, which of course it was.

THE MEN TAKE OVER, AND IOWA GOES OFF THE WAGON

Electorally, Iowa Republicans were in a bind. Supporting prohibition regained most drys' votes, but also alienated many Republicans, especially

German-Americans.[60] Typical was Horace Boies, who had been a Republican legislator in New York before moving his law practice to Waterloo. Boies was so incensed by what he saw as the harsh penalties of the 1885 law that he became a Democrat. The move proved fortunate for his political ambitions; Boies embodied those German ex-Republicans willing to vote out a dry Republican party, and in 1889, despite Senator Dolliver's confidence expressed in the epigraph above, Boies was elected governor as a Democrat.[61] Reports on the religious census in hell for that year were not available.

The 1894 Mulct Law, an elaborate edifice that basically brought back the local option, was the basis for liquor law for the next decade and a half in Iowa but did not resolve the controversy.

Republicans, capable of learning contradictory lessons about the wisdom of supporting prohibition based on the most recent election results, resumed their waffling. While Francis Drake, patron of Drake University and prominent Iowa Disciple, had been involved in controversy before (see chapter 10), he set off an unprecedented firestorm in the denomination after his 1896 election as governor. Regarded by Iowa Disciples as a reliable temperance man, he had also made a campaign promise not to veto any bills. So, when the legislature passed a bill legalizing and licensing distilleries and breweries, Drake signed it. One denominational paper, the *Christian Standard,* in an editorial breathlessly headlined "A Crime Against Civilization," fulminated that Drake had "sinned against God, against the church, against patriotism, and against civilization" and called for his removal from the board of Drake University and disfellowshipping by his Centerville congregation. The rival *Christian Evangelist* found this attack extreme, as did the Iowa-based *Christian Oracle* (which, full disclosure, was partly owned by Drake).[62]

The politicization of temperance into prohibition meant that the religiously based movement had to develop legal and electoral strategies. One indication of the importance of Iowa in the national picture was the title of an 1898 US Supreme Court case, *Rhodes v. Iowa.* The case pitted railroad and retail interests against the state's interest in limiting the

---

60. The Dutch also often resented prohibition. Klumpp, "Colony before Party," 9.

61. "Boies, Horace," BDI, 54. On Methodist, Baptist, and Presbyterian bodies' support for Prohibition during the 1889 election, see Jensen, *Winning of the Midwest,* 106–7.

62. Harrell, *Social Sources of Division,* 231–36.

liquor trade. Business interests and the principle of interstate commerce prevailed.[63]

That Iowa women temperance advocates achieved what they did, without access to the vote, is remarkable. That their victories were ephemeral is not. That the WCTU was undermined, not just by male wets, but also by male drys, is predictable but depressing.

In 1897 the lead organizing by the WCTU was supplanted by a male-dominated counterpart, the Anti-Saloon League. Hiram Price, the Methodist Davenport storekeeper who had joined the Sons of Temperance in the 1840s and kept agitating in the decades thereafter, had risen in status to banker, railroad executive, and Congressman, and continued his advocacy for prohibition. His reputation and Iowa's relative success were such that he was elected the first national president of the Anti-Saloon League.[64] Also crucial to the founding of the national Anti-Saloon League were two other Iowans, Howard Russell and A. J. Kynett.

Russell was an Iowan from 1870 to 1883. Son of a Minnesota Episcopalian minister, he attended Griswold College in Davenport, becoming an educator and then a lawyer in Adams County until 1883, when a conversion experience led him to the Congregational ministry and prohibition advocacy. He became adept at flipping wet counties dry, subsequently founding the Anti-Saloon League. His successful tactic of winning local referenda, though, soon seemed outdated as the league sought a more national strategy.[65]

Perhaps even more important to the founding of the ASL was A. J. Kynett, arguably the male J. Ellen Foster in Iowa. As a Methodist minister, he had early shown the instincts of an organizer and strategist and employed those talents not just for the Iowa Conference but also on the governor's staff during the Civil War. Later he established the national Board of Temperance within Methodism. And he moved to consolidate his Ohio and Pennsylvania operations with Russell's, abetting the ASL's founding. He died in 1899, before the League started scoring its major victories.[66]

63. Hamm, *Shaping the Eighteenth Amendment*, 176.

64. Lender, *Dictionary of American Temperance Biography*, 408. Price attended the founding convention of the Prohibition party in 1869 to argue against its founding. Blocker, *Retreat from Reform*, 256.

65. Lender, 424–25; Odegard, *Pressure Politics*, 15. Odegard flubs the biography of Hiram Price, describing him as a minister from Washington, when he was neither.

66. Lender, 283–85; Hoehnle, "A. J. Kynett and Iowa Methodism," presentation at Iowa Heritage Expo, Des Moines, Jun. 12, 1998.

Using the Progressive wing of the Republican Party, the league guided the statewide re-prohibition campaign. Iowa went dry again in 1915, five years before the national Eighteenth Amendment took effect.[67] But even that 1915 victory for the drys would be short-lived.

In Frank Luther Mott's elegiac but realistic memoir, he portrayed the usual state of affairs in an Iowa town:

> There were saloons in What Cheer when I was a young child there; it had begun as a coal-mining town, and the "wet" element was strong enough to defeat the "drys" in a state allowing "local option" but dominated by a prohibition policy. But in the more typical Iowa towns in which I lived later, liquor was procurable only from drugstores or bootleggers or from supplies laid up on occasional visits . . . to Chicago or Kansas City. Yet there was always the town drunkard . . . There was also a good deal of drinking by some people on festival occasions, as though red figures on the calendar were invitations to intoxication.[68]

In the prolonged debate over alcohol,[69] each side indulged in religious stereotyping of the other.[70] Like most stereotypes, there is some basis in fact to distinguish the voting patterns between what Richard Jensen called Confessional and Pietist religious groups.[71]

Just before the final drive for a national constitutional amendment, Iowa held another vote on a statewide prohibition amendment in 1917. In an extremely close vote, the amendment failed, with 49.9 percent voting in favor. In his analysis of the outcome, Thomas Ryan suggested reasons for the differences between the 1917 and the 1882 referenda. Party affiliation was not as significant, but religious affiliations, especially in the two largest denominations, Catholic and Methodist, had become even more polarized.[72]

67. Timberlake, *Prohibition and the Progressive Movement*, 129, 166.

68. Mott, *Time Enough*, 39–40.

69. The most complete study of nineteenth-century prohibition legislation is a three-part article by Clark, "History of Liquor Legislation in Iowa," together with its prequel, "Beginning of Liquor Legislation in Iowa." A handier summary is in Sage, *History of Iowa*, 203–4, 249–50. See also Wines and Koren, *Liquor Problem*. Chapter 2 is "The History of Prohibition in Iowa."

70. Ehrstine, 2–5, 74.

71. Jensen, *Winning of the Midwest*. Chapter 4 is entitled, "Iowa: Wet or Dry?," republished in IHR . . .

72. Ryan, "Supporters and Opponents of Prohibition: Iowa in 1917," *AI* 46, 515,

NATIONAL PROHIBITION AND ITS AFTERMATH

With the onset of nationwide Prohibition, some Iowa communities stood out in their open defiance—as had been the case during previous prohibitions in the state. Noteworthy were German Catholics in Carroll County, including a monsignor. A local man of German Methodist extraction, bearing the surprising name of Herbert Hoover, concocted a whiskey recipe that received renown and was sold as Templeton Rye, with a revival in the next century.[73]

While the bootlegging in Carroll County was fairly "gentlemanly," Prohibition did lead to an increase in crime more generally, especially in urban areas. And as some drys encouraged enforcement by publicizing suspected bootleggers, Iowa drys had another martyr to mourn: Vinton WCTU leader Myrtle Cook was shot and killed in her own home on September 7, 1925. Her murder was never prosecuted. Although she clearly was killed for informing on liquor traffickers, apparently that motive did not sufficiently pare the suspects.[74]

Just as several Iowa prohibitions and repeals had preceded the national ban, the argument in the state did not end with repeal of the Eighteenth Amendment in 1933. For some, it meant returning to the older temperance model of individual persuasion; for others, both temperance and prohibition emerged tainted by the failure of state-enforced abstinence to achieve its stated goal. Perhaps more insidious was the expansion of state and federal law enforcement powers, which repeal did not significantly prune back.[75]

Iowans had an outsized leadership role in the Prohibition movement, with its legislative statutes and with such figures as Annie Wittenmyer, Ellen Foster, A. J. Kynett, and Hiram Price. This leadership role continued after repeal, in the person of Ida Belle Smith. Smith, from Des Moines, was one of the first women to be ordained by the Disciples of Christ. She diligently and effectively worked for the Iowa WCTU, and that diligence rewarded her with election as president of the national WCTU. The only problem was the timing: she was elected in 1933, simultaneously with

---

517–18, 521.

73. Bauer, *Gentlemen Bootleggers*, chapter 5. See also Sage, *History of Iowa*, 96.
74. McCann, *Prohibition in Eastern Iowa*, 20–21; CRG, Sep. 7, 2000.
75. McGirr, *War on Alcohol*, especially chapter 7.

repeal. Her vigorous efforts at repealing the repeal proved not just fruitless but increasingly irrelevant.[76]

Smith was not the only Iowan to fight rearguard actions. The Quaker Virgil Hinshaw, born in 1876 in Woolson in Jefferson County, became active in temperance causes while attending Penn College in Oskaloosa. He served as organizer for the Intercollegiate Prohibition Association after his time in college and became leader of the Prohibition Party just as the passage of the Eighteenth Amendment made it seem irrelevant.[77]

In Iowa, the effects of the prohibition movement had a long hangover. The struggle in Iowa to legalize liquor by the drink continued into the 1960s, until a Methodist recovering alcoholic named Harold Hughes was elected governor promising to end the hypocrisies, which included skirting the law by establishing "key clubs," and to tap a new revenue stream for the state.[78] Hughes was not insensitive to the dangers of alcohol, however; he pushed for treating alcoholism as a disease, not a character flaw, and as United States senator, he shepherded through the Comprehensive Alcohol Abuse and Alcoholism Prevention, Treatment, and Rehabilitation Act into law in 1970.[79]

The repeal of Prohibition was a blow to Protestant supremacy; the continued restrictions in Iowa reflected its lingering ascendancy. Prohibition was, over the decades, a conflict that entangled a melange of issues and identities, all important: class, ethnicity, feminism, and the ability of religious leaders to steer society in directions they thought were crucial to society's survival and flourishing. That others had different views about priorities made for an intriguing story that revealed much about the interaction of religion and governance in Iowa. While Protestants could set the agenda, in the long run, they could not control it.

---

76. Lender, *Dictionary of American Temperance Biography*, 454–55; "Smith, Ida B.," BDI, 470–71; Ward, 57–65.

77. Lender, *Dictionary of American Temperance Biography*, 228–29; Andersen, *Politics of Prohibition*, 218, 262, 264.

78. Babe Bisignano, oral history interview, 1972, tape in Des Moines Public Library; Hughes, *Man from Ida Grove*, chapter 13; King, "Harold E. Hughes"; Harrington, "Iowa's Last Liquor Battle."

79. Lender, 244; Ensign, "From Iowa to the Nation."

Social Justice and Holiness

Prohibition was explicitly racialized in Tama County in the nineteen-fifties when local ordinances attempted to bar Meskwakis from local bars.[80]

By the twenty-first century, a gradual acceptance of social drinking among mainline Protestants is evident in public radio coverage of a brewpub theology discussion group sponsored by a church in Altoona in 2008.[81] A decade later, such meetings were commonplace, and even among some evangelicals, the old strictures against alcohol eroded.

The prohibition of alcohol was not unique in trying to impose religious standards on personal behavior. Iowans also contended over gambling,[82] and in the somewhat more secular war on drugs. While the grand social experiment to regulate individual behavior by banning alcohol failed, the religious and political dynamics of the movement remain crucial in understanding Iowa.

The fervor with which Methodists like George Haddock and Judith Ellen Foster attacked that demon rum and the ways in which diverse religious movements like Holiness and the Social Gospel intersected to try to reform individuals and communities shaped an Iowa that increasingly was less urbanized than the country as a whole and more apt to arrive at a Protestant consensus about regulating morality. But that consensus faced new challenges, ranging from theological to demographic to staying relevant, as conversations shifted away from personal morality and towards topics like war and small-town viability.

---

80. Foley, *Heartland Chronicles*, 20–23.

81. "Speaking of Faith," National Public Radio, May 4, 2008; cf. DMR, Mar. 21, 2008.

82. DMR, Aug. 30, 2001.

CHAPTER 13

The Landscape of Fin de Siècle Iowa Religion[1]

"Our debt to the twentieth century consists in preserving unimpaired for it all the links in the chain of progress which have been entrusted into our care, and in the welding on a link of our own."

—JOHN R. MOTT, COLLEGE ESSAY, UPPER IOWA UNIVERSITY, 1885[2]

"I have long thought that it was the life on those boundless plains which profoundly kindled my imagination and was a great factor in making me responsive in later years to worldwide visions and plans."[3]

—JOHN R. MOTT, 1946 NOBEL PEACE PRIZE WINNER[4]

AT PRECISELY THE TURN of the century, in an already old house in Davenport, the protagonists of the play *Alison's House* tried to manage their religious doubts. The house seemed haunted by a dead poet who

---

1. The portion of this chapter dealing with the 1893 Chicago fair was presented in an earlier form at the April 2017 Iowa Interfaith Exchange conference at Drake University sponsored by the Des Moines Area Religious Council and Drake's Comparison Project. I am grateful to the sponsors, attendees, and commentators.

2. Mathews, *John R. Mott*, 19; cf. Buxbaum, "John R. Mott," 138.

3. Mathews, *John R. Mott*, 13.

4. Hopkins, *John R. Mott,*, 695–96. On Mott changing his mind, see Putney, *Muscular Christianity*, 136.

The Landscape of Fin de Siècle Iowa Religion

resembled Emily Dickinson.[5] Most of the characters did not have the ghost's stamina in struggling with religious uncertainty. But uncertainty haunts the play—and by implication the new century. Susan Glaspell won a surprise Pulitzer Prize for the play in 1931, despite critics' dismissal of it as "literary."[6]

Glaspell was a Davenport native, Drake alumna, and birthright Disciple,[7] who also became privy to the doings of upper-class Davenportians upon her liaison with (and eventual marriage to) George Cram Cook. The new century would provide ample reasons for doubts, but the primary tone at its inception seemed closer to confidence.

How did turn-of-the-twentieth-century Iowans experience religion? The considerable evidence suggests multiple answers. From the lens of Iowa diversity, it can seem kaleidoscopic; through the lens of Protestant hegemony, a more monochromatic picture emerges.[8] Iowa in 1900 mixed images of small-town homogeneity with a hearty if not unequivocal dose of acceptance of diversity.

BEING IN SMALL-TOWN IOWA

There are numerous worthwhile memoirs that plow the ground of rural and small-town life in Iowa in the 1890s but none with a more sympathetic and perceptive eye to religion than that of the Quaker-born but Methodist-raised Frank Luther Mott.[9] Mott's father was a newspaper

---

5. On Dickinson's spirituality, see Lundin, *Emily Dickinson and the Art of Belief.*
To support the plausibility of Glaspell's claim for transposing a Dickinson-like poet to Iowa, see the Transcendentalist connections: Hoeltje, "Ralph Waldo Emerson in Iowa."

6. Mantle, *Best Plays*, 223. Glaspell's prominence as a feminist author is suggested by her short story title *A Jury of Her Peers* being also title for an anthology of feminist writing.

7. She mined this vein lightly in her novel *Brook Evans.*

8. Sarah Boyle, in her dissertation on the Women's Christian Temperance Union, seeks to explain Iowa WCTU's divergent course from the WCTU majority by distinguishing Iowa as singularly homogeneous and rural, as opposed to the rest of the Midwest. Boyle, "Creating a Union of the Union," 83, 126. Looking at the same issue of prohibition from a slightly wider lens, Ballard Campbell, seeking to vindicate the legislative outcome(s), describes Iowa: "Similar to many states, Iowa contained an ethnic polyglot in the nineteenth century. Yankees, Southerners, Germans, 'Bohemians,' Scandanavians, and Irishmen comprised sizable segments of the state's population." Campbell, "Did Democracy Work," 91.

9. Mott, *Time Enough.*

editor who worked successively in What Cheer, Tipton, and Audubon. Mott would become a Pulitzer Prize-winning historian of American magazines. Mott's neglected autobiography is a reliable guide to small town Iowa lived religion[10] in the nineties. Here are some excerpts:

> No lying late abed of a Sunday morning! Up bright and early we were, to get our chores done . . . all in plenty of time to wash and dress carefully for Sunday School at ten . . . At Sunday School we received cards bearing colored pictures of Bible scenes for attendance prizes and papers to bring home for Sunday reading.
> Of these, the *Classmate,* to which some of the *Youth's Companion* writers sometimes contributed, seemed to me to be far the best . . . After Sunday School, we were usually allowed to run home and read our papers and await the return of our elders for Sunday dinner.
> Evening services were chiefly for the younger members and the popular audience and became important to me only after I began 'going with girls' and singing in the choir.[11]

Mott was attentive to another trend prevalent in small-town Iowa: revivalism. The ambitious Billy Sunday would make it a big-city phenomenon. An Iowa orphan turned Major League baseball player turned energetic revivalist, Sunday started his revivalistic career in Garner, Iowa, in 1896,[12] tweaking a template that would work well for much larger venues, including Des Moines and Cedar Rapids. As Mott portrays Sunday's rally in Audubon:

> The greatest church effort of the year . . . was the revival meeting . . . I went through a series of meetings led by William A. ("Billy") Sunday. This was in the years when the great evangelist, newly recruited from the ranks of professional baseball, was still visiting the smaller towns . . . In my hometown his meetings had to be a "union effort," in which the Methodists and Presbyterians joined. There was at first much objection to taking in the Presbyterians, many of whom (it was whispered) played cards and danced. But the Reverend Mr. Sunday would come to Audubon, Iowa, only if the churches would join forces . . .
> His acrobatic homiletics were a sight to behold: with one foot on the seat of the chair and the other on the top of the

---

10. For more on the lived religion trend in American religious history, see, e.g. Orsi, *Gods of the City,* and Hall, *Lived Religion in America.*

11. Mott, *Time Enough,* 22–23.

12. For more on Sunday, see also the references in chapter 18.

The Landscape of Fin de Siècle Iowa Religion

lectern, he would shake both fists in the faces of his gaping congregation and call them hypocrites and liars . . .

There was some disillusion in the aftermath of a series of Billy Sunday meetings. I remember the quarreling . . . about whether the Methodists or the Presbyterians would get this or that new convert . . . Also, after he was gone, with the money in his pocket, a feeling grew that it was not a very nice thing to have so much cash taken out of town so easily. Then, too, there was the inevitable backsliding. Billy Sunday's athletic figure had scarcely disappeared . . . when word got about that the star convert of the whole meeting was on a sensational bender.[13]

The pious atmosphere that permeated most Iowa small towns was bolstered by an educational system[14] and a cultural milieu that provided an intellectual foundation for the Protestant ethos. In her study of library usage in Osage, Iowa, Christine Pawley found that the small-town library acted as a decentralized cultural center that connected to broader national conversations. Reading in Osage often meant being on the receiving end of national conversations about topics like prohibition, missions, and the Social Gospel.[15]

Not all future authors were as impressed by the Iowa religion of their youth as Frank Luther Mott. In Davenport, Harry Hansen recalled that

> I had rewarding Sunday School experiences, but they did not ripen into affiliation with any church. My parents were Lutheran . . . [but] when a Lutheran pastor refused to officiate at the funeral of a suicide, [my mother] ended her attendance. As a little fellow, I was taken by other children to Sunday School of the First Presbyterian Church, where Bible stories were told with verbal literalness. When I asked for plausible explanations, I was told I must accept them as the Word of God. This left me unsatisfied.

---

13. Mott, *Time Enough*, 27–29. Another rural revival (slightly later) is recalled by Floyd A. Robinson, *This Is Home Now*, 55–61. Fictionalized accounts of the aftermath of revivals include Paul Corey, *Three Miles Square*, 277, 378; and Sigmund, "Converts."

14. On the general ascendancy of a cultural Protestantism in US public schools in the nineteenth century, see Green, *Bible, the School, and the Constitution*. The Iowa court decision upholding "non-sectarian", i.e., Protestant Bible reading in public schools is mentioned on page 239.

15. Pawley, *Reading on the Middle Border*, chapter 4.

Nonetheless, Hansen appreciated the intellectually stimulating atmosphere of the Unitarian Church, pastored by Arthur Judy, and the beauty and uplifting spirit of Grace Episcopal Cathedral.[16]

One other relationship between religion and small-town culture is worth noting: the conflation of class differences. Historians and novelists alike have observed this;[17] particularly interesting is a 1984 archaeological study of gravestones in Story County, which found religious symbolism most prevalent in graveyards in neighborhoods between the extremes of wealth and destitution.[18] If death is the great equalizer, this study suggests that while religious symbols were widely available, they were less accessible to the destitute and more optional for the wealthy.

IOWA IN THE WORLD PARLIAMENT OF RELIGIONS

Another way to observe Iowa religion at the turn of the century is to leave the state and attend the 1893 World's Fair in Chicago. In the exposition, Iowans saw the opportunity to display their attributes, and it had the added advantage of proximity. But in the showcasing, we should simultaneously remember that most Iowans did not attend, and some looked askance at the spectacle. Benjamin Irwin was decrying the consumption of Coca-Cola, after all.

Chicago hosted one of the earliest, largest, and most spectacular world fairs, the Columbian Exposition. Meant to celebrate the four-hundredth anniversary of Columbus's first voyage to America, political squabbling in Congress over which city would host it, and then construction delays, pushed back the opening. That it was obviously a year late for the quadricentennial did not spoil the festivities; over twenty-seven million people attended.[19] Des Moines newspapers and other businesses chartered their own trains to ferry customers to Chicago for Iowa Day, Thursday, September 21, coinciding with day eleven of the World's Parliament of Religions.[20]

---

16. "Davenport Boyhood," *Pal* 37, 190–92.
17. Atherton, *Main Street on the Middle Border*, 100–105, 278–80.
18. Nulty, "Cemetery Symbolism of Prairie Pioneers," 129.
19. The documentary *Expo: The Magic of the White City* (2003), narrated by Gene Wilder, is an engaging introduction to the fair. See also Larson, *Devil in the White City*, Shaw, *World's Fair Notes*, and Kittelstrom, "International Social Turn."
20. See Swaim, "Iowans At the 1893 World's Columbian Exposition."

The Landscape of Fin de Siècle Iowa Religion

Of all the exposition's gatherings, the most ambitious and successful was the World's Parliament of Religions, which first introduced East Asian religions to a wide American public.[21] The organizers brilliantly encouraged the many American religious groupings to meet and to display their accomplishments during the larger gathering, ensuring a large attendance both of the faithful and the curious. The Iowa Presbyterian Synod, for example, extensively planned for the parliament a year in advance.[22]

Several Iowans gave presentations at the parliament and its congresses, and several exotic parliament speakers visited Iowa after the conference. Mary Newbury Adams of Dubuque (see also chapter 10) exulted that the opening day of the parliament was "the greatest day the world ever saw" in a letter to her son.[23] The statement is open to disputation.

The *Iowa State Register*'s reporter was also effusive in her praise. She may have been the *Register*'s fashion editor, as her longest observations were sartorial, e.g., "The Occident in severely plain garments touched elbows not only on the platform but in the great audience with the brilliantly costumed Orient in picturesque commingling." Or (writing on the Catholic Congress,) "it was quite startling—this gorgeous garbing of men— . . . these long, flowing robes seemed to transfigure the very common-faced men with something approaching deity."[24]

But Maria Oewig's gushing was not confined to clothing; her descriptions of the convocation included words like *beautiful*, *unique*, *unequaled*; "in all my life I have never been so impressed, so strangely moved, as during the wonder scene of brotherhood! . . . and to the readers of the REGISTER who failed to attend, I can only say 'I am sorry for you.'" The event was also "this foretaste of the millennium."[25] It's safe to characterize the *Register*'s coverage as positive.

At least ten Iowans were on the stage of the World's Parliament of Religion[26] or its denominational and interdenominational congresses,

---

21. The three general secondary accounts I have depended upon are Seager, *World's Parliament of Religions*; Lancaster, *Parliament of Religions*; Ziolkowski, *Museum of Faiths*.

22. Hinkhouse, *One Hundred Years*, 380.

23. Adams Family Papers, Box 2, Folder 1, Mary Adams to Eugene Adams, Sep. 12, 1893, MS 10, Special Collections Department, Iowa State University Library.

24. *Iowa State Register*, Sep. 10, 1893; Sep. 9, 12, 1893.

25. *Iowa State Register*, Sep. 17, 1893. This is her only signed article; I'm assuming the other *Register* articles were also hers.

26. There are three primary sources for the parliament; none of them are complete, and each has its strengths and limitations: Houghton, *Neely's History of the Parliament*

along with a person with an intimate impact on twentieth-century Iowa religion Three Asian leaders visited the state in the wake of the event. Taken together, they can suggest some of the contours of Iowa religion and the state of interreligious awareness in 1893.

Of the ten Iowans, only two presented papers at the Parliament proper, presenting a decided contrast: Martin Wade, a male Catholic layman rooted in conservative values and Catholic superiority, and Rev. Ida Hultin, a female Unitarian minister committed to progressivism and religious equity. They spoke on different subjects, in different tones, apparently to different intended audiences, and did not intentionally interact, but reconstructing the debate that did not take place between them seems irresistible.

Wade set down his judgment on the seventh day of the Parliament; Hultin dispensed her wisdom on the tenth. (From statements Wade made elsewhere opposing the role of women in public life, such a debate with Hultin would have been unlikely.)

Both Wade and Hultin are memorable. In 1893 Martin J. Wade, a brilliant lawyer, was a law professor at the State University of Iowa in Iowa City, specializing in family law. A lifelong Democrat and one-term Congressman from Iowa's Second District from 1903 to 1905, the Wilson administration appointed him to the federal bench, where he was best known for his harsh treatment of anti-war advocates during World War I. He continued advocating for Catholic and anti-radical causes after the war.[27]

The Rev. Ida Hultin was part of the "prophetic sisterhood," women ministers who served Iowa Unitarian parishes. Small-town parishes were the least desirable posts, and women ministers had the least bargaining power, but they collectively found ways to cope with those disadvantages. Hultin had served churches in Algona and Des Moines; in 1893, she was stationed across the river in Rock Island, Illinois.[28]

For his part, on the seventh day of the parliament, Professor Wade spoke on "The Catholic Church and the Marriage Bond." Ignoring the

---

of Religions; Barrows, *World's Parliament of Religions*; Hanson, *World's Congress of Religions*.

27. "Wade, Martin Joseph," BDI, 525–26; Miller, *From Prairie to Prison*, 149–55, 190; Douglas, "Summer of Discontent"; Mills and Peterson, *No One Is Above The Law*, 44–47. (Eggers does not discuss Wade's World War I experience.)
Wade continued his anti-radical activism after the war, authoring pamphlets against Sacco and Vanzetti.

28. Tucker, *Prophetic Sisterhood*, 31–34, 97, 126–27, 237.

concept of a world parliament and the transnational character of the Catholic Church, he sought instead to preach to his largely American audience on the dangers of rising divorce rates in the United States and the importance of the Catholic doctrine against remarriage. He based his case partly on the assumption of a "Christian America." Somewhat histrionically, he declaimed, "Oh, shades of the Christian founders of this Christian land: didst thou ever foresee this threatening evil?" Wade maintained that laws restricting divorce would reverse the decadence responsible for the fall of Greece and Rome.[29]

In marked contrast to Wade, on the tenth day of the proceedings Hultin gave a briefer, more general speech on "The Essential Oneness of Ethical Ideas Among All Men." Not surprisingly from the title, she fully engaged other traditions in attendance. She was vehemently anti-creedal and anti-ecclesiastical in contrasting established religious institutions and belief systems with what she called the human striving toward "an eternal moral purpose."

Like Wade, Hultin also evoked American history, but unlike Wade's myth of Christian founders, she focused on the anti-slavery struggle. She was right to condemn church justifications of slavery, but her suggestion that religious institutions were not also engaged in its abolition seems as far afield as Wade's misrepresentations of the American Revolution. Her advocacy of women's emancipation also involved a critique of ecclesiasticism.

"The men and women belonging to all countries and all races, who perhaps have not had time to formulate their beliefs about unity, are busy working for it, who have never known how to define God, are finding him in their daily lives." "When the ethical intent has been removed from a theological system it is a dead faith." "We need to learn humility. We are only beginners, all of us." These representative quotes give a sense of Hultin's message: religion ought to concentrate on ethics rather than dogma, and modest claims are better than extravagant ones.[30]

It is a leap too far to see in the contrasts between Wade and Hultin the bifurcated American religious situation of the twenty-first century—and yet, there are hints. Wade's essay did not engage other perspectives; instead he laid out the Catholic perspective on marriage and expected

---

29. Barrows, *World's Parliament of Religions*, 743–51; Houghton, *Neely's History of the Parliament of Religions*, 339–45.

30. Barrows, *World's Parliament of Religions*, 1003–1005; Houghton, *Neely's History of the Parliament of Religions*, 474–77.

The People Are Kind

reverence for it. In contrast, Hultin sought a unifying force animating all the assembled religions; her approach was much closer to the dominant spirit of the proceedings.

Except for the Jewish Women's Congress, most of the Iowans participating in the denominational conferences looked inward rather than engaging in interfaith dialog: their theological pavilions highlighted their own distinctive qualities. The Iowa participants of the subsidiary congresses suggest additional clues about *fin de siècle* Iowa religion:

Archbishop John Hennessy of Dubuque did not have a speaking role; he processed with other Catholic hierarchy in the pre-parliament Catholic Congress.[31] His raiments were undoubtedly among those the *Register* correspondent raved about. He had to scoot back to Dubuque for a celebration in his honor: he was receiving his pallium (an ornamental symbol of his rank). His administrative deficiencies in terms of financial and personnel management have been documented elsewhere.[32]

Frank J. Sheridan, a layperson from the Archdiocese of Dubuque, addressed the Catholic Congress with a concrete and detailed proposal: that the Church tackle issues of its working-class members. He called for a parish-based voluntary arbitration system that could mediate labor disputes. The proposal was approved but referred to a committee for implementation; I have not located evidence that a parish-based arbitration system was enacted, although Sheridan may have continued pursuing labor arbitration through a federal program.[33]

Mrs. Kate Klinefelter Bowman of Des Moines addressed the Evangelical Association Congress on "The Heroines of the Evangelical Association." The Evangelical Association was a German Methodist precursor of the United Methodist Church. She was probably a member of the Salem Evangelical Association Church on the east side of Des Moines, at 1217 E. Grand,[34] (now part of the Capitol complex.) The lovely image of

---

31. Houghton, *Neely's History of the Parliament of Religions*, 890.

32. Coogan, "Redoubtable Archbishop John Hennessy"; *Davenport Democrat*, Sep. 18, 1893. See also my book review on archdiocesan histories in the Fall 2013 *AI 72*, 388–89: "Seed/Harvest." Hennessy's successor in Dubuque, theologian John Keane of Catholic University, did present a paper. Burg, *Chicago's White City of 1893*, 267; Barry, *Catholic Church and German Americans*, 220–23.

33. Hanson, *World's Congress of Religions*, 1020–21, 1023; Houghton, *Neely's History of the Parliament of Religions*, 892.

34. *Des Moines City Directory, 1893, 1899, 1900*. By 1900, it had moved to 1234 E. Garfield, a site replaced by a strip mall at East 14th and East University that used to be anchored by a SuperValue grocery store, and now a Walgreens, and about the

The Landscape of Fin de Siècle Iowa Religion

Mrs. Bowman holding forth on the Evangelical Association's illustrious past is somewhat undercut by the fact that another eruption of divisiveness in the denomination had begun with church trials in Iowa in 1889. A civil court battle over which national conference was legitimate, filed in Polk County district court in April 1892, was wending its way to the Iowa Supreme Court as Bowman spoke.

Bowman was also the name of the bishop who was central to the division; whether Mrs. Bowman was related to him, I have not ascertained. The court weighed in on May 11, 1894, but did not end the bitterness of the dispute, which split the denomination in two. Probably Holiness issues precipitated that division. But nothing in the Evangelical Association's upbeat presentations in Chicago hinted at that churning dissension.[35] C. C. Pumpf of Des Moines also gave a short address.[36]

Rev. H. D. Jenkins, pastor of the First Presbyterian Church of Sioux CIty, lectured the Presbyterian congress on missions. He boasted that "between the Golden Gate and Plymouth Rock we [Presbyterians] are preaching the Gospel of the Son of God in upwards of twenty languages," and suggested that "the cure for mere sectarianism is evangelism."[37]

Sioux City, it will be recalled from chapter 9, was a natural place for Presbyterians to focus on missions: in 1868, on Prospect Hill, Sheldon Jackson had looked across the Missouri River and solemnly proclaimed that all the land west to the Pacific Ocean was under the jurisdiction of the Western Iowa Presbytery.[38]

George Augustus Gates, president of Iowa College, and the college's professor of Applied Christianity, George Herron, gave papers to the interdenominational congress of the Evangelical Alliance, which the notetaker for the event dismissed as "sociological."[39]

---

same time, moved denominationally from the Evangelical Association to the United Brethren. (The two groups did not merge nationally until 1946. Olson, *Handbook of Denominations*, 191.)

35. Houghton, *Neely's History of the Parliament of Religions*, 949; Hanson, 1149; *Des Moines City Directory*, 1893; Behney and Eller, *History of the Evangelical Brethren Church*, 283–84; Richey et al., *Methodist Experience in America*, vol. 1, 332; *Auracher v. Yerger*, 58 NW 893, 90 Iowa 558. On Iowa as a hub of Evangelical Association presence in 1890, see Gaustad and Barlow, *New Historical Atlas of Religion in America*, Fig. 2.140.

36. Hanson, *World's Congress of Religions*, 1149.

37. Barrows, *World's Parliament of Religions*, 1498–1500; Hanson, *World's Congress of Religions*, 1042; Hubbard, *Presbyterian Church in Iowa, 1837–1900 History*, 205.

38. Heartland Presbyterian Church newsletter, Clive, IA, February 2013.

39. Houghton, *Neely's History of the Parliament of Religions*, 969. The links between

The People Are Kind

Perhaps the most significant of the congresses was the Jewish Women's Congress. The ever helpful *Register* correspondent pointed to the greater attendance at women's congresses than at men's; if she also listed the Jewish Women's Congress as among those at which "Christian fellowship" predominated, that can charitably be chalked up as more clueless than insensitive. (Admittedly, there is an overlap.) Louise Mannheimer of Cincinnati, poet, educator, inventor, and mother of the future rabbi of Temple B'nai Jeshurun of Des Moines, Eugene Mannheimer, gave a major address on Jewish women of biblical and medieval times.[40]

Mary Newbury[41] Adams of Dubuque, who was in charge of the history committee of the Women's Committee on Literary Congresses at the exposition, lectured on "How The Discovery of America Influenced the Jews." Her religious trajectory arced through Transcendentalism and Theosophy. She had hosted both Bronson Alcott and Ralph Waldo Emerson in Dubuque and maintained close ties to Alcott, who, not atypically, had rapturous things to say about Adams's spirituality and her work to re-spark educational efforts in the West, which was without the lingering detrimental detritus of tradition that affected even New England. According to Alcott, Adams was "the representative woman of the West . . . reminding me of Margaret Fuller."[42]

Also a panel respondent on the topic which was not called anti-Semitism, but "protesting and interfering" against Jewish persecution, was Ida Hultin. She seemed to be everywhere at the parliament, also

---

the establishment-oriented Evangelical Alliance and the radical-leaning Kingdom Movement were short-lived; by 1895 the Evangelical Alliance board had forced General Secretary Josiah Strong to resign from the editorial board of the *Kingdom*. Jordan, *Evangelical Alliance*, 164–65.

40. Hanson, *World's Congress of Religions*, 970–972; Barrows, *World's Parliament of Religions*, 1466, Houghton, *Neely's History of the Parliament of Religions*, 876. If the modern claim to fame is to have a Wikipedia article about one, she qualifies. On Eugene Mannheimer, see Douglas, "Making Iowa Safe For Differences."

41. The spelling of her maiden name varies. In parliament proceedings, it was spelled "Newberry."

42. Barrows, *World's Parliament of Religions*, 1466; Lex, "Mary Newbury Adams"; "Adams, Mary Newbury," *BDI*, 3–4; Stein, "Mrs. Alcott"; Noun, *Strong-Minded Women*, 113–15, 263–64. Houghton, *Neely's History of the Parliament of Religions*, 871, lists a different speaker, Pauline H. Rosenberg, giving this address; perhaps it was a collaborative effort, or perhaps Adams was enlisted as a last-minute fill-in.

For more on Adams's position of influence within the Women's Department, see Weimann, *Fair Women*, 70–72, 219, 263, 546.

The Landscape of Fin de Siècle Iowa Religion

chairing a session of the Unitarian congress.[43] Certainly the Jewish Women's Congress showed most clearly the first glimmers of Iowans engaging in interreligious dialog.

Even events that are "a taste of the millennium" must come to an end in this world, and the world parliament was supposed to be temporary. But the variety and intensity of Iowa manifestations of religion documented by the parliament give us a sense of the diversity and rigor of *fin de siècle* Iowa religion.

NOVELISTIC IMPRESSIONS

The World's Fair was not the only gauge of Iowa religion. Increasingly, Iowa writers were leaving their impressions. Susan Glaspell, a Davenport native raised in a Disciples of Christ Church (and later one of the twentieth century's foremost feminist playwrights),[44] explored the territory of new vistas in theology and biblical criticism in her short story "For Tomorrow: The Story of an Easter Sermon."[45] Glaspell believed the effects of an honest embrace of the new theology would be liberating.

A little later in the century, Ellis Parker Butler wrote a paean to a small-town pastor, *Dominie Dean*. The sales of his book were affected negatively by the sudden entry of the United States into World War I (and that the book had a negative view of the horrors of war). Butler's book painted a sympathetic portrait of a Presbyterian minister in Butler's[46] hometown of Muscatine for the latter half of the nineteenth century. As the critic John Frederick put it, "In the portrayal of David Dean, Butler achieved something rare in fiction: a character who is wholly and consistently a good man, and yet both credible and interesting."[47]

The book follows a gentle pastor through troubled times, only to retire impoverished. Butler's book was a plea for systematizing ministerial pensions; it coincided with the establishment of a pensions fund in the Northern Presbyterian Church, although it is unclear what effect *Domine Dean* had.[48]

43. Barrows, *World's Parliament of Religions*, 1467; Hultin, "Extracts from 'Women and Religion,'" 788–89.
44. See, e.g., Noe, *Susan Glaspell*; Ozieblo, *Susan Glaspell*; Ben-Zvi, *Susan Glaspell*.
45. Glaspell, "For Tomorrow."
46. Burns, *Kinship with the Land*, 90–93.
47. Frederick, "Town and City in Iowa Fiction," 58.
48. Brackenridge and Boyd, *Presbyterians and Pensions*; Baird, *Horn of Plenty*.

DEMOGRAPHIC CHANGES

While urbanization has often been associated with an increase in Catholics, that did not happen in many Iowa cities in the early twentieth century. The beginnings of the exodus from the countryside (see chapter 14) instead meant an influx of mostly Protestant rural residents to Des Moines, Davenport, and Sioux City.[49]

Taking a church census became a relatively popular undertaking, although sometimes controversy accompanied the task.[50]

OTHER SIGNS OF CHANGE

Anticipating other national religious conventions held in Iowa's capital city during the twenties (see chapters 14 and 19), in 1908, the "Dunkard Hosts Swarm[ed] to City For Big Meet."[51] Translated from journalese, Brethren met in national convention in Des Moines. Anticipating the larger movement away from ethnic religion, at the Des Moines national conference the "Dunkard"-nicknamed German Baptist Brethren changed their name to the Church of the Brethren.[52]

While the Meskwaki continued to thrive on their settlement, it is important to acknowledge that this was in the context of racist assumptions. In Truman Douglass's 1911 history of Iowa Congregationalists, he avers that

> Of these early proprietors of Iowa, all that remains is a little remnant of the Sac and Foxes—the Masquawkees (squaw men), about three hundred in number, located on the reservation on the Iowa River near Tama City.[53]

The geographical details are correct, but it is hard to know where to start with the rest of this appalling, ignorant, racist, and sexist sentence.

---

49. Christiano, *Religious Diversity and Social Change*, 173–74. Of the four Iowa cities Christiano looked at, only heavily Catholic Dubuque became more Catholic between 1890 and 1906, and then only slightly so.

50. Hurto, "1910 Church Census of Colfax."

51. DMT, June 2, 1908.

52. *Two Centuries of the Church of the Brethren*; Fitzkee, *Moving Toward the Mainstream*, 33.

53. Douglass, *Pilgrims of Iowa*, 11.

Suffice it to say that, aside from the fact that the words "Meskwaki" and "squaw" both are found in Algonquin languages, the connections between the two words stop there. And the settlement is not a reservation.

The erosion of small-town culture was not always obvious, although signs of rural decline that small towns were already showing (see chapter 15). The twentieth century would bring an agricultural revolution and a concomitant decline in rural population, the jarring effects of world wars, new challenges to a dominant if divided Protestantism from new immigration, a newly assertive Catholicism, a new insistence on a return to an imagined past purity of belief, and new ways of looking at the religious project. Iowa values would react and adapt accordingly. The challenges and opportunities created by diversity would remain, and the divergent views articulated by Martin Wade and Ida Hultin at the World Parliament of Religions would be reprised in new contexts. Susan Glaspell wanted to live in the twentieth century, but the weights of the previous century also intruded. When her play stroked the hour of midnight into the next century, much was left unresolved.

CHAPTER 14

From Farmland as Eden to "Badly Overchurched"

From Promise to Rural Decline

"When James Stuart returned again home, the night was deepening and he drove slowly, looking again towards Stuart's Hill. The walls had fallen and the flames crept lower now, so that the shadows of their burning moved hither and yon among the oaks and hickories, as spirits lingering until the chapel which Brother Baird had visioned would pass completely away."

—Eleanor Saltzman[1]

"In Clay County [Iowa] there is one church for every 474 people . . . According to the standard recommended by the interdenominational organizations, one to 1,000 people, it is obvious that each one of these communities [in Clay County] is overchurched."

—Benson Y. Landis[2]

"For [Henry A.] Wallace, concerned as he was with the decline of the rural culture of his Iowa youth, it went without saying that involvement with the land, especially farming, was as much a spiritual endeavor as a practical one."[3]

 1. Saltzman, *Stuart's Hill*, 142.
 2. Landis, *Rural Church Life in the Middle West*, 51.
 3. Kleinman, *World of Hope*, 30.

From Farmland as Eden to "Badly Overchurched"

"Milo [Reno] and young Henry [A. Wallace] had argued about many things, including interpretations of the Bible."

—Dale Kramer[4]

"Men come and men go, but earth lies there cool, capable, willing to be made to serve. Earth is good because man is good and tells it what to do. Earth has a human, personal quality borrowed from man, and it is rich because it manages to provide for him in at least a poor way."

—Leo R. Ward[5]

In September 1929, members of the Methodist Episcopal Church of Wapello gathered one Sunday, left the sanctuary, closed the doors, and walked several blocks to the other Methodist church in town to merge the two congregations.[6] The process was repeated, if not always so ritually or consensually, in countless other communities in the state, as consolidation became the order of the day. In the case of Wapello, both congregations belonged to the same denomination, with the language barrier resolved a decade earlier when the German Methodist Episcopal Church converted to English and for good measure rebranded as Grace.[7]

Consolidation touched many congregations. Salem Church of Lincoln (Tama County), for example, in a much smaller community, devised an elaborate federation of German Reformed and Presbyterian churches that withstood multiple national mergers and remained a viable congregation in 2024.[8]

To be Iowan was to be rural, until it wasn't. But the state certainly made a good run of it; an early professor of humanities at Iowa State College in Ames listed among his courses "Agricultural Theology."

---

4. Kramer, *Wild Jackasses*, 236. For the nuts and bolts of the disagreements pertaining to agricultural policy, see Choate, *Disputed Ground*.

5. Ward, *Holding Up the Hills*, 95. The neighborhood in question was the rural one around Melrose in Monroe County, composed of Irish Catholics. James Stevens, in his short story "The Downfall of Elder Barton," described an overlapping neighborhood (see chapter 17).

6. Personal communication from Gene Matthews to author, March 2, 2019.

7. "Move into the Future."

8. Martin, "History of Salem Church."

Accordingly, he also led chapel services.[9] Exactly what the syllabus contained I have been unable to determine.

In Ruth Suckow's 1934 novel *The Folks*, the protagonists Fred and Annie Ferguson returned from visiting their daughter in California to find that their beloved but struggling Presbyterian Church in Belmond[10] had voted to merge with the Congregationalists. Their Congregationalist neighbor Mr. Viele broke the news:

> "Well, Fred, I know how you feel, but if you look at it in this way—it's pretty nice after all to know we're all united. For my part," Mr. Viele said boldly, "I'd like to see even the Methodists join in!" He looked triumphantly around the table. And it did seem to be true, Fred couldn't think of a good argument against it—in this way, all who believed in the churches and the work they were doing could make a real stand against all the forces that were trying to overtake them. It made them feel that the older people and their ideals weren't, after all, a thing of the past. Of course, Mr. Viele added hastily, that didn't include the Catholics. The Methodists were as far as he would go.

The critic Margaret Omrcanin saw Suckow as describing an Iowa "that is not static but is shifting . . . [with] a gradual breakdown of the ideals of domestic and religious life." She summarized the doubts cast by the novel's events:

> By the time Fred Ferguson is ready to retire he has been sad witness to the alteration of everything he cherished. The beautiful family life Annie had tried to keep was cracking and straining. Through some strange force with which his children seemed allied everything of value was slipping away. The old folks were no longer on the farm; the Presbyterian membership had disbanded to unite with the Congregational Church; bank failures were threatening his financial security, and there was no Ferguson child at home to continue in his home or his business. The faith of his fathers was gone, which they had come to found in a new land . . . His faith had been the church, which his father had left to him. It was the church he had helped build . . . Now that it was gone, what did he believe? Anything more than his

---

9. Ross, *Democracy's College*, 109.

10. Suckow's habit was to fictionalize the names of towns she was familiar with by giving them the names of other Iowa towns. She grew up moving around Iowa as the daughter of a Congregationalist minister, William Suckow. Her "Belmond" most closely resembles Algona.

own children? . . . Now at the end of his life based on trust, he was coming into uncertainty.[11]

That uncertainty would continue to haunt rural Iowa.

Iowa's rural population peaked around 1910. World War I helped keep agricultural prices high for another decade, but by 1920 a long rural depression began, anticipating the more general one and accelerating the exodus from farms and rural communities and the consolidation of farms that would characterize twentieth century Iowa. As mechanization, chemicalization, and genetic modifications increasingly transformed agriculture, fewer and fewer farmers could produce more and more of fewer kinds of crops, and rural and small-town churches were increasingly unsustainable, although their decline was a lagging indicator. Serial overextension of credit increased the impetus for consolidation.[12] Increasingly, the debate between seeing farming as a business or farming as a way of life was won by the former.

Even groups as agriculturally oriented as the Mennonites saw their farmers' numbers decline. One study of Mennonites near Donnellson in southeast Iowa found that before 1925, 50 percent of those who left the area moved to continue farming; after that, the percentage fell to 28 percent.[13]

With the shrinking distances that automobiles enabled, weekly worship in town became more feasible. As mechanization further depopulated the countryside, small towns whose primary economic purpose was to serve rural customers also retrenched.

By 1907 the Iowa Baptist Convention was in a panic over the "removal epidemic." But besides those leaving the state, church leaders identified an additional factor: increasingly rural people were disinclined to attend. "We can not neglect our rural population and retain our position as an intelligent, moral, and religious people," thought State Secretary S. E. Wilcox.[14]

Church closures continued throughout the century and beyond. Sometimes the decision was made high-handedly, causing alienation from the institutional church. Ethnographer Kristy Nabhan-Warren

---

11. Omrcanin, *Ruth Suckow*, 65, 64, 85.

12. The question of land ownership could even take on a specifically religious overtone, as the Cedar Rapids *Gazette* reported (June 11, 2023) that the Mormon Church had become a major landowner in Iowa.

13. Raid, "Donnellson Migrations Analyzed," 63. See also Avella, *Catholic Church in Southwest Iowa*, 127–28.

14. Blanchard, "Introduction and Acknowledgement," 411–12.

reported that "all of the Catholics I interviewed and spent time with became emotional when we talked about parish closures." As late as 2017, the Diocese of Sioux City's major consolidation reduced the number of parishes from 108 to 61.[15]

Towns were also subject to decline. Keokuk had Iowa's first synagogue, and in the nineteenth century had the most Jews, but "the Jewish community in Keokuk . . . went into decline when that town's role as a key Mississippi River port diminished."[16]

A historian for the United Brethren summarized both the dilemma and the realities, after its Iowa membership peaked at 11,636 in 1917:

> Some said the decline was caused by departure from old ways and others stated that it was caused by failure to adopt new methods promptly. As well, however, the correct question is "What is the will of God?" That will always prospers.

The changes in the rural scene in Iowa were at heart the cause of the decline.[17] Of course, looked at from a purely economic perspective, with no recognition of the environmental toll or of the potential cultural advantages of small-town life, the consolidation of rural Iowa has been a major success.

THE USES AND LIMITATIONS OF NOSTALGIA

The iconic Little Brown Church in the Vale outside of Nashua was fortunate enough to have a famous hymn written memorializing it (by William S, Pitts),[18] but most rural congregations could not depend on income from tourism or strangers' weddings to sustain them. Nostalgia was a powerful argument for holding on to the old ways, but it did not pay the pastor's salary or keep the lights on.

In fact, even the story of "The Church in the Wildwood" does not hold up under historical examination, as Christopher Cantwell has done. Pitts wrote the song as a ballad of a fictional lost love interest *before* the church was even built (let alone painted brown). As the song morphed

---

15. Warren, *Meatpacking America*, 19–20, 24–25. See also Kilen, "Last Mass."
16. Weissbach, *Jewish Life in Small Town America*, 49; Schuessler, "Last of Iowa's Small-town Synagogues."
17. MacCanon, *Short History of the United Brethren in Christ in Iowa*, 6
18. *History of the Little Brown Church*; Ellis, *Parish of the Little Brown Church*; DMR, July 21, 2009; Williams, *Houses of God*, 213.

into a hymn (that, perhaps uniquely, made no reference to God), the backstory filled in. And an enterprising local group turned that story into a destination wedding locale.[19]

Marvin Cone, *Storm Clouds over Church*. Permission Stephen Cone Weeks and thanks to Cedar Rapids Art Center.

Nostalgia could be used to affirm the superiority of the rural ideal. In studying congregational histories written in the 1950s, historian David Zwart found an eagerness to embrace a past that idealized the strivings of forebears to build a religious environment that was able to protect against the many threats posed by the outside world.[20]

William Pitts was not the only Iowan who mined nostalgia to create hymns. Charles Gabriel of Wilton was Iowa's most prolific hymn composer; his gospel-infused hits included "Will the Circle Be Unbroken," "His Eye is on the Sparrow," "He Lifted Me," and "Higher Ground."[21] Other Iowans with popular hymns that spoke to those uprooted from the land included George Bennard, a Methodist who grew up in the coalfields

19. Cantwell, "'No Place Is So Dear to My Childhood.'"
20. Zwart, "Telling Heartland Histories."
21. DMR, *Jan.* 30, 2006; NYT, Sep. 15, 1932; Mungons and Yeo, *Homer Rodeheaver*, 24–27, 223–24.

around Albia and Lucas, who contributed "The Old Rugged Cross," and Adelaide Addison Pollard of Bedford, who moved from Presbyterian to Pentecostal and composed "Have Thine Own Way."[22]

Sometimes the heroic narrative could be over the top. Agricultural journalist and Keokuk County native Wallace E. Sherlock flourished his pen with "A Church That Refused to Die" to immortalize the Lancaster Church of Christ. Seven decades later, the congregation was still a viable institution.[23]

STUDYING THE PROBLEM

Decline was already apparent by 1900. Or perhaps, given the rural revolt of the 1870s, decline was chronic, given a system inherently unsustainable, although capable of elongation if enough nonrenewable resources were used on an uncommonly rich soil. Responding to early glimmers of decline, President Theodore Roosevelt appointed a Commission on Country Life in 1908, which included Iowan Henry Wallace.[24]

Wallace, who has already appeared in multiple roles, was a United Presbyterian minister turned agricultural editor, and the father and grandfather of US secretaries of agriculture, one of whom would become vice president. The eldest Wallace's most enduring column in *Wallace's Farmer* was a commentary for Sunday School lessons, which remained a fixture in the paper—the column was in reruns decades after his death in 1915.[25] He died in the pulpit of First Methodist Church in Des Moines, while giving an ecumenical invocation in support of Protestant missions.[26]

Despite Wallace's religiosity—or because of the historical context of it—he was scrupulous about how the commission should approach religion without breaching the wall of separation between church and state. He got into a dispute with another commissioner about surveying rural churches and used his pull with his pal James "Tama Jim" Wilson, the Secretary of Agriculture, to ensure that the proposed survey wouldn't happen. (Wilson refused to authorize the postal payments for mailing

22. Mungons, "Iowa Hymn Writers"; email from Mungons, Mar. 15, 2022. I am grateful to Kevin Mungons for sharing from his vast knowledge of Iowa hymnody.
23. Sherlock, "Church that Refused to Die"; "Lancaster Christian Church."
24. Lord, *Wallaces of Iowa*, 7, 155–56; *Tributes to Henry Wallace*.
25. Kirkendall, *Uncle Henry*, 138–39; Lord, *Wallaces of Iowa*, 163–64.
26. Reynolds, "Making of Buck Creek," 354–55; Bowers, *Country Life Movement*.

the surveys.)²⁷ The Scottish disestablishmentarian heritage of the United Presbyterian Church that had been so formative for Wallace and Wilson prevailed over any sociological curiosity.²⁸

The Country Life Commission sparked a wider Country Life movement eagerly applying Progressive techniques to the countryside, foremost among them the tool of consolidation. But this strategy dealt with symptoms, not the cause.

If Social Gospelers sometimes felt they lagged behind the urban working class, their cohorts in the Country Life movement were confident that they were ahead of the curve in dealing with rural issues and only needed to be listened to.²⁹

Harlan Paul Douglass was the son of a prominent Iowa Congregationalist minister, Truman Douglass, who in the early twentieth century wrote a history of Iowa Congregationalism, *Pilgrims of Iowa*. The younger Douglass was a student of George Herron (unlike his father, Paul was a fan) and a graduate of Iowa College. After a stint teaching in the South, he became an eminent sociologist, specializing in studies of religion in the US that meshed with Progressive ideas of ecumenism and consolidation.³⁰

While such sociological data-gathering appealed to the American spirit of community improvement and commonsense reliance on facts, counting church programs had its limitations.³¹

LIVING THE PROBLEM AND MAKING DO

For countless Iowans, whether they stayed on the land, moved into town, or moved away, the recurring upheavals and consolidations were unsettling. Modernity sowed progress but reaped uncertainty. Modernization promised agricultural success but only for some; it also pushed many off

---

27. Swanson, "Country Life Movement and the American Churches," 361.

28. United Presbyterians came from the Free Church tradition of Seceders and Covenanter in Scotland. On Wilson, see Wilcox, *Tama Jim*, 107–8, 171.

29. Madison, "Reformers and the Rural Church"; Swanson, "'Country Life Movement' and the American Churches," 358–73. Swanson also demonstrates that what was accomplished by the Country Life movement amounted mostly to a denominational revival rather than a rural resurgence in the larger community.

30. Douglass, *Some Iowa Rural Churches*; Wall, *Grinnell College*, 252–53. Douglass was an 1891 graduate who returned to study with Herron as a graduate student in 1894.

31. For one critique of equating pastoral longevity with success in bringing new members, see Bauer, "Progress of Churches and Length of Pastorates."

the land. The mystical aspects of farming as communion with the land were increasingly bulldozed away by a "Get Big or Get Out" philosophy touted by government, banks, and corporations.

Competing with this business plan was an older mysticism that found common cause with a creator in close relationship with the land. Communion with the land need not even require institutional religious intercession. Frederick Manfred's freethinking character Pedersen, in dialogue with his son-in-law Pier about Pedersen's not going to church, had this defense:

> Pier, I know what you fellows call me. The Old Dreamer. I don't mind . . . . [I've] taken to the land like most men take to religion, or a sweet wife. Pier, I have no church but this land. I have no woman but this soil.[32]

In 1942, Thomas Lutman, a pastor from Sheldon, offered this defense of the small town to a sympathetic audience, the Iowa Retail Hardware Association convention:

> Main Street has grown the wheat and the corn and the men that have nourished America. Just as the city draws its water from the hills beyond, it also draws its leadership.[33]

But Rev. Lutman's tribute to Main Street could also be read as evidence of a brain drain.

The Fergusons and Viehls in Suckow's novel could see the silver lining in merging congregations, with the results of increasing Christian (Protestant) unity and the strength of more viable congregations.[34] Congregants and church workers could count other advantages in keeping up with the times. Even as new technology transformed and upended rural religion, many Iowans found the new technologies could be harnessed for religious ends. For example, Lois Crawford was the first woman in the country granted a license for a radio station by the Federal Communications Commission, in 1922. She ran a religious station in Boone, KFGQ, the third station to be licensed in Iowa.[35]

---

32. Manfred, *This Is the Year*, 24.
33. Quoted in Ossian, *Home Fronts of Iowa*, 90.
34. See Swanson, "'Country Life Movement,'" 363.
35. Balmer, *Encyclopedia of Evangelicalism*, 162; Crawford, *Papa and I*; Erickson, *Religious Radio and Television*, 64. Crawford was the daughter and successor to J. Charles Crawford, the founder of Boone Biblical Ministries. His works have been collected in Crawford, *Holy Spirit and Holy Living*. See also, for the ministry's demise,

From Farmland as Eden to "Badly Overchurched"

Another early radio practitioner was temperance preacher James Pearson of the "Radio Mission Church" KFNF of Shenandoah.[36] And most famously, the "Little Minister" Edythe Stirlen's "Send Out Sunshine" (later, "Gospel on the Air") program comforted thousands on KFNF's more powerful sister station KMA for over six decades.[37] Not all her listeners were rural, of course,[38] but the chatty "Down on the Farm with Rosalee" was a long-running column in her monthly newsletter, *S. O. S. Signal*.[39] Radio became an important way for religious leaders to overcome isolation and build community in rural areas.

THE PROSPECT OF LAND AS ALTERNATIVE TO MODERNITY

Even some of the more traditional religious communities adapted. Two communities on the Iowa River are cases in point. The Amana Colonies in 1932 famously ended communal ownership. The church survived as a small, independent entity.[40] A bit upstream, the Meskawki, who had had cordial relationships with their fellow communal society, were bewildered by the Inspirationists' abandonment of that economic arrangement.[41] But the Meskwaki also faced a challenge from the Bureau of Indian Affairs, which wielded some power on the settlement even though it was not a reservation.[42] Any threat to Meskwaki autonomy was also perceived as a threat to Meskwaki religion. That the Presbyterian mission had trouble gaining traction on the settlement[43] can also be viewed as evidence of the persistence and resilience of indigenous religious practices.

DMR May 10, 2004; May 19, 2004.

36. Hangen, *Redeeming the Dial*, 134–35.

37. Birkby, *Neighboring on the Air*, 32–34; Edythe Stirlen Papers, IWA; Birkby, *KMA Radio*, 94–96, 199, 224, 225.

38. On the Jan. 12, 1970, broadcast, Stirlen thanked the listeners who had written in recently. Six were from Des Moines and one from West Des Moines, and seventeen had small-town Iowa addresses: Lovilia, Anita, Bondurant, Winterset, Humboldt, Casey Boone, Creston, Washington, Marshalltown, Pella, Albion, Bayard, Carlisle, Murray, and Dawson. Box 9, F. 1, Stirlen Papers, IWA.

39. Box 14, F. 6, Stirlen Papers, *S. O. S. Signal*, April 1948.

40. Yambura and Bodine, *Change and a Parting*; Hoehnle, *Amana People*.

41. Hoehnle, "*Colonstein und die Indianer*," 98.

42. Zimmer, "Settlement Sovereignty," 3.

43. Baker, *Study of the Presbyterian Mission*. The study was probably prompted by the denominational merger of the United Presbyterian and the larger northern

The People Are Kind

And then there were religious groups unbending to modernity. The Old Order Amish witness to a simpler life was doctrinaire, exclusive,[44] and sometimes rigid or even abusive,[45] but it also had alluring aspects in its thoroughgoing rejection of the equivalence of convenience with progress. Beachy Amish also rejected modernity.[46]

John Hostetler, a Mennonite who had grown up Old Order Amish in Iowa, proclaimed the Amish ideal to the larger society—or more precisely, "domesticated the Amish to confer value to rural life in an age of rural decline."[47]

Perhaps no group was more committed to rural organizing than the Catholics. The National Catholic Rural Life Conference came to be headquartered in Des Moines in 1943.[48]

Key to that connection was Monsignor Luigi Ligutti.[49] Born of peasant parents in Italy in 1895, he emigrated to Des Moines as a teenager, graduating from St. Ambrose College, and becoming the youngest priest in the country. Assigned to rural parishes in the Diocese of Des Moines, he empathized with parishioners whose livelihoods were threatened by the agricultural depression of the nineteen-twenties, and later with out-of-work coal miners, victims of the wider-scale depression of the nineteen-thirties. In 1933, with federal loans newly available through the Division of Subsistence Homesteads of the New Deal, he organized

---

Presbyterian churches, with a more sociological, pragmatic, and bureaucratic approach being favored in the merger's wake. The mission was continued for another decade and a half and then abruptly ended by the local presbytery. Personal interview with Loren Soth, Toledo, IA, Jun. 24, 2018.

44. That the "English" were an outside group was brought home to me when an Amishman refused to cooperate in a boycott of a farm auction called by Iowa Family Farm Coalition in Keokuk County in 1983.

45. Burkholder, *Amish Confidential*; Garrett, *Crossing Over*.

46. Schwieder and Schwieder, "Beachy Amish in Iowa," 41–51.

47. Weaver-Zercher, *Amish in the American Imagination*, 136. Cf. another Iowa Mennonite intellectual, Hershberger, "Maintaining the Mennonite Rural Community," 14, 214–23.

48. Bovee, *Church and the Land*, 133, 139, 152, 157; Witte, *Twenty-five Years of Crusading*, 133.

49. Yzermans, *People I Love*; Miller, *Monsignor Ligutti*; "Ligutti, Luigi Gino," BDI, 357–58; Kosek, "American Capitalism and Agrarian Spiritual Dissent," 43–49; Conkin, *Tomorrow a New World*, 294. Ligutti elaborated his distributist philosophy most completely in Ligutti and Rawe, *Rural Roads to Security*.

an agricultural cooperative of laid-off miners to do subsistence farming outside of Granger, one of the more successful rural projects of the New Deal, and "only in the case of Granger . . . did the agrarian, distributist school of thought remain important."[50]

Fr. Herbert Duren also organized an array of co-operative enterprises in his Shelby County parish of Westphalia, based on the Rochdale cooperative model. For example, he pioneered the building of "Villa Nova" homes to ease the rural housing crisis.[51]

The energetic Ligutti soon outgrew the limitations of the first two words in the NCRLC; "Catholic," in that he was a pre-Vatican II proponent of ecumenical cooperation with Protestants, sometimes to the frustration of his bishop; and "National," in that he soon was representing the Vatican in many international capacities related to land and hunger.[52]

At the other end of the ecclesiastical spectrum, during the farm uprising of the thirties, the Farm Holiday Movement was led by a farmhand-turned-agitator from Agency, Milo Reno, a Church of Christ minister.[53] Reno's exhortations to direct action by farmers were laced with biblical references.[54] While the Farm Holiday did not transform the agricultural pricing system, it did leave a legacy among some farmers who sought parity or a just return on farmers' investments.

THE LARGER QUESTIONS OF LAND

Closeness to the land might lead to an instrumentalism justifying its exploitation, but it could also lead to an appreciation of nature and to an ethic of conservation. In his history exploring the religious roots of environmentalism, Mark Stoll suggested that most early environmentalists had a Presbyterian background. But his mentions of Iowans complicate

50. Bovee, *Church and the Land*, 152; Duggan, *Federal Resettlement Project*.
51. Avella, *Catholic Church in Southwest Iowa*, 116–19.
52. Miller, *Ligutti*, passim.
53. Curtis, *Like Ordinary People*, 305–8; "Reno, Milo," BDI, 421–23.
The rough-and-tumble Reno had a reputation around Wapello County for brawling, drinking, and womanizing, but also for preaching. According to an associate's account, he got ordained only after a particularly effective sermon led to a successful altar call, and the new converts asked for immediate baptism, which he was not authorized to do. He managed a postponement but got ordained to prevent a recurrence of such embarrassment. Kramer, *Wild Jackasses*, 194–95.
54. Stewart, 423. For a radio transcript in which Reno discusses "Religious and Civil Ideas," see White, *Milo Reno*, 133–38.

his assertion. Aldo Leopold, who grew up in Burlington, was raised German Lutheran. William Temple Hornaday, who grew up Seventh-day Adventist in Mahaska County, was instrumental in saving the bison from extinction and was the first director of the Bronx Zoo. Ding Darling, long-time cartoonist for the Des Moines *Register* and an avid conservationist, was a Methodist minister's son.[55] Love of nature, at least in Iowa, seems to have seeped beyond denominational boundaries.

That aesthetic, arguably sown by Iowa landscapes, and perhaps cross-fertilized by religious traditions, was put to the test as Iowa became the state most transformed by human endeavors.[56] Certainly one of the obstacles to a clear ethic for conservation was a countervailing argument, which also had some biblical sanction, that the land was for humans, and especially chosen humans, to exploit.

THEOLOGIZING

Surrounded by sky and land, hoping for a crop dependent upon weather and the absence of plagues, and yet profoundly grateful when the land yielded its bounty, a somewhat fatalistic theology could develop among farmers. On the one hand, gratitude when the harvest was bountiful was understandable; on the other hand, when drought and pestilence interfered, doubt and questions about evil might bubble up.

Among the novelists who developed this theme, the Dutch Reformed-raised Frederick Manfred of "Siouxland," or Northwest Iowa and parts of Minnesota and South Dakota, stands out. In *This Is the Year,* devout farmers come very close to years that they'll break even but always fall just short or deal with disaster. A reckoning with the divine seemed in order; what was God saying?[57]

A new agrarian crisis would flare up with the contraction of credit in the economically troubled 1980s, and once again religious leaders responded, notably from Catholic bishop Maurice Dingman and the Protestant-led

---

55. Stoll, *Inherit the Holy Mountain,* 270–71.

56. Mutel, *Emerald Horizon,* 76–111; Connerly, *Green, Fair, and Prosperous,* 36–44. See also Cronon, *Nature's Metropolis,* on how Iowa fit into the larger regional economy.

57. Manfred, *Frederick Manfred Reader,* 496–505.

Iowa Family Farm Coalition; we will discuss that later development in chapter 23, but those laments were of a piece with earlier iterations.

It would be easy to survey the triumph of monoculture so evident on the Iowa landscape and to see in consolidation, population decline, and the consequent embrace of nostalgia the mirror image of that economic reality in Iowa rural religion. The reality is more complex, and many Iowans continued to believe in the special graces of creation even as economic realities suggested otherwise.

In his 1919 book calling for renewed attention to the countryside, *The Fairview Idea*, Iowa novelist and reformer Herbert Quick considered the agrarian issue from the perspective of the recently prosecuted war:

> Soldiers, if they fight well, must be proud and happy. Our soldiers in France astonished the world with their wonderful morale . . . This book is a plea for a better morale in rural life. With a better morale, our farmers will fight their battles to a victory which will [also] amaze the world . . . In the absence of morale we face a future of rural decay.[58]

Sadly, Quick's optimism was misplaced on both counts, as this chapter has argued regarding rural decline, and the upcoming chapter about the Great War. Morale, an upcoming chapter partially on New Thought (chapter 19) will maintain, is an inadequate substitute for physical health, material prosperity, and inner peace. While working the land could be therapeutic, it might not be restorative.

---

58. Quick, *Fairview Idea*, xiii.

CHAPTER 15

"We Had To Create Our Own"

The Creations of Jews, Muslims, Southern European and Orthodox Christians, and Edward Steiner's Applied Christianity

"Perhaps I am, for I believe in the teachings of Jesus."

—EDWARD STEINER, RESPONDING TO THE QUESTION OF WHETHER HE WAS A RADICAL[1]

"On all these journeys . . . I have come in touch with the heart of humanity and found it good. Neither Schopenhauer nor Nietzsche nor my Calvinistic theology . . . have weaned me from this conviction, begotten of experience . . . .I have preached the one message I have—the inner kinship of the human."

—EDWARD STEINER[2]

IN 1991, HELENE BARRACKS described what it was like to grow up in the only Jewish household in Emmetsburg in the early twentieth century. When asked how they preserved Jewish religious customs in such an environment, she said, "We had to create our own." The family observed

---

1. Drake, "Steerage," Aug. 15, 2008, presentation to Grinnell Fortnightly Club. I appreciate the diligence of the Grinnell College Library staff in confirming the authorship of this piece.

2. Drake, *Steerage*, 29.

religious days with single families living east, south, and north of Emmetsburg, probably from the adjacent county seats of Estherville, Algona, and Pocahontas, so they could attain the quorum for a minyan—the traditional requirement of ten adult males. More remarkably, she also remembered nuns from the Catholic school in Emmetsburg visiting her grandparents to learn Torah.[3]

Such stories complicate the dominant narrative that Iowans were Christian and Northern European. Immigrants' starting points shifted in the late nineteenth century from Northern to Eastern and Southern Europe. For the first time, it was economically feasible to make the return journey as well, providing a disincentive for acculturation among a minority planning to return to Europe. And with the widening array of different cultures and languages came different ways of approaching religion, just as earlier immigrant groups had often balked at assimilating their religious traditions into the American mainstream. Old World languages were often clung to for worship—although outside forces would threaten that separatism. But the assimilationist impetus accelerated by World War I contended with countervailing forces.

NEW ETHNIC CATHOLICS

Recollecting at the same time as Helene Barracks, at St. Joseph's Catholic parish in Sioux City, Hope and Monica W. remembered the missions to the bottoms and the east side, and how Germans and Irish made room for Poles, Lithuanians, Syrians, and Italians.[4]

Drawn to work in the Iowa coalfields, Italian and Croatian Catholics sometimes settled out to Des Moines, with Italians on the south side[5] and the Croats on the near east side.[6] St. Mary's parish in Waterloo made special efforts to keep the Croatians there practicing Catholics.[7] The settling out doubtless also occurred in smaller south-central Iowa towns.

Mexican Catholics, lured to the state by railway work after 1900, also started settling out.[8] Disruptions from the Mexican Revolution soon

3. Griff, "Toldot Iowa Diary."
4. Women's Project, Diocese of Sioux City, Folder 1, Box 1, IWA.
5. Italian American Cultural Center of Iowa, *2004 St. Joseph Day Celebration*.
6. Email from David Polich, Jan. 9, 2021; Schwieder, *Black Diamonds*, 148; McMurry, *Centerville*, 199.
7. Bresson, "Contemporary Iowa Opinions," 8–9.
8. Otjen, "Creating a Barrio."

pushed refugees north. Farm work in sugar beets around Mason City, tomatoes near Muscatine, and nurseries in Shenandoah provided incentives for Spanish speakers to move to the state, bringing their specific devotion to Our Lady of Guadalupe.

EASTERN ORTHODOX CHURCHES IN IOWA

Greek Orthodox congregations in Iowa were not founded until the twentieth century: in Waterloo (1914), Sioux City (1917), Mason City (1918), Des Moines (1928), Cedar Rapids (1938), and Dubuque (1956).[9] Other national Orthodox churches in the state include a Western Rite Russian Orthodox in Sioux City[10] and Antiochan (Syrian/Lebanese) Orthodox in Cedar Rapids and Sioux City. In this century, Coptic and Serbian Orthodox churches sprang up around Des Moines, and a new interest in Orthodoxy outside traditional ethnic groups planted congregations in Pella, Ames, and Iowa City.

Greek immigrants gathered from as far away as Fort Dodge and Ottumwa to organize the congregation in Des Moines. The relative newness of Orthodoxy in the state and the tightening of immigration laws in 1924 made establishing congregations more challenging. St. George Greek Orthodox Church in Des Moines had to battle immigration authorities before they could install their first priest, Fr. Meletio Kestekides, who came directly from Greece.[11]

NEW JEWISH POPULATIONS

After 1870, Jewish immigration trends paralleled those of non-Jewish immigrants; Germans were largely replaced by Eastern Europeans. The religious, ethnic, linguistic, and class differences between German-American Jews and more recent Jewish immigrants often led to tensions, and these conflicts created the divisions between Reform or Conservative Jews and the Orthodox. Sometimes the gulf was astonishing; as late as the 1950s, Latvian-American Jews in Muscatine were unaware of a

---

9. Cunning, "Ethnicity in a Midwestern City."
10. "Orthodox Christianity in Iowa" (St. George Greek Orthodox Church).
11. "Our Parish History" (St. George Greek Orthodox Church).

"We Had To Create Our Own"

German-Jewish cemetery there.[12] Orthodox Jews in Davenport refused to bury their dead in the Reform cemetery and bought their own.[13]

Oscar Littlefield was struck by the variety within the late-nineteenth century Jewish community in Sioux City:

> [There was] infinitely richer and more varied Jewish cultural life than any being witnessed today... By no means a heterogeneous community, the Sioux City immigrant generation included Chasadim, Yeshiva-trained scholars, free-thinkers, labor-Zionists, Marxists, atheists, scoffers, some who embraced Reform.[14]

This is startlingly confirmed by the fact that the only Soviet spy on the Manhattan Project who was never caught, George Koval, was born and raised in Sioux City; his father was involved in a rival group to the Zionists who sought to make a Jewish homeland in the Soviet Union.[15]

Thomas Yoseloff, who grew up in Sioux City in the 1910s, recalled

> To a Jewish child growing up in "the bottoms" in those years, the synagogue was a symbol of mystery and awe. The Reform movement—even the Conservative—had made no impact on Sioux City's bottom lands, and there was only one religion—the stark, awesome orthodoxy of the patriarchs.[16]

Latskivah, Lithuania, "seems to have had a direct pipeline to Muscatine."[17] Joseph Bleeden arrived in 1892 from Lithuania and served as rabbi-surrogate until his death in 1916.[18] Such micro-histories would be replicated.

Muscatine elected several Jews to local office in the 1870s and 1880s.[19] Similarly, Moses Bloom, the first Jewish settler in Iowa City, was elected mayor in 1873, the first Jewish mayor in the country.[20]

---

12. Weissbach, *Jewish Life in Small Town America*, 247–48.

13. Weissbach, *Jewish Life in Small Town America*, 249.

14. Littlefield, "Point of View," in Shuman, *History of the Sioux City Jewish Community*, 163. See also Sorin, *Tradition Transformed*, 94.

15. smithsonianmag.com/history/george-koval-atomic-spy-unmasked-12504622 s3. Thanks to Duncan Stewart for this information. See also Hagedorn, *Sleeper Agent*.

16. Yoseloff, *Time of My Life*, 19.

17. Weissbach, *Jewish Life in Small-Town America*, 65, 371, fn 32.

18. Weissbach, *Jewish Life in Small-Town America*, 208.

19. Weissbach, *Jewish Life in Small-Town America*, 225.

20. Weissbach, *Jewish Life in Small-Town America*, 245; "About Us" (Agudas Achim). For another glimpse of a Jewish family in small-town Iowa in the 1870s, see Gradwohl, "Samuel Gradwohl," 5.

Life was not always easy for religious minorities in the state. While the majority of Iowa Jewish histories are silent on the issue of anti-Semitism, the novelist Edna Ferber recalled with bitterness her experience of persecution as a child in Ottumwa in the 1890s:

> Through the seven years of living in Ottumwa I know I never went out on the street without being subjected to some form of devilment . . . The little trip [delivering lunch to her father on Saturdays] from the house on Wapello Street to the store on Main Street amounted to running the gauntlet . . . As I approached the Main Street corner there sat a row of vultures perched on the iron railing at the side of Sargent's drug store. They were not children, they were men . . . " Sheeny! Has de gusak de Isaac! De Moses! De Levi! Hey, Sheeny, what you got?" Good Old Testament names. They doubtless heard them in their Sunday worship, but they didn't make the connection, quite . . .[21]

Ansel Chapman reported similar harassment from Irish Catholic children in Iowa City in the 1920s, so severe that he stopped going to Hebrew school.[22]

The Barish brothers gave up their lucrative Ford dealership in 1924 rather than distribute Henry Ford's anti-Semitic newspaper and bought a full-page ad in the Sioux City *Journal* to explain their decision.[23]

On the other hand, some Jews were pleasantly surprised by their reception. One who settled in Dubuque around 1907 wrote, "There is no feeling against us . . . The Jews and people of other religions live together quietly and comfortably."[24] (But Dubuque has long had a deserved reputation for racism against African Americans.)[25]

For Orthodox Jews, maintaining kosher in an isolated community was (and sometimes remains)[26] a major obstacle. Local leaders and scrap dealers the Cohn Brothers in Waterloo wrote the Industrial Removal Office in New York in 1908, interceding for Jacob Bobrov who needed financial help to get to Waterloo to become the Jewish community's kosher butcher.[27]

21. Ferber, *Peculiar Treasure*, 31–33.
22. Weissbach, *Jewish Life in Small-Town America*, 276.
23. Hagedorn, *Sleeper Agent*, 23.
24. Weissbach, *Jewish Life in Small-Town America*, 76–77.
25. Chaichian, *White Racism on the Western Urban Frontier*.
26. DMR, Jul. 2, 1997.
27. Weissbach, *Jewish Life in Small-Town America*, 218.

OTHER ETHNIC GROUPS

World War brought the fraught question of what language to use in worship to crisis for most immigrant groups in Iowa (see chapter 16). But ethnic minorities within larger English-speaking denominations continued as an issue; for example (see chapter 6), the Central West Bohemian Presbytery of the Synod of Iowa was set up to accommodate Czech speakers in 1910 and survived until 1948.[28] Similarly, the Synod of the West survived as a German non-geographical entity in the Presbyterian Church into the fifties, also centered in Iowa.[29]

The religious makeup of immigrant Syrians and Lebanese was particularly complex, including Eastern Rite Catholic and Orthodox Christians and Sunni, Shi'a, and Druze Muslims.[30] The "Mother Mosque" in Cedar Rapids, the oldest continuously occupied mosque in North America, is a fairly well-known story.[31] Muslims have been a respected religious minority in Cedar Rapids for well over a century, with one source tracing them back to 1885.[32] More probably, individual Muslims were in Cedar Rapids by 1895, and formed a religious community by 1901.[33] Less well-known is that, emanating from Lebanese Christian and Muslim kinship networks in Cedar Rapids, Shi'a Muslims were reported in Ft. Dodge, although it is unwise to suggest that this was more than an ephemeral presence.[34] Even more obscurely, the first and probably only US settlement of Metualay, a heterodox Syrian Shi'a group, gathered in Sioux City.[35] The nomadic peddling culture waned, with Muslims occupying a

---

28. Straatmeyer, *Synod of the West*, 49–50.
29. Brass, "German Presbyterians"; Straatmeyer, *Synod of the West*, 57–61, 102–6.
30. Tesdell et al., *Way We Were*.
31. Sheronick, "History of the Cedar Rapids Muslim Community"; Khan, "In the Name of Allah," 73–74; Judge, "Mother Mosque"; Daley, "Mosque That Is As American As Apple Pie"; Williams, "Religion and Recent Immigrants," 139, 153. The latest word is Curtis, *Muslims of the Heartland*, chapters 3 and 6.
32. Rugg, "Will America's Oldest Muslim Community Survive."
33. Sheronick, "History of the Cedar Rapids Muslim Community," 28–30.
34. Eck, *New Religious America*, 244–45; CRG, Oct. 11, 1959; email from Edward Curtis, Apr. 25, 2023.
35. Naff, *Becoming American*, 155.

considerable portion of the grocery business in early twentieth-century Cedar Rapids—and even a dairy farm in Fayette.[36]

Aleck Sheronick, a founding member of the Mother Mosque. Photo permission: The History Center, Cedar Rapids.

Even before Muslims started arriving, Iowa had a link to the Muslim world. In 1846 Elkader, the county seat for Clayton County, was named in tribute to Emir Abd El-Kader, an Algerian resistance leader to French colonization.[37]

---

36. Curtis, *Muslims of the Heartland*, chapter 6.
37. Gross, "Emir Abd El-Kader"; Kiser, *Commander of the Faithful*, xiii-xiv; NYT, May 3, 2013.

Another microgroup with a relatively long history in Iowa was the Chinese, who began arriving in small numbers by 1879. Most probably some practiced traditional religion; others sought some measure of refuge from vicious racist assaults by attending or joining Protestant churches. Presbyterian congregations in Des Moines, Dubuque, and Perry, a Baptist church in Council Bluffs, and a Methodist church in Davenport welcomed Chinese members in the late nineteenth century.[38] Reports of brutal treatment of Chinese immigrants could be counterproductive to the burgeoning Protestant missionary enterprise in China.[39]

EDWARD STEINER AND THE MODELING OF AN IMMIGRANT AS AMERICAN

Christian Americanization can be a troubling concept. In accepting new immigrants on their own terms, "Americanization" could be both challenged and redefined. The liberal Protestant goal of accepting, and perhaps assimilating, new immigrants found its advocate extraordinaire in Edward Steiner. Steiner's autobiography[40] explains his passion and his mission.

Steiner, who succeeded George Herron to the Rand Chair of Applied Christianity at Iowa College (soon to become Grinnell),[41] was both an advocate for and a model of Eastern European immigrants. Born Jewish in the Austrian-Hungarian Empire, in an area with strong Slovak separatist sentiments, he self-exiled for his sympathies with Slovak nationalism and disinclination to be drafted, with the authorities not far behind, came to this country, and converted from atheism to Christianity as a result of kindness shown to him when he was an impoverished new immigrant.[42] (It turned out his degree in philology was not marketable.) His conversion has become controversial; actually, it was at the

---

38. Miller, "Pioneers, Sunday Schoolers, and Laundrymen"; Mitchell, *Century of Iowa Baptist History*, 415–16.

39. Miller, "Pioneers, Sunday Schoolers, and Laundrymen," 140–41. In 1954, William Ng of Cedar Rapids became the first Chinese-American to be ordained as a United Presbyterian pastor. DMR, Oct. 3, 1954.

40. Steiner repeatedly told his story in his books but most comprehensively in *From Alien to Citizen*.

41. On Steiner as a teacher, see Sherwood, *Roosevelt and Hopkins*, 18.

42. [Drake], "Steerage," Aug. 15, 2008, grinnell.edu/news/steerage?v2node. I am basing the authorship on my email exchange with Burling Library, Jan. 12, 2021.

time within his family, as his brother, a Zionist activist, never spoke to him again.[43]

In over a dozen books published mostly before World War I, he told his own story and generalized from it, arguing that immigrants strengthened the country, that each ethnic group had its own strengths, and that recent arrivals could assimilate if given a chance—and treated with the same kindness he had been.[44]

"Dr. Steiner's accurate picture of conditions at Ellis Island motivated reforms that brought him recognition as an authority on the immigration problem," the *New York Times* observed in his obituary.[45]

Steiner was tireless in putting forth arguments for the acceptance of immigrants. He was attacked, despite his support for the war, during World War I. (See chapter 16 for more on intolerance of minority religious opinions during the Great War.) But the reason for the vandalism of his home (part of a larger pattern in the county) surely had less to do with his Tolstoyan ideals and friendship with the Russian nonviolence advocate[46] than with his work advocating for immigrants in an environment demanding "hundred percent Americanism."[47]

Even though the highest profile advocate of Americanism, Teddy Roosevelt, vouched for his loyalty,[48] Steiner never regained his pre-war prominence, and immigration politics shifted. The exclusionary acts of 1921 and 1924 effectively locked out immigrants from Southern and Eastern Europe whose cause Steiner had championed. The war to make the world safe for democracy had made it more tenuous at home, and took some of the sunniness from Social Gospelers' visions about the closeness of the kingdom.

---

43. For discussions of Steiner's conversion, see the introduction "About the Author," Steiner, *St. Peter and I*, vii-ix; Haas, "Conversion of Edward A. Steiner."

44. Spitzer, "Edward A. Steiner."

45. NYT, Jul. 2, 1956.

46. Steiner, *Tolstoy the Man*. The foreword to the University of Nebraska edition by Tolstoy biographer A. N. Wilson misidentifies Steiner as a professor of literature.

47. Jordan, "Edward A. Steiner and the Struggle for Toleration." *Sanctus Spiritus and Company* was Steiner's thinly fictionalized account of the attack on his home.

48. Roosevelt disagreed with Steiner's championing of "hyphenated Americans," but he telegraphed Steiner on January 2, 1918, that "from all I know of you and your writing I am sure you are entirely loyal." Jordan, "Edward A. Steiner and the Struggle for Toleration," 534-35. For Steiner's framing, see his *Confession of a Hyphenated American*.

Steiner was not the sole religious advocate for immigrants in Iowa. The University of Dubuque, in addition to being a hub for Frisian-American Presbyterians, in 1906 began recruiting Latin American students and students from Eastern European countries. The missions were linked, claimed college and seminary dean William O. Ruston: the goal was the "Christian Americanization" of both German-speaking Presbyterians and foreign and immigrant students.[49]

What are the implications of "Christian Americanization"? Equating Americanization with Christianity is inherently dangerous, Jews, Muslims, and ethnic Christians would concur. The patronizing tone is evident, but it is important to separate much of the benign aspects of assimilation from the more strident tones of Christian nationalism that would appear during the Great War, be pushed by nativist groups like the Klan in the twenties, and still have resonance in some quarters today. The nationalist impulses aroused by war would have corrosive effects on the state.

---

49. Mihelic, "Survey of the History of the University of Dubuque"; Straatmeyer, *Child of the Church*, 49–50, 79–80, 94; Pruitt, *Open Hearts, Closed Doors*, 30.

CHAPTER 16

"Unprogressive, Peaceful, and Religious Habits"

The Moral Crisis of the Great War[1]

"The First World war produced in Dubuque, as in the nation, a curious outpouring of hatred and hope that in the end, went sour."
—William E. Wilkie[2]

"As one who was brought up to think of the Middle West as the liberal, democratic part of the land, in contrast to the aristocratic and effete East, this [repression of dissent] shocked me. A pacifist and nonconformist felt, and actually was, safer in the East during World War I."
—A. J. Muste[3]

"I had never before, in matters involving religion, felt myself deeply at variance with my father. Now for the first time in my whole knowledge of him, my father threw aside his eminently sane viewpoint, his quality of disinterested judgment, and his independence of thought, and stood for what seemed

---

1. Among the sources consulted dealing with the national religious response to the war were Abrams, *Preachers Present Arms*; Piper, *American Churches in World War*; Heath, *American Churches in the First World War*; and Jenkins, *Great and Holy War*.

2. Wilkie, *Dubuque on the Mississippi*, 393.

3. Muste, "Sketches for an Autobiography," 49. Muste lived in Orange City for a year and was married there. Robinson, *Abraham Went Out*, 12.

"Unprogressive, Peaceful, and Religious Habits"

completely opposed to the intent of his life and preaching. He became one of those preachers who ardently presented arms."

—Ruth Suckow

"The winter of 1917–1918 will long be remembered by the 'oldest inhabitant', and the record of its fierce biting blasts will be recalled whenever the survivors of that period tell the story of the bitterness and rancor which filled human hearts, for they were as cruel as the weather."

—Edward Steiner[4]

"What we called foundations . . . have been found to be shifting sand."

—John R. Mott[5]

On May 1, 1918, ebullient after the long hard winter, Rev. John A. Robinson of the First Church of the Brethren of Des Moines was out visiting parishioners, normally an unremarkable pastoral activity. But he was arrested and charged with violating the Espionage Act. How a pastoral errand could become a federal felony charge suggests how the climate of World War I affected religious activity.

Robinson had grown up in the Iowa church, preaching his first sermon at nineteen in Muscatine, where his father pastored. He had stumped Brethren churches in Iowa in the past two years for Prohibition and was serving as moderator of the central district conference in 1918.[6]

The Church of the Brethren was a historic peace church, and as such its conscripted members were entitled to conscientious objector status, according to the draft law. Since Robinson's parish was near Camp Dodge, Brethren objectors at the camp attended his church, as did many of the more numerous Mennonites (those not confined to the guardhouse).[7]

---

4. Steiner, *Sanctus Spiritus and Company*, 289.
5. Quoted in Hopkins, *John R. Mott*, 598.
6. Hamer et al., *History of the Northern Plains*, 53, 25, 72, 89, 158.
7. *Des Moines Capital*, May. 2, 1918; Moomaw, *Christianity Versus War*, 311; Hamer et al., *History of the Northern Plains*, 53, 25, 72, 89, 158; *Plain Talk*, May. 9, 1918; DMT, May 6, 1918; DMR, May 14, 1918.
The best source on Mennonite absolutists, who refused to put on a uniform or work for the war, is Roy Buchanan, "World War I Experience, 1917–18," Roy Buchanan

The People Are Kind

Robinson had contacted Mennonite leader Sanford Yoder of Kalona the previous fall, proposing cooperation. If Yoder responded, the correspondence is not extant. Yoder would subsequently be privately critical of Robinson for lack of finesse in dealing with camp guards.[8]

When Robinson presented his credentials to the sentries, he was drawn into a conversation about his stance on the war. The garrulous minister obliged, showing the soldiers copies of the Brethren's Goshen Statement explaining its conscientious objection to war. Evidently, it was a trap. He found himself under arrest for violating the Espionage Act.[9] Despite its name, the Espionage Act dealt primarily with outlawing anti-war activity, or whatever might be construed as discouraging soldiers from performing their duties.[10]

The Espionage Act did have the effect of getting Americans to spy on one another. Federal prosecutors felt overwhelmed by the complaints and had to set priorities. The freedom of religion and entrapment defenses that a good lawyer could have presented were probably not why the government dropped Robinson's case after the war; more likely was the overwhelming caseload and the disappearance of the imminent threat.

In fact, while Mennonite national leader Aaron Loucks and his Iowa liaison Yoder were critical of Robinson's clumsiness, their own work at Camp Dodge left them perilously close to their own indictments—unbeknownst to them. We now know that the head of the Army's Military Intelligence Department referred a seven-page transcript of Loucks's talk to Camp Dodge Mennonites to the Justice Department, claiming Loucks was "in direct violation of the law." He followed up, insisting, "There is absolutely no question . . . that the activities of the Mennonites and Amish religious organizations are doing as much harm with their pacifist

---

Collection, Hist. Mss. 1–360, Archives of the Mennonite Church, Goshen, IN, 15–17. I featured Buchanan prominently in a talk on Iowa conscientious objection for PEACE Iowa in 2017: youtube.com.watch?v=BtoKecW.as&t+187s.

On Brethren ministers appointed to visit Camp Dodge draftees, see Rodabaugh and Brower, compilers, *History of the Church of the Brethren in Southern Iowa*, 273, 276; James L. Goughnor, Ankeny, to W. J. Swigart, May 8, 1918, CSCC Camp Visiting Commission Box 1, Brethren Historical Library and Archives, Elgin, IL.

8. John Robinson to Sanford Yoder, Nov. 20, 1917, Sanford C. Yoder papers, Hist. Mss. 1–162, Box 13, Folder 6, Archives of the Mennonite Church, Goshen, IN. Yoder was usually conscientious about making copies of outgoing correspondence.

9. Goughner to Swigarrt, May 8, 1918; Galen B. Royer to Bishop Bonsack, May 22, 1918, CSCC files, Box 2, Brethren Historical Library and Archives, Elgin, IL; J. A. Robinson to Rufus D. Bowman, Feb. 16, 1943, Rufus D. Bowman papers, Box 32, BHLA.

10. See, e.g., Polenberg, *Fighting Faiths*.

and anti-war views as an[y] similar organization in the country today, and the[y] ... ought to be silenced at once."[11]

What was the reaction of Robinson's congregation to his arrest? The minutes are silent. Except that the same week as the arrest, the congregation voted to put an American flag in the sanctuary.[12] The pull for religious groups to conform to the government's view of the war was strong—and unexpected.

THE IMPOSSIBILITY OF WAR

Benjamin Franklin Trueblood, president of the Quaker Penn College from 1879 to 1890, left Oskaloosa to pursue a career with the American Peace Society, advocating for arbitration of international disputes as a civilized alternative to war.[13] By the twentieth century, many Americans conflated civilization and Christianity and believed that humankind was finally ready to take up the challenge of the Prince of Peace. Many also believed that modern society was too advanced, and technological advances in warfare had become too devastating, for large-scale war to be fought in Europe ever again. They were wrong. (Perhaps the devastating wars of conquest on those considered less civilized could have served as clues.)

Even so, for almost three years, Americans viewed the incessant carnage from a distance, although also through a lens filtered through Britain, which had cut the communications cable between the US and the Continent early on.[14]

President Wilson's reelection campaign in 1916 was close, but he won with the slogan "He kept us out of war." While the implication was that he would continue to do so, he carefully evaded that promise.

Before the US Congress voted on Good Friday, 1917, to join the hostilities, Iowans had been solidly against involvement. Three of Iowa's eleven congresspeople voted against the declaration, and Iowa's two Progressive Republican senators had backed their anti-war ally Wisconsin

---

11. Homan, *American Mennonites in the Great War*, 113; Teicherow, "Military Surveillance of Mennonites," 100, 114; National Archives, Record Group 165, 10902–18.

12. Minutes, First Church of the Brethren, Des Moines, May 7, 1918. Robinson was also reticent about talking about the arrest when interviewed later in life by church historian Rufus Bowman. Bowman Papers, Box 32. Brethren Historical Library and Archives, Elgin, IL.

13. Watson, *William Penn College*, 283.

14. Fleming, *Illusion of Victory*, 43–45.

senator Robert LaFollette in preliminary votes before abandoning him on the final one.[15]

THE REALITY OF WAR

The suddenness of the shift to war left many peace advocates with the psychological equivalent of whiplash. For example, Drake University's Charles Medbury was bewildered. The Disciples minister, who had traveled from Des Moines to Washington to lobby against the war, left "sickened by the thought of the bloodshed . . . but he said, 'Well, we are in the war and we must all stand by our government.'"[16]

Similarly, Congregationalist and immigrant rights activist Edward Steiner of Grinnell (see chapter 15) put his Tolstoyan ideals on hold for the duration of the war.[17] However, this did not save him from being targeted by pro-war vigilantes, who threw yellow paint on his house after the jingoistic *Des Moines Capital* accused him of giving patriotic speeches that were, while clearly not subversive, insufficiently patriotic.[18] Nuance was not in vogue.

In Davenport, Unitarian minister Joseph Addison Kyle was unready to abandon the cause of peace. According to one newspaper account, he advocated that "all battleships should be sunk and all soldiers dismissed." It cost him his job. His replacement cheered on the war.[19]

As support for the war became the only option permissible in public discourse, a range of degree of support was still available. To be sure, few were as vehement in their patriotism as Catholic layman Martin Wade. (The Iowa Citian Wade, it will be recalled, spoke for American Catholics at the World Parliament of Religions in 1893.) Speaking to the American Federation of Catholic Societies in August 1917, Wade fulminated that "the opinions of citizens are puerile; the fist of the government is vital.

---

15. Holbo, "They Voted against War." When informed that Iowa Senator Kenyon estimated that two-thirds of Iowans were against the war, President Wilson snapped that if the Germans were to invade New York, Iowans would applaud. Fleming, *Illusion of Victory*, 135.

16. Dowell, "Charles S. Medbury," 44.

17. Steiner had been on personal terms with Tolstoy, visited him several times, and wrote a biography,

18. Jordan, "Edward A. Steiner and the Struggle for Toleration."

19. Gorsche et al., *Davenport, Iowa Unitarian Church*, 38–41; *Oskaloosa Herald*, May 15, 1917.

There is but one law: instant and unquestioning obedience to the voice of authority."[20]

While obedience to authority in time of war was a common theme for religious leaders, most were not so strident. More typical was "War Time Discipline of the Private Citizen," a speech by a Des Moines Episcopalian rector, instructing Iowans that "to obey orders . . . right or wrong . . . is the duty of every American."[21] His bishop Theodore Morrison agreed, maintaining, "We are American citizens and we are pledged to loyalty, as well as by conviction to win the war."[22]

Also representative was Samuel Zane Batten, a Baptist theologian who would move to Iowa shortly after the war to teach at Des Moines University. In "The Moral Meaning of the War," he spilled a lot of ink denouncing European imperialism generally but then pivoted to denounce Germany specifically, arguing that

> Sin is a matter of degree. The blackness of the sin depends on the intensity of the light. In the past all nations have been guilty of great wrongs against their weaker neighbors . . . But in these modern times the great nations have moved toward the light . . . But one great nation has refused the modern light.[23]

Batten thought that the Germans had sinned most egregiously, but his assertion that sin is a matter of degree may have been conjured from thin air.

Religion during wartime can best be viewed through the lens of those who sought to be consistent with principles that seemed suddenly abandoned by the majority. Pacifists and drafted peace-church members often gave a lonely witness, but ethnic language speakers and those who came back from the war disillusioned would also shape how the war was remembered and bear testimony to its lasting effects.

---

20. *Ottumwa Courier*, Aug. 27, 1917. While Wade's comments would have been problematic under any circumstances, the fact that his day job was a federal judge, overseeing defendants charged with speaking out against the war and violating the draft law, made his comments particularly inappropriate.

21. DMR, Oct. 26, 1917.

22. Horton, *Beautiful Heritage*, 70. Morrison's Bishop Coadjutor Harry Longley was even more forceful: "Never have great armies gone forth to fight for more noble and higher purposes." Horton, *Beautiful Heritage*, 76.

23. Batten, "New Conviction of Sin."

THE WAR ON GERMAN-AMERICANS AND HYPHENS

In Iowa, the war unleashed pent-up resentments against German-Americans, and more broadly, revealed grievances that Anglo-Americans had against "hyphenated-Americans." In Iowa,[24] German Catholics and Lutherans[25] were unlikely to publicly oppose the war; the Evangelical and Reformed, and sometimes the German Methodists, more often did. Anti-draft agitation by the League of Humanity in August of 1917 resonated in parts of Hardin and Benton counties corresponding to Evangelical and Reformed presence.[26] A northside church in Burlington was also deemed suspect by patriotically zealous and spying neighbors.[27]

Wilhelm Schumann was the most intransigent of the religious dissenters. He served a small German Evangelical[28] church in Pomeroy until he was convicted under the Espionage Act of expressing his dissenting opinion on the war. He served two and a half years of a five-year sentence in the federal prison at Leavenworth.[29] After serving his sentence, he returned to Pomeroy and resumed his pastorate, serving until 1932.[30]

Helen Zurbriggen of Elgin recalled, "The [First German Baptist] church . . . when I was small, the services were in German. They sang German songs. When WWI came, it wasn't popular to be German so

---

24. There were places such as New Ulm, Minnesota, where the German-American opposition to the war seemed nearly universal.

25. Of course, not all Lutherans were German. The Rev. Carl Schmidt of Fertile, Iowa, had a German-sounding name, but he seems to have pastored a Norwegian Lutheran congregations. He was one of the few non-Unitarians, and the only Iowan, to have signed the "Those Willing To Be Counted" anti-war statement. *Unity* 79 (Jun. 1917) 238.

26. Derr, "Iowa During World War I," 226–27; DMR, Aug. 22, 1917; *Des Moines Capital*, Aug. 22, 23, 24, 1917; *Ottumwa Daily Courier*, Aug. 21, 22, 1917.

27. Herbert J. Metcalf Papers, Box 7, Folder 9, SHS-IC; *Burlington Gazette*, Sep. 20, 1917. It is not clear whether the church in question was the German (now Oak Street) Baptist Church or Zion Evangelical Church.

28. Schumann was misidentified as a Lutheran in the state press, much to the chagrin of Lutherans. *Algona Upper Des Moines Republican*, Jul. 10, 1918; *Des Moines Capital*, Jun. 21, 1918; Jul. 12, 1918. Cf. Abrams, *Preachers Present Arms*, 211–13.

29. Thomas, *Unsafe for Democracy*, 14–16; Kohn, *American Political Prisoners*, 131; Peterson and Fite, *Opponents of War*, 84. While Kohn claims Schumann served a three and a half year sentence, he apparently was not aware that Schumann was out pending appeal until 1920.

30. Allen, "Anti-German Sentiment in Iowa During World War I."

that [First German Baptist name] was changed completely to the North American Baptist Church."[31]

Attacks on those who were not viewed as "100 percent American" were not confined to German-Americans. With an insufficient number of German-Americans in the neighborhood to attack, and as Dutch-Americans seemed to be breaching an invisible boundary and settling east of the Skunk River,[32] arson to Dutch churches and schools was reported in Peoria and other Mahaska and Jasper County towns. The fires so unnerved the pastor that he abruptly left town for northwest Iowa, seeking safety in Hull.[33]

In 1918 Iowa governor William Harding issued what came to be known as the Babel Proclamation, outlawing the public use of any language other than English.[34] Its effect on foreign language speakers was profound. Most ethnic churches complied with the Babel Proclamation order, quickening the pace of acculturation. Typical was St. Paul's German Evangelical Lutheran Church in Sioux City, which switched its service to English, providing private services for those few elderly members who still only spoke German.[35] Sometimes county councils of defense or other entities granted waivers.[36] Within the Augustana Lutheran Church, the Fort Dodge congregation was the center of the controversy about giving up Swedish.[37]

In addition to pressures to adopt the English language, the suppression of all things German extended to churches. The First German Presbyterian Church of Dubuque had "German" chiseled out of its

---

31. Blockhaus et al., *Echoes from the Valley*, 87.

32. Van Hinte, *Netherlanders in America*, 753, 761.

33. Dahm and Van Kooten, *Peoria, Iowa*, 78–100; Bratt, *Dutch Calvinism in Modern America*, 258; Swierenga, "Disloyal Dutch," 29; Van Hinte, *Netherlanders in America*, 760–763; "Dutch or Deutsch" sidebar in Schaap, *Our Family Album*, 223.

34. Derr, "Babel Proclamation"; Peterson, "Language and Loyalty"; DMR, May 20, 2018; "Young, Lafayette," BDI, 573–74; *North Central Iowa Presbytery Bicentennial History*, 66, 96, 123.

35. *Sioux City Volksfreund*, Jun. 6, 1918, accessed via germansiniowa.lib.uiowa.edu.

36. Butler County Council of Defense Waiver.

37. Barton, "Conrad Bergendoff and the Swedish-American Church Language Controversy," 49–50. Gronlid, "Lutheran Pastor Addressing Babel."

At the Christian Reformed Church in Parkersburg, one prominent member wanted English retained after the war and joined the Baptists when it was not. He was coaxed back into the fold only with great difficulty. Norman, *Henry's Daughter*, 45.

cornerstone. The word was restored after the war, but the congregation became and remained the First Presbyterian Church.[38]

Of course, English was not the only issue involved in the contentious process of assimilation and Americanization of immigrant-based denominations. In the twenties, a conflict flared in the Christian Reformed congregation of Sioux Center over the seemingly innocuous question of Sunday school. For most American Christians, this dispute would seem baffling, but Sunday school was an American institution[39] alien to the Dutch and would be teaching children in English. The new structure also seemed to threaten the authority of the consistory, the ruling congregational body. A tense *twenty-nine hour* meeting failed to resolve the dispute, and the congregation split in two.[40]

THE WAR ON PACIFISTS

In addition to John Robinson, other peace church leaders faced perils during the war. Vigilantes threatened Bishop Simon Gingerich of Wayland with bodily harm if he did not write Mennonite draftees at Camp Dodge and instruct them to wear a uniform. An American flag was also placed on his residence.[41] He complied, leading to consternation and confusion among Mennonite resisters at the camp who knew him, but he began backpedaling as soon as the duress was lifted.[42]

Special Agent A. P. Sherwood of the Justice Department, stationed in Des Moines, thought he had "one of the strongest Espionage cases ever produced by this office" after investigating a sermon by Mennonite Daniel Kaufman. Kaufman argued that selling farm produce or horses to the military was inconsistent with the Mennonite ideal of nonresistance. Sherwood had several sources aiding him in his investigation. Wayland doctor and Methodist layperson J. C. Stone initially led the accusers,

---

38. "History of the First Presbyterian Church in Dubuque, Iowa."

39. To be more precise, its origins were English, which was a source of opposition to it in this country a century earlier. Petersen, *Brief History of the American Sunday-School Union*, 1–2.

40. Schaap, *Our Family Album*, 227–30.

41. National Archives, RG 165:10902–18 (7–9, 11.4, 14, F/W); Simon Gingerich to Guy F. Hershberger, Simon Gingerich Collection, Hist. Mss. 1–382, Box 1, Archives of the Mennonite Church), Goshen, IN; Sanford C. Yoder Papers, 13/3, 13/7, AMC; Hist. Mss. 1–171, Guy F. Hershberger Collection, AMC; *Ottumwa Courier*, Feb. 25, 1918; *Burlington Hawkeye*, Feb. 19, 1918; *Oskaloosa Herald*, Feb. 21, 1918.

42. DMR, Mar. 5, 1918; *Des Moines Capital*, Mar. 5, 1918.

joined by Mennonite-born lawyer Henry Eicher of Washington, Iowa, who had a clear conflict of interest since he was also representing Simon Gingerich. Stone egged on local vigilantes and then seemed shocked by vigilantism. Despite the variety of informants, Sherwood could not obtain an indictment in the Kaufman case.[43]

"The corn looks good around here," wrote Mennonite draftee and farm furlough recruit Earling Kinsinger to Sanford Yoder from Versailles, Missouri, in the fall of 1918.[44] His experience with farm furlough, and that of objectors sent to the Adams Ranch in Odebolt,[45] was better than what happened in eastern Iowa. As part of the compromise with absolutists who refused War Department directives to wear the uniform and cooperate with the military, a farm work option was offered. Many Mennonite draftees were sent to farms in Johnson and Washington Counties. Non-Mennonites were not happy. A convoy of from thirty-eight to seventy cars (eyewitness accounts varied) descended upon Mennonite farms in Johnson County to force relocation of alternative service workers.[46]

THE MORAL CONSEQUENCES OF THE WAR

The moral crisis of the Great War was articulated on a national scale in Des Moines at the 1919 conference of the Student Volunteer Movement, with great anguish by those who had witnessed the war in and behind the

---

43. National Archives, RG 165: 10902–18 (F/W). Derr, in "Iowa during World War I," 258–65, mistakes Stone's eventual rejection of vigilantism for a pro-Mennonite stance, but the military intelligence documents clearly do not support that view. Stone's practice in Wayland did not long survive the war, as Mennonite patients stopped using him as a doctor. In fact, Stone also agitated against the use of Mennonite objectors at the Mount Pleasant state mental hospital. Simon Gingerich to Guy Hershberger, Sep. 20, 1962, Hist. Mss. 1–171, Guy Hershberger Collection: WWI, Box 65, F. 55, AMC.

44. Sanford C. Yoder correspondence, 13/3, Yoder Papers, AMC. An Iowa Quaker in France with the American Friends Service Committee couldn't help commenting on the crops in his letters home, either. Standing, *One Man's Story,* 200.

45. William Leitzel to "Friend," Sep. 26, 1918, Yoder Papers, 13/19, AMC; *Gospel Herald,* Oct. 31, 1918.

46. Jesse Schwartzendruber interview, *Sourcebook,* 176; Yoder Papers, Box 13, F.11 (9–10), AMC; *Iowa City Republican,* Sep. 13, 1918; *Des Moines Capital,* Sep. 10, 11, 1918; DMT, Sep. 12, 1918; *Camp Dodger,* Sep. 13, 1918; L. Lasher, Iowa Adjutant General, to Col. W. C. Bennett, Commanding Officer, Camp Dodge, RG 165 10902–51 (13), National Archives.

trenches, and to the great surprise of the older generation. The occasion was the quadrennial national conference of the SVM, dedicated to "winning the world for Christ in our generation." Almost all of Des Moines' Protestant churches were mobilized to host the occasion and welcome the 6,890 participants.[47]

Emphasizing the international thrust of the conference, the *Tribune* headlines noted attendees from "all parts of *civilized* globe" [emphasis added]. "Kipling Never Attended a Student Volunteer Convention When That Remark Was Made About East and West," it contended. The *Register* was confident that Des Moines was "ready for the greatest of its conventions."[48]

John R. Mott, a Methodist layperson who hailed from Postville and Upper Iowa University,[49] returned to Iowa for the conference, eager to resume the worldwide missionary crusade that had been interrupted by the shooting. By this time, Mott was arguably the most preeminent leader of that enterprise, having founded the World's Student Christian Federation in 1895. He was in leadership in the Young Men's Christian Association and SVM. (In fact, the SVM in the United States functioned as the mission recruitment arm of the YMCA.) As General Secretary of the National War Work Council of the YMCA, Mott had been intensely involved in maintaining the troops' morale.[50]

The combustible mix pitted elder statesmen of the missionary movement, eager to get the mission train back on the rails, with the younger generation, incredulous that it could be assumed that nothing had changed. In addition to Mott, who spoke ebulliently about the thirty-three-year history of the SVM, missionary legend Robert Speer, later in the conference, spoke defiantly about the danger of isolationism. Still later, Sherwood Eddy of the YMCA abandoned his prepared remarks, entitled "Have We a Gospel Indispensable and Adequate for All Mankind?" and was reduced to questioning the sexual purity and academic integrity of the students.[51]

47. DMT, Dec. 29, 30, 31, 1919; DMR, Dec. 28, 29, 30, 31, 1919; Warren, *Theologians of the New World Order*, 25–26, 33; "Statistics of the Convention," in St. John, *North American Students*, 624.

48. DMT, Dec. 29, 1919; DMR, Dec. 28, 1919.

49. Hopkins, *John R. Mott*; Mathews, *John R. Mott*; Hopkins, "Legacy of John R. Mott," *International Bulletin*, Apr. 1961, 70–73; Fisher, *John R. Mott*; Buxbaum, "John R. Mott, World Citizen."

50. Mott, *Criticism About Y.M.C.A.*

51. Showalter, *End of a Crusade*, chapter 6. For a view of a younger generation

But many of the students were not deterred by such gaslighting. In light of the recent war, they wanted to discuss the whole nature of the Western Christian enterprise, not just how to get the missionary tide flowing again. A prominent religious historian posited that "the long bombardment with war propaganda had probably served to cheapen and degrade popular idealism."[52]

The war turned out to have been more than an interruption to the campaign to Christianize the world in the current generation, as the pervasive pessimism in the wake of the war had two very different effects that both slowed mainline Protestant missionary activity. One was a new premillennialist theology that challenged the missionary assumptions that conversions would lead to a postmillennial kingdom. Fundamentalists were soon challenging mainline missionary enterprises directly, battling the clock against doomsday instead of striving for a new heaven.

The other effect was an even more existential questioning—did Westerners any longer have the moral authority to lecture others on issues of social morality? That question could creep closer to the justifications for religion itself. Along with the exhilarating effects of modernization, concerns about its accompanying secularization began to be raised by some religious observers.

EFFECT ON THE AMANAS

Iowans who just wanted to be left alone during the Great War were not. Perhaps precipitating the Great Change of the Amana Society of 1933 was conscription of young Amana men, sending them to Camp Pike, Arkansas. Conditions at the camp were less than adequate, although perhaps comparable to conditions of conscientious objectors at other camps. Nonetheless, Governor Harding intervened on their behalf. That Inspirationists voted, and voted Republican, might have influenced his uncharacteristic response.[53]

Amana was founded in Iowa County, it may be remembered, because the Inspiriationists' previous North American location was too

---

participant in the conference, see Carter, "These Wild Young People," *Atlantic Monthly* 126, 301–4. For a wider lens on the failure of ambitious post-war projects, see Ernst, *Moment of Truth for Protestant America*.

52. Sydney Ahlstrom, quoted in Showalter, *End of a Crusade*, 90.

53. Richling, "Amana Society"; Derr, "Iowa during World War I," 246–53. When Mennonites voted, they tended Democratic. Gingerich, *Mennonites in Iowa*, 161.

close to a city and outside influence. Having the colony's young males sent off to a military camp out of state (combined with the shrinkage of distances caused by automobiles) had the similar effect of bringing the outside world into the villages. In 1933, the colonists formally dissolved their communal structure.[54]

On March 14, 1918, a Cedar Rapids deputy US marshal filed a report on Selective Service as it affected Amana. Draft-eligible men in the communal, religious pacifist villages had at first been given agricultural exemptions, but this meant undue burdens for the rest of Iowa County's draft pool, and appeals by non-Amana citizens resulted in young Amana males' reclassification as conscriptable (a result an unsympathetic newspaper blamed on their communism,)[55]

But the marshal's observation was remarkable, in that he thought outside the strictures created by the war. "There is no question that they would make poor soldiers with their unprogressive, peaceful and religious habits."[56]

Most Iowans had at least some combination of those traits, if those who are featured in the next three chapters are representative. Catholics were mostly staunch patriots during the war, and sought and achieved social advancement in a way that African-Americans, who sought the same bargain, did not. Fundamentalists were less unanimous about the war and generally interpreted the conflict more apocalyptically. As we have seen, mainline Protestants seemed in disarray as a result of the war, which left an opening for alternative religions. The two decade respite between world wars was a fertile time for Iowa religion in many ways.

In 1920, while dismantling Camp Dodge, a building was moved to Merle Hay Road and Douglas Avenue in Des Moines, where it (and a sturdier successor brick building) served as the site of St. Gabriel's Monastery for over three decades.[57] The conversion of the wartime building to a reli-

---

54. Hoehnle, *Amana People*, 66–74; Yambura, *Change and a Parting*, 271–94.

55. DMR, Dec. 27, 1917.

56. Mar. 14, 1918, report on the Amanas, National Archives, RG 165: 10902–18 (F/W) B16.

57. "St. Gabriel's Monastery," Des Moines Historical Society Historygram, Aug. 21, 2021, DesMoinesHistoricalSociety.org; Avella, *Catholic Church in Southwest Iowa*, 97–98, 263.

St. Gabriel's was not the only religious entity to salvage from Camp Dodge. For

gious purpose represented not just a general refocusing on religion, but specifically the newfound assertiveness of Catholicism, the topic of the next chapter.

---

example, the Log Cabin Church built by Presbyterians in the Tama County hamlet of Lincoln also benefited. Martin, "History of Salem Church," 35–37.

CHAPTER 17

The New Assertiveness of Roman Catholicism

"The Daughters of Isabella, the women's counterpart of the Knights of Columbus, was in a flourishing enough condition to host the state convention in Dubuque in 1917. They sponsored an address by Father Hoffman[n] of Columbia College on 'Americanization[,]' indicating that citizenship was part of their reason for being, just as it was in the men's group."

—David Salvaterra[1]

"[Bishop Gerald Bergan] had the reputation of being an extraordinarily witty public speaker. Des Moines at that time had a small Catholic population in the center of a largely Protestant state . . . Some country clubs were closed to Catholics. The charming and funny young bishop became a frequently sought-after speaker for any function, secular or religious. Through humor he worked against prejudice and changed the climate for Catholics in Iowa."

—Thomas O'Meara[2]

"Monsignor Skahill's sermons on sin are remembered today. On more than

---

1. Gallagher, *Seed/Harvest*, 70. Columbia College was renamed for Bishop Loras in 1939. See below for the variant spellings of Mathias Hoffmann's last name.
2. Quoted in Avella, *Catholic Church in Southwest Iowa*, 154.

The New Assertiveness of Roman Catholicism

one occasion to make his point he would say, 'Most of you here today are too dumb to commit a mortal sin.' This always woke the congregation."

—WENDELL R. BENSON[3]

ONE OF MONROE COUNTY native James Stevens's most memorable short stories is "The Downfall of Elder Barton." The main antagonists are Elder Dewberry Barton, a horsetrader and Hardshell (Primitive) Baptist preacher from Tyrone, and the Methodist pastor Pearl Yates from Moravia, who "kept hatred of Romanism going like a bonfire in the town."[4] Yates's jealousy of Barton's popularity found its moment when in an act of kindness, Barton delivered the priest in Tyrone to the deathbed of the only Catholic in Moravia—and drove him *back!* Yates denounced Barton for his wanton ways, and Barton lost his pulpit.

Two aspects of this story bear examination: First, anti-Catholicism was a vehicle for social control of the larger populace, not just the Catholic minority. And second, in the story the Catholics have no agency; aside from the dying widow, they are barely mentioned.

After World War I, Iowa Catholics began to claim their agency, and the larger community began to recognize it.

Much immigration in the early twentieth century had new points of origin. Newer nationalities arrived, to be assimilated, rejected, or left alone. Among the Catholic groups arriving in Iowa were Italians,[5] Croatians,[6] Lebanese,[7] and Mexicans.[8] Roma, or Gypsies, also seem to have been Catholic; some of them settled out to Waterloo during World War II.[9]

But over and above those new infusions was a new assertiveness among Catholics that they belonged in mainstream America, an assertion

---

3. *Century of Service*, 108.

4. Stevens, "Downfall of Elder Barton"; Andrews, *Literary History*, 235.

5. Schwieder, *Black Diamonds*, 74–78, 104–5; Offenburger, *Babe*, 3–4; Avella, *Catholic Church in Southwest Iowa*, 39–41, 96.

6. Schwieder, *Black Diamonds*, 104; email from Fr. David Polich, Jan. 9, 2021.

7. Eastern Rite Catholics generally assimilated into the larger Roman Catholic milieu. Lee S. Tesdell et al., *Way We Were*; Gallagher, *Seed/Harvest*, 53–56.

8. Valerio-Jimenez, "Racializing Mexican Immigrants," 2, 42.

9. *Waterloo Courier*, Jan. 8, 1986; Apr. 4, 1943. I want to thank Barbara Morrison and Robert Neymeyer for calling my attention to this group, who also had ties to Eastern Orthodox churches, and later to evangelical Protestant ones.

bolstered by their loyalty during World War I. While that strategy had not been successful in improving the position of African-Americans, Catholics had more success.[10] Helpful to their cause was the fact that most Catholics in Iowa were white.

But Catholics' new assertiveness and claims to mainstream Americanness was not uncontested, and first struggled with contradictory definitions of "Americanism."

AMERICANISM AS HERESY

Iowa Catholics entered the twentieth century with limited room to maneuver on questions of theology and the relation of the church to a democratic society. Their most high-profile representative, Archbishop of Dubuque John J. Keane, had been rebuked by Pope Leo XIII while Keane was leading Catholic University in Washington, DC. Keane had tried to update the medieval relationship between church and state to fit democratic realities in the religiously pluralistic United States.[11] But in the European context, the Vatican had pinned its waning hopes for continued temporal power on the forces of monarchy and against republican and democratic movements. "Americanism" was the convenient name for what the Vatican declared a heresy.

In the long run the Vatican's support for monarchism was a losing bet. In the short term American Catholics advocating for rapprochement with democracy faced institutional headwinds. Keane was summoned to Rome, and after a two-year exile, when he was appointed archbishop but given no responsibilities or geographical jurisdiction, he was sent back to the United States but kept far from the national centers of power, with a sort of internal exile as archbishop of Dubuque.[12] The forces of "Americanism" had been temporarily beaten, although with Vatican II what had been heresy would become Church doctrine.

---

10. Carey, "First World War and Catholics," 41–43, 48–50; Schmidt, *Seasons of Growth*, 169–72; Avella, *Catholic Church in Southwest Iowa*, 105.

11. McAvoy, *Americanist Controversy*; Tentler, *American Catholics*, 194–206; Dolan, *In Search of American Catholicism*, 95–112; Cross, *Emergence of Liberal Catholicism*, 187.

12. Ahern, *Life of John J. Keane*, 318–56; Cross, *Emergence of Liberal Catholicism*, 187, 191–99, 203–4; Gleason, *Contending with Modernity*, 8–11.

PUBLIC AND PAROCHIAL SCHOOLS AS ILLUSTRATIVE OF OUTSIDER STATUS

Public schools in the nineteenth century had a generic Protestant patina unacceptable to the Catholic Church, which responded by proliferating parochial schools. The funding burdens represented a continual challenge. One local incident in Marshalltown can stand in for a whole panoply of resentments and counter-resentments.

In 1898 Marshalltown had a talented priest, Fr. Mathias Lenihan, the scion of a wealthy Dubuque family who would soon be elevated to bishop (the first native Iowan to be consecrated). He reasoned that since Catholics paid taxes for public schools they did not use, the city of Marshalltown could reciprocate by granting the parochial school free water. The city council initially agreed, but what had not been communicated was that the school would also use the water for heating. This proved too much, and the deal was rescinded.[13] The competing interests of public and private schools continue to absorb the attention of Iowa politicians.

ANTI-CATHOLICISM, AGAIN (OR STILL)

Ironically, the new Catholic assertiveness came at the same time as a resurgence of anti-Catholicism. Or perhaps it was more a persistence than a resurgence, as suggested by a series countering anti-Catholic tropes published in the diocesan Davenport *Messenger* in 1915.[14] As a Marshalltown historian put it, over-alliteratively, "Stories of gun caches, rectory-convent affairs, were all popular parts of a perverted public panoply."[15]

Or perhaps the new Catholic assertiveness triggered the reaction. For example, Iowa poet laureate Mary Swander had family memories of her grandparents' house being threatened by the Ku Klux Klan in Perry in 1920:

> A horse gallops into my grandparents' yard in Perry, Iowa, a man in a long, flowing white gown carrying a torch. Other men, in white hoods, their eyes peering out of holes as in Halloween costumes, erect a huge cross wrapped in straw, quickly pounding its point into the ground. It is near midnight, the fall sky dark, the air clear, a breeze blowing the rag my grandmother

---

13. Benson, *Century of Service*, 21, 44–45, 54.
14. Reprinted as Appendix D of Schmidt, *Seasons of Growth*, 385–86.
15. Benson, *Century of Service*, 70.

uses to clean the line still clothespinned to the rope. The man with the torch bends down and sets fire to the cross, flames bursting into the night. "Papists! Foreigners," he yells.[16]

Swander was writing creative nonfiction, not history, so some of the details of this story must have been imagined, given the author's birthdate. But the story's outlines clearly were etched into the family's collective memory.

Pushing back against that new assertiveness of Catholics was a reactionary strain of Protestantism that coalesced into the second manifestation of the Ku Klux Klan. In Iowa, the target of the Klan was Catholicism. Partially this was because of their relative ubiquity; Catholics were much more likely to be a visible minority in Iowa than Black people or Jews. One can emphasize either the breadth of the Klan power in the twenties or its ephemerality. For example, parts of the city government of Des Moines, including the police force, were effectively under Klan control in 1925.[17]

Ties between the Klan and segments of Protestantism were clear. For example, the leader of the Des Moines KKK was Rev. N. C. Carpenter, pastor of Capitol Hill Church of Christ. Disciples historian Charles Blanchard lamented the association, seeing the Klan's twenties roots not in anti-Catholicism or racism but in "the microbe of militarism—misnamed 'Americanism,'" the result of a "hang-over" of the Great War.[18]

Why was Klan power so ephemeral? The answer must be speculative, but include its overreach, Catholic pushback, and a general distaste for intolerance, at least in such an explicit form.[19]

Presbyterian minister James Moody of Cottage Grove Church in Des Moines opposed Roman Catholic Al Smith's candidacy for the presidency in 1928, but he was careful to distance himself from a more intemperate anti-Catholicism, insisting that it was Smith's opposition to Prohibition, not his Catholicism, that was objectionable.[20]

The case of Centerville is instructive but complex. The Klan took Appanoose County by storm in 1924, taking over both the Democratic and the Republican parties. In Centerville, its primary target was not Catholics, who were numerous in the surrounding coalfields, but the small

16. Swander, *Out of This World*, 220–21.
17. Johnson, "Ku Klux Klan in Iowa," 126, 137–38; Jackson, *Ku Klux Klan and the City*, 162–63; Neymeyer, "In the Full Light of Day," 62.
18. Jackson, *Ku Klux Klan and the City*, 163.
19. Blanchard, "'Pioneers' of a Great Cause," 203.
20. DMR, Sep. 10, 1928; DMT, Sep. 20, 1928.

The New Assertiveness of Roman Catholicism

mercantile Jewish community. The Klan was also focused on obtaining and maintaining political power locally. All but one of the white Protestant pastors endorsed the Klan, and the Christian Church minister, J. Roy Wright, became the local leader. The exception was the Presbyterian minister, Rev. Mott Sawyers, who sought to rally an opposition. (A Baptist minister also refused to go along but was fired by his congregation.)

The Klan drew crowds of hundreds in the rural county and set its sights on taking over the municipal government of Centerville. A cleverly staged electoral counter-attack, which included organizing by the African American congregation in town, the Second Baptist Church, resulted in rejection of the Klan-backed ticket, and Klan organizers soon left for more hospitable climes.[21]

An incident in the Wayne County town of Humeston, just west of Appanoose County, is illustrative both of Klan tactics and newfound assertiveness of Iowa Catholics. Bishop Drumm saw the Klan as an existential threat to Catholicism in the rural sections of his southwestern Iowa see, and wanted to confront it directly with missions to small towns. He arranged with the Church Extension Society in Chicago for the use of a chapel railway car, and sent Fr. Appleby to evangelize in the southern tier of counties. Once again, the most vocal foes were Christian Church pastors.

Appleby was met with hostility, especially in Humeston, where the Christian Church pastor first heckled him and then returned to burn a cross. But despite threats of violence, Appleby persisted in his mission and gained some respect locally for his courage in being willing to persist. But he also felt panicked during his week in the town, given the continued death threats.[22]

By mid-century, threats of violence were gone, but microaggressions could still sting. In an Irish-Catholic pocket of Muscatine County, "Corrine remembered being teased about her religion and being called a 'papist' in her grade school, and her children reported that the Protestant kids at school were mean."[23] The move toward the mainstream was steady but also slow.

---

21. An intriguing letter seeking advice from the Centerville National Association for the Advancement of Colored People to the national office asked if it would condemn a hundred dollar donation the Klan had given to a local African American church, with the *quid pro quo* that they join ranks against the Jewish synagogue. The national office obliged. Brigham and Wright, "Civil Rights Organizations in Iowa," 320.

22. Avella, *Catholic Church in Southwest Iowa*, 131–35. For a detailed view of the 1920s-era Klan in nearby Centerville, see McMurry, *Centerville*, 273–92.

23. Nabhan-Warren, *Meatpacking America*, 1, 18, 34. But sometimes, Catholicism's

MOVING TOWARD THE MAINSTREAM: AMERICANISM AS ASPIRATION

Catholics, emboldened by their inclusion in the pro-war consensus and as a more urban institution less affected by rural decline than many Protestant denominations, hit the ground running after World War I. For example, when novelist Edna Ferber (who recalled bitterly being bullied by Catholics as a Jewish child in Ottumwa) referred to convents as "prisons," Catholics were quick to react and push back.[24]

The Catholic men's service and fraternal organization the Knights of Columbus exemplified the lay male portion of this new assertiveness. On one day alone in 1927, the *Des Moines Register* reported on an expected "show of faith" march of thousands of Catholics in Des Moines and announced the Knights' state convention in Sioux City the next day.[25] While Iowa Catholics edged closer to being in the mainstream, some parochialism was still extant. In 1940, several "national parishes" of ethnic identity persisted: a Polish parish in Sioux City, and a German one in Carroll, where it hardly seemed necessary, as German and Catholic were practically synonymous in the county.[26]

Another way of measuring the degree of minority integration is the rate of intermarriage. By that yardstick, Catholics were still outsiders into the 1960s.[27]

THE HISTORICAL RENAISSANCE OF IOWA CATHOLICISM

No one epitomized the Catholic resurgence in Iowa better than Monsignor Matthias Hoffmann (Hoffmann changed his name to Hoffman during World War II; to the frustration of future catalog librarians, he sacrificed the last letter of his last name for the war effort.)[28] Indefatiga-

---

relative exoticism could lead to envy; in her memoir of growing up in mid-twentieth-century Burlington, Lisa Knopp found her neighbors' Catholic ways enviable. Knopp, *Flight Dreams*, 27–29.

24. DMR, Oct. 20, 1926.

25. DMR, May 22, 1927.

26. Gaustad, *New Historical Atlas*, Fig. 3–26, 3–28.

27. Burchinal and Chancellor, "Proportion of Catholics, Urbanism, and Mixed-Catholic Marriage Rates."

28. Eulberg, *Rt. Rev. Mathias Hoffman*. Hoffmann's name appears both with two n's and one in the pages of the *Iowa Catholic Historical Review*, which published from 1930 to 1935.

bly raising the Catholic case for inclusion, and arguing for Catholicism's influence on Iowa history from his pastoral assignments in and around Dubuque, Hoffmann even found time to write a historical novel, *Young and Fair Is Iowa*. The historical romance was a tale of boy meets girl, boy meets Catholics, boy loses girl, boy marries girl, and they live happily Catholic ever after. That all of the Catholics were heroic some critics found grating.[29]

Hoffmann also edited and published the *Iowa Catholic Historical Review* from 1930 to 1936. He probably borrowed the idea from a similar effort in Illinois. While some articles were rather tedious recitations of dates, Hoffmann himself spiced up the journal with claims about Fr. Samuel Mazzuchelli's architectural contributions to the territorial capitol in Iowa City. Hoffmann continued to argue for Mazzuchelli's claim to designing the building, finally conceding that only "three outstanding features of the Old Capitol—the unsupported winding stair-case, the cupola and the dome must be accredited to Father Mazzuchelli."[30]

Federal Judge Martin Wade, the most prominent Catholic jurist in the state, was the first honorary president of the Iowa Catholic Historical Society.[31] We have already encountered Wade at the World Parliament of Religions in 1893 (chapter 12) and as a ferocious opponent of dissenters during World War I (chapter 16). Remembering fondly his childhood in rural Butler County, Wade brought a thick layer of nostalgia to the society.[32]

Occasionally Hoffmann's enthusiasms outpaced those of his ecclesiastical superiors. In 1950, while stationed in the overwhelmingly Catholic town of Dyersville, Hoffmann proposed that Catholics offer space for a public school instead of running their own parochial system.[33] While this idea combined Hoffman's enthusiasm for promoting Catholicism with his generosity in sharing its benefits with the state, not all of the constitutional questions involving the separation of church and state had been thought through, and more importantly, the archdiocese was blindsided. The notion died quietly (although not before the national Protestant journal the *Christian Century* raised an alarm.)

29. Andrews, *Literary History of Iowa*, 33–34.

30. Griffith, "H. V. Gildea," 24. Two of the early authors of histories of Iowa, Cyrenius Cole and Benjamin F. Gue, made similar claims of Mazzuchelli's involvement, although Mazzuchelli does not mention it in his memoir.

31. Wade, "Message from the President," 3–5; "Late Judge Wade," 35–36.

32. Wade, "Message from the President," 4.

33. Eulberg, *Hoffman*, 235; DMR, Feb. 6, 24, 1950; *Christian Century*, Feb. 20, 1950.

Another novel featuring Iowa Catholics was more warmly received by the critics than Hoffman's. Josephine Donovan's 1930 *Black Soil* was set in O'Brien County, near Donovan's native Sioux County. With a theme familiar to readers of Rolvaag, Garland, and Quick, limning the challenges of pioneer settlement but with Irish Catholic characters, Donovan's narrative helped normalize Catholics' place in the state in a way that Hoffmann's more exotic plot did not.[34]

A CATHOLIC DAILY

Another indication of the dominance of Catholics in Dubuque was the publication of the only English-language daily Catholic newspaper in the country,[35] *The Daily American Tribune,* from 1920 to 1942.[36] Starting in 1934, it also published a national edition, proclaiming itself "the First and Only English Catholic Daily in the World."[37]

The publication had its roots in the nationalism of Luxembourger immigrants to Iowa and Minnesota and specifically Prussia's 1871 threat to the independence of the Grand Duchy of Luxembourg.[38] Nicholas Gonner moved from Cape Girardeau to Dubuque County to start up a newspaper in the German language and the Catholic voice.[39]

When the German language and American Catholicism were in conflict, Gonner opted for the former. He supported the founding of Catholic University of America but demurred when it failed to establish

---

34. Andrews, *Literary History of Iowa,* 34–35; Burns, *Kinship with the Land,* 83.
   Two later Iowa novelists with Catholic themes may be noted. Panned by Garry Wills in *Bare Ruined Choirs* as of the third rank, Wills simultaneously lauded Robert Byrne for his ability "to fascinate when they draw on the [Catholic] subculture and its folkways." See Byrne, *Memories of a Non-Jewish Childhood,* and *Always a Catholic.* For a visceral view of Sioux City Catholicism, see McHale, *Dooley's Delusion.*

35. Stuart, "History of the Catholic Press in Iowa."

36. Gallagher, *Seed/Harvest,* 70, 77; Library of Congress, chroniclingamerica.loc.gov/lccn/sn83045559. The *Tribune* had its roots in the German language *Luxemburger Gazette;* when publisher Nicholas Gonner, Jr. was forced during World War I to cease publication due to the excessive costs associated with wartime censorship of foreign language publications, he turned his attention to an English publication. Wilkie, *Dubuque on the Mississippi,* 397.

37. Masthead, *Daily Catholic Tribune.* But as Anne Meysembourg Stuart pointed out, the Springfield [MA] *Daily News* was "a Puritan-owned but Catholic motivated newspaper." p. 12).

38. Stuart, "History of the Catholic Press of Iowa," 16.

39. Gebhardt, "History of the *Catholic Daily Tribune,*" 2, 3, 8.

a chair of German language and subsequently referred to the school as that "Irish University in Washington."[40]

Nonetheless, when the Sedition Act of 1918 made publishing a newspaper in German prohibitively costly during World War I, Gonner shifted his emphasis to starting up a Catholic daily in English.

Gonner recognized his brashness in going daily in such a small market, and after negotiations with the archbishop about merging with the new diocesan paper failed, he attempted to relocate in St. Louis or Detroit. Milwaukee seemed an even more promising locale, but Gonner was killed in an automobile accident in late 1922, while returning to Milwaukee during negotiations, and this also killed the deal. Dubuque would remain the publication site of the *Tribune* until its demise in 1942.[41]

One of Gonner's most trusted employees was Charles Nennig, who served as editor for almost four decades. Like his employer and mentor, he was originally from Luxembourg. This description, printed in the paper to mark the thirty-third anniversary of his hiring, captures the essence of a politically active lay Catholic of the period:

> Mr. Nennig has been a member of St. Mary's parish since 1905. He is a member of the Holy Name Society and the Knights of Columbus. He is a firm believer in constitutional government, civic and religious freedom, private property rights, cooperation between labor and capital and Americanization as carried on by the Legion. He has always been in the forefront against foreign "isms," and has helped along every progressive measure that was aimed at a better and bigger Dubuque.[42]

Nennig's career at the *Tribune* ended sadly. After thirty-six years of service, as the newspaper increasingly struggled financially, he was summarily fired. After that, he spent some time trying to organize a union of Catholic editors. (The union printers of the *Tribune* had already been laid off to cut costs, with the printing moved to Winona, Minnesota.) His organizing efforts were unsuccessful.[43]

---

40. Gebhardt, "History of the *Catholic Daily Tribune*," 10.

41. Gebhardt, "History of the *Catholic Daily Tribune*," 21, 23, 29–40. Late in the Tribune's life, a Mr. Bruce of New York made inquiries about starting an East Coast edition. Probably he was affiliated with the Catholic book publisher Bruce Company. That avenue also proved a dead end. Gebhardt, "History of the *Catholic Daily Tribune*," 68.

42. *Catholic Daily Tribune*, Jul. 21, 1938.

43. Gebhardt, "History of the *Catholic Daily Tribune*," 49–52.

The *Tribune*'s circulation rarely exceeded 20,000 subscribers; the average was 14,000. It faced several identity problems. As a local paper, it competed with a secular daily. As an independent Catholic paper, it faced competition from official diocesan publications. While no other Catholic dailies existed, increasingly the *Tribune* was challenged by chains like the Denver-based *Register* and outlets such as *Our Sunday Visitor,* which had closer connections to dioceses.[44]

Several editorial decisions that can be justified morally turned out to be disastrous financially. In 1936, somehow thinking it would reap a bonanza in new advertising, the *Tribune* printed a six-part series by Catholic University researcher Clarence Enzler that was extremely critical of the popular radio priest Fr. Coughlin. Publishing the critique cost the paper 1,500 subscribers, or about 10 percent of its readership.[45] Similarly, an editorial endorsing municipal ownership of utilities raised the ire of the Dubuque Chamber of Commerce, cutting into local advertising.[46]

The *Tribune* was much more sympathetic to the New Deal than Coughlin, and while it shared some of Archbishop Beckman's isolationism before the US entry into World War II (see chapter 20), it was less strident than the archbishop. Its last issue in 1942 represented more of a whimper than a bang. The *Tribune* was a tribute to audaciousness as well as a cautionary tale about the financial realities of journalism.

After the *Tribune's* demise, the national magazine *Commonweal* waded into the controversy that the daily paper's remaining Catholic rivals had roiled up over its post-mortem.[47] Responding to Monsignor Smith of the Denver *Register* chain of official diocesan newspapers, *Commonweal* admitted the *Tribune's* editorial and "typographical" deficiencies but praised its spirit of perseverance. While Smith maintained that official publications represented the future of American Catholic journalism, *Commonweal* saw the diocesan papers "dispensing strictly ecclesiastical news," while independent outlets had a financial incentive to attract readers by "having something stimulating to say."[48]

44. Gebhardt, "History of the *Catholic Daily Tribune*," 1, 29, 117, 126–27.

45. Gebhardt, "History of the *Catholic Daily Tribune*," 69–70; *Catholic Daily Tribune,* Oct. 27–Nov. 1, 1936.

46. Gebhardt, "History of the *Catholic Daily Tribune*," 118.

47. *Commonweal,* Jul. 17, 1942; Aug. 14, 1942. For commentary on a twenty-first century parallel to the *Tribune's* closing, the US Bishops Conference closing of the domestic portion of the Catholic News Service, see the *National Catholic Reporter,* Jun. 14, 2022.

48. *Commonweal,* Jul. 17, 1942.

But, summarizing a flurry of protests in other Catholic press outlets to Smith's statement, *Commonweal* resurrected the old Americanist question in a new context: how top-down could the American Catholic press be in a politically democratic milieu? Quoting an authorized publication, *Commonweal* affirmed,

> And now the *Catholic Messenger,* "the Official Catholic Newspaper of Texas," has this to add on Monsignor Smith's observations: "It is not easy to place these singular expressions into proper intellectual focus: to the 'justification' propounded by Msgr. Smith, its implications are frightening in the similarity to the 'justification' used by the totalitarian powers which have all but eliminated the Church in the majority of countries in Europe."[49]

In the dark days of 1942, the *Texas Messenger* may have conflated the prospects for democracy and the situation of the Catholic Church in Europe. But the *Daily Tribune,* in its afterlife, had become a stand-in for a new independence as well as assertiveness among American Catholics.

ARTS

Some Catholics also asserted themselves in the arts. With a seeming obsessiveness, Fr. Paul Dobberstein gathered rocks from around the world for decades to build the world's largest grotto, the Grotto of the Redemption, in West Bend.[50]

"Into the construction of the Grotto has gone the most beautiful of precious stones, ores, minerals, fossils, petrifications, corals, crystals, and shells gathered literally from all over the world. The Andes of South America, the Alps of Europe, the underground caverns of Dakota and New Mexico, the Rockies of the West, have each yielded of their treasures for the realization of a dream . . . "[51]

---

49. *Commonweal,* Aug. 14, 1942.

50. Hutchinson, *Grotto Father*; Greving, *Pictorial History of the Grotto*; *Explanation of the Grotto of the Redemption.*
Another architectural curiosity, chronicled in *Ripley's Believe It Or Not*, was Waterloo's "Boulder Church," the third of four structures of the First Presbyterian Church, which was constructed entirely from a single boulder from a farm in Black Hawk County. "Our Story" (First Presbyterian Church of Waterloo).

51. McAvoy, "History of the Church in Northwest Iowa," *Iowa Catholic Historical Review* 8, 36–37.

Perhaps in whimsical counterpoint, Iowa also has claim to the world's smallest grotto, at 520 South Governor Street in Iowa City.[52]

DAVENPORT AND DES MOINES AS CENTERS OF AMERICAN LIBERAL CATHOLICISM

Iowa Catholics expressed their newfound assertiveness in more than one way. Speaking broadly, the northern two dioceses, Dubuque[53] and its offshoot, Sioux City, tended to express that assertiveness conservatively, building and shoring up Catholic institutions; the two southern dioceses, Davenport and its offshoot, Des Moines, trended more liberal, negotiating how Catholics could function in the larger society, being more open to ecumenical endeavors and more apt to initiate efforts for social justice.

Demography drove much of the difference. The city of Dubuque is heavily German Catholic and tends to insularity. Davenport and Des Moines had much more religiously mixed populations, hence more of an incentive to get along with other religious groups.[54]

One early ecumenical endeavor involved not just Protestants but also Jews. The Brotherhood Trio of the National Conference on Christians and Jews, based in Des Moines, traversed the state from 1936 to 1942, barnstorming in high school gymnasiums and other venues on behalf of religious tolerance. Rabbi Eugene Mannheimer, Congregationalist minister Stoddard Lane, and Father Robert Walsh cajoled and teased each other in a way that let small-town audiences in on the joke that differences need not lead to enmity. Their success, and their existence, was only possible because of the support of Bishop Gerald Bergen of Des Moines.[55] The program introduced thousands of curious Iowans to alternative expressions of religion by those who were their neighbors.

---

52. "World's Smallest Grotto." Festina also claims to have the world's smallest church. This claim has been recently challenged by a tiny church in Alabama. Kazek, "Alabama Chapel."

53. This is obviously a generalization; a recent counterexample was Archbishop Michael Jackels's criticism of the San Francisco prelate who banned a Catholic politician from communion for her support of reproductive rights. Jackels called the decision misguided, argued for the healing power of the Eucharist, and pointed to a long list of social issues that Catholics should also address positively. Crary, "AP-NORC Poll Details Rifts."

54. Avella suggests this about southwest Iowa in *Catholic Church in Southwest Iowa*, xix-xxiii.

55. See my "Making Iowa Safe for Differences."

The New Assertiveness of Roman Catholicism

Not all US bishops welcomed the idea of ecumenical cooperation or interreligious dialog,[56] as the young Davenport priest William O'Connor discovered to his chagrin when the archbishop of New York forbade him to lecture at the Jewish Theological Seminary in 1943.[57] Although combating anti-Catholicism was clearly in Catholics' interest, some bishops thought that purity had a higher priority.

The State University of Iowa School of Religion was a groundbreaking ecumenical endeavor within the boundary of the Davenport diocese. Iowa became the first American public university to grant degrees in religion. Its original model depended on financing and support from the religious groups of the state.[58]

Theological differences between the southern and the northern dioceses would grow more pronounced in the fifties, as Davenport's diocesan newspaper, *The Catholic Messenger*, became a national voice for liberals in the church.[59] Its popular columnist, J. D. Conway, churned out books based on his "Question Box" columns, many of them with titles starting, *What They Ask About . . .* He was eventually syndicated in over fifty diocesan newspapers as well as *The National Catholic Reporter*.[60]

The *Messenger's* editor in the fifties, Donald McDonald, gathered a talented staff and spoke out on the issues of the day. He later became editor of *The Center Magazine*, voice of the Center for the Study of Democratic Institutions in Denver, Colorado.[61]

---

56. On some of the Catholic hierarchy's reluctance to participate fully in the NCCJ project, see Athans, "Courtesy, Confrontation."
Sometimes, of course, the message was mislaid. Morris Ketzer, who sometimes replaced Mannheimer, recalled with considerable glee a woman in Clinton who accosted him afterwards with "Rabbi! I'm not of your faith, but I sure appreciate your loud voice. My ears have gone bad and I didn't hear a word of those two Christian gentlemen. Why do our Christian preachers always mumble? I don't care too much about your religion, but you rabbis sure come through loud and strong." Kertzer, *Tell Me, Rabbi*, 13–14.

57. O'Connor to Bishop Francis McIntyre, Oct. 8, 1943, Box 2, Rev. William T. O'Connor Papers, IWA.

58. Lampe, *Story of an Idea*; Bach, *Of Faith and Learning*; Folder 32, Box 5, William Francis Riley Papers, SC-UI.

59. Wills, *Bare Ruined Choirs*, 53.

60. Topics in the *What They Ask About* series included titles on marriage, the church, morals, sin, and divorce. *National Catholic Reporter*, Feb. 15, 1967. Conway also served on the board of the School of Religion at the State University of Iowa.

61. Wills, *Bare Ruined Choirs*, 53; Schmidt, *Seasons of Growth*, 209–10, 214. Like many Catholic liberals, McDonald traced what he saw as the unraveling of the sixties to the assassination of President Kennedy. Ellis, *American Catholicism*, 222.

Catholic Action in Davenport worked on race relations in the Quad Cities during the fifties. With a growing population of Mexican-Americans, most of whom were Catholics, the diocese had both moral and strategic reasons for supporting their civil rights.[62]

But, despite the imprimatur of social justice by modern papal encyclicals, such work could be controversial. Labor priest William O'Connor, who taught sociology at St. Ambrose College until he was fired, had a knack for antagonizing the local business establishment. For college administrators, that meant alienating potential donors. "Every time you open your mouth, you cost the college $15,000," O'Connor recalled the college president accusing him after he endorsed Case farm implement workers' unionizing.[63]

Maurice Dingman, originally of the Davenport Diocese, was elevated to bishop of Des Moines in 1968. His work to implement the new vision distilled by the Second Vatican Council on the diocesan level and within the US Council of Bishops will be examined in chapter 22.

Shifting theology and new liturgy confronted Catholics by mid-century. The monastery first constructed from surplus World War I materials in northwestern Des Moines was sold, becoming the site of Merle Hay Mall.[64] That transition foretold a decline in what Catholics call religious vocations. Combined with professionalization of Catholic hospitals and the disinclination of post-Vatican II nuns to work for minimal pay in parochial schools, much of the landscape of Catholic presence would have to be renegotiated. The depopulation of rural Iowa would also take its toll on Iowa Catholicism.

It would be easy for critics of modern mass society to see in the transformation of this property from monastery to mall the signs of encroaching commercialism and secularism threatening traditional religion. And "old-time religion" would be celebrated by fundamentalists (in a very different way than in Catholic tradition),[65] even when some of

---

62. McDaniel, "Catholic Action in Davenport"; Hinojosa, "Catholic Interracial Council."

63. Matthew Perosky, President of the Associated Industries of the Quad Cities to Bishop Ralph Hayes, Aug. 10, 1953; O'Connor to William J. Collins, Jun. 28, 1956, Box 1, O'Connor Papers, IWA.

64. Avella, *Catholic Church in Southwest Iowa*, 201.

65. Bishop Maurice Dingman of the Des Moines Diocese, for example, more out of

The New Assertiveness of Roman Catholicism

their tenets were actually very new. Fundamentalists also tried to assert themselves in the state in the twenties (sometimes by bullying Catholics), but they stumbled, as the next chapter will show. Any alliance between conservative Catholics and Protestants would be decades distant (see chapter 23), due in large part to the anti-Catholic prejudices outlined earlier in this chapter, but also to lingering Catholic isolation.

Whatever the merits of finding meaning in a monastery morphing into a shopping mall—and the temptation is strong—it is clear that as Iowa Catholics tacked toward the mainstream, they were also pulled by the tides of secularism and ecumenism. As a consequence, late twentieth-century Catholicism would look very different from the Catholicism at the century's start. Those changes as much as the Catholic Church's vaunted continuity would serve to define contemporary Iowa Catholicism.

---

ecumenism and admiration for the reconciliation of political enemies than sympathy for the cause, would endorse a Harold Hughes-Chuck Colson event in 1977 but went into contortions to do so: "However, even though I am encouraging attendance, I do wish to point out briefly some of my concerns . . . Catholics attending the "Evening with Hughes and Colson" may become exclusively attracted to Scripture and overlook the other aspects of their Catholic faith. For the Scriptures to be fully effective, the fuller vision provided by the Catholic tradition is essential . . . In saying this I do not intend to demean the importance of the Scriptures . . . " *Catholic Mirror*, Jul. 14, 1977.

CHAPTER 18

The Counter-Narrative

Fundamentalism[1]

Science says that the oldest rocks in Iowa are between one and two billion years old, but these are not my rocks to understand. I attended the high school in Monticello, eight miles from my grandmother's house, from 1954 to 1959. There we were not allowed to learn about evolution because the superintendent saw it as antithetical to biblical truth.

"Nonsense," said my mother, whose own Christian faith saw no contradiction between science and religion . . . "The Hebrews were an ancient people who recorded their religious faith in the symbols they understood. The truth of the Bible isn't challenged simply because the stories reflect the limited scientific knowledge of their time."

—Barbara J. Scot[2]

"In coming here I was not entirely ignorant of the difficult task to which I came. I knew something of the history of the church in recent years, and something of the unfortunate re-action from the Billy Sunday campaign, a re-action which was said to make religious work in Des Moines much harder than before the campaign was held.

—Rev. H. J. Bryce[3]

    1. Some of this chapter is adapted from my article "'Serious Nature of the Division.'"
    2. *Prairie Reunion*, 30.
    3. Resignation letter, October 1919, Box 1, Book 2, 18–22, Oct. 5, 26, 1919, Calvary Baptist Church (Des Moines) Papers, SHSI-DM.

The Counter-Narrative

"Des Moines Christians are the laziest, good-for-nothing[est] bunch I've ever met."

—Billy Sunday[4]

"Nine new churches were established in Ottumwa between 1922 and 1939: the Fundamentalist Baptist Church, Community Christian Church, Chapel of the Church of God, Pentecostal Church of God, Church of the Nazarene, North Church of the Nazarene, Central Addition Pentecostal Church, First Church of the Open Bible, and Harding Park Open Bible Church."[5]

Susan Glaspell, Davenport and Disciples native who became a prominent American feminist playwright, wrote a short story, "Finality in Freeport," based on her experience battling the Davenport Public Library over its refusal to order a work of modernist theology by University of Chicago professor George Burman Foster, *The Finality of the Christian Religion.*[6]

Marcia Noe has explored the factual basis of that story: Glaspell lightly fictionalized a controversy sparked by the Monist Society[7] over the library board's refusal to stock the book.[8] The Monists, philosophical heirs to Davenport's freethinking Forty-Eighters, were joined by progressive Unitarian, liberal Baptist, and Reform Jewish leaders in fighting against censorship. The concluding scene may be fictional, but it is plausible: after censorship fails, the book sits for months unread on the library's shelves. Then the agitator-protagonist bumps into her chief opponent holding the book, who sheepishly explains it is now required reading for his Sunday School class.

---

4. DMT, Nov. 28, 1914. This statement may have been intended as a motivational device, and also served to deflect blame onto the volunteers for his relative lack of success at that point in the Des Moines crusade.

5. Warren, *Struggling with "Iowa's Pride,"* 47.

6. "Religion and Ethics"; Arnold, *Near the Edge of Battle*, 24–35.

7. Glaspell, "Finality in Freeport"; Noe, *Susan Glaspell*, 25–27; Noe, *Three Midwestern Playwrights*, 2, 92–98. On Rabbi Fineshreiber, see Wolfe, *Century with Iowa Jewry*, 203–4; Fleishaker, "Illinois-Iowa Jewish Community," 129.

8. Noe, *Glaspell*, 26, 89; Ozieblo, *Susan Glaspell*, 32, 49–50; *Davenport Democrat and Leader*, Feb. 16, 18, 1910. Glaspell also explored the issue of theological modernism in the short story "Tomorrow: The Story of an Easter Sermon," in *Booklovers Magazine*, Mar. 5, 1905, 563.

Framing the discussion of fundamentalism in the context of Davenport's Monist Society,[9] with Theosophists, free-thinking Socialists, Unitarians and a Reform rabbi challenging small-minded decisions, illuminates the constellation of perceived threats that bedeviled fundamentalism: a modern movement claiming to be anti-modernist, an anti-Social Gospel group that had its own political agenda, with a call for biblical literalism that elided much of the Gospel message.

In the popular mind, fundamentalism was associated with the movement against teaching evolution in public schools, led memorably by William Jennings Bryan. More intellectually, it claimed that a literal reading of the Bible was necessary for orthodoxy. Often, this reading was done with dispensationalist glasses, which led to pessimism about the world and found consolation in savoring its imminent end.

In sketching how fundamentalism looked in Iowa, we will limn the Billy Sunday phenomenon, examine the controversy in Northern Baptist and Presbyterian conventions, assess the fundamentalist Baptist Bible Union experiment with higher education in Des Moines, take note of a literary relic, and mention Iowa as an exporter of fundamentalist leadership to the West Coast. Had Glaspell stayed in Iowa, she would not have lacked for material.

THE GEOGRAPHICAL AND SOCIAL LOCATION OF SUNDAY'S BRAND

Emblematic of fundamentalism in many ways was the Iowa-born revivalist Billy Sunday. A major league baseball player with a dramatic conversion experience, he returned to Iowa to begin his career as a revivalist, starting in Garner in 1896.[10] He tried to make every sinner's conversion as dramatic as his own, drawing freely on his previous career for sermon illustrations, even pantomiming baseball plays on stage.

Sunday's inward-looking theology had been shaped by his hardscrabble early life. Born in Ames as the Civil War began, his father died of

---

9. For Susan Glaspell's recollections of the Monist Society, see her *Road to the Temple*, 190–99. See also Humphrey, "Children of Fantasy," 36.

10. The secondary literature on Sunday is vast. See, e.g., Martin, *Hero of the Heartland*, which situates Sunday in his native Midwest; Dorset, *Billy Sunday*; Bruns, *Preacher*; and Wiard, "Gospel of Efficiency."

disease in a training camp in 1862, just a month after Billy was born. Sunday spent part of his youth in orphanages in Glenwood and Davenport.[11]

Sunday's evangelistic career peaked in the first two decades of the twentieth century, paralleling the growth of fundamentalism. But Sunday depended on the broad participation of local Protestant churches for his rallies' saturation efforts. Newspapers and Sunday's public relations machine had a symbiotic relationship. Sunday sold copy; newspaper reports sustained the campaign with daily reminders of his presence. A gushing *Des Moines Tribune* even pointed to a surge in cigar sales as indicative of Sunday's salubrious effect on the local economy.[12]

Looking at Sunday's 1914 Des Moines crusade illustrates the breadth of Sunday's influence and the limitations of his methods.[13] Sunday came into Des Moines for a seven-week revival in November 1914, at the peak of his prominence. Expectations were huge, a scenario his well-oiled public relations department did nothing to discourage. As an Iowa native son, no news angle was too trivial for the evening *Tribune*; each issue had at least two stories on the campaign, and as many as nine.[14]

Sunday's organizational juggernaut split the city into eight divisions, with "almost block-by-block" neighborhood prayer meetings and city-wide events. Of the eight divisions, Division 6, on the working-class east side, had the most neighborhood meetings.[15] As Sunday and his crew masterfully built the tension forward toward his most famous sermon, "Booze" (he was against it), cracks appeared in the carefully managed stagecraft. Perhaps it was just part of the show when he called Des Moines

---

11. Martin, *Hero of the Heartland*, 4–6.

12. DMT, Dec. 23, 1914.

13. Particularly helpful for understanding the local campaign in Des Moines was Margaret Bendroth, *Fundamentalists in the City*, whose chapter six covers Sunday's campaign in Boston two years after Des Moines, and Baldwin, "When Billy Sunday 'Saved' Colorado." The Denver revival immediately preceded Des Moines's. A popular account of Sunday in Iowa, Holston, "Billy Sunday: The Calliope of Zion," *The Iowan* (Spring 1985), 19–23, 48–53, was also useful.

14. DMT, Oct. 28–Dec. 23, 1914. Readers learned, for example, that he had a housekeeper who prepared his meals; but "Ma" Sunday herself went to market for Thanksgiving. Inquiries about his future availability from Kansas City, St. Paul, Chicago, and Japan were not only fielded by his staff but used as fodder for a voracious press. The *Tribune*'s morning partner, the *Des Moines Register and Leader*, often ran the same stories, but at a less intense rate, as it focused more on being a statewide newspaper. See Nov. 2, 1914. The weekly African American *Iowa State Bystander* also provided favorable coverage: Nov. 20, 1914.

15. DMT, Nov. 5, 1914.

Christians "the laziest, good for nothin' bunch" he'd ever met," but they were just gullible enough to believe it, and as hard as they had worked, they were just big-city enough to express resentment.

Perhaps Sunday was just being coy when he threatened to cut short the revival, citing inadequate results, but "personal workers" (volunteers who counseled those responding to Sunday's altar calls) promised to improve if he would stay on. He did. One of Sunday's aides also expressed disappointment that many of the city's prominent citizens were absent.[16]

Conversion numbers are extremely slippery. Contradicting the projections when Billy threatened to pull out early, Sunday's campaign claimed at the close that Des Moines had done better than Denver, the previous campaign, a city twice as big. But sometimes church members came forward to rededicate themselves; a third of the converts were children, ineligible for full membership in most churches; 2,400 had been from out of town. (The ever cheerful *Tribune* pointed to increased tourism.)[17] Divvying up the actual new converts caused friction among congregations.

But if the *Tribune* did its best to elide any differences between Sunday and the sponsoring churches, the rival *Capital* thought it smart journalism to exploit conflicts. While it didn't report Sunday's threat to leave (being less attentive to local religious sensibilities), it did suggest Sunday's baiting of local churches, with headlines like "Sham Religion"; "What Ails Church"; "Church People, Get Right With God"; "Devil Likes a Church Scrap"; "Modern Prayer Meetings a Farce"; "Preachers Chase Fads Instead of Souls"; and "Bogus Christians Denounced."[18] A *Capital* reader might have surmised that Sunday was dissatisfied with Des Moines religion, even if the revival was a homecoming.

Sunday's emphasis on personal conversion, his moralism, and his support for a literal interpretation of the Bible meant that he fit well into the emerging fundamentalist movement.

THE DENOMINATIONAL CONTEXT

Northern Presbyterian and Northern Baptist national conventions in Des Moines in the early twenties proved to be ground zero in the culture war.

16. DMT, Nov. 28, 1914; Dec. 3, 1914.
17. DMT, Dec. 23, 1914; Firstenberger, *In Rare Form*, 122.
18. *Des Moines Capital*, Nov. 4, 7, 10, 14, 18, 19, 1914; Dec. 2. On November 5, a *Capital* editorial offered this assessment: "Everybody wants to hear Billy—all those, at least, who love the sight of power. The matter of religion may be beside the question."

In both denominations, fundamentalists were outmaneuvered by the more irenic rhetoric of moderates and progressives. Much more so for Iowa Baptists than Iowa Presbyterians, this would result in schism, with fundamentalists leaving the mainline and forming new associations.

At the 1921 national convention of the Northern Baptist Convention in Des Moines, fundamentalists proposed imposing a creed on the denomination. They hoped to offer a "Des Moines Confession," although it never actually came to the floor. That initiative was outmaneuvered and a moderate was elected president—and not just a moderate, but the first woman to serve as leader of a major Protestant denomination: Helen Barrett Montgomery,[19] the warmly pious leader of the Women's Missionary Society.[20]

The Northern Presbyterian General Assembly in Des Moines in 1922 produced a similar outcome.[21] The next year, fundamentalists hoped to install William Jennings Bryan as moderator. Bryan, after a long political career as a populist and progressive politician, had come to believe that liberal tendencies in German theology, and belief in the Darwinian theory of evolution were responsible for World War I. As a pacifist—who had been fired by Woodrow Wilson as secretary of state for opposing US entanglement in the war—Bryan saw modernism as akin to nihilism. Of course, the denouement of his career, the Scopes Trial, was several years in the future.[22]

Perhaps it was only that most Northern Presbyterians were Republicans, but the lifelong Democrat Bryan did not win the post of moderator. Since he was a national figure, to save face the General Assembly elected him to the newly created position of vice moderator.[23] But the message

---

19. Presidential Address," *Annual of the Northern Baptist Convention*, v. 15, 38–39; Hill, *World Their Household*, 175, 181–90. For an intriguing study of the fundamentalist-liberal contestation over the concept of piety, see Ostrander, "Practice of Prayer in a Modern Age."

20. DMT, Jun. 20, 21, 1921; *Annual of the Northern Baptist Convention*, v. 14, 23, 55–60, 100–102; Bartlett, *History of Baptist Separatism*, 13; Stowell, *History of the General Association of Regular Baptist Churches*, 21–22.
On the Des Moines Confession, see Bauder and Delnay, *One in Hope and Doctrine*, 100–101. The text of the confession can be found in Mould, "Conflict between the Modernists and the Fundamentalists," Appendix 6, 290–91.

21. Longfield, *Presbyterian Controversy*.

22. Levine, *Defender of the Faith*, 282–86; Kazin, *Godly Hero*, 9, 277; Longfield, *Presbyterian Controversy*, 62–68.

23. Longfield, *Presbyterian Controversy*, 73–75; Kazin, *Godly Hero*, 276–77.
Bryan was not the only political figure to seek denominational office. In 1884, US

was clear: the majority was uninterested in joining the crusade against modernism.[24] While there was a schism, few Iowans left for the Orthodox Presbyterian Church.[25]

THE BAPTIST BIBLE UNION'S BID FOR POWER

While national convention battles provide context, a better way to examine the fundamentalist scene in Iowa in the twenties is to review the Baptist Bible Union takeover of Des Moines University and its subsequent spectacular collapse.[26] In reaction to their failure to capture the Northern Baptist Convention, and blaming a slightly more moderate faction,[27] in 1924 militant fundamentalists formed the Baptist Bible Union and began a strategy of withholding financial support from the denomination.

As the BBU started to make inroads within the Iowa Baptist Convention, the state Baptist institution of higher education, Des Moines University, was teetering financially.[28] The fact that the BBU had called for a financial boycott of the institution until it was purged of modernist influences factored in, but the school's fiscal woes were chronic. At the crucial Iowa convention in 1926, when the university proposed merging with the financially viable Disciples-backed Drake University across the Des Moines River, moderates and fundamentalists locked arms in denominational solidarity to reject the merger.[29] This did not pay the bills.

Supreme Court Justice Samuel Freeman Miller, of Keokuk, was elected president of the national conference of the Unitarian Church. Ross, *Justice of Shattered Dreams*, 239.

24. Longfield, *Presbyterian Controversy*, 227–30.

25. Of the three Iowa OPC churches listed in the national directory, only one seems to have been organized in the thirties, in Waterloo; it is now in Cedar Falls ("About" [Covenant Presbyterian Church]). Longfield emphasizes the theological differences between a Pietist like Bryan, who came out of the Cumberland Presbyterian tradition, and a dogmatist like J. Gresham Machen, for whom correct doctrine was paramount.

26. May, "Des Moines University and T. T. Shields," is still a reliable guide, but see also my "'Serious Nature of the Division." My article "Culture War Gets Physical" muses on the ongoing political ramifications of fundamentalist tendencies in Iowa.

27. Hummel, *Rise and Fall of Dispensationalism*, 162.

28. The Northern Baptists had consolidated their colleges in the state in 1906. Burlington Collegiate Institute (1852–1901) did not last until then; the Central College (1865–1906) campus in Pella became Reformed, reflecting Pella's natural demographics. Cedar Valley Seminary (1863–1906) and Sac City Institute (1894–1906) were also folded into what became Des Moines University. Abernethy, *History of Iowa Baptist Schools*; Brackney, *Congregation and Campus*, 227–29.

29. DMR, Oct. 20, 22, 1926; *Waterloo Evening Courier*, Oct. 22, 1926. One of the

Rev. H. O. Meyer of Calvary Baptist Church of Des Moines and Des Moines layman Frank Foulkes conceived a plan: the Baptist Bible Union should take over the struggling institution. It would remain Baptist, and the BBU would acquire an institutional presence. The upshot was, after a purge of faculty members unwilling to sign a loyalty oath to fundamentalism, the Union had its beachhead in academia. (As long as the pledge was signed, a certain flexibility in theological expression was allowed: when the football coach was asked if he had been saved, he replied, "Sure, lots of times."[30] That this did not quite square with the Calvinist doctrine of irresistible grace was apparently insufficient grounds to bar the coach from the performance of his duties.)

The three titans of Baptist fundamentalism converged on Des Moines to christen their new possession. Biographical sketches seem in order for the triumvirate assembling in the chapel of Des Moines University in October 1927, the last time they would share a stage.[31] Each had a slightly different ecclesiastical strategy: Frank Norris of Ft. Worth would become known for Baptist separatism,[32] T. T. Shields of Toronto for purity at all costs,[33] and William Bell Riley of Minneapolis for a regional strategy, and also for a pan-denominational fundamentalism that might marginalize Baptist purity.[34]

They also had differing primary prejudices: Shields, in his anti-Catholicism, would break with Norris in the forties over Norris's visit to the pope to promote anti-Communism; Riley (who would abandon the DMU project when he believed reports about the marital infidelity of Shields)[35] embraced anti-Semitism. (This may help explain why his protege Billy Graham would, decades later, listen to Richard Nixon's

---

most successful departments, pharmacy, survived the school's demise, and after operating independently for about a decade, did merge with Drake University.

30. Wiggins, *Iowa Tragedy*, 73.

31. May, "Des Moines University and T. T. Shields," 206.

32. Barry Hankins, *God's Rascal*; Moody, "Conversion of J. Frank Norris."

33. Shields is profiled in Russell, *Voices of American Fundamentalists*, and Lippy, *Twentieth Century Shapers*, 393–402.

34. Trollinger, *God's Empire*. On Riley's anti-communism, see Zubovich, *Before the Religious Right*, 51.

35. In a letter from Riley to George Mould, April 22, 1940, he also stated that he "could no longer approve the character and methods of T. T. Shields and J. Frank Norris." Mould, 260–69. On the question of separatism dividing Riley and Shields, see Delnay, *History of the Baptist Bible Union*, 149–50, and Bauder, "Biography of O. W. Van Orsdahl," 46–47.

anti-Semitic rants without protest.) But two of the three withdrew from active involvement before the denouement: Norris, distracted by a murder trial in which he was the defendant,[36] and Riley, disillusioned with Shields, would let Shields play out the drama—or melodrama.

Baptist Bible Union control of Des Moines University lasted only two years. It is likely the only institution of higher learning in the United States to have been permanently closed by a student riot.

Personality clashes, accusations of adultery directed at Shields, dueling Canadian and American patriotisms, the suspicion that Shields aide Edith Rebman was spying on everyone on campus, and accusations by Shields that the administration was insufficiently vigilant in rooting out modernist heresy all boiled over in a tumultuous board of trustees meeting in May 1929. Shields's opponents (fundamentalists all) overplayed their hand, accusing Shields and Rebman of having an adulterous affair but without sufficient evidence. When Shields won a vote of confidence from the board, he characteristically also overplayed his hand, firing all the faculty and staff.

News of this coup outraged the students, who besieged the building where the trustees were meeting with rocks and rotten eggs. The police were conveniently tardy. The resulting bitterness and bad publicity, along with the fact that now the school had no staff, and that the debt remained an insoluble problem, all combined to make a return to academic business as usual impossible. The grand experiment of a Baptist fundamentalist university lay in shambles, with no modernist in sight to shoulder the blame.

Iowa Baptists had at least one fundamentalist president in the thirties, Richard Clearwaters,[37] but many of the Iowa Baptist churches involved in the Baptist Bible Union seceded in the thirties and joined the newly formed General Association of Regular Baptists, especially in a belt from Waterloo to south of Des Moines. The GARB did develop a healthy suspicion of charismatic pastors, probably as a reaction to the Des Moines University debacle.[38] Other congregations, such as Calvary in Des Moines, remained within the Northern (now American) Baptist fold, perhaps chastened by the bitterness of the Des Moines University experience.[39]

---

36. Stokes, *Shooting Salvationist*. It being Texas, with a self-defense argument and the only other witness being dead, Norris was acquitted.

37. Bendroth, *Good and Mad*, 81.

38. Whiteman, "General Assembly of Regular Baptist Churches," 143.

39. Douglas, "'Serious Nature of the Division,'" 43–44.

FUNDAMENTALISM AND FICTION

Davenport novelist Elizabeth Knauss was championed by William Bell Riley, and she reflected his superdenominational fundamentalist and anti-Semitic perspectives in her two novels.[40] Neither literary effort recommends itself for the canon; the first, *The Conflict,* is a sedate romance that argues against modernism and for a post-denominational alliance of fundamentalist churches; the second is an attempt at a thriller with the premise that a Bolshevik takeover of the country is imminent and being abetted by religious modernists. Spoiler alert: late in the book, the virulently anti-Semitic (and fake) *The Protocols of the Elders of Zion* is evoked as evidence for the pending Communist coup.

Joel Carpenter's observation that fundamentalism was not ready for prime time[41] seems apt in Knauss's case. As he also pointed out, the retreat into quietism by the larger movement turned out to be strategic. And for those with ambitions within the fundamentalist movement, Iowa was often just a way station.

IOWA CONNECTIONS TO THE FUNDAMENTALIST UPSURGE

During her short-lived marriage in the forties, future charismatic faith-healing megastar Kathryn Kuhlman shared preaching duties at Mason City's Radio Chapel with her husband, who had just divorced his previous wife. The optics of that situation needed editing for one with ambitions to make the big time in evangelistic circles. Kuhlman was up to the challenge.[42]

Herbert W. Armstrong was born in Des Moines in 1892 and raised in the First Friends Church.[43] He achieved success after moving to the

---

40. Knauss, *Conflict*; Knauss, *Rising Tide*; Wenger, *Social Thought in American Fundamentalism*, 278; *Berkeley Daily Gazette*, Dec. 9, 1932; *Davenport Democrat and Leader*, Dec. 9, 1927. In November 1931 Knauss lectured in New England; in 1932 she started editing on a projected series of twelve pamphlets on Communism, the first being *Communism of Today in Light of the Past Experiments* by Gleason Archer (in which the French utopian Fourier's name is misspelled as "Fournier.")

41. Carpenter, *Revive Us Again*, xi-xiv.

42. Artman, *Miracle Lady*, 40-44.

43. Lippy, *Twentieth-Century Shapers of American Popular Religion*, 9-14; Armstrong, *United States and Britain in Biblical Prophecy*; Lupo, "Advancing the Time of the End"; Sumner, *Armstrongism*; Hopkins, *Armstrong Empire*; Walker, *World in Flames*.

West Coast and parlaying radio evangelism into the media-based Worldwide Church of God, which stressed premillennialism combined with British Israelism, the belief that Britons were the lost tribes of Israel. In Armstrong's case, this seemed more cockamamie than virulently racist, as the Christian Identity movement would develop it. But undertones could be detected. Remarkably, after Armstrong's death, the Worldwide Church of God swung back to a more traditional evangelicalism.[44]

Thomas Wyatt, born and raised in Jasper County, moved through Methodism and to the West Coast, establishing a healing ministry he called Wings of Faith.[45]

Healing evangelist Maria Woodworth-Etter brought repeated revivals to the Quad Cities, Sioux City, Sidney, Grand River, Des Moines, Muscatine, and Ottumwa. In Ottumwa in 1922 a young boy died of lockjaw when his parents eschewed medical help in favor of Woodworth-Etter's.[46]

Robert Schuller, still another Iowan who succeeded in conservative religion in California, we will discuss in the next chapter. While conservative in theology, he was better known for his devotion to positive thinking, or New Thought.

In 1922, the Cedar Falls Bible Conference began its annual gatherings at Riverview Park. The conference had its roots in the Evangelical Association, a German Methodist predecessor to the United Methodist Church. Attendance peaked in 1946 at 11,000.[47]

While the fundamentalist movement had interdenominational and sometimes post-denominational dimensions, there was also usually a denominational bending. Paul Burgdoff was a small-town Iowa minister who attempted to recall the Lutheran Church-Missouri Synod to true confessionalism via fundamentalism.[48] But Burgdoff was isolated from denominational power. His goal would be unmet until it was fused with a broader, more political message in the seventies. Even after the 1976 purge of moderates, though, the Missouri Synod brand of conservatism still bore a more European tint, simultaneously less provincial and more isolated.

---

44. Nichols and Mather, *Discovering the Plain Truth*.

45. Balmer, *Encyclopedia of Evangelicalism*, 645–46; Miller, *Grappling With Destiny*.

46. Warner, *Woman Evangelist*, 152, 264–66, 275–77; Hastie, *History of the West District Central Council*, 75–84.

47. *Waterloo Courier*, Jun. 22, 2000; Jul. 12, 29, 2001; *Riverview Remembers*.

48. Burkee, *Power, Politics, and the Missouri Synod*.

THE INCREASING FUSION OF THEOLOGY AND POLITICS

As fundamentalism began to emerge from its self-imposed shell after World War II, it took on a more political tone that matched the times. Australian transplant Frederick Schwarz first surfaced as an anti-Communist advocate in the United States in 1953, apparently at the invitation of Waterloo pastor W. E. Pietsch. His trip abroad was instigated by a 1950 visit to Australia from T. T. Shields, of Des Moines University notoriety, and Carl McIntyre, who had led a right-wing split from the fundamentalist Orthodox Presbyterian Church, accusing it of being insufficiently anti-Communist.[49] While in Waterloo, Schwarz found Walnut Street Baptist Church (affiliated with the GARB), and radio station KXEL congenial.[50] He founded the Christian Anti-Communism Crusade in Waterloo, and although he soon moved its headquarters to sunnier climes in Southern California, his associate Pietsch maintained a branch office in Waterloo.[51]

From such roots can be traced right-wing politicians like Chuck Grassley, a member of The Family,[52] who is also a member of the GARB congregation in New Hartford, and support for his immediate predecessor in the congressional district, the less religious but infamously parsimonious thirteen-term Congressman H. R. Gross,[53] who thrived in the conservative atmosphere of east-central Iowa that such fundamentalism produced or reproduced.

Such connections depended on the fact that fundamentalism would reemerge as a political force and as a more visible presence on the religious landscape later in the century. Chapter 23 will explore that phenomenon as it both adapted to and critiqued American society in the seventies.

---

49. Clabaugh, *Thunder on the Right*, 88, 89; Thayer, *Farther Shores of Politics*, 246–56; Edwards, *Missionary for Freedom: The Life and Times of Walter Judd*, 270–71.

50. W. E. Pietsch, preface to Schwarz, *Heart, Mind, and Soul of Communism*; Clabaugh, *Thunder on the Right*, 107; *Waterloo Courier*, May 29, 1953; DMT, Mar. 27, 1954.
The Bible Presbyterian Church is tiny and in 2021 did not list any Iowa churches in its directory.

51. Schwarz, *Beating the Unbeatable Foe*, 4, 41–42, 104–7; Walker, *Christian Fright Peddlers*, chapter 3. Schwarz was at first an ally and then a rival of the John Birch Society. Dallek, *Birchers*, 53, 63, 99.

52. Sharlet, *Family*, 18, 54, 281; Garrison, "2021 National Prayer Breakfast."

53. Kaufmann, "H. R. Gross." Gross's motto was, "There is always free cheese in a mousetrap." (Dennominationally, Gross was a Presbyterian.) Gross got his start in the Farmers' Holiday Association of the thirties, aiding Church of Christ minister Milo Reno in the militant blockades by farmers seeking fair prices for their products.

Any chapter-long sketch of fundamentalism necessarily leaves out much of the complexity of Iowa religion at the time. The Holiness movement and the Pentecostal movement had close affinities with fundamentalism and provided some synergy. Given the kinetic potential, when fundamentalism started rolling again, the effect of the snowball is surprising only because of the relative dormancy for decades.

In Jane Smiley's Iowa family trilogy, set in the fictional town of Denby (probably in Marshall County, judging from distances to the real towns mentioned), the Langdon family moves temporarily during the twenties from their inherited bland Methodism to a fiery Pentecostalism. But when they leave that church they do not return to Methodism, and, significantly, religion is not a topic of the century-spanning trilogy again until volume three.[54]

Certainly fundamentalism cannot be blamed for the "religious depression" of the thirties, but the trend hit conservative and liberal churches alike, and the restlessness provided fertile ground for less orthodox religious alternatives.

---

54. Smiley, *Some Luck*, 66–67, 92–96, 132, 141, 171–74. The other volumes of the trilogy are *Early Warning* (2015) and *Golden Age* (2015).

CHAPTER 19

Alternative Counter-Narratives

"[M]ost important I shall be seeking an opportunity to find the religious keynote of the new age."

—Henry A. Wallace, 1931[1]

"The Century of Progress has turned to ashes in our mouths. Is it possible that the world is finally ready for the realization of the teachings of Jesus, the appreciation of the teachings of the Sermon on the Mount, the bringing of the kingdom of heaven to earth?"

—Henry A. Wallace, 1934[2]

"[I] . . . had a reputation for eccentricity in the West which began when I was five years old, and it was like finding my home again [in Kashmir] after a long exile to be where [I] was understood. The things for which I had been considered unconventional and queer in the West were regarded as piety in India, and from one end of the country to the other I was received by people of all classes with a devout kind of love."

—Nilla Cram Cook

---

1. Quoted in White and Maze, *Henry A. Wallace*, 23–24, 317.
2. Wallace, *Statesmanship and Religion*, 71.

The People Are Kind

"Iowa comes here and goes crazy."

—WALTER DURANTY, EXPLAINING THE PROLIFERATION OF RELIGIOUS SECTS IN SOUTHERN CALIFORNIA[3]

JUST AS FUNDAMENTALISM ENGAGED American culture by feeding on suspicion of elites that was arguably democratic while embracing a pessimism about the future that seemed confirmed by rural declension and world war, so too, more exotic explanations of the universe, even when they were or claimed to be Asian in origin, usually adapted to the American vernacular and mood.

Much in Iowa's collective character made it susceptible to blandishments of smooth talkers like Professor Harold Hill and his Think Method, the invention of Mason City-born playwright Meredith Willson.[4] (Skeptics would suggest that the entire religious enterprise deserves such scrutiny.) Small-town values like self-reliance and natural curiosity about the larger world, nourished by missionary narratives, could combine in seemingly endless exciting arguments for a superior alternative to an increasingly bland master narrative about God blessing America.

In his combination of scientific rigor, boundless curiosity, naivete in evaluating character, and a heritage of employing religion for good, no Iowan exceeded Henry A. Wallace in his experimentations with varieties of religion—while keeping one foot firmly planted in mainstream Protestantism.

In exploring alternative religions, interrogating why they are outside the norms is a fruitful line of questioning. Geographical, class, and philosophical differences may play a part. Asian religions were foreign by definition. While Holiness and Pentecostal enthusiasms challenged middle-class norms from below, such beliefs as Theosophy and Christian Science tended to appeal to upper classes less confined by middle-class norms.

Many groups also claimed a scientific basis for their beliefs, which had a certain cache in secularizing America. We need not doubt the sincerity of a scientific experimenter like Henry A. Wallace in his quixotic search for truth, but mere mortals might feel incomprehension at the

---

3. Quoted in Jenkins, *Mystics and Messiahs*, 93.

4. Willson's religious background was solidly mainstream Protestant. He endowed a fellowship wing of the Mason City Congregational Church after making it as a playwright. Skipper, *Meredith Willson*, 139–40.

claims of Alfred Lawson and reserve judgment about the contested scientific claims of Transcendental Meditation.

Escape from Iowa was a theme featured in life stories of positive thinker Robert Schuller and yoga innovator Pierre Bernard, but this tendency was balanced by new religions finding their home in Iowa, notably Lawsonomy and Transcendental Meditation. Sometimes God is found in exploration; sometimes God is found nearby. And for all of this chapter's subjects, God is to be found within.

RELIGION, MENTAL ILLNESS, AND THE QUESTION OF THE FRINGE

Two more aspects to factor in when discussing alternative religions include the intersection of religion and mental illness, and the overarching question of what constitutes a religious fringe.

Street corner preaching has a long history. Consider this item from the 1870 Prairie City *Gleaner and Herald*: "A crazy preacher appeared in our streets last Sunday, and harangued a crowd in front of the Post Office. He is a traveling missionary for a very vague kind of a religion of his own. He remarked that Geo. Washington, George Francis Train, and his (the speaker's) father were about the three greatest men this country ever saw—which is rather hard on Geo. Washington."[5]

As I worked on this book in 2015, a preacher appeared daily, for at least a week, on the steps of what some time ago had been the Mondamin Avenue Church of Christ in the near northside neighborhood of Des Moines (that building had several more congregational iterations before its abandonment). While I was a block away, his lung power was considerable, his persuasive powers less so. The simple message of repentance fell on deaf ears, although no one called the police, either.

Arguably the most bizarre religious episode in Iowa was the possession and exorcism of a Catholic woman in Earling in 1928. She had been a victim of incest and sexual and psychological abuse. The one account we have relies on the testimony of the exorcist;[6] when diocesan historian Fr. Steven Avella recently tried to examine the case's Vatican files, they were still unavailable.[7] While the psychological diagnosis of dissociation

---

5. Jun. 11, 1870. (George Francis Train was a railroad entrepreneur.)
6. Vogl, *Begone Satan!*
7. Avella, *Catholic Church in Southwest Iowa*, 129–30.

is helpful in explaining this episode, historians should withhold judgment without a fuller record.

The mental disorder need not be so extreme to be remarkable. With equal parts affection and irritation, a parish priest in Tama County recalled "the most eccentric person in 100 years of parish history":

> Jennie Tory[8] is a recluse . . . [who] spent more time at church than at home. An inveterate reader of devotional literature, she carried her books and personal effects in a large tin pail that was always at her side together with her crude single crutch. Beside the warm church radiator she sat all day, breaking the monotony by ringing the angelus bell and going about as a self-appointed door-keeper, sacristan, and floral arranger. One might find the altar adorned with a weird assortment of stuffed birds, twigs, herbs, and other horticultural oddities that pleased her peculiar aesthetic taste. Even the most vigorous pleadings of the pastor could never dissuade her from carrying out her self-styled duties as a deaconess . . .
>
> The coming of the electric bell in 1956 marked the end of the Jennie era. She became too feeble to care for herself and since that time has lived in a Nursing Home . . .

The parishioner's need to have a part in the common ritual seems important, and her replacement by an electric bell symbolic of the redundancy caused by mechanization. The pastor's routine was doubtless smoothed but at what cost to an anguished parishioner?

Of course, "fringe religion" was not an exclusively twentieth-century phenomenon. Frontier figures such as Abner Kneeland and the prophet Mathias certainly worked beyond the ken of the average Iowan, and many found Mormon doctrine and practice bewildering and some Mormon offshoots—say the Baheemyites—even more bizarre. What constitutes the religious fringe, and how that changes over time, are issues that this chapter will attempt to address.[9] Of course, this is a matter of public perception; all the chapter's subjects would argue for their place within the universe of normality.

---

8. She was taunted by neighborhood children with the cry "Jennie Tory Jennie Towquay," which I have been reliably informed is from the Latin mass benediction, "Genitori Genitoque," or "The Father and the Son." Email communication from Fr. David Polich, Nov. 17, 2021.

9. Useful books include McCloud, *Making the American Religious Fringe*; Bednarowski, *New Religions and the Theological Imagination*; Jenkins; and Albanese, *A Republic of Mind and Spirit*.

ASIAN RELIGIONS INTRODUCED

Interest in East Asian religions was evident in the state by the 1890s. Theosophy, a Westernized brand of Hinduism, had adherents in Davenport and Dubuque by then.[10] Burcham Harding, a lecturer for the Theosophical Society in America, spoke in Des Moines in 1897.[11] At least by 1919, Theosophists had an office in downtown Des Moines. While its downtown location shifted, an office existed at least until 1928, when the headline "Theosophist to Talk Here" promoted a lecture by Nina Pickett.[12]

The Hindu leader Vivekananda, after his combative but successful appearance at the World Parliament of Religions of 1893, included several Iowa stops on his subsequent tour. The Parliament's Christian sponsors had sought to show, in summary, how all the best tendencies of world religions pointed to Christ. Not surprisingly, representatives of non-Christian religions demurred. "Brethren all, yet they indulged in sharp words," reported the *Davenport Democrat* regarding the refusal to capitulate to Christianity.[13] Surprisingly, among Vivekananda's defenders was John Keane, later Archbishop of Dubuque.[14]

Vivekananda's Des Moines visit was sponsored by Rev. Harvey O. Breeden of the Central Church of Christ, a leader of progressive thought in the city.[15] Breeden probably attended the Parliament when Swami Vivekananda made what the Davenport paper called "a savage attack on Christian nations;" or what we might better call an anti-imperialist critique of early Prosperity Gospel theology:

> We who have come here from the east have sat here day after day and have been told in a patronizing way that we ought to accept Christianity because Christian nations are the most

---

10. Ben-Zvi, *Susan Glaspell*, 70; Cook, "What Religion Means to Me," 72; "Adams, Mary Newbury (or Newberry)," BDI, 4. According to the *Hand Book of Iowa*, (p. 110), there were two chapters and twenty members in the state in 1893.

11. *Des Moines Leader*, Mar. 9, 1897.

12. DMT, Sep. 20, 1928. According to city directories, the Theosophical Society had offices in various downtown Des Moines locations from at least 1920 to 1928.
A good short guide is in Miller, *America's Alternative Religions*, 315–24.

13. *Davenport Democrat*, Sep. 29, 1893.

14. Burg, *Chicago's White City of 1893*, 327; Ahern, *Life of John J. Keane*, 144–47, 169.

15. Coffman, *Christian Century and the Rise of the Protestant Mainline*, 16–17; deGroot, *Central of Des Moines*, 63–83; Burke, *Swami Vivekananda in the West*, 198–215; Stavig, *Western Admirers of Ramakrishna*, 300–303. Central Church of Christ merged with the University Place Christian Church to form First Christian Church.

prosperous. We look about us and see England as the most prosperous Christian nation in the world, with her foot on the neck of 350,000,000 Asiatics. We look back into history and see that the prosperity of Christian Europe began with Spain. Spain's prosperity began with the invasion of Mexico. Christianity wins its prosperity by cutting the throats of its fellow men. At such a price the Hindoo will not have prosperity.[16]

While the *Democrat* described Vivekananda as cantankerous, the adjective *incisive* might also be apt.

Breeden, the most active Protestant minister in Des Moines during the nineties, founded the influential Prairie Club and ran a lecture series. From the Parliament speakers, he also obtained for his lectures the Greek Orthodox Dionysius Latos, archbishop of Zante (decades before Des Moines had an Orthodox congregation).[17]

All three Des Moines dailies gave prominent coverage to Vivekananda's weeklong visit. The December 3 *Register* is representative:

> It has done no harm to Christianity to have some of its weaknesses of so-called Christians pointed out as they have been so clearly and mercilessly during the past week by Swami Vivekananda . . . But it was also woe to any man who undertook to combat the monk on his own ground . . . His replies came like flashes of lightning, and the venturesome questioner was sure to be impaled on the Indian's shining intellectual lance . . . but . . . he said nothing unkind . . . Vivekananda and his cause found a place in the hearts of all true Christians. It is to the credit of Dr. Breeden that, knowing what he would say, he brought him here to address the members of his congregation . . .
>
> Another effect of the Eastern influence will be, or at least ought to be, to make us treat our dumb animals better . . .
>
> His visit to Des Moines, where he became at once the chief subject of discussion in intellectual circles has had a permanent good effect in broadening the views of a great many people, and compelling them, by force of his intelligence and character, to see things from a different standpoint.[18]

---

16. *Davenport Democrat*, Sep. 29, 1893.

17. Houghton, *Neely's History of the Parliament of Religions,* 140; deGroot, *Central of Des Moines,* 73. Henry George and Julia Ward Howe rounded out the lecture series ticket for the year. On Breeden, see Putz, "Building a City on a Hill."

18. Cf. Burke, *Swami Vivekananda in the West,* 210–14.

Alternative Counter-Narratives

As Vivekananda was leaving town, the Unitarian Church hosted B. B. Nagarkar of Mumbai, of the Brahmo-Samaj movement. This movement, arguably post-Hindu, had links with Unitarian missionaries and attempted to make Hinduism monotheistic—and palatable to colonial masters.[19] Vivekananda and Nagarkar disagreed on many counts. While the *Register* was hearty in its praise of Vivekananda, it also looked forward to a representative of "the more advanced class." But aside from a perfunctory notice among weekly church announcements, the local press did not cover Nagarkar's visit, having perhaps had its quota of Eastern religion. About the timing of Nagarkar's visit fresh on the heels of Vivekananda's, a skeptic might wonder if a rivalry existed between Breeden's popular lecture series and the Unitarians.[20]

The rivalry underlying the competing visits of Vivekananda and Nagarkar to Des Moines is invisible to the casual observer. But Vivekananda continues to be resented for his prominence at the parliament.[21] Indian religion was at least as complicated as Iowa religion.

Even more interesting than Vivekananda's lectures in Des Moines and Iowa City is his chance encounter on the train. He describes the person—and perhaps he had as little understanding of the Midwest as his hosts at Chicago had of India—as a "Presbyterian cowboy." This gregarious Iowan apparently held cognitively dissonant positions on theology. He confidently told Vivekananda that anyone not believing in Jesus would go to hell but also affirmed his belief in reincarnation.[22] (I have been unable to find this doctrine anywhere in the Westminster Confession.) This combination of clinging to ancient truths handed down with openness to alternative visions of ultimate reality seems American—and perhaps Indian as well. Vivekananda appreciated the visit.

Two other early Iowa connections to Asian religion deserve mention. The second convention of the "International" Metaphysical League,

---

19. Doniger, *Hindus*, 597, 639; Barrows, *World's Parliament of Religions*, 767–79.

20. DMR, Dec. 3, 1893.

21. Chattopadhaya's book is an attempt to argue that Vivekananda's presence is overrepresented. His argument that Dharmapala was equally important, for example, seems a stretch, not because of his prominence but because the Sri Lankan Buddhist was neither Indian nor Hindu. Jains at the centennial conference in 1993 also felt this resentment; their pamphlet *We Were There as Well* is described in Braybrooke, "Pan-Asian Participation." Dharmapala did visit Iowa in 1896 and 1897, speaking in Davenport, Iowa City, and Des Moines. Sangharakshita, *Anagarika Dharmapala*, 72.

22. Burke, *Swami Vivekananda in the West*, 198–99.

held in New York in 1900, had George Herron of Iowa College speaking on "The Nature of Power."[23]

The American popularizer of yoga, Pierre Bernard, was born with the somewhat less prepossessing name of Perry Baker in Leon, Iowa, in 1876, and grew up in Humeston. He also spent time with relatives in Lamoni, becoming acquainted with the Reorganized Church of Latter-day Saints.[24] But if an Iowa boy taking the name Pierre Bernard seemed pretentious, he also called himself, with no lack of confidence, "Oom the Omnipotent."[25] As Bernard came onto the national spiritual scene at the turn of the century, dominant alternative groups like the Theosophists and Vivekananda's Vedanta Society were leery of hatha yoga as a physical exercise, preferring more cerebral alternatives.[26] But Bernard could make complex realities seem simple. A master of reinvention, he floated through early twentieth-century upper-class America, blithely pontificating on universal spiritual themes.

HOMEGROWN RELIGIOUS INNOVATION: D. D. PALMER AND CHIROPRACTIC

Not all heterodox religious beliefs and practices came from Asia. Canadian-born D. D. Palmer moved to Iowa as a young man, opening up a grocery store in What Cheer and starting a mail-order operation selling raspberries, among other jobs, selling goldfish from a wheelbarrow being the most eccentric. He operated a clinic for "magnetic healing" in Burlington in the 1880s; after moving to Davenport, Palmer opened the Palmer College of Chiropractic in 1897, introducing a new approach to health that also had religious undertones unlikely to meet orthodoxy tests. Palmer envisioned his healing as halfway between New Thought, which was all about mind, and medicine, which admitted only the physical.[27]

While D. D. Palmer and his son and successor B. J. Palmer became bitter rivals, they shared a skepticism towards Christianity. For D. D., chiropractic was a discovery within the broader world of mesmerism,

---

23. Meyer, *Positive Thinkers*, 35.

24. Love, *Great Oom*, 9–11, 13. One need look no further than the local library or recreation center to document the widespread acceptance of yoga as exercise.

25. Albanese, 362–66.

26. Love, *Great Oom*, 70–74.

27. Albanese, 405–9; Folk, *Religion of Chiropractic*, 50–70; Moore, *Chiropractic in America*, 11, 19, 45–47, 50–54.

spiritualism, Theosophy, and energy patterns that could be deciphered and controlled. His son was more materialistic, seeing chiropractic as a science that needed no metaphysical explanation; he was even less cautious about offending Christian sensibilities.[28] But as chiropractic moved in the twentieth century from the fringes to acceptance, the Christian Chiropractors Association, also founded in Davenport, worked to drop the early hostility to organized religion.[29]

NEW THOUGHT

Overlapping with Theosophy and kindred movements, New Thought, with more indigenous roots in Transcendentalism, proclaimed an appealing message to many Americans: if you think it, you can do it. This belief in mind over matter did not necessarily require a religious infrastructure, but organizations were forthcoming.[30]

The connections between Eastern thought and New Thought were clearest in the I Am movement.[31] This "I Am" derived from Sanskrit, not Hebrew. The Iowa connection is also clear; Edna Wheeler Ballard was born in Burlington in 1886 and cofounded the movement along with her husband Guy Ballard.[32] The "I Am" movement peaked in the 1930s, with the Ballards attracting thousands. Guy Ballard's death in 1939 was untimely, in that he had not expected to die at all but to "ascend." Indictments for fraud and a decade of appeals further dimmed the movement's prospects.[33]

Christian Science was an extreme form of New Thought, positing that mind was all and the physical world was illusory, but it caught on. In 1890, a Christian Science advocate named Rebecca Morrison was "arrested for disorderly conduct and committed for one day" while visiting McGregor. An unsympathetic newspaper opined that Morrison "is

---

28. Moore, *Chiropractic in America*, 102; Albanese, 405–9.

29. Brown, "Chiropractic and Christianity"; Hultgren, *Against All Odds . . . But God*; Moore, *Chiropractic in America*, 100–103.

30. Braden, *Spirits in Rebellion*, 9–13.

31. On I Am's blending of the two, see Albanese, 467–71.

32. Bowden, "Ballard, Edna Wheeler," *Dictionary of American Religious Biography*, 2d ed., 29–30; Albanese, *Republic of Mind and Spirit*, 467–70.

33. Campbell, *Ancient Wisdom Revived*, 161–63.

insane on the issue of Christian science, having attended their meetings for quite some time."[34]

By 1889, Christian Scientists were gathering in Des Moines and Cedar Rapids. Currently there are also congregations in Cedar Falls and Davenport.[35]

An early practitioner of Christian Science, Mary Collson was a native Iowan, born and raised in the Unitarian stronghold of Humboldt. For a time she was part of the "Prophetic Sisterhood" of women Unitarian ministers (see chapter 10). But the studious Collson was a poor fit for the small-town Ida Grove congregation and suffered a nervous breakdown. After recovering, she ministered at Cherokee and Washta before moving on, working as a social worker at Hull House, eventually finding healing in the doctrines of Christian Science:

> I accepted Christian Science through the will to believe and not [through] the exercise of reason . . . I submerged myself in [its teachings] in order to escape from my world, which had become too difficult a proposition for me.[36]

Collson, with a liberal Unitarian background and experience in cosmopolitan Chicago, was not entirely at home with strict adherence to Mary Baker Eddy's precepts. She ultimately rejected Christian Science but could not find a publisher for her book explaining why.[37]

Divine Science was a similar early New Thought group with Iowa connections. In the 1880s, William McKendree Brown moved from Iowa to Denver to help merge the Denver and San Francisco streams of the young movement. As late as 1938, the group was active in Cedar Rapids.[38]

Most of New Thought was less sectarian but vaguer. Some common aspects can be described.[39] With its emphasis on looking inward, New Thought tended towards individualism. Followers could pull themselves up by their own mental bootstraps. This meant that New Thought was often conservative—but not always. For example, in books with titles like *Handles of Power* and *Power to Become*, Iowa City Methodist minister

---

34. Colfax, *Weekly Clipper*, Feb. 8, 1890.
35. "Welcome to First Church of Christ, Scientist."
36. Tucker, *Prophetic Sisterhood*, 67.
37. Tucker, *Prophetic Sisterhood*, 153–67.
38. Melton, *Encyclopedia of American Religions*, 244; Curtis, *Muslims of the Heartland*, 146–47.
39. A couple of present-day critiques of the movement are Crookford, "How 'Positivity' Can Lead to Conspiratorial Thinking'" and Ehrenreich, *Bright Sided*.

Alternative Counter-Narratives

Lewis L. Dunnington provided a progressive version of positive thinking, one endorsed by social evangelist Kirby Page.[40]

Another progressive proponent of New Thought was Glenn Clark, who grew up in Des Moines and graduated from Grinnell College. He was a Presbyterian elder and Congregationalist Sunday School teacher whose workshops on spirituality and prayer were popular with religious people of all stripes. His Camps Farthest Out promoted the training of "spiritual athletes."[41] Even more than Dunnington, with his Presbyterian and Congregationalist credentials, Clark translated New Thought into mainline Protestant language[42]—and well beyond it.

After the publication of the article that won him fame, and the subsequent publication of his book, *The Soul's Sincere Desire*, by Atlantic Monthly Press, he relates that

> the Quakers claimed him; the Catholics thought the book breathed the spirit of Brother Lawrence and Saint Francis; and New Thought joined the chorus. The Swedenborgians said, "He may never have read Swedenborg," but that he "states the law of correspondence better than any of our writers have done"; while a New England Bahai was certain that he was a Bahai.[43] Clark's skill at developing a prayer technique that could mainstream New Thought theory into conventional religion opened many doors for him.

Robert DePatten's self-help church, claiming an Ethical Culture affiliation, brought a message of positivity to inner-city Des Moines African Americans.[44]

The ambitious and innovative Robert Schuller of Crystal Cathedral fame was born and raised in Sioux County. His autobiography perhaps does not do Iowa justice: "I was born at the dead end of a dirt road that had no

---

40. Braden, *Spirits in Rebellion*, 381–84, 519. For another side of Dunnington, see chapter 20.

41. Balmer, *Encyclopedia of Evangelicalism*, 145; Braden, *Spirits in Rebellion*, 258, 376, 383, 391–96; Clark, *Man's Reach*; DMR, Oct. 5, 2008.

42. A work that places Clark centrally in twentieth-century American Protestant book culture, both in connection with the Religious Book Club and Harper & Row, is Hedstrom, *Rise of Liberal Religion*, 100–106.

43. Braden, *Spirits in Rebellion*, 395.

44. *Unity Call*, Jan. 1929; Chase, *Outside In*, 205.

name and no number . . . You can go anywhere from nowhere," he said not just inside his memoir but on the dustjacket.[45] A Reformed Church minister, he called his version of New Thought "possibility thinking." Schuller also thought outside the church box, pioneering such innovations as the drive-in church, a perfect fit for Southern California culture, and anticipating the culturally adaptable megachurches. But his story did not end happily, as the Crystal Cathedral's financial foundations were built on sand, and after bankruptcy proceedings, the Roman Catholic diocese of Los Angeles bought the building.[46] Possibly, possibility thinking needed more thought.

THE APPEAL OF MYSTICISM: THE CASE OF HENRY A. WALLACE

Iowa agricultural editor, hybrid seed mogul, New Deal cabinet member, and Vice President Henry A. Wallace[47] epitomized the early twentieth century yearning for something beyond. One biography summarized his religious viewpoint thusly:

> Wallace was attracted to that religious thought which emphasized religious unity and the brotherhood of all men. He admired the Amana Society of Iowa, which he regarded as a perfect "sociological and economic laboratory" because its members actually lived their religion . . . He eventually joined the Episcopal Church but simultaneously delved into theosophy and oriental beliefs.[48]

Another commentator described Wallace's religiosity more genetically:: "The sturdy Scottish Calvinism of his grandfather and father had been tempered by a streak of stubborn independence . . . He insisted upon approaching religion in a personal way, which led him to stray from the strict bounds of denominational orthodoxy."[49]

---

45. Schuller, *My Journey*, 3, and back dustjacket.
46. DMR, Jul. 5, 2011; Apr. 3, 2015; Jan. 6, 2006.
47. Kleinman, "Searching for the 'Inner Light.'"
48. Schapsmeier and Schapsmeier, *Henry A. Wallace of Iowa*, 137. In their article "Religion and Reform," they connect Wallace's agricultural politics and religion, although I am unpersuaded by their cyclical theory of political change.
49. Schapsmeier and Schapsmeier, "Religion and Reform." Persons, "Comment." Persons seems wrong about the Calvinism of Henry A.'s father Henry C. Wallace, but that is a minor point.

Grandson of a United Presbyterian minister (Henry) and son of a rather unreligious father (Henry C.), the youngest Wallace wanted to explore Asian and native American spirituality. He left Westminster United Presbyterian Church in Des Moines after objections to his using William James's *Varieties of Religious Experience* as a Sunday School text.[50] In exploring Asian religions he was not unique, but his later prominence left him vulnerable to religious con artists and to political opponents out to discredit him.[51] And in the throes of enthusiasm, he could make unguarded remarks. Calling for a "new religion," for example, did not endear him to guardians of already established ones.[52]

Writing to a friend in 1931, Wallace hinted at the range of his religious curiosity: "Is my esoteric hookup best through Chas Roos of Taylor Falls, Dr. Wm H. Dower of Halcyon, Calif, and L. Edward Johnson or through the Esoteric section of Theosophical Society of Ojai California?"[53]

Wallace's first fling with Eastern religion was with Theosophy, encountering it in 1919, and then with an offshoot, the Liberal Catholic Church, with which he was affiliated from 1925 to 1929.[54] He probably left the church when the charismatic Indian Krishnamurti renounced Theosophy, the Liberal Catholic Church, and all institutions.[55] The Liberal Catholic Church put Theosophical doctrine into a Christian setting. Wallace subsequently joined the rest of his immediate family in the Episcopal Church,[56] but settling into a mainline Protestant denomination did not quench his thirst for the more exotic. Notably, in 1931 he joined another offshoot of Theosophy, the California-based Society of

---

50. Kleinman, *World of Hope*, 24.

51. Culver and Hyde, *American Dreamer*, 81–82; White and Maze, *Henry A. Wallace*, 64–73.

52. DMR, Jan. 14, 1932; correspondence between John W. Todd, Shenandoah, and Henry A. Wallace, Jan. 19, 20, 21, 1932, Henry A. Wallace Papers, SC-UI, Box 12-94, 107, 136; Schapsmeier and Schapsmeier, *Henry A. Wallace*, 137.

53. White and Maze, *Henry A. Wallace*, 23–24.

54. Olson, *Handbook of Denominations*, 318–19. A congregation of the LCC currently exists in Fairfield: see "St. Gabriel and All Angels."

55. Email correspondence with LCC Presiding Archbishop William S. Downey, Jul. 31, 2021; Campbell, *Ancient Wisdom Revived*, 129–30, 147–50.

56. Cf. Henry A. Wallace Papers, SC-UI, MsC 177, Series III, Box 1A, Folder 1, Feb. 26, 1938, letter from Franklin D. Roosevelt to Henry A. Wallace, in which he invited his Secretary of Agriculture to private services on Fridays at 10:30 a.m. at St. John's Church on Lafayette Square.

the Temple of the People, taking correspondence classes with its leader William Dower.[57]

The temple leader's ties to Native American religion particularly attracted Wallace. Both Dower and Native American Theosophist Charles Roos encouraged Wallace to meet with Iroquois spiritual leaders in upstate New York. Roos coached Wallace on how to pray for rain, a useful skill for an agriculturalist to have.[58]

Wallace's eccentric dabblings would become irresistible material for his political opponents. In his 1947 "hatchet job"[59] *Henry Wallace: The Man and the Myth*, the left-wing[60] critic Dwight Macdonald devoted a whole chapter to "The Cornfed Mystic."

More spurious than Macdonald's book, but more widely distributed, right-wing columnist Westbrook Pegler divulged the "guru letters."[61] What made the accusations credible was Wallace's association with Nicholas Roerich, which blew up into a scandal during Wallace's tenure as secretary of agriculture.[62] Roerich, a Russian emigre, artist, Theosophist, and power player on the New York philanthropic scene, was tapped by Wallace to lead an agricultural delegation to Mongolia to investigate ways to mitigate drought. The failure of the mission was overshadowed by Roerich's diplomatic disasters, managing to insult officials of several Asian countries.

From Theosophy, Wallace acquired an ongoing belief in pantheism. His views reincarnated those of Abner Kneeland, although I have not found evidence that Wallace knew of Kneeland. He preferred to attribute his pantheism to his friend and mentor George Washington Carver:

> I know that I'm often called a mystic, and in the years following my leaving the United Presbyterian Church, I would probably

---

57. Kleinman, *World of Hope*, 30–31

58. White and Maze, 17–31.

59. The phrase is that of Macdonald's biographer: Wreszin, *Rebel in Defense of Tradition*, 200.

60. Macdonald's Third Camp position on the Cold War differed significantly from Wallace's accommodationism during the 1948 campaign. See Frank A. Warren, review of Mark Kleinman, *A World of Hope, A World of Fear*, in *Annals of Iowa* 60, 194–96.

61. Macdonald, *Henry Wallace*, 120–23, argues both for their spuriousness, since the Republican Party could not get anyone to release them in the 1940 campaign, and for their plausibility, given Wallace's religious interests.

62. For wildly different takes on the episode, see the appendix to Markowitz, *Rise and Fall of the People's Century*, 333–42; and Culver and Hyde, *American Dreamer*, 130–46. See also Kleinman, *World of Hope*, 31–34.

Alternative Counter-Narratives

say that I was a practical mystic. I've always believed that if you envision something that hasn't been, that can be, and bring it into being, that is a tremendously worthwhile thing to do. I'd go this far—I'd say I was a mystic in the same sense that George Carver was, who believed that God was in everything, and therefore, if you went to God, you could find the answers.

Maybe that belief is mysticism. I don't know.[63]

Henry A. Wallace, approving Freedom from Want. Photo permission: Wallace House Foundation, Des Moines.

63. Columbia University Oral History 1951 interview, quoted in Culver and Hyde, *American Dreamer*, 78.

In citing the eminent scientist Carver as a model, Wallace was playing it safe: Carver was an orthodox if experiential Christian.[64] Strains of New Thought "envisioning" can also be detected. Wallace's coyness about whether to claim a word that is nearly indefinable encapsulates both his interest in alternative ways to experience God and his political instinct not to publicly veer too far from accepted norms.[65]

In his 1934 book *Statesmanship and Religion*, Wallace sought to synthesize his religious and political beliefs. It was a project that few US cabinet secretaries attempted while in office—or ever. Based on lectures to the Chicago Theological Seminary and the Federal Council of Churches, it is best read as a Social Gospel text, as Theodore Wilson has suggested—perhaps the last book in the canon.[66]

In a politically important personage like Wallace, we can clearly see the ways that alternative religion is pilloried or defended. Was Henry A. a visionary or a dupe? The answer often seems to depend less on views of Theosophy and more on views of Wallace's politics. Marginalizing Wallace's religious views could help marginalize him as a politician.

FROM DAVENPORT TO GANDHI TO ISLAM: THE SAGA OF NILLA CRAM COOK

While ambitious religious entrepreneurs like Pierre Bernard and Robert Schuller quickly and eagerly left Iowa, Davenport native Nilla Cram Cook strayed farthest from the state. Cook was the granddaughter of a Theosophist and daughter of author George Cram Cook, one of a circle of early twentieth-century Davenport writers that included Floyd Dell and Susan Glaspell. Cook divorced Nilla's mother and married Glaspell when Nilla was four.[67]

---

64. On George Washington Carver's religious views, which are better described as panenthestic than pantheistic, see McMurry, *George Washington Carver*, 268–71; Kremer, *George Washington Carver in His Own Words*, chapter 7; Hersey, *My Work Is That of Conservation*.

65. Wallace was not the only Iowa politician whose religious curiosity obstructed their ambitions. On Harold Hughes's interest in alternative religion and the paranormal, see Harrington, *Thunder from the Prairie*, 236–38.

66. Wilson, "Henry Agard Wallace and the Progressive Faith." See also Mills, *Judge and a Rope*, 86–87.

67. See., e.g., Ozieblo, *Susan Glaspell*. The Pulitzer Prize-winning Glaspell wrote a book about George Cram Cook after his death, *The Road to the Temple*, exploring his religious impulses. George Cook identified with the religion of ancient Greece and is

In his diary, George Cook wrote of the Monist Society, to which the *avant garde* of Davenport belonged:

> Modern thought is forced to discard dualism. There are not two worlds, there is one. Modern thought believes, that is, in monism (one-ism.) At first, when it was seen that there was only one world, men said: 'Then there is only the natural world and there is no spiritual world.' That was materialism—the practical, working faith of the world today, a faith that is woven into nearly every action of nearly every man. But a few have looked deeper and seen this: 'The natural world *is* the spiritual world, and the spiritual world *is* the natural world.'[68]

Growing up in such a milieu, not surprisingly Nilla Cook turned to the East for meaning. Her somewhat manic account of her time at Mohandas Gandhi's ashram in the thirties is *My Road to India*. A glance at other accounts suggests she exaggerated her importance to the cause. At any rate, her departure from the ashram had drama, as she rolled the car after accelerating to seventy miles per hour. Temporarily back in the States, she produced a charming article that documented her spiritual wanderings from childhood to date.[69]

Cook was not quite done with non-Western religions. She resurfaced in 1945, in a one-off *New York Times* article datelined Tehran that touted her project to reform Islam. "Iowa Woman The Luther of Islam," proclaimed the headline. Her translation of the Qur'an into English stressed the tolerant side of Muhammad.[70] The plausibility of the headline can be questioned, with no response from Islam and the improbability of a Western woman affecting such a change.

Cook returned to the subcontinent in the fifties; Guha found her "working with Kashmiri craftsmen" in 1954.[71] She died in Austria in 1982,[72] able to claim a remarkable if not a productive career. Perhaps the lesson to be learned is that life is a pilgrimage.

---

buried at the Delphic Temple (as is his daughter).

68. Quoted in Noe, *Susan Glaspell*, 23.

69. Cook, *My Road to India*; Cook, "What Religion Means to Me," *Forum and Century*, Feb. 1936, 69–75; NYT, Nov. 29, 1933.

70. NYT, Mar. 12, 1945.

71. Guha, *Rebels Against the Raj*, 305, 392.

72. NYT, Oct. 13, 1982; DMR, May 21, 2006.

THE (LIMITED) APPEAL OF A UNIFIED THEORY

Alfred Lawson was an experienced salesman of the unconventional.[73] His long and variegated resume listed professional baseball player, commercial airline pioneer, social security advocate, and philosopher able to explain the universe in a rarefied theory that he modestly called Lawsonomy.

Lawson became associated with Iowa when he purchased the long dormant campus of Des Moines University in 1944. (See chapter 18.) At first, neighboring Highland Park merchants were ecstatic at the prospect of the college reopening. Their mood soured, however, upon learning that the few students who matriculated at the Des Moines University of Lawsonomy were confined to campus. Lawson adopted a similar policy regarding outside academia: students were to read only books by Lawson. Lawson's logic was clear: when one has discovered the transcendent truth, other ideas are distractions.[74]

A taste of Lawsonomy can be gleaned from this excerpt (which could easily have been chosen at random):

> LAWSONOMY teaches that there is an opposite to everything. So the opposite of constructive MENORGS are destructive DISORGS. The MENORGS are cellular organizers, inventors, designers, builders, and scholars. The DISORGS are cellular disorganizers, disturbers, wreckers, and destroyers.[75]

A trivial but telling anecdote helps explain Lawson's *modus operandi*. City inspectors cited the college's heating system for inadequate filtering. In response, Lawson promised to invent a pollution-free furnace, a "smoke evaporator." And when inspectors returned, they could discern no smoke. A decade later, as the campus was being dismantled to make way for Parkfair Mall, workers discovered a diffuse system of tunnels, hidden by plants, that diverted smoke from the chimney.[76]

The institution of highest learning did not long outlast its founder, folding in 1954, but Lawsonomy still has a handful of acolytes today, if not in Iowa.[77]

---

73. Henry, *Zig-Zag-and-Swirl*; Lawson, *Lawsonian Religion*.
74. Henry, *Zig Zag and Swirl*, 206–9, 227–28.
75. Lawson, *Lawsonian Religion*, 129.
76. Henry, *Zig Zag and Swirl*, 274–76.
77. "Lawsonomy."

NEW AGE AND IOWA: TRANSCENDENTAL MEDITATION AND FAIRFIELD

Alternate spirituality did not end in the thirties. The consciousness-expanding 1960s fostered new searches, many leading to the East. While elites might not be trusted, the quest for a new self still needed guidance, and Transcendental Meditation promised it both through science and a guru. The celebrity[78] guru Maharishi claimed that yogic meditation could be proven beneficial in any number of situations.[79] The organization's purchase of a defunct Presbyterian college in Fairfield meant that that county seat town would be the North American center of TM. The town versus gown conflict could flare extreme.[80] The new suburb of Vedic City was incorporated in 2001, renamed Maharishi Vedic City by referendum two years later.[81]

Transcendental Meditation aggressively marketed its techniques as scientific, boosted by the interest of celebrities as big as the Beatles,[82] while reserving religious teachings for more advanced practitioners. In Transcendental Meditation's claim that meditation can affect world events, from the stock market to peace in the Mideast, its connection to New Thought is most evident.[83]

The scientific argument for Transcendental Meditation has been contested,[84] and internal contradictions exist. Maharishi University im-

---

78. Olson, *Maharishi at '433'*; Shumsky, *Maharishi and Me*; Lapham, *With the Beatles*.

79. Orme-Johnson, "International Peace Project in the Middle East"; Fales and Makovsky, "Evaluating Heterodox Theories"; see also Russett, "Editor's Comment," in the same issue,

80. Weber, *Transcendental Meditation in America*; Hoffman, *Greetings from Utopia Park*; Gilpin, *Maharishi Effect*; Wren, "Iowa Town Where Marianne Williams Is Already President."

81. Weber, *Transcendental Meditation in America*; DMR, Feb. 7, 2008; *Burlington Hawkeye*, Aug. 7, 2000; Kennedy, "Field of TM Dreams."

82. *Look Magazine*, Feb. 6, 1968; DMR, Jan. 12, May 21, 23, Nov. 15, 2001, Nov. 20, 2003, Jun. 24, Jun. 25, Oct. 19, 2007; CRG, Oct. 18, 2007.

83. Like TM, Theosophy has denied being a religion. McGuire, "Don't Call It a Religion," *Wall Street Journal*, May 17, 2002.

84. Fales and Markovsky, "Evaluating Heterodox Theories." For the pro-Maharishi argument, see Orme-Johnson et al., "International Peace Project," and see also Russett, "Editor's Comment," in the same issue, 773–75.

On the question of whether Transcendental Meditation is a science or a religion, see Rose, "Transcendental Meditation Movement" and "Is TM a Religion?" *Daily Iowan*, Oct. 9, 10, 1975. I am grateful to Geneva Community pastor Jason Chen for unearthing

ported pandits from India to do mass meditation, on passports claiming they were doing religious, not scientific, work. Widespread public awareness of this contradiction occurred only after the dissatisfaction of the pandits with their living conditions in a fenced-off facility boiled over into a riot in 2014.[85]

While TM advocates sometimes worked for peace, many seemed more inclined to pursue prosperity. But one scholar has suggested that their meditative techniques influenced the spirituality of American Catholicism.[86] And another has credited them with sustaining the anti-GMO movement.[87]

Did Iowa, as it might appear, have a greater propensity than other states to produce or attract practitioners of alternative religions? The answer is hard to quantify. A more fruitful question to ask is, Is there a quintessentially Iowan perspective?

Glenn Clark qualifies. While he left Iowa, he settled nearby, in St. Paul, Minnesota. What is striking about his avowed mysticism is its practical streak. Like Henry A. Wallace, there is a scientific quality to his explorations, but Wallace mostly explored alone; Clark's vocations as teacher and coach led in a more communal direction. And Clark was more sure-footed than Wallace regarding mainstream religion—arguably, a more attuned politician. Wallace's gaffes seem attributable to his isolation, not taking predictable public reactions into account; Clark was thoroughly engaged with icons of mainline Protestantism, from Charles Sheldon[88] to George Washington Carver to Toyohiko Kagawa.[89] Nonetheless, his scheme to supplement the New Deal Brain Trust with a Spiritual Trust did not come to fruition. Wallace probably would have voted for it, had it come up for a cabinet vote.[90]

---

this. See also Bainbridge and Jackson, "Rise and Decline of Transcendental Meditation," in Wilson, *Social Impact of New Religious Movements*, 135–58.

85. DMR, Jun. 7, 2007, Mar. 12, 14, 17, 23, 28; Dec. 30, 2014.
86. Porterfield, *Transformation of American Religion*, 86.
87. Grohman, "Transcending Transgenics."
88. DMR, Oct. 5, 2008.
89. Clark, *Man's Reach*, 244–47, 249.
90. Clark, *Man's Reach*, 254–56. Clark proposed that Rufus Jones, George Washington Carver, and E. Stanley Jones would be in the trust, along with representatives from the Catholic, Jewish, and Christian Science traditions.

Alternative Counter-Narratives

The presence of alternative religions has enriched our state—materially, in the case of Fairfield, if not so much for Lawsonomy, provoking expanded horizons, and adding colors when the scene may have seemed too drab. Heterodoxy is only a threat to orthodoxy when the latter feels insecure. Of course, life presents numerous reasons for insecurity. In the twentieth century, prominent among those reasons was world war.

CHAPTER 20

Leaving the Porch Light On

Chastened Rhetoric, Total War

"The idea of freedom . . . is derived from the Bible with its extraordinary emphasis on the dignity of the individual. Democracy is the only true political expression of Christianity."

—HENRY A. WALLACE[1]

"After their victories in two world wars, Americans have more to fear than ever before."

—FERNER NUHN, CEDAR FALLS, 1947[2]

"The [Jehovah's] Witnesses predicted that history just before the end would be exciting."

—MULFORD Q. SIBLEY AND PHILIP E. JACOB[3]

"I wonder whether as business and professional men we are really big enough to deal with the grand and awful times we are in."

—REV. DALE WELCH, DUBUQUE, 1941[4]

    1. Quoted by French Catholic personalist in exile in the United States Jacques Maritain. See Jacobs, *Year of Our Lord 1943*, 189.
    2. Box 48, Ruth Suckow Papers, SC-UI.
    3. Sibley and Jacob, *Conscription of Conscience*, 33.
    4. Quoted in Ossian, *Home Fronts of Iowa*, 50. Welch, president of the

A NEW SOBRIETY ABOUT the costs of war was evident in the Great War's aftermath but did not prevent the recurrence of a global conflagration. This general statement also applied to Iowa, as the state increasingly felt itself entwined in national politics and a global economy, even as there were countervailing calls for isolationism. World War II's transformative effects would include challenges to Iowa religion.

In 1942, Lucy B. Dexter of Montezuma breathlessly wrote the *Iowa Fellowship* about her intended act of civil disobedience. When the air raid drill called for lights out, apparently to befuddle a Japanese or German aerial attack on Poweshiek County, she was going to leave her porch light on. "Three churches in this town and I'm the only heretic," she claimed defiantly.[5]

It's unclear whether Dexter followed through with her threatened defiance. Somehow Montezuma survived unscathed and unbombed. But the metaphor of leaving the porch light on resonates with a panoply of Iowans' emotions and actions surrounding the war, from greeting refugees to praying for loved ones to return unharmed. It might also, as Dexter suggested, question the embrace of darkness.

THE PEACE MOVEMENT(S) BETWEEN THE WARS

The broad peace movement of the thirties did not prevent US involvement in World War II, but it did help shape its domestic parameters (except when it involved treatment of Japanese-Americans). Movement may be too imprecise—the political and religious roots were so diverse that it might better be described in the plural. Historic peace church members, mainline Protestants, and conservative Roman Catholics (and politically, libertarians, fascists, and leftists), for different reasons, all found temporary ground in common in opposing the impending war, although temporary isolationism or vague internationalism would not withstand the sudden jagged reality of an attack on American territory.

Edward Steiner had been skeptical that isolationism was possible. "No nation lives to itself or dies to itself, and [America's] influence upon

---

Presbyterian-affiliated University of Dubuque, was speaking to the Iowa Taxpayers Association.

5. *Iowa Fellowship*, Dec. 1942; *Montezuma Republican*, Dec. 17, 1942.

the future of mankind will continue to be a blessing or a curse, as she herself decrees."[6]

Particularly significant among isolationists was the Catholic antiwar movement, in Iowa centered in Dubuque and associated with Archbishop Francis Beckman, who was also the most prominent isolationist Catholic nationally. The tenor of the Catholic movement was not politically progressive; it had strong strains of anti-communism and sometimes an indifference to state terrorism carried out by fascist governments, and an unholy alliance with anti-Semites like Fr. Charles Coughlin, who spoke at a peace rally in Dubuque in 1941, sharing the stage with the archbishop.[7] Berkman did not further his own reputation when he used coded phrases, advocating in defense of "Christian America" and attacking "masters of international finance."[8]

The experience of University of Iowa campus minister and Catholic professor at the School of Religion Donald Hayne is instructive. In his memoir, Hayne recalled his commitment to isolationism and illustrated its temporary character:

> The clouds of war, dark over Europe, were coming closer to us. I was strongly isolationist. The first letter I ever wrote to a Congressman was a protest against either Lend-Lease or Selective Service, I forget which. When Archbishop Beckman came down from Dubuque . . . I cornered him alone in St. Mary's rectory and obtained his willing promise to back me up in support of any Catholic student who wanted to register as a conscientious objector to war . . .
>
> But when war came, I am afraid I shocked my classes, the morning after Pearl Harbor, by the vigor of my assertion that it was now the duty of all of us to prosecute the war ruthlessly. The same morning, however, I had made it a point to invite to breakfast in a much-frequented restaurant the only Japanese national in the student body. He was, naturally, a very troubled boy that day; I wanted to give him the remembrance of a moment of an

---

6. Quoted in Pruitt, *Open Doors*, 55.

7. McKenzie, "Archbishop Beckman and the Dubuque Anti-War Movement." See also *Dubuque Catholic Daily Tribune*, May. 28, 29, 1940. An inside banner headline, apparently sponsored by advertisers, proclaimed "Dubuque Extends a Sincere Welcome to Father Charles E. Coughlin and His Sincere Endeavor to Maintain the Peace." The *Tribune* had earlier lost subscribers when it ran a series critical of Coughlin. See chapter 17.

8. McKenzie, "Archbishop Beckman and the Dubuque Anti-War Movement," 25; *Time*, Aug. 4, 1941.

American's friendship and to give anyone who saw us together an example of how I felt a Christian should act with an "enemy."[9]

Haynes's contradictory impulses of ruthlessness and friendship portray well how many religious Iowans suddenly felt torn. But the mass nature of the anti-war movement, already shaken on the left by the collapse of the Hitler-Stalin pact, did not outlast the attack on Pearl Harbor.

Some mainline Protestants embraced pacifism in response to the disillusionment occasioned by World War I. Prominent among them was Kirby Page, a Disciples minister and Drake Divinity School graduate. Describing his vocation as "social evangelist," Page criss-crossed the country, logging thousands of miles a year, proclaiming that Christianity and war were incompatible.[10]

While the Catholic anti-war movement fell apart after Pearl Harbor, some of the liberal Protestant pacifists continued their opposition. Two other prominent pacifist Protestant pastors deserve mention. Stoddard Lane preached a gentle message of reconciliation from his pulpit at Plymouth Congregational Church in Des Moines.[11] Also maintaining his pacifism for the duration was Sam Nichols, pastor of Collegiate Methodist Church in Ames. Nichols was such a spell-binding preacher that the pews of Collegiate were always crowded and sometimes overflowing, and congregants included military personnel taking courses at Iowa State. His preaching was cited as exemplary by *The Christian Century*.[12]

The historic peace churches, such as Mennonites, Brethren, and Quakers, were in a much more secure position legally than they had been in World War I, thanks to that negative experience and to the fact that the rollout of the draft occurred before the war's start. Most of the peace churches' members eligible for conscription were satisfied with the options of noncombatant or alternative service. Seventh-day Adventists, particularly keen on noncombatant service within the military, preferred the term "conscientious cooperators" to conscientious objectors.

---

9. Hayne, *Batter My Heart*, 193.

10. Page, *Social Evangelist*, 19–22, 69–70, 106, 137; Chatfield and DeBenadetti, *Kirby Page and the Social Gospel*, 20–33; Crain, *Development of Social Ideas among the Disciples of Christ*, 136.

11. Lane, "Challenge to Disarmament"; *Iowa Fellowship News*, Feb. 1942; Lane, "There Are Things that Abide Always"; DMR, May 18, 1943.

12. "Great Churches of America," *Christian Century*, Nov. 29, 1950; *Iowa Fellowship*, Aug. 11, 1941, Apr., Aug., 1942; Aug. 1943; Ames *Daily Tribune*, Mar. 29, 1960.

Iowa Mennonites set up one of the first Civilian Public Service camps, No. 12, at a former Civilian Conservation Corps site near Denison in August of 1941, months before the attack on Pearl Harbor. The camp crew drew praise from Council Bluffs city leaders for work combating the Missouri River flood in the spring of 1943.[13]

Later in the war, Mennonites sponsored work at the state mental hospital in Mt. Pleasant. Two mainline Protestant churches followed suit, with Methodists sponsoring one of their two units nationally at Cherokee and the Evangelical and Reformed Church sponsoring their only unit at Independence.[14] These units would have a significant effect on the treatment of mental health in Iowa after the war.

THE NEW REALITY OF A TOTAL WAR

While Pearl Harbor came as a jolt, in fact, the coming of war wasn't quite so sudden. The nation's first peacetime draft was instituted over a year before Pearl Harbor. Iowa's first draft registration resister of the era, James Ball, a Quaker from Des Moines, was convicted and completed his one-year prison sentence before the US entry into the war.[15]

As a Marshalltown historian put it,

> After Pearl Harbor, all life changed. War was uppermost in everyone's mind and deed. St. Mary's Sunday Masses and parish activity bore mute evidence of this total commitment. There were few young men at services or about town. Those who were seen usually wore military uniforms, or held jobs necessary to the war effort. Only older men and the physically impaired were left to keep the home front going. This, too, was a supreme effort . . .
>
> St. Mary's parish saw nearly 300 of its sons and daughters enter military service. Five never returned.[16]

---

13. DMR, Aug. 29, 1941; Apr. 8, 1943; Gingerich, *Service for Peace*, 114–21; *Iowa Fellowship*, Sep. 29; Dec. 13, 1941; Mar. 27, 1942; Oct. 1942; May 1943; Jul. 1944; Sep. 1944; *Council Bluffs Nonpareil*, Apr. 7, 9, 1943; Uriah Mast, oral interview, in Frazier and O'Sullivan, *We Have Just Begun To Not Fight*, 44–45.

14. See below.

15. DMT, Oct. 21, Nov. 30, 1940; DMR, Oct. 22, 1940; *Iowa Peace News*, Jul. 14, 1941; *Iowa Fellowship*, Jan. 1943, Aug. 1943. [*Iowa Peace News* was soon renamed *Iowa Fellowship*.] Ball also wrote his master's thesis on *satyagraha*. Ball, "Beginnings of Satyagraha."

16. Benson, *Century of Service to God and Community*, 100.

An Iowan was one of the first two American chaplains killed during World War II, during the Japanese attack on Pearl Harbor. Fr. Aloysius Schmitt of Dubuque, aboard the USS Oklahoma, perished while trying to save other crew members.[17]

The five Sullivan brothers all died after their ship went down near the Solomon Islands in the Pacific, early in the war. In his requiem Mass at their home parish, St. Mary's of Waterloo, Archbishop Beckman rather oddly talked about the benefits of large families, and also oddly, given that the Soviet Union was an American ally, about the dangers of Communism.[18]

Many Iowa clergy sought to serve as military chaplains.[19] Probably the most dramatic story was that of Fr. Francis Sampson, born in Cherokee and who served briefly in the Des Moines diocese. After volunteering for the Airborne Division without realizing the implications of that term, Sampson became celebrated in the press as the "paratrooper padre." He parachuted into Normandy on D-Day and was captured. After the war, he stayed in the chaplaincy, and from 1967 to 1971 was chief of Army chaplains. The Steven Spielberg film *Saving Private Ryan* is based partially on his D-Day story.[20]

Sampson, finding himself a prisoner of war, continued his chaplaincy duties. He sought to console his fellow prisoners by getting them to recite the Lord's Prayer. His anecdote about the recitation belies the dire situation they were in:

> Of all the times and places for a religious argument! When one of the boys finished with 'for Thine is the Kingdom, and the Power, and glory forever and ever,' one of the Catholic men said it didn't belong there. The Protestant men insisted that it did. The other Catholic men joined in to insist it didn't belong. I told them each to say it in whatever way he had learned it. Scared as I was, this argument struck me [as] so funny at the time that I almost became hysterical.

Sampson was not the only Des Moines diocese priest who found himself a prisoner of war. During the North African campaign, soldiers

---

17. Gallagher, *Seed/Harvest*, 92; Tallahassee *Democrat*, Dec. 6, 2021; Piehler, *Religious History of the American GI*, 127.

18. Gallagher, *Seed/Harvest*, 92. For more on Beckman's funeral sermon and on the circumstances surrounding the brothers' deaths, see also Ossian, *Home Fronts*, 114–16.

19. Sampson, *Look Out Below*; Avella, *Catholic Church in Southwest Iowa*, 171, 219.

20. DMR, Feb. 4, 2008.

The People Are Kind

from southwestern Iowa sustained particularly high losses. Montgomery County had the highest per capita casualty rate in the country during the war due to that campaign, and journalists from *Life*, the *Des Moines Register*, and the *Saturday Evening Post* all descended on Red Oak to report on the somber mood.[21] Initially included in the Missing in Action column of casualties was Fr. Stephen Kane of Red Oak, who spent over two years in captivity, refusing to be released separately because he felt "my obligation is with my boys." He wrote his bishop that

> 1943 has brought me the experiences of a hundred lives. Prison life may be one of petty tyrannies, but it is assuredly one of good fellowship. There is a hidden wealth in humans that only suffering will reveal. This life is not one of jaded emptiness and hours passed recapturing the past and planning for the future. Here men are most themselves, so poor creatures of circumstance in defiant, patient waiting the dawn of the Great Day.

Another Iowan who has left his story is Rabbi Morris Kertzer of Iowa City. Kertzer left the Jewish chair in the School of Religion in 1943 to become a chaplain. Kertzer was sent to Italy directly from New York for Passover in 1944 so that Jewish soldiers on the Anzio beachhead could have a seder service. Kertzer also witnessed the reopening of synagogues in Rome and Marseilles after those cities' liberation.[22]

One other small but significant consequence of religious Iowans going to war was the expansion of the varieties of religious choices on the "dog tags" that soldiers were issued as identification. After the war, Muslim veteran Abdullah Igran of Cedar Rapids petitioned President Dwight Eisenhower to allow the tags to include "I" for Islam, along with P, C, and H (later J). This was the president who had famously called for every American to have a "deeply held religious faith, and I don't care what it is." In keeping with that pronouncement, Eisenhower expanded the religious options.[23]

---

21. Ossian, *Home Fronts*, 107–12; Cross, *Soldiers of God*, 209; Lingeman, *Noir Forties*, 22–26; Senden, *Red Oak*, 91; Atkinson, *Army at Dawn*, 660–65; Janeway, "Midwest's Mood," *Life*, Sep. 13, 1943. The mental breakdown of the priest at Red Oak who succeeded Kane can be at least partially attributed to the town's wartime trauma. Douglas, "Making Iowa Safe for Differences," 242.

22. Kertzer, *With an H on My Dog Tag*. Jones's chronology, "A Century of Jewish Life at Iowa," notes 1833–1994. See also Kertzer's historian son's acknowledgement: Kertzer, *Pope at War*, 483–84.

23. Rugg, "Will America's Oldest Muslim Community Survive President Trump"; Curtis, *Muslims of the Heartland*, 160–61; Stark, "Looking for Leadership," 229; Kyle

Not every clergyperson could volunteer as a chaplain. On the home front, ministers sometimes replaced the drafted farmhands to ease the labor shortage.[24]

Missionaries' lives were often disrupted by the war's tumult. Darlene Deibler (Rose) of Boone, stationed at a Christian and Missionary Alliance outpost in New Guinea, endured four years of Japanese internment, suffering malnutrition and disease and separation from her husband, who died in another camp.[25]

The war mobilization was often too rapid for ecclesiastical institutions to keep up. While the Iowa Conference of the Methodist Church had proclaimed itself pacifist between the wars, in practice that designation did not fit the realities after the declaration of war, given most Iowa Methodists wholeheartedly supported it. On paper, however, the conference remained officially pacifist for several annual conferences into the war. It seemed more a case of bureaucratic inertia than pacifist finesse.[26] "That's the Iowa Conference!" Ames pastor and pacifist Sam Nichols proclaimed cheerfully about the big-tent atmosphere of the denomination when he was denounced for his pacifism and given an honorary doctorate at the same graduation ceremony of Iowa Wesleyan College.[27]

REFUGEES AND OUTCASTS

The US internal response to the Japanese attack on Pearl Harbor included the mass incarceration of Japanese-Americans residing on the West Coast (although not in Hawaii). But college-age Nisei could be diverted from concentration camps if institutions outside the zone admitted them as students. While Iowa's public universities (unlike the University of

---

Gassiott, *For Memorial Day*. Someone apparently more of a contrarian than a Muslim successfully got an M for "Mohammaden" (!) on his dog tag during World War II, but that did not change policy. Piehler, *American GI*, 133–35.

24. Ossian, "Home Fronts," 49.

25. Rose, *Evidence Not Seen*; Bremer, *New History of Iowa*, 265.

26. Ward, "Must the Christian Church Condemn"; *Year Book of the Iowa-Des Moines Annual Conference*, 261; Miller, *How Will They Hear Without a Preacher*, 460–70.

27. *Iowa Fellowship*, Aug. 11, 1941; Aug. 1942; Aug. 1943.

Nebraska)[28] were mostly uninterested in accommodating Nisei, many religiously affiliated colleges in the state welcomed them.[29]

Grinnell College had an inside track. Sociology professor and Quaker activist Laetitia Conard's nephew was working for the American Friends Service Committee in San Francisco as the roundup of Japanese Americans began, so Grinnell became among the first colleges to host college-eligible Nisei. In addition to Grinnell, eight other colleges in Iowa were listed as hosting Nisei students in 1943. Drake had by far the most students, with thirty-three, but St. Ambrose, Loras, Parsons, Simpson, Cornell, Central, and William Penn Colleges all participated. Morningside and Dubuque appear on another list, probably for a different semester.[30]

West Coast Nisei were not the only ones in need of refuge from concentration camps. Quakers turned Scattergood School near West Branch into a hostel that sheltered refugees from the Nazis.[31] However, after those refugees were successfully transplanted into American society and Friends floated the idea of making Scattergood a refuge for Nisei, strong local opposition torpedoed the project.[32]

When fascist forces in Spain and Ethiopia had engaged in aerial bombing of civilian populations in the thirties, the actions had faced widespread condemnation as contrary to the laws of war. But the moral question of indiscriminate bombing was submerged into pragmatic war aims as the conflict dragged on and Allies sought the upper hand.

---

28. Wertheimer, "Admitting Nebraska's Nisei."

29. Austin, *From Concentration Camp to Campus*, 23, 90–91, 98, 155; *Directory of American Students of Japanese Ancestry*, 46–48; Hall, "Japanese-American College Students," 66; Virgil M. Hancher to John W. Nason, President of Swarthmore College, Mar. 22, 1943, Virgil Hancher Papers, SC-UI, Box 57, F. 73; Iowa Board of Regents Minutes, Apr. 14, 1942, SHSI-DM, RG 079, Box 230, vol. 16; DMR, Feb. 26, 1943; Iowa State Teachers College *College Eye*, Apr. 19, 1943.

30. Okihiru, *Storied Lives*, 32–33, 78–79; *Iowa Fellowship*, Apr. 1943; Jun., 1943; Grinnell College *Scarlet & Black*, Mar. 19, 1943; Carroll, "Japanese-American Student Relocation."

31. Curtis, "Place of Peace in a Time of War," *Pal* 65, 42–52; Luick-Thrams, *Out of Hitler's Reach*.

32. Fredericksen, "Proposed Japanese-American Relocation Center," 4; *Iowa Fellowship*, Mar. 1943; DMR, Feb. 13, 20, 1943.

The change in strategy culminated with the incineration of cities of dubious military value such as Dresden and Nagasaki. Iowa pacifists, led by Ames Quaker Minne Allen, sought to challenge this cognitive dissonance between what had been beyond the pale in the thirties and what was routine in the forties, raising the issue in the state's newspapers.[33] While the course of the war was not altered, the points they raised would have a continued relevance as this world war, too, would not be the war to end all wars.

THE END OF THE WAR

For many, the specter of Hiroshima and Nagasaki clouded the jubilation felt at the Allied victory. The specter intensified as what seemed to follow victory turned out not to be peace but something called a Cold War.

Among the larger flow of refugees from the Nazi persecution of Jews, another grim reminder of the war was the resettlement of Holocaust survivors.[34] In the former category was Kurt Lewin, who fled the Hitler regime in 1933 and brought his Gestalt tenets to the psychology department at the State University of Iowa, where he applied them, in what he called "action research,"[35] to problems of democracy and authoritarianism. Working with the American Jewish Congress, Lewin pioneered experiments showing links between prejudice and environment. Not surprisingly, studying anti-Semitism was a priority for him, but his work would also help challenge segregation in the fifties, figuring in the *Brown v. Topeka Board of Education* Supreme Court case that overturned school segregation.[36]

In the latter category of refugees, many Holocaust survivors felt that telling their stories was important to prevent a recurrence and that it honored its victims. One survivor was Celina Karp Biniza, who

---

33. Biographical information on Allen is in the introduction to Allen and Allen, *Tenderness and Turmoil*, xi-xiii. See also Douglas, "Bombing Civilians Fosters Fear, Hatred," DMR, May 18, 1999. The Minne Allen quotes are not extended far enough in the *Register*'s rendition.

34. "Jewish Oral Histories." See also Cumberland, "Albert Hirsch"; DMR, Oct. 20, 2006; Mar. 20, 2008; May 26, 2010.

35. By the 1940s, "action" seems to have replaced "applied" as a preferred descriptor among progressive American scholars.

36. Heinze, *Jews and the American Soul*, 160–62; Marrow, *Practical Theorist*, 84, 97, 100–101. Lewin was only marginally involved in his Iowa colleagues' efforts to counter eugenics-based IQ tests. Brookwood, *Orphans of Davenport*, 169.

graduated from North High School in Des Moines and from Grinnell College after her ordeal as a teenager at Auschwitz. She spoke eloquently about how being on Oskar Schindler's list saved her life.[37]

The presence of survivors incarnated the complications to Jewish theology, amplifying the age-old questions about suffering and the role of God.[38] But for David Wolnerman, who moved to Des Moines after his retirement because his children had settled there, surviving was a matter of "being lucky—and believing in God." As a teenager, he was transferred from Auschwitz to a labor camp in his native Poland by chance. He realized that the evil of the Holocaust led some people not to believe anymore, but his faith became stronger. "If I wouldn't believe, maybe I wouldn't be alive," he asserted.[39]

The historical fact of the Holocaust (and the consequent establishment of the state of Israel) brought Zionism into ascendancy within American Judaism.[40] Eugene Mannheimer of Temple B'nai Jeshurun in Des Moines found himself in the last generation of prominent rabbis to be non-Zionist.[41]

Other religious minorities faced war-related challenges. Jehovah's Witnesses had served long prison sentences rather than participate in the war. Their provocative stance on war, their anti-Catholicism, and their penchant for self-defense boiled over soon after the war in the mostly Catholic town of Lacona. Some Witnesses had been locals; a subtext of settling scores can be surmised. Witnesses were partial to soapbox sermonizing in small towns, particularly Catholic ones.[42] Witness eschatology[43] was especially vivid in identifying the papacy as the Whore of

37. Sep. 13, 2017, speech at Caspe Terrace, Waukee, jewishdesmoines.org. See also Friedricks, *Saved by Schindler*, and Anolik, *Liberation of the Concentration Camps*.

38. Bell, "'True Israelites of America.'"

39. "Celina Karp Biniaz." Jewish Federation of Greater Des Moines. https://www.jewishdesmoines.org/our-pillars/iowa-jewish-historical-society/virtual-programs/celina-karp-biniaz/.

40. Bell, "'True Israelites of America,'" 122.

41. Mannheimer, "Reminiscences," I:5, typescript, SHSI-DM; Kertzer, *With an H*, 190–92.

42. Peters, *Judging Jehovah's Witnesses*, 147–52, 243. For other Iowa episodes of local opposition to Witness witnessing, see Peters, 68, 103–4, 126–28; Allen, *Freedom in Iowa*, 86–88.

43. Cumberland, "History of Jehovah's Witnesses,".

Babylon depicted in Revelation, which did not sit well with Catholics.[44] One measure of Catholicism's mainstreaming is that in the 1920s Catholics proselytized in southern Iowa via railcar (see chapter 17), but by the forties they were defending their turf.

With First Amendment law on their side and seeing (and seeking) persecution as proof of righteousness, the Jehovah's Witnesses gathering at the war memorial municipal park seemed combustible. Strong but contradictory ideas about what constituted a legal assembly were exchanged.[45] Something akin to a riot broke out, with punches thrown, noses bloodied, and, reportedly, brass knuckles brandished, until, about forty-five minutes later, Warren County deputies arrived and squelched the standoff.

The September riot had an extraordinary result: on the following Sunday, the Sheriff's Department, bolstered by state police and neighboring counties' deputies, roadblocked all outside traffic into Lacona. Unwilling to discriminate against one religious group, anyone seeking to attend Catholic, Christian, Methodist, Nazarene, or Lutheran services from outside the cordoned-off area was also prohibited. Extending the ban on worship to all groups would not ultimately help the legal case. While Southern District of Iowa federal judge Charles Dewey upheld the action of Warren County law enforcement, citing the imminent threat of bloodshed, he was reversed on appeal, with the appellate court somewhat appalled at the implication that First Amendment rights could be revoked by threatening violence against unpopular practitioners.[46]

When Witnesses returned to Lacona after the appellate court decision, Lacona tried a very different response: near total indifference. Only "a dozen small boys perched on a second-story fire escape across from the park" witnessed the Witnesses' return.[47] Shunning turned out to be a more effective tactic than open hostility in preventing a Witness permanent presence. It was a painful lesson in tolerance, or at least toleration.

---

44. On the debate within American Catholicism as to how to deal with the provocation, see Butler, "Right of Free Listening"; *Newsweek*, Mar. 12, 1945, 88. The priest in Lacona, Fr. Dower, unsuccessfully urged his parishioners to stay away from the conflict.

45. Douglas, "'Religion as Peacemaker,'" 124–29.

46. *Sellers v. Johnson*, 163 F. 2d 848, 69 F. Supp. 778; Peters, *Judging Jehovah's Witnesses*, 147–52; Allen, *Freedom in Iowa*, 87–88; *Indianola Record-Herald*, Sep. 3, 10, 12, 26; Oct. 9, 31, 1946; DMT, Sep. 12, 1946; DMR, Sep. 9, 16, 1946; Oct. 21, 1947; Jan. 13, 1948; Jun. 7, 1948; *Indianola Tribune*, Sep. 10, 17, 1946.

47. DMR, Jun. 7, 1948.

Down the road from Lacona, another countercultural drama was playing out in Oskaloosa: the Hinshaw era at William Penn College.[48] Cecil Hinshaw was a Quaker minister who had become the nation's youngest college president in 1943 and sought to steer the college away from its financial precarity by making it the center of radical pacifism in the country. The experiment would ultimately prove too out-of-step with small-town Iowa Friends Church sensibilities, but while the Hinshaw era lasted, it modeled what an institution committed to racial equality and resistance to the threat of nuclear war could be.[49]

THE WAR AND MENTAL HEALTH REFORM IN IOWA

An unintended consequence of conscientious objectors working in state mental hospitals was the beginning of a movement to reform mental hospitals in the state, a baton picked up flawlessly by ecumenical Protestants as objectors departed after the war.

The need for reform fell into three categories: First, there was the specific problem of sexual predation by the staff. This was exacerbated by wartime labor shortages, creating an opportunity for sadists to prey on patients and move on to another institution with impunity if they were found out.[50] Second was the issue of hospital conditions. Third, the issue of warehousing rather than healing inmates surfaced after the war, coinciding with breakthroughs in medical treatment.[51]

The first attempt by Iowa church people to bring attention to state hospital conditions was a public relations disaster. In July 1944, the peripatetic social evangelist Kirby Page led a workshop in Mt. Pleasant on the social dimensions of the gospel, and one of the field trips was to the state hospital in Mt. Pleasant, visiting with the Mennonite conscientious objectors working there. They expressed concerns about their fellow employees but given their tenuous position, wanted the visitors to be discreet about the objectors' role in any exposé. Unfortunately, the person

---

48. Douglas, "Penn in Technicolor."

49. A growing body of work links World War II dissent with sixties ferment. See, e.g., Kisek, *Acts of Conscience*; Appelbaum, *Kingdom to Commune*; Akst, *War by Other Means*.

50. Saroyan, *Turning Point*, 240–43; Sulek, "Analysis of the Role of a Ward Therapist," 7, 17–18, 20; DMR, Mar. 25, 1947.

51. I am indebted to L. K. Berryhill, MD, of Ft. Dodge for his insights on this era of psychiatry.

who volunteered to make public their concerns, Rev. L. L. Dunnington of the First Methodist Church of Iowa City, was tone deaf on the discretion necessary. Moreover, he issued his press release as he was leaving town for vacation; the Iowa Board of Control had little trouble parrying charges when the accuser was unavailable for comment.[52]

The fiasco set back, but did not stop, setting up the two other conscientious objector units at state hospitals.[53] At the Methodist unit in Cherokee and the Evangelical and Reformed unit in Independence, objectors worked closely with local churches in documenting conditions and setting up an infrastructure to campaign for reform in the state legislature.

The outsiders able to observe and report on state institutions' conditions and seasoned reformers in mainline churches, especially in Church Women United, proved a winning combination. Bipartisan consensus was hardly necessary in a legislature where 107 of 112 representatives were Republican, although a caucus that large proved unruly and resulted in several alternate reform proposals. But this only fed the momentum for reform. By the 1950s, statistics on turnover suggested that healing was overtaking warehousing as a priority, and there were anecdotal testimonies as well.[54]

Whatever its underlying causes, most religious groups in Iowa did experience a post-war boost in numbers and interest. In some respects, the post-war period can be seen as a golden age for religion in Iowa. Viewed from other lenses, a popular religion that served to mask anxieties seems

---

52. *Mt. Pleasant Free Press*, Jul. 13, 1944; *Iowa City Press-Citizen*, Jul. 31, 1944; Aug. 1, 1944; DMR, Aug. 4, 1944; *Iowa Fellowship*, Sep. 1944.

53. While the Methodist-sponsored Cherokee unit was already underway (*Iowa Fellowship*, May 1944), the Evangelical and Reformed unit in Independence experienced a delay. "As a consequence of a recently developed bad public relations situation in Iowa, Selective Service has postponed the establishment of an additional unit in that state," the Commission on Christian Social Action of the Evangelical and Reformed Church reported. *Christian Social Action Bulletin*, Aug. 1944; Jul. 15, 1945; Nov. 15, 1945; Jan. 15, 1946; Minutes of the Commission on Christian Social Action, Jan. 5, 1944; Aug. 16, 1944; Apr. 4–5, 1945; Jan. 16, 1946; Sep. 4–5, 1946; Jan. 28–29, 1947. Newsletters from the Cherokee CPS unit (*Release*) are compiled in Rosheim, *Four Sisters*.

54. Comparing the population and turnover statistics of the reports of the institutions suggest this, as well as anecdotal evidence. 27th *Biennial Report, Board of Control, 1950*, 8–10; 28th *Biennial Report*, 95; 29th *Biennial Report*, 11–12, 15, 17, 19, 20; Rogers, *Time and the Human Robot*.

The People Are Kind

less ideal. Coming back from the war and venturing into fifties Iowa was a relief, but there were unresolved aspects of the postwar situation that did not seem settled. The seeds of the sixties had been planted.

CHAPTER 21

Protestantism at Zenith

"Washington Prairie Lutheran Church . . . stands as monument to Scandinavian industry and dogged persistence . . . Its very survival as a country church in an era of rampant urbanization and suburbanization in American culture offers eloquent testimony to the sense of community parishioners feel at Washington Prairie."

—*Christian Century*[1]

"Two large stained-glass windows frame the Gothic-style sanctuary of Collegiate United Methodist Church in Ames . . . The window in the east transept shows Jesus confounding the learned scholars in the temple. The west window offers a more traditional Methodist scene: Jesus praying in the Garden of Gethsemane.

These windows, backlit by the autumn sun, illustrate well the twin fulcrums of intellect and piety in Christianity . . .

Collegiate Methodist Church was able to carry off that balancing act, catering to both the spiritual and intellectual demands of the university, in 1950."

—*Christian Century*[2]

---

1. Balmer, *Grant Us Courage*, 25. The church is near Decorah.
2. *Christian Century*, Nov. 20, 1950; Balmer, *Grant Us Courage*, 89.

The People Are Kind

WE HAVE SEEN IN chapters 17 and 18 that the 1950s were a time of ferment for Catholics and fundamentalists. The post-war period in Iowa was also in many ways a high-water mark for mainline Protestants. Despite geopolitical, racial, and theological unrest, the relative prosperity of the decade lent itself to a certain self-satisfaction, a sense of arrival for many. And the somewhat widespread nature of that prosperity seemed to affirm the small-town ethos so compatible with much of mainline Protestantism.

Suburbanization often added a modernizing gloss to such small-town sensibilities. Technological progress and old-fashioned morality often seemed in tension, but mainline Protestantism was there to apply oil to that friction. On the other hand, sometimes that tension seemed existential, as religious Iowans struggled to make sense of the new nuclear reality.

IMAGINING THE END OF THE WORLD

In 1954, the United States exploded the world's first hydrogen bomb, multiplying the dangers of the nuclear age and making the acronym for the "doctrine" of Mutually Assured Destruction altogether too apt.

The *Des Moines Tribune,* always on the pulse of mainline Protestant leadership, polled six ministers for their reactions. Four of them, Lewis Jacobsen of First Baptist, Maynard Smith of Douglas Avenue Presbyterian, Orlando Dick of First Friends, and Warner Muir of University Christian, expressed alarm. C. T. B. Yeates of Westminster United Presbyterian observed, probably correctly but perhaps irrelevantly, that it would not change the moral order. The most banal response came from Charles Houser of Plymouth Congregational, whose answer his predecessor Stoddard Lane may have found deficient: "Religion is working for peace, brotherhood and understanding so this power can be used for constructive purposes."[3] If soothing words could allay nuclear anxieties, Rev. Houser was there to oblige.

A glance at ads and notices on a typical religion page of a fifties newspaper confirms the angst of living with Mutually Assured Destruction, although expressed in very different ways. In reassurance, the First

---

3. DMT, Apr. 3, 1954. For the general tendency to meld premillennialism with post-war current events, see Boyer, *When Time Shall Be No More.* The tiny Baha'i community ("about 60 [congregants] in Iowa, and eight in Des Moines") also got its statement opposing the H-Bomb into the *Tribune,* Jul. 10, 1954.

Seventh-day Adventist Church advertised, "When God Destroys All H-Bombs: The Resurrection of Christ Is a Promise of the End of War." More ominously, the First Assembly of God warned, "Wake Up or Blow Up[!]" The Fellowship Tabernacle joined the chorus; Rev. Peter Varnof was dubbed a "Crusader for Peace, . . . [but] Millions Wondering Will Russia Invade America? How Close Is War With Russia[?]"[4]

But the Rev. C. W. Phillips of the Unitarian Society approached the issue theologically rather than eschatologically in a New Year's sermon reprinted in the *Tribune*, "Are We Carrying Banners Of a God Named Security?" He questioned the motivation behind the religious revival of the 1950s: "I don't think this is any 'revival of religion,' but rather a symptom of the same low-level quest for security which has suffused us in nearly all areas of livin[g]."[5]

Enfolding and enabling the nuclear angst was fear of Communism. For fundamentalists especially, opposition to atheistic Communism became an article of faith (see chapter 18.) One of the more unexpected stories of Cold War Iowa is that of Helen W. Wood, sent to Iowa by the Communist Party to advocate for an African American prisoner. Encountering opposition to her work by local Communists, she had a change of heart and became a born-again Christian.[6]

The story is startling in at least three ways: it features an actual Communist, as opposed to the phantoms Senator McCarthy and others were chasing. The black prisoner gets obscured in the controversy. And the central character's veering from Communist organizer to fundamentalist American Soul Clinic propagandist can only be called stunning. Much in this story is unsettling, and yet somehow perfectly in tune with the times.

IMAGINING IOWA AS QUINTESSENTIALLY RELIGIOUS AMERICA

But it was hard to focus on totalitarianism or human extinction when things were going so well, for white Americans not suffering from poverty or polio. And there was much to celebrate in mid-century Iowa. When *Life Magazine* went looking for the prototypical American minister, its

---

4. DMT, May 1, 1954; Apr. 17, 1954; Oct. 29, 1955.
5. DMT, Jan. 1, 1955.
6. Wood, *America: Look and Live*.

search ended at the First Methodist Church in Boone.[7] In a photo essay, Alfred Eisenstadt followed Rev. Edwin S. Briggs around for a week, culminating with the Sunday service. Briggs exuded busyness, calm, efficiency, and an inoffensive spirituality that affirmed the townspeople.

Life's search for the model minister was probably spurred by Hartzell Spence's humorous but fond 1940 novelistic tribute to his Iowa Methodist minister father and the 1941 movie adaptation of his *One Foot in Heaven* starring Fredric Marsh and Martha Scott. The elder Spence served just a county north of Boone in Fort Dodge. (Hartzell had been born in nearby Clarion.)[8] Both the *Life* piece and the Spence novel refracted a sunny confidence that belied the tempestuous century seemingly outside the immediate experience of an idyllic Iowa.

Of course, the fact that Iowa was (mostly) religious did not address the quality of the religious experience. In 1950, *Christian Century* did a series examining what the editors deemed the top twelve (mainline Protestant) congregations in the nation. Of the twelve, only Iowa had more than one "great" church. They were Collegiate Methodist of Ames and Washington Prairie Lutheran in rural Decorah.[9]

Washington Prairie figured prominently in the diary of pioneer Norwegian-American pastor's wife Elisabeth Koren (see chapter 6). For Collegiate Methodist, see chapter 20's discussion of its World War II pastor Sam Nichols and his preaching abilities. The *Century* saw Collegiate Methodist and Washington Prairie Lutheran as models of student and rural parishes.

MARCUS BACH'S ARC AS EMBLEMATIC OF TWENTIETH-CENTURY PROTESTANTISM

Others took up the search for quintessentially religious Iowa. State University of Iowa School of Religion professor (from 1942 to 1961) Marcus Bach was a prolific popularizer of American religion. His several dozen books embraced many differing forms of Protestantism and provided him with multiple vantage points to view his theme. His books tended

---

7. "Practical Man of God," *Life*, Feb. 3, 1941, 55–63.

8. Spence, *One Foot in Heaven*. Spence also wrote a 1942 sequel, *Get Thee Behind Me*.

9. *Christian Century*, Nov. 20, 1950; Randall Balmer, *Grant Us Courage*. Balmer revisited the congregations fifty years later for clues on change and stability in American Protestantism.

to dwell on the unusual aspects of American religion. He was fond of retelling his personal story in many of those books.[10]

While many of the books Bach churned out are forgettable, what is remarkable is how his personal religious arc mirrored so closely many changes in twentieth-century American religion. Bach grew up as an ethnic Protestant in the German Reformed Church. Early in his adulthood, he converted to Pentecostalism. That did not last, although he claimed he could practice glossolalia at will throughout his life.[11] He did report with embarrassment his zealous but failed attempt as a guest preacher to convince his Reformed pastor brother's stolid congregation to try speaking in tongues.[12]

Bach's next reincarnation was as graduate student in Iowa City, where he specialized in writing religious pageants and plays.[13] His appointment at the School of Religion led to the advocacy for mainline Protestantism that characterizes most of his books, although he also loved to explore more esoteric groups. But as more exotic breezes began to blow again in the sixties, Bach once again transformed, affirming a gentle New Age consciousness, sometimes akin to Unity Christianity, sometimes to Shoghi Effendi, and often just groovy.[14]

Marcus Bach was more emblematic than prophetic. His work popularizing American religion in the 1950s seems, when not self-referential, then fluffy and ethereal. His prose had captured the staccato of a *Time* piece, and it is unlikely that he caused offense after the ill-fated episode in his brother's pulpit. Bach's journey was not unique but illustrative of the century: from ethnic Protestantism through Pentecostalism and mainline Protestantism to something more ephemeral, less institutional, and more personal. Others traversed similar arcs.

Bach had another legacy, less obvious than his books but arguably more important for Iowa religious history. He hosted a WSUI radio show that highlighted various Iowa religious groups, primarily their music. Working with SUI music professor Addison Albach, among the groups

---

10. On Protestantism, see Bach, *Report to Protestants*. On more esoteric groups, see, e.g., *They Have Found a Faith, Faith and My Friends, Strange Sects and Curious Cults*.

11. Bach, *Inner Ecstasy*.

12. Bach, *Report to Protestants*, 140–47.

13. Bach, *Vesper Dramas*. Bach also wrote pageants celebrating the centenaries of Iowa Baptists and Methodists, but I have been unable to track those down. But I do thank Public Library of Des Moines librarian Ashley Molzen for her efforts.

14. *Unity Way*; *Meeting with Shoghi Effendi*; *I, Monty*.

Bach recorded singing hymns and psalms or preaching sermons were Norwegian and German Lutherans, Welsh Congregationalists, Czech and Associate Reformed Presbyterians, African American Methodists, Dutch Reformed, Reorganized Latter-day Saints, and, somewhat astonishingly, even Old Order Amish. The result is a remarkable snapshot of Iowa lived religion that confirms the continued importance of faith in many eastern Iowans' lives in the middle decades of the twentieth century and also affirms and celebrates its diversity.[15]

THE SCHOOL OF RELIGION

The University of Iowa's School of Religion had its roots in the 1920s, the first public university to attempt such a project,[16] and was an interfaith endeavor. While founded earlier, it epitomized the *zeitgeist* of the fifties. In fact, by then the unwieldiness of its original structure was showing signs of fissure. A dishy letter from a Catholic board member reveals a resentment to "radical" Protestants perceived to be in control of the decision-making process, and an angling for Lutherans to get a seat at the table.[17]

Indeed, the professorship of George Forell, who was certainly an asset to the religion faculty, was also an indication of a new Lutheran public presence. Lutherans had been preoccupied with internal matters, slowly consolidating their ethnically and theologically diverse denominations. By the 1950s, Lutherans were consolidated enough, primarily in the German-dominated American Lutheran Church (which incorporated the Iowa Synod) and the Scandinavian-heavy Lutheran Church in America, to begin to pull the weight their numbers allowed. (The two, and an expelled faction of Missouri Synod Lutherans, would unite into the Evangelical Lutheran Church in America in 1988.)

The school venture also became an ongoing struggle for the small Jewish population in the state to keep up their fundraising commitments to the interreligious enterprise.[18]

15. WSUI audio tapes by Marcus Bach, SC-UI.
16. Douglas, "Making Iowa Safe for Differences."
17. William Francis Riley Papers, Box 5, Folder 32, SC-UI. George Forell became a Lutheran member of the faculty in 1954. Although irenic, he may not have been the antidote to Protestant "radicalism" that the board member was yearning for. But his scholarship did lift the school's prestige.
18. Mannheimer, "Reminiscences," 2:283–88, typescript, SHSI-DM.

THE CONTINUED BUSYNESS OF IOWA PROTESTANTISM

The political influence and concerns of Iowa churchgoers, exemplified by the postwar work to reform Iowa's mental health system (see previous chapter) continued in the decade, and religious folk continued to find ways to keep busy. One ecumenical project had "Catholics, Protestants Plan[ning a] Church Census."[19]

No one was busier in the fifties than Church Women United.[20] In pushing through mental health reform, it had shown it was a force to be reckoned with. When the Greater Des Moines Council of Churches held its founding meeting in 1952, one of the local CWU leaders could not keep from observing, with an uncharacteristic lack of modesty, that "she was glad the men were catching up with the women, who had been organized for 60 years."[21]

The Disciples of Christ, founded on the principle of Christian unity, was particularly anxious to effect greater organizational unity among Protestants. One Drake graduate Disciple who was focused on ecumenism was Jesse M. Bader.[22] Bader was particularly adept at finding ways to keep the mainline Protestant tent as large as possible. As one colleague put it,

> When the major emphasis of the Federal Council [of Churches] seemed to be not only social Christianity but social Christianity to the disparagement of evangelism, Dr. Bader, always with 'sweetness and light' but also with an unfaltering purpose, sought to restore the balance. Perhaps he, more than any other man, saved the Federal Council from the loss of evangelical support. This also he will humbly deny.[23]

For a multiplicity of reasons, including the passing of a generation of leaders like Bader, who had already died when this tribute appeared,

---

19. *Des Moines Tribune*, Jan. 9, 1954. On the national level, a proposal to include questions on religion in the 1960 federal census proved divisive. Catholics thought that such a survey would underline their numerical strength, while Jews worried that it would show the opposite for their religion. Schultz, *Tri-Faith America*.

20. DMR, Feb. 15, 1954; Scrapbooks, Box 8, Church Women United of the Des Moines Area papers, SHSI-DM; Johnson, "Building Bridges," 120–23.

21. DMR, Feb. 18, 1952. Earlier ecumenical endeavors among the males were intermittent.

22. Dahlberg, *Herald of the Evangel*, 196–213, 214–21.

23. Dahlberg, *Herald of the Evangel*, 218.

that irenic spirit would not hold, and the lines the first generation of fundamentalists drew in the twenties would harden by the late seventies.

Illustrative of institutional religion's forays into social services was the Lutheran Social Services of Iowa. With roots in services to orphans, by the forties LSSI had become the largest private human services agency in the state.[24]

African American Protestantism continued somewhat apart. Exemplary was African Methodist Episcopal pastor George Singleton, of St. Paul A.M.E. in Des Moines and president of the local NAACP, who would become a bishop, editor of the denominational paper, and historian of the denomination in his *Romance of African Methodism*.[25]

And, as much by default as by design, black churches continued to be social service agencies for their congregants. A stark reminder of the church as employment agency was the circa 1942 business card of Rev. H. J. Parker of Bethel A.M.E. of Des Moines, which read, "For Colored Help, Call the Pastor."[26]

Illustrative of the post-World War II migration of African Americans to Iowa is the career of the longest serving bishop of the largest Black Pentecostal denomination in Iowa, the Church of God in Christ. Hurley Bassett, a native of Memphis, moved to Davenport after military service in World War II, where he was converted. In 1958 he moved to Cedar Rapids to found New Jerusalem COGIC (which would purchase the Czech Presbyterian Hus Memorial building).[27]

ALTERNATIVE PROTESTANTISMS

While mid-century was the zenith for mainline Protestantism, fundamentalists were busy too, with some rebranding as evangelicals. In hindsight, notable was the cameo appearance of Billy Graham, then working as an evangelist for Youth for Christ. Graham came to Des Moines in

24. Lagerquist, "Being Lutheran in Public"; Hanusa, *Hope for All Generations*.

25. Singleton, *Romance of African Methodism*. The biographical information is from the dust jacket cover; "St. Paul AME Church."

26. Box 3, F.[7] "African-American Churches of Des Moines," Frances Hawthorne Papers, IWA. The photocopy of the card has "1942" in the background, and a city directory confirms that Parker was pastor at Bethel then.

27. DMR, Oct. 10, 2017; CG, Oct. 8, 2010; Black Iowa podcast, May 2, 2023.

that capacity immediately after World War II, two years before going solo with his own crusade. Rev. Frank Smith of the Church of the Open Bible served as Graham's local sponsor as he organized a Youth For Christ chapter in the capital city.[28]

Smith was himself a leader in Pentecostal and evangelical circles. He helped found both the National Association of Evangelicals and the Pentecostal Fellowship of North America, serving as president of the latter.[29]

Perhaps because of the long history in Iowa of groups such as the Church of the Open Bible, the largest predominantly white Pentecostal denomination, the Assemblies of God, does not dominate as much as in some states. A map of denominational dominance of Pentecostals by county shows a wide variation of groups.[30]

Among the complaints conservatives lodged against the mainline was a new translation of the Bible. Sometimes the accusations leveled against the Revised Standard Version seemed calculated more toward whipping up controversy than maintaining accuracy.[31]

Conservative Protestants were also establishing educational institutions. In 1956, the General Association of Regular Baptists approved the Omaha Baptist Bible Institute as in keeping with its principles. (As ultra-congregationalists, they were reluctant to establish a denominational entity.) It moved to Ankeny and became Faith Baptist Bible College and Seminary in 1965.[32]

In 1955 in Sioux Center, members of the Christian Reformed Church established Dordt College, which became an outpost for the Reformed thought of Dutch philosopher Herman Dooyeweerd.[33] This was an intellectual accomplishment that had little resonance in the rest of the state.

Among the college-plantings of Vernon Newland, Christian Church leader and former missionary to Tibet and prisoner of war in the Philippines during World War II, was Iowa Christian College in Des Moines. This seed was apparently planted in poor soil, as the college never thrived.[34]

28. Grem, *Blessing of Business*, 48; private Facebook group.
29. DMR, Oct. 4, 1997.
30. Gaustad, Fig. 2.127.
31. *S. O. S. Signal*, v. 18:4 (Apr.-May 1953), in Box 9, F. 5, Edythe Sterlin Papers, IWA.
32. "History of Faith"; Hummel, *Rise and Fall of Dispensationalism*, 317.
33. McIntire, "Herman Dooyeweerd in North America," 58.
34. *Dubois County Herald*, Apr. 5, 2016; Garrett, *Stone-Campbell Movement*, 4, 475.

Other mentions of conservative religion are extant. Perhaps the scariest of *Life*'s photographs of Iowa ministers was of the Rev. Haan of First Christian Reformed Church of Sioux Center, with hands ominously outstretched, exhorting parishioners not to attend movies.[35] This particular crusade did not enjoy long-term success.

THEOLOGICAL RUMBLINGS

Iowans continued to try to make sense of the scars of the recent war, struggling with the meaning of the Holocaust and indiscriminate bombing and filtering its meaning through their religious understanding. German Lutheran pastor Martin Niemöller, famous for his lament for being too late in speaking up against the Nazi regime, spoke in Cedar Rapids in 1947.[36]

While most theological change in Iowa was gradual, it could be dramatic. The transformation of the Luther College religion department was one such case. In the forties the department was so conservative that J. A. O. Preuss, who as denominational president would steer the Lutheran Church Missouri Synod from conservative to ultraconservative, was comfortable as a student (even though it was not a Missouri Synod school).[37] In 1961, the rest of the religion department threatened to quit if the new faculty member, the moderate Robert Jenson, remained on staff. The administration called this bluff and accepted the resignations; only Jenson remained. Ironically, by the nineties, well after his stay in Decorah, Jenson himself had moved to a more conservative position, albeit not one as hidebound as his faculty opponents in the fifties.[38] And the religion department at Luther had moved into the mainstream of American Lutheran thought.

While the impulse for Iowa laypersons to write theological treatises was hardly new, starting with the 1839 imprint by Joseph Kirkpatrick (see introduction),[39] Mary McDermott Shideler brought a new sophisti-

---

35. Schaap, *Our Family Album*, 261–63; *Life*, Apr. 19, 1948.
36. Kuhns, "Evangelical and Reformed Church in Iowa," 181.
37. Balmer, *Encyclopedia of Evangelicalism*, 465.
38. *Christianity Today*, Sep. 7, 2017.
39. Other published attempts at theology, for which some enterprising scholar might some day find redeeming value, include Thayer, *Morning Star*; Whitcomb, *Meditations on the* Via Crucis; Crawford, *Holy Spirit and Holy Living*; Espey, *Minor Heresies*; Goodwin, *Prophecy Concerning Babylon*; Bechtold, *From Hostility to Nobility*;

cation to the task; drawing upon the Inklings group, she devised *A Creed for a Christian Skeptic* from the Apostles' Creed.[40]

The theological rumblings in fifties Iowa suggest a certain dissatisfaction with the *de facto* mainline Protestant consensus, a rumbling that would become louder in the next decade and lead to a reckoning about whether a gospel of conciliation, reconciliation, or challenge might best fit the times.

THE TRIUMPH OF BUREAUCRACY IN PROTESTANT DENOMINATIONS

As early as Social Gospel times, an insistence on conceding to experts on rural issues and deferring to professional expertise in reforming society was present. By the fifties, bureaucratization was entrenched in most Protestant denominations, with the American ideal of efficiency raised to the level of a Christian imperative, abetted by appeals to stewardship.[41]

For both ecumenical and efficient reasons, the decade saw a time of consolidation. German Reformed and Congregationalists formed the United Church of Christ, becoming the third largest Protestant denomination in Iowa. Northern Presbyterians and United Presbyterians merged; each had a significant presence in the state. Lutherans continued their long march toward merging almost all of the non-Missouri Synod Lutherans into the Evangelical Lutheran Church in America, finally accomplished in 1988, and Methodists and their German kin, the Evangelical United Brethren, would merge in 1968.

The Methodist merger provided an opportunity to undo the segregation of Methodist African Americans who had been confined to a non-geographic "Central Jurisdiction" since Northern and Southern Methodists merged in 1938. Ancillarily, with a consequent surplus of African American bishops, the Iowa Conference experienced the leadership of several African American bishops, starting with James Thomas in 1964.[42] Charles Jordan and Gregory Palmer continued that tradition,

---

McNellus, *Unveiling of the Great Whore and the Diverse Beast*.

40. See also Mary McDermott Shideler Papers, IWA; and *Consciousness of Battle* and *Visions and Nightmares: Ends and Beginnings*. (5 vols.)

41. For the national picture, see Bendroth, *Good and Mad*, chapter 2; Moorhead, "Presbyterians and the Mystique of Organizational Efficiency."

42. Thomas, *Methodism's Racial Dilemma*; Nye, *Between the Rivers*, 146–49; Shockley, *Heritage and Hope*, 211; Andrews, *Tradition of Grace*, 57.

The People Are Kind

with Palmer also serving as president of the worldwide Council of Bishops in 2007.[43]

Consolidation generally privileged efficiency above community. But sometimes new communities could be forged. And, importantly, Protestants increasingly began conversations across denominational lines; for small churches in small towns, like the Fergusons' congregation in Suckow's *The Folks*, merging congregations across denominational lines was often a less painful alternative than simply closing the doors.

JUNIOR PARTNERS

Arguably the preeminent Jewish contribution to American popular culture[44] was made by twins from Sioux City, Esther Pauline Lederer and Pauline Esther Phillips, advice columnists known to millions of devoted readers as Ann Landers and Abigail Van Buren.

> Landers and Van Buren accurately represented the values of the average American Jew in the 1950s, 1960s, and early 1970s. They believed in God and Country, espoused liberal Judaism and liberal politics, frowned on public expressions of religious and racial intolerance but disliked traditionalist forms of Christianity, accepted sexual drives as good (i.e., not sinful), tolerated abortion, and, though not endorsing homosexuality, attacked homophobic intolerance.[45]

But growing up as a Jew in Des Moines in the 1950s, Marlene Booth felt more conflicted. Her film *Yidl in the Middle: Growing Up Jewish in Iowa* portrayed a childhood torn between her Jewish and her larger environments, which she and almost all of her twenty-two cousins resolved by leaving the state in adulthood.[46]

---

43. DMR, Aug. 21, 2000; Nov. 10, 2007.

44. University of Northern Iowa professor Harry Brod made the case for another popular icon, this one fictional, in *Superman Is Jewish?*

45. Heinze, *Jews and the American Soul*, 303.

46. Marlene Booth Papers, IWA; *Yidl in the Middle* trailer, available on YouTube (youtube.com/watch?v=u1cC4stXJcw); *Best of Living in Iowa*; DMR, Mar. 21, 1999; *The Scene*, Spring 1999; *Cityview*, Dec. 1, 1999.

THE VIEW FROM THE SETTLEMENT

Both anthropologists and Presbyterians were interested in reexamining Meskwakis (still referred to as Fox, or Sac and Fox). In typical gung-ho 1950s fashion, Action Anthropology felt that all that was necessary for Meskwakis to forge ahead (in which direction, it wasn't entirely clear) was a proper infusion of sociological insight.[47] The University of Chicago anthropologists were dismayed at the (apparent) Meskwaki lethargy, especially when they were disinterested in the academics' suggestions.[48] Many Meskwakis, however, had other, often religious, perspectives that made them resistant to a progressive transformation of their nation.

Sociology also foregrounded Presbyterian bureaucratic[49] analysis of the settlement, although more narrowly focused on the viability of the Presbyterian mission there.[50] Reading between the lines, after the merger with the smaller United Presbyterian Church (which was dominant in Tama County),[51] Northern Presbyterians hoped to withdraw from evidently futile conversion efforts. But the study's conclusions about options were listed neutrally, and the mission at Tama lasted for another decade and a half, only to be abruptly terminated then.[52]

While the report ended up shelved, the sociological analysis does give us insight into the religious situation on the settlement in 1959. While Meskwaki agency may be missing from the conclusions, both the anthropological and sociological studies do limn religious practice there. Paul Baker found four religious groupings on the settlement: the traditionalist "Cult of the Sacred Bundle," the Drum Society, Christians, and "Peyote Cult" practitioners of the Native American Church. Ironically, all but members of the pan-Indian Native American Church were invited to

---

47. Tax et al., *Documentary History of the Fox Project*.

48. Daubenmeier, *Meskwaki and Anthropologists*; Foley, *Heartland Chronicles*; McTaggart, *Wolf That I Am*.

49. "The Iowa Board of National Missions requested a survey of the Mesquakie Indian Work at Tama, Iowa, in May, 1959, through the Department of Town and Country Church—Indian Work, of the Board of National Missions, UPUSA in New York . . . " Baker, *Study of the Presbyterian Mission Among the Mesquakie*, iv.

50. Baker, *Study of the Presbyterian Mission Among the Mesquakie*. While Baker cited Applied Anthropology works in his reports, subsequent works on the movement have ignored his study.

51. See Wilcox, *Tama Jim*, 16; Murray, *They Came to North Tama*, 192–93.

52. Interview with Loren Soth, Toledo, IA, Jun. 21, 2018.

participate in the annual powwow. Advocating universality meant exclusion by particularists.

SETTING UP THE SIXTIES

Perhaps the partial vision that Protestants had about Meskwaki culture has something to say about the limits of Protestantism,[53] even at its zenith.

Moving from the staidness of the fifties to the boldness of the sixties would not, of course, resolve the existential nuclear question that hovered overhead. And yet a bubbling up of questions and challenges that was sometimes barely perceptible in the former decade often boiled over in the latter, not just in Protestantism but in the vibrancy of Vatican II Catholicism and in increased interest in other faiths—and increased skepticism about all faiths. And an Iowa religious entity would, for the first time nationally, challenge the nuclear consensus. Iowans approached the new decade with an increasingly familiar mixture of hope and angst, but largely oblivious to its expansive possibilities and concomitant threats. (Of course, that is always the case.)

---

53. There was a brief unsuccessful attempt at a Catholic mission to the Meskwakis in the early twentieth century. Goodman, *Century of Catholicity in Southwest Tama County*, 15.

CHAPTER 22

Complicating the Consensus
The 1960s

"The world is not only changing. It has always been doing that. What is new in our world is the speed at which everything is changing . . . The church cannot be seen as a peaceful asylum for those who wish to escape from the vicious cycles of change in the world."
—CARL E. BRAATEN, LECTURING IN DECORAH, 1963[1]

"Jesus loves our President,
Even though he is a Catholic.
There's a lot for a boy to think about . . ."
—GREG BROWN[2]

"The challenge to the old institutions became the subtle, incremental effects of time and growing material well-being that focused on secular and personal matters. Individuals were taking more control over their lives. Families were smaller, Separation from the grind of labor-intensive farming created fewer but more prosperous farmers . . .

Religion still had a central place, of course, but people had more choices . . . This was an era when people were asking more questions, and even the

---

1. Braaten, "Dynamics of a Responding Church," in *Challenge of Change*, 29, 30.
2. Brown, "Brand New '64 Dodge."

authority of the church was not as strong as it had been. Fewer young persons were joining the priesthood or entering the convent. It is easier to run a parochial school when the faculty has taken an oath of poverty."

—Kenneth Pins, on growing up in the Catholic enclave of Dyersville[3]

"Our time is a time of erasing the lines that divided things neatly."
—Sr. Corita[4]

"I had a grower once tell me, 'Sister Irene, what business do you have here with these migrant workers? You should be in your chapel with your rosary.' I thought, oh, God. I said, 'Have you ever heard of Vatican II? We've changed. Isn't that something?'"
—Sr. Irene Munoz[5]

Most Protestants were blindsided by evidence that the coalition between God and America was unstable or conditional. Catholics were likewise jolted by Vatican II, which upended much that had been taken for granted: some in the hierarchy now sometimes argued against the primacy of hierarchy, and a church that had based its superiority on its changelessness suddenly embraced change. In 1965, a new, less racist immigration law increased the possibility that newcomers might have belief systems different from those two dominant traditions.

The destabilization of the sixties, grounded in the insistent and visceral religious call for racial justice that had so long been ignored, reshaped Iowa and Iowa religion in ways that most observers in the fifties could not have imagined. (Those attending William Penn College in the late 1940s might have seen inklings.)[6] And the quagmire that became the US war in Indochina further challenged received wisdom. Of course, received wisdom was always selective. Young people usually did not realize past precedents for change, without knowledge of the Student

3. Pins, "In the Steeple's Shadow," 141.
4. Kent, "Art and Beauty in the Life of the Sister," 11.
5. Oral History Interview with Sr. Irene Munoz, Aug. 3, 2003, 23, IWA.
6. See my "Penn in Technicolor."

Volunteer Movement convention in Des Moines in 1920 or the anti-war movement around Dubuque in the 1930s, to cite just two examples of generational upheaval.

Emblematic of a new sense of social responsibility was the story of Joe Fagan. He grew up in rural Catholic Dubuque County, attended public school, and became a life-long Dodger fan after learning of Jackie Robinson's breaching of the color barrier. After college at Loras, he became a priest, but he felt stifled at his assignment at Oelwein, where the senior priest held up fastidiousness as the principle virtue, and he was shocked when no one else seemed disturbed by Martin Luther King's assassination in 1968. Transferred to Waterloo, Fagan with other priests founded the community organizing group Citizens for Community Improvement, which became a statewide force.[7] He continued to work for CCI after leaving the priesthood and marrying.

The combination of questioning received opinion and assertiveness on behalf of the underprivileged was a touchstone of religious experience in the sixties. The previous decade's anxiety about atomic destruction also, finally, provoked pushback.

NUCLEAR DISARMAMENT

The 1960 Dubuque Statement against nuclear weapons began the decade on a progressive note. On January 12, 1960, seven of the twelve faculty members at the Presbyterian-affiliated University of Dubuque Theological Seminary issued a statement formally titled "Mass Extermination as a Means of Waging War." They were against it.

Arthur Cochrane, the Canadian-born theologian who drafted the statement,[8] was an unreconstructed Barthian; when later given the guest column in the *Christian Century* on "How My Mind Has Changed," he maintained that it hadn't.[9] More to the point, his study of the Barmen Declaration, a Barth-influenced document in which German church

---

7. Fagan, "How One Opportunity Led to Another."
8. Healey, "Arthur Cochrane and the Church-Confessing."
9. Cochrane, "Whether Karl Barth Has Changed My Mind."

people challenged the Nazi state's encroaching power over the German church, gave him a vantage point to critique nationalist politics.[10]

Here are two of the most salient points of the Dubuque Statement:

> 4 . . . .the threat and exercise of the means of mass extermination in waging war is blasphemy against God the Creator, Preserver, and Redeemer of human life and is sin against the creature for whom Christ died and rose again. It defeats the very purpose for which war may lawfully be waged . . .
>
> 15. As "fruit that befits repentance" (Lk. 3:8), we declare that we can no longer support the government's policy of the threat and exercise of the means of mass extermination, whether nuclear, chemical, or biological. We cannot sanction the production, testing, and application of the means of extermination, nor can we approve of any military service that involves the use of such instruments of warfare.[11]

The statement's publication made only a minor splash; it did not make statewide news and was only a one-day story in Dubuque. On campus, the political science department at the university hotly debated it. But it was reported in denominational and pan-Protestant periodicals, and, tellingly, was translated into Japanese and German.[12]

The statement also sent ripples of nervousness through the Northern Presbyterian bureaucracy, which found funding to send some of the signers to New York for instruction from the State Department on why the possession of nuclear weapons was necessary. The Dubuque professors enjoyed the excursion but remained unpersuaded by government propaganda.[13]

The Dubuque Statement was probably the first American religious institutional statement critical of nuclear weapons, but it was followed

---

10. Cochrane, *Church's Confession Under Hitler*, 9–49, 206, 210; Cochrane, "Barmen and the Confession of 1967." See also his *Christian Century* article, "John Calvin and Nuclear War," Jul. 4, 1962.

11. The statement was reprinted in Cochrane, *Mystery of Peace*, xiii-xiv.

12. *Dubuque Telegraph-Herald*, Jan. 13, 1960; *Christian Century*, Mar. 19, 1960; *Presbyterian Life*, Mar. 15, 1960; May 1, 1960; *Presbyterian Outlook*, Feb. 29, 1960; *Pulpit* 31, 9–11.

13. Interview with Howard Wallace, Dubuque, Nov. 9, 1999; letters from Donald Bloesch, Charles E. Carlston, Bill Jamison, Robert M. Healey, Nov. 1999. It should be noted that as a pacifist, Jamison did not sign the statement because it was not pacifist enough.

closely by a more widely circulated statement initiated at Andover Seminary and was folded into it.[14]

Other events at Dubuque Seminary deserve mention. In 1962, the eminent Swiss theologian Karl Barth made his only trip to the United States. Thanks to his friendship with Cochrane, Dubuque was one of five theological centers where Barth spoke, along with Chicago, New York, Princeton, and San Francisco.[15]

Barth's influence on Christian theology can hardly be overstated, but his work was so dense that its effects were diffuse. His critique of nineteenth-century liberalism was more easily assimilated, and his stand against Nazi idolatry too easily appropriated for patriotic purposes by an American audience, although his dogged insistence on wedding a theology of revelation with a democratic socialist ethics may prove enduring.[16]

In 1965, the seminary joined with the Aquinas Institute, Wartburg Seminary, and the School of Religion in Iowa City to form a groundbreaking ecumenical cooperation, the Association of Theological Faculties in Iowa.[17]

In 1974, Dubuque Seminary would be the first in the country to sign a collective bargaining agreement with its faculty.[18] In 1980, Dubuque Seminary would again make headlines, in what the press hailed as the first labor strike of seminary professors since the Middle Ages. Professors struck for three days, returning partially victorious.[19]

From a relatively protected vantage point,[20] religious Iowans drew on ethical reserves to critique the status quo.

---

14. *Worldview*, Feb. 1961; Gottwald, "Nuclear Realism or Nuclear Pacifism?" *Christian Century*, Aug. 3, 1960.

15. Busch, *Karl Barth*, 391, 459; *Time*, Apr. 30, 1962. Barth was not the only European religious luminary to speak in Dubuque in the early sixties; the year previous, World Council of Churches leader Visser T'ooft spoke at Wartburg Seminary. *Dubuque Telegraph-Herald*, May 2, 6, 1962.

16. See, e.g., Hunsinger, *Karl Barth and Radical Politics*. "Barth's . . . influence on [Martin Luther] King has been underappreciated." Marsh, *Beloved Community*, 226n47.

17. *Christian Century*, Sep. 29, 1965.

18. Mihelic, "Survey of the History of the University of Dubuque," 61–62.

19. Straatmeyer, *Child of the Church*, 188–89; *Des Moines Register*, Sep. 2, 6, 1980.

20. According to Healey, both the dean, Calvin Schnucker, and the president, Gaylord Couchman, "sta[u]nchly defended our right to speak out on the issues," despite strong pressure. Neither of them signed the statement, Schnucker because he saw it as "a failure of nerve in which our fear of mass extermination had triumphed," and Couchman gave no explanation. Robert M. Healey to author, Roseville, MN, Nov. 19, 1999.

CIVIL RIGHTS

The obvious religious roots, moral means, and ethical implications of the civil rights struggle that began in the American South resonated with many religious Iowans. Some Iowa church people participated directly in the civil rights revolution, overthrowing segregation in the South. Frazer and Loris Thomason of Wakonda Christian Church in Des Moines answered the call,[21] as did Milton Cole, who became an Episcopalian pastor and moved to West Des Moines,[22] and Lutheran pastor Larry Stumme of Cedar Falls, who participated in the voting rights march from Selma to Montgomery in 1965.[23]

Rims Barber of Iowa served as pastor for Delta Ministry in Canton, Mississippi from 1964 to 1966, and John Else, a Disciples minister, was in the Gulfport area working for Delta for a year. Barber remained in Mississippi as an activist; Else later taught social work at the University of Iowa.[24] The list is certainly much longer, as the civil rights movement had a profound effect on religious Iowans.

Rev. Waldo Mead, a Methodist minister from Cedar Rapids studying in North Carolina, challenged Jim Crow laws in 1962, inviting a black friend to join him at a Durham restaurant. Mead was arrested for trespassing and chose jail, working on a road gang, over a fine. His punishment was more than he bargained for; he was deliberately nicked by axes of fellow prisoners clearing brush. After ten days of constant hostility by prisoners and guards alike, he paid his fine.[25]

More locally but just as crucially was the involvement of St. Paul Methodist Church of Cedar Rapids in desegregating its neighborhood in 1961, on behalf of a professional couple, Dr. Percy and Lileah Harris. (Percy Harris would later become the long-term coroner of Linn County.) The church served as an intermediary, buying the house without the seller's knowledge that a racial compact was being breached. But the action proved internally divisive as a disgruntled minority left to join the just-formed Lovely Lane Methodist Church, where they also found little sympathy for their views.[26]

---

21. Frazer and Loris Thomasen Papers, SHSI-DM.
22. DMR, Mar. 26, 2017.
23. Waterloo-Cedar Falls *Courier*, Aug. 2, 2014; Jan. 19, 2015; Apr. 5, 2018.
24. Findlay, *Church People*, 119–20, 134n23.
25. Mills, *Judge and a Rope*, 175–77.
26. Box 2, Lileah Harris Papers, IWA; Lake, "Manuscript Collections," AI 63, 185;

Later on in the decade, with St. Paul Methodist in the lead, Linn County formed a Cousin County Project with Holmes County, Mississippi, providing material aid to that poverty-stricken area. Grundy and Cerro Gordo Counties also set up programs.[27]

Another thread connecting Iowa to the movement was Rev. Martin Luther King, Jr's frequent visits. He first spoke in Iowa in April 1959, preaching at the University Christian Church in Des Moines. He returned that November, to Cedar Falls, Waterloo, Davenport, Des Moines, Iowa City, and Cedar Rapids.[28] He preached in Ames on January 22, 1960, participated at a week-long religious colloquium at Simpson College in February 1962 and spoke at Coe and Cornell Colleges on October 15, 1962. In 1965 he received the Pacem in Terris award from the Diocese of Davenport.[29] He also spoke at Central College on March 22, 1967, and at Grinnell College in October 1967. The honoraria helped replenish the coffers of the chronically underfunded Southern Christian Leadership Conference.

Religious leadership in lobbying for the Civil Rights Act had a determinative effect in the Midwest, where reluctant Republican representatives needed reassurance that a white constituency for racial justice existed. Political strategists realized Midwestern votes were crucial in overcoming a Southern-led filibuster.

Archbishop James Byrne, energized by the Second Vatican Council, doggedly lobbied Catholic Senator Jack Miller until Miller committed to the bill.[30] Senator Bourke Hickenlooper and Congressman James Bromwell of Cedar Rapids were two Iowa Republicans somewhat bewildered by the groundswell of public opinion, with many constituents touting their religious affiliations. When B'nai Brith organized its Iowa

---

Redlining Exhibit, African American Museum of Iowa, Cedar Rapids, 2021; Brigham and Wright, "Civil Rights Organizations," OI, 317-18; Brigham, "Places," 120-23; phone interview with Scott Meador, Cedar Rapids, Jun. 22, 2023.

27. Brigham, "Places," 200, 371-74, 382-87.

28. KWWL News, Jan. 20, 2020. Iowapublicradio.org, Jun. 27, 2022; "Ames History Museum"; "Search Online King Records Access (OKRA)."

29. DMR, Jan. 15, 2008; Brigham, "Places," 129-30.

30. Risen, *Bill of the Century*, 4, 223, 230; Gallagher, *Seed/Harvest*, 134-36; Brigham, "Transforming Places," 133-40.

attorney members to visit Congressional offices, the lobbyists included Hickenooper's former law partner. Presbyterians seem to have been particularly ardent petitioners to Bromwell.[31]

> The local organizing was in many respects unprecedented: A certain spontaneity suggested how unusual the efforts were for the people involved. A large gathering organized by the local clergy in Delaware County, Iowa, in September 1963, was described by a local politician as 'quite unique' because none of the organizers 'had ever been involved in a rally on a public issue so they were not quite sure how to conduct it, but they went ahead anyway.'[32]

The Iowa Council of Churches, though often constrained by a constituency resistant to controversy, was struck by the moment. "Suddenly our nation awoke last year in the midst of an intense fight over civil rights. Seldom have the churches and denominations been so unanimous in demanding positive action,"[33] its newsletter proclaimed. Notable as the local organizing was, it did have direction from the state's religious leaders. On September 12, 1963, the founding conference of the Iowa Commission on Religion and Race was called to order by three of its four co-chairs, Bishop Daly of the Des Moines Diocese; Rabbi Irving Weingart, president of the Iowa Board of Rabbis; and Judson Fiebiger, conference minister of the United Church of Christ. (The fourth co-chair, Methodist Bishop Gerald Ensley, was out of the country.) Attendance estimates varied from seven hundred to one thousand, with three-quarters coming from outside of Des Moines.[34]

But not all civil rights work was received positively by white churches. Rev. Leonard Tinker was forced out of the Methodist Church in Atlantic in 1957 after calling for desegregation of the public swimming pool. Reassigned to Epworth in Des Moines, he and his wife Lorena again came under fire for inviting blacks to worship there. Tinker pivoted to become regional peace secretary for the American Friends Service Committee in Des Moines in 1961.[35]

31. Findlay, *Church People*, 56–61, 73n51.
32. Findlay, *Church People*, 60.
33. *Councilor*, Jan. 1964, in Box 8, F. "*Councilor*, Iowa Council of Churches Newsletter, 1962–1970," Iowa Council of Churches Records, SHSI-IC. See also *Councilor*, Jun. 6, 1964.
34. DMR, Sep. 12, 13, 1963; Risen, *Bill of the Century*, 107.
35. Johnson, *Struggle for Student Rights*, 12–13; *American Friends Service Committee North Central Region 50th Anniversary*, 11.4. I have also benefited by talking to

Complicating the Consensus

One civil rights activist, emblematic if not representative, was Martha Nash of Waterloo. Nash, as a doctor's wife, was part of a small black middle class, and also distinctive in the African American community as an active Roman Catholic. From the fifties into the nineties, she worked with a dizzying array of activities and organizations: "Organizations she has participated in have dealt with education, health planning, racial justice, political activism, religion, mental health, developmental disabilities, welfare programs, and recreation," one newspaper breathlessly reported.[36] Civil rights organizations included the NAACP, a 1963 Black Hawk County conference on religion and race, the Waterloo Human Rights Commission, the black radio station KBBG, and the Martin Luther King, Jr Center, where she was director for a decade.

Nash's work within the Archdiocese of Dubuque with the Council of Catholic Women spilled out nationally and internationally, on the National Council of Catholic Women board from 1970 to 1973, and as chair of its International Relations Committee. In that capacity she attended a conference on Women and Peace in Nicosia, Cyprus in 1972 co-sponsored by the World Council of Churches and the Pontifical Commission on Justice and Peace.[37]

In early 1968, Governor Harold Hughes spoke to local churches at "Crisis Convocations" across the state, sharing his experiences listening to Iowa inner city residents.[38]

The civil rights movement viewed from the vantage point of Iowa could be inspiring, yet unsettling when the subject turned to racism within the state. But much as the issue of nuclear weapons was crowded out by the urgency of the civil rights struggle, later in the decade race was often overshadowed by war.

David Foster of Ankeny, who is writing a book on the Tinker case and its background.

36. Young, "Woman of Opinions," *Waterloo Courier*, Feb. 12, 1995.

37. Series 2, "Catholic Church, Society, and Reform," Box 1, Martha Nash Papers, IWA: Pew Research Center, "Black Catholics in America," Mar. 15, 2022.

38. Harrington, *Thunder from the Prairie*, 170–72; Wilson and Hedlund, *In His Own Words*, 135–40.

THE WAR IN INDOCHINA

As civil rights legislation gained traction in the mid-sixties, a new issue emerged. Slowly but perceptibly, the United States escalated its participation in a war in Southeast Asia. Patriotism, anti-Communism, isolationism, and anti-colonialism all had deep roots in the Midwest, but their coexistence was fragile, and particularly combustible in the context of US involvement in Vietnam. The self-immolation of Buddhist monks on American television screens was a religious reality that few in Iowa could comprehend.

Korean War-era draft resister Herbert F. Hoover, a Quaker farmer from Oskaloosa (and independent candidate for president in 1964), chartered a bus in November 1965 for Iowans to attend the first major anti-war rally in Washington, DC. Most Americans would have been befuddled by the sign he carried, "A Sign of Jonah," as more likely to evoke whales than a call to repentance.[39]

An early chapter of Clergy and Laity Concerned About Vietnam formed in 1966 in Grinnell.[40] Thousands of Iowans would eventually express their misgivings about the foreign misadventure. On the front lines were groups such as the Association of Campus Ministers in Iowa City, who helped fund the Center for Peace and Justice. The center housed various peace groups; sponsored speakers and debates on peace issues; organized the weekly silent vigils on the corner of Clinton and Washington Streets; and mediated between angry anti-war protesters and angry police.[41]

Bob Hartzler, a Mennonite pastor in Des Moines, was typical of a newfound activism around social justice and peace. He traveled to Europe in 1971 to monitor the peace conference in Paris, sponsored by the Urban Religious Council locally and by several national peace groups.[42] Hartzler was guardedly optimistic about the effects of their trip but readily admitted that public opinion was not unanimous.[43]

---

39. DMR, Nov. 28, 1965.

40. Hall, *Because of Their Faith: CALCAV*, 21.

41. Box 1, F. "History," F. "Newsletters," F. 6, "Reports and Press Releases," Box 2, F. 2, "Clergy and Laity Concerned," F. 4, "International Assembly of Christians," Center for Peace and Justice records, SHSI-IC; Hudson, *Diverse Community of Seekers*, 114.

42. Hartzler, *Memoir*, photocopy in author's possession, 66–68.

43. Hartzler, *Memoir*, 68.

THE COUNTERCULTURE AND ITS MIXED RESULTS

Much of what came to be known as the counterculture sought to remake religious experience from scratch. Of course, that was impossible, but importing from Eastern religions and from what seemed a simpler American past was not just possible but groovy.

One incident at Grinnell College suggests both rebellion and a new frankness about sex. Ten students stripped to protest a *Playboy* representative on campus. They employed biblical language to confront the exploitation: "Playboy Magazine is a money-changer in the temple of the body."[44]

Two young Iowans whose trajectories suggested the possibilities of the New Age were Ina May Gaskin of Marshalltown[45] and Donald Engstrom of Polk City. Gaskin, writing from a New Age commune, The Farm, almost single-handedly revolutionized Americans' views of childbirth with her *Spiritual Midwifery*, framing childbirth as a natural, earth-affirming event rather than a medical procedure.[46]

Engstrom celebrated the first flush of gay liberation with a combination of paganism and rural communal living, especially in the periodical *R.F.D.*, from Iowa City and Grinnell.[47]

An early indication that all was not well within mainline Protestantism became evident in Fairfield. A struggling Parsons College was remade, for a time, as a last chance college by Millard Roberts, a Presbyterian minister who pursued a high-risk strategy that increased enrollment but increased debt faster, a business model that would not outlast the end of the draft. The national publicity attendant with *Life* publishing an article entitled "The Wizard of Flunk Out U" did not help matters.[48]

After Parsons closed, Fairfield tried to adapt to a new reality: the town unwittingly had become the new American center of a New Age empire.

---

44. Miller, *Hippies and American Values*, 61.
45. Miller, *America's Alternative Religions*, 372–75; NYT, Jul. 2, 2014.
46. Gaskin, *Spiritual Midwifery*; salon.com/1999/06/01/gaskin.
47. LGBT Religious Archive Network.
48. Koerner, *Parsons College Bubble*; *Life*, Jun. 3, 1966.

THE CATHOLIC REVOLUTION OF VATICAN II

As noted in chapter 17, progressive Catholicism found a home in Davenport even before Vatican II. The early fifties League for Social Justice and later, the Catholic Interracial Council, focused Catholics' attention on local racial issues,[49] while the liberal-leaning diocesan paper *The Messenger* had developed a national reputation. But nothing prepared most Catholics for the seismic changes of the Second Vatican Council. Liturgical, ecumenical, and social justice initiatives all vied for parishioners' attention, and even more fundamentally, the council replaced a long-standing top-down vision of the Church with a horizontal one, stressing the concept of the People of God.

Beginning in 1964, the diocese of Davenport embraced "the constitutive dimension of the Gospel" of social justice by inaugurating the Pacem in Terris Peace and Justice award, given annually to a prominent, often globally famous activist. Martin Luther King, Jr., Dorothy Day, and Dom Helder Camara have been among the most famous recipients.[50]

Interviewed in 1991, parishioners in Sioux City had mixed feelings about the changes wrought by Vatican II but were mostly positive. For nuns, giving up the habit was at first "like parting with part of you." But the restrictions some orders had, for the BVM requiring two to be together in public at all times, or—for the Congregation of the Humility of Mary, allowing visits to family only once every three years—were rules happily discarded. The liturgical changes were the most popular. Most were happy to give up the Latin mass; comprehensibility increased their sense of participation in worship.[51]

Implementing Vatican II's new directions was the mission of Bishop Maurice Dingman in Des Moines. Appointed bishop in 1968, arriving from the progressive diocese of Davenport, Dingman would become the face of Vatican II Catholicism for most Iowans. He was active in drafting US Conference of Bishops statements on agriculture, *Strangers and Guests*, and on US nuclear weapons policy, *The Challenge of Peace*.

More problematically, he was the US bishops' point person on women's ordination. But he was disappointed to discover that his colleagues

---

49. McDaniel, "Catholic Action in Davenport"; Hinojosa, "Catholic Interracial Council."

50. "Social Action."

51. Interviews with Frances Marie Wetz, Sr. Mary Joel Kramer, Evelyn Rose Courey, Women's Project, Diocese of Sioux City, IWA; *Ottumwa Courier*, Jul. 14, 2006.

used his listening skills to deflect and delay, and that he had not been empowered to negotiate or advocate for change. The pope reined him in further, shutting down the discussion.[52]

Moving in the opposite direction to Bishop Dingman in terms of proximity to power within the church was Fr. Michael Colonnese. As head of the Inter-America division of the Catholic Conference of Bishops, he championed the liberation theology movements of Latin America. But as Catholic hierarchy drifted away from progressivism in the seventies, he found himself in what amounted to internal exile, pastoring a tiny parish in Holbrook (Iowa County). He continued to protest US intervention in El Salvador from that remote location.[53]

Sometimes, of course, liberalization had unintended negative effects, at least according to anecdotal accounts from Dubuque. While it would be wrong to attribute age-old clerical sexual indiscretions to Vatican II, the sexual liberalization taking place in society simultaneously could present added temptations.[54]

Nowhere was the conflict between joy and stodginess more starkly portrayed than in the biography of Sister Corita Kent. Born near Fort Dodge, she became an acclaimed artist in the trippy sixties mold and also a participant in the Los Angeles Immaculate Heart Sisters' rebellion against archdiocesan authoritarianism.[55] Her art suffused the classic Christian ethic of hope with the contemporary ethos that a better world was possible. The archbishop loathed it.

Sister Corita's art in 1985 was recognized by a US postage stamp, an indication that she had won the aesthetic battle with the archbishop, at least in popular culture.[56]

---

52. For a summary of Dingman's life, see "Dingman, Maurice," BDI, 130–31. For a booklength biography, see Crisler and Mosle, *In the Midst of His People*. Thanks to the Des Moines Catholic Worker, a collection of his social justice writings is online at bishopdingman.tumblr.com. Mary Lynch, leader of the Deaconess Movement, actually moved its headquarters to Des Moines because of her friendship with Dingman. Henold, *Catholic and Feminist*, 107–8.

53. Colonnese, *Human Rights and the Liberation of Man in the Americas*; Nabhan-Warren, *Meatpacking America*, 24; "We Cannot Remain Silent."

54. For a dishy account of post-Vatican II Catholicism in Dubuque, see Mulgrew, *How To Forget*, 179–82.

55. Barnett, "Nun Inspired By Andy Warhol"; Wills, *Bare Ruined Choirs*, 90–91, 95, 119; *Rebel Nuns*, film documentary, 2020; Winston, "'Flying Nun' and 'Painting Nun,'" 110–11; McDannell, *Spirit of Vatican II*, 132–38, 146, 169.

56. NYT, Sep. 19, 1986.

The People Are Kind

Controversial art was not the only connection linking Iowa and California. Both, as major agricultural states, needed to heed the kosher mandate that food be produced in a just manner. Some of the workers involved questioned whether this religious requirement was being followed.

FARMWORKERS

Vatican II-inspired Catholics (and many liberal Protestants and Jews) found inspiration and occasion for solidarity with the cause of the United Farm Workers, who were mostly Chicano and Filipino Catholics struggling for a union in an industry exempted from basic federal labor law. And the issue rebounded to Iowa, where migrant farmworkers were working and living in inferior conditions in places like Muscatine, Mason City, and Shenandoah.

In 1958, an enthusiastic and persistent college student, Skip Andrews, was determined to help migrant workers in Muscatine. A member of the Christian Church and president of UCYM of Iowa, the Disciples of Christ youth group, he approached the Iowa Council of Churches, who responded positively and in turn contacted the Muscatine County Ministerial Alliance. With backing from the National Council of Churches, the Muscatine Migrant Committee formed.[57]

The Iowa Council of Churches made its migrant ministry a priority, and despite strong pushback from the Iowa Farm Bureau, stood by its decision to call on Iowans to support the UFW boycotts of grapes and lettuce.[58]

Catholic women religious with Iowa connections were active in the movement supporting farmworker unionization. Franciscan sister Patricia Drydyk, a Wisconsin native who taught for a few years in Algona, and another Franciscan, Margaret Kruse, an Iowa native, worked with the National Farm Worker Ministry.[59] Sisters Irene and Molly Munoz (both nuns and siblings) from West Des Moines, joined the Muscatine Migrant Committee's medical clinic as nurses and advised migrant tomato

---

57. Muscatine Migrant Committee Papers, Box 1, "General Report for Season of 1962," IWA.

58. Box 8, F. "*Councilor* Newsletter, 1960–971," Iowa Council of Churches Records, 18–1976, SHSI-IC.

59. Murray, *Seeing Jesus in the Eyes of the Oppressed*; email from Murray, Apr. 27, 2020.

pickers of their rights.⁶⁰ As Latino migrant workers began to settle out into small Iowa communities, they had welcoming as well as challenging experiences with the majority white culture.

A NEW RESPECT FOR NATIVE AMERICANS

The civil rights movement, the movement against the war in Indochina, environmentalism, and a resulting skepticism about received wisdom, all contributed to reevaluating the status of Native Americans. (While tensions simmered in Tama County, this time the action was elsewhere.)⁶¹ In 1963, children playing at a West Des Moines construction site found human bones, evidently Indian. They displayed them widely, until State Historical Society officials intervened, confiscated them—and displayed the remains themselves. Only in the seventies could American Indian Movement activists persuade the state that displaying human remains was inappropriate.⁶²

If such callousness now seems unthinkable, we can thank Maria Pearson of Sioux City. In 1971, a decade after the Historical Society display, a highway project near Glenwood unearthed bodies of both whites and Native Americans. The whites' remains were reburied; native remains were sent to a museum. Pearson, or Running Moccasin, her Yankton Sioux name, was outraged by the differential treatment, and she persuaded Governor Robert Ray that native American remains were worthy of the same respect as those of others. Iowa became the first state to protect indigenous people's gravesites.⁶³ (Nor was respect for the dead a new issue; one of Black Hawk's first protests lodged against whites was the desecration of native graves. And his own grave was robbed.)⁶⁴

A new awareness and respect for other humans signaled that the new agitations could have positive consequences.

60. DMR, Jun. 4, 2005; IWA

61. Hoyt, "Tama"; Foley, *Heartland Chronicles*, 5.

62. Landis and Thompson, "History with Humanity"; DMR, Mar. 19, 2022; Jul. 24, 1963.

63. Treuer, *Heartbeat of Wounded Knee*, 337, 481; Gradwohl et al., "Still Running," 52; Foster, *Indians of Iowa*, 12, 51, 81; Whittaker et al., *Archaeological Guide*, 72–73; Pearson, "Give Me Back My People's Bones."

64. Harlan, *Narrative History*, v. 2, 381; Foster, *Indians of Iowa*, 51.

CHURCH-STATE CONFLICT

On November 20, 1965, Iowans opened their *Des Moines Registers* to a compelling front-page photograph by Thomas De Feo, of Amish boys running into cornfields to avoid truant officers. The image likely struck several chords, some of them discordant: playing hooky had a certain romantic appeal, whether or not one had actually ever followed through. The Amish voluntary renunciation of modern values increasingly resonated in a hectic world, harkening back to a simpler, rural idyllic society, a compelling if imaginary daydream, so the image of escaping into corn seemed perfect.

On the other hand, as *Register* readers reversed their breakfast reveries to gird for the day's realities, public education was an Iowa ideal, too, with Iowa educational standards close to topping the nation at the time. And the rule of law would have to be factored in. The competing legal values of separation of church and state versus compulsory public education may have occurred to the more litigiously minded.[65]

The resolution of the Hazleton Amish compulsory school controversy was mediated rather than enforced. Political pressures in Iowa in the sixties generally worked to mitigate rather than inflame tensions.[66] And the solution was not far away, as the neighboring Wapsie Valley school district, unencumbered by hostility against the Amish, had avoided contentiousness. Governor Harold Hughes, recognizing both the explosive political potential and the religious issues involved, was instrumental in forging the compromise, and would be keynote speaker at the founding meeting of the The National Committee for Amish Religious Freedom.[67]

---

65. To contemporary eyes, the image evokes a scene from *Field of Dreams,* but the movie and W. P. Kinsella's novel *Shoeless Joe* had yet to be produced.

66. Erickson, "Showdown at an Amish Schoolhouse," 5, 43–83. Schwieder, *Peculiar People*, 94–112; Evans, "Iowa's Amish Have Some Lessons for Us." Both Erickson and the Schwieders also explore the complicated backstory; the Amish were generally cooperative with the school district until the 1961 consolidation vote, when they unexpectedly voted, and voted for consolidation, infuriating the antis.

In 1972 the US Supreme Court decided in *Wisconsin v. Yoder* that Amish children could be exempted from attending high school on religious freedom grounds. Justice Douglas produced an interesting dissent, chiding the majority for not adequately considering the rights of the children involved. See also Franklin H. Littell, "State of Iowa vs. the Amish."

67. Meyers, "Education and Schooling," 97–100, and Lindholm, "National Committee for Amish Religious Freedom," 112, 115, both in Kraybill, *Amish and the State*.

TWO MAINLINE PROTESTANT GOVERNORS

The continued influence of mainline Protestantism is shown by the compelling religious biographies of the two dominant Iowa governors of the sixties and seventies, Harold Hughes and Robert Ray. Hughes, a recovering alcoholic, was a devout Methodist who left his US Senate seat in 1974 for full-time evangelistic work.[68]

Ray's steady and emphatic moderate Republican credentials dovetailed seamlessly with his active lay leadership in the Disciples of Christ, most famously at their national convention proposing state sponsorship of Vietnamese refugees.[69] The end of the political careers of the two governors from opposing parties underlined the decline of influence of mainline Protestantism, and was a harbinger of the harsher religious climate that began in the seventies. Not only was mainline Protestantism in decline; the new affirmations of Vatican II became open to debate. Soon, conservative Catholics and conservative Protestants would negotiate a new alignment, with an ease that would have astonished their early twentieth-century predecessors—and would have infuriated some of them!

The alliance would have consequences for all Iowans regardless of religious affiliation, given the combustible political combination that reconfiguration would command. In strange ways, questioning authority could lead to accepting whatever felt good, and this divorce of morality from reality might be problematic.

---

68. "Hughes, Harold Everett," BDI, 262, 263; King, "Harold E. Hughes"; Hughes, *Man from Ida Grove*. The best description of Hughes's part in the controversy is in Larew, *Party Reborn*, 96–109.

69. Walsh, *Good Governor*, 7; Bowermaster, *Governor*, 239; Gradwohl, "In Memoriam."

CHAPTER 23

The Counter-Narrative Strikes Back
This Dark World

"The selection of my father to deliver the invocation [at Balmer's Des Moines Hoover High School graduation] struck both of us as significant because we, as evangelicals, never felt part of the establishment. We were the outsiders, the religious insurgents engaged in a hopeless struggle against the Protestant mainline, which had the wealth, the influence, and the status that we simultaneously resented and coveted."

—Randall Balmer[1]

"We lay down on a stretch of dusty plywood in the back of the truck with the daylight knocking against our eyelids and the fragrance of alfalfa thickening on our tongues.
'I want to go to church,' Georgie said.
'Let's go to the county fair.'
'I'd like to worship. I would.'
'They have those injured hawks and eagles there. From the Humane Society,' I said.
'I need a quiet chapel about now.'"

—Denis Johnson[2]

    1. Balmer, "'Great Excess of Undenominationalism.'"
    2. Johnson, *Jesus' Son*, 85–86. The short story follows two lumpenproletariat workers at Iowa City's Mercy Hospital in 1973. Spoiler alert: they opted for the secular alternative.

The Counter-Narrative Strikes Back

THE ICONIC PHOTOGRAPH OF the Amish school-age boys near Hazleton fleeing the enforcers of Iowa's mandatory public education system starkly illustrated how many Iowans were coming to see political authority: not as representative but as aloof and unresponsive.[3] This attitude had both radical and reactionary sources. Sometimes religious authority came under the same skeptical glare.

Change was swirling in the air—swirling because change seemed to blow in multiple directions at once. Bishop Maurice Dingman came to Des Moines in 1968 committed to embodying the changes Vatican II proclaimed, but he braced to confront the new realities of suburbia, whose denizens could be forward-looking in supporting vague notions of progress but also tended to nostalgia regarding religious practice and to recalcitrance when proclamations of social justice seemed aimed too close. The relocation of Dowling High School from the inner city to West Des Moines was already underway when Dingman arrived from Davenport, too late to stop it but recognizing the social and moral implications of abandoning the inner city. Dingman's personal response was to open the bishop's south-of-Grand mansion for diocesan use and move into an inner-city apartment.[4] But many of his flock viewed the intertwined subjects of race and suburbanization very differently.

The unrest and uncertainty of the sixties also produced reactions leading to the culture wars dominating recent politics in Iowa. Often those reactions had religious roots, or at least religious justifications. The challenge to gender norms sparked by third-wave feminism and gay rights activism produced a countervailing defensiveness by biblical literalists who equated patriarchal order with God's design. Spurred on by political agendas, traditionalists would not go gentle into what was a good night for those trapped outside gender norms. Increasingly, religious institutions were

---

3. As late as 2005, Buchanan County still publicly opposed one-room schools for the Amish, according to Des Moines preservationist Bill Sherman, *Talk of Iowa*, Oct. 17, 2005.

A similar controversy erupted in Mitchell County in 2010, when the Old Order Groffdale Mennonites' practice of placing steel cleats on their tractors collided with the county's objection that the practice was destructive to the county roads and illegal. DMR, Feb. 19, 2010; Jun. 6, 2010; Jul. 9, 2010.

4. *Catholic Mirror*, Jul. 10, 1969; Sep. 5, 1969; Crisler and Mosle, *In the Midst of His People*, 121–23; Avella, *Catholic Church in Southwest Iowa*, 201, 246, 298–305.

caught up in competing narratives about who was an elite; the only consensus to come out of the sixties was that elites were untrustworthy.

JESUS PEOPLE, THE LAST DAYS, AND NEW FUNDAMENTALISMS

Sometimes what seemed to be new and youthful about the sixties easily morphed into older forms of religion. Linda Meissner was raised in rural Iowa and infused with Pentecostal values. When she called out to God and felt healed at age twelve, she promised to devote her life to God. Meissner first worked for Campus Crusade for Christ and then more dramatically with David Wilkerson in his evangelistic efforts to confront gang violence in New York City. But when young people started converting to a new brand of Christianity that encompassed both New Age ecstasy and old-fashioned apocalypticism, she moved to Washington State to organize them into the Jesus People Army.

But she found the army insufficiently organized and reached out to the Children of God for help. The Children of God did provide structure in abundance, which appealed to Meissner but not to most of her troops. After following the Children of God on their forced march to Europe, she exited the group, and more recently has been evangelizing Eastern Europe from Scandinavia.[5]

Illustrative of the new wave of fundamentalist and Pentecostal churches were the Gospel Assemblies (Sowders/Goodwin), a group based in Des Moines.[6] (While claiming to be nondenominational, the Assemblies are linked.) Pentecostal churches had been divided on the question of the trinitarian nature of God. William Sowder tried to square the triangle, arriving at an intermediate position between trinitarian and Oneness Pentecostalism. Following Sowder, Lloyd Goodwin of Des Moines broke with other Gospel Assemblies in 1972.

The Goodwin branch of the Gospel Assemblies also spiritualized the sacraments, much as Quakers do, downplaying the physical acts of communion and baptism. The group has been criticized for aggressive

---

5. Balmer, *Encyclopedia of Evangelicalism*, 370–71.

6. Melton, *Encyclopedia of American Religions*, 425–26; Kerns, "Gospel Assembly Church"; "Gospel Assembly: Des Moines, Iowa."

"shepherding," or trying to control basic aspects of their congregants' lives.[7] But those choosing the group found comfort in having all the correct answers to life's persistent problems.

The economic malaise of the seventies, the generation-old nuclear anxiety, and the military and political setbacks of Vietnam and Watergate had all darkened the country's mood The frightening prospect of impending doom was captured exquisitely if luridly in a premillennialist film by Donald Thompson and Des Moines's Mark IV Pictures, *The Thief in the Night*. To the extent that one can get frightened into salvation, this picture met its goal, but perhaps its real success was in graphically reinforcing beliefs already held.[8]

The starkness of the new religious intensity is portrayed vividly in Carolyn Briggs's memoir *This Dark World*.[9] Briggs grew up poor in central Iowa in "Allendale," a fictionalized town between Iowa Falls and Marshalltown. She was pregnant and married just out of high school when her bridesmaid introduced the couple to a religious revival centered at Iowa State University, and they were eager to find a larger purpose.

Soon they were part of a new church in Des Moines made up of young, "hippie" trending couples, "hyper-Calvinist," patriarchal, and countercultural, into natural foods and averse to medicinal drugs, leery of consumer culture, critical of established churches, sex-positive within heterosexual marriage, and having an intrusive accountability ritual that perhaps drew from the criticism/self-criticism practices of Maoism or from the New Age techniques of Synanon,[10] filtered through a charismatic leader controlling the process.[11]

With an unsparing eye, Briggs described her infatuation and disillusionment with the attempt to model a New Testament church. Most of the energy was directed inward. A generation plus later, Lyz Lenz would limn a similar experience of her evangelical disenchantment in *God Land*.[12] Lenz

---

7. Schmitt, "Heaven or Hell?" *Cityview*, Feb. 28, 2001.

8. Balmer, *Encyclopedia of Evangelicalism*, 45, 354–55, 577–78. Cf. Briggs, *This Dark World*, 119. Briggs fictionalizes the film's title as *I Wish We'd All Been Ready*.

9. DMR, Feb. 24, 2002. The book was made into a film, *Higher Ground*. DMR, Jan. 30, 2011; Oct. 21, 2011, and the book was also reissued under that title.

10. Bardacke, *Trampling Out the Vintage*, 541–53.

11. Briggs, *This Dark World*.

12. Lenz, *God Land*.

went on to be a prominent journalist and activist in Cedar Rapids.[13] For those who did not fit into the expected heterosexual mold, like Jeanna Kadac, the exodus from evangelicalism felt even more urgent.[14]

The new fundamentalism could take many forms, but it increasingly coalesced along patriarchal and hierarchical lines.

THE OLD-TIME RELIGION REDUX

Representative Iowans illustrate the shifting sands of Iowa religion. Vic Eliason, born in Fort Dodge, a culture warrior who attended Open Bible College in Des Moines, mounted his challenge to the liberal status quo on the radio airwaves in Milwaukee, a local representative of the national trend of televangelists preaching an emergent Christian nationalism.[15]

In contrast, Storm Lake native, Cornell College alumna, and University of Iowa writing workshop attendee Marjorie Holmes represented a gentler past, pouring out devotionals and religious novels that harkened more to the pastoral stylings of someone like the radio maven Edythe Stirlin, suggesting that God leading us to green pastures was a spiritually rewarding metaphor.[16] But the past was a powerful sedative and for readers of Holmes, a refreshing alternative to present anxieties.

A debate rages among historians about the extent that legalizing abortion was originally a motivating factor in organizing a religious right. Randall Balmer has suggested that evangelicals had little to say about the Supreme Court's *Roe v. Wade* decision at the time, and that the major politicizing factor was the desegregation of public schools.[17] Gillian Frank has argued that patriarchy has been integral to the religious right from its inception.[18] What is clear is that the issue of abortion "became a symbolic surrogate for

13. Men Yell at Me (lyz.substack.com).
14. Kadlec, *Heretic*; Kadlec, "How a Tarot Reader Spends Her Sunday."
15. Balmer, *Encyclopedia of Evangelicalism*, 190.
16. Balmer, *Encyclopedia of Evangelicalism*, 283; Holmes, *You and I and Yesterday*.
17. Balmer, *Bad Faith*: Congregational Library and Archives video, "Author Interview with Dr. Randall Balmer" (https://www.youtube.com/watch?v=8H-_J7q7sjs). See also Kadlec, *Heretic*, 20–21.
18. www.politico.com/news/magazine/2022/05/10l Lenz, interview with Frank, "What About the Babies," May 11, 2022; Curtis, "Bad History of Randall Balmer's "Bad Faith."

cultural misgivings that already existed" and intertwined the Catholic and fundamentalist right in a way unimaginable to their forebears.[19]

Iowa-born historian Kristin Kobes Du Mez has analyzed the roots of the white Evangelical pact with Christian nationalism in patriarchy by referencing another Iowan, John Wayne.[20]

The Family Leader, led by Bob Vanderplaats, engineered the religious right's control of much of the Republican Party in the state.[21] The surprise victory of televangelist Pat Robertson in the 1988 Republican presidential caucus made clear that newly politicized evangelicals would henceforth play a major role in the state's politics.[22]

THE FARM CRISIS

The farm crisis of the 1980s seemed a piece with the otherworldly pessimism of latter-day premillennialists. The suddenness with which economic catastrophe descended upon overextended farmers did approach the apocalyptic for many rural communities, and religious Iowans searched for ways to help.

> Thousands of clergy in rural Iowa parishes worked to make their responses to the rural crisis as utilitarian as possible.
> One of the most powerful and best organized denominations was the Catholic church. The Catholic hierarchy . . . was alerted to the dangerous Implications of change in the structure of American agriculture in the 1970's. The Catholic clergy, therefore, were able to be more outspoken than those of other denominations early in the crisis. The rural life directors of the four Catholic dioceses of Iowa were determined to help their congregations and the farm population in general . . .[23]

Particularly outspoken was Bishop Dingman. Raised on a family farm in Lee County, he was a driving force behind the Midwestern bishops' 1978 pastoral letter on farm issues, *Strangers and Guests*, and often spoke at rallies protesting the debt structure that forced many farmers off of their land in the 1980s.[24] Protestants and Jews were also involved in

---

19. Mohr, "Iowa's Abortion Battles," 430, 425, 427.
20. Du Mez, *Jesus and John Wayne*, See also Wills, *John Wayne's America*.
21. Du Mez, *Jesus and John Wayne*, 253.
22. Meyer and Nesmith, "Iowa," 191–210.
23. Friedberger, *Shake-Out*, 94–95.
24. Riney-Kehrberg, *When a Dream Dies*, 51, 95, 116 ("The crowd responded most

the Iowa Farm Unity Coalition, which advocated for structural change in the farm economy.[25]

Local religious organizations also provided material aid and counseling for the distraught. One counselor remembered the depth of despair some farmers felt:

> A desperately frightened woman called to tell [the counselor] that her husband had taken his high-powered rifle and gone for a drive. "I'm a good shot. I'll only get the banker." [The counselor] called a local minister, who enlisted his parishioners to form a human chain across the road and stop the truck. The man returned home peacefully.[26]

The overtly religious symbol of the protest movement was the brandishing of white crosses representing lost family farms. The net result of the crisis was a further consolidation of farmland and hollowing out of rural Iowa.

Photo permission: Linda Nelson.

---

enthusiastically to Bishop Dingman.")

25. Harl, *Farm Debt Crisis*, 197, 247, 250; Friedberger, *Shake-Out*, 83–86, 92, 95; Berry, "Story of the Farm Crisis," 204; Comstock, *Is There a Moral Obligation to Save the Family Farm*, 325–33.

26. Riney-Kehrberg, *When a Dream Dies*, 73.

THE PROSPECT OF NUCLEAR ANNIHILATION

An increasing awareness about the threat of nuclear annihilation added to the gloom. Alarm had been raised before, but it now became a mass issue. Once again, Bishop Dingman offered leadership, this time on a national stage, helping to draft the US bishops' statement, *The Challenge of Peace*. With Dingman's prodding, the bishops condemned even possessing nuclear weapons. On this count, the government seemed guilty.

Grassroots activists, Catholic and otherwise, fueled this questioning. On Iowa's doorstep was the Strategic Air Command (later STRATCOM) headquarters in Bellevue, Nebraska, which targeted nuclear weapons. Regular—even ritual—acts of nonviolent civil disobedience took place at the base, usually around Nagasaki Day and the Feast of the Holy Innocents. The Des Moines Catholic Worker was a core organizer of those actions.[27]

The mass protests helped lead to tamp-downs on the nuclear arms race and arguably even to the fall of the Soviet Union, though not to nuclear disarmament.

THE UNCERTAIN STATE OF MAINLINE PROTESTANTISM

Competition from fundamentalism and secularism, along with the population drain away from the rural places that had formed a solid base for many denominations, made the last quarter of the twentieth century a difficult period for ecumenical Protestantism, which had so recently basked in what now seemed to be the twilight summer sun of popularity.

Iowans experimented with ecumenical and interfaith efforts that were less tied to national efforts than the Iowa Council of Churches had been. The Iowa Inter-Church Forum and its Agency for Peace and Social Justice was the first such experiment, and its structure reflected the perceived desire of denominations to pick and choose which policy positions and programs they would endorse. The forum spent considerable time in the 1980s trying to expand its support. But smaller denominations like the African Methodist Episcopal Church often did not have the time or staff to participate,[28] and the largest, the Roman Catholic Church, was

---

27. Strabala and Palecek, *Prophets without Honor*, 129–42, 358–59. Hiroshima Day was slotted for local actions.

28. Box 15, F. African Methodist Episcopal Church, Ecumenical Ministries of Iowa

wary. While the Des Moines diocese favored[29] ecumenical work, the other three dioceses demurred, and Des Moines declined to proceed alone.[30]

The most successful project of the Forum was a four-day peace caravan of Iowa Christian leaders, who crisscrossed the state with a surprisingly strong message against nuclear weapons in the fall of 1984. Signed by twenty-two church leaders (all men!)[31] from eleven different denominations,[32] ranging ecclesiastically from Roman Catholic to Mennonite and theologically from United Church of Christ to Southern Baptist! But this project marked the high point for the forum: the withdrawal of the Catholics, the widening gap between ecumenical and fundamentalist Protestants, and increasing internal financial and membership woes of mainline denominations all contributed to the forum's retrenchment in 1986 and demise in 1991.[33] The forum's structure, meant to be accommodating to a wide range of religious opinion, turned unwieldy, and the core of ten mainline Protestant denominations[34] was all that could be counted on for most programs.

In 1989, a structural study committee, following a proposal by Church of the Brethren layperson Wanda Button of Conrad, recommended that the forum disband and be replaced by a more streamlined Ecumenical Ministries of Iowa.[35] At the turn of the century, the group described its constituents as "10 denominations, 16 judicatories, 1423 small town and country congregations and 926 large town and city

---

Records, SHSI-DM.

29. Cf., in Linn County, the Council of Churches was replaced by Churches United. Brigham, "Transforming Places," 270–72.

30. *Des Moines Catholic Mirror*, Feb. 23, 1989; Box 15, Fs. Dioceses of Des Moines, Dubuque, Davenport, Sioux City, EMI Records, SHSI-DM.

31. Iowa Inter-Church Forum, *Our Faith Compels Us*, Box 1, F. 3, Marilyn O. Murphy Papers, IWA.

While the signatories were all male, it is clear from the planning that much of the organizing work was done by women, from agency staffer Suzanne Peterson to local and regional social justice staffers like Marilyn Murphy of Catholic Charities in Sioux City. Murphy Papers, Box 1, Folders 3 and 4.

32. Presbyterian, Lutheran, Roman Catholic Methodist, American Baptist, Mennonite, United Church of Christ, Disciples of Christ, Episcopalian, Southern Baptist, and Reformed. Iowa Inter-Church Forum, *Our Faith*, 2.

33. Box 6, F. F Communications, EMI records, SHSI-DM.

34. The ten were American Baptist, Christian (Disciples of Christ), Church of the Brethren, Episcopal, Evangelical Lutheran Church in America, Presbyterian, Reformed, United Church of Christ, United Methodist Church, and Reorganized Church of Latter-day Saints, which was in the process of renaming itself Community of Christ.

35. Box 1, EMI records; phone interview with Sarai Schmucker Rice, Dec. 16, 2022.

The Counter-Narrative Strikes Back

congregations, with memberships totaling 644,374. We are [also] 25 ethnic congregations in 11 communities serving 2135 ethnic congregants."[36]

The financial situation at EMI became untenable, and it ceased operations in 2005.[37]

Ecumenical statements on matters of public concern were still possible, but EMI's demise made them more difficult logistically.

Most mainline denominations also felt the sting of retrenchment, and by the second decade of the twenty-first century, many conservative churches were also experiencing membership declines.[38] The specter of secularization, which had been lurking earlier, reemerged as a preoccupation for institutional religions. There was no consensus, however, as to how to respond; the respective attitudes of being socially relevant or doubling down on a traditional American emotionalism continued as competing options. Moreover, the impulse to act collectively was eroded by internal diversions.

THE CRISIS OF TRUST IN THE CATHOLIC CHURCH

The sapping of mainline Protestant strength was difficult but explainable. More bewildering were revelations of sexual abuse and cover-up that rocked the Catholic Church.[39] The abuse was enabled by a culture of secrecy and denial that perpetuated the cycle and recycled abuser priests to other parishes. Financial setbacks, such as the declaration of bankruptcy by the Diocese of Davenport,[40] seemed secondary to the moral bankruptcy involved. Integrity in leadership at the parish and diocesan levels began to repair the breaches, but the process of regaining trust is a slow one. Victim support groups took the lead in the healing process.[41]

Other, mostly hierarchical, religious institutions had challenges to their authority based on abuse. Two exiles from the Amish who wrote

---

36. *Ecumenical Ship*, V. 9, #4, 12/2000, Box 8, F. Newsletters, EMI records.

37. Box 18, f. Board of Director Minutes, Nov. 16, 2004, EMI records.

38. "U.S. Public Becoming Less Religious."

39. Concerned Catholics of the Davenport Diocese, *Toward Hope and Understanding*. The scandal was the subject of over a hundred articles in the *Register* between 2003 and 2007. For a summary of the legal cases, see DMR, May 10, 2010.

40. *Quad City Times*, Dec. 3, 2007; *National Catholic Reporter*, Jul. 5, 2012.

41. DMR, Jun. 19, 2003, Jan. 24, 2004; Feb. 12, 2005; Jun. 14, 2005.

tell-all memoirs were Ruth Garrett of Kalona[42] and Chris Burkholder of Wayne County.[43]

GAY ORDINATION, MARRIAGE EQUALITY, AND BACKLASHES

Unitarians and the United Church of Christ were early supporters of ordaining gay people. Other denominations, such as the Disciples, Presbyterians, and Lutherans, took longer to recognize that civil rights should extend into church settings.[44] Episcopalians faced a crisis when retired Iowa bishop Walter Righter was tried for heresy for ordaining a gay man.[45] Mennonites[46] and Methodists have had recent divisions on the subject.[47] Some denominations, such as Catholics, tried to balance rejection of gay marriage with a reconciling approach to individuals. For Methodists, the struggle was drawn-out and the denomination was reduced, although not as much as anticipated.

The gains made by gay rights activists triggered a response from the religious right, often expressed electorally. Two cases stand out. In 2006, Jonathan Wilson was an outstanding Des Moines school board member, an attorney, a United Church of Christ layperson, and—as he announced in order to support LBGT students—was gay. And he was up for reelection; the religious right mounted a campaign against him. In the highest turnout ever in a school board election, he was defeated. The victorious candidates, though, seemed surprised that their commitment would continue through their terms of office and, uninterested in the mundane details of running a school district, did not seek reelection.[48] Wilson became a trusted consultant to the district.

---

42. Garrett and Farrant, *Crossing Over*; Garrett and Morse-Kahn, *Born Amish*.

43. Burkholder, *Amish Confidential*.

44. For Presbyterians, see DMR, Nov. 14, 2003; Dec. 2, 7, 18, 2004; Oct. 21, 2005. On Lutherans, DMR, Nov. 30, 2000; Aug. 23, 28, 2010.

45. Righter, *Pilgrim's Way*; NYT, Nov. 5, 2023; DMR, Jul. 29, 2023; Nov. 7, 2023; Nov. 8, 2003; Aug. 14, 2006.

46. DMR, Jul. 3, 2009.

47. DMR, Jun. 5, 2012; Dec. 11, 2016; May 11, 2017; Jun. 7, 2017. In May 2023, eighty-three United Methodist congregations announced they were leaving the Iowa Conference. DMR, May 28, 2023; CRG, May 28, 2023.

48. Witosky and Hansen, *Equal Before the Law*, 11–12.

The Counter-Narrative Strikes Back

When the Iowa Supreme Court handed down its landmark ruling that gay marriage was protected by the Iowa Constitution, a similar effort went statewide, and the justices who were up for retention also faced the wrath of religious right voters, losing their positions.[49]

On May 21, 2011, the end of the world did not happen. (The American Atheists, at their national convention in Des Moines earlier in the month, had foretold this.)[50] Of course, this was only the latest in a string of erroneous predictions among Christians, based on readings of Scripture that seemed self-evident to believers except in retrospect. It was too late for a Coralville couple who had sold their house, believing the prophecy. For them, the prophecy was close to self-fulfilling.[51] The larger question, why people of faith would fervently hope for the end of this existence, was mostly left unexplored.[52] This dark world seemed too close to home.

The defensiveness that many Christian Iowans felt about a seeming loss of status was illustrated stunningly by an incident in Knoxville in 2015, when a veterans' memorial was placed in a city park, without official permission, that depicted a soldier kneeling to a cross. Non-Christian veterans objected that they were excluded; a large rally defended the display. White crosses became a divisive sore point in the community for several years.[53]

The darknesses caused by the pessimism of premillennialism, by insecurities aroused in some by feminism and marriage equality, by the starkness of the farm crisis and the resultant exodus from rural Iowa, by the prospect of a nuclear winter, by an increasing gulf between mainline and fundamentalist Christians that played out bitterly in political arenas, and by the uncertainties when seemingly solid religious organizations retrenched and faced crises of trust, could all weigh down on Iowans

---

49. Witosky and Hansen, *Equal Before the Law*, 170–73.
50. Briggs, "Waiting for Lightning to Strike."
51. DMR, May 17, 2011.
52. But see Davis, *Left Behind and Loving It*. Davis pastored Heartland Presbyterian Church in Clive.
53. "In Depth"; "Large Crowd in Knoxville Supports Memorial Near Freedom Rock"; Robert Leonard, email correspondence and phone interview, Feb. 21, 2014.

seeking to maintain or discover their religious identities. But glimmers of light could also be ascertained by those charged to be hopeful. We will turn to such signs in the conclusion. Prophecy will also be cited.

CHAPTER 24

After All

The Blessings of Diversity

"The Creator of Europe made her small and even split her up into little parts, so that our hearts could find joy not in size but in plurality."
—Karl Capek[1]

"No one knows for certain
So it's all the same to me;
I think I'll just let the mystery be.
—Iris DeMent, Iowa City folk singer

"Civilizations they crumble and fall;
We're just here in the middle of it all."
—William Elliott Whitmore, Lee County folksinger

THE SIGN WELCOMING VISITORS to Postville used to bill it as "Hometown of John R. Mott." The Nobel Prize-winning Mott is no longer a household name, but his religious significance is substantial, and the missionary vision of his ambition to evangelize the world for Christ in one generation bears multiple ironies in a hometown beset by religious diversity, often in

---

1. Quoted in Judt, *Postwar*, 749.

unenviable ways. Mott's hopes for the twentieth century went unrealized, and Postville's for the twenty-first seem similarly complicated.

Nowadays, Postville is "Hometown to the World." In 1987, the Chalad-Lubavitcher Rubashkin family from Brooklyn, New York bought an abandoned meatpacking plant in Postville and transformed it into the largest kosher meat processing plant in the world.[2] Kosher meat must be supervised by rabbis. Soon Postville had the highest concentration of Hasidic rabbis in the country, not just Lubavitcher[3] but also Sighet,[4] Belz, and Vizhnitz,[5] all with slightly different garb and loyalties.

Hasidim have been compared to the Amish in their distinctive dress, beards, and self-imposed isolation from the outside world. The Lutherans, Catholics, and Presbyterians who had dominated Postville found dealing with the newcomers challenging.

The meatpacking industry by the 1990s had broken the union's power and relied on low-wage labor obtainable from immigrants. Turnover was extremely high; Ukrainian and Russian immigrants were soon replaced by Guatemalans and Mexicans. In 2008, the Immigration and Naturalization Service conducted its largest ever raid up until then, at the Postville plant.[6]

St. Bridget's Catholic Church became a sanctuary for those families torn asunder by the raid. In the wake of the raid, the Rubashkins were charged and convicted of multiple federal charges. The scorched-earth appeal strategy of accusing the judge of anti-Semitism was mostly unsuccessful. A less publicized but more thought-provoking scandal occurred in 2004, when news broke that not just kosher but USDA slaughter laws were violated by animal abuse at the plant. In a reflection, Jewish theologian Aaron Gross mused about what our religious connection to animals should be.[7] His meditation recalled the indigenous religious reformers

---

2. Grey et al., *Postville, U.S.A.*; Bloom, *Postville*. For a defense of the Lubavitchers, see Feldman, *Lubavitchers as Citizens*.

3. Melton, *Encyclopedia of American Religions*, vol. 3, 151; Sarna, *American Judaism*, 297–301; Kaplan, 71; Queen et al., *Encyclopedia*, vol. 1, 279; Kaplan, *Cambridge Companion*, 71.

4. Grey et al., *Postville, U.S.A.*, 21–22; Melton, *Encyclopedia of American Religions*, vol. 3, 151.

5. *Jerusalem Post*, Jul. 30, 2022. Belz and Vizhnitz Hasidim were both originally Ukrainian, and sometimes allied.

6. Grey, *Postville, U.S.A.*, 78–84.

7. Gross, *Question of the Animal*.

After All

who called on native nations caught up in the commodification of hunting by the fur trade to return to an ethic of gratitude.

In a non-Postville postscript, most of the major religious groups in Iowa arrived at the twenty-first century in somewhat of disarray and still jockeying for position, even if alliances had changed. But, as in early Iowa, religious diversity would have a new blooming. This bloom was less exceptional than the first compared to other states, but it has begun to form new religious realities on the ground.

Davenport Catholics continued their traditional liberalism in 2023 with a (mostly) celebratory national conference at St. Ambrose University, marking the tenth anniversary of Francis's papacy.[8]

Thoughtful theists continued to appreciate both science and religion and look for ways to reconcile them. Harvard astronomer Owen Gingerich, Washington, Iowa-born and Mennonite-raised, contributed *God's Universe* to the discussion.[9]

Islam was long established in Iowa (see chapter 15), but it became more diverse in the twenty-first century, as Bosnian and Somali refugees moved in. By 2008, Iowa Muslims could worship in twenty-three mosques, and there were an estimated sixty thousand adherents. A chapter of the Council on Islamic-American Relations was set up to defend Muslim Americans' civil rights.[10] Workplaces such as the IPB meatpacking plant in Tama worked to accommodate the religious needs of their Somali and Sudanese Muslim workers, with part of the break area set aside for daily prayers.[11] While in the 1930s Cedar Rapids Muslims were almost entirely of Lebanese/Syrian origin, in 1978, the Mother Mosque in Cedar Rapids agreed to adopt several Muslim refugee families from Cambodia.[12] By 2017, nine Muslim congregations served greater Des Moines, including Bosnian, Somali, Mideastern, and African American congregations.[13]

8. *National Catholic Reporter*, Mar. 23, 2023.

9. NYT, Jun. 10, 2023; *Anabaptist World*, Jun. 28, 2023; Owen Gingerich, *God's Universe*. His father Melvin wrote an early history of Iowa Mennonites.

10. Iowa Interreligious Exchange conference, "Islam in Iowa" workshop, Drake University, Apr. 17, 2017; "In Iowa, Campaign Season Finds Muslims."

11. Nabhan-Warren, *Meatpacking America*, 165–66.

12. Sheronick, "History of the Cedar Rapids Muslim Community," 45.

13. Knepper, *Spectrum of Faiths*, 1–8, 57–64, 97–108.

The People Are Kind

Twenty-first century Buddhists resembled nineteenth-century Lutherans in being divided along national lines and to a lesser extent, by theology.[14] In 2010, the Dalai Lama visited Cedar Rapids. In 2014, a traveling collection of Buddhist relics, known as the Loving Kindness tour, was displayed in Des Moines. In 2021, Marshalltown Buddhists unveiled the largest statue of Buddha in the country,[15] installed by the Theravada Dhamma Society of Iowa.[16]

Photo permission: Marshalltown Times-Republican.

Hindus also became a presence in parts of the state, most notably completing a temple outside of Madrid.[17] In 2022, the Bhutanese Hindu community opened a temple on the south side of Des Moines,[18] and a temple was completed in Robbins in 2023.[19] Also marking Hinduism's

14. DMR, Aug. 16, 1998; Feb. 24, Mar. 20, 1999; Oct. 19, 2002; Apr. 14, 2003; Apr. 16, May 18, 2006; Jan. 17, Mar. 24, Apr. 11, Jan. 17, 2011; Mar. 7, Mar. 19, 2017.

15. DMR, May 16, May 19, 2010; Aug. 10, 2014; Marshalltown *Times-Republican*, Aug. 9, 2021.

16. Marshalltown *Times-Republican*, Nov. 26, 2021.

17. *Iowa State Daily*, Nov. 12, 2007.

18. Email from Timothy Knepper, The Comparison Project, Drake University, Sep. 20, 2022.

19. CRG, Nov. 9, 2023.

developing roots, in 2022 the first Hindu, Megan Srinivas of Des Moines, was elected to the state legislature.[20]

Sikhs also energetically promoted their faith and vision of coexistence in Central Iowa.[21] The Chinese meditation sect Falun Gong, banned in China, had a presence in the state.[22]

The Tai Dam represented an aspect of refugee religion unique to Iowa. The Tai Dam were an ethnic and religious minority from northwestern Vietnam. Unlike most Vietnamese, they were not Buddhist or Catholic; they practiced a form of ancestor worship that contributed to their social cohesiveness. Unfortunately, too near their ancestral home was Dien Bien Phu, site of the crucial battle between Vietnamese nationalists and French colonialists in 1954. The Tai Dam backed the losing side, and consequently many Tai Dam sought refuge in Laos, where they remained for a generation, until the war followed them there, whereupon they relocated to Thailand and began lobbying for refugee status in the United States.

The Tai Dam pleas coincided with Governor Robert Ray's singular response to refugee resettlement. Unlike other Indochinese refugees, the Tai Dam were mostly resettled as a group and ended up in Des Moines.[23]

But immigrants did not necessarily bring along an exotic religion. Many Vietnamese refugees were Catholic. Some new Iowans carried with them a Christianity that had been exported by western missionaries, or even earlier, by conquistadors. Chin and Karen Burmese were often Baptist; they took over abandoned church buildings in Des Moines, Marshalltown, and Waterloo.[24] South Sudanese, Congolese, and Liberians were often Christian,[25] as were most Latin Americans. In 2008, Vietnamese refugees and their descendants in Des Moines who were Catholic got a parish of their own, St. Peter Vietnamese Catholic Community.[26]

20. Belin, "Elections Bringing More Diversity to Iowa Legislature."
21. DMR, Feb. 27, 1999; Aug. 6, 13, 2012; Oct. 3, 2012; Jul. 1, 2014; Apr. 18, 2015; Oct. 9, 2017; *Talk of Iowa*, Iowa Public Radio, Jun. 7, 2016.
22. DMR, May 1, 2001.
23. Walsh, *Good Governor*, 7–9, 83–108.
24. *River to River*, Iowa Public Radio, Aug. 17, 2012; DMR, Jul. 4, 2011.
25. DMR, Aug. 30, 2003; Dec. 8, 2004.
26. DMR, Oct. 6, 2008; Dec. 5, 2008; *River to River*, Iowa Public Radio, Aug. 17, 2012.

While the legal category of refugee did not exist in the nineteenth century, the current definition would retrofit easily to cover exiles who had a long history in Iowa, Hendrik Scholte and his followers and the exiles from the 1848 European revolutions being prime examples. What seemed different a century and a half later was the degree of globalization.

Iowa had an unusual convergence of visits from transnational prelates in the late 1970s/early 1980s, with visits from the Roman Catholic pope,[27] the Episopal/Anglican archbishop of Canterbury,[28] and the Greek Orthodox patriarch.[29]

The improbable success of football hero and evangelical icon Kurt Warner proved a morality tale for those immersed within that religious subculture and provided vicarious vindication for those feeling the buffetings of a perceived outside culture hostile to old-fashioned values.[30]

Wallace Short, the iconoclastic Sioux City minister and member of the Bartenders Union, would have felt vindicated by the national *Speaking of Faith* broadcast reporting on the Altoona, Iowa, Theology on Tap discussion group discussing religious issues over beer.[31] A decade later, the practice had become commonplace.

Echoing the conflict between Sister Corita's order and the Archdiocese of Los Angeles in the sixties, American nuns came under official church scrutiny in 2012. Representing the Leadership Conference of Women Religious for a crucial period during that inquiry was Dubuque Franciscan Pat Farrell.[32] Farrell used nonviolent skills she had learned in Latin America to be simultaneously forthright and respectful. American nuns outlasted their accusers, as the new Pope Francis dismissed accusations of their supposed unorthodoxy.[33]

27. LemMon, *John Paul II*; DMR, Nov. 3, 2005.
28. *Celebration: The Archbishop of Canterbury*.
29. DMR, Jun. 1, 2004.
30. Balmer, *Encyclopedia of Evangelicalism*, 604.
31. National Public Radio, *Speaking of Faith*, May 4, 2008.
32. *National Catholic Reporter*, Aug. 3, 2012; *Morning Edition*, National Public Radio, Aug. 21, 2009; *Fresh Air*, National Public Radio, Jul. 17, 2012; iobserve.org, Jul. 19, 2012; Sanders, *However Long the Night*, 45–54, 160; *Christian Century*, Dec. 16, 2014.
33. Hall, "Sister Elizabeth Johnson."

After All

The Meskwaki prophecy that white people will be destroyed, and that Meskwakis will regain the land now called Iowa, is understandably disturbing to many whites. Perhaps, if we overcome the sustainability crises that Native friends have predicted, we might all end up assimilated into the Meskwaki Nation. Which means we will be having an argumentative, and indirect, discussion about where the Great Spirit wants us to go from here. Indirectness might be a step forward, a step toward a people being kind.

Bibliography

AI citations are Third Series unless otherwise indicated.

BOOKS AND ARTICLES

86th Annual Report of the American Board of Commissioners for Foreign Missions at Toledo, Ohio, October 6–9, 1896. Boston, 1896.

Aarek, Hans Eirik. "A Short History of the Troms Quakers and Their Emigration to America." *Norwegian-American Studies* 35 (2000).

Abernethy, Alonzo. *A History of Iowa Baptist Schools*. Osage, IA: Self-published, 1907.

"About Catholic Daily Tribune." Library of Congress. https://chroniclingamerica.loc.gov/lccn/sn83045559/.

"About Us: A Brief History of Agudas Achim." Agudas Achim Congregation. https://agudasachimic.org/about-us.

Abrams, Ray H. *Preachers Present Arms*. Scottdale, PA: Herald, 1969.

Acton, Richard, and Patricia Nassif Acton. *To Go Free: A Treasury of Iowa's Legal Heritage*. Ames, IA: Iowa State University Press, 1995.

Adams, Ephraim. *The Iowa Band*. Boston: Congregational, 1870.

———. *Sketch Book*. San Francisco: Sorg, 1968.

Adams, Michael. "A Trail of Hope." *Iowan* 54.2 (Nov. 2005) 27–32.

Adway, John R. "Who Was Father Mazzuchelli?" *AI* 39.7 (Winter 1969) 552–60.

African American Museum of Iowa. Redlining Exhibit. Cedar Rapids, IA, 2021.

Ahern, Patrick Henry. *The Life of John J. Keane, Educator and Archbishop*. Milwaukee: Bruce, 1954.

Ahlstrom, L. J. *Eighty Years of Swedish Baptist Work in Iowa*. Des Moines: Swedish Baptist Conference of Iowa, 1933.

Akst, Daniel. *War by Other Means*. Brooklyn, NY: Melville, 2022.

Albanese, Catherine L. *Nature Religion in America from the Algonquian Indians to the New Age*. Chicago: University of Chicago Press, 1990.

———. *A Republic of Mind and Spirit: A Cultural History of American Metaphysical Religion*. New Haven: Yale University Press, 2007.

Albertson, Ralph. "A Survey of Mutualistic Communities in America." *IJH* 34 (1936) 375–444.

Bibliography

Alex, Lynn M., ed. *From the Great Lakes to the Great Plains: Meskwaki Archeology and Ethnohistory*. Wisconsin Archeologist 89.1–2 (Jan-Dec 2008).

———. *Exploring Iowa's Past: A Guide to Prehistoric Archaeology*. Iowa City, IA: University of Iowa Press, 1980.

Allchin, A. M., et al., eds. *Heritage and Prophecy: Grundtvig and the English-Speaking World*. Norwich: Canterbury, 1994.

Allen, Edward S. *Freedom in Iowa: The Role of the Iowa Civil Liberties Union*, Ames, IA: Iowa State University Press, 1977.

Allen, Edward S., and Minne Allen. *Tenderness and Turmoil: Letters to a German Mother, 1914–1920*. Edited and translated by Julius W. Allen. Santa Ana, CA: Seven Locks, 1998.

Allen, Leola. "Anti-German Sentiment in Iowa During World War I." *AI* 42 (1974) 426–47.

Allen, Mary. *The Rooms of Heaven: A Story of Love, Death, Grief, and the Afterlife*. New York: Alfred A. Knopf, 1999.

"Amana." *Pal* 11:7 (July 1921).

Amana Church Society. *The Morning Star: Words of Inspiration as Presented to the Community of True Inspiration*. Edited by Janet W. Zuber. Middle Amana, 2005.

American Friends Service Committee North Central Region. *50th Anniversary Celebration, Sep. 12, 1998*. Des Moines: AFSC, 1998.

"Americanism." *The Catholic Encyclopedia*. Edited by Robert C. Broderick. Nashville: Thomas Nelson, 1975.

"Ames History Museum." https://ameshistory.org.

Andelson, Jonathan G. "Tradition, Innovation, and Assimilation in Iowa's Amana Colonies," *Pal* 69:1 (Spring 1988), 2–15.

Andersen, Lisa M. F. *The Politics of Prohibition: American Governance and the Prohibition Party, 1869–1933*. New York: Cambridge University Press, 2013.

Anderson, Charles A., ed. "Letters of William Hamilton, 1811–1891." *Journal of the Presbyterian Historical Society* 35 and 36 (1957 and 1958) 157–70 and 53–65.

Anderson, Chester G. *Growing Up in Minnesota: Ten Writers Remember Their Childhood*. Minneapolis: University of Minnesota Press, 1976.

Anderson, Douglas Firth. "Reconceptualizing Protestantism and Minorities: A Review Essay." *AI* 74 (2015) 314–20.

Anderson, Joseph A. "The Swedish Lutheran Church in Iowa." *AI* 11 (1915) 590–93.

Andrews, Clarence. *A Literary History of Iowa*. Iowa City: University of Iowa Press, 1972.

———. *A History of the First Presbyterian Church of Iowa City, Iowa on the Occasion of its 125th Anniversary in 1965, with Particular Concern for the Years 1940–1965*. Iowa City, 1966.

Andrews, Lorenzo F. *Pioneers of Polk County, Iowa, and Reminiscences of Early Days*. Des Moines, 1908.

Andrews, Tamara. *A Tradition of Grace Yesterday, Today, and Tomorrow: A History of Grace United Methodist Church, Des Moines, Iowa, 1885–2000*. Des Moines: Grace United Methodist Church, 2001.

Angell, Stephen W., and Anthony B. Pinn, eds. *Social Protest in the African Methodist Episcopal Church, 1862–1938*. Knoxville, TN: University of Tennessee Press, 2000.

Anolik, Adele. *The Liberation of the Concentration Camps, 1945: The Des Moines, Iowa Survivors*. North Liberty, IA: Ice Cube, 2008.

Bibliography

Appelbaum, Patricia. *Kingdom to Commune*. Chapel Hill: University of North Carolina Press, 2009.

Armstrong, Gary W. "Utopians in Clayton County, Iowa." *AI* 41 (1974) 923–38.

Armstrong, Herbert W. *The United States and Britain in Prophecy*. N.p.: 1980.

Arnold, Charles Harvey. *Near the Edge of Battle: A Short History of the Divinity School and the "Chicago School of Theology,"* 1866–1966. Chicago: Divinity School Association, 1966.

Aron, Elaine, and Arthur Aron. *The Maharishi Effect: A Revolution Through Meditation*. Walpole, NH: Dutton, 1986.

Artman, Amy Collier. *Miracle Lady: Kathryn Kuhlman and the Transformation of Charismatic Christianity*. Grand Rapids: Eerdmans, 2019.

Athans, Mary Christine, BVM. "Courtesy, Confrontation, Cooperation: Jewish-Christian/Catholic Relations in the United States." *U.S. Catholic Historian* 28 (Spring 2010) 107–34.

Atherton, Lewis. *Main Street on the Middle Border*. Bloomington, IN: Indiana University Press, 1954.

Atkinson, Rick. *An Army at Dawn: The War in North Africa, 1942–1943*. Detroit: Holt, 2002.

Auge, Thomas F. "The Dream of Bishop Loras: A Catholic Iowa." *Pal* 61:6 (Nov. 1980) 170–79.

———. *Man of Deeds: Bishop Loras and the Upper Mississippi Valley Frontier*. Dubuque, IA: Loras College Press, 2008.

———. "The Priest Behind the Legend: Father John Alleman," *Pal* 74:2 (Summer 1993) 84–96.

Aumann, F. R. "A Minor Prophet in Iowa," *Pal* 8:7 (July 1927) 253–60.

Auracher v. Yerger, 58 NW 893, 90 Iowa 558.

Austin, Allan W. *From Concentration Camp to Campus*. Urbana, IL: University of Illinois Press, 2004.

Avella, Steven M. *The Catholic Church in Southwest Iowa: A History of the Diocese of Des Moines*. Collegeville, MN: Liturgical, 2018.

Avelos, Hector. *Fighting Words: The Origins of Religious Violence*. Amherst, NY: 2005.

Aveni, Anthony. *People and the Sky: Our Ancestors and the Cosmos*. New York: Thames & Hudson, 2008.

Babb, Laura Longley. "Iowa's Enduring Amana Colonies." *National Geographic* 148 (1975) 862–78.

Bach, Marcus. *Adventures in Faith*. Minneapolis: T. S. Denison, 1959.

———. "Baha'i: A Second Look." *Christian Century* (Apr. 10, 1957) 449–51.

———. *The Chiropractic Story*. Los Angeles: DeVorss, 1968.

———. *Had You Been Born in Another Faith*. Englewood Cliffs, NJ: Prentice Hall, 1961.

———. "In the Church's Back Yard." *Christian Century* (Jan. 8, 1958) 45–46.

———. *The Inner Ecstasy: The Power and the Glory of Speaking in Tongues*. Nashville: Abingdon, 1969.

———. *Let Life Be Like This!* Englewood Cliffs, NJ: Prentice Hall, 1963.

———. "Life and Death of Psychiana." *Christian Century* (Jan. 2, 1957) 11–14.

———. *Major Religions of the World*. Nashville: Abingdon, 1959.

———. *A Meeting with Shoghi Effendi*. Oxford: Oxford University Press, 1993.

———. *Of Life and Learning: The Story of the School of Religion at the State University of Iowa*. Iowa City: University of Iowa Press, 1952.

Bibliography

―――. "Pioneer in 'Positive Thinking.'" *Christian Century* (Mar. 20, 1957) 357–59.
―――. *The Power of Perception*. Garden City, NY: Doubleday, 1971.
―――. *The Power of Total Living*. New York: Dodd, Mead & Co., 1977.
―――. *Report to Protestants*. Indianapolis: Bobbs-Merrill, 1948.
―――. *Spiritual Breakthroughs for Our Time*. Garden City, NY: Doubleday, 1965.
―――. *They Have Found a Faith*. Indianapolis: Bobbs-Merrill, 1946.
―――. *The Unity Way*. Unity Village, MO: Unity, 1986.
―――. *Vesper Dramas*. Chicago: Willett, Clark and Company, 1938.
―――. *What's Right with the World*. Englewood Cliffs, NJ: Prentice Hall, 1973.
Bader, Jesse M. "Heralds of the Evangel." In Edward T. Dahlberg, *Herald of the Evangel: 60 Years of American Christianity*, 196–214. St. Louis: Bethany, 1959.
Baird, John. *Horn of Plenty: The Story of the Presbyterian Ministers' Fund*. Wheaton, IL: Tyndale, 1982.
Baker, Paul E. *A Study of the Presbyterian Mission Among the Mesquakie Indians in Tama, Iowa*. New York: Board of National Missions, 1960.
Baker, Thomas R. *The Sacred Cause of Union: Iowa in the Civil War*. Iowa City: University of Iowa Press, 2016.
Balakian, Peter. *The Burning Tigris: The Armenian Genocide and the American Response*. New York: Harper, 2003.
Baldwin, David A. "When Billy Sunday 'Saved' Colorado." *Colorado Heritage* 2 (1990) 34–44.
Baldwin, Lewis V. *There Is a Balm in Gilead: The Cultural Roots of Martin Luther King, Jr*. Minneapolis: Fortress, 1991.
Ball, James W. "The Beginnings of Satyagraha: A Natural Growth of India." Master's thesis, Drake University, 1940.
Ballou, Hosea. *A Series of Letters, in Defence of Divine Revelation, in Reply to Reverend Abner Kneeland's Serious Inquiry into the Authenticity of the Same*. Boston: Henry Bowen, 1820.
Balmer, Randall. *Bad Faith: Race and the Rise of the Religious Right*. Grand Rapids, MI: Eerdmans, 2021.
―――. *Encyclopedia of Evangelicalism*. Louisville: WJK, 2002.
―――. *Grant Us Courage: Travels Along the Mainline of American Protestantism*. Oxford: Oxford University Press, 1996.
―――. "'A Great Excess of Undenominationalism': Religion in Iowa at the Sesquicentennial." In *Family Reunion: Essays on Iowa*. Ames, IA: Iowa State University Press, 1995.
―――. *Growing Pains: Learning to Love My Father's Faith*. Grand Rapids: Eerdmans, 2001.
―――. *Mine Eyes Have Seen the Glory: A Journey into the Evangelical Subculture in America*. New York: Oxford University Press, 1993.
―――. *Thy Kingdom Come: An Evangelical's Lament*. New York: Oxford University Press, 2000.
Bardacke, Frank. *Trampling Out the Vintage: Cesar Chavez and the Two Souls of the United Farm Workers*. London: Verso, 2011.
Barge, Scott. "Renegotiating the Goshen College-Mennonite Church Relationship: Faculty Development at Goshen College, 1931–1944." *MQR* 81 (2007) 549–76.
Barlow, Philip. "Demographic Profile." In *Religion and Public Life in the Midwest: America's Common Denominator?*, edited by Philip Barlow and Mark Silk, 21–48. Walnut Creek, CA: AltaMira, 2004

Bibliography

Barnes, Gregory A. *A Biography of Lillian and George Willoughby, Twentieth- Century Quaker Peace Activists.* Lewiston, NY: Edwin Mellen, 2007.

Barnett, David C. "A Nun Inspired by Andy Warhol: The Forgotten Pop Art of Sister Corita Kent." National Public Radio, *All Things Considered*, Jan. 8, 2015.

Barnhart, Cornelia Mallett. "Church Foundations in Iowa." *Pal* 27:4 (Apr. 1946) 97-115.

Barrows, John Henry, ed. *The World's Parliament of Religions: An Illustrated and Popular Story of the World's Parliament of Religions, Held in Chicago in Connexion with the World's Columbian Exposition.* Chicago: Parliament, 1893.

Barry, Colman J. *The Catholic Church and German Americans.* Milwaukee: Bruce, 1953.

Barth, Karl. *On Religion: The Revelation of God as the Sublimation of Religion.* London: T&T Clark, 2006.

Barthel, Diane L. *Amana: From Pietist Sect to American Community.* Lincoln, NE: University of Nebraska Press, 1984.

Bartlett, Billy Vick. *A History of Baptist Separatism.* Springfield, MO: Bible Baptist Fellowship, 1972.

Barton, H. Arnold. "Conrad Bergendoff and the Swedish-American Church Language Controversy of the 1920's." In *Aspects of Augustana and Swedish America: Essays in Honor of Dr. Conrad Bergendoff on His 100th Year,* edited by Raymond Jarvi, 46–56. Dexter, MI: Augustana Historical Society, 1995.

———., ed. *Peter Cassel and Iowa's New Sweden.* Chicago, 1995.

———. et al., eds. *Swedish Roots: The Legacy of George M. Stephenson, Pioneer and Patriot.* Swedesburg, IA: Swedish Heritage Society, 2001.

Bascom, Tim. *Chameleon Days: An American Boyhood in Ethiopia.* Boston: Mariner, 2006.

———. "Visionquest," *DSM* 11 (Nov. 2009) 130–46.

Bataille, Gretchen M., et al., eds. *The Worlds between Two Rivers: Perspectives on American Indians in Iowa.* Expanded ed. Iowa City: University of Iowa Press, 2000.

Batten, Samuel Zane. "New Conviction of Sin." *Biblical World* 52 (Nov. 1918) 270–279.

———. *The Social Task of Christianity.* New York: Revell, 1911.

Battey, Thomas C. *The Life and Adventures of a Quaker among the Indians.* Norman, OK: University of Oklahoma Press, 1968.

Bauder, Kevin. "Biography of O. W. Van Orsdel." ThM. thesis, Denver Baptist Seminary, 1983.

Bauder Kevin, and Robert Delnay. *One in Hope and Doctrine: Origins of Baptist Fundamentalism, 1870–1950.* Schaumberg, IL: Regular Baptist, 2014.

Bauer, Bryce T. *Gentlemen Bootleggers: The True Story of Templeton Rye, Prohibition, and a Small Town in Cahoots.* Chicago: Chicago Review, 2014.

Bauer, E. Theodore. "Progress of Churches and Length of Pastorates: A Study of 36 Churches from Different Denominations in Des Moines." M.A. thesis, Drake University, 1935.

Bechtold, Paul F. *From Hostility to Nobility.* Montezuma, IA: Sutherland, 1984.

Beck, Paul N. *Inkpaduta: A Dakota Leader.* Norman: University of Oklahoma Press, 2008.

Beck, Peggy V., et al. *The Sacred: Ways of Knowledge, Sources of Life.* Tsaile, AZ: Navajo Community College Press, 1992.

Bedell, L. Frank. *Quaker Heritage: Friends Coming into the Heartland of America. A Story of Iowa Conservative Yearly Meeting.* Cedar Rapids, IA: Cono, 1984.

Bibliography

Bederman, Gail. "'The Women Have Had Charge of the Church Work Long Enough': The Men and Religion Forward Movement of 1911–1912 and the Masculinization of Middle-Class Protestantism." *American Quarterly* 41 (1989) 432–65.

Bednarowski, Mary Farrell. *New Religions and the Theological Imagination in America*. Bloomington, IN: Indiana University Press, 1989.

Behney, J. Bruce, and Paul H. Eller. *The History of the Evangelical Brethren Church*. Edited by Kenneth W. Krueger. Nashville: Abingdon, 1979.

Beisel, Suzanne. "Henry Clay 'Dirty' Dean." *AI* 36 (1963) 505–24.

Belin, Laura. "Elections Bringing More Diversity to Iowa Legislature." *Iowa Capital Dispatch*, Nov. 17, 2022.

Bell, Michael J. "'True Israelites of America': The Story of the Jews in Iowa." *AI* 53 (1994) 65–127.

———. "To Light Out for the Territories Ahead of the Rest." *Pal* 71:4 (Winter 1990) 146–53.

Ben-Zvi, Linda. *Susan Glaspell: Her Life and Times*. Oxford: Oxford University Press, 2005.

Bender, Norman J. "Sheldon Jackson's Crusade to Win the West for Christ, 1869–1880." *Midwest Review* 4 (2nd series, 1982) 1–12.

Bendroth, Margaret Lamberts. *Fundamentalism in the City: Conflict and Division in Boston's Churches, 1885–1950*. New York: Oxford University Press, 2005.

———. *Good and Mad: Mainline Protestant Churchwomen, 1920–1980*. New York: Oxford University Press, 2023.

———. "Why Women Loved Billy Sunday: Urban Revivalism and Popular Entertainment in Early Twentieth Century American Culture." *Religion and American Culture* 14 (2004) 251–71.

Benedict, Lovina. *Woman's Work for Woman*. Des Moines: Iowa Printing, 1892.

Benedict, Philip. *Christ's Churches Purely Reformed: A Social History of Calvinism*. New Haven: Yale University Press, 2002.

Bennett, John C. *The History of the Saints: Or, An Expose of Joe Smith and the Mormons*. Boston: Leland & Whiting, 1842.

Bennett, Richard E. *Mormons at the Missouri: Winter Quarters, 1846–1852*. Norman, OK: University of Oklahoma Press, 2004.

Benson, Wendell. *A Century of Service to God and Community: The Story of St. Mary's Church, Marshalltown, Iowa, 1869–1969*. Marshalltown, IA: Marshall, 1970.

Berry, Dorothy G. "The Story of the Farm Crisis: Kansas as a Case Study." In *A Tapestry of Justice, Service, and Unity: Local Ecumenism in the United States, 1950–2000*, edited by Arleon L. Kelley. Tacoma: NAIES, 2004.

Berry, Jason. *Spirit of Black Hawk: A History of Africans and Indians*. Jackson: University of Mississippi Press, 1995.

Best of Living in Iowa. Episode 125. Iowa PBS.

Betts, Rev. Frederick W. *Billy Sunday: The Man and Method*. Boston: Murray, 1916.

"Beauty and Building." *Iowan* 4.2 (Dec. 1955) 42–43, 60.

Bianco, Fran. *Voices of Silence: Lives of the Trappists Today*. New York: Anchor, 1991.

"Bible School at St. Mark's." *Radical Religion* 4 (1979) 87–90.

Bicha, Karel D. "Prairie Radicals: A Common Pietism." *Journal of Church and State* 18 (1976) 79–94.

Biddle, Conley J. *Trails Trials Triumphs*. West Des Moines, IA: Rob Lee Hill, 1972.

Billington, Ray Allen. *The Protestant Crusade: A Study of the Origins of American Nativism*. Chicago: Quadrangle, 1964.

Bibliography

Birkby, Evelyn. *Neighboring on the Air: Cooking with the KMA Radio Homemakers.* Iowa City: University of Iowa Press, 1994.

Birkby, Robert. *KMA Radio: The First Sixty Years.* Shenandoah, IA: May, 1985.

Black Hawk. *An Autobiography.* Edited by Donald Jackson. Urbana, IL: Prairie State, 1990.

Black, Susan Easton, and William G. Hartley, eds. *The Iowa Mormon Trail: Legacy of Faith and Courage.* Orem, UT: Helix, 1997.

Blaine, Martha Royce. *The Ioway Indians.* Norman, OK: University of Oklahoma Press, 1979.

Blair, A. R. "Reorganized Church of Latter Day Saints: Moderate Mormons." In *The Restoration Movement: Essays in Mormon History.* Edited by Blair, et al. Lawrence, KS: Coronado, 1973.

Blanchard, Charles. *History of Drake University.* Des Moines: Drake University, 1931.

———. "Introduction and Acknowledgement to the History of Religion in Iowa." In Edgar Rubey Harlan, *A Narrative History of the People of Iowa,* vol. 2, 372–474. Chicago: American Historical Society, 1931.

———. "'Pioneers' of a Great Cause: A History of the Disciples of Christ in Iowa." Des Moines, 1931, typescript. Special Collections, Cowles Library, Drake University, Des Moines.

———. "Religion in Iowa: The Presbyterians." *AI* 36 (1962) 401–13.

Bliss, Edwin Munsell. *Turkey and the Armenian Atrocities.* N.p., 1896.

Blocker, Jack S., Jr. "'Give to the Winds Thy Fears': The Women's Temperance Crusade, 1873-1874." Westport, CT: Greenwood, 1985.

———. *Retreat from Reform: The Prohibition Movement in the United States, 1890–1913.* Westport, CT: Greenwood, 1976.

Blockhaus, Harriet, et al. *Echoes from the Valley: Stories from Clermont and Elgin.* Clermont, IA: Country Heritage Community, 1999.

Bloesch, Donald G. *The Christian Witness in a Secular Age: An Evaluation of Nine Contemporary Theologians.* Minneapolis: Augsburg, 1968.

———. *Jesus Is Victor! Karl Barth's Doctrine of Salvation.* Nashville: Abingdon, 1976.

———. "Vain Hope for Victory: The State Must Not Play God," *Pulpit* 31:11 (Nov. 1961), 329–32.

———. *Wellsprings of Renewal: Promise in Christian Communal Life.* Grand Rapids: Eerdmans, 1974.

Bloom, Stephen G. *Postville: A Clash of Cultures in Heartland America.* New York: Mariner, 2000.

Bloomer, D. C., ed. *Life and Writings of Amelia Bloomer.* New York: Schocken, 1975.

Blumhofer, Edith L. *Aimee Semple McPherson: Everybody's Sister.* Grand Rapids: Eerdmans, 1993.

Boeck, George Albert. "An Early Iowa Community." PhD. diss., State University of Iowa, 1961.

Bohach, Leona J. "Settlement of St. Ansgar: A Miniature Melting Pot." *IJH* 46:3 (July 1948) 296–315.

Bonney, Margaret Atherton. "The Salubria Story." *Pal* 56:2 (Mar. 1975) 34–45.

Bonney, Edward. *Banditti of the Prairies.* Norman, OK: University of Oklahoma Press, 1963.

Bonomi, Ferne G., and Robert F. *Show Me a Man . . . Ellis I. Levitt.* Des Moines: Penny, 1969.

Bibliography

Bonvillain, Nancy. *The Sac and Fox.* New York: Chelsea, 1995.
Booth, Howard J. *Edwin Diller Starbuck: Pioneer in the Psychology of Religion.* Washington, D.C.: University Press of America, 1981.
Booth, Marlene. *Yidl in the Middle: Growing Up Jewish in Iowa.* VCR, 1999.
Borden, Ruth. *Women and Temperance: The Quest for Power and Liberty, 1873-1900.* Philadelphia: Temple University Press, 1981.
Borich, Michael. *Black Hawk Songs.* N.p., 2016.
Boulding, Elise. *The Small Plot of Heaven: Reflections on Early Life by a Quaker Sociologist.* Wallingford, PA: Pendle Hill, 1989.
Bourret, Joan Liffring-Zug, compiler. *Life in Amana 1867-1935: Reporters' Views of the Communal Way.* Iowa City: [Penfield], 1998.
Bovee, David S. *The Church and the Land: The National Catholic Rural Life Conference and American Society, 1923-2007.* Washington, D. C., 2010.
Bowden, Henry Warner. "Ballard, Edna Wheeler." *Dictionary of American Religious Biography.* 2nd ed. Westport, CT: Greenwood, 1993.
Bower, Robert K. "Joseph Dugdale: A Friend of Truth." *Pal* 56:6 (Nov. 1975) 170-83.
Bowermaster, Jon. *Governor: An Oral Biography of Robert D. Ray.* Ames, IA: Iowa State University Press, 1987.
Bowers, William L. *The Country Life Movement in America, 1900-1920.* Port Washington, NY: Kennikat, 1974.
Bowie, Mary Ella. *Alabaster and Spikenard: The Life of Dr. Iva Durham Vennard.* Chicago: Chicago Evangelistic Institute, 1947.
Boyd, Myron F., and Merne A. Harris. *Projecting Our Heritage: Messages from the Centennial Convention of the National Holiness Convention.* Kansas City: Beacon Hill, 1969.
Boyd-Bayly, Elisabeth. *A Brief Memoir of Ida Mellinger.* London: Jarrold, [1900].
Boyle, Sarah. "Creating a Union of the Union: The Women's Christian Temperance Union and the Creation of a Political Female Reform Culture, 1880-1892." PhD. diss., Binghamton University, 2005.
Braaten, Carl E. "The Dynamics of a Responding Church in a Changing World." In *The Challenge of Change: To Serve and To Share.* Symposium Lectures. Decorah, IA: Luther College Press, 1964.
Brackenridge, R. Douglas and Lois A. Boyd. *Presbyterians and Pensions, 1717-1988.* Atlanta: John Knox, 1988.
Brackney, William H. *Congregation and Campus: North American Baptists in Higher Education.* Macon, GA: Mercer University Press, 2008.
Braden, Charles S. *Spirits in Rebellion: The Rise and Development of New Thought.* Dallas: Southern Methodist University Press, 1963.
Brass, Maynard F. "German Presbyterians and the Synod of the West." *Journal of Presbyterian History* 56 (1978) 237-51.
Bratt, James D. *Dutch Calvinism in Modern America: A History of a Conservative Subculture.* Grand Rapids: Eerdmans, 1984.
Brauer, Jerald C. "Regionalism and Religion in America." *CH* 54 (1985) 366-78.
Braybrooke, Marcus. "Pan-Asian Participation in the 1893 Parliament." *Interfaith Observer*, Nov. 15, 2012.
Breckbill, Laban T. *History Old Order River Brethren.* N.p.: Breckbill & Strickler, 1972.
Bremer, Fredrika. *America of the Fifties: Letters of Fredrika Bremer.* Edited by Adolph B. Benson. London: Scandinavian Classics, 1924.

Bibliography

Bremer, Jeff. *A New History of Iowa*. Lawrence, KS: University Press of Kansas, 2023.

Bresson, Mary Alfred. "Contemporary Iowa Opinions Regarding the Influence of Croatians in Waterloo and Vicinity, 1907–1949." Master's thesis, Catholic University, 1951.

"A Brief History of First Presbyterian Church, Iowa City." https://firstpresiowacity.org/a-brief-history/.

Brinton, Howard H., ed. "The Revival Movement in Iowa: A Letter From Joel Bean to Rufus M. Jones." *Quaker History* 50 (1961) 102–10.

Britton, Essie M. "The Negro in Iowa: History of the Colored Race of People Residing in Keokuk and Vicinity." Typescript in Box 3, F., "1830–1867," Frances Hawthorne Papers, IWA.

Brigham, Jeremy John. "Transforming Places." PhD. diss., University of Iowa, 1998.

Brigham, Johnson. *Des Moines: The Pioneer of Municipal Progress and Reform of the Middle West*. Chicago: Clarke, 1911.

Briggs, Carolyn. *This Dark World: A Memoir of Salvation Found and Lost*. New York: Bloomsbury, 2002.

———. "Church of the Snake." In *Beyond Belief: The Secret Lives of Women in Extreme Religions*, edited by Susan Tive and Cami Ostman, 265–67. Berkeley: Seal, 2013.

———. "Waiting for Lightning to Strike: A Wobbly Agnostic among the Atheists." ReligionDispatch, Oct. 20, 2011.

Bringhurst, Newell G., and John C. Hamer, eds. *Scattering of the Saints: Schism within Mormonism*. Independence, MO: John Whitmer, 2007.

Brinks, Herbert J. *Dutch American Voices: Letters from the United States, 1850–1930*. Ithaca: Cornell University Press, 1995.

Brock, Peter. *Against the Draft: Essays on Conscientious Objection from the Radical Reformation to the Second World War*. Toronto: University of Toronto Press, 2006.

Brod, Harry. *Superman Is Jewish?* New York: Free, 2012.

Broihahn, "Meskwaki Mining Metamorphosis." *Wisconsin Archeologist* 89 (2008) 98–118.

Brondahl, Jorn. *Ethnic Leadership and Midwestern Politics: Scandinavian-Americans and the Progressive Movement in Wisconsin, 1890–1914*. Northfield, MN: Norwegian-American Historical Association, 2004.

Brooks, Juanita, ed. *On the Mormon Frontier: The Diary of Hosea Stout, 1844–1861*. Salt Lake City: University of Utah Press, 1964.

Brookwood, Marilyn. *The Orphans of Davenport: Eugenics, the Great Depression, and the War over Children's Intelligence*. New York: W. W. Norton, 2021.

Brown, Candy Gunther. "Chiropractic and Christianity: The Power of Pain to Adjust Cultural Alignments." *CH* 79 (2010) 144–81.

Brown, Greg. "Brand New '64 Dodge." *The Poet Game*. Red House Records, 1994.

Brown, Nicholas A., and Sarah E. Kanouse. *Re-Collecting Black Hawk: Landscape, Memory, and Power in the American Midwest*. Pittsburgh: University of Pittsburgh Press, 2015.

Bruns, Roger A. *Preacher: Billy Sunday and Big-Time Evangelism*. Urbana, IL: University of Illinois Press, 1992.

Bucko, Raymond A. *The Lakota Ritual of the Sweat Lodge*. Lincoln: University of Nebraska Press, 1998.

Buffalo, Johnathon Lantz. "Oral History of the Meskwaki." *Wisconsin Archeologist* 89 (2008) 3–6.

Bibliography

Bull, Malcolm, and Keith Lockhart. *Seeking a Sanctuary: Seventh-day Adventism and the American Dream.* New York: HarperCollins, 1989.

Bunkers, Suzanne L. *In Search of Susanna.* Iowa City: University of Iowa Press, 1996.

Burchinal, Lee G., and Loren E. Chancellor. "Proportions of Catholics, Urbanism, and Mixed-Catholic Marriage Rates among Iowa Counties." *Social Problems* 9 (1962) 359–65.

Burg, David F. *Chicago's White City of 1893.* Lexington: University Press of Kentucky, 1976.

Burke, Mary Louise. *Swami Vivekananda in the West: New Discoveries,* Calcutta: Ramakrishna, 1983.

Burkee, James C. *Power, Politics, and the Missouri Synod.* Minneapolis: Fortress, 2011.

Burkholder, Chris. *Amish Confidential: The Bishop's Son Shatters the Silence.* Argyle, IA: Argyle, 2006.

Burkholder, J. R., and Calvin Redekop, eds. *Kingdom, Cross and Community: Essays in Honor of Guy F. Hershberger.* Scottdale, PA: Herald, 1976.

Burns, E. Bradford. *Kinship with the Land: Regionalist Thought in Iowa, 1894–1942.* Iowa City: University of Iowa Press, 1996.

Burns, Helen Marie. "Active Religious Women on the Iowa Frontier: A Study in Continuity and Discontinuity." PhD. diss, University of Iowa, 2001.

Busby, Allie B. *Two Summers among the Musquakies.* Vinton, IA: Herald, 1886.

Busch, Eberhardt. *Karl Barth: His Life from Letters and Autobiographical Texts.* Philadelphia: Fortress, 1976.

Bushman, Richard Lyman. *Joseph Smith: Rough Stone Rolling.* New York: Knopf, 2005.

Butchert, Ronald E., and Amy F. Rolleri. "Iowa Teachers among the Freedpeople of the South, 1862–1876." *AI* 62 (2003) 1–29.

Butler, Diane Hochstedt. *Standing against the Whirlwind: Evangelical Episcopalians in Nineteenth Century America.* New York: Oxford University Press, 1995.

Butler, Ellis Parker. *Dominie Dean.* New York: Revell, 1917.

Butler, William J. "The Right of Free Listening." *Catholic World* 168 (Dec. 1948).

Buxbaum, Katherine. *Iowa Outpost.* Philadelphia: Dorrance, 1948.

———. "John R. Mott, World Citizen." *AI* 40 (1969) 137–41.

———. "The Pommey Piling." *AI* 38 (1936) 309–12.

Byrd, James P. *A Holy Baptism of Fire and Blood: The Bible & the American Civil War.* Oxford: Oxford University Press, 2021.

Byrne, Robert. *Always a Catholic.* New York: Pinnacle, 1981.

———. *Memories of a Non-Jewish Childhood.* New York: L. Stuart, 1970.

———. *Once a Catholic.* New York: Pinnacle, 1970.

Cada, Joseph. "The Pioneers, Czech-American Catholics after 1850." In *The Other Catholics,* edited by Keith P. Dyrud, et al, 1–46. New York: Arno, 1978.

"Cain, Richard Harvey." https://history.house.gov/People/Detail/10470.

Cajka, Peter. "The French Revolution and American Catholicism: Five Questions with Mitchell Oxford." Cushwa Center, May 19, 2020. https://cushwa.nd.edu/news/the-french-revolution-and-american-catholicism-five-questions-with-mitchell-oxford/.

Campbell, Ballard C. "Did Democracy Work? Prohibition in Late Nineteenth-Century Iowa: A Test Case." *Journal of Interdisciplinary History* 8 (1977) 87–116.

Campbell, Bruce F. *Ancient Wisdom Revived: A History of the Theosophical Movement.* Berkeley: University of California Press, 1980.

Bibliography

Campbell, Will D. *Providence*. Atlanta: Longstreet, 1992.

Cantwell, Christopher D. "'No Place Is So Dear to My Childhood': Evangelicalism, Nostalgia, and the History of an American Hymn." Paper delivered at Cushwa Center Forum, Apr. 1, 2022.

Carey, Isaac E. "The War an Occasion for Thanksgiving: A Discourse for Thanksgiving." Preached at the First Presbyterian Church, Keokuk, Iowa, Nov. 28, 1861.

Carey, Patrick. "The First World War and Catholics in the United States." In *American Churches and the First World War*, edited by Gordon L. Heath. Eugene, OR: Pickwick, 2016.

Carmody, Denise Lardner, and John Tully Carmody. *Native American Religions: An Introduction*. Mahwah, NJ: Paulist, 1993.

Carpenter, George Thomas. *A Debate on the Destiny of the Wicked*. Oskaloosa, IA: Christian, 1875.

Carpenter, Joel. *Revive Us Again: The Reawakening of American Fundamentalism*. New York: Oxford University Press, 1997.

Carpenter, M. F. "The Episcopalians in Iowa." *Pal* 34:10 (Oct. 1953) 433–80.

Carroll, George. "Japanese-American Student Relocation: The Grinnell College Experience." Undergraduate thesis, Grinnell College, 2004.

Carter, John F., Jr. "These Wild Young People." *Atlantic Monthly* 126 (Sep. 1920) 301–4.

Carton, Evan. *Patriotic Treason: John Brown and the Soul of America*. New York: Free, 2006.

Case, Clarence M. *Non-Violent Coercion*. New York: Century, 1923.

———. "Passive Resistance." In *Nonviolent Direct Action*, edited by A. Paul Hare and Herbert H. Blumberg, 319–27. Washington, DC: Corpus, 1968.

Case, Jay Riley. *An Unpredictable Gospel: American Evangelicals and World Christianity, 1812–1920*, Oxford: Oxford University Press, 2012.

Casteel, Joshua. *Letters From Abu Ghraib*. N.p., 2008.

Celebration: The Archbishop of Canterbury Visits Iowa. Des Moines, 1981.

Chaichian, Mohammad. "Getting Settled in the Heartland: Community Formation among First- and Second-Generation Iranians in Iowa City, Iowa." *Immigrants Outside Megapolis: Ethnic Transformation in the Heartland*, edited by Richard C. Jones, 213–35. Lanham, MD: Africa World Press, 2008.

Chamber of Commerce, *St. Ansgar*, n.p., n.d.

Chancellor, Loren E., and Thomas P. Monahan. "Religious Preferences and Interreligious Mixtures in Marriages and Divorces in Iowa." *American Journal of Sociology* 61 (1955) 233–39.

Chapin, E. N. *Iowa Cranks, or, the Beauties of Prohibition: A Political Novel*. Marshalltown, IA: Hartwell Bros., 1893.

Chase, Hal, et al., eds. *Outside In: African-American History in Iowa, 1838–2000*. Des Moines: State Historical Society of Iowa, 2001.

Chase, Rachelle. *Creating the Black Utopia of Buxton, Iowa*. Charleston, SC: History, 2019.

Chatfield, Charles, and Charles DeBenadetti, eds. *Kirby Page and the Social Gospel: An Anthology*. New York: Garland, 1976.

Chaves, Mark. *Ordaining Women: Culture and Conflict in Religious Organizations*, Cambridge: Harvard University Press, 1997.

Chiat, Marilyn J. *America's Religious Architecture: Sacred Places for Every Community*. New York: Wiley, 1997.

Bibliography

Chitty, Arthur Ben. "Griswold College, 1859-1897 Davenport, Iowa." *Historical Magazine of the Protestant Episcopal Church* 37 (Mar. 1968) 73-75.

Choate, Jean. *Disputed Ground: Farm Groups That Opposed the New Deal Agricultural Program*. Jefferson, NC: McFarland, 2002.

Christensen, Thomas P. "Denmark—An Early Stronghold of Congregationalism." *IJH* 24 (1926) 108-43.

———. "Fredrik Lange Grundtvig." *AI* 25 (1943) 105-11.

Christian Churches of Iowa. Des Moines, 1956.

Christiano, Kevin J. *Religious Diversity and Social Change: American Cities, 1890-1906*. Cambridge: Cambridge University Press, 1987.

"Christian Union." https://www.christianunion.com/.

Chu, Jonathan M. *Neighbors, Friends, or Madmen: The Puritan Adjustment to Quakerism in Seventeenth-Century Massachusetts Bay*. Westport, CT: Greenwood, 1985.

"Churches." Boone County. https://web.archive.org/web/20200218123937/iagenweb.org/boone/churches.html.

Cistercians of the Strict Observance. Peosta, IA: New Melleray Abbey, 1947.

City of Vedic City, Iowa. "Application to Vision Iowa: Maharishi Vedic Land," 2001.

Clabaugh, Gary K. *Thunder on the Right: The Protestant Fundamentalists*. Chicago: Nelson Hall, 1974.

Clampitt, Amy. *The Collected Poems of Amy Clampitt*. New York: Alfred A. Knopf, 1997.

Clampitt, Roy J. *A Life I Did Not Plan: An Autobiography*. Des Moines: Wallace-Homestead, 1966.

Clark, Daniel Elbert. "History of Liquor Legislation in Iowa," *IJH* 6 (1908) "1846-1861," 55-87; "1861-1878," 339-74; "1878-1908," 503-68; "Beginning of Liquor Legislation in Iowa" (1907) 193-212.

Clark, Frank. *The Country Parson*. Des Moines, n.d.

Clark, Glenn. *God's Voice in the Folklore*. St. Paul, MN: Macalester Park, 1956.

———. *A Man's Reach*. Austin, MN, 2004.

Clarkson, James S. "General Grant's Des Moines Speech." *Century Illustrated Monthly Magazine* 55 (Mar. 1898) 785-88.

Clemmons, Linda M. "'The Young Folks [Want] to Go in and See the Indians': Davenport Citizens, Protestant Missionaries, and Dakota Prisoners of War, 1863-1866." *AI* 77 (2018) 121-50.

Clough, John E., and Emma Rauschenbusch Clough. *Social Christianity in the Orient: The Story of a Man, a Mission, and a Movement*. New York: Macmillan, 1914.

Clyde, J. F., and H. A. Dwelle, eds. *History of Mitchell and Worth Counties*. Chicago: S. J. Clarke, 1918.

Cochrane, Arthur C. "Barmen and the Confession of 1967." *McCormick Quarterly* 19 (1966) 135-48.

———. *The Church and the War*. Toronto: Nelson, 1940.

———. *The Church's Confession under Hitler*. Philadelphia: Westminster, 1952.

———. *Eating and Drinking with Jesus: An Ethical Inquiry*. Philadelphia: Westminster, 1974.

———. *The Existentialists and God*. Dubuque, IA: University of Dubuque Press, 1956.

———. "John Calvin and Nuclear War." *Christian Century*, July 4, 1962.

———, ed. *Reformed Confessions of the 16th Century*. Philadelphia: WJK, 2003.

———. "Karl Barth's Doctrine of the Covenant." In *Major Themes in the Reformed Tradition*, edited by Donald K. McKim, 108-16. Grand Rapids: Eerdmans, 1992.

Bibliography

———. *The Mystery of Peace*. Elgin, IL: Brethren, 1986.

———. "Whether Karl Barth Changed My Mind." In *How Karl Barth Changed My Mind*, edited by Donald K. McKim, 15–18. Grand Rapids: Eerdmans, 1986.

Coffman, Elesha J. *The Christian Century and the Rise of the Protestant Mainline*. Oxford: Oxford University Press, 2013.

"Collier, Ada Langworthy." Encyclopedia Dubuque. https://www.encyclopediadubuque. org/index.php/COLLIER,_Ada_Langworthy.

Collier, Ada Langworthy. *Lilith: The Legend of the First Woman*. Boston: D. Lothrop, 1885.

Collins, Hubert E., ed. "The Story of Mahlon Day Collins." *IJH* 28.1 (Jan. 1930) 55–131.

Colman, John Park. "In Pursuit of Harmony: A Study in the Thought of Jesse Macy." PhD dissertation, State University of Iowa, 1968.

Colonnese, Louis M. *Human Rights and the Liberation of Man in the Americas*, Notre Dame, IN: Notre Dame Press, 1970.

Colton, Kenneth E. "Father Mazzuchelli's Iowa Mission." *AI* (1938) 297–315.

———. "The Coming of the Norwegians to Iowa." *IJH* 3 (1905) 381–82.

Colyer, Elmer M. *Evangelical Theology in Transition: Theologians in Dialogue with Donald Bloesch*. Downers Grove, IL: InterVarsity, 1999.

Commager, Henry Steele. "The Blasphemy of Abner Kneeland." *New England Quarterly* 8 (1935) 29–41.

Comstock, Gary, ed. *Is There a Moral Obligation to Save the Family Farm?* Ames, IA: Iowa State University Press, 1987.

Conard, Laetitia Moon. "A Word Picture of Iowa Conditions." In *Prosperity?*, edited by Harry W. Laidler and Norman Thomas, 106–8. New York: Vanguard, 1927.

Concerned Catholics of the Davenport Diocese. *Toward Hope and Understanding: Stories of Survivors of Clergy Sexual Abuse in the Davenport Diocese*. Iowa City, [2005?].

Congregational Library and Archives. "Author Interview with Dr. Randall Balmer." Video.

Conkin, Paul K. *American Originals: Homemade Varieties of Christianity*. Chapel Hill: University of North Carolina Press, 1997.

———. *Tomorrow a New World: The New Deal Community Program*. Ithaca, NY: Cornell University Press, 1959.

Conner, Susan Marks, ed. *I Remember When: Personal Recollections and Vignettes of the Sioux City Jewish Community, 1869–1984*. Sioux City, IA: Jewish Federation, 1985.

Connerly, Charles R. *Green, Fair, and Prosperous: Paths to a Sustainable Iowa*. Iowa City: University of Iowa Press, 2020.

Conway, Monsignor J. D. *Facts of the Faith*. New York: All Saints, 1961.

———. *Modern Moral Problems*, Notre Dame, IN: Fides, 1961.

———. *Times of Decision: Story of the Councils*. Notre Dame, IN: Fides, 1962.

———. *What the Church Teaches*. New York: Harper, 1962.

———. *What They Ask About Divorce*. Notre Dame: Ave Maria, 1964.

———. *What They Ask About Marriage*. Chicago: Fides, 1955.

———. *What They Ask About Morals*. Notre Dame: Fides, 1960.

———. *What They Ask About Sin*. Notre Dame: Fides, 1962.

Coogan, M. Jane. "The Redoubtable John Hennessey, First Archbishop of Dubuque." *MidAmerican* 62 (1980) 21–34.

———. *The Price of Our Heritage: History of the Sisters of Charity of the Blessed Virgin Mary, 1831–1869 and 1869–1920*. 2 vol. Dubuque: Mount Carmel, 1975, 1978.

Bibliography

Cook, Nilla Cram. *My Road to India*. New York: Lee Furman, 1939.

———. "What Religion Means to Me." *Forum and Century* (Feb. 1936) 69–75.

Cook, Reverend Robert C. *When the Sun Comes Up in the West: A Missionary's New Song of Justice and Peace*. Bloomington, IN: WestBow, 2011.

Cordaro, Fr. Frank. "Dorothy Day's Des Moines Visit November, 1952." *Via Pacis* 27.2 (May 2003) 1.

Corey, Paul. *Three Miles Square*. Indianapolis: Bobbs-Merrill, 1939.

Cowman, Mrs. Charles E. *Streams in the Desert*. Grand Rapids: Zondervan, 1965.

Cox, Jeffrey. *Imperial Fault Lines: Christianity and Colonial Power in India, 1818–1940*. Stanford: Stanford University Press, 2002.

Cozzens, Peter. *Tecumseh and the Prophet: The Shawnee Brothers Who Defied a Nation*. New York: Knopf, 2020.

Crain, James. *The Development of Social Ideas Among the Disciples of Christ*. St. Louis: Bethany, 1969.

Crary, David. "AP-NORC Poll Details Rifts between Lay Catholics and Bishops." AP, June 3, 2022. https://apnorc.org/ap-norc-poll-details-rift-between-lay-catholics-and-bishops.

Crawford, J. Charles. *The Holy Spirit and Holy Living*. Boone, 1934.

Crawford, Lois. *Papa and I: The Story of J. Charles Crawford*. N.p., n.d.

Crisler, Shirley, SFCC, and Mira Mosle, BVM. *In the Midst of His People: The Authorized Biography of Bishop Maurice J. Dingman*. Iowa City: Rudi, 1995.

Cronon, William. *Nature's Metropolis: Chicago and the Great West*. New York: W. W. Norton, 1994.

Crookford, Suzannah. "How 'Positivity' Can Lead to Conspiratorial Thinking." Religion Dispatches, Jan 4, 2021.

Cross, Christopher. *Soldiers of God: True Story of the U.S. Army Chaplains*. New York: Dutton, 1945.

Cross, Robert D. *The Emergence of Liberal Catholicism in America*. Chicago: Quadrangle, 1968.

Crumden, Robert. "George D. Herron: A New Frame of Reference for the 1890's." *AI* 42 (1973) 81–113.

Cullen, Art. "Iowa Is the Thumping Heart of the Midwest." https://iowacapitaldispatch.com/2022/08/17/iowa-is-the-thumping-heart-of-the-midwest.

Culver, John C., and John Hyde. *American Dreamer: The Life and Times of Henry A. Wallace*. New York: W. W. Norton, 2000.

Cumberland, William H. "Albert Hirsch: From Frankfurt to Storm Lake." *Iowa Heritage* 83 (2002) 178–86.

———. *History of Buena Vista College*. Ames, IA: Iowa State University Press, 1991.

———. "A History of Jehovah's Witnesses." PhD. diss., State University of Iowa, 1958.

———. "Plain Honesty: Wallace Short and the I.W.W." *Pal* 61 (1980) 146–60.

———. "The Red Flag Comes to Iowa." *AI* 39 (1968) 441–53.

———. *Wallace Short: Iowa Rebel*. Ames, IA: Iowa State University Press, 1983.

Cummins, D. Duane. *The Disciples Colleges: A History*. St. Louis: Chalice, 1987.

Cunning, Virginia K. Fisher. "Ethnicity in a Midwestern City: An Anthropological Investigation of the Greeks in Des Moines." M.S. thesis, Iowa State University, 1975.

Cunningham, Lawrence S., and John Kelsay. *The Sacred Quest: An Invitation to the Study of Religion*. Upper Saddle River, NJ: Pearson, 1995.

Bibliography

Currie, Roxana. "Log Cabin Captures a Moment in History." *Mennonite Historical Bulletin* 57.4 (Oct. 1996) 7–8.

———. *Polk City's Early History: Before 1900.* Ames, IA: Cyclone, 2000.

Curtis, Bruce. *Like Ordinary People: An Illustrated Iowa Social Biography of Josephine Mae Teeter Curtis and Her Times, 1903–2007.* East Lansing: Little Stomach, 2008.

Curtis, Edward E., IV. *Muslims of the Heartland: How Syrian Immigrants Made a Home in the American Midwest.* New York: New York University Press, 2022.

Curtis, Jesse. "The Bad History of Randall Balmer's 'Bad Faith.'" Substack, Oct. 14, 2022. https://jessecurtis.substack.com/p/the-bad-history-in-randall-balmers-bad-faith.

Curtis, Peter H. "A Place of Peace in a World of War: The Scattergood Refugee Hostel, 1939 to 1943." *Pal* 65.2 (Mar. 1984) 42–52.

Curtis, Susan. *A Consuming Faith: The Social Gospel and Modern American Culture.* Baltimore: Johns Hopkins University Press, 1991.

Dahl, Orin L. *Des Moines: Capital City.* Tulsa: Continental Heritage, 1978.

Dahm, J. P., and D. J. Van Kooten. *Peoria, Iowa: A Story of Two Cultures, With an Indepth Look at the "Hollander Fires," 1863–1993.* Pella, IA: Self-published, 1993.

Daley, Michael. "The Mosque That Is as American as Apple Pie." *Daily Beast*, June 26, 2017. https://www.thedailybeast.com/the-mosque-that-is-as-american-as-apple-pie.

Dallek, Matthew. *Birchers: How the John Birch Society Radicalized the American Right.* New York: Basic, 2022.

Daubenmier, Judith M. *The Meskwaki and Anthropologists: Action Anthropology Reconsidered.* Lincoln: University of Nebraska Press, 2008.

Davidson, Osha. "A Question of Conscience." *Iowa Alumni Review* (May/Jun. 1986) 20–23.

Davis, D. Mark. *Left Behind and Loving It: A Cheeky Look at the End Times.* Eugene, OR: Cascade, 2011.

———. *Talking About Evangelism.* Cleveland: Pilgrim, 2007.

Dawes, Gil. "Liberation Theology in the Bible Belt." *Monthly Review* 36 (July 1984) 81–91.

———. "Working People and the Church: Portrait of a Liberated Church in Reactionary Territory." In *Churches in Struggle: Liberation Theologies and Social Change in North America,* edited by William K. Tabb, 223–39. New York: Monthly Review, 1986.

Day, Beth. *The Little Professor of Piney Woods: The Story of Professor Laurence Jones.* New York: Messner, 1955.

De Cailly, Rev. Louis, ed. *Memoirs of Bishop Loras, First Bishop of Dubuque.* New York: Christian Press Association, 1897.

Delbanco, Andrew. *The War before the War: Fugitive Slaves and the Struggle for America's Soul from the Revolution to the Civil War.* New York: Penguin, 2018.

Delnay, Robert George. *History of the Baptist Bible Union.* Winston-Salem: Piedmont Bible College Press, 1974.

DeGroot, A. D., ed. *Central of Des Moines: The Story of Central Christian Church (Disciples).* Des Moines, 1945.

Dehler, Gregory J. *The Most Defiant Devil: William Temple Hornaday & His Controversial Crusade to Save American Wildlife.* Charlottesville: University of Virginia Press, 2013.

Bibliography

Delloff, Linda-Marie, et al. *A Century of The Century*. Grand Rapids: Eerdmans, 1984.

Den Hartog, Egbert. *Tramp Preacher*. N.p., 1949.

Derr, Nancy R. "Iowa during World War I: A Study of Change under Stress." PhD diss., George Washington University, 1979.

———. "The Babel Proclamation." *Iowa Heritage Illustrated* 85 (2004) 128–45.

DeSmet, Fr. Pierre-Jean. *Life, Letters and Travels in North America Among the Natives, 1821–1873*. New York: Harper, 1905.

"Des Moines River Primitive Baptist Church." https://iowaprimitivebaptist.org/index.html.

Desroche, Henri. *The American Shakers: From Neo-Christianity to Presocialism*. Amherst: University of Massachusetts Press, 1971.

DeYoung, Garry. *The Meaning of Christianity*. Hull, 1982.

Dibble, J. Birney. *Outlaw for God: The Esther Bacon Story,* Hanover, MA: Christopher, 1992.

Dieter, Melvin Easterday. *The Holiness Revival of the Nineteenth Century*. Metuchen, NJ: Scarecrow, 1980.

Dieterich, H. R. "Radical on the Campus: Professor Herron of Iowa College, 1893–1899." *AI* 37:6 (Fall 1964) 401–15.

Dilts, Harold E. *From Ackley to Zwingle: The Origins of Iowa Place Names*. 2nd ed. Ames, IA: Iowa State University Press, 1993.

"Directory." NAB Conference. https://nabconference.org/directory/.

Directory of American Students of Japanese Ancestry in the Higher Schools, Colleges, and Universities of the U.S.A. Philadelphia, June 1943.

Dixon, Thomas, Jr. *The One Woman*. New York: Doubleday, 1903.

Dobson, Melanie. *Love Finds You in Amana, Iowa*. Minneapolis: Summerside, 2012.

Dolan, Jay P. *In Search of American Catholicism: A History of Religion and Culture in Tension*. Oxford: Oxford University Press, 2002.

Dolezal, Joshua. *Down From the Mountaintop: From Belief to Belonging,* Iowa City: University of Iowa Press, 2014.

Dombrowski, Jamesi. *The Early Days of Christian Socialism in America*. New York: Columbia University Press, 1936.

Doniger, Wendy. *The Hindus: An Alternative History,* New York: Penguin, 2009.

Donovan, Josephine. *Black Soil*. Boston: Stratford, 1939.

Dorrien, Gary. *The New Abolition: W. E. B. DuBois and the Black Social Gospel*. New Haven: Yale University Press, 2015.

Dorsett, Lyle W. *Billy Sunday and the Redemption of Urban America*. Grand Rapids: Eerdmans, 1991.

Dostal, W. A. "Bohemian Czech Catholics in Iowa." *Iowa Catholic Historical Review* 5 (Oct. 1932) 1–10.

Douglas, Andy. *The Curve of the World: Into the Spiritual Heart of Yoga*. Huron, OH: Bottom Dog, 2013.

Douglas, Bill R. "Bombing Civilians Fosters Fear, Hatred." DMR, May 18, 1999.

———. "The Culture War Gets Physical: Des Moines University, 1929." *Wapsipinicon Almanac* 18, 118–22.

———. "Hoping Against Hope: The 1891 State-Wide Strike for an Eight-Hour Day in the Iowa Coal Mines." Unpublished paper.

———. "Insurgent Religion in Iowa from Statehood to the Civil War." *Wapsipinicon Almanac* 14, 108–14.

Bibliography

———. "Making Iowa Safe for Differences: Barnstorming Iowa on Behalf of Religious Tolerance, 1936–1943." *AI* 75 (2016) 234–59.

———. "Penn in Technicolor: Cecil Hinshaw's Radical Pacifist-Perfectionist Experiment at William Penn College, 1944–1949." *Quaker History* 96 (2007) 54–68.

———. "Iowa Protestantism of 1911." In *Trinity United Methodist Church Building Centennial, 1911–2011*. Des Moines, 2011.

———. "'Religion as Peacemaker': The Lacona Riot of 1946." *Wapsipinicon Almanac* 8, 124–29.

———. "Seed/Harvest: A History of the Archdiocese of Dubuque/Archdiocese of Dubuque 1837–2012: Jesus Alive Through 175 Years." *AI* 72 (2013) 388–89.

———. "'The Serious Nature of the Division': Calvary Baptist Church of Des Moines and the Fundamentalist Challenge of the 1920's." *Baptist History & Heritage* 52.2 (Summer 2017) 32–48.

———. "Summer of Discontent: The Davenport Espionage Act Trials." Unpublished paper presented at Gateway History Conference, Clinton, IA, Apr. 29, 2017.

Douglass, Paul. *Some Iowa Rural Churches*, Chicago: Iowa Interchurch Council, 1945.

Douglass, Paul F. *The Story of German Methodism: The Biography of an Immigrant Soul*, Cincinnati: Methodist, 1939.

Douglass, Truman. *Pilgrims of Iowa*, Boston: Pilgrim, 1911.

Dow, James R. "Toward an Understanding of Some Subtle Stresses on Language Maintenance among the Old Order Amish of Iowa." *International Journal of the Society for Language* 69 (1988) 19–31.

Dowd, Gregory Evans. *A Spirited Resistance: The North American Indian Struggle For Unity, 1745–1815*. Baltimore: Johns Hopkins University Press, 1992.

Dowell, Cassius. "Charles S. Medbury—The Citizen." In *Charles S. Medbury: Preacher and Master Workman for Christ*, edited by Raphael H. Miller, 41–46. St. Louis: Christian, 1933.

Dorsett, Lyle W. *Billy Sunday and the Redemption of Urban America*. Grand Rapids: Eerdmans, 1991.

Drake, George A. *Steerage: From Alien to Citizen: The Story of Edward Steiner: Grinnell College Professor of Applied Christianity 1903–1941*. Grinnell, 2021.

Draper, Mark. "Jacob Albrecht: An Evangelical Conversion and an Evangelical Ministry." *MH* 56 (2018) 222–34.

Duchaine, R. Mark. *Living Stones: Priests of the Diocese of Sioux City: 1856–2004*. N.p., 2004.

Dudiak, Jeffrey. "The Meaning of 'Quaker History.'" *Quaker History* 106 (Spring 2017) 1–21.

Duggan, Raymond P. *A Federal Resettlement Project: Granger Homesteads*. Washington, DC: Catholic University of America, 1937.

Du Mez, Kristin Kobes. *Jesus and John Wayne: How White Evangelicals Corrupted a Faith and Fractured a Nation*. New York: Liveright, 2020.

Dungan, D. R. *On the Rock; Or, Truth Stranger Than Fiction: A Story of Souls Whose Pathway Began in Darkness, But Brightened to the Perfect Day*. St. Louis: Christian, 1914.

———. *Rum and Ruin: The Remedy Found*, Oskaloosa, IA: Central, 1879.

Dunlap, Flora. "Roadside Settlement of Des Moines." *AI* 21 (1938) 161–205.

Dunnington, Lewis L. *Power to Become*. New York: MacMillan, 1956.

———. *Handles of Power*. New York: Abingdon, 1942.

Bibliography

Durkin, Mary-Cabrini, and Miguel Berzosa. *A Journey of Faith: Archdiocese of Dubuque, 1837–2012*. Strasbourg: du Signe, 2011.

Durnbaugh, Donald F. *Church of the Brethren: Yesterday and Today*. Elgin, IL: Brethren, n.d.

DuVal, F. Alan. *Christian Metz: German-American Religious Leader and Pietist*. Iowa City: Penfield, 2003.

Dykstra, Robert R. *Bright Radical Star: Black Freedom and White Supremacy on the Hawkeye Frontier*. Cambridge: Harvard University Press, 1993.

———. "The Know-Nothings Nobody Knows: Political Nativists in Ante-Bellum Iowa." *AI* (1994) 5–24.

Eby, Cecil. *"That Disgraceful Affair": The Black Hawk War*. New York: W. W. Norton, 1973.

Eck, Diana L. *A New Religious America: How a "Christian Country" Became the World's Most Religiously Diverse Nation*. New York: HarperCollins, 2001.

Edmunds, R. David, ed. *Enduring Nations: Native Americans in the Midwest*. Urbana: University of Illinois Press, 2008.

Edmunds, R. David, and Joseph L. Peyser. *The Fox Wars: The Mesquakie Challenge to New France*. Norman: University of Oklahoma Press, 1993.

Edwards, Lee. *Missionary for Freedom: The Life and Times of Walter Judd*. New York: Paragon, 1990.

Edwards, Paul M. "The Restoration History Manuscript Collection." *AI* 47 (1984) 377–81.

Egge, Sara. *Woman Suffrage and Citizenship in the Midwest, 1870–1920*. Iowa City: University of Iowa Press, 2018.

Eisenach, George J. *A History of the German Congregational Churches in the United States*. Yankton, SD: Pioneer, 1938.

Ehrenreich, Barbara. *Bright Sided: How the Relentless Promotion of Positive Thinking Has Undermined America*. New York: Henry Holt, 2009.

Ehrstine, Glenn, and Lucas Gibbs. "Iowa's Prohibition Plague: Joseph Eiboeck's Account of the Battle Over Prohibition, 1846–1900." *AI* 78 (2019) 1–74.

Elliott, Errol T. *Quaker Profiles from the American West*. Richmond, IN: Friends United, 1972.

———. *Quakers on the American Frontier,* Richmond, IN: Friends United, 1969.

Ellis, Clyde, Luke Eric Lassiter, and Gary H. Dunham, eds. *Powwow*. Lincoln: University of Nebraska Press, 2005.

Ellis, John Tracy. *American Catholicism*. Chicago: University of Chicago Press, 1969.

Ellis, Mina Walleser. *The Parish of the Little Brown Church in the Vale*. Grinnell, IA: Walleser, 1936.

Ellis, William T. *"Billy" Sunday: The Man and His Message*. N.p, 1914.

Elmen, Paul. *Wheat Flour Messiah: Eric Jansson of Bishop Hill*. Carbondale, IL: Southern Illinois University Press, 1997.

Emerson, Dorothy May, ed. *Standing Before Us: Unitarian Universalist Women and Social Reform, 1776–1936*. Boston: Beacon, 2000.

Engel, Eugene. *Gracehill's One Hundred Years, 1866–1966*. N.p, n.d.

Engle, Paul. "'Those Damn Jews.'" *American Heritage* 30.1 (1978) 72–79.

Ensign, Kelsey. "From Iowa to the Nation: Harold Hughes and the Politics of Alcoholism Treatment." *AI* 81 (2022) 203–38.

Epstein, Barbara Leslie. *The Politics of Domesticity: Women, Evangelism, and Temperance in Nineteenth Century America*. Middletown, CT: Wesleyan University Press, 1981.

Bibliography

Erickson, Donald A. "Showdown at an Amish Schoolhouse." In *Compulsory Education and the Amish: The Right Not To Be Modern*, edited by Albert N. Keim, Boston: Beacon, 1975, 43–83.

Erickson, Hal. *Religious Radio and Television in the United States, 1921–1991: The Programs and the Personalities*. Jefferson, NC: McFarland, 1991.

Erickson, Lori. "Bending the Rule." *The Iowan* 57.2 (Nov. 2008) 52–57.

Ernst, Eldon G. *Moment of Truth for Protestant America: Interchurch Campaigns Following World War I*. Missoula: American Academy of Religion, 1972.

Espey, John. *Minor Heresies*. New York: Knopf, 1949.

Etcheson, Nicole. *The Emerging Midwest: Upland Southerners and the Political Culture of the Old Northwest, 1787–1861*. Bloomington: Indiana University Press, 1996.

Eulberg, Sister Mary Thomas, OSF. *The Rt. Rev. Mathias M. Hoffman V. F. Whose World Was Others*. Dubuque, IA, 1989.

Evans, Bernard F., and Gregory D. Cusack, eds. *Theology of the Land*. Collegeville, MN: Liturgical, 1987.

Evans, Christopher H. *The Kingdom Is Always but Coming: A Life of Walter Rauschenbusch*. Grand Rapids: Eerdmans, 2004.

Evans, Mary Ellen. *The Seed and the Glory: The Career of Samuel Charles Mazzuchelli, O.P., on the Mid-American Frontier*. New York: McMullen, 1950.

Evans, Randy. "Iowa's Amish Have Some Lessons for Us about Today's COVID Controversies." https://iowacapitaldispatch.com/2021/08/21/iowas-amish-have-some-lessons-for-us-about-todays-covid-controversies/.

An Explanation of the Grotto of the Redemption. West Bend, n.d.

Expo: The Magic of the White City (2003), dir. Mark Bussler.

Fagan, Joe. "How One Opportunity Led to Another." Unpublished paper, copy at Iowa CCI, Des Moines.

Faldet, David S. *Oneota Flow: The Upper Iowa River and Its People*. Iowa City: University of Iowa Press, 2009.

Fales, Evan, and Barry Markovsky. "Evaluating Heterodox Theories." *Social Forces* 76.2 (Dec. 1997) 511–25.

Fankhauser, Craig Charles. "The Heritage of Faith: An Historical Evaluation of the Holiness Movement in America." Master's thesis, Pittsburg State University, 1983.

Farrell, Pat. "The Gift and Challenge of Communal Discernment." In *However Long the Night: Making Meaning in a Time of Crisis*, edited by Annmarie Sanders, 45–54. N.p., 2018.

Fate, Tom Montgomery. *The Long Way Home: Detours and Discoveries*. North Liberty, IA: Ice Cube, 2022.

Feazell, J. Michael. *The Liberation of the Worldwide Church of God*. Grand Rapids: Zondervan, 2001.

Fehrenbacher, Don E. *The Dred Scott Case: Its Significance in American Law and Politics*. Oxford: Oxford University Press, 1978.

Feinman, Peter. "The Upper Iowa Conference: From Wilderness to Melting Pot." *MH* 47.4 (July 2009) 226–41.

Feldman, Jan. *Lubavitchers as Citizens: A Paradox of Liberal Democracy*. Ithaca: Cornell University Press, 2003.

Fellows, Stephen Norris. *History of the Upper Iowa Conference of the Methodist Episcopal Church, 1856–1906*. Cedar Rapids, 1906.

Fenton, Elizabeth. *Old Canaan in a New World: Native Americans and the Lost Tribe of Israel*. New York: New York University Press, 2020.

Bibliography

Ferber, Edna. *A Peculiar Treasure*. New York: Doubleday, 1969.

Ferris, John N. (Jake). *Mary Jane Whiteley Coggeshall, Hicksite Quaker, Iowa/National Suffragette and Her Speeches*. Milton, IN: Kids at Heart, 2017.

Fialka, John J. *Sisters: Catholic Nuns and the Making of America*. New York: St. Martins, 2003.

Ficke, Charles August. *Memories of Fourscore Years*. Davenport, IA: Graphic, 1930.

Findlay, James F., Jr. *Church People in the Struggle: The National Council of Churches and the Black Freedom Movement, 1950–1970*. New York: Oxford University Press, 1993.

Finney, Daniel. "Reaching For the Peak." *Drake Blue* (Fall 2005) 15–19.

First Congregational Church, Cedar Rapids, Iowa: A History of Its First 120 Years, 1879–1999. Decorah, [1999?].

"First Presbyterian Church Near Ely, Iowa." http://www.elypres.org/history.html.

Firstenberger, W. A. *In Rare Form: A Pictorial History of Baseball Evangelist Billy Sunday*. Iowa City: University of Iowa Press, 2005.

Fisher, Allen, and David Hay. *In the Heart of the City: A History of First Presbyterian Church Cedar Rapids, Iowa, 1847–1997*. Cedar Rapids, IA: First Presbyterian Church, 1997.

Fisher, Galen M. *John R. Mott: Architect of Co-operation and Unity*. New York: Association, 1952.

Fitzkee, Donald R. *Moving Toward the Mainstream: 20th Century Change among the Brethren of Eastern Pennsylvania*. Intercourse, PA: Good, 1995.

Fitzmeier, J. R. "Old School Presbyterians." In *The Dictionary of the Presbyterian and Reformed Tradition in America*, edited by D. G. Hart, 180–82. Downers Grove, IL: InterVarsity, 1999.

Fix, Andrew C. *Prophecy and Reason: The Dutch Collegians in the Early Enlightenment*. Princeton: Princeton University Press, 1991.

Flanders, Robert Bruce. *Nauvoo: Kingdom on the Mississippi*. Urbana, IL: University of Illinois Press, 1965.

Fleishaker, Oscar. *The Illinois-Iowa Jewish Community on the Banks of the Mississippi River*. [New York], 1957.

Fleming, Thomas. *The Illusion of Victory: America in World War I*. New York: Basic, 2003.

Florman, Jean. *Moments in Iowa History*. Cedar Falls: KUNI, 1997.

Foerstner, Abigail. *Picturing Utopia: Bertha Shambaugh and the Amana Photographers*. Iowa City: University of Iowa Press, 2000.

Foley, Douglas E. *The Heartland Chronicles*. Philadelphia: University of Pennsylvania Press, 1995.

Folk, Holly. *Religion of Chiropractic: Populist Healing from the American Heartland*. Chapel Hill: University of North Carolina Press, 2017.

Folmar, John Kent, ed. *"This State of Wonders": The Letters of an Iowa Frontier Family, 1858–1861*. Iowa City: University of Iowa Press, 1986.

Foner, Philip S., ed. *Black Socialist Preacher*. San Francisco: Synthesis, 1983.

Forell, George W. *Faith Active in Love*. Minneapolis: Augsburg, 1954.

Forem, Jack. *Transcendental Meditation: Maharishi Mahesh Yogi and the Science of Creative Intelligence*. New York, 1973.

Foster, Lance M. *The Indians of Iowa*. Iowa City: University of Iowa Press, 2009.

———. "Sacred Bundles of the Ioway Indians." Master's thesis, Iowa State University, 1994.

Bibliography

———. "The Ioway and the Landscape of Southeast Iowa." *Journal of the Iowa Archaeological Society* 43 (1996) 1–5.
Fox, H. Clifford. *German Presbyterianism in the Upper Mississippi Valley*. Ypsilanti, MI, 1941.
Frederick, John T. "Town and City in Iowa Fiction." *Pal* 35 (Feb. 1954) 49–96.
Frederick, Peter J. *Knights of the Golden Rule: The Intellectual as Social Reformer in the 1890s*. Lexington: University of Kentucky Press, 1976.
Fredericksen, Carl L. "The Proposed Japanese-American Relocation Center at Scattergood Hostel: An Idea and Its Rejection. West Branch, Iowa, January–March, 1943." Seminar paper, University of Iowa, 1984.
Freer, Hamline Hurlburt. "Laity and Education: A Paper Presented at the Annual Association of the Laymen's Association of the Upper Iowa Conference of the Methodist Episcopal Church Held at Cedar Falls, Iowa, Thursday, October 10, 1907." Iowa Bible Training School and Bidwell Deaconess Home, 1916–17.
Fridsma, Bernard J. "Frisians to America, 1880–1914, With the Baggage of the Fatherland." *Origins* 15.1 (1997) 36–40.
Friedberger, Mark. *Shake-Out: Iowa Farm Families in the 1980s*. Lexington: University of Kentucky Press, 1989.
Friedricks, William B. *Saved by Schindler: The Life of Celina Karp Biniaz*. North Liberty, IA: Ice Cube, 2022.
"Friends Historical Association Past Events." Friends Historical Association. https://www.quakerhistory.org/past-events.
Fulton, A. R. "Baneemyism," *Howe's AI* 3:1 (1884) 17–20.
Gallagher, Mary Kevin, BVM, ed. *Seed/Harvest: A History of the Archdiocese of Dubuque*. Dubuque, IA: Archdiocese of Dubuque, 1987.
Gallaher, Ruth A. "Abner Kneeland—Pantheist." *Pal* 20:7 (Jul. 1939) 209–25.
———. "Adventure in Faith." *Pal* 13:3 (Mar. 1932) 93–102.
———. *A Century of Methodism in Iowa 1844–1944*, Mt. Vernon, 1944.
———. "The First Church in Iowa." *Pal* 7:1 (Jan. 1926) 1–10.
———. "Hummer's Bell." *Pal* 3:5 (1922) 155–64.
———. "Indian Agents in Iowa." *IJH* 14 (1916) 1–16.
———. "Methodists in Conference." *Pal* 25.8 (Aug. 1944) 225–33.
———. "The Methodist Episcopal Church of Iowa City." *IJH* 37 (1939) 379–422.
———. "The Methodists in Iowa." *Pal* 32.2 (Feb. 1951) 57–120.
———. "Religion and Morality." *Pal* 8:1 (Jan. 1927) 28–33.
———. "The Tama Powwow." *Pal* 58:7 (Jul. 1967) 289–99.
Garrett, Clarke. *Origins of the Shakers: From the Old World to the New World*. Baltimore: Johns Hopkins University Press, 1987.
Garrett, Leroy. *The Stone-Campbell Movement: The Story of the American Restoration Movement*. Abilene, [TX]: College, 1994.
Garrett, Ruth, with Rick Farrant. *Crossing Over: One Woman's Exodus from Amish Life*. Allen, TX: Thomas More, 2001.
Garrett, Ruth Irene, and Deborah Morse-Kahn. *Born Amish*. Paducah, KY: Turner, 2004.
Garrison, Becky. "2021 National Prayer Breakfast: A Kinder Gentler Christian Capitalism." Religion Dispatches, Feb. 8, 2021. https://religiondispatches.org/2021-national-prayer-breakfast-a-kinder-gentler-form-of-christian-capitalism.

Bibliography

Gassiott, Kyle. *For Memorial Day, An "I" for Islam*. Public Radio Exchange, May 28, 2007.

Gaskin, Ina May. *Spiritual Midwifery*. Summertown, TN: BPC, 1975.

Gaston, Paul M. *Coming of Age in Utopia: The Odyssey of an Idea*. Montgomery: Black Belt, 2010

———. *Man and Mission: E. B. Gaston and the Origins of the Fairhope Single Tax Colony*. Montgomery: Black Belt, 1993.

Gately, M. Louise. *Pursuit of a Dream: James Jordan, His Life and His Legacy*. West Des Moines, IA: Donning, 2018.

Gates, Isabel Smith. *Life of George Augustus Gates*. Boston: Pilgrim, 1915.

Gaustad, Edwin Scott, and Philip L. Barlow. *New Historical Atlas of Religion in America*. Oxford: Oxford University Press, 2001.

Gauthier, Paul S. *Quest for Utopia: The Icarians of Adams County*. Corning, IA: Gauthier, 1992.

[Gaylord, Mary W.]. *Life and Labors of Reuben Gaylord*. Omaha: Rees, 1889.

Gearing, Frederick O. *The Face of the Fox*. Chicago: Sheffield, 1970.

———., et al., eds. *Documentary History of the Fox Project, 1948–1959: A Program in Action Anthropology*, dir. Sol Tax. Chicago, 1960.

Gebhard, David, and Gerald Mannheim. *Buildings of Iowa*. New York: Oxford University Press, 1993.

Gebhardt, Daniel Francis. "A History of the *Catholic Daily Tribune*." Master's thesis, Marquette University, 1953.

Geiger, Erika. "The Biography of William Loehe: Insights into His Life and Work." Translated by Craig L. Nessan. Paper presented at International Loehe Society conference, Dubuque, IA, July 11, 2005. Copy in possession of author.

George, Paul R., Jr. "Selfhood and the Search for Identity: Exploring the Emergence of the Holiness Movement and the Early Church of the Nazarene." PhD diss., Western Michigan University, 2004.

Gill, Sam D. *Native American Religions: An Introduction*. Belmont, CA: Wadsworth, 1982.

Gilpin, Geoff. *The Maharishi Effect: A Personal Journey Through the Movement That Transformed American Spirituality*. New York: Penguin, 2006.

Gingerich, Melvin. "Bibliographical and Research Notes: An Iowa Mennonite Church Constitution of 1865." *MQR* 28 (Jul. 1954) 223–27.

———. "The First Mennonite Settlement in Iowa." *MQR* 42 (1968) 193–202.

———. *Mennonites in Iowa*. Iowa City: Kalona, 1974.

———. "The Mennonites in Iowa." *Pal* 40:5 (May 1959) 161–223.

———. "Mennonites in Lee and Davis Counties, Iowa." *Mennonite Life* (Apr. 1960) 51–52, 56.

———. "Mennonites in Mount Pleasant." *Pal* 23:12 (Dec. 1942) 373–80.

———. "Sebastian Gerig (1838–1924): His Life and Times." *MQR* 35 (1961) 297–308.

———. "Service for Peace: A History of Mennonite C. P. S." Akron, PA: Herald, 1949.

Gingerich, Owen. *God's Universe*. Cambridge, MA: Belknap, 2006.

Girvin, Rev. E. A. *Phineas F. Bresee: A Prince in Israel*. Kansas City: Nazerene, 1981.

Gjerde, Jon. *Catholicism and the Shaping of Nineteenth-Century America*. Edited by S. Deborah Kang. Cambridge: Cambridge University Press, 2012.

———. *The Minds of the West: Ethnocultural Evolution in the Rural Middle West, 1830–1917*. Chapel Hill: University of North Carolina Press, 1997.

Bibliography

Glaspell, Susan Keating. *Allison's House*. In *The Best Plays of 1930–31*, edited by Burns Mantle, 222–53. New York: Dodd, Mead, 1932.

———. "Finality in Freeport." *Pictorial Review*, July 17, 1916.

———. "For Tomorrow: The Story of an Easter Sermon." *Appleton's Booklovers' Magazine* 5 (Mar 1905) 559–70.

———. *The Road to the Temple*. New York: Stokes, 1927.

Glazer, Rabbi Simon. *The Jews of Iowa*. Des Moines: Koch Brothers, 1904.

Gleason, Philip. *Contending with Modernity: Catholic Education in the Twentieth Century*. Oxford: Oxford University Press, 1995.

Godfrey, Kenneth W. "Crime and Punishment in Mormon Nauvoo, 1839–1846." *BYU Studies* 32 (1992) 194–227.

Goen, C. C. *Broken Churches, Broken Nation: Denominational Schisms and the Coming of the Civil War*. Macon: Mercer University Press, 1985.

Goff, James R., Jr. *Fields White unto Harvest: Charles F. Parham and the Missionary Origins of Pentecostalism*. Fayetteville: University of Arkansas Press, 1988.

Goldenstein, Erwin H., and Royce R. Ronning. *The Heart of the ALC: A History of the American Lutheran Church, 1960–1987*. N.p., 1989.

Goodman, Joseph Raphael. *Century of Catholicity in Southwest Tama County, Iowa, 1864–1964*. Tama, IA, [1964?].

Goodwin, Lloyd L. *Prophecy Concerning Babylon*. Des Moines: Gospel Assembly Church, 1976.

———. *Prophecy Concerning the Church*. Des Moines: Gospel Assembly Church, 1978.

Goodykoontz, Colin Brummitt. *Home Missions on the American Frontier*. Caldwell, ID, 1939.

Gorsche, Betty Kopp, et al. *Davenport, Iowa Unitarian Church: For 125 Years, A Place to Grow*. [Davenport, IA], 1993.

"Gospel Assembly: Des Moines, Iowa." https://dmgac.org/.

Gottwald, Norman K. "Nuclear Realism or Nuclear Pacifism?" *Christian Century*, Aug. 3, 1960.

Graber, William B. "An Amish Farmer Chooses Iowa." *Pal* 69 (1988) 154–62.

Gradwohl, David M., and Nancy M. Osborn. *Exploring Buried Buxton: Archaeology of an Abandoned Iowa Coal Mining Town with a Large Black Population*. Ames, IA: Iowa State University Press, 1984.

Gradwohl, David M. "In Memoriam: Governor Robert D. Ray, A Strong Proponent of Human Rights." *Journal of the Iowa Archeological Society* 65 (2018) 53–55.

———. "Samuel Gradwohl, A Jewish Merchant in Mt. Pleasant, Iowa, in the 1870s. *CHAIowan: Newsletter of the Iowa Jewish Historical Society*, Spring 2005.

———., Joe B. Thomson, and Michael J. Perry. "Still Running: A Tribute to Maria Pearson, Yankton Sioux." *Journal of the Iowa Archeological Society* 52 (2003).

Graham, Ronald W., and Sarada Galindo. *The Christian Churches in the Upper Midwest 1972–1998: A Brief History*. Des Moines, 1998.

Grant, H. Roger, ed. "The Amana Society of Iowa: Two Views." *AI* 43 (1975) 1–23.

Grasso, Christopher. *Skepticism and American Faith from the Revolution to the Civil War*. Oxford: Oxford University Press, 2018.

Green, James N. *We Cannot Remain Silent: Opposition to the Brazilian Military Dictatorship in the United States*. Durham: Duke University Press, 2010.

Green, Stephen K. *The Bible, the School, and the Constitution: The Clash That Shaped Modern Church-State Doctrine*. Oxford: Oxford University Press, 2012.

Bibliography

———. *The Second Disestablishment: Church and State in Nineteenth-Century America*. Oxford: Oxford University Press, 2010.
Greenberg, Amy S. *A Wicked War: Polk, Clay, Lincoln and the 1846 U.S. Invasion of Mexico*. New York: Knopf, 2012.
Gregurich, Avery. "The Old College Try." *The Iowan* 69.6 (2021) 50–53.
Grem, Darren E. *The Blessing of Business: How Corporations Shaped Conservative Christianity*. New York: Oxford University Press, 2016.
Greving, Father Louis H. *A Pictorial Story of the Grotto of the Redemption*. West Bend, n.d.
Grey, Mark, et al. *Postville, U.S.A.: Surviving Diversity in Small-Town America*. Boston: Gemma, 2009.
Grey, Wood. *The Hidden Civil War: The Story of the Copperheads*. New York: Viking, 1942.
Griff, Hanna. "Toldot Iowa Diary." *Jewish Folklore and Ethnology Review* 13:2 (1991) 13–19.
Griffith, C. F. "H. V. Gildea: Pioneer Church Builder." *Iowa Catholic Historical Review* 1 (1930) 18–25.
Griffith, Martha E. "The Czechs in Cedar Rapids." *IJH* 33 (1944) 114–61, 266–315.
———. *The History of Czechs in Cedar Rapids*. Cedar Rapids, IA: Lilly, 1970.
Grohman, Gregory. "Transcending Transgenics: Transcendental Meditation, Natural Law, and the Campaign to Ban Genetically Engineered Food." *AI* 80 (2021) 1–34.
Gronlid, J. M. "Lutheran Pastor Addressing Babel." *German Iowa and the Global Midwest*. germansiniowa.lib.uiowa.edu/items/show/823.
Gross, Aaron S. *The Question of the Animal* and *Religion: Theoretical Stakes, Practical Implications*. New York: Columbia University Press, 2015.
Gross, Jan. "Emir Abd El-Kader: A 19th Century Muslim Hero Is Celebrated in an Unlikely Place: Iowa." Des Moines *Register*, Jul. 6, 2014.
Grundtvig, N. F. S. *Selected Writings*. Edited by Johannes Knudsen. Philadelphia: Fortress, 1976.
Guengerich, S. D. "Brief History of the Amish Settlement in Johnson County, Iowa." *MQR* 3 (1929) 243–48.
Gugel, Lois Brenneman Swartzendruber. *Amish and Mennonites Celebrate 150 Years 1846–1996*. Kalona: [Mennonite Historical Society of Iowa], 1996.
Guha, Ramachandra. *Rebels Against the Raj: Western Fighters for India's Freedom*. New York: Knopf, 2022.
Guinn, Lisa. "Annie Wittenmyer and Nineteenth-Century Women's Usefulness." *AI* 74 (2015) 351–77.
Gullen, Karen, ed. *Billy Sunday Speaks*. New York: Chelsea, 1970.
Gustafson, J. Glenn, et al. *A Century of Grace: The One Hundred Years of the Evangelical Covenant Church*. Des Moines, 1971.
Gutjahr, Paul. "'Hundreds of Souls Lie in the Balance': An Eastern Congregational Minister Ponders Moving West to Iowa." *Pal* 74:2 (Summer 1993) 54–61.
Haas, Dennis W. "The Conversion of Edward A. Steiner." Grinnell College, Jun. 15, 2004. https://www.grinnell.edu/news/conversion-edward-steiner.
Haas, Stewart, and Leo Ponsar. "The Plain People." *Iowan* 7.3 (Feb. 1959) 4–9.
Haddock, Frank Channing. *Life of Rev. George C. Haddock*. New York: Funk & Wagnalls, 1887.
Hafen, Mary Ann. *Recollections of a Handcart Pioneer of 1860*. Lincoln, NE: Bison, 1983.

Bibliography

Hafen, Leroy R., and Ann W. Hafen. *Handcarts to Zion: The Story of a Unique Western Migration, 1856–1860*. Lincoln, NE: Bison, 1992.

Hagan, William T. *The Sac and Fox Indians*. Norman: University of Oklahoma Press, 1958.

Hagedorn, Ann. *Sleeper Agent: The Atomic Spy in America Who Got Away*. New York: Simon & Schuster, 2021.

Hagen, Monys A. *The Worldly Game: The Story of Baseball in the Amana Colonies*. Iowa City: Penfield, 2024.

Haines, Aaron W. *The Makers of Iowa Methodism*. Cincinnati: Jenning & Pye, 1900.

Hall, David D., ed. *Lived Religion in America: Toward a History of Practice*. Princeton: Princeton University Press, 1997.

Hall, Heidi. "Sister Elizabeth Johnson: 'The Waste of Time on This Investigation Is Unconscionable.'" Religion News, Aug. 16, 2014. https://religionnews.com/2014/08/16/sister-elizabeth-johnson-waste-time-investigation-unconscionable.

Hall, Jennis Evelinel. "Japanese-American College Students During the Second World War: The Politics of Relocation." PhD diss., Indiana University, 1993.

Hall, Mitchell K. *Because of Their Faith: CALCAV and Religious Opposition to the Vietnam War*. New York: Columbia University Press, 1990.

Hallwas, John E. "Black Hawk: A Reassessment." *AI* 45.8 (Spring 1981) 599–619.

Hamer, Maryanna, et al. *History of the Great Plains District of the Church of the Brethren 1844–1977*. N.p., [1977].

Hamilton, J. Taylor. *History of the Church Known as the Moravian Church*. New York: AMS, 1900.

Hamm, Richard F. *Shaping the 18th Amendment: Temperance Reform, Legal Culture, and the Polity, 1880–1920*. Chapel Hill: University of North Carolina Press, 1995.

Hamm, Thomas D. "The Divergent Paths of Iowa Quakers in the Nineteenth Century." *AI* 61 (2002) 125–50.

———. "Joel Bean and the Revival in Iowa." *Quaker History* 76 (1987) 33–49.

———. *The Transformation of American Quakerism*. Bloomington: Indiana University Press, 1988.

Hamre, James S. "J. A. Bergh: The Nestor of Norwegian American Lutheran Historians." *Concordia Historical Institute Quarterly* 79 (2009) 94–96.

Handy, Robert T. "George D. Herron and the Kingdom Movement." *Church History* 19 (1950) 97–115.

Hangen, Tona J. *Redeeming the Dial: Radio, Religion, and Popular Culture in America*. Chapel Hill: University of North Carolina Press, 2002.

Hankins, Barry. *God's Rascal: J. Frank Norris and the Beginnings of Southern Fundamentalism*. Lexington: University of Kentucky Press, 1996.

Hansen, Harry. "A Davenport Boyhood." *Pal* 37 (Apr 1956) 190–92.

Hansen, Rev. H. N. "An Account of a Mormon Family's Conversion to the Religion of the Latter Day Saints and of their Trip from Denmark to Utah." *AI* 41 (1971) 684–708 and 765–79.

Hansen, Thorvald. *Church Divided: Lutheranism Among the Lutheran Immigrants*. [Des Moines, 1992].

———. "Danish Immigrant Materials: The Archives at Grand View College." *AI* 45 (1980) 313–18.

———. *That All Good Seed Take Root: A Centennial History of Grand View College*. Des Moines: Grand View, 1996.

Bibliography

———. *We Laid a Foundation Here: The Early History of Grand View College*. Des Moines: Grand View College, 1972.

Hanson, John Wesley. *The World's Congress of Religions: The Addresses and Papers Delivered before the Parliament, and the Abstract of the Congresses Held in the Art Institute, August 25 to October 15, 1893*. Chicago: Monarch, 1894.

Hanusa, George R. *Hope for All Generations: Lutheran Social Services of Iowa--125 Years, 1870-1995*. Minneapolis: Kirk, 1996.

Hargis, Mina Davis. "History of the Disciples of Christ in Iowa Before the Civil War." Master's thesis, State University of Iowa, 1937.

Harl, Neil. *The Farm Debt Crisis of the 1980s*. Ames, IA: Iowa State University Press, 1990.

Harlan, Edgar Rubey. *Narrative History of the People of Iowa*, vol. 2. Chicago, 1931.

Harley, William G. "Mormons and Early Iowa History (1838 to 1858): Eight Distinct Connections." *AI* 59 (2000) 217–60.

Harnack, Curtis. *Gentlemen on the Prairie*. Ames, IA: Iowa State University Press, 1985.

Harrell, David Edwin, Jr. *The Social Sources of Division in the Disciples of Christ, 1865–1900*. Atlanta: Systems, 1973.

Harrington, Ann M. *Creating Community: Mary Frances Clarke and Her Companions*. Dubuque, IA: Mount Carmel, 2004.

Harrington, Jerry. "Iowa's Last Liquor Battle: Harold E. Hughes and the Liquor-by-the-Drink Conflict." *AI* 76 (2017) 1–46.

———. *Thunder from the Prairie: The Life of Harold E. Hughes*. Lawrence: University Press of Kansas, 2023.

Harrington, M. R. *Sacred Bundles of the Sauk and Fox Indians*. Philadelphia: Alpha, 1914.

Harris, Faye. "A Frontier Community: The Economic, Social, and Political Development of Keokuk, Iowa from 1820 to 1866." PhD diss., State University of Iowa, 1965.

Harris, Merne A. *The Torch Goeth Forward: Tested but Triumphant*. University Park, IA, 1985.

Harris, Paul William. "The Social Dimensions of Foreign Missions: Emma Rauschenbusch Clough and Social Gospel Ideology." In *Gender and the Social Gospel*, edited by Wendy J. Deichmann Edwards and Carolyn De Swarte Gifford, 87–100. Urbana, IL: University of Illinois Press, 2003.

Harrison, Ida Withers. *Forty Years of Service: A History of the Christian Woman's Board of Missions, 1874–1914*. N.p., 1914.

Harsha, William Justin. *The Story of Iowa*. Omaha: Central West, 1890.

Hart, D. G. *Calvinism: A History*. New Haven: Yale University Press, 2013.

Hartzler, Robert. *Memoir*. Privately printed, 2006.

Harvey, R. E. "Hail and Farewell! The Methodist Protestant Church in Iowa." *AI* 24 (1942) 168–80.

——— "The Local Preacher." *AI* 22:1 (July 1939) 54–63.

Hastie, Eugene N. *History of the West District Central Council of the Assemblies of God*. Fort Dodge, IA: Walterick, 1948.

Hatch, Nathan. *The Democratization of American Christianity*. New Haven: Yale University Press, 1989.

Haury-Artz, Cherie E. *A River of Unrivaled Advantages: Life along the Lower Des Moines River*. [Des Moines]: DNR, n.d.

Hawley, Charles Arthur. "Asa Turner and the Welsh." *Pal* 18 (Jan. 1937) 10–19.

———. "A Communistic Swedenborgian Colony in Iowa." *IJH* 33.1 (Jan. 1935) 3–26.

Bibliography

———. "Congregationalists in Iowa City." *Pal* 18.1 (Jan. 1937) 20–30.

———. "Correspondence between John Greenleaf Whittier and Iowa." *IJH* 35 (1937) 115–41.

———. "The Historical Background of the Attitude of the Jasper Colony toward Slavery and the Civil War." *IJH* 34.2 (Apr. 1936) 172–97.

———. "The New Church in Iowa: The Jasper Colony and Later Developments." *New Church Review* 41 (1934) 195.

———. "Some Aspects of Congregationalism in Relation to the Early Cultural Development of Iowa." *IJH* 35 (1937) 181–205.

———. "Salem," *Pal* 16:11 (Nov. 1935) 337–72.

Haws, Dick. *Iowa and the Death Penalty: A Troubled Relationship, 1834–1965*. Self-published, 2010,

Hawthorne, Frances. "The Church," in Bill Silag, et al. *Outside In: African-American History in Iowa, 1838–2000*. Des Moines: State Historical Society, 2001.

Hayne, Donald. *Batter My Heart*. London: Hutchinson, 1963.

Haynes, Fred Emory. *James Baird Weaver*. Iowa City: State Historical Society of Iowa, 1919.

———. *Third Party Movements Since the Civil War, With Special Reference to Iowa*. New York: Russell & Russell, 1966.

Healey, Robert M. "Arthur Cochrane and the Church-Confessing." *Scottish Journal of Theology* 49.4 (1996) 466–81.

Heath, Gordon L., ed. *American Churches in the First World War*. Eugene, OR: Wipf & Stock, 2016.

Hedstrom, Matthew S. *The Rise of Liberal Religion: Book Culture and American Spirituality in the Twentieth Century*. Oxford: Oxford University Press, 2013.

Heffern, Colman, O.C.S.D. "Clement Smyth (1810–1865): A Founder of New Melleray Abbey and Civil War Bishop." *American Benedictine Review* 21 (1970) 351–72.

Heideman, Eugene P. *Hendrik P. Scholte: His Legacy in the Netherlands and in America*. Grand Rapids: Eerdmans, 2015.

———. *The Practice of Piety: The Theology of the Midwestern Reformed Church in America, 1866–1966*. Grand Rapids: Eerdmans, 2009.

Heintzen, Erich H. *Love Leaves Home: Wilhelm Loehe and the Missouri Synod*. St. Louis: Concordia, 1972.

Heinze, Andrew R. *Jews and the American Soul: Human Nature in the 20th Century*. Princeton: Princeton University Press, 2004.

Henderson, Gertrude. "An Epic of Early Iowa: Father Trecy's Colonization Scheme." *Iowa Catholic Historical Review* 3 (Oct. 1931) 3–13.

Hennessey, Dorothy Marie, OSF, and Rebecca Rosemeyer, OSF. *Rooted/En Route: Two Decades With the Dubuque Franciscans, 1954–1975*. Dubuque, IA: Union-Hoermann, 1978.

Henning, Barbara Beving Long, and Patrice K. Beam. *Des Moines and Polk County: Flag on the Prairie*. Sun Valley, CA: American Historical, 2003.

Henning, Dale R., and Gerald E. Schnepf. *Blood Run: The "Silent City."* Des Moines: DNR, 2014.

Henold, Mary J. *Catholic and Feminist: The Surprising History of the American Catholic Feminist Movement*. Chapel Hill: University of North Carolina Press, 2008.

Henry, Lyell D., Jr. *Zig-Zag-and-Swirl: Alfred W. Lawson's Quest for Greatness*. Iowa City: University of Iowa Press, 1991.

Bibliography

[Henry, Mary Gertrude]. *The Life of the Most Reverend Clement Smyth, D. D., O.C.S.O: Second Bishop of Dubuque*. Peosta, IA: New Melleray Abbey, 1937.

"Heritage." Vennard College Alumni Association. https://vcaa.net/heritage.html.

Herold, Elaine Bluhm. "Hopewell: Burial Mound Builders." *Pal* 51:12 (Dec. 1970).

Herron, George D. *Between Caesar and Jesus*. New York: T. Y. Crowell, 1899.

———. *The Call of the Cross: Four College Sermons*. New York: Revell, 1892.

———. *The Larger Christ*. New York: Revell, 1891.

———. *The Menace of Peace*. New York: Mitchell Kennerley. 1917.

———. *The New Redemption*. New York: T. Y. Crowell. 1893.

Hersey, Mark D. *My Work Is That of Conservation: An Environmental Biography of George Washington Carver*. Athens: University of Georgia Press, 2011.

Hershberger, Guy. "Maintaining the Mennonite Rural Community." *MQR* 14 (1940) 214–23.

Higginbottom, Daniel K. *Foundation and Early Years of the United Brethren in Christ in Central Iowa*. Des Moines: Iowa State Historic Preservation Office, 2014.

Hill, Patricia R. *The World Their Household: The American Women's Foreign Mission Movement and Cultural Transformation, 1870–1920*. Ann Arbor: University of Michigan Press, 1985.

Hinkhouse, Rev. J. F., ed. *"The Beloved": An Iowa Boy in the Jungles of Africa: Charles Warner McCleary, His Life, Letters and Work*. Fairfield, IA: Friends, 1909.

———. *One Hundred Years of the Iowa Presbyterian Church*. Cedar Rapids IA: Laurance, 1932.

Hinojosa, Felipe. "The Catholic Interracial Council and Mexican-American Civil Rights in Davenport, Iowa, 1957–1974." In *The Religious Left in Modern America: Doorkeepers of a Radical Faith*, edited by Leilah Danielson, et al. New York: Palgrave, 2018, 163–84.

Hinshaw, Cecil E. "An Apology for Perfection." *Pendle Hill Pamphlets*, 1964.

———. "Toward Political Responsibility," *Pendle Hill Pamphlets*, 1954.

"History." Aplington Baptist Church. https://web.archive.org/web/20230305215441/www.aplingtonbaptistchurch.com/history.aspx

"History." Divine Word College. https://www.dwci.edu/about-dwc/history.

"History of Faith." Faith Baptist Bible College. https://faith.edu/history.

"History of Johnson County." *AI First Series* 6.4 (Oct. 1868) 302–3.

A History of the Evangelical and Reformed Church. New York: Pilgrim, 1990.

History of the Iowa Church of God and Conference: "Those People Called Restitutionists," 1855–1987. Belle Plaine, IA, [1987?].

History of the Iowa Synod of the Lutheran Church in America, 1962–1987. Des Moines: Iowa Synod, 1987.

History of the Little Brown Church in Story and in Song. Mason City, IA, n.d. [>1994].

"History of the First Presbyterian Church in Dubuque, Iowa." http://www.firstpresdbq.org/about-us/history-of-our-church.

Hocking, William Ernest. *The Meaning of God in Human Experience*. New Haven: Yale University Press, 1912.

Hoehnle, Peter. *The Amana People: The History of a Religious Community*. Iowa City: Penfield, 2003.

———. "Communal Bonds: Contact Between the Amana Society and Other Communal Groups, 1843–1932." *Communal Studies* 20 (2000) 59–80.

Bibliography

———. "*Die Colonstein und die Indianer*": The Unusual Relationship between the Meskwaki Nation and the Amana Society." *Iowa Heritage Illustrated* 92 (2013) 90–99.

———. "With Malice Toward None: The Inspirationist Response to the Civil War, 1860–1865." *Communal Societies* 18 (1998) 72–76.

Hoek, Albert Llewellyn. *The Pilgrim Colony: The History of Saint Sebald Congregation, the Two Wartburgs, and the Synods of Iowa and Missouri*. Minneapolis: Lutheran College Press, 2004.

Hoeltje, Hubert H. "Ralph Waldo Emerson in Iowa." *IJH* 25.2 (Apr. 1927) 236–76.

Hoffman, Claire. *Greetings from Utopia Park: Surviving a Transcendent Childhood*. New York: Harper, 2016.

Hoffman, M. M. *Arms and the Monk: The Trappist Saga in Mid-America*. Dubuque, IA: W. C. Brown, 1952. [Hoffmann dropped the last letter of his name during World War II.]

———. *Centennial History of the Archdiocese of Dubuque, 1837–1937*. Dubuque, IA: Columbia College Press, 1938.

———. *The Church Founders of the Northwest*. Milwaukee: Bruce, 1937.

———. "Europe's Pennies and Iowa's Missions." *Iowa Catholic Historical Review* 5 (Oct. 1932) 39–45.

———. "Letters and Documents." *Iowa Catholic Historical Review* 9 (1932)

———. *Franciscans under Fire: Twenty Nuns, a Girl, and a Dog*. Edited by Duane Hutchinson. Lincoln: Foundation, 1990.

———. *Young and Fair Is Iowa*. Dubuque, IA: Loras College Press, 1946.

Holbo, Paul Sothe. "They Voted against War: A Study of Motivations." PhD diss., University of Chicago, 1961.

Holbrook, John C. *Discourses, Dedicatory and Historical*. Dubuque, IA: W. J. Gilbert, 1860.

———. *Prairie Breaking: Or, Scenes in the Work of a Western Pastor*. Boston: H. Hoyt, 1863.

———. "'The Worst That I Had Yet Witnessed': Mormon Diarists Cross Iowa in 1846." *Pal* 77.2 (Summer 1996) 70–73.

———. *Reflections of a Nonagenerian*. Boston, 1897.

Holden, David E. W. *Friends Divided: Conflict and Division in the Society of Friends*. Richmond, IN: Friends United, 1988.

Hollinger, David A. *Protestants Abroad*. Princeton University Press: Princeton, 2017.

Holmes, Marjorie. *You and I and Yesterday: A Woman's Nostalgic Reminiscences of a Small-Town Childhood*. New York: Morrow, 1973.

Holmgren, David G. *Abolitionists and Freethinkers with the Underground Railroad in Clinton County, Iowa*. Des Moines, 2017.

Holston, Jim. "Billy Sunday: The Calliope of Zion." *The Iowan* (Spring 1985) 19–23, 48–53.

Homan, Gerlof D. *American Mennonites in the Great War*. Scottdale, PA: Herald, 1994.

Hopkins, C. Howard. *John R. Mott: A Biography*. Grand Rapids: Eerdmans, 1979.

———. "Legacy of John R. Mott." *International Bulletin* (Apr. 1961) 70–73.

———. *The Rise of the Social Gospel in American Protestantism, 1865–1915*. New Haven: Yale University Press, 1967.

Horton, Loren. *Beautiful Heritage: A History of the Diocese of Iowa, 1853–2003*. Des Moines: Diocese of Iowa, 2003.

Bibliography

Houf, Walter R., ed. "American Home Missionary Letters from Iowa." *AI* 37 (1968) 95–120.

Houghton, Walter R., ed. *Neely's History of the Parliament of Religions and Religious Congresses of the World's Columbian Exposition.* Chicago, 1894.

Howard, Barbara, and Junia Braby. "The Hodges Hanging." *Pal* 60 (Mar. 1979) 48–58.

Howard, Victor B. *Religion and the Radical Republican Movement, 1860–1870.* Lexington: University of Kentucky Press, 1990.

Hoyt, Elizabeth E. "Tama: An American Conflict." Typescript, Ames, 1964.

Hubbard, Ethel Daniels. *Under Marching Orders: A Story of Mary Porter Gamewell.* New York: Board of Foreign Missions, 1909.

Hubbard, Joseph W. *History: Presbyterian Church in Iowa, 1837–1900.* Cedar Rapids, IA: Superior, [1900].

Hudson, David. *A Diverse Community of Believers and Seekers: A History of the First Christian Church in Iowa City, Iowa, 1863–2013.* Coralville: Lulu, 2013.

Hudson, David, et al. *The Biographical Dictionary of Iowa.* Iowa City: University of Iowa Press, 2008.

Huff, Sanford W. "Hummer's Bell." *AI First Series* 1 (1869) 69–75.

Hughes, Harold E. *The Man from Ida Grove.* Waco: Word, 1979.

Huizenga, John. "Pella, Iowa: Tulips in a Crumbled Castle." *Origins* 15.1 (1997) 15–21.

Hultkrantz, Ake. *Native Religions of North America: The Power of Visions and Fertility.* San Francisco: HarperCollins, 1987.

———. *The Religions of the American Indians.* Berkeley: University of California Press, 1967.

Hulme, William E. "Dubuque's Experiment in Ecumenism." *Christian Century*, Sep. 29, 1965, 1187–90.

Hultgren, Glenn M. *Against All Odds . . . But God: The History of the First 50 Years of the Christian Chiropractors Association.* Ft. Collins, CO: CCA, 2003.

Hultin, Ida C. "Extracts from 'Women and Religion.'" *The Congress of Women: Held in the Woman's Building, World's Columbian Exposition, Chicago, USA, 1893*, edited by Mary Cavanaugh Oldhaus Eagle, 788–89. Chicago: International, 1894.

Hummel, Daniel. *The Rise and Fall of Dispensationalism: How the Evangelical Battle over the End Times Shaped a Nation.* Grand Rapids: Eerdmans, 2023.

"Hummer, Rev. Michael J." *Melissa's World.* https://www.beadles.org/schuyler-presbytery/hummer-rev-michael-j/.

Humphrey, Robert E. "Children of Fantasy: The Rebels of Greenwich Village, 1910–1920." PhD diss., University of Iowa, 1975.

Hunsinger, George, ed. *Karl Barth and Radical Politics,* Philadelphia: Westminster, 1976.

Hunter, Jane. *The Gospel of Gentility.* New Haven: Yale University Press, 1984.

Hurto, Larry R. "1910 Church Census of Colfax." Unpublished paper.

———., ed. *A History of Newton, Iowa.* Dallas: Curtis, 1992.

———. "Oldest Czech Church in U.S. Creates Spillville Pride." *Iowa History Journal* 5.2 (Mar.-Apr. 2013) 31–36.

Hussman, Benedict J. "Voices from the Cloister: Oral Perspectives on the Recent History of New Melleray Abbey." Master's thesis, University of Northern Iowa, 1989.

Hutchinson, Duane. *Grotto Father: Artist-Priest of the West Bend Grotto.* Lincoln: Foundation, 1989.

Hyde, Anne F. *Born of Lakes and Prairies: Mixed Descent Peoples and the Making of the American West.* New York: W. W. Norton, 2022.

Bibliography

Impressions of New Melleray: Living the Life of a Trappist for Twenty-Four Hours. Peosta, IA: New Melleray Abbey, 1929.

"In Depth: Americans United for Separation of Church and State." KNIA-KRLS. https://www.kniakrls.com/2015/09/02/in-depth-americans-united-for-separation-of-church-and-state/.

Ingersol, Stan. "Methodism and the Theological Identity of the Church of the Nazarene." *MH* 43 (2004) 17–32.

Iowa Bible Training School and Bidwell Deaconess Home, 1916–1917.

Iowa Board of Immigration. *Iowa: The Home for Immigrants.* Iowa City, 1970.

Iowa Catholic Historical Review, vols. 1–9, 1930–36.

Iowa College Quinquennial, 1897.

"Iowa Cumerland [sic] Presbyterian Churches Past and Present." https://cumberland.org/hfcpc/churches/Iowa.htm.

Iowa Inter-Church Forum. *Our Faith Compels Us To Speak: A Pastoral Message on the Challenge of Peace from Christian Leaders of Iowa to Their Churches and All Iowans.* [Des Moines, 1984].

Iowa Interreligious Exchange Conference. "Islam in Iowa" workshop, Drake University, Apr. 17, 2017.

Iowa Official Register, 1900.

Iowa Public Radio. "In Iowa, Campaign Season Finds Muslims Caught in a Harsh Spotlight." Jan. 31, 2016.

———. "River to River." Aug. 17, 2012.

Iowa Public Television. *Iowa Places of Worship.* VCR, 2007.

Ireland, John. "The Coming of Bishop Loras." *AI* [2nd Ser.] 5 (1902) 532–34.

Italian American Cultural Center of Iowa. *2004 St. Joseph's Day Celebration.* DVD. Des Moines, 2004.

Jackson, David B. *Iowa's Talley War: An Incident in Keokuk County, August 1, 1863.* North English, IA: English Valleys History Center, 2013.

Jackson, Holly. *American Radicals: How Nineteenth-Century Protest Shaped the Nation.* New York: Crown, 2019.

Jackson, Kenneth T. *The Ku Klux Klan and the City.* New York: Ivan R. Dee, 1967.

Jacobs, Alan. *The Year of Our Lord 1943: Christian Humanism in an Age of Crisis.* Oxford: Oxford University Press, 2018.

Jacobsen, Douglas G. *An Unprov'd Experiment: Religious Pluralism in Colonial New Jersey.* Brooklyn: Carlson, 1991.

Jacobsen, James. National Register of Historic Places application, 1983.

Jacobson, Thomas E., ed. "Introduction to Claus Lauritz Clausen's Reply." *Journal of the Lutheran Historical Conference* 2017, 56–77.

Jagnow, Albert A., et al. "Some Iowa Lutheran Centennials." *Pal* 35:6 (June 1954).

Jaher, Frederic Cople. *Doubters and Dissenters: Cataclysmic Thought in America, 1885–1918.* New York: Free, 1964.

Jamison, Wallace N. *The United Presbyterian Story: A Centennial Study, 1858–1958.* Pittsburgh: Geneva, 1958.

Janeway, Elliott. "The Midwest's Mood." *Life,* Sep. 13, 1943.

Jenkins, Philip. *The Great and Holy War: How World War I Became a Religious Crusade.* New York: HarperOne, 2014.

———. *Mystics and Messiahs: Cults and New Religions in American History.* Oxford: Oxford University Press, 2000.

Bibliography

Jensen, Richard. *The Winning of the Midwest: Social and Political Conflict, 1888–1896.* Chicago: University of Chicago Press, 1971.
Jensen, Theodor I. "United Danish (1884): The Prairie Sod Was Hard." In *Church Roots: Stories of Nine Immigrant Groups That Became the American Lutheran Church,* edited by Charles P. Lutz, 143–63. Minneapolis: Fortress, 1985.
Jenson, Robert W. *A Religion against Itself.* Richmond: John Knox, 1967.
Jepsen, Dee. *What's Happening to My World?* Ann Arbor: Servant, 1989.
"Jewish Oral Histories." https://www.jewishdesmoines.org/our-pillars/iowa-jewish-historical-society/jewish-oral-histories/.
Job, Reuben P. *Life Stories.* Nashville: Abingdon, 2010.
"John Brown among the Quakers." *Pal* 41:1 (Jan. 1960)
Johnson, Christopher Jay. "An Oral History Study of the Religiosity of Fifty Czech-American Elderly." PhD diss., Iowa State University, 1981.
Johnson, Denis. "Emergency." In *Jesus' Son: Stories,* 69–90. New York: Perennial, 1982.
Johnson, Hildegard Binder. "German Forty-Eighters in Davenport." *IJH* 44:1 (Jan. 1946) 3–53.
Johnson, John W. *The Struggle for Student Rights: Tinker v. Des Moines and the 1960s.* Lawrence: University Press of Kansas, 1997.
Johnson, Kay. "The Ku Klux Klan in Iowa: A Study in Intolerance." Master's thesis, University of Iowa, 1967.
Johnson, Melinda Marie. "Building Bridges: Church Women United and Social Reform Work Across the Mid-Twentieth Century." PhD diss., University of Kentucky, 2015.
Johnson, P. Adelstein. *The First Century of Congregationalism in Iowa, 1840–1940.* Cedar Rapids, IA: Congregational Christian Conference of Iowa, 1945.
Johnson, Paul E., and Sean Wilentz. *The Kingdom of Matthias.* New York: Oxford University Press, 1994.
Johnson, Russell. "Are Vaccine Exemptions Actually Religious?" *Sightings,* Feb. 2, 2022.
Johnson, Russell L. *Warriors into Workers: The Civil War and Social Formation in a Northern City.* New York: Fordham University Press, 2003.
Jones, Charles Edwin. "The Holiness Complaint with Late-Victorian Methodism." In *Rethinking Methodist History,* edited by Russell E. Richey and Kenneth E. Rowe, 59–63. Nashville: Kingswood, 1985.
———. *Guide to the Study of the Holiness Movement.* Metuchen, NJ: Scarecrow, 1974.
Jones, Douglas W. "A Brief History of Judaism in Iowa." *Little Village,* Apr. 17, 2019.
Jones, Laurence C. *Piney Woods and Its Story.* New York: Revell, 1922.
Jones, Louis T. *The Quakers of Iowa.* Iowa City: State Historical Society of Iowa, 1914.
Jordahl, Leigh D. "Contemporary Worship: The Adiaphoristic Controversy Revisited." *Dialog* 33.4 (1995) 300–304.
———. "Stability and Change." *Pal* 67 (1986) 102–17.
———. "Norwegian (1853): The Gentry Tradition—Men and Women of a Leadership Class." In *Church Roots: Stories of Nine Immigrant Groups That Became the American Lutheran Church,* ed. Charles P. Lutz. Minneapolis: Fortress, 1985.
Jordahl, Leigh D., and Harris E. Kaasa. *Stability and Change: Luther College in Its Second Century.* Decorah, IA: Luther College Press, 1986.
Jordan, David W. "Edward A. Steiner and the Struggle for Toleration During World War I." *AI* 46 (1983) 523–42.
Jordan, Philip D. *The Evangelical Alliance for the United States of America, 1847–1900.* New York: Edwin Mellen, 1982.

Bibliography

———. "The Iowa Pioneer Phalanx." *Pal* 16 (1935) 211–30.
———. "The Missionary Who Fled Iowa." *Books of Iowa* 30 (1979) 13–31.
———. "Notes on the Salter-Shackford Correspondence." *AI* 18 (1932) 413–19.
———., ed. "William Salter's 'My Ministry in Iowa, 1843–1846.'" *AI* 20 (1935) 26–49.
———. *To Thy Trust*. Burlington, IA: First Congregational Church, 1973.
———. "William Salter and the Slavery Controversy." *IJH* 33.2 (Apr. 1935) 99–122.
———. *William Salter, Western Torchbearer*. Oxford, OH: Mississippi Valley, 1939.
Jordan, Ryan. The Dilemma of Quaker Pacifism in a Slaveholding Republic, 1833–1865." *Civil War History* 53 (2007) 5–28.
Jorgensen, Danny L. "Back to Zion: The Emergence of the Church of Jesus Christ (Cutlerite) and Its Return to Independence, Missouri." in Newell G. Bringhurst and C. Hamer, ed., *Scattering of the Saints*. Independence, MO: John Whitmer, 2007. 161-176
———. "The Scattered Saints of Southwestern Iowa: Cutlerite-Josephite Conflict and Rivalry, 1855–1865." *John Whitmer Historical Association Journal* 13 (1993) 80–97.
Judd, Peter, and Bruce Lindgren. *An Introduction to the Saints Church*. Independence, MO: Herald, 1976.
Judge, Michael. "Mother Mosque." *Wall Street Journal*, Dec. 21, 2006.
"The Judges and the Judged." *Christian Century*, May 1, 1957, 51–52.
Judson, Katherine B., ed. *Myths and Legends of the Mississippi Valley and the Great Lakes*. Chicago: A. C. McClurg, 1914.
Judt, Tony. *Postwar: A History of Europe since 1945*. New York: Penguin, 2005.
"Just Say Om." *Time*, August 4, 2003, 48–56.
Kaag, John. *American Philosophy*. New York: Farrar, Straus, & Giroux, 2016.
Kadlec, Jeanna. *Heretic: A Memoir*. New York: HarperCollins, 2022.
———. "How a Tarot Reader Spends Her Sunday." *New York Times*, Jan 8, 2023.
Kaiser, Daniel K. *Grinnell Stories: African Americans of Early Grinnell*. Grinnell, IA: Grinnell Historical Museum, 2020.
Kaplan, Dana Evan. *The Cambridge Companion to American Judaism*. Cambridge, UK: Cambridge University Press, 2005.
Kaufmann, Bill. "H. R. Gross, R. I. P." *Reason*, Dec. 1987.
Kazek, Kelly. "Alabama Chapel Billed as 'Smallest Church on Earth.'" https://www.al.com/life/2022/06/alabama-chapel-billed-as-smallest-church-on-earth.html.
Kazin, Michael. *A Godly Hero: The Life of William Jennings Bryan*. New York: Knopf, 2006.
Keith, LeeAnna. *When It Was Grand: The Radical Republican History of the Civil War*. New York: Hill & Wang, 2021.
Keller, Dorothy Birge, and Robert S. Keller. "American Board Missions in Turkey." In *The Role of the American Board in the World*, edited by Clifford Putney and Paul T. Burlin, eds.,Eugene: Wipf & Stock, 2012.
Kellison, Walter. "The Symbolic World of the Mound Builders." *Wapsipinicon Almanac* 4, 96–102.
———. "Prisoner of State." *Wapsipinicon Almanac* 10, 113–18.
Kelly, Mary Ellen. *But With the Dawn Rejoicing*. Milwaukee: Bruce, 1959.
Kelly, Sister Mary Gilbert, OP. *Catholic Immigrant Colonization Projects, 1815–1860*. New York: United States Catholic Historical Society, 1939.
Kempker, Rev. John F. "Catholic Missionaries in the Early and in the Territorial Days of Iowa." *AI* 10 (1911) 54–62.

Bibliography

Kennedy, John W. "Field of TM Dreams." *Christianity Today*, Jan 8, 2001.
Kennedy, Earl William. "Northwestern College." *Origins* 19 (2001) 39–46.
Kenny, Kevin. *Peaceable Kingdom Lost: The Paxton Boys and the Destruction of William Penn's Holy Experiment*. Oxford: Oxford University Press, 2009.
Kent, M. Corita, et al. *Sister Corita*. Philadelphia: Pilgrim, 1968.
Kerns, Travis S. "Gospel Assembly Church." Watchman Fellowship. https://www.watchman.org/profiles/pdf/gospelassemblychurchprofile.pdf.
Kerr, K. Austin. *Organized for Prohibition: A New History of the Anti-Saloon League*. New Haven: Yale University Press, 1985.
Kerr, Robert Y. "The Wittenberg Manual Labor College." *IJH* 24 (1926) 290–304.
Kertzer, Morris N. *Tell Me, Rabbi*. New York: Bloch, 1976.
———. *With an H on My Dog Tag*. New York: Behrman, 1947.
Khan, Mohamad. "In the Name of Allah, Most Gracious, Most Merciful: Being a Muslim in Iowa." In *Family Reunion*, edited by Thomas J. Morain, 72–80. Ames: Iowa State University Press, 1995.
Kilbourne, Margotann. "A Time Apart." *Iowan* 14 (Summer 1966), 42–45, 52.
Kilen, Mike. "The Last Mass." Des Moines *Register*, May 9, 2009.
Kimball, Stanley B. "Nauvoo West: The Mormons of the Iowa Shore." *BYU Studies* 18 (1978) 132–42.
King, Larry L. "Harold E. Hughes: Evangelist From the Prairies." *Harper's*, Mar. 1969, 50–57.
Kinzer, Donald L. *An Episode in Anti-Catholicism: The American Protective Association*. Seattle: University of Washington Press, 1964.
Kipnis, Ira. *The American Socialist Movement, 1897–1912*. New York: Monthly Review, 1972.
Kirkendall, Richard S. *Uncle Henry: A Documentary History of the First Henry Wallace*. Ames: Iowa State University Press, 1993.
Kirkpatrick, Ellis Lore. *English River Congregation of the Church of the Brethren*. Iowa City: State Historical Society of Iowa, 1930.
Kirkpatrick, Joseph S. *Private Thoughts on Theology: To the Serious Enquirer after Truth*, Dubuque, IA: Russell & Reeves, 1839.
Kiser, John W. *Commander of the Faithful: The Life and Times of Emir Abd el-Kadir*. Rhinebeck, NY: Monkfish, 2008.
Kisker, Scott T. "Unpopular Religion: Bishop Milton Wright and the United Brethren Schism of 1889." *MH* 57 (2018) 45–63.
Kittelstrom, Amy. "The International Social Turn: Unity and Brotherhood at the World's Parliament of Religions, Chicago, 1893." *Religion and American Culture* 19 (2009) 243–74.
Klein, Robert F., ed. *Foundations: The Letters of Mathias Loras, D.D., Bishop of Dubuque*. Dubuque: Loras College Press, 2004.
Kleinman, Mark L. "Searching for the 'Inner Light': The Development of Henry A. Wallace's Experimental Spiritualism." *AI* 53 (1994) 195–218.
———. *A World of Hope, A World of Fear*. Columbus: Ohio State University Press, 2000.
Klumpp, Andrew. "Colony before Party: The Ethnic Origins of Sioux County's Political Tradition." *AI* 79 (2020) 1–34.
———. "From Prairie to Parsonage: The Changing Role of Women in a Frontier Conference." *MH* 55 (2016) 161–72.

Bibliography

Knauss, Elizabeth. *The Conflict: A Narrative Based on the Fundamentalist Movement*. Los Angeles: Bible Institute of Los Angeles, 1923.

———. *Rising Tide*. New York: Christian Alliance, 1927.

Knepper, Timothy, ed. *A Spectrum of Faiths: Religions of the World in America's Heartland*. Des Moines: Drake Community, 2017.

Knopp, Lisa. *Flight Dreams: A Life in the Midwestern Landscape*. Iowa City: University of Iowa Press, 1998.

Knudsen, Johannes. *Danish Rebel: The Life of N. F. S. Grundtvig*. Philadelphia: Muhlenberg, 1955.

Koerner, James D. *The Parsons College Bubble: A Tale of Higher Education in America*. New York: Basic, 1970.

Kohn, Stephen M. *American Political Prisoners: Prosecutions under the Espionage and Sedition Acts*. Westport, CT: Praeger, 1994.

Kooi, Muriel Byers. "An Elusive Peace in Pella." *Origins* 10.1 (1992) 35–37.

Kosek, Joseph Kip. *Acts of Conscience: Christian Nonviolence and Modern American Democracy*. New York: Columbia University Press, 2011.

———. "American Capitalism and Agrarian Spiritual Dissent in the 1930s." In *Religion and Politics Beyond the Culture Wars: New Directions in a Divided America*, edited by Darren Dochuk, 37–55. Notre Dame, IN: University of Notre Dame Press, 2021.

Kostlevy, William. *Holy Jumpers: Evangelicals and Radicals in Progressive Era America*. Oxford: Oxford University Press, 2010.

———., ed. *Historical Dictionary of the Holiness Movement*. 2nd ed. Lanham, MD: Scarecrow, 2009.

Kramer, Dale. *The Wild Jackasses: The American Farmers in Revolt*. New York: Hastings, 1956.

Kraybill, Donald B., ed. *Amish and the State*. 2nd ed. Baltimore: Johns Hopkins University Press, 2003.

Krehbiel, John C. "Early Years at West Point, Iowa: The Founding of the General Conference Mennonite Church." *Mennonite Life* (Apr. 1960) 53–56.

Kremer, Gary R., ed. *George Washington Carver in His Own Words*. Columbia: University of Missouri Press, 1987.

Kuhns, Frederick I. *The American Home Missionary Society in Relation to the Antislavery Controversy in the Old Northwest*. Billings, MT: [Kuhns?], 1959.

———. "The Baptists in Iowa." *Pal* 36:9 (Sep. 1953) 333–88.

———. "The Evangelical and Reformed Church in Iowa." *Pal* 33:6 (Jun. 1952) 161–92.

———. "The Presbyterians in Iowa," *Pal* 33:4 (Apr. 1952)

———. "Religion on the Iowa Frontier to 1846." *IJH* 51 (1953) 37–56.

Kujawa-Holbrook, Sheryl A., ed. *Freedom Is a Dream: A Documentary History of Women in the Episcopal Church*. New York: Church Pub, 2002.

Lacey, Margaret. *Silent Friends: A Quaker Quilt*. Urbana, IL: Stormline, 1992.

Lagerquist, L. DeAne. "Being Lutheran in Public: Contributions to Social Capital in the Midwest." *Anglican and Episcopal History* 74 (2005) 94–116.

———., *The Lutherans*. Westport, CT: Praeger, 1999.

Lair, Loren E. *From Restoration to Reformation*. Des Moines, 1970.

Lake, Sharon M. "Manuscript Collections: The Iowa Women's Archives." *AI* 63 (2004) 170–202.

Lampe, M. Willard. "The Story of an Idea." *State University of Iowa Extension Bulletin* 764 (Mar. 1, 1960) 3–15.

Bibliography

"Lancaster Christian Church." https://www.facebook.com/SigourneyLCC/.

Landis, Benson Y. *Rural Church Life in the Middle West, As Illustrated by Clay County, Iowa and Jennings County, Indiana.* New York: G. H. Doran, 1922.

Landis, Leo, and Jerome Thompson. "History With Humanity: American Indian Burials in Iowa." https://medium.com/iowa-history/history-with-humanity-american-indian-burials-in-iowa-81a81d38a7f9.

Lane, Belden C. *Landscapes of the Sacred: Geography and Narrative in American Spirituality.* Mahwah, NJ: Paulist, 1988.

Lane, Ortha May. *Missions in Magazines: An Analysis of the Treatment of Protestant Foreign Missions in American Magazines since 1910.* Tientsin: Tientsin, 1935.

———. *Under Marching Orders in North China.* Tyler, TX: Story-Wright, 1971.

Lane, Stoddard. "The Challenge to Disarmament." Grinnell College. *Tanager* 8.2 (Nov. 1932) 37.

———. "It's Hard to Believe in Christmas." Typescript sermon, Plymouth Congregational Church, Des Moines, Dec. 22, 1940.

———. "Labor Troubles and the Local Church." *Social Action,* Jan 15, 1939.

———. "There Are Things That Abide Always." Sermon. August 30, 1942. In *Stoddard Lane, 1887–1943.* Des Moines, 1943.

Lapham, Lewis. *With the Beatles.* Hoboken, NJ: Melville, 2005.

Larew, James C. *A Party Reborn: The Democrats of Iowa 1950–1974.* Iowa City: State Historical Society, 1980.

Larson, Erik. *Devil in the White City.* New York: Random House, 2003.

Lasch, Christopher. "Anti-Imperialists." *Journal of Southern History* 24 (Aug 1958) 319–31.

Launius, Roger D. "The Mormon Quest for a Perfect Society at Lamoni, Iowa, 1870–1890." *AI* 47 (1984) 325–42.

Launius, Roger D., and John E. Hallwas, eds. *Kingdom on the Mississippi Revisited.* Urbana: University of Illinois Press, 1996.

Lawlor, Kathryn. *Your Affectionate: Commentary on Mary Frances Clarke's Writings.* Dubuque: Mount Carmel, 2003.

Lawrence, Noah. "'Since It Is My Right, I Would Like to Have It': Edna Griffin and the Katz Drug Store Desegregation Movement." *AI* 67 (2008) 298–330.

Lawson, Alfred. *Lawsonian Religion.* Detroit: Humanity Benefactor Association, 1949.

"Lawsonomy." https://web.archive.org/web/20240825225438/https://www.lawsonomy.org.

Lazell, J. Arthur. *Alaskan Apostle: The Life Story of Sheldon Jackson.* New York: Harper, 1960.

Leavelle, Tracy Neal. *The Catholic Calumet: Colonial Conversions in French and Indian North America.* Philadelphia, 2012.

Lee, Bishop Henry W. *Third Annual Address.* Davenport, IA, 1857.

Lee, J. W. *History of Hamilton County.* Chicago: S. J. Clarke, 1912.

Lee, Jacob F. *Masters of the Middle Waters: Indian Nations and Colonial Ambitions along the Mississippi.* Cambridge, MA: Harvard University Press, 2019.

Legried, Ann M. "'By the Oaks of Mamre': Swedish Lutheran Colonization on the Frontiers of Southwestern Iowa, 1870–1900." *Swedish-American Historical Quarterly* 44 (1993) 68–83.

Lehman, James O., and Steven M. Nolt. *Mennonites, Amish, and the American Civil War.* Baltimore: Johns Hopkins University Press, 2007.

Bibliography

LemMon, Jean, ed. *John Paul II Visits Rural America.* Des Moines: Meredith, 1979.

Lenehan, Rev. B. C. "Rt. Rev. Mathias Loras, First Bishop of Dubuque." *AI* 3.8 (Jan. 1899) 577–600.

Lender, Mark Edward. *Dictionary of American Temperance Biography: From Temperance Reform to Alcohol Research, the 1600s to the 1980s.* Westport, CT: Greenwood, 1984.

Lendt, David L. "The Copperhead Movement in Iowa." *AI* 40 (1970) 412–27.

Lenz, Lyz. *God Land: A Story of Faith, Loss, and Renewal in Middle America.* Bloomington: Indiana University Press, 2019.

Levine, Lawrence W. *Defender of the Faith: William Jennings Bryan: The Last Decade, 1915–1925.* Cambridge, MA: Harvard University Press, 1987.

Lex, Louise Moede. "Mary Newbury Adams: Feminist Forerunner From Iowa." *AI* 43 (1976) 323–41.

Liffring-Zug, Joan. *The Amanas Yesterday: A Religious Communal Society.* Iowa City: Penfield, 1975.

Ligutti, Luigi, and John C. Rawe. *Rural Roads to Security: America's Third Struggle for Freedom.* Milwaukee: Bruce, 1940.

Lindberg, Carter, ed. *Piety, Politics, and Ethics: Reformation Studies in Honor of George Wolfgang Forell.* Kirksville, MO: Truman State University Press, 1984.

Lingeman, Richard. *The Noir Forties: The American People from Victory to Cold War.* New York: Bold Type, 2012.

Linker, Damon. "Why Can't the *New York Times* Religion Columnist Define Religion?" *The Week*, Dec. 2, 2015.

Lippy, Charles H., ed. *Twentieth-Century Shapers of American Popular Religion.* New York: Bloomsbury, 1989.

"A Listing of Public Debates in Which Primitive Baptist Ministers Have Participated." http://pblib.org/Debates.html.

Littell, Franklin H. "The State of Iowa vs. the Amish." *Christian Century*, Feb. 26, 1966, 234–35.

Little, Lawrence S. *Disciples of Liberty: The African Methodist Episcopal Church in the Age of Imperialism, 1884–1916.* Knoxville: University of Tennessee Press, 2000.

Lodwick, Kathleen L. *Educating the Women of Hainan: The Career of Margaret Moninger in China, 1915–1942.* Lexington: University of Kentucky Press, 1995.

Logan, Wilfred D., and G. Earl Ingmanson. "Effigy Mounds National Monument." *Pal* 50:5 (May 1969).

Long, Kathryn T. "Consecrated Respectability: Phoebe Palmer and the Refinement of American Methodism." In *Methodism and the Shaping of American Culture*, edited by Nathan O. Hatch and John H. Wigger, 281–307. Nashville: Kingswood, 2001.

Longenecker, Stephen L. *Piety and Tolerance: Pennsylvania German Religion, 1700–1850.* Metuchen, NJ: Scarecrow, 1994.

Longfield, Bradley J. *The Presbyterian Controversy: Fundamentalists, Modernists, & Moderates.* New York: Oxford University Press, 1991.

———. *Presbyterians and American Culture: A History.* Louisville: WJK, 2013.

Lohrmann, Martin J. "Prairie Royalty: Auguste von Schwartz (1807–1877) and the Baltic Noblewomen Who Supported the Iowa Synod." *Journal of the Lutheran Historical Conference* 2017, 78–87.

Lord, Russell. *The Wallaces of Iowa.* Boston: Houghton Mifflin, 1947.

Love, Robert. *The Great Oom: The Improbable Birth of Yoga in America.* New York: Penguin, 2010.

Bibliography

Lucas, Henry S. "The Beginnings of Dutch Immigration to Iowa, 1845–1847." *IJH* 23 (1924) 483–531.

———. *Netherlanders in America*. Grand Rapids: Eerdmans, 1955.

Lucke, Susan K. *The Bellevue War*. Ames: McMillen, 2002.

Luick-Thrams, Michael. *Out of Hitler's Reach: The Scattergood Hostel for European Refugees, 1939-43*. [Mason City, IA]: Goodfellow, 1996.

Luker, Ralph E. *The Social Gospel in Black and White: American Racial Reform, 1885–1912*. Chapel Hill: University of North Carolina Press, 1985.

Lundin, Roger. *Emily Dickinson and the Art of Belief*. Grand Rapids: Eerdmans, 1998.

Lupo, Michael Scott. "Advancing the Time of the End: Herbert W. Armstrong and Modern American Culture." PhD diss., University of Nevada Reno, 2002.

Lyftogt, Kenneth L. *Iowa and the Civil War, Volume 1: Free Child of the Missouri Compromise*. Iowa City: Camp Pope, 2018.

———. *Iowa and the Civil War, Volume 2: From Iuka to the Red River, 1862–1864*. Iowa City: Camp Pope, 2020.

"Luxembourg Heritage Society of Northwest." https://www.nwialux.org/.

Lyttle, Charles H. *Freedom Moves West: A History of the Western Unitarian Conference*. Boston: Beacon, 1952.

MacCanon, Robert R. *A Short History of the United Brethren in Christ in Iowa*. N.p., 1975.

Macdonald, Dwight. *Henry Wallace: The Man and the Myth*. New York: Vanguard, 1947.

McArraher, Eugene. *Enchantments of Mammon*. Cambridge, MA: Belknap, 2019.

McAvoy, E. L. "History of the Church in Northwest Iowa." *Iowa Catholic Historical Review* 8 (1935) 36–37.

McAvoy, Thomas T. *The Americanist Controversy in Roman Catholicism, 1895–1920*. Notre Dame: University of Notre Dame Press, 1963.

McBride, Spencer W. *Joseph Smith for President: The Prophet, The Assassins, and the Fight for American Religious Freedom*. New York: Oxford University Press, 2021.

McCann, Linda Betsinger. *Prohibition in Eastern Iowa*. Des Moines: Iowan, 2014.

McCloud, Sean. *Making the American Religious Fringe: Exotics, Subversives, & Journalists, 1955–1993*. Chapel Hill: University of North Carolina Press, 2004.

McCreery, J. L., ed. *Theological Discussion Held at Des Moines, June 22, 1868, between W. W. King, Pastor of the Universalist Society of Des Moines, Iowa, and Alvin I. Hobbs, Pastor of the Church of Christ, on Cherry Street, Des Moines, Iowa*. Des Moines, 1868.

McDannell, Colleen. *Picturing Faith*. New Haven: Yale University Press, 2004.

———. *The Spirit of Vatican II: A History of Catholic Reform in America*. New York, 2011.

McDaniel, George William. *A Great and Lasting Beginning: The First 125 Years of St. Ambrose University*. Davenport, IA: St. Ambrose University Press, 2006.

———. "Catholic Action in Davenport: St. Ambrose College and the League for Social Justice." *AI* 55 (1996) 239–72.

McDonnold, Benjamin Wilbur. *History of the Cumberland Presbyterian Church*. Nashville: Board of Publication, 1888.

McElroy, John M. *Men of the Past*. N.p., 1905.

McElroy, W. O. "Wittenberg Manual Labor College" and "Wittenberg Congregational Church." *History of Jasper County, Iowa*. Chicago: Western Historical, 1878.

Bibliography

McFarland, Milton Robert. "Congregationalism and Its Contribution to the Educational Development of Iowa: The First Fifty Years." Master's thesis, Drake University, 1966.

McGirr, Lisa. *The War on Alcohol: Prohibition and the Rise of the American State*. New York: W. W. Norton, 2016.

McGovern, Rev. James J., D.D. *The Life and Writings of the Most Reverend John McMullen, D.D. First Bishop of Davenport, Iowa*. Milwaukee: Bruce, 1888.

McGreal, Mary Nona, O.P. *Samuel Mazzuchelli, American Dominican*. Notre Dame, IN: Ave Maria, 2005.

McGuire, Brian. "Don't Call It a Religion." *Wall Street Journal*. May 17, 2002.

McHale, Tom. *Dooley's Delusion*. Atlanta: Droke House/Hallux, 1971.

McIntire, C. T. "Herman Dooyeweerd in North America." In *Dutch Reformed Theology: Reformed Theology in America*, edited by David F. Wells. Grand Rapids: Eerdmans, 1989.

McIntosh, Lois A. "Biography of a Church." *Pal* 29 (1945) 129–44.

McKenzie, Betty. "After the Mormon Exodus." *Pal* 77:2 (Summer 1996) 86–87.

McKenzie, Thomas. "Archbishop Beckman and the Dubuque Anti-War Movement 1939–41." Unpublished paper, copy in author's possession, 1986.

McKiernan, F. Mark. *Voice of One Crying in the Wilderness: Sidney Rigdon, Religious Reformer, 1793–1896*. Independence, MO: Herald, 1979.

McLean, Hulda Hoover. *Hulda's World: A Chronicle of Hulda Minthorn Hoover, 1848–1884*. West Branch, IA: Herbert Hoover Presidential Library Association, 1989.

McLeister, Ira F., and Roy S. Nicholson. *Conscience and Commitment: The History of the Wesleyan Methodist Church of America*. Rev. 4th ed. Marion, IN: Wesley, 1976.

McLoughlin, William G. *Billy Sunday Was His Real Name*. Chicago: University of Chicago Press, 1955.

McMillan, James E. "Central College." *Origins* 19 (2001) 47–53.

McMurray, Enfys. *Centerville: A Mid-American Saga*. Charleston, SC: History, 2012.

McMurry, Linda O. *George Washington Carver: Scientist and Symbol*. Oxford: Oxford University Press, 1981.

McNellus, James. The Unveiling of the Great Whore and the Diverse Beast. N.p., 1997.

McTaggert, Fred. *Wolf That I Am: In Search of the Red Earth People*. Boston: Houghton Mifflin, 1976.

Macy, Jesse. *An Autobiography*. Springfield, IL: Charles C. Thomas, 1933.

———. "Union of Church and State at Springdale, Iowa." *AI* 7 (1905) 34–37.

Madison, James H. "Reformers and the Rural Church, 1900–1950." *Journal of American History* 73 (1986) 645–68.

Magill, Samuel. "Hummer's Bell." *AI Second Series* 1 (Jan. 1883) 26–28.

Magnuson, Jon. "Marquette's Bones." *Christian Century*, Jun. 15, 2022.

Magoun, George F. *Asa Turner: A Home Missionary Patriarch and His Times*. Boston: Congregational, 1897.

Mahan, Bruce E. "New Melleray." *Pal* 3:9 (Sep. 1922) 265–312.

Main, Elaine. "The Fraulein Chooses Backwoods Iowa." *Pal* 59 (Nov. 1978) 162–67.

Manfra, Jo Ann. "Hometown Politics and the American Protective Association, 1887–1890." *AI* 55 (1996) 138–66.

Manfred, Frederick. *The Frederick Manfred Reader*. Edited by John Calvin Rezmerski. Duluth: Holy Cow, 1996.

———. *No Fun on Sunday*. Norman: University of Oklahoma Press, 1990.

Bibliography

———. *This Is the Year.* Boston: Gregg, 1979.
Manfred, Freya. *A Daughter Remembers.* St. Paul: Minnesota Historical Society, 1999.
"March to Zion." marchtozion.com.
Margaret, Helene. "Father Pierre Jean DeSmet." *Pal* 20 (June 1939) 177–90.
Markowitz, Norman D. *The Rise and Fall of the People's Century: Henry A. Wallace and American Liberalism, 1941–1948.* New York: Free, 1973.
Marlett, Jeffrey. *Saving the Heartland: Catholic Missionaries in Rural America, 1920–1960.* DeKalb: Northern Illinois University Press, 2002.
Marrow, Alfred J. *The Practical Theorist: The Life and Work of Kurt Lewin.* New York: Basic, 1969.
Marsden, George. *The Evangelical Mind and the New School Presbyterian Experience.* New Haven: Yale University Press, 1970.
Marsh, Callie. *A Lively Faith: Reflections on Iowa Yearly Meeting of Friends (Conservative).* Philadelphia: FGC Quaker, 2011.
Marsh, Charles. *The Beloved Community: How Faith Shapes Social Justice, from the Civil Rights Movement to Today.* New York: Basic, 2005.
Martin, Donald, J. "History of Salem Church." Typescript, copy in possession of Salem Church of Lincoln, IA, 1966.
Martin, Joel A., and Mark A. Nicholas, eds. *Native Americans, Christians, and the Reshaping of the American Religious Landscape.* Chapel Hill: University of North Carolina Press, 2010.
Martin, Robert F. "Billy Sunday and the Mystique of the Middle West." *AI* 55 (1996) 345–60.
———. *Hero of the Heartland: Billy Sunday and the Transformation of American Society, 1862–1935.* Bloomington, IN: Indiana University Press, 2002.
———. "Wittenmyer, Sarah Ann ("Annie") Turner." *BDI*, 565–66.
Mathews, Basil. *John R. Mott, World Citizen.* New York: Harpers, 1934.
May, George S. "Des Moines University and T. T. Shields." *IJH* 54 (1956) 192–232.
Mazzuchelli, Samuel. *The Memoirs of Father Samuel Mazzuchelli, O. P.* Chicago: Priory, 1967.
Melloh, Ardith K. "New Sweden, Iowa." *Pal* 59 (1978) 2–19.
Melton, J. Gordon. *Melton's Encyclopedia of American Religions.* Tarrytown, NY: Triumph, 1991.
Melville, Thomas R. *Through a Glass Darkly: The U.S. Holocaust in Central America.* N.p.: Xlibris, 2005.
Merrill, Christopher. *Things of the Hidden God: Journey to the Holy Mountain.* New York: Random, 2005.
Merry, John F. *History of Delaware County, Iowa, and Its People,* vol. 2. Chicago: S. J. Clarke, 1914.
The Mesquakies of Iowa, A Summary of the First Five Years The University of Chicago—State University of Iowa Mesquakie Indian Project. N.p, n.d. [1953?].
"Methodists in Iowa." *Pal* 32.2 (Feb. 1951).
Meyer, Carl S., ed. *Moving Frontiers: Readings in the History of the Lutheran Church-Missouri Synod.* St. Louis: Concordia, 1962.
Meyer, Donald. *The Positive Thinkers: Religion as Popular Psychology from Mary Baker Eddy to Oral Roberts.* New York: Knopf, 1980.
Meyer, Jeremy D., and Bruce Nesmith. "Iowa: Everything Comes Up Rosy." In *God at the Grass Roots: The Christian Right in the 1994 Elections,* edited by Mark J. Rozell and Clyde Wilcox. Lanham, MD: Routledge, 1995.

Bibliography

Meyer, Sabine N. *We Are What We Drink: The Temperance Battle in Minnesota*. Urbana, IL: University of Illinois Press, 2015.

Michelsen, Truman. "White Owl Sacred Pack." *U.S. Bureau of American Ethnology Bulletin* #72 (1921).

Mihelic, Joseph L. "A Survey of the History of the University of Dubuque, 1846–1979." Unpublished manuscript, University of Dubuque Theological Seminary archives.

Miles, Austin. *Setting the Captives Free: Victims of the Church Tell Their Stories*. Buffalo: Prometheus, 1990.

Miller, Anthony J. "Pioneers, Sunday Schoolers, and Laundrymen: Chinese Immigrants in Iowa in the Chinese Exclusion Era, 1870–1890." *AI* 81 (2022) 113–48.

Miller, Benjamin L. *In God's Presence: Chaplains, Missionaries, and Religious Space during the American Civil War*. Lawrence: University Press of Kansas, 2019.

Miller, Brian Craig, ed. *A Punishment on the Nation: An Iowa Soldier Endures the Civil War*. Kent: Kent State University Press, 2012.

Miller, Jeremy. "Through a Glass, Brightly." *Earth Island Journal* 33 (Winter 2018) 30–34.

Miller, Raphael H. *Charles Medbury: Preacher and Master Workman for Christ*. St. Louis: Christian, 1932.

Miller, Raymond W. *Monsignor Ligutti: The Pope's County Agent*. Lanham, MD: University Press of America, 1981.

Miller, Robert J. *Both Prayed to the Same God: Religion and Faith in the American Civil War*. Lanham, MD: University Press of America, 2007.

Miller, Robert Moats. *How Will They Hear without a Preacher? The Life of Ernest Fremont Tittle*. Chapel Hill: University of North Carolina Press, 1971.

Miller, Sally M. *From Prairie to Prison: The Life of Social Activist Kate Richards O'Hare*. Columbia, MO: University of Missouri Press, 1993.

Miller, Timothy. *America's Alternative Religions*. Albany: SUNY Press, 1995.

———. *The Hippies and American Values*. Knoxville: University of Tennessee Press, 1991.

———. *Following in His Steps: A Biography of Charles M. Sheldon*. Knoxville: University of Tennessee Press, 1987.

Miller, William Lee. *Arguing about Slavery: The Great Battle in the United States Congress*. New York: Knopf, 1996.

Mills, George. *A Judge and a Rope and Other Stories of Bygone Iowa*. Ames, IA: Iowa State University Press, 1994.

Mills, George A., and Richard W. Peterson. *No One Is Above The Law: The Story of the Southern Iowa's Federal Court*. N.p., n.d.

Milner, Clyde A. *With Good Intentions: Quaker Work among the Pawnees, Otos, and Omahas in the 1870s*. Lincoln: University of Nebraska Press, 1982.

Milner, George R. *The Moundbuilders: Ancient Peoples of Eastern North America*. London: Thames & Hudson, 2004.

Milner, Virginia Voorhies. *La Doctorcita: Memoirs of Virginia Voorhies Milner, M.D.* Albuquerque: Albuquerque, 1989.

Minutes, First Church of the Brethren, Des Moines, 1918.

Minutes of the General Association of Congregational Churches and Ministers of Iowa, 1863, 1864, 1877.

Minutes of the General Association of Iowa at Its Session in Grinnell, June 1864.

Minutes of the Ninety-Ninth Annual Meeting of the Iowa Baptist Convention, Pella, IA, 1940.

Bibliography

Mitchell, Bennett. *History of the Northwest Iowa Conference 1872–1903*. Sioux City: Perkins, 1904.

Mitchell, Don. *The Longest Way Home*. N.p., 1974.

Mitchell, G. P. *A Century of Iowa Baptist History, 1834–1934*. Pella, IA: Baptist Record, 1934.

Mitchell, Robert B. *Skirmisher: The Life, Times, and Political Career of James B. Weaver*. Roseville, MN: Edinborough, 2008.

Mitchell, Robert Bryant. *Heritage and Horizons: The History of Open Bible Standard Churches*. Des Moines: Open Bible, 1982.

Moffitt, Alexander. "A Checklist of Iowa Imprints, 1837–1860." *IJH* 36 (1938) 7–8.

Mohler, John E. "Dunkers in Iowa." *AI* 7 (1906) 260–82.

Mohr, James C. "Iowa's Abortion Battles of the 1960s and 1970s: Long-Term Perspectives and Short-Term Analyses." In *Iowa History Reader*, edited by Marvin Bergman, 411–31. Ames: Iowa State University Press, 1996.

[Montgomery, Helen Barrett]. "Presidential Address." *Annual of the Northern Baptist Convention*, v. 15 (1922) 38–39.

Moody, Dwight A. "The Conversion of J. Frank Norris: A New Look at the Revival of 1910." *Baptist History and Heritage* 46 (2010) 48–64.

Moomaw, D. C., ed. *Christianity Versus War*. Ashland, OH: Brethren, 1924.

Moore, Deborah Dash, et al. "Roundtable." *American Jewish History* 93 (2007) 113–28.

Moore, J. Stuart. *Chiropractic in America: The History of a Medical Alternative*. Baltimore: Johns Hopkins University Press, 1993.

Moorhead, James H. "Presbyterians and the Mystique of Efficiency, 1870–1936." In *Reimagining Denominationalism: Interpretive Essays*, edited by Robert Bruce Mullin and Russell E. Richey, 264–87. New York: Oxford University Press, 1994.

Morain, Thomas J., ed. *Family Reunion: Essays on Iowa*. Ames: Iowa State University Press, 1995.

———. "Mormons and Nineteenth Century Iowa Historians." *John Whitmer Historical Association Journal* 1 (1981) 34–42.

Morgan, David. *Protestants and Pictures: Religion, Visual Culture, and the Age of American Mass Production*. Oxford: Oxford University Press, 1999.

Morgan, Douglas. *Adventism and the American Republic: The Public Involvement of a Major Apocalyptic Movement*. Knoxville, TN: University of Tennessee Press, 2003.

Morgans, James Patrick. *John Todd and the Underground Railroad*. Jefferson, NC: McFarland, 2006.

Morrill, Allen C., and Eleanor D. "Launcelot Graham Bell: 'The Lengthened Shadow of One Man.'" *Journal of the Presbyterian Historical Society* 40 (1964) 225–35.

Morris, Jim, W. "Beginnings of the Methodist Protestant Church in Iowa." *MH* 7 (1969) 45–51.

———. "History of the Methodist Protestant Church in Iowa," B.D. thesis, Drake University, 1966.

Morrison, Peter A., ed. *A Taste of the Country: A Collection of Calvin Beale's Writings*. University Park, MD: Pennsylvania State University Press, 1990.

Mortensen, Enok. *The Danish Lutheran Church in America: The History and Heritage of the American Evangelical Lutheran Church*. Philadelphia: Lutheran Church of America, 1967.

Bibliography

Moseley, Edward. "The Christian Church (Disciples of Christ) and Overseas Ministries." In *The Christian Church (Disciples of Christ): An Interpretive Examination in the Cultural Context*, edited by George G. Beazley, Jr., 237–52. St. Louis: Bethany, 1973.

Mott, David C. "Judith Ellen Foster." *AI* 19 (1935) 126–38.

Mott, Frank Luther. "Quaker Boy." *Pal* 43:7 (Jul. 1962) 305–26.

———. *Time Enough: Essay in Autobiography*. Chapel Hill: University of North Carolina Press, 1962.

Mott, John R. *Addresses and Papers*. New York: Association, 1947.

———. *Criticisms About Y.M.C.A.: War Work and Answers*. N.p., 1918.

———. *Five Decades and a Forward View*. New York: Harper, 1939.

———. Foreword to Jashwant R. Chitambar, *Mahatma Gandhi: His Life, Work and Influence*. Chicago: John C. Winston, 1933.

———. *Methodists United for Action*. Nashville: Board of Mission, 1939.

Moudry, Susan Lynn. "'A Society of Our Own': Methodists, Coeducation, and the Founding of the P. E. O." *MH* 52 (2013) 33–42.

Mould, George. "The Conflict between the Modernists and the Fundamentalists in the Northern Baptist Convention since 1920." Master's thesis, State University of Iowa, 1940.

Moulton, Candy. *The Mormon Handcart Migration: "Tongue Nor Pen Can Never Tell the Sorrow."* Norman: University of Oklahoma Press, 2019.

Mousel, Sister Mary Eunice, OSF. *They Have Taken Root: The Sisters of the Third Order of St. Francis of the Holy Family*. New York: Bookman, 1954.

"Move into the Future by Saving the Past: Churches of Louisa County, Iowa." http://iagenweb.org/louisa/churches/wapello_unitedmethodist.htm.

Mulder, William. "Norwegian Forerunners among the Early Mormons." *Norwegian-American Studies and Records* 19 (1956) 46–61.

Mulgrew, Kate. *How to Forget: A Daughter's Memoir*. New York: William Morrow, 2019.

Mullin, Robert Bruce. *Episcopal Vision/American Reality: High Church Theology and Social Thought in Evangelical America*. New Haven: Yale University Press, 1986.

Mungons, Kevin, and Douglas Yeo. *Homer Rodeheaver and the Rise of the Gospel Music Industry*. Urbana: University of Illinois Press, 2021.

Mungons, Kevin. "Iowa Hymn Writers." Unpublished manuscript.

Munson, Kyle. "Which Black Church Is Iowa's Oldest?" *Des Moines Register*, Jan. 20, 2016.

Murphy, Andrew R. *Conscience and Community: Revisiting Toleration and Religious Dissent in Early Modern England and America*. University Park: Pennsylvania State University Press, 2001.

Murray, Janette Stevenson. "Sabbath at the Kirk/A Beloved Dominie." *Pal* 17.12 (Dec. 1936) 404–9.

———. *They Came to North Tama: A Historical Account of North Tama, Iowa*. Lake Mills, IA: Graphic, 1973.

Murray, Janette, and Janet Murray Fiske. *Bonnie Iowa Farm Folk*. Ames: Iowa State University Press, 1966.

Murray, Paul T. *Seeing Jesus in the Eyes of the Oppressed: A History of Franciscans Working for Peace and Justice*. Oceanside, CA: Academy of American Franciscan History, 2021.

Bibliography

Muste, A. J. "Sketches for an Autobiography." In *The Essays of A. J. Muste*, edited by Nat Hentoff, 1–174. New York: Clarion, 1967,

Mutel, Cornelia F. *The Emerald Horizon: The History of Nature in Iowa*. Iowa City: University of Iowa Press, 2008.

Nabhan-Warren, Kristy. *Meatpacking America: How Migration, Work, and Faith Unite and Divide the Heartland*. Chapel Hill: University of North Carolina Press, 2021.

Nabokov, Peter. *When the Lightning Strikes: The Lives of American Indian Sacred Places*. New York: Penguin, 2006.

Naff, Alixa. *Becoming American: The Early Arab Immigrant Experience*. Carbondale: Southern Illinois University Press, 1985.

Nash, Sister Mary Borromeo. "The Sisters of Mercy in Iowa Founded from the Davenport Motherhouse." Master's thesis, State University of Iowa, 1931.

National Catholic Rural Life Conference. *Manifesto on Rural Life*. Milwaukee: Bruce, 1944.

Natte, Roger B., ed. "'A Reckless Life of Three Years in Iowa': The Diary of a Young Attorney, John Duncombe, 1856–1859." *Iowa Heritage Illustrated* 83 (2002) 58–108.

Neely, Mark E., Jr. *The Fate of Liberty: Abraham Lincoln and Civil Liberties*. New York: Oxford University Press, 1991.

Nefzger, Ben, and Peter Kivisto. "Conditions of Jewish Life in a Middle-sized American City." *Sociological Focus* 23.3 (Aug. 1990) 177–201.

Nelson, David T., ed. *The Diary of Elisabeth Koren, 1853–1855*. Northfield, MN: Norwegian-American Historical Association, 1955.

Nelson, E. Clifford, and Eugene L. Fevold. *The Lutheran Church among Norwegian-Americans*. Minneapolis: Augsburg, 1960.

Nelson, O. N. *History of the Scandinavians and Successful Scandinavians of the United States*. Minneapolis: Haskell, 1901.

Nelson, Paul C. "The Norwegian Lutheran Churches of Northern Story County, Iowa: A History of Their Synodical Differences." *Concordia Historical Institute Quarterly* 48 (1973) 112–34.

Nelson, Phyllis A. "George D. Herron and the Socialist Clergy, 1890–1914." PhD diss., State University of Iowa, 1952.

Nessan, Craig L. "Missionary Theology and Wartburg Theological Seminary." *Currents in Theology and Mission* 31.2 (Apr. 2004) 85–95.

Neufeld, Vernon. "Mennonites Settle in Lee County, Iowa." *Mennonite Life* (Oct. 1953) 170–73.

"New Melleray Abbey." *Pal* 42.3 (Mar. 1961). [Updates 1922 article.]

Newby, James R. *Elton Trueblood: Believer, Teacher & Friend*. New York: HarperCollins, 1990.

Newton, Joseph Fort, ed. *My Idea of God*. Boston: Little, Brown, 1927.

———. *River of Years*. Philadelphia: J. B. Lippincott, 1946.

———. *Sermons Delivered at the Liberal Christian Church Cedar Rapids, Iowa*. Cedar Rapids: 1916.

———. *Some Living Masters of the Pulpit: Studies in Religious Personality*. New York: George H. Doran, 1923.

Neymeyer, Robert J. "In the Full Light of Day: The Ku Klux Klan in 1920s Iowa." *Pal* 76 (1995) 56–63.

Nguyen, Thoi V. *The Making of a Believer: From the Rice Paddies of Viet Nam to the Cornfields of Iowa*. Baltimore: America Star, 2005.

Bibliography

Nichol, Todd. "Wilhelm Lohe, the Iowa Synod and the Ordained Ministry." *Lutheran Quarterly* 4 (Spring 1990) 11–29.

———. "United Norwegian (1890): A Church and a College for the World; Can the Church Be United for Mission?" In *Church Roots: Stories of Nine Immigrant Groups that Became the American Lutheran Church*, edited by Charles P. Lutz. Minneapolis: Fortress, 1985.

Nichols, Larry, and George Mather. *Discovering the Plain Truth: How the Worldwide Church of God Encountered the Gospel of Grace*. Downers Grove, IL: InterVarsity, 1998.

Nichols, Roger L. "Black Hawk and the Historians: A Review Essay." *AI* 75 (2016) 61–79.

Nielsen, Ernest D. *N. F. S. Grundtvig: An American Study*. Rock Island, IL: Augustana, 1955.

Niewenhuis, Nelson. "A New Colony in Northwestern Iowa." *Pal* 59 (Nov. 1978) 182–93.

Niezen, Ronald. *Spirit Wars: Native North American Religions in the Age of Nation Building*. Berkeley: University of California Press, 2000.

Noe, Marcia. *Susan Glaspell: Voice from the Heartland*. Macomb, IL: Western Illinois Press, 1983.

———. *Three Midwestern Playwrights: How Floyd Dell, George Cram Cook, and Susan Glaspell Transformed American Theatre*. Bloomington: Indiana University Press, 2022.

Nofziger, Jacob. "A Further Account of Noah Troyer." In Noah Troyer, *Sermons Delivered by Noah Troyer*, Second Book. Tampico, IL, 1950.

Noll, Mark A. *The Old Religion in the New World*. Grand Rapids: Eerdmans, 2002.

Nollen, John Scholte. *Grinnell College*. Iowa City: SHSI, 1953.

Nolt, Steven M. *A History of the Amish*. Intercourse, PA: Good, 1992.

Nordhoff, Charles. *The Communistic Societies of the United States, From Personal Observations*. New York: Dover, 1966.

Norelius, Eric. *The Pioneer Swedish Settlements and Swedish Lutheran Churches in America 1845–1860*. Translated by Conrad Bergendoff. Rock Island, IL: Augustana Historical Society, 1984.

Norman, Mildred. *Henry's Daughter: My Journey through the 20th Century*, Chandler, AZ: Five Star, 2007.

North, James Brownlee. "The Fundamentalist Controversy among the Disciples of Christ 1890–1930." PhD diss., University of Illinois, 1973.

North Central Iowa Presbytery Bicentennial History. N.p., 1989.

"North Central Presbytery's Congregations." https://web.archive.org/web/20190422095651/ncpwebsite.com/Congregations.htm.

Noun, Louise Rosenfield. "Amelia Bloomer: A Biography." *AI* 47 (1985) 576–621.

———. *Journey to Autonomy: A Memoir*. Ames: Iowa State University Press, 1990.

———. *Strong-Minded Women: The Emergence of the Woman-Suffrage Movement in Iowa*. Ames, IA: Iowa State University Press, 1969.

Noyes, Katherine Macy, ed. *Jesse Macy: An Autobiography*. Springfield, IL: Charles C. Thomas, 1933.

Nutty, Colleen L. "Cemetery Symbolism of Prairie Pioneers: Gravestone Art and Social Change." *Journal of the Iowa Archaeological Society* 31 (1984) 1–36.

Nye, John G. *Between the Rivers: A History of the United Methodist Church in Iowa*. Commission on Archives and History. Lake Mills, IA: 1986.

Bibliography

O'Connor, Father Jim, OCSO. "The Story of an Iowa Monk." *The Iowan* 49.2 (Nov. 2000) 68–69.

Odegard, Peter H. *Pressure Politics: The Story of the Anti-Saloon League.* New York: Columbia University Press, 1928.

Offenburger, Chuck. *Babe: An Iowa Legend.* Ames: Iowa State University Press, 1989.

Ogburn. Carl. "The Pioneer Religious Revival." *AI* 15 (Jan. 1927) 483–506.

Okihiru, Gary Y. *Storied Lives: Japanese-American Students and World War II.* Seattle: University of Washington Press, 1999.

"Old Order River Brethren Counties (2010)." ARDA. https://web.archive.org/web/20220729163649/www.thearda.com/ql2010/QL_C_2010_2_1131c.asp.

Olson, Oscar N. *The Augustana Lutheran Church in America, Pioneer Period, 1846–1860.* Rock Island, IL: Augustana, 1950.

Olson, Roger E., et al. *Handbook of Denominations in the United States,* 14th ed. Nashville: Abingdon, 2018.

Olsson, Karl A. *By One Spirit.* Chicago: Covenant, 1962.

Omrcanin, Margaret Stewar. *Ruth Suckow: A Critical Study of Her Fiction.* Philadelphia: Dorrance, 1972.

Oostendorp, L. H. P. *Scholte, Leader of the Secession of 1844 and Founder of Pella.* Eastmanville, MI, n.d.

Oppedal, Al. "The Scandinavian Heritage in Our Country Churches." *Iowan* 20 (Summer 1972) 25–27.

Orme-Johnson, David W., et al. "International Peace Project in the Middle East: The Effects of the Maharishi Technology on the Unified Field." *Journal of Conflict Resolution* 32 (1988) 773–812.

Orsi, Robert, ed. *Gods of the City.* Bloomington: Indiana University Press, 1999.

"Orthodox Christianity in Iowa." St. George Greek Orthodox Church. stgeorge.ia.goarch.org/about/orthodox-christianity-in-iowa

Osborn, Cal. "The Pioneer Religious Revival." *AI* 15 (1927) 483–506.

Ossian, Lisa. *The Home Fronts of Iowa, 1939–1945.* Columbia, MO: University of Missouri Press, 2009.

———. "The Home Fronts of Iowa, 1940–1945." PhD. diss., Iowa State University, 1998.

Ostergren, Robert C. "The Immigrant Church as a Symbol of Community in the Upper Midwest." *Great Plains Quarterly* 1 (1981) 225–38.

Ostler, Jeffrey. *The Plains Indians and U.S. Colonialism from Lewis and Clark to Wounded Knee.* Cambridge: Cambridge University Press, 2004.

———. *Prairie Populism: The Fate of Agrarian Radicalism in Kansas, Nebraska, and Iowa, 1880-1892.* Lawrence, KS: University Press of Kansas, 1993.

———. *Surviving Genocide: Native Nations and the United States from the American Revolution to Bleeding Kansas.* New Haven, 2019.

Ostling, Richard. "Ask Any Church-State Lawyer and You'll Hear That This Is a Hard Question: What Is Religion?" Religion Unplugged, February 27, 2021.

Ostrander, Rick. "The Practice of Prayer in a Modern Age: Liberals, Fundamentalists, and Prayer in the Early Twentieth Century." In *Practicing Protestants: Histories of Christian Life in America 1630–1965,* edited by Laurie F. Maffly-Kipp, et al., 177–95. Baltimore: Johns Hopkins University Press, 2006.

Otjen, Nathaniel. "Creating a Barrio in Iowa City, 1916–1936: Mexican Section Laborers and the Chicago, Rock Island, and Pacific Railroad Company." *AI* 76 (2017) 406–32.

Bibliography

Ottersberg, Gerhardt. *Wilhelm Loehe and Wartburg Theological Seminary.* Waverly, IA: 1972.

Otting, Rev. Loras, ed. *Letters to a Pioneer Bishop, Correspondence to Mathias Loras, D.D., First Bishop of Dubuque.* Dubuque, IA: Loras College Press, 2009.

Our First 100 Years of Serving Our Lord: First Presbyterian Church Near Ely, Iowa. Ely, IA, 2015.

"Our History." WesternHome Communities. https://westernhomecommunities.org/history.

"Our Story." First Presbyterian Church of Ft. Dodge. http://fpcfd.org/about-us/our-story.

"Our Story." First Presbyterian Church of Waterloo. http://www.1stpresby.org/our-story.html.

"Our Story." Pentecostal Church of God. https://www.pcg.org/about/our-story.

Ozieblo, Barbara. *Susan Glaspell: A Critical Biography.* Chapel Hill: University of North Carolina Press, 2000.

Page, Kirby. *Social Evangelist: The Autobiography of a Twentieth-Century Prophet for Peace.* Nyack, NY: Fellowship, 1975.

Pals, Daniel L. *Seven Theories of Religion.* New York, 1996.

Pannabecker, Samuel Floyd. *Open Doors: A History of the General Conference Mennonite Church.* Newton, KS: Faith & Life, 1975.

Papa, Stephan. *The Last Man Jailed For Blasphemy.* Franklin, NC, 1998.

"Papua New Guinea Museum." Wartburg Seminary. https://www.wartburgseminary.edu/papua-new-guinea-museum-2.

Park, Benjamin E. *Kingdom of Nauvoo: The Rise and Fall of a Religious Empire on the American Frontier.* New York: Liveright, 2020.

Parsons, Elaine Franz. "Slaves to the Bottle: Smith's Civil Damage Liquor Law." *AI* 59 (2004) 347–73.

Pasquier, Michael, ed. *Gods of the Mississippi.* Bloomington: Indiana University Press, 2013.

Passet, Joanne. "Yours for Liberty: Women and Freethought in Nineteenth-Century Iowa." *AI* 63 (2004) 137–69.

Pawley, Christine. *Reading on the Middle Border: The Culture of Print in Late Nineteenth Century Osage, Iowa.* Amherst: University of Massachusetts Press, 2001.

Pearson, B. H. *The Vision Lives: A Profile of Mrs. Charles E. Cowman, Author of "Streams in the Desert."* Ft. Washington, PA: OMS, 1972.

Pearson, Maria D. "Give Me Back My People's Bones: Repatriation and Reburial of American Indian Remains in Iowa." In *The Worlds Between Two Rivers: Perspectives on American Indians in Iowa, Expanded Edition,* edited by Gretchen M. Bataille, et al., 131–34. Iowa City: University of Iowa Press, 2000.

Pegram, Thomas P. *Battling Demon Rum: The Struggle for a Dry America, 1800–1933.* Chicago: Ivan R. Dee, 1998.

Pehl, Matthew. *The Making of Working-Class Religion.* Urbana: University of Illinois Press, 2016.

Perkins, George D. "Two Lay Sermons," *Pal* 5:8 (Aug. 1924) 305–17.

Perkins, William Rufus. *History of the Trappist Abbey of New Melleray, in Dubuque County, Iowa.* Iowa City: University of Iowa, 1892.

Perkins, William, and Barthinius L. Wick. *History of the Amana Society.* Iowa City: University of Iowa Press, 1891. (Facsimile reprint, New York: Arno, 1975.)

Bibliography

Persinger, Michael A., Normand J. Carrey, and Lynn A. Suess. *TM and Cult Mania*. North Quincy, MA, 1980.

Persons, Stow. "Comment." *AI* 47 (1983) 157.

Peters, Shawn Francis. *Judging Jehovah's Witnesses: Religious Persecution and the Dawn of the Rights Revolution*. Lawrence: University Press of Kansas, 2000.

Petersen, William J. *A Brief History of the American Sunday-School Union*. Philadelphia: ASSU, 1969.

———. *Methodist Almanac 1866*. Facsimile reproduction. Iowa City, 1965.

———. "Mormons on the March." *Pal* 27.5 (May 1946) 142–57.

———. "Religion and Morality." *Pal* 19.6 (Jun. 1938) 215–29.

———. "Scattergood School in 1962." *Pal* 43.7 (Jul. 1962) 334–36.

———. *The Story of Iowa: The Progress of an American State*. New York: Lewis Historical, 1952.

Peterson, Derek, and Darren Walhof, eds. *The Invention of Religion: Rethinking Belief in Politics and History*. New Brunswick, NJ: Rutgers University Press, 2002.

Peterson, H. C., and Gilbert C. Fite. *Opponents of War, 1917–1918*. Seattle: University of Washington Press, 1957.

Peterson, James A. *Slater of Iowa*. Chicago: Hinckley & Schmitt, 1958.

Peterson, Peter L. "Language and Loyalty: Governor Harding and Iowa's Danish-Americans during World War I." *AI* 42 (1974) 404–43.

Peterson, Walter F. "Burns Chapel: The Little White Church and the Westward Movement." *AI* 36 (1963) 605–9.

Pettys, Todd E. *The Iowa State Constitution*. 2nd edition. Oxford: Oxford University Press, 2018.

Pfeifer, Michael J. "The Making of a Midwestern Catholicism: Identities, Ethnicity, and Catholic Culture in Iowa City, 1840–1940." *AI* 76 (2017) 290–315.

———. *The Making of American Catholicism: Regional Culture and the Catholic Experience*. New York: NYU Press, 2020.

Phillips, Ruth B. ""Clothed in Blessing: Meaning in Mesquakie Costume." *AI* 51 (1991) 1–25.

Phipps, Barry. *Between Gravity and What Cheer: Iowa Photographs*. Iowa City: University of Iowa Press, 2018.

Pickett, Clarence E. *And Having Done All, to Stand*. Philadelphia: Young Friends, 1951.

———. *For More Than Bread: An Autobiographical Account of Twenty-two Years' Work with the American Friends Service Committee*. Boston: Little, Brown, 1953.

———. *God's Faith in Us*. Philadelphia: American Friends Fellowship Council, 1953.

Piehler, G. Kurt. *A Religious History of the American GI in World War II*. Lincoln: University of Nebraska Press, 2021.

Piper, John F., Jr. *The American Churches in World War I*. Athens: Ohio University Press, 1985.

Pins, Kenneth. "In the Steeple's Shadow: The Parish Town in a Secular World." In *Family Reunion: Essays on Iowa*, edited by Thomas J. Morain, 136–44. Ames, IA: Iowa State University Press, 1995.

Pitcher, Milo. *My Heritage on Hominyridge*. [Marshalltown, IA], 1977.

Plumb, Beatrice. *"The Goodwill Man": Edgar James Helms*. Minneapolis: T. S. Denison, 1965.

Polenberg, Richard. *Fighting Faiths*. New York: Penguin, 1987.

Pope-Levison, Priscilla. "A 'Thirty Year War' and More: Exploring Complexities in the Methodist Deaconess Movement." *MH* 47 (2009) 111–33.

Bibliography

Porterfield, Amanda. *The Transformation of American Religion: The Story of a Late Twentieth-Century Awakening*. Oxford: Oxford University Press, 2001.
Postal, Bernard, and Lionel Koppman. *American Jewish Landmarks: A Travel Guide and History, Volume III: The Middlewest*. New York: Fleet, 1984.
Power, Richard Lyle. *Planting Corn Belt Culture: The Impress of the Upland Southerner and the Yankee in the Old Northwest*. Indianapolis: Bobbs-Merrill, 1953.
"A Practical Man of God: Here Is the Life of a Typical U.S. Parson," *Life*, Feb. 3, 1941, 55–63.
Pratt, LeRoy G. *From Cabin to Capital City*. [Johnston, IA], 1990.
Prichard, Robert. *A History of the Episcopal Church*. Harrisburg, PA: Morehouse, 1991.
Proescholdt, Kevin. "New Sweden, Iowa: A Narrative History, 1845–1880." Undergraduate thesis, Iowa State University, 1977.
Prohibition in Iowa. New York: National Temperance Society, 1889.
Pruitt, Nicholas T. *Open Hearts, Closed Doors: Immigration Reform and the Waning of Mainline Protestantism*. New York: NYU Press, 2021.
Pryor, Mrs. J. C. *History of the First Congregational Church, Burlington, Iowa*. 1957.
Public Religion Research Institute. 2020 Census of American Religion. "American Religious Identity at the County Level." July 8, 2021.
Putney, Clifford. *Muscular Christianity*. Cambridge: Harvard University Press, 2001.
Putz, Paul Emory. "Building a City on a Hill: Evangelical Protestant Men and Moral Reform Under the Des Moines Plan, 1907–1916." *AI* 77 (2018) 1–40.
Qualey, Carlton C., ed. "Claus L. Clausen: Pioneer Pastor and Settlement Promoter." *Norwegian-American Studies and Records* 6 (1931) 12–29.
Queen, Edward, et al. *The Encyclopedia of American Religious History*. New York: Facts on File, 1996.
Quick, Herbert. *The Fairview Idea*. Indianapolis: Bobbs-Merrill, 1919.
———. *One Man's Life*. Indianapolis: Bobbs-Merrill, 1925.
———. *Vandemark's Folly*. New York: A. L. Burt, 1922.
Quinn, Michael D. *Mormon Hierarchy: Origins of Power*. Salt Lake City: Signature, 1994.
Quinter, Mary N. *Life and Sermons of Elder James Quinter*. Mt. Morris, IL: Brethren, 1891.
Quinton, Mrs. Harlan B. "Early Denmark and Denmark Academy." *AI* 7 (1905) 16–29.
Rabben, Linda A. "The Utopian Vision of George D. Herron: The History of a Life after Grinnell." *Grinnell Magazine* (Apr.-May 1981) 23–26.
Rabin, Shari. *Jews on the Frontier*. New York: NYU Press, 2017.
———. "'A Nest to the Wandering Bird': Iowa and the Creation of American Judaism, 1855–1877." *AI* 73 (2014) 101–27.
Rable, George C. *God's Almost Chosen Peoples: A Religious History of the American Civil War*. Chapel Hill: University of North Carolina Press, 2010.
Radin, Paul. *The Winnebago Tribe*. Lincoln: University of Nebraska Press, 1990.
Raid, Howard. "Donnellson Migrations Analyzed: The Migration from a Rural Community." *Mennonite Life* (Apr. 1960) 62–63, 91.
———. "Farm Succession at Donnellson, Iowa." *Mennonite Life* (Apr. 1960) 60–61.
Ratke, David C. *Confession and Mission, Word and Sacrament: The Ecclesial Theology of Wilhelm Lohe*. St. Louis: CPH, 2001.
Ready to Harvest. YouTube channel. https://www.youtube.com/c/ReadyToHarvest.
Redford, M. E. *The Rise of the Church of the Nazarene*. Kansas City: Nazarene, 1961.

Bibliography

Reed, Julius. *Reminiscences of Early Congregationalism in Iowa.* Grinnell, IA: Herald, 1885.

Reformed Church in America. *Minutes of the Particular Synod of Iowa.* Prairie City, IA, 1950.

"Religion and Ethics: The Latest Heretic—George Burman Foster." *Current Literature* 47 (Aug. 1909) 174–79.

Reschly, Steven R. *The Amish on the Iowa Prairie: 1840 to 1910.* Baltimore: John Hopkins Univerrity Press, 2000.

———. "'The Parents Shall Not Go Unpunished': Preservationist Patriarch and Community." In *Strangers at Home: Amish and Mennonite Women in History,* edited by Kimberly D. Schmidt, et al., 160–81. Baltimore: Johns Hopkins University Press, 2002, .

Rettig, Lawrence. *Amana Today: A History of the Amana Colonies from 1932 to the Present.* South Amana, IA: Amana, 1975.

Reu, M. *An Explanation of Dr. Martin Luther's Small Catechism.* Columbus, OH: Wartburg, 1946.

Reymon, Ronald. "David Lowry and the Winnebago Indian School, 1833–1848." *Journal of Presbyterian History* 56 (1978) 108–18.

Reynolds, David R. "The Making of Buck Creek: Country Life Reform, Religion, and Rural School Consolidation." *AI* 58 (1999) 351–87.

Reynolds, David S. *John Brown: Abolitionist.* New York: Knopf, 2005.

Richey, Russell E., et al. *Methodist Experience in America: A History, Vol. I.* Nashville: Abingdon, 2010.

Richling, Barnett. "The Amana Society: A Study of Change." *Pal* 58.2 (Summer 1977) 34–47.

Richman, Irving B. "Congregational Life in Muscatine." *IJH* 21.3 (July 1923) 347–72.

———. *Ioway to Iowa: The Genesis of a Corn and Bible Commonwealth.* Iowa City: State Historical Society of Iowa, 1931.

Rietveld, Ronald D. "Hendrick Peter Scholte and the Land of Promise." *AI* 48 (1986) 135–54.

Rigal, Laura. "No Place to Call Home: The Winnebago Removal of 1848." *Wapsipinicon Almanac* 25, 104–11.

Righter, Walter C. *A Pilgrim's Way.* New York: Knopf, 1998.

Riley, Rachel Katherine Daack. "BVM Catholic Schools and Teachers: A Nineteenth Century U.S. School System." PhD. diss., University of Iowa, 2009.

Riney-Kehrberg, Pamela. *When a Dream Dies: Agriculture, Iowa, and the Farm Crisis of the 1980s.* Lawrence: University Press of Kansas, 2022.

Risen, Clay. *The Bill of the Century: The Epic Battle for the Civil Rights Act.* New York: Bloomsbury, 2014.

Ritchey, Charles J. *Drake University Through Seventy-Five Years, 1881–1956.* Des Moines: Drake University, 1956.

Riverview Remembers 1917–1982. [Cedar Falls, IA? 1982?]

Roba, William. "Einwanderung: Germans Forced Out of Their Homeland in the 1850s." *German-Iowan Studies: Selected Essays.* New York: Lang, 2004.

Robert, Dana. *American Women in Mission.* Macon, GA: Mercer University Press, 1996.

Roberts, David. *Devil's Gate: Brigham Young and the Great Mormon Handcart Tragedy.* New York: Simon & Schuster, 2008.

Roberts, Ron. "Ammon Hennacy in Des Moines." *Via Pacis* 28.4 (Dec. 12, 2004) 1, 4.

Bibliography

———., ed. *Iowa's Ethnic Roots*. Dubuque, IA: Kendall/Hunt, 1993.
Robeson, Geo. F. "Henry Clay Dean." *Pal* 5.9 (Sep. 1924) 321–33.
Robinson, Floyd A. *This Is Home Now*. Ames, IA: Iowa State University Press, 1983.
Robinson, Joann Ooiman. *Abraham Went Out: A Biography of A. J. Muste*. Philadelphia: Temple University Press, 1981.
Robinson, Marilynne. *Death of Adam*. New York: Houghton Mifflin, 1998.
———. *The Givenness of Things*. New York: Farrar, Straus & Giroux, 2015.
———. *Gilead*. New York: Farrar, Straus & Giroux, 2004.
———. *Home*. New York: Farrar, Straus & Giroux, 2008.
———. *Jack*. New York: Farrar, Straus & Giroux, 2020.
———. *Lila*. New York: HarperCollins, 2014.
———. *When I Was a Child I Read Books*. New York: Picador, 2012.
Rodabaugh, Willis P., and A. H. Brower. *History of the Church of the Brethren in Southern Iowa*. Elgin, IL: Brethren, 1924.
Roder, Richard J. *Frontiers of Faith: A History of the Diocese of Sioux City*. Sioux City: Catholic Diocese, 2001.
Rogers, Hope. *Time and the Human Robot*. Vinton, IA: Inkspot, 1975.
Rohne, J. Magnus. *Norwegian-American Lutheranism up to 1872*. New York: Macmillan, 1926.
Rohrer, James R. "German Presbyterians or Christian Americans? Intercollegiate Sports and the Identity Crisis at the University of Dubuque, 1902–1927." *American Presbyterians* 74 (1996) 183–94.
———. *Keepers of the Covenant: Frontier Missions and the Decline of Congregationalism, 1774–1818*. New York: Oxford University Press, 1995.
Rohrer, S. Scott. *Wandering Souls: Protestant Migrations in America, 1630–1985*. Chapel Hill: University of North Carolina Press, 2010.
Ronk, Albert T. *History of the Brethren Church*. Ashland, OH: Brethren, 1968.
Rorabaugh, W. J. *Alcoholic Republic: An American Tradition*. Oxford: Oxford University Press, 1979.
Rose, Darlene Deibler. *Evidence Not Seen: A Woman's Miraculous Faith in a Japanese Prison during World War II*. San Francisco: Harper & Row, 1988.
Rose, Donna. *Transcendental Meditation Movement: The Creation, Development and Institutionalization of a World View*. PhD. diss., Southern Illinois University, 1976.
Rosenberg, Morton M. *Iowa on the Eve of the Civil War: A Decade of Frontier Politics*. Norman: University of Oklahoma Press, 1972.
Rosenthal. Erich. "Studies of Jewish Intermarriage in the U.S." *American Jewish Yearbook* 64 (1963) 3–53.
Rosenthal, Frank. *The Jews of Des Moines: The First Century*. Des Moines: Jewish Welfare Federation, 1957.
Rosheim, David, ed. *The Four Sisters: Iowa's State Psychiatric Hospitals, Vol. 3: Journals and Articles*. Maquoketa: Andromeda, 2015.
Ross, Earle D. *Democracy's College: The Land Grant College in Its Formative Stage*. New York: Arno, 1969.
Ross, Michael A. *Justice of Shattered Dreams: Samuel Freeman Miller and the Supreme Court during the Civil War Era*. Baton Rouge: LSU Press, 2003.
Ross, Russell M. "The Development of the Iowa Constitution of 1857." *IJH* 55 (1957) 97–114.
Roth, Sister Mary Augustine, R.S.M. *Written in His Hands: The Sisters of Mercy of Cedar Rapids, Iowa, 1875–1975*. Cedar Rapids, IA: Laurance 1976.

Bibliography

Roth, Robert. *The Natural Law Party: A Reason to Vote.* New York: St. Martins, 1998.

———. *Transcendental Meditation.* New York: Plume, 1988.

Rothermund, Dietmar. *The Layman's Progress: Religious and Political Experience in Colonial Pennsylvania, 1740–70.* Philadelphia: University of Pennsylvania Press, 1961.

Rozendaal, Neal. *Duke Slater: Pioneering Black NFL Player and Judge.* Jefferson, NC: McFarland, 2012.

Ruff, Henrietta. *Seasons to Remember: Recollections of an Amana Childhood.* Deep River, IA: Brennan, 1996.

Rugg, Peter. "Will America's Oldest Muslim Community Survive President Trump?" *Rolling Stone*, Feb. 22, 2017.

Rupp, Joyce. *Fresh Bread and Other Gifts of Spiritual Nourishment.* Notre Dame, IN: Ave Maria, 1985.

———. *Open the Door: A Journey to the True Self.* Notre Dame, IN: Ave Maria, 2008.

Russell, C. Allyn. *Voices of American Fundamentalism: Seven Biographical Studies.* Philadelphia: WJK, 1996.

Russell, Charles Edward. *Bare Hands and Stone Walls: Some Recollections of a Side-Line Reformer.* New York: Scribner, 1933.

Ryan, Thomas G. "Supporters and Opponents of Prohibition: Iowa in 1917." *AI* 46 (1983) 510–22.

Saathoff, John A. "Eastfriesen in the United States." Master's thesis, State University of Iowa, 1930.

Sage, Leland L. *A History of Iowa.* Ames, IA: Iowa State University Press, 1974.

"St. Gabriel and All Angels." http://stgabe.org/.

"St. Gabriel's Monastery." DMHS Historygram email, August 21, 2021.

St. John, Burton, ed. *North American Students and World Advance: Addresses Delivered at the Eighth International Convention of the Student Volunteer Movement for Foreign Missions, Des Moines, Iowa, December 31, 1919 to January 4, 1920.* New York: SVM, 1920.

Salter, Mary Jo. "Foreword." In *Collected Works of Amy Clampitt.* New York: Alfred A. Knopf, 1999.

Salter, William. "1821–1910, A Memorial." *AI* 9:8 (Jan. 1911)

———. "Early Days with the Christian Commission: A Diary." Edited by Philip D. Jordan. *IJH* 33 (1935) 123–54.

———. *A Sermon Preached at the Congregational Church of Burlington, Iowa, in Commemoration of the Fiftieth Anniversary of Its Original Formation.* Burlington, IA, 1888.

———. *Sixty Years,* Boston: Pilgrim, 1907.

Saltzman, Eleanor. *Stuart's Hill.* New York: Bernard Ackerman, 1945.

"The Salvation Army." Historical Marker Project. https://historicalmarkerproject.com/markers/HMNFN_backtoHMNFN.html.

Sampson, Francis L. *Look Out Below! A Story of the Airborne by a Paratrooper Padre.* Washington, DC: CUA, 1958.

Sandberg, Carl. *Billy Sunday and Other Poems.* Orlando: Harcourt, 1993.

Sanders, Annmarie, ed. *However Long the Night: A Spiritual Journey of the Leadership Conference of Women Religious (LCWR).* N.p., 2018.

Sangharakshita, Bhiksu. *Anagarika Dharmapala: A Biographical Sketch.* Kandy, Ceylon: Buddhist, 1964.

Bibliography

Sarna, Jonathan D. *American Judaism: A History.* New Haven: Yale University Press, 2004.

Saroyan, Alex. *The Turning Point: How Men of Conscience Brought About Major Change in the Care of America's Mentally Ill.* Washington, 1994.

Schaap, James Calvin. *Crossing Over: Stories of Asian Refugee Christians.* Sioux Center, IA: Dordt College Press, 2006.

———. *Fifty-Five and Counting: Essays and Stories.* Sioux Center: Dordt College Press, 2004.

———. *Finding Christmas.* Grand Rapids: Revell, 2005.

———. "Frederick Manfred: An Elegy for the Man." *Origins* 24.2 (2006) 4–15.

———. *Intermission.* Grand Rapids: CRC, 1987.

———. *Our Family Album: The Unfinished Story of the Christian Reformed Church.* Grand Rapids, 1998.

———. *The Secrets of Barneveld Calvary,* Grand Rapids: Baker, 1997.

———. *Sign of a Promise,* Sioux Center: Dordt College Press, 1979.

———., ed. *Speaking of Pastors: Parishioners Tell Their Stories.* Grand Rapids: Christian Reformed Church in North America, 2006.

———. *Thirty-Five and Counting: Essays and Stories.* Sioux Center, IA: Dordt College Press, 1985.

———. *Touches the Sky.* Grand Rapids: Revell, 2003.

Schapsmeier, Edward L., and Frederick H. Schapsmeier. *Henry A. Wallace: The Agrarian Years, 1910–1940.* Ames, IA: Iowa State University Press, 1968.

———. "Religion and Reform: A Case Study of Henry A. Wallace and Ezra Taft Benson." *Journal of Church and State* 21 (1979) 525–35.

Scheumer, Gottlieb. *Inspirations-Historie.* 3 vol. Translated by Janet W. Zuber. Amana: Amana Church Society, 1987.

Schlabach, Theron F. *Peace, Faith, Nation: Mennonites and Amish in Nineteenth-Century America.* Scottdale, PA: Herald, 1988.

Schmidt, Leigh Eric. *Village Atheists: How America's Unbelievers Made Their Way in a Godly Nation.* Princeton: Princeton University Press, 2016.

Schmidt, Madeleine M. CHM, *Seasons of Growth: History of the Diocese of Davenport, 1881–1981.* Davenport, IA: Diocese of Davenport, 1981.

Schmitt, Tim. "Heaven or Hell?" *Cityview*, Feb. 28, 2001.

Schmitt, Tom. *Places of Prayer and Celebration: The Diocese of Des Moines.* N.p., 2006.

Schneider, Carl. *German Church on the American Frontier.* St. Louis: Eden, 1939.

Schneider, Paul. *Old Man River: The Mississippi River in North American History.* New York: Holt, 2013.

Schnieder, Hans. *German Radical Pietism.* Lanham, MD: Routledge, 2007.

Schnucker, George. *The German Element in the Reformed Church in America.* Aplington, IA, 1928.

Scholte, H. P. "Two Letters from Pella." *Origins* 4:2 (1986) 24–27.

Scholte, Leonora. *A Stranger in a Strange Land.* Iowa City: State Historical Society of Iowa, 1985.

The School of Religion at the University of Iowa: The First Seventy Years. Iowa City, 1997.

Schrader, Gus. "Duke Slater: Helmetless Star Was an All-American on, off Field." In *Greatest Moments in Iowa Hawkeyes Football History,* ed. Mark Dukes and Gus Schrader. Chicago: Triumph, 1998.

Schuller, Robert H. *My Journey.* San Francisco: HarperCollins, 2001.

Bibliography

Schultz, Kevin M. *Tri-Faith America: How Catholics and Jews Held Postwar America to Its Protestant Promise.* Oxford: Oxford University Press, 2011.

Schuessler, Ryan. "The Last of Iowa's Small-town Synagogues: Seven Members Still Praying." *Guardian*, Feb. 24, 2016.

Schwalm, Leslie A. *Emancipation's Diaspora: Race and Reconstruction in the Upper Midwest.* Chapel Hill: University of North Carolina Press, 2009.

Schwartz, Hillel. *The French Prophets: The History of a Millenarian Group in Eighteenth Century England.* Berkeley: University of California Press, 1980.

Schwartz, Sally. *"A Mixed Multitude": The Struggle for Toleration in Colonial Pennsylvania.* New York: New York University Press, 1988.

Schwarz, Fred. *Beating the Unbeatable Foe: One Man's Victory over Communism, Leviathan, and the Last Enemy.* Washington, DC: Regnery, 1996.

———. *Heart Mind, and Soul of Communism.* [Waterloo, IA?]: Christian Anti-Communism Crusade, 1952.

Schwieder, Elmer, and Dorothy Schwieder. "The Beachy Amish in Iowa: A Case Study." *MQR* 51 (1977) 41–51.

Schwieder, Dorothy. *Black Diamonds: Life and Work in Iowa's Coal Mining Communities, 1895–1925.* Ames, IA: Iowa State University Press, 1983.

———. *Buxton: Work and Racial Equality in a Coal Mining Community.* Ames, IA: Iowa State University Press, 1987.

———. "The Paradox of Change in the Life Style of Iowa's Old Order Amish." *International Review of Modern Sociology* 6 (Spring 1976) 65–74.

———. *A Peculiar People: Iowa's Old Order Amish.* Ames, IA: Iowa State University Press, 1975.

———. "A Rare Visit to an Amish Home." *Iowan* 25.1 (Fall 1976) 18–21.

———. "Utopia in the Midwest: the Old Order Amish and the Hutterites." *Pal* 54.3 (May 1973) 9–23.

"Scotch Grove Presbyterian Church, Scotch Grove, Iowa" and "Center Junction Presbyterian Church, Center Junction, Iowa." *Journal of Presbyterian History* 19.2 (Fall 2013), 94, 95.

Scot, Barbara J. *Prairie Reunion.* New York: Farrar, Straus & Giroux, 1996.

Scott, James Leander. *A Journal of a Missionary Tour.* Providence: Self-published, 1966.

Scott County Historical Society. *Early Churches of Scott County Prior to 1900.* N.p., 1981.

Scott v. Thompson. 21 Iowa 799–603.

Seager, Richard Hughes. *The World's Parliament of Religions: The East/West Encounter, 1893.* Bloomington: Indiana University Press, 1995.

"Search Online King Records Access (OKRA)." https://okra.stanford.edu.

Seariac, Hanna. "Mormon Group Digging for Scriptural City of Zarahemla in Iowa is a Portrait of Religious Nationalism." Religion Dispatches, Dec. 15, 2021. https://religiondispatches.org/mormon-group-digging-for-scriptural-city-of-zarahemla-in-iowa-is-a-portrait-of-religious-nationalism.

Sellers v. Johnson. 163 F. 2d 848, 69 F. Supp. 778.

Senden, S. M. *Red Oak.* Charleston: History, 2008.

Senik, Troy. *A Man of Iron: The Turbulent Life and Improbable Presidency of Grover Cleveland.* New York: Threshold, 2022.

Shambaugh, Benjamin F. *The Constitution of Iowa.* Iowa City: State Historical Society, 1934.

Bibliography

Shambaugh, Bertha. *Amana: The Community of True Inspiration*. Iowa City: Penfield, 1908, 1988.

Sharlet, Jeff. *The Family: The Secret Fundamentalism at the Heart of American Power*. New York: Harper, 2008.

Shaw, Marian. *World's Fair Notes: A Woman Journalist Views Chicago's 1893 Columbian Exposition*. N.p., 1992.

Shepard, Bill. "Stealing at Mormon Nauvoo." *John Whitmer Historical Association Journal* 23 (2003) 99–110.

Sherlock, Wallace E. "A Church That Refused to Die." *AI* 32 (1954) 376–79.

Sherman, Bill. *Talk of Iowa*, Oct. 17, 2005.

Sheronick, Hussien Ahmed. "A History of the Cedar Rapids Muslim Community: The Search for an American Islamic Identity." Honors paper, Coe College, 1988.

Sherwood, Robert E. *Roosevelt and Hopkins: An Intimate History*. New York: Harper, 1948.

Shideler, Mary McDermott. *Consciousness of Battle: An Interim Report on a Theological Journey*. Grand Rapids: Eerdmans, 1979.

Shockley, Grant S. *Heritage and Hope: The African American Presence in United Methodism*. Nashville: Abingdon, 1991.

Short, Mrs. Wallace M. [Mary Eliza Morse]. *Just One American*. [Sioux City], 1943.

Short, Wallace M. *The Deeper Meaning of the "Temperance" Question*. Kansas City: Hyde Park, 1915.

———. *Let There Be Light: A Study in Freedom and Faith[,] Being a Review of Six Years Ministry in Sioux City, Iowa*. Kansas City: Hyde Park, 1916.

Showalter, Nathan D. *The End of a Crusade: The Student Volunteer Movement for Foreign Missions and the Great War*. Lanham, MD: University Press of America, 1998.

Shroder, Tom. *The Greatest Novelist Who Ever Lived*. New York: Blue Rider, 2016.

Shuman, Bernard. *A History of the Sioux City Jewish Community, 1869–1969*. Sioux City, IA: Jewish Federation, 1969.

Shumsky, Susan. *Maharishi and Me: Seeking Enlightenment with the Beatles' Guru*. New York: Skyhorse, 2018.

Sibley, Mulford Q., and Philip Jacob. *Conscription of Conscience*, Ithaca: Cornell University Press, 1952.

Siegel, Aryeh. "Why Did Chicago Public Schools Just Quietly Drop Transcendental Meditation?" Religion Dispatches, June 24, 2020. https://religiondispatches.org/exclusive-why-did-chicago-public-schools-just-quietly-drop-transcendental-meditation.

Sigmund, Jay G. "The Converts." In *Wapsipinicon Tales*, 33–42. Cedar Rapids, 1927.

Sillanpa, Tom. *Annie Wittenmyer: God's Angel*. Hamilton, IL: Signal, 1972.

Silverberg, Robert. *The Mound Builders*. Athens, OH: Ohio University Press, 1986.

Simon, Ed. "Why Are U.S. Borders Straight Lines?" JSTOR Daily, Oct. 20, 2018.

Singleton, George. *Romance of African Methodism*. New York: Exposition, 1952.

Sinha, Manisha. *The Slave's Cause: A History of Abolition*. New Haven: Yale University Press, 2016.

Skipper, John C. *Meredith Willson: The Unsinkable Music Man*. El Dorado Hills, CA: Savas, 2003.

Skjelver, Mabel C. "Randall's Congregational Church in Iowa City." *AI* 42 (1974) 361–70.

Smiley, Jane. *Early Warning*. New York: Anchor, 2015.

Bibliography

―――. *Some Luck*. New York: Anchor, 2014.

Smith, Andrew F. *The Saintly Scoundrel: The Life and Times of Dr. John Cook Bennett*. Urbana: University of Illinois Press, 1997.

Smith, Brett H. "Reversing the Curse: Agricultural Millennialism at the Illinois Industrial University." *CH* 73 (2004) 759–91.

Smith, Hazel. "The Negro Churches in Iowa." Master's thesis, State University of Iowa, 1926.

Smith, Martha Browning. "The Story of Icaria." *AI* 38 (1965) 36–64.

Smith, Page. *The Rise of Industrial America: A People's History of the Post-Reconstruction Era*. New York: Penguin, 1984.

Smith, Seymour A. *Religious Cooperation in State Universities: An Historical Sketch*. Ann Arbor: University of Michigan, 1957.

Smith, Timothy L. *Called unto Holiness: The Story of the Nazarenes: The Formative Years*. Kansas City: Nazarene, 1962.

Smith, Thomas S. "A Martyr for Prohibition: The Murder of Reverend George C. Haddock." *Pal* 62.6 (Nov. 1981) 186–93.

Smoak, Gregory C. *Ghost Dances and Identity: Prophetic Religion and American Indian Ethnogenesis in the Nineteenth Century*. Berkeley: University of California Press, 2006.

Snavely, Ida B. *Orange Township Lore, Pieced into a Patchwork*. 3rd ed. [Waterloo, IA, 2002].

Snyder, Charles E. "Unitarianism in Iowa." *Pal* 30:11 (Nov. 1949) 345–76.

Snyder, Lillian M. *The Search for Brotherhood, Peace & Justice: The Story of Icaria*. Deep River, IA, 1996.

"Social Action." Diocese of Davenport. https://davenportdiocese.org/past-recipients.

Soderstrom, Hugo. *Confession and Cooperation: The Policy of the Augustana Synod and the Synod's Relations with other Churches up to the Beginning of the Twentieth Century*. Lund, Sweden: CWK Gleerop, 1973.

Soike, Lowell J. *Necessary Courage: Iowa's Underground Railroad in the Struggle against Slavery*. Iowa City: University of Iowa Press, 2013.

Soland, Martha Jordan. "William Salter: Portrait of a Pioneer Preacher." *Pal* 54:4 (Jul. 1973) 2–15.

Sorin, Gerald. *Tradition Transformed: The Jewish Experience in America*. Baltimore: Johns Hopkins University Press, 1997.

Souvenir of Presbyterian Iowa, in Commemoration of the 118th General Assembly in Des Moines, Iowa, May 17, 1906.

Special Commemorative Issue: Mormon Handcart Trek. *AI* 65.2–3 (2006).

Spence, Hartzell. *Get Thee Behind Me: My Life as a Preacher's Son*. New York: McGraw Hill, 1942.

―――. *One Foot in Heaven: The Life of a Practical Parson*. New York: Grosset & Dunlap, 1940.

―――. *The Story of American Religions*. New York: Abingdon, 1960.

Spence, Mary Crowther. *The Preacher's Wife*. Fairmont, MN: Ruth Barnes, n.d.

Spencer, Carole D. "Evangelism, Feminism and Social Reform: The Quaker Woman Minister and the Holiness Revival." *Quaker History* 80 (1991) 24–48.

Spencer, Dick, III. "Powwow Time." *Pal* 48 (1967) 260–80.

Spiegelman, William, ed. *"Love, Amy": The Selected Letters of Amy Clampitt*. New York: Columbia University Press, 2005.

Bibliography

Spinka, Matthew. "Francis Kun, A Czechoslovak Pioneer." *Journal of the Presbyterian Historical Society* 12.2 (Oct. 1924) 115–21.

Spitzer, Yanni. "Edward A. Steiner: A Writer on Immigration." Aug 24, 2021. yannayspitzer.net/2012/08/24/edward-a-steiner-a-writer-on-immigration.

Standing, Arthur C. *One Man's Story: A Conscientious Objector in World War I*. Edited by Reva Griffith. Kansas City: John & Reva Griffith, 1997.

Stanford, Robert D., ed. *Sketches: The Baptist Churches in Minnesota and Iowa*. N.p., 1994.

"Stanton, Bloomer, Truth, and Tubman." St. Alban's Episcopal Church. http://www.saintalbansepiscopal.org/2021/07/stanton-bloomer-truth-and-tubman.html.

Starbuck, Edwin Diller. *The Psychology of Religion*. London: Walter Scott, 1900.

Starbuck, Winifred. "The Scattergood Seminary." *Pal* 43:7 (July 1962) 327–33.

Stark, Harvey. "Looking for Leadership: Discovering American Islam in the Muslim Chaplaincy." PhD diss., Princeton University, 2015.

Stark, Jack. *Iowa State Constitution: A Reference Guide*. Westport, CT: Greenwood, 1998.

Stark, Rodney, and William Sims Bainbridge. *The Future of Religion: Secularization, Revival, and Cultural Formation*. Berkeley: University of California Press, 1985.

State of Iowa. 27th Biennial Report, Board of Control, 1950.

———. 28th Biennial Report, Board of Control, 1952.

Stavig, Gopal. *Western Admirers of Ramakrishna and His Followers*. Kolkata: Vedanta, 2010.

Stein, Madeleine B. "Mrs. Alcott of Concord to Mrs. Adams of Dubuque." *New England Quarterly* 50 (1977) 331–40.

Steiner, Edward A. *Against the Current: Simple Chapters from a Complex Life*. New York: Revell, 1910.

———. *The Confession of a Hyphenated American*. New York: Revell, 1916.

———. *The Eternal Hunger*. New York: Revell, 1925.

———. *From Alien to Citizen: The Story of My Life in America*. New York: Revell, 1914.

———. *The Immigrant Tide: Its Ebb and Flow*. New York: Revell, 1909.

———. *The Mediator*. New York: Revell, 1907.

———. *Old Trails and New Borders*. New York: Revell, 1921.

———. *On the Trail of the Immigrant*. New York: Revell, 1906.

———. *Sanctus Spiritus and Company*. New York: Doran, 1919.

———. *Tolstoy the Man*. Lincoln: University of Nebraska Press, 2005.

Stelcik, Charlotte. *History of the Hus Memorial Presbyterian Church, Cedar Rapids, Iowa*. Cedar Rapids: Superior, 1949.

Stellingwerff, Johann. *Iowa Letters: Dutch Immigrants on the American Frontier*. Edited by Robert P. Swierenga. Grand Rapids: Eerdmans, 2004.

Stentzel, Jim, ed. *More Than Witnesses: How a Small Group of Missionaries Aided Korea's Democratic Revolution*. Seoul, Korea: Mng, 2006.

Stephens, Randall J. *The Fire Spreads: Holiness and Pentecostalism in the American South*. Cambridge: Harvard University Press, 2008.

Stephenson, George M. "Nativism in the Forties and Fifties, with Special Reference to the Mississippi Valley." *Mississippi Valley Historical Review* 9 (1922) 185–202.

———. *The Religious Aspects of Swedish Immigration*. New York: Arno, 1969.

Stevens, James. "The Downfall of Elder Barton." *American Mercury*, Dec. 1931, 461–71.

Stevens, Peter F. "The Paratrooper Padre: 'Father Sam' of Cherokee." *The Iowan* 47.4 (1999) 28–31.

Bibliography

Stiles, C. C. "The Skunk River War (Or Tally War)." *AI* 19 (1935) 614–43.

Stoeffler, F. Ernest, ed. *Continental Pietism and Early American Christianity*. Grand Rapids: Eerdmans, 1976.

Stoker, Kevin, and James Arrington. "Weekly Sabbath School: The Farm Press as a Pulpit for 'Uncle Henry' Wallace's Progressive Moral Reform and Instruction." *Journal of Media and Religion* 9 (2011) 30–46.

Stokes, David R. *The Shooting Salvationist: J. Frank Norris and the Murder Trial That Captivated America*. Hanover, NH: Steerforth, 2011.

Stoll, Mark R. *Inherit the Holy Mountain: Religion and the Rise of American Environmentalism*. Oxford: Oxford University Press, 2015.

Stolz, Karl Rof. *Pastoral Psychology*. New York: Cokesbury, 1932.

Stowell, Joseph. *History of the General Association of Regular Baptist Churches*. Haywood, CA: 1949.

"St. Paul AME Church." https://www.stpauldesmoines.org.

Straatmeyer, Alvin J. *Child of the Church: University of Dubuque, 1852–2008*. Cedar Rapids: WDG, 2008.

Straatmeyer, H. Gene. *The Synod of the West: A History of the Presbyterian German Synod of the West and Its Churches*. N.p., 2016.

Strabala, William M., and Michael J. Palacek. *Prophets without Honor: A Requiem for Moral Patriotism*. New York: Algora, 2002.

Strassburg, James. "Reviving the Heartland: American Lutherans, Post-War Internationalism, and the Crisis of Germany, 1940–1949." *Journal of the Lutheran Historical Conference* (2015) 62–84.

Steiner, Edward A. *St. Peter and I: A Collection of Autobiographical Essays*. Grinnell, IA: Grinnell College, 1959.

Strong, Douglas M. *Perfectionist Politics: Abolitionism and the Religious Tensions of American Democracy*. Syracuse: Syracuse University Press, 1999.

Stuart, Anne Meysenbourg. "History of the Catholic Press in Iowa." *Iowa Catholic Historical Review* V (October 1932) 11–38.

Suckow, Ruth. *The Bonney Family*. New York: Alfred A. Knopf, 1933.

———. *The Folks*. Iowa City: University of Iowa Press, 1992.

———. *The John Wood Case*. New York: Viking, 1959.

———. *New Hope*. New York: Farrar & Rinehart, 1942.

———. *Some Others and Myself: Seven Stories and a Memoir*. New York: Rinehart, 1952.

Suelflow, August R. *The Heart of Missouri*. St. Louis: Concordia, 1954.

Sulek, James W. "An Analysis of the Role of a Ward Therapist in the Treatment of Patients at Mount Pleasant State Mental Hospital, Mt. Pleasant, Iowa." M.S.Ed. Thesis, Drake University, 1951.

Sullivan, Winnifred Fallers. *Prison Religion: Faith-Based Reform and the Constitution*. Princeton: Princeton University Press, 2009.

Sumner, Robert L. *Armstrongism: The "Worldwide Church of God" Examined in the Searching Light of Scripture*. Brownsburg, IN: Biblical Evangelism, 1974.

Sutton, Robert P. *Les Icarians: The Utopian Dream in Europe and America*. Urbana: University of Illinois Press, 1994.

Swaim, Ginnalie. "Iowans At the 1893 World's Columbian Exposition." *Pal* 74.1 (Winter 1993) 160–87.

Swander, Mary. *Desert Pilgrim: En Route to Mysticism and Miracles*. New York: Penguin, 2003.

Bibliography

———. *Out of This World: A Journey of Healing*. New York: Penguin, 1993.

Swansen, H. Fred. *The Founder of St. Ansgar: The Life Story of Claus Laurits Clausen*. Blair, NE: Lutheran, 1949.

Swanson, Merwin. "The 'Country Life Movement' and the American Churches." *CH* 46 (1977) 358–73.

Swierenga, Robert P. "Disloyal Dutch? Herman Hoeksema and the Flag in the Church Controversy during World War I." *Origins* 25 (2007) 28–35.

———. *Faith and Family: Dutch Immigration and Settlement in the United States, 1820–1920*. New York: Holmes & Meier, 2000.

———. "The Little White Church: Religion in Rural America." *Agricultural History* 71 (1997) 415–39.

———. *Pioneers and Profits: Land Speculation on the Iowa Frontier*. Ames, IA: Iowa State University Press, 1968.

———. "Van Raalte and Scholte: A Soured Relationship and Personal Rivalry." *Origins* 17.1 (1999) 21–33.

Swisher, Jacob A. "Beginnings of Salem." *Pal* 21.5 (May 1940) 140–50.

———. "Old Zion Church." *Pal* 13.7 (Jul. 1932) 274–84.

Synan, Vinson. *The Holiness-Pentecostal Movement in the United States*. Grand Rapids: Eerdmans, 1971.

Szasz, Ferenc Morton. *The Divided Mind of Protestant America, 1880–1930*. University of Alabama Press, 1982.

———. "The Episcopal Bishops and the Trans-Mississippi West, 1865–1918." *Anglican and Episcopal History* 67 (2000) 348–63.

———. *The Protestant Clergy in the Great Plains and Mountain West, 1865–1915*. Albuquerque: University of New Mexico Press, 1988.

Taft, Fred H. *An Empire Builder of the Middle West*. Los Angeles: Parker, Stone & Baird, 1929.

"The Tai Dam Bible." Des Moines Mennonite. http://www.desmoinesmennonite.org/tai-dam-bible.html.

Tatum, Lawrie. *Our Red Brothers and the Peace Policy of President Grant*. Lincoln, NE: University of Nebraska Press, 1899, 1970.

Taves, Ann. "Is It the Job of Religion Journalists To Define 'Religion'?" Religion Dispatches, Dec. 3, 2015. https://religiondispatches.org/is-it-the-job-of-religion-journalists-to-define-religion/.

Tax, Sol, et al. *Documentary History of the Fox Project, 1948–1959: A Program in Action Anthropology*. Chicago: University of Chicago Press, 1960.

Taylor, Archibald Alexander Edward. *Israel against Benjamin: A Sermon For the Times*. Dubuque, IA, 1861.

Taylor, Landon. *The Battlefield Reviewed*. Chicago: Self-published, 1881.

———. "Pioneer Ministry." *Pal* 25:1 (Jan. 1944)

Taylor, Samuel W. "The Nauvoo Everyone Should Know." *Restoration Trail Forum* 14.2 (Oct. 1988) 2–10.

Teakle, Thomas, ed. "History and Constitution of the Icarian Community." *IJH* 15 (1917) 214–86.

Teicherow, Allan. "Military Surveillance of Mennonites during World War I." *MQR* 55 (1979) 95–127.

Tentler, Leslie Woodcock. *American Catholics: A History*. New Haven: Yale University Press, 2020.

Bibliography

tenZythoff, Gerrit J. *Sources of Secession*. Grand Rapids: Eerdmans, 1987.

Terrell, John Upton. *Black Robe: The Life of Pierre-Jean DeSmet, Missionary, Explorer, Pioneer*. Garden City, NY: Doubleday, 1964.

Tesdell, Lee S., et al. *The Way We Were: Arab-Americans in Central Iowa, An Oral History*. Des Moines: Grand View College, 1993.

Thanet, Octave. "One of the Congregation." *Sunday Afternoon* 3 (Mar. 1879) 193–204.

Thayer, George. *The Farther Shores of Politics: The American Political Fringe Today*. New York: Simon & Schuster, 1967.

Thayer, William M. *The Morning Star; or, Symbols of Christ*. Philadelphia: John E. Potter, 1896.

Thomas, James S. *Methodism's Racial Dilemma: The Story of the Central Jurisdiction*. Nashville: Abingdon, 1992.

Thomas, Paul Westphal, and Paul William Thomas. *The Days of Our Pilgrimage: History of the Pilgrim Holiness Church*. Marion, IN: Wesleyan, 1976.

Thomas, William H., Jr. *Unsafe for Democracy: World War I and the U.S. Justice Department's Covert Campaign to Suppress Dissent*. Madison: University of Wisconsin Press, 2008.

Thompson, Era Bell. *American Daughter*. Chicago: University of Chicago Press, 1967.

Thompson, J. Earl, Jr. *Congregational Dissent Against the War of 1812*. [Cleveland]: Pilgrim, 1976.

Thompson, Patricia J. "'Against the Odds, They Did Preach': The First Four Women in the Methodist Protestant Church to be Ordained as Elders in Full Connection." *MH* 59 (2021) 135–48.

Thorne, Tanis C. *The Many Hands of My Relations: French and Indians on the Lower Missouri*. Columbia, MO: University of Missouri Press, 1996.

Throne, Mildred Throne, ed. "Letters From Shiloh." *IJH* 52 (1952).

Thuesen, Peter J. *Tornado God: American Religion and Violent Weather*. Oxford: Oxford University Press, 2020.

Timberlake, James H. *Prohibition and the Progressive Movement, 1900–1920*. New York: Atheneum, 1970.

"Timeline of History of Baptist Work in Iowa." Baptist Convention of Iowa. https://bciowa.org/about/history/convention-history/.

Tinker, George E. *Missionary Conquest: The Gospel and Native American Cultural Genocide*. Minneapolis: Fortress, 1993.

Tjernagel, N. "Pioneer Church Fathers." *AI* 32 (1954) 217–25.

Tjossem, Wilmer L. *Quaker Sloopers: From the Fjords to the Prairies*. Richmond, IN: Friends United, 1984.

———. "History of Des Moines Friends Meeting." Typescript, 1956.

"The TM Craze: Forty Minutes to Bliss." *Time*, Oct. 13, 1975, 71–74.

Todd, Mary. *Authority Vested: A Story of Identity and Change in the Lutheran Church—Missouri Synod*. Grand Rapids: Eerdmans, 2000.

Tooker, Elisabeth, ed. *Native North American Spirituality of the Eastern Woodlands*. New York: Paulist, 1979.

Torrence, Gaylord, and Robert Hobbs. *Art of the Red Earth People: The Mesquakie of Iowa*. Seattle: University of Iowa Museum of Art, 1989.

Toulouse, Mark. "The Origins of the *Christian Century*, 1884–1914: A Climate of Optimism." *Christian Century*, Jul. 12, 2012.

Tracy, Shannon M., Glen M. Leonard, and Ronald G. Watt. "The Nauvoo Temple Bells." *BYU Studies* 58.2 (2019) 113–70.

Bibliography

Trask, Kerry A. *Black Hawk: The Battle for the Heart of America.* New York: Henry Holt, 2006.
Treuer, David. *The Heartbeat of Wounded Knee: Native America From 1890 to the Present.* New York: Penguin, 2019.
Tributes to Henry Wallace. Des Moines: Wallace, 1919.
Trollinger, William. *God's Empire: William Bell Riley and Midwestern Fundamentalism.* Madison: University of Wisconsin Press, 1990.
Troyer, Noah. *Sermons.* 2nd book. Tampico, IL: Fairfield A. M. Church, 1950.
Trueblood, Elton. *While It Is Day: An Autobiography.* New York: Harper & Row, 1974.
Trumbo, Jean. "Orson Hyde's *Frontier Guardian:* A Mormon Editor Chronicles the Western Movement through Kanesville, Iowa." Pal 77.2 (Summer 1996) 74–85.
Tucker, Cynthia Grant. *Prophetic Sisterhood: Liberal Women Ministers of the Frontier, 1880–1930.* Boston: Beacon, 1990.
―――. *A Woman's Ministry: Mary Collson's Search for Reform as a Unitarian Minister, a Hull House Social Worker, and a Christian Science Practitioner.* Philadelphia: Temple University Press, 1984.
Turner, Jean B. "The Christian Women's Board of Missions: Service and Sisterhood." Discipliana 49.4 (1984) 26–36.
Tuthill, William H. "The Garry Owen Vote." AI First Series (1870) 217–20.
Tuttle, A. H. *Mary Porter Gamewell and Her Story of the Siege in Peking.* New York: Eaton & Mains, 1997.
Twain, Mark. *Life on the Mississippi.* New York: Harper & Row, 1961.
Twedt, Arlen. *The Central Iowa Norwegians: Histories, Memoirs, and Studies of their Settlement from 1855–1905.* Three volumes. Ankeny: CINP, 2017.
Two Centuries of the Church of the Brethren: Bicentennial Addresses at the Annual Conference Held at Des Moines, Iowa, June 3–11, 1908. Elgin, IL: Brethren, 1908.
Tyler, Robert Llewellyn. "Migrant Culture Maintenance: The Welsh in Mahaska County, Iowa, 1870–1920." AI 81 (2022) 45–76.
Tyrell, Charles W. "Primitive Methodism: The Midwestern Story." MH 15 (Oct. 1976) 22–51.
Tyrell, Ian R. *Sobering Up: From Temperance to Prohibition in Antebellum America, 1800–1860.* Westport, CT: Greenwood, 1979.
Ulrich, Laurel Thatcher. *A House Full of Females: Plural Marriage and Women's Rights in Early Mormonism, 1845–1870.* New York: Vintage, 2017.
"U.S. Public Becoming Less Religious." Pew Research Center. https://www.pewresearch.org/2015/11/03/u-s-public-becoming-less-religious.
"US States by Mainline Protestant Population." WorldAtlas. https://www.worldatlas.com/articles/us-states-by-mainline-protestant-population.html.
Valbracht [misspelled "Valbracth" on cover], Louis H. *Matters of Life and Death.* Lima, OH: CSS, 1973.
Vail, Thomas H. *Sermon Preached at the Consecration of the Chapel of Griswold College.* Davenport, IA: Luse & Griggs, 1865.
Valerio-Jimenez, Omar. "Racializing Mexican Immigrants in Iowa's Early Mexican Communities." AI 75 (2016) 1–46.
Van Buren, Janis Bennington. *Susan Angeline Collins: With a Hallelujah Heart.* Bloomington, IN: WestBow, 2021.
Van der Zee, Jacob. "History of Presbyterianism in Iowa City." IJH 13 (1915) 529–50.
VanderVelde, Lea. *Mrs. Dred Scott: A Life on Slavery's Frontier.* Oxford: Oxford University Press, 2009.

Bibliography

Van Hinte, Jacob. *Netherlanders in America: A Study of Emigration and Settlement in the 19th and 20th Centuries in the United States of America.* Grand Rapids: Baker, 1985.

Van Wagoner, Richard S. *Sidney Rigdon: A Portrait of Religious Excess.* Salt Lake City: Signature, 1994.

Vassady, Bela. "New Buda: A Colony of Hungarian Forty-Eighters in Iowa." *AI* 51 (1991) 26–52.

Vavra, Edwin J. *Our First 50 Years of Serving Our Lord: First Presbyterian Church Near Ely, Iowa.* Ely, IA, 2008.

Veblen, A. A. "At Luther College, 1877–1881." *Pal* 56 (1975) 150-60.

Vecsey, Christopher. *Imagine Ourselves Richly: Mythic Narratives of North American Indians.* San Francisco: HarperCollins, 1991.

Visser T'Hooft, Willem. *The Background of the Social Gospel in America.* Haarlem, Netherlands: H. D. Tjeenk Willink & Zoon, 1928.

Vogel, Dan. *Indian Origins and the Book of Mormon.* Salt Lake City: Signature, 1986.

Vogel, Geo. A. W., and Walter S. Wendt. *Seventy-Five Years of God's Grace: A History of the Lutheran Church-Missouri Synod in Iowa, 1879–1954.* Ogden: [Ogden Reporter], 1954.

Vogel, Virgil J. *Iowa Place Names of Indian Origin.* Iowa City: University of Iowa Press, 1983.

Vogl, Rev. Carl. Translated by Rev. Celestine Kapsner, OSB. *Begone Satan! An Account of Diabolical Possession.* Collegeville, MN: Celestine Kapsner, 1935.

Von Rohr, John. *The Shaping of American Congregationalism, 1620–1957,* Cleveland: Pilgrim, 1992.

Voskuil, Dennis. *Mountains into Goldmines: Robert Schuller and the Gospel of Success.* Grand Rapids: Eerdmans, 1983.

Waddilove, Alan. "Grundy College: Undying Legacy or Broken Promises?" *Origins* 19 (2001) 54–68.

Wagler, Ira. *Growing Up Amish.* Carol Stream, IL: Tyndale, 2011.

Wagoner, John, with Martha Riordan. "William Penn University." In *Founded by Friends: The Quaker Heritage of Fifteen Colleges and Universities,* edited by John W. Oliver, Jr., 109–23. Lanham, MD: University Press of America, 2007.

Walch, Timothy. *Irish Iowa.* Charleston, SC: History, 2019.

———. "Man of Deeds: Bishop Loras and the Upper Mississippi Valley Frontier." *AI* 71 (Spring 2012) 174–75.

Waldrop, G. C. "The New Order Amish and Para-Amish Groups: Spiritual Renewal within a Tradition." *MQR* 82 (2008) 395–426.

Walker, Brooks B. *The Christian Fright Peddlers: The Radical Right and the Churches.* Garden City, NY: Doubleday, 1964.

Walker, James R. *Lakota Belief and Ritual.* Lincoln, NE: University of Nebraska Press, 1991.

Walker, Jerald. *World in Flames.* Boston: Beacon, 2016.

Walker, Marietta Hodges. *With the Church at an Early Day.* Lamoni, IA: Herald, 1942.

Wall, James M. "A Senator's Faith and Vocation." *Christian Century,* Sep. 26, 1973, 931–32.

Wall, Joseph Frazier. *Grinnell College in the Nineteenth Century: From Salvation to Service.* Ames, IA: Iowa State University Press, 1997.

———. *Iowa: A History.* New York: W. W. Norton, 1978.

Wallace, Henry. *The Fast That God Has Chosen.* Davenport, 1863.

Bibliography

———. *Uncle Henry's Own Story of His Life*. Des Moines: Wallace, 1917.
Wallace, Henry A. *Statesmanship and Religion*. New York: Round Table, 1934.
Walls, Andrew F. *The Missionary Movement in Christian History: Studies in the Transmission of Faith*. Maryknoll: Orbis, 1996.
Walsh, Matthew R. *The Good Governor: Robert Ray and the Indochinese Refugees of Iowa*. Jefferson, NC: McFarland, 2017.
Ward, Harry W. *Western-Leander-Clark College, 1856–1911*. Dayton, OH: Otterbein, 1911.
Ward, Leo R. *Holding Up the Hills: The Biography of a Neighborhood*. New York: Sheed & Ward, 1941.
Ward, Marilyn S. "'Must the Christian Church Condemn All Use of Military Force?' The Methodist Episcopal Church and the Endorsement of World War II." *MH* 35 (1997) 162–68.
Ward, Sarah F. *The White Ribbon Story: 125 Years of Service to Humanity*. Evanston, IL: Signal, 1999.
Wanatee, Donald. "Effects of Euroamerican Incursions on the Social, Linguistic, Economic and Religious Aspects of the Meskwaki throughout the Great Lakes Region." *Wisconsin Archaeologist* 89 (2008) 200–2.
Waring, Edmund H. "Old Zion Church, Burlington, Iowa." *AI* 9.6 (July 1910) 524–34.
———. *History of the Annual Conference of the Methodist Episcopal Church*. N.p., 1909.
Warren, Frank A. "Review of Mark Kleinman, *A World of Hope, A World of Fear*." *AI* 60 (2001) 194–96.
Warren, Heather A. *Theologians of the New World Order: Reinhold Niebuhr and the Christian Realists, 1920–1948*. New York: Oxford University Press, 1997.
Warren, Louis S. *God's Red Son: The Ghost Dance Religion and the Making of Modern America*. New York: Basic, 2017.
Warren, Stephen. "'To Show the Public That We Were Good Indians:' Origins and Meanings of the Meskwaki Powwow." *American Indian Culture and Research Journal* 33.4 (2009) 1–28.
Warren, Wilson J. *Struggling with "Iowa's Pride": Labor Relations, Unionism and Politics in the Rural Midwest since 1877*. Iowa City: University of Iowa Press, 2000.
Watson, S. Arthur. *William Penn College: A Product and a Producer*. Oskaloosa, IA: William Penn College, 1971.
Watt, Ronald G. "A Tale of Two Bells: Nauvoo Bell and Hummer's Bell." *Nauvoo Journal* 11 (1999) 31–46.
Watts, Edward. *An American Colony: Regionalism and the Roots of Midwestern Culture*. Athens: Ohio University Press, 2002.
Weaver, Janet. "Barrio Women: Community and Coalition in the Heartland." In *Breaking the Wave: Women, Their Organizations, and Feminism, 1945–1985*, edited by Kathleen A. Laughlin and Jacqueline L. Castledine, 173–88. New York: Routledge, 2011.
Weaver-Zercher, David. *Amish in the American Imagination*. Baltimore: Johns Hopkins University Press, 2001.
Weber, Joseph. *Transcendental Meditation in America: How a New Age Movement Remade a Small Town in Iowa*. Iowa City: University of Iowa Press, 2014.
Webber, Philip E. *Kolonie-Deutsch: Life and Language in Amana*. Ames, IA: Iowa State University Press, 1993.
———. "Crossing Colony Lines: Moves From Two Families From Pella to the Amana Colonies in the 1860s." *Pal* 73:1 (1992) 6–17.

Bibliography

———. *Pella Dutch: The Portrait of a Language and Its Use in One of Iowa's Ethnic Communities*. Ames, IA: Iowa State University Press, 1988.

"We Cannot Remain Silent: Opposition to the Military Dictatorship." Brown University Library. https://library.brown.edu/create/wecannotremainsilent/biographies.

Weimann, Jeanne Madeline. *The Fair Women*. Chicago: Academy Chicago, 1983.

Weissbach, Lee Shai. *Jewish Life in Small Town America*. New Haven: Yale University Press, 2005.

"Welcome to First Church of Christ, Scientist." http://christiansciencedesmoines.com.

"Welcome to Immaculate Conception Parish, Wexford." https://icwexford.org/.

Wenger, Robert E. *Social Thought in American Fundamentalism, 1918–1933*. Eugene, OR: Wipf & Stock, 1974.

Wenger, Tisa. *Religious Freedom: The Contested History of an American Ideal*. Chapel Hill: University of North Carolina Press, 2017.

Wertheimer, Andrew B. "Admitting Nebraska's Nisei: Japanese American Students at the University of Nebraska, 1942–1945." *Nebraska History* 83 (2002) 58–72.

"The West Grove Debate." The Primitive Baptist Library of Carthage, Illinois. http://pblib.org/RWThompsonDebates.html.

Westminster's Century of Progress: 100 Years of Christian Service 1858–1958. [Des Moines, 1958.]

Westchester Evangelical Free Church. 100 Years of Service, 1883–1983. Des Moines, 1983.

Whalen, Rev. Charles W. *The Trappist Way*. Rev. ed. N.p., 1947.

"What Price Syncretism?" *Time*, May 6, 1957, 89.

Wheaton, Elizabeth R. *Prisons and Prayer, or, A Labor of Love*. Tabor, IA, 1900.

Whitcomb, Mary R. "Abner Kneeland, His Relations to Early Iowa History." *AI* 6 (1904) 340–63.

Whitcomb, Selden M. *Meditations on the Via Crucis*. Cedar Rapids: Torch, 1915.

White, Ellen G. *Testimonies for the Church*. Mountain View, CA: Pacific, 1948.

White, Graham, and John Maze. *Henry A. Wallace: His Search for a New World Order*. Chapel Hill: University of North Carolina Press, 1995.

White, Roland A. *Milo Reno: Farmers Union Pioneer*. New York, 1975.

White, Ronald C., Jr. *Liberty and Justice For All: Racial Reform and the Social Gospel (1877–1925)*. San Francisco: HarperCollins, 1990.

White, Ronald C., Jr., and C. Howard Hopkins. *The Social Gospel: Religion and Reform in Changing America*. Philadelphia: Temple University Press, 1976.

White, Trumbell. "Does Prohibition Pay? [Part] III." *Appleton's Magazine* 12 (1908) 343.

Whiteman, Curtis Wayne. "The General Assembly of Regular Baptist Churches, 1932–1970." PhD diss., St. Louis University, 1982.

Whitlatch, Forrest E. *On Good Soil: A History of the Iowa District Church of the Nazarene*. Shoal, IN: Country Pines, 2003.

Whittaker, William E., Lynn M. Alex, and Mary C. de la Garcia. *The Archaeological Guide to Iowa*. Iowa City: University of Iowa Press, 2015.

Whittlesey, Wellington W. "The Friends Pastoral System." Master's thesis, Drake University, 1955.

Wiard, Jennifer. "The Gospel of Efficiency: Billy Sunday's Revival Bureaucracy and Evangelicalism in the Progressive Era." *CH* 85 (2015) 587–616.

Wiggins, David. *An Iowa Tragedy: The Fall of Old Des Moines U*. Mt. Horeb, WI: Historical-Midwest, 1988.

Wilcox, Earley Vernon. *Tama Jim*. Boston: Stratford, 1930.

"Wilhelm Loehe and His Legacy." *Currents in Theology and Mission* 33.2 (Apr. 2006)

Bibliography

Wilkie, William E. *Dubuque on the Mississippi, 1788-1988*. Dubuque, IA: Loras College Press, 1987.

Willard, Frances E. "American Imperialism." *Social Forum* 1 (1899) 1-18.

Willems, Nate. "Lutheran Funeral." *Wapsipinicon Almanac* 25, 33-35.

Williams, Charles C. "Who Is My Neighbor?" *Unity* 79 (May 17, 1917).

Williams, Daniel Day. *Andover Liberals*. New York: Octagon, 1971.

Williams, David. *A People's History of the Civil War*. New York: New, 2001.

Williams, Peter W. *Houses of God: Region, Religion, and Architecture in the United States*. Urbana: University of Illinois Press, 1997.

Williams, Raymond Brady. "Religion and Recent Immigrants: New Ferment in American Civic Life." In *Religion and Public Life in the Midwest: America's Common Denominator?*, edited by Philip Barlow and Mark Silk, 135-58. Walnut Creek: AltaMira, 2004.

Williams, Walter L. *Black Americans and the Evangelization of Africa, 1877-1900*. Madison: University of Wisconsin Press, 1982.

Williams, William Appleman. *Tragedy of American Diplomacy*. 2nd ed. New York: Dell, 1972.

"William Salter's Letters to Mary Ann Mackenzie." *AI* 2 (1943) 103-85.

Wills, Garry. *Bare Ruined Choirs: Doubt, Prophecy and Radical Religion*. Garden City, NY: Doubleday, 1971.

———. *John Wayne's America: The Politics of Celebrity*. New York: Simon & Schuster, 1997.

Wilson, Aaron M. *Our Story: The History of the Pentecostal Church of God, 1919-2001*. Joplin, MO: Messenger, 2001.

Wilson, Bryan, ed. *The Social Impact of New Religious Movements*. Barrytown, NY: Unification Theological Seminary, 1981.

Wilson, E. Raymond. *Thus Far on My Journey*. Richmond, IN: Friends United, 1976.

———. *Uphill for Peace: Quaker Impact on Congress*. Richmond, IN: Friends United, 1975.

Wilson, Margaret. *The Able McLaughlins*. New York: Grosset & Dunlap, 1923.

———. *Daughters of India*. New York: Harper, 1929.

———. *The Law and the McLaughlins*. Garden City, NY: Sun Dial, 1936.

Wilson, Russell, and William Hedlund. *In His Own Words: The Harold Hughes Story*, Bloomington, IN: LifeRich, 2020.

Wilson, Theodore A. "Henry Agard Wallace and the Progressive Faith." In *Three Progressives from Iowa: Gilbert N. Haugen, Herbert C. Hoover, Henry A. Wallace*, 37-50. Iowa City: Center for the Study of the Recent History of the United States, 1980.

Windsor, William. *Justice and Mercy: A Sermon Preached at a United Service Held at the Methodist Episcopal Church in Davenport, Iowa, on the National Fast Day, June 1st, 1865*. [Davenport?, 1865?].

Wines, Frederic H., and John Koren. *The Liquor Problem in its Legislative Aspects*, Boston: Houghton Mifflin, 1898.

Winslow, Brady G. "David W. Kilbourne: The Creation of an Iowa Anti-Mormon." *AI* 78 (2019) 241-67.

Winston, Diane. "'The Flying Nun' and 'The Painting Nun': Gender, Conflict, and Representation in Los Angeles." In *Religion in Los Angeles: Religious Activism, Innovation, and Diversity in the Global City*, edited by Richard Flory and Diane Winston, 110-21. London: Routledge, 2021.

Bibliography

Witosky, Tom, and Mark Hansen. *Equal before the Law: How Iowa Led Americans to Marriage Equality.* Iowa City: University of Iowa Press, 2015.

Witte, Raymond Philip. *Twenty-Five Years of Crusading: A History of the National Catholic Rural Life Conference.* Des Moines: National Catholic Rural Life Conference, 1948.

Wittke, Carl. *The Utopian Communist: A Biography of William Weitling, Nineteenth Century Reformer.* Baton Rouge: Louisiana State University Press, 1950.

Wolfe, Jack. *A Century with Iowa Jewry, 1833–1940.* Des Moines: Iowa, 1941.

Wood, Gordon. *The Radicalism of the American Revolution.* New York: Vintage, 1992.

Wood, Helen W. *America: Look and Live.* Los Angeles: American Soul Clinic, 1952.

———. *The Broken Wall.* Waterloo, IA: Christian Anti-Communism Crusade, 1954.

Wood, Richard E. "Evangelical Quaker Acculturation in the Upper Mississippi Valley." *Quaker History* 76 (1987) 128–44.

Woods, Fred E., and Douglas Atterberg. "The 1853 Mormon Migration through Keokuk." *Annals of Iowa* 61 (2002) 1–23.

Woodworth, Steven E. *While God Is Marching On: The Religious World of Civil War Soldiers.* Lawrence: University Press of Kansas, 2001.

Worcester, Mark W. *Master Key: The Story of the Hephzibah Faith Missionary Association.* Kansas City, 1966.

Work, John M. *What Is and What Isn't.* Chicago: Charles H. Kerr, 1905.

"The World's Smallest Grotto." Society of Architectural Historians. sah-archipedia.org/buildings/IA-01-CE288.

WPA Historical Records Survey Project. *American Imprints Inventory No. 15: A Checklist of Iowa Imprints, 1838–1860.* Chicago, 1940.

Wren, Adam. "The Iowa Town Where Marianne Williamson Is Already President." *Politico*, Jan. 6, 2020. https://www.politico.com/news/magazine/2020/01/06/marianne-williamson-fairfield-iowa-093590.

Wreszin, Michael. *Rebel in Defense of Tradition: The Life and Politics of Dwight Macdonald.* New York: Perseus, 1994.

Wright, Edward Needles. *Conscientious Objectors in the Civil War.* New York: A. S. Barnes, 1961.

Wright, Louis B. *Culture on the Moving Frontier.* Bloomington: Indiana University Press, 1955.

Wright, Luella. *Peter Melendy: The Mind and the Soul.* Iowa City: State Historical Society of Iowa, 1943.

Wubben, Hubert H. "Dennis Mahony and the Dubuque *Herald*, 1860–1863." *IJH* 56 (1958) 289–320.

Wuerffel, L. C. "The Lutheran Church Missouri Synod." *Pal* 29.11 (Nov. 1948) 321–52.

Wyman, Mark. *Immigrants in the Valley: Irish, Germans, and Americans in the Upper Mississippi Country, 1830–1860.* Chicago: Nelson-Hall, 1984.

Yambura, Barbara S., with Eunice Wills Bodine. *A Change and a Parting: My Story of Amana.* Ames, IA: Iowa State University Press, 1986.

Year Book of the Iowa-Des Moines Annual Conference. The Methodist Church, 1942.

Yeast, William E. "The Mesquakie Memorial Feast." *AI* 36 (1963) 591–98.

Yoder, Franklin L. *Opening a Window on the World: A History of Iowa Mennonite School.* Kalona, IA: Iowa Mennonite School, 1994.

Yoder, Holly Blosser. *The Same Spirit: History of Iowa-Nebraska Mennonites.* Freeman, SD: Central Plains Mennonite Conference, n.d.

Bibliography

Yoder, James D. *The Yoder Outsiders*. Newton, KS: Faith and Life, 1988.
Yoder, Michael L. "Anabaptists and Calvinists Four Centuries Later: An Iowa Case Study." *MQR* 67 (1993) 49–72.
Yoder, Rhonda Lou. *Amish Agriculture in Iowa: Indigenous Knowledge for Sustainable Small-Farm Systems*. Ames, IA: Iowa State University Press, 1990.
Yoder, Sanford Calvin. "The Amish in Wright County." *Pal* 43.9 (Sep. 1962).
———. *The Days of My Years*. Scottdale, PA: Herald, 1959.
———. "My Amish Boyhood." *Pal* 39.3 (Mar. 1958).
Yoseloff, Thomas. *The Time of My Life*. South Brunswick, NJ: A. S. Barnes, 1979.
"Young Center for Anabaptist and Pietist Studies." Elizabethtown College. https://www.etown.edu/centers/young-center.
Yzermans, Vincent A. *The People I Love: A Biography of Luigi G. Ligutti*. Collegeville, MN: Liturgical, 1976.
Zelley, Ed. "Working for Justice and Understanding." *engage/social action* 2 (Oct. 1974) 7–13.
Zeilinger, G. J. *A Missionary Synod with a Mission, 1854–1929*. Chicago: Wartburg, 1929.
Zerin, Edward. *The Birth of the Torah*. New York: Appleton-Century-Crofts, 1961.
Zielinski, John M. *Mesquakie and Proud of It*. Kalona, IA: Photo-Art, 1976.
Zikmund, Barbara Brown, ed. *Hidden Histories in the United Church of Christ*. New York: Pilgrim, 1984.
Zikmund, Barbara Brown, et al. *Clergy Women: An Uphill Calling*. Louisville: WJK, 1998.
Zimmer, Eric Steven. "Settlement Sovereignty: The Meskwaki Fight for Self-Governance, 1856–1937." *AI* 73 (2014) 311–47.
Zink-Sawyer, Beverly. *From Preachers to Suffragists: Women's Rights and Religious Conviction in the Lives of Three Nineteenth-Century American Clergywomen*. Louisville: WJK, 2003.
Ziolkowski, Eric J., ed., *Museum of Faiths: Histories and Legacies of the 1893 World's Parliament of Religions*. Atlanta: American Academy of Religion, 1993.
Zollmann, Mary Ann, and Margaret Cain McCarthy. *The Power of Sisterhood Women Religious Tell the Story of the Apostolic Visitation*. Lanham, MD: University Press of America, 2014.
Zuba, Wendy Mercy. "The Sense of Place: The Many Horizons of Martin E. Marty." *Christian Century*, Nov. 23, 2002.
Zuber, Janet W., trans. *Barbara Heinemann Landmann Biography. E. L. Gruber's Teaching on Divine Inspiration and Other Essays*. Middle Amana, IA: Amana Church Society, 1981.
Zubovich, Gene. *Before the Religious Right: Liberal Protestants, Human Rights, and the Polarization of the United States*. Philadelphia: University of Pennsylvania Press, 2022.
Zug, Joan, and John Zug. *The Amanas Today: Seven Historic Iowa Villages*. Monticello, IA: Amana Society, 1974.
Zwart, David. "Telling Heartland Histories: Rural Iowa Protestant Congregations in the Mid-Twentieth Century." *AI* 77 (2018) 384–415.

Bibliography

ARCHIVES

Archives of the Mennonite Church, Goshen, IN
    Guy Hershberger Collection
    Roy Buchanan Papers
    Sanford C. Yoder Papers
    Simon Gingerich Collection
Brethren Historical Library and Archives, Elgin, IL
    CSCC Camp Visiting Commission Files
    Rufus D. Bowman Papers
Evangelical and Reformed Church Archives, Lancaster, PA
    Minutes of the Commission on Christian Social Action
LGBT Religious Archive Network
National Archives, Washington, DC
    Record Group 165
State Historical Library, Des Moines
    Calvary Baptist Church (Des Moines) Papers
    Church Women United of the Des Moines Area Papers
    Ecumenical Ministries of Iowa Records
    Eugene Mannheimer Papers
    Frazer and Loris Thomason Papers
    Iowa Board of Regents Minutes
    Mahlon Day Collins Papers
    Mary Elizabeth Walton Journal
State Historical Society Library, Iowa City
    Center for Peace and Justice Records
    Herbert J. Metcalf Papers
    Iowa Council of Churches Records
Special Collections, Cowles Library, Drake University
    H. O. Breeden, et al., *Iowa Clergymen for Woman Suffrage*
Special Collections, Grinnell College
    Foreign Missions Folder
Special Collections, University of Iowa Libraries
    Adams Family Papers
    Henry A. Wallace Papers
    Ruth Suckow Papers
    Virgil Hancher Papers
    William Francis Riley Papers
    WSUI audio tapes by Marcus Bach, currently unprocessed.
Iowa Women's Archives, University of Iowa Libraries
    Anna Marie Mitchell Papers
    Edythe Stirlen Papers
    Frances Hawthorne Papers
    Irene Munoz Papers
    Lileah Harris Papers
    Leona Ruppel Papers
    Marianne Michael Papers
    Marilyn O. Murphy Papers

Bibliography

    Marion Farquhar Papers
    Marlene Booth Papers
    Martha Nash Papers
    Mary McDermott Shideler Papers
    Myrle Olive Ward Papers
    Muscatine Migrant Committee Papers
    Ortha Lane Papers
    Rev. William T. O'Connor Papers
Sr. Mary Dominica Urbany Papers
    Women's Christian Temperance Union Papers
    Women's Project, Diocese of Sioux City

NEWSPAPERS

Algona *Upper Des Moines Republican*
Ames *Iowa State Daily*
Appleton's Magazine
Bridgeport, CT *Post*
Brooklyn, NY *Daily Eagle*
Burlington *Hawkeye*
Cedar Rapids *Gazette*
Christian Century
Christian Social Action Bulletin
Christian Socialist
Christianity Today
Clinton *Herald*
Colfax *Weekly Clipper*
Commonweal
Council Bluffs *Nonpareil*
Davenport *Daily Gazette*
Davenport *Democrat*
Davenport *Times*
Des Moines *Capital*
[Des Moines] *Catholic Mirror*
[Des Moines] *Cityview*
Des Moines *Leader*
[Des Moines] *Pointblank*
Des Moines *Register*
Des Moines *Tribune*
DeWitt *Observer*
Drake *Delphic*
[Dubuque] *Daily Catholic Tribune*
Dubuque *Telegraph-Herald*
Dubois County *Herald*
Ecumenical Ship
Free Flowing
Grinnell *Herald*

Grinnell *Scarlet and Black*
Gospel Herald
Home Missionary
Indianapolis *Journal*
Indianola *Record-Herald*
Indianola *Tribune*
Iowa Bystander
Iowa City *Daily Iowan*
Iowa City *Little Village*
Iowa City *Press-Citizen*
Iowa Fellowship
Iowa State Teachers College *College Eye*
Jerusalem *Post*
Keokuk *Daily Gate City*
The Kingdom
Life Magazine
Look Magazine
Montezuma *Republican*
Mt. Pleasant *Free Press*
National Catholic Reporter
Newsweek
New York *Times*
North Tama *Telegraph*
Montezuma *Republican*
Mt. Pleasant *Free Press*
National Catholic Reporter
Newsweek
Millennial Harbinger
Oskaloosa *Herald*
Ottumwa *Courier*
Plain Talk
Prairie City *News*
Presbyterian Life

Bibliography

Presbyterian Outlook
Pulpit
The Scene
Sioux City *Journal*
Sioux City *Volksfreund*
Social Crusader
Social Forum
Social Gospel
Tallahassee *Democrat*
Wallace's Farmer
Williamsburg *Journal-Tribune*
Worldview

INTERVIEWS & CORRESPONDENCE

Kari Bassett
L. K. Berryhill
David Barton-Liles
Sarai Schmucker Rice
David Foster
Rich Houseall
Robert M. Healey
Tim Knepper
Bob Leonard
David McCartney
Scott Meador
Robert Neymeyer
David Polich
Lauren Soth
Howard Wallace
Felecite Wolfe

Index

Iowa place names are in bold.

The Able McLaughlins (Wilson) 91, 134
Abolitionism 83, 85, 95–99, 103,112, 123, 130–31. 139–44, 200, 202
Ackley 64, 65
Action Anthropology 343
Action Research 325
Adams County 43, 209
Adams, Ephraim 33, 35–45, 73, 79
Adams, Mary Newbury 170–71, 171, 202, 219, 224
Adams Ranch 261
Adaville 66
Alaska 153
Albach, Addison 335
Albia 131, 177, 230
Albrechtians 51
Alden, Ebenezer 85
Alexander 65
Alison's House (Glaspell) 214
Algona 220, 230, 243, 258
Algonquian language group 23, 27, 227
Allen, Minne 325
Alsace 68
Altoona 213, 380
Amana Colonies—see Inspirationists
American Atheists 373
American Federation of Catholic Societies 256
American Friends Service Committee 163, 261, 324, 352

American Home Missionary Society 67, 79, 82–85, 96, 98, 136
American Indian Movement 359
American Jewish Congress 325
American Peace Society 255
American Protective League 8
Americanism 13, 250, 268, 270
Ames 284, 310, 323, 325, 331, 334, 351
Amish 10, 55, 57,68, 69, 132, 140, 142–43, 254, 363
   Beachy Amish 69, 239
   Old Order Amish 68–69, 142, 239, 336, 360
Amman, Carl 81
Anderson, Dan 112
Anderson, George 163
Anderson, Jeremiah 123
Andersonville (Kantor) 135
Andhra Pradesh, India 160
Andover Seminary 83–84, 181, 349
Andrews, Skip 358
Anglican Catholic Church 11
Anglicans 13, 159, 380
Angola 158
Ankeny, Henry 127
Anthony, Susan B. 196
Anti-Saloon League 209
Aplington 64, 65
Appanoose County 71
Appleby, William 271

Index

Appleseed, Johnny 70
Aquinas Institute 349
Argentina 155, 162
Armenians 155–56, 184
Armstrong, Herbert W. 291–92
Army of the Tennessee 134
Asbury, Francis 111
Ashland Seminary 111
Ashton 65
Association of Campus Ministers, Iowa City 354
Association of Theological Faculties in Iowa 349
Atlantic 352
Attica 47
Audubon 216
Auschwitz, Poland 326
Austinville 65
Australian Lutheran Church 151
Avalonian Catholic Church 11
Aylesworth, Barton 190
Azusa Street Revival 145

Babel Proclamation 259
Baccam, Ha 4
Baccam, La 4
Bach, Marcus 334–36
Bader, Jesse M. 357
Badger Hill—see Gladbrook
Ba'hais 305
Baileyville, IL 64
Baker, Paul 343
Baker, Perry—see Pierre Bernard
Ball, James W. 320
Ballard, Edna Wheeler 303
Ballard, Guy 303
Balmer, Randall 362, 366
Bangor 141
Baptist Bible Union 288–91
Baptists ix, 8, 13, 40, 41, 51, 64, 82, 102, 105, 107–10, 118, 120, 130–31, 133, 152, 160–61, 171–77, 185–86, 191, 208, 231, 249, 257–59, 271, 284–91, 297, 332, 335, 339, 370, 379
    African-American Baptists/National Convention 108–9, 175–77, 271, 286
    Danish Baptists 108

General Association of Regular Baptists 293, 339
North American Baptist Conference 64
Primitive Baptists 109, 267
Southern Baptists 109, 370
Swedish Baptists 102, 108
Barber, Rimson 350
Barracks, Helene 242–43
Barrett, Mary Elizabeth 117
Barish brothers, 246
Bartenders Union 191
Barth, Karl 4, 347, 349
Barton, Dewberry 267
Bascom, Tim 163
Bassett, Hurley 338
Basilicas 78
Basinger, Bill 167
Basinger, Jean 167
Batten, Samuel Zane 182, 191, 257
Battey, Thomas 153
Bean, Hannah 141
Bean, Joel 141
Bear Creek Friends Meeting 138
Beatles 313
Beckman, Francis 318, 321
Bedford 234
Bellevue 85
Bellevue, NE 369
Belmond 65
Benedict, Lovina 203, 206
Benkert, William 189
Bennard, George 233
Bennett, John 45
Benson, Wendell R. 267
Benton Barracks, MO 127
Benton County 255
Bergan, Gerald 266, 278
Bernard, Pierre 297
Berne, Switzerland 160
Bethel A. M. E. Church, Des Moines 338
Bhutanese 378
Big Canoe 124
Biniaz, Celina Karp 325–26
Bird, Thompson 97–98
Bixby, Ruby 108, 175
Black Hawk 24–25, 31–32, 34
Black Hawk War 25, 30–32
Black Soil (Donovan) 274

Index

Blaine, Martha Royce 21
Blairstown 71
Blanchard, Charles 270
Blood Run 21
Bloom, Moses 245
Bloomer, Amelia Jenks 171, 196
Bloomfield 106, 166–67, 188
Blooming Prairie, MN 50
Bloomington—see Muscatine
B'nai Jeshurun Temple, 224, 326
B'nai Brith, 351
Bobrov, Jacob 246
Bohemians—see also Czechs 5, 58, 114, 215, 247
Boies, Horace 208
Book of Mormon 20, 48, 49
Boone 112. 172, 236, 237, 323, 334
Booth, Marlene 342
"Booze" sermon (Sunday) 285
The Bonney Family (Suckow) 172
Borich, Michael 24
Bosnians 377
Boston College 161
Bowman, Kate Klinefelter 222–23
Boxer Rebellion 158
Boyd, Cyrus 125, 127, 128, 133, 134
Boyd, Jane 192
Boyle, Sara 193
Braaten, Carl 345
Breeden, Harvey O. 172, 190, 299–301
Bremer County 50, 60
Bresee, Phineas F. 139, 143, 147
Brethren (see also United Brethren, Evangelical United Brethren) 10, 56, 68–70, 131–32, 162, 188, 226, 253–55, 319, 370
Brewer, Mary E. 155–56
Briggs, Carolyn 365
Briggs, Edwin S. 334
Bristow 65, 66
British Israelitism 292
Bromwell, James 351
Brotherhood Trio 278
Brown, Greg 345
Brown, John 123, 131, 132
Brown, Nicholas 32
Brown v. Topeka Board of Education 325
Brown, William 175–77
Brown, William McKendry 304
Bryan, William Jennings 283, 287–88
Bryce, H. J. 282
Buchanan, Amos 131
Buchanan, Roy 253
Buchanan County 69, 363
Budde, Dietrich 52
Budde-Stump, Christine 65, 136
Buddhists 6, 301, 354, 375–79
Buffalo Center 64, 65
Buffalo Dance 25
Buffalo, NY 57
Bull Run, VA 129
Burgdoff, Paul 292
Burkholder, Chris 372
Burlington 35, 36, 46, 52, 54. 59–61, 64–65, 84–86, 97, 102, 106, 107, 110, 112, 114, 121, 128, 130, 179–80, 196, 204, 240, 258, 272, 289, 302–303
Burlington Railroad 102
Burmese 4, 160, 161, 379
Bussey 188
Butler County 259, 273
Butler, Ellis Parker 134, 285
Button, Wanda 370
BVM—see Sisters of Charity of the Blessed Virgin Mary
Byrne, James 351

Cabet, Etienne 43
Cain, Richard Harvey 112
Calhoun County 68
California 51, 141, 194, 230, 282, 290–91, 308, 328
Calvary Baptist Church, Des Moines 282, 289
Camanche 14, 162
Camara, Helder 356
Cambodians 377
Camp Dodge 253–55, 260–61, 264
Camp Pike, AR 263
Campbell, Alexander 105–6
Campbell, John Quincy Adams 126
Campbellites—see also Disciples of Christ, Church of Christ, Christian Church 2–3, 91, 105–10, 153, 338

Index

Camps Farthest Out 305
Campus Crusade for Christ 364
Cantwell, Christopher 232
Capitol Hill Church of Christ, Des
    Moines 270
Carey, Isaac E. 120, 133
Carpenter, George Thomas 106
Carpenter, Joel 291
Carpenter, N. T. 270
Carr, Ella 188
Carroll County 115, 211, 272
Carroll Kuemper High School 159
Cartright, Peter 110
Carver, George Washington 309,
    310, 314
Case farm implement union 280
Castalia 65
Catholic Interracial Council, Davenport
    356
Catholic Total Abstinence Union 199
Catholic University 222, 268, 274, 276
Catholics—see Roman Catholics
Catt, Carrie Chapman 172, 175
Cedar County 85
Cedar Falls 64, 66, 67, 96, 101, 288,
    292, 304, 316, 350, 351
Cedar Falls Bible Conference 282
Cedar Rapids 5, 13, 58, 66, 83, 97, 115,
    148, 162, 192, 203, 216, 244,
    247–49, 264, 304, 322, 338,
    340, 350, 351, 366, 377, 378
Center for Peace and Justice 354
Centerville 107, 208, 270–71
Central College 40, 288, 351
Central Christian Church, Waterloo 185
Central Church of Christ, Des Moines
    172, 190, 299
Central Jurisdiction, Methodist Church
    341
Central Presbyterian Church, Des
    Moines 97
Central West Presbytery 93
Cerro Gordo County 351
Challenge of Peace (pastoral letter) 356,
    369
Chambers, John 121
Chapel of the Church of God, Ottumwa
    283
Chapin, Edwin 201–2
Chapman, Ansel 246
Charles CIty 67, 115
Charles City College 67
Chatterton, Aaron 107
Cherokee 304, 320, 321
Chicago 297
Children of God 364
Children of Zion—see Mormons:
    Rigdonites
China 158–59
Chinese 249
Christ-Platonism 55
Christian Century 13, 106, 191, 273,
    319, 331, 334, 347
Christian Chiropractic Association 303
Christian Churches 91, 106, 131, 140,
    154, 188, 234, 271, 339
Christian Standard newspaper 208
Christian Socialist newspaper 187
Christian Oracle 107, 191, 208
Christian Science 296, 303–4
Christian Union 140
Church Extension Society 271
Church of God in Christ (COGIC) 338
Church of the New Jerusalem—see
    Swedenborgians
Church Women United 329, 337
Churches of Christ 12, 45, 106–7, 140,
    199, 234, 239, 293, 297
Citizens for Community Improvement
    347
Civil Bend 123
Civil Rights Act 351–52
Civil War, US 33, 56, 92, 95, 113, 118,
    120–37
Civilian Public Service 320
Clampitt, Amy 17, 142
Clarinda 95, 143, 161, 188
Clarion 322
Clark, Daniel 156
Clark, Glenn 305, 314
Clarke, Mary Frances 111
Clarke College 86
Clarksville 6
Classmate 216
Clausen, Claus Laurits 50, 124–25,
    127–28

Index

Clay County 171, 228
Clayton County 10, 81, 108, 248
Clergy and Laity Concerned About Vietnam 354
Clinton 11, 101, 136, 186, 201, 203, 279
Clough, Emma Rauschenbusch 160
Clough, Harriet 160
Clough, John 152, 160
Cochrane, Arthur 347–49
Coe College 16, 66, 351
Coffin, Levi 121
Coffin, Lorenzo 189
Coggeshall, Mary Jane Whiteley 172
Cohn Brothers, Waterloo 246
Cole, Milton 350
Colfax 169
College Springs 160
Collegiate Methodist Church, Ames 319, 331, 334
Collier, Ada Langworthy 171
Collins, Mahlon Day 161
Collins, Susan Angeline 158
Collson, Mary 304
Colonnese, Michael 13, 357
Colporteur 111
Columbia College—see Loras College
Commager, Henry Steele 47
Commission on Country Life 234
Commonweal 276–77
Communia 43, 58
Communist Party 333
Community of Christ 10, 49, 370
Community of True Inspiration—see Inspirationists
Conard, Laetitia 324
The Conflict (Knauss) 291
Congo 155, 157, 379
Congregation of the Humility of Mary 356
Congregationalists (see also United Church of Christ) 14, 24, 33, 35–36, 42–43, 46, 51, 54–55, 59, 61–62, 65, 67, 74, 79, 81–87, 90–92, 96–99, 104, 108, 118, 122–23, 134, 136, 153, 155–56, 172, 179–85, 187, 191, 198, 205, 226, 230, 235, 256, 278, 296, 305, 332, 336, 341

Conscientious objectors 132, 253–54, 263, 318, 319, 328–29
Conway, J. D. 279
Cook, George Cram 215, 310
Cook, Myrtle 211
Cook, Nilla Cram 295, 310–11
Coon Rapids 144
Copperheads 130, 131, 134
Coppoc, Barclay 132
Coppoc, Edwin 132
Coralville 64, 373
Corita—see Kent, Corita
Cork, Ireland 77
Cornell College 324, 351
Corning 161
Corydon 188, 202
Coston, William Hillary 177
Cottage Grove Presbyterian Church, Des Moines 270
Coughlin, Charles 271, 284, 318
Council Bluffs 29, 48, 143, 161, 166, 171, 186, 196, 249
Council of Catholic Women 353
Council on Islamic-American Relations 377
Cousin County Project 351
Cox, Jeff 159
Crawford, Lois 236
Crawfordsville 157
Creed for a Christian Skeptic (Shideler) 340
Croatians 243, 267
Crystal Cathedral 305–6
Curry, C. G. 146
Cutler, Alpheus 47–48
Cylinder 162
"Czech Athens" 58
Czech Reformed 97
Czechs—see also Bohemians 58, 93, 97, 115, 336, 338

Daily American Tribune 274
Dalai Lama 373
Dallas County 10, 69, 138
Dalits 160
Daly, Edward 352
Danes 100–101
Danville 84, 107
Danville, IL 187

Index

Darlington, Brinton 153
Darling, Ding 240
Daubenmier, Judith 27
Daughters of India (Wilson) 160
Davenport 4, 5, 54, 58, 85, 90, 104, 106–7, 120–21, 131, 133, 148, 154, 166, 189, 196–97, 214–15, 217, 225, 245, 256, 269, 278–80, 283–85, 291, 299, 301–4, 310–11, 338, 351, 356, 371, 377
Davenport *Democrat* 299
Davenport Public Library 283
Davis, Jefferson 130, 136
Davis County 10, **68**, 168
Dawes, Gil 162
Day, Dorothy 168, 356
Deaconess Movement 144, 189, 357
Dean, David 225
Dean, Henry Clay 113
Death penalty 36
Decatur County 49, **58**
Decorah 1, **100**, 123, 331, 334, 340, 345
"The Deeper Meaning of the Temperance Question" sermon (Short) 198
De Feo, Thomas 360
Deindoerfer, Johannes 81
Delaware County 352
Dell, Floyd 320
DeMent, Iris 375
Denison 104, **161**, 320
Denmark 83, **98**
Denver, CO 279, 285–86, 304
Denver *Register* 276
DePatten, Robert 305
Des Moines 4, 11, 13, **60–61**, 68, 70, 75, 78, 97–98, 101–102, 106–107, 112–13, 134, 143–44, 148. 161–63, 166, 169–70, 172, 176, 186, 188, 190–92, 196, 200, 202, 205, 211, 216, 218, 220, 222–24, 233–34, 237, 243, 248–49, 254–57, 260–62, 264–66, 270, 272, 278–80, 282–83, 285–91, 297, 299–301, 304–307, 312, 319–21, 326, 332, 337–39, 342, 350–52, 354, 356–57, 360, 363–66, 369–70, 372–73, 377–79

Des Moines Catholic Worker 369
Des Moines Confession 287
Des Moines River 29, 74, 102, 108–11
Des Moines University
Deseret [UT] 46–47
DeSmet, Pierre-Jean 29
Detroit, MI 75, 275
Dewey, Charles 327
Dexter, Lucy B. 317
Dick, Orlando 337
Dickinson, Emily 215
Diekhonner, Dietrich 70–71
Dien Bien Phu 379
Dingman, Maurice x, 12, 240, 280, 356–57, 363, 367–69
Disestablishment 39, 42, 87, 235
Disciples of Christ 2, 8, 10, 43, 91, 106–7, 116, 118, 131, 133, 140, 154–55, 169–70, 174, 188, 190–91, 200, 206, 208, 211, 227, 256, 270, 299, 319, 337, 350, 358, 361, 370, 372
Divine Science 304
Divine Word College 158
Dobberstein, Paul 277
Dog tags 322–23
Dolliver, Jonathan 158, 209
Dominie Dean (Butler) 55, 134, 221
Donaldson, Oscar F. 187
Donnellson 231
Donovan, Josephine 274
Dooyevwaad, Herman 339
Dordt College 330, 339
Dordt Confession 38–39
Douglas Avenue Presbyterian Church, Des Moines 332
Douglass, Harlan Paul 67, 153–54
Douglass, Truman 67, 153, 185, 226
Dove, William 166
Dower, William H. 307–8
Dowling High School, Des Moines and West Des Moines 363
"The Downfall of Elder Barton," (Stevens) 267
Drake, Francis Marion 107, 190, 208
Drake University 107, 157, 169, 190, 208, 214, 215, 256, 288–89, 319, 324, 337

Index

Drakesville 106, 199
Dresden, Germany 325
Dresel, Theodore 61
Drumm, Thomas 271
Drydyk, Patricia 358
Dubuque 2, 8, 10–11, 13, 29, 36, 50, 54, 59, 62–63, 67, 71, 75–80, 83, 86, 106, 110–12, 114–16, 120, 131, 151–52, 170–71, 197, 202, 219, 222, 226, 244, 246, 249, 252, 259, 261, 266, 269, 273–76, 278, 299, 316–18, 320, 347–49, 357, 380
Dubuque County 10, 61, 162
Dubuque Seminary, University of, 63, 86, 251, 324, 347–49
Dull, Rev. 145
DuMez, Kristin Kobes 367
Dumont 65, 66
Duncombe 114
Duncombe, John 118–19
Dungan, David R. 206
Dunkards—see Brethren
Dunlap, Florence 192
Dunnington, Lewis L. 329, 334
Duren, Herbert 239
Dutch Reformed 10, 38–41, 54, 58, 63, 65, 118, 140, 162, 240, 288, 306, 336, 370
    Christian Reformed 11, 40, 64, 259–60, 339–40
    Reformed Church in America—see main heading
    United Reformed 11
Dvorak, Antonin 115
Dyersville 78, 273, 346
Dykstra, Robert 92

Earling 297
East End Presbyterian Church, Ottumwa 14
Eastern Orthodox 6, 13, 244, 247, 267, 300, 380
Eastern Woodland people 25, 30
Ebenezer, NY 57
Ecumenical Ministries of Iowa 370
Eddy, Mary Baker 304
Eddy, Sherwood 282
Effendi, Shoghi 335

Effigy Mounds National Monument 17, 19
Eiboech, Joseph 196, 202, 205
Eicher, Henry 261
Eighteenth Amendment 195, 210–11
Eisenstadt, Alfred 334
Eisenhower, Dwight 322
El Salvador 13, 162, 357
Elat, Cameroun 157
Eliason, Vic 366
Elgin 258
El-Kader, Abd 248
Elkader 248
Elkhorn 101
Ellefson, Erik 124
Ellis Island, NY 250
Ellyson, Edgar 144
Elm Grove Church, Madison County 140
Else, John 350
Ely 97
Emerson, Ralph Waldo 42, 224
Emmet County 8
Emmetsburg 114, 242–43
English language 39, 138, 259
English River 76, 131
Engstrom, Donald 355
Ensley, Gerald 352
Episcopalians 91, 102–5, 125, 142, 171, 189, 209, 218, 253, 350, 370, 372
Epworth 158
Epworth Methodist Church, Des Moines 352
Espionage Act 253–54, 258
Estherville 114, 242
Ethical Culture 305
Ethiopia 63, 324
Evangelical and Reformed Church—see also United Church of Christ 258, 320–21, 329, 340
Evangelical Alliance 233–34
Evangelical Association 55, 65, 67, 140, 222–23, 292
Evangelical Covenant Church 102
Evangelical Free Church 102
Evangelical Lutheran Congregation of the Unaltered Augsburg Confession of Story and Hamilton County 100

459

Index

Evangelical United Brethren 114, 158, 341
Exorcism 29

Fagan, Joe 347
Fairfield 5, 84, 157, 307, 313–15, 355
Fairhope, AB 170
Faith Bible Theological Seminary, Ankeny 339
Falgetter family 67
Falun Gong 379
The Family 263
The Farm 355
Farmington 43. 46, 146, 196
Farquhar, Marion 161
Farrell, Pat 380
Father Ephraim—see Thompson, Charles
Fayette 66
Fayette County 69
Feast of the Holy Innocents 369
Fellowship Tabernacle, Des Moines 332
Ferber, Edna 246, 272
Ferguson, Annie 230
Ferguson, Fred 230
Ficke, August 54
Fiebiger, Judson 352
Fifer, Oren 169
Finality of the Christian Religion (Foster) 283
"Finality in Freeport," (Glaspell) 283
Finnell 66
Finney, Charles 139
Fire-Baptized Holiness Association of Southern Iowa 144–45
First African Baptist Church, Keokuk 177
First Baptist Church, Des Moines 191, 332
First Christian Reformed Church, Sioux Center 340
First Church of the Brethren, Des Moines 253
First Congregational Church, Burlington 85, 179–80
First German Baptist Church, Elgin 255
First Methodist Church, Des Moines 169, 234
First Methodist Church, Iowa CIty 334

First Methodist Episcopal Church, Sioux CIty 194
First Presbyterian Church, Davenport 217
First Presbyterian Church, Dubuque 120, 260
First Presbyterian Church, Sioux City 203
Fisk College 184–85
Fitzmaurice, Charles 75
Fleury, Peter 62
Flint Hills—see Burlington
Florenceville 71
Foley, Douglas 27
The Folks (Suckow) 230
"For Tomorrow" (Glaspell) 225
Forell, George 336
Ft. Dodge 11, 64, 80, 118, 145, 189, 244, 247, 264, 322, 357, 366
Ft. Madison 106
Ft. Smith, AR 77
Ft. Worth, TX 168, 289
'Forty-Eighters 58, 70, 83, 123
Foster, J. Ellen 203–6, 209, 212, 213, 259
Foster, George Burman 283
Foster, Lance 18
Fourierists 59
Fox—see Meskwakis
Frank, Gillian 366
Frazier, Thomas Clarkson 122
Frederick, John 225
Freethinkers 6, 37, 57–59, 61, 243
Fremont, John 92, 98, 103, 104, 107, 110, 114, 116
Fremont County 48
French 23, 26, 28, 32, 43, 54, 68, 72, 74, 79, 199, 248, 291, 316, 379
French Revolution 31, 79
Friends, Society of, and Friends Church, Friends Yearly Meeting—see Quakers
Frischel Hall, Dubuque 151
Frisians 63–65, 251
Fundamentalism 11, 24, 70, 140, 145, 153, 191, 280–294, 333, 338, 364, 366–67, 373
Fundamentalist Baptist Church, Ottumwa 283

Index

Gabriel, Charles 233
Gage, Harry Morehouse 16
Gage, William 191
Galena, IL 67, 75
Galesburg 143
Gamewell, Mary Porter 158
Gandhi, Mohandas 184, 310–11
Garden Grove 46
Garland, Hamlin 274
Garnavillo 62
Garner 216, 284
Garrett, Ruth 372
Garryowen 77
Garwick, Noah 188
Garwin 66
Gaskin, Ina Mae 355
Gaston, E. B. 170
Gates, George Augustus 153, 156, 178–85, 223
Gaylord, Reuben 84
George 64, 65
George, Henry 170, 300
Gerig, Sebastian 68
German Evangelicals—see also Evangelical and Reformed Church 55, 61, 71, 110, 258
German Methodist—see Evangelical Association, United Brethren, Evangelical United Brethren
German Reformed—see also Evangelical and Reformed, United Church of Christ 36, 55, 61, 63, 86, 229, 331, 341
Germans 8, 10, 36, 41, 49, 54–72, 74, 77–78, 80–81, 86, 91, 97, 100–101, 108, 110, 114–15, 138, 151, 196, 208, 211, 215, 222, 226, 227, 240, 243–45, 251, 256, 258–59, 272, 274–76, 292, 336, 340–41, 347–48
Ghost Dance 148
Gilead (Robinson) 99
Gingerich, Simon 260–61
Gingrich, Owen 377
Gladbrook 65
Glandon, Clara 131
Glaspell, Susan 215, 225, 227, 283–84, 310
Glenwood 21, 289, 359

God's Universe (Gingrich) 377
Gonner, Nicholas 274–75
Goodwin, Lloyd 364
Goshen 66
Goshen Statement (Church of the Brethren) 254
Gospel Assemblies (Sowder/Goodwin) 364–65
Gospel Missionary newspaper 157
Graham, Billy 289, 338–39
Grace Episcopal Cathedral, Davenport 218
Gracehill 77
Graceland College 49
Grain Millers union 14
Grand View College 101
Grant, Ulysses 134
Grassley, Charles 263
Greater Des Moines Council of Churches 337
Green Earth (Manfred) 41
Greenback Party 168–69, 205
Greene County, AB 93
Griffin, Edna 186
Grimes, James 85, 131
Grinnell 143, 355
Grinnell, Josiah 85
Grinnell College 67, 85, 104, 156, 159, 170, 180–85, 189, 202, 205, 249, 256, 302, 305, 324, 326, 351, 354–55
Griswold College 104, 209
Gross, H. R. 283
Grotto of the Redemption 277
Grundy Center 64
Grundy County 10, 63, 64, 65, 70, 351
Grundtvig, Frederike 101
Grundtvig, N. F. S. 101
Guatemala 151, 162, 376
Guthrie Center 144
Guthrie County 162

Haan, B. J. 340
Haddock, George 194
Hakansson, Magnus 102
"Half Breed Tract" 68
Hall, Claybourne 131
Halland, Bengt Magnus 102
Halsey, A. W. 150

461

Index

Hamburg 155
Hamilton, William 33
Handles of Power (Dunnington) 304
Hansen, Harry 217–18
Hanson, Howland 190–91
Hardin County 10, 141, 258
Harding, Burcham 299
Harding, William 259, 263
Harding Park Open Bible Church, Ottumwa 283
Hargis, Mina Davis 137
Harmony—see Zwingle
Harnack, Curtis 104
Harpers Ferry, WV 123, 132
Harris, Lileah 350
Harris, Percy 350
Hartzler, Bob 354
Hastings 188
Hatch, Nathan 105
"Have Thy Own Way" (hymn) 234
Haven, Silas 129
Hawaii 185, 323
Hawthorn Hill—see Iowa Bible Training School
Hayne, Donald 318–19
Haynes, George 184–85
Hazleton 360, 363
"He Lifted Me" (hymn) 233
Hedstrom, Jonas 102
Hempstead, Stephen 197
Hennessey, Ronald William 151, 162
Hennessy, John 114, 116, 122
Henry County 121
Henry Wallace: The Man and the Myth (Macdonald) 308
Hephzibah Faith Missionary Association 11, 146
Herron, George Davis 153, 178–83, 223, 235, 240, 297
Hickenlooper, Bourke 351
"Higher Ground" (hymn) 233
Highland Park, Des Moines 191, 312
Hill, Harold 296
Hill, James J. 73
Hill, Kate Alexander 160
Hindus 5, 6, 299, 301, 378–79
Hinshaw, Cecil 328
Hinshaw, Virgil 211

Hiroshima Day 369
"His Eye Is on the Sparrow" (hymn) 233
Hiteman 177
Ho Chunks 16, 22, 29, 32–33
Hoag, Enoch 153
Hoar, Thomas 77
Hobbs Grove 130
Hocking, William 162
Hodge brothers 5, 36–37, 45
Hoffman(n), Matthias 135, 266, 272–74
Holbrook 14, 357
Holbrook, John 83, 86
Holiness 8, 11, 87, 138–49, 195, 223, 294, 296
Holland 65
Holmes, Marjorie 366
Holmes County, MS 351
Holocaust 325–26, 340
Home Missionary magazine 79
Honey Creek 141
Hoover, Herbert 211
Hoover, Herbert F. 354
Hoover High School, Des Moines 362
Hornaday, William Temple 240
Horton, Loren 101
Hospers, Henry 35, 40
Hostetler, John 238
Houser, Charles 332
Howard County 67
Hubbard, Ethel Daniels 150, 158
Hudson 65
Hughes, Harold 211, 281, 310, 353, 360–61
Hughes, John 106, 131
Hull 64, 259
Hull House, Chicago 192
Hultin, Ida 220–222
Humboldt 51, 304
Humboldt College 59
Humeston 271, 297
Hummer, Michael 95–96
Hurst, John 205
Hus Memorial Presbyterian Church, Cedar Rapids 97, 338

I Am Movement 303
Icaria 42–44, 170
Ida Grove 114, 212, 304

Index

Igran, Abdullah 322
Illinois 31, 46, 49, 56, 61, 64, 65, 67, 75, 84, 98, 102, 110, 186, 187, 220, 273, 284
Illinois Confederation 22, 29
Immaculate Heart Sisters 357
Independence 71, 320, 329
Independence, MO 44, 49, 103
India 152, 155, 159–60, 299–301
Indiana 25, 56, 65, 141, 180, 204
Indiana Yearly Anti-Slavery Meeting 122
Indiana Yearly Meeting of Orthodox Friends 122
Indochina War 142, 346, 354
Industrial Removal Office 246
Industrial Workers of the World 191
Inkpaduta 33
Inspirationists 11, 42, 52, 56–57, 132, 170, 237, 263–64, 306
International Bible Students Association—see Jehovah's Witnesses
International Metaphysical League 297
Ioka 130
Ion 32
Iowa Band 15, 33, 43, 73, 83–86, 88, 179, 181
Iowa Bible Training School 189
Iowa Board of Rabbis 352
Iowa Catholic Historical Review 277
Iowa Christian College, Des Moines 339
Iowa CIty 11, 46,, 60, 90, 65–96, 108, 111, 114, 154, 167, 200, 220, 244–46, 273, 278, 301, 304, 322, 329, 335, 349, 351, 354–55, 362, 375
Iowa City Women's Missionary Society 154
Iowa College—see Grinnell College
Iowa Commission on Religion and Race 352
Iowa Congregational Association 183, 198
Iowa Council of Churches 352, 358, 369
Iowa Cranks (Chapin) 201
Iowa Falls 365
Iowa Farm Bureau 358
Iowa Farm Unity Coalition 368

Iowa Inter-Church Agency for Peace and Justice 369
Iowa Inter-Church Forum 369
Iowa Retail Hardware Association 236
Iowa Staats-Anzeiger 196
Iowa State Historical Society 359
Iowa State University 162, 175, 229, 319, 365
The Iowa Story (Harsha) 98
Iowa Supreme Court 48, 204, 223, 373
Ioways 18, 21, 22, 33
Irish 8, 51, 77–78, 114–16, 151, 215, 229, 243, 246, 271, 274–75
Irish Emigrant Society 77
Irwin 6
Irwin, Benjamin Hardin 11, 144–45, 147, 218
Italy, Intalians 233, 243, 267, 322

Jackson, Sheldon 75, 152, 223
Jackson County 47, 115
Jacobsen, Lewis 332
Jamaica 152, 155
James, William 308
Janes, Martha 165, 171
Japan 151, 161, 285, 318, 323, 348
Jasper Colony 70–71
Jasper County 96, 123, 143, 239, 292
Jehovah's Witnesses 4, 316, 326–27
Jenkins, H. D. 223
Jensen, Richard 210
Jenson, Robert 340
Jesuits 29–30, 74
Jesus People Army 364
Jewish Theological Seminary 279
Jews 6, 56, 72, 180, 189, 222, 224–25, 232, 242–46, 249, 251, 270–72, 278–79, 281, 314, 322, 325–26, 336–37, 342, 358, 367, 376
  Belz 376
  Chalad-Lubavitcher 376
  Conservative 244
  Hasidic 245, 376
  Orthodox 244–46
  Reform 244, 283
  Sighet 376
  Vizhnitz 376
  Zionists 245, 250, 326
Johnson, Denis 362

Index

Johnson County 66, 68, 78, 142, 261
Joliet, Louis 39
Jones, George 113
Jones, Laurence 154
Jordan, Charles 341
Jordan, James 113–14
Jordan, Philip D. 24, 84
Josephites—see Community of Christ
Judy, Arthur 218

Kadac, Jeanna 366
Kalona 68–69, 254, 372
Kane, Stephen 322
Kanesville—see Council Bluffs
Kanouse, Sarah 32
Kansas 22, 32–33, 48, 52, 99, 123, 141, 173
Kansas City, MO 145
Kantor, MacKinlay 135
Karens 161, 379
Kashmir 295, 311
Kasson, Caroline 129
Kasson, John 129, 151
Katz Drug Store, Des Moines 186
Kaufman, Daniel 260
KBBG Radio 353
Keane, John J. 13, 199, 268, 299
Kellerton 188
Kelley's Army 190
Kellum, Samuel 121
Kemper, Jackson 163
Kent, Corita 357
Keokuk 50, 72, 96, 106, 108, 112–13, 117, 120, 126, 128, 166, 175, 177, 202, 232, 288
Keokuk (Sauk leader) 31
Keokuk County 60–61, 70, 130–31, 142. 197, 234, 238
Keosauqua 29
Kertzer, Morris 279, 322
Kesley 65
Kestekides, Melitio 244
Keswick Movement 139
KFGQ 236
KFNF 237
Kierkegaard, Soren 101
King, Martin Luther, Jr. 169, 347, 351, 356

King, Steve 8
Kinsinger, Earling 261
Kirkpatrick, Joseph 2, 3
Klumpp, Andrew 174
KMA 237
Knauss, Elizabeth 291
Kneeland, Abner 37–38, 41–43, 82, 298, 308
Knights of Columbus 266, 272, 275
Know-Nothing Party 8, 113, 116
Knoxville 131, 373
Korea 151, 162–63
Koren, Elisabeth 1, 89, 100, 103
Koren, Vilhelm 1, 100
Kosher 246, 358, 376
Koszta 143
Koval, George 245
Kramer, Dale 229
Krishnamurti 307
Kruse, Margaret 358
Ku Klux Klan 8, 269–71
Kuhlman, Kathryn 291
Kuhns, Frederick 104
Kun, Frantisek 48, 97
KXEL 253
Kyle, Joseph Addison 256
Kynett, A. J. 209

Labor Party 191, 200
Lacona 326–27
LaFollette, Robert 256
Lake Mills 100
Lamanites 20–21
Lamoni 47, 49, 297
Lancaster Church of Christ 234
Landers, Ann 342
Landis, Benson V. 228.
Lane, Ortha May 138–39
Lane, Stoddard 14, 218, 319, 332
Lansing 66
Larrabee, William 194, 205–7
Latos, Dionysius 300
Latskiva, Lithuania 245
Latter-Day Saints—see Mormons
Latvia 244
Lawson, Alfred 4, 312
Lawsonomy 297, 312

464

Index

Leadership Conference of Women Religious 380
League for Social Justice, Davenport 356
League of Humanity 258
Leander Clark College 66
Lebanese 244, 247, 267, 377
Lederer, Esther Pauline—see Ann Landers
Lee, Henry Washington 104, 125
Lee County 29, 51, 55, 66, 68, 83, 96, 98, 367, 375
LeMars 67
Lenihan, Mathias 269
Lenz, Lyz 365–66
Leo XIII 268
Leon 297
Leopold, Aldo 246
Leopoldine Society 76, 78
Levi, Alexander 72
Lewin, Kurt 325
Liberal Catholic Church 307
Libby, John 111
Liberation Theology 162
Libertyville 69
Life Magazine 322, 334, 340, 355
Life Story of Rev. Wm Brown 1930 (Brown) 175
Ligutti, Luigi 233
Lilith (Collier) 165, 171
Lincoln 229, 265
Lincoln, NE 144
Lincoln, Abraham 121, 130–31, 135–37
Linn County 66, 106, 350–51, 370
Lisbon 66
Lithuanians 243, 245
Littell, Franklin 56
Little Brown Church in the Vale, Nashua 232–33
Little Rock 65
Littlefield, Oscar 245
Living Word Fellowship 11
Lochner, Frederick 59, 60
Loehe, Wilhelm 80–81, 86–87
Long Creek Baptist Church, Danville 107
Long Remember (Kantor) 135
Loras, Mathias 74–79, 86–87, 114, 116, 117, 152, 199, 266
Loras College 86, 266, 324, 347
Lost Creek 106
Loucks, Aaron 254
Lovely Lane Methodist Church, Cedar Rapids 350
Loving Kindness tour 378
Lowry, David 32–33
Lucas County 11, 144, 234
Lucas, Robert 46
Luker, Ralph 185
Lundgren 66
Luther College 100, 163, 300
Luther Valley, WI 50
Lutheran Social Services of Iowa 338
Lutherans 1, 10–11, 36, 50–51, 55, 59–61, 65, 74, 79–81, 87, 91–92, 99–103, 108, 124–25, 127, 139, 151, 162–63, 172, 204, 217, 240, 258–59, 292, 327, 331, 334, 336, 338, 340–41, 350, 370, 372, 376
    American Lutheran Church 60, 101, 336
    Augsburg Lutherans 11
    Augustana Lutheran Church 102–3
    Evangelical Lutheran Church in America 99, 163, 336
    Evangelical Lutheran Synod 100
    Frankean Lutherans 103. 122, 123
    Hauge Synod 100
    Iowa Synod 50, 60, 80–82, 336
    Lutheran Church in America 101, 336
    Missouri Synod 56–60, 80, 99, 125, 292, 336, 340–41
    Norwegian-Danish Evangelical Lutheran Church ("The Conference") 50
    United Lutheran Synod 100
Lutman, Thomas 236
Luxembourgers 159, 274–75
Lynch, Mary 357
Lyon County 10, 64
Lyons—see Clinton
Lyons, France 75

McCabe, Charles Cardwell 206
McCarthy, Joseph 333
McCleary, William 157

Index

McClintock, J. C. 89
McCraven, Henry 172
McDonald, Donald 279
McGregor 66, 303
McIntire, Carl 253
McPherson, Aimee Semple 11, 147
McTaggert, Fred 26
Macdonald, Dwight 308
Macedonia 46
Macy, Jesse 185, 189
Madoulet, Jean Baptiste 54–68
Madrid 102, 378
Magnetic healing 302
Magoun, George 136, 205
Maharishi 313
Maharishi Vedic City 5, 313
Mahaska County 59, 131, 240
Mahony, Dennis 77, 131, 136
Maine 195
Mamrelund Lutheran Church, Stanton 103
Manchester 201, 202
Manfred, Frederick 41, 236, 244
Manitoba 47
Mannheimer, Eugene 224, 278, 326
Mannheimer, Louise 224
Manti 48
Maquoketa 77, 84, 146
Maquoketa River 77
Marion County 10
Mark IV Pictures 365
Marquette, Jacques 29
Marsh, Fredric 334
Marshall County 10, 141, 148, 159, 294
Marshalltown 51, 66, 93, 144, 161, 193, 207, 237, 269, 355, 365, 378, 379
Martin Luther King, Jr. Center 353
Martindale, Pauline Williams 173
Marty, Martin 6
Mason City 244, 291, 296, 358
"Mass Extermination as a Means of Waging War" statement 347
Massachusetts 20, 38, 42
Matthews, Gene 163
Matthias 52
Maxfield 60
Maytag 14

Mazzuchelli, Samuel 32–33, 75, 79, 90, 273
Mead, Waldo 350
Medbury, Charles 256
Meisner, Linda 364
Melville, Thomas 151
Men and Religion Forward Movement 172, 188
Men of the Past (McElroy) 98
Mennonites 4, 10, 36, 47, 55–56, 68–69, 71, 132, 140, 142, 238, 253–55, 260–61, 263, 319–20, 328, 354, 363, 370
    Evangelical Mennonites 11
    General Conference Mennonites 55
Mental Illness 297
Merle Hay Mall, Des Moines 264, 280
Meservey 65
Meskwakis 5–6, 15, 22–33, 51, 53, 148–49, 163, 213, 226–27, 237, 343–44, 381
"The Message of Jesus to Men of Wealth," (Herron) 179
Messenger 269, 277, 279, 358
Methodists 2, 8, 10–12, 36, 41, 43, 51, 55, 59–61, 65–66, 75, 82, 86, 88, 90–91, 102–3, 105–6, 110–15, 117–18, 128–29, 131, 139–40, 143–44, 147, 154, 158, 161–63, 166, 169, 173–76, 188–89, 193–94, 197, 200, 203–12, 215–17, 222–23, 229–30, 233–34, 240, 249, 258, 260, 262, 267, 292, 304, 319–20, 323, 327, 329, 331, 334–36, 338, 341, 350–52, 361, 369–70, 372
    African Methodist Episcopal 112, 158, 177, 185, 338, 369
    African Methodist Episcopal Zion 113
    Christian Methodist Episcopal 113
    Methodist Protestants 90, 111–12, 114, 173
    Primitive Methodists 90, 111–12
    Swedish Methodists 102
    Wesleyan Methodists 118, 123, 144, 146
Methodist Reporter 173

Index

Metis 68, 74
Metropolitan Church Association 145
Metz, Christian 57
Mexican Revolution 243
Mexican War 183
Mexicans 243, 267, 280, 370
Mexico 155, 300
Meyer, H. O. 289
Michael, Marianne 162
Miller, Jack 351
Miller, John
Miller, Samuel 298, 361
Millerites 40, 91
Milner, Virginia Voorhies 162
Milwaukee, WI 235
Minneapolis, MN 179, 289
Minnesota 33, 50, 75, 179, 209, 246, 258, 274, 275, 314
Minyan 242
Missionverein 76
Mississippi 130, 154, 175, 350–51,
Mississippi River 18, 20, 22, 29, 31, 44, 50, 75, 79, 83–84, 90, 230
Missouri 8, 32, 44, 46, 49
Missouri River 21, 33, 75, 132, 223, 320
Missouris 22
Mitchell, Anna Marie 162
Mitchell County 363
Moingwenas 29
Mondamin Avenue Church of Christ, Des Moines 297
Moninger, Margaret 159
Monist Society 283
Monona County 47
Monroe County 109, 229, 267
Montezuma 173, 317
Montgomery, AB 350
Montgomery, Helen Barrett 287
Montgomery County 322
Mooar 106
Moody, Dwight 139
Moody, James 270
Moravia 71
Moravians 71
Mormon Creek 46
Mormons 5, 6, 20–21, 35, 36–37, 39, 44–49, 51, 96, 102, 231, 298
  Baneemyites 47–48
  Cutlerites 48
  Hedrickites 47
  Rigdonites 47
Morning Sun 95
Morningside College 67, 324
Morrell, John 14
Morrison, Charles Clayton 107, 191
Morrison, Rebecca 303
Morrison, Theodore 257
Mother Mosque 247–48, 377
Mott, Frank Luther 210, 215–17
Mott, John R. 214, 253, 262, 375
Mott, Lucretia 172
Moundbuilders 17, 19–20
Mount Ayr 188
Mount Pleasant 65, 67, 84–85, 106, 113, 200, 261 320, 328
Moville 66, 114
Muhammed 311
Muir, Werner 332
Mulct Law 194, 208
Mumbai, India 301
Munich, Germany 76
Munoz, Irene 358–59
Munoz, Molly 358–59
Murphy 66
Murphy, Dennis 127
Murphy, Marilyn 370
Muscatine 99, 112, 117, 134, 145, 153, 196, 225, 244–45, 253, 271, 292, 358
Muscatine County Ministerial Alliance 358
Muscatine Migrant Committee 358
Muslims 6, 155, 247–48, 304, 311. 322, 377
  Druze 247
  Metualay 247
  Shia 247
  Sunni 247
Muste, A. J. 252
Mutually Assured Destruction doctrine 332
My Road to India (Cook) 311

Nabhan-Warren, Kristy 231
Nagarkar, B. B. 301
Nagasaki, Japan 325

Index

Nafziger, Jacob 138
Napoleonic Wars 30, 51
Nash, Martha 353
Nashville, TN 184
National Association of Evangelicals 339
National Association for the Advancement of Colored People (NAACP) 271
National Catholic Reporter 279
National Conference of Christians and Jews 278
National Council of Catholic Women 353
National Council of Churches 358
National Fast Day 120–21
National Temperance Society 206
Native American Church 26, 149, 343
Native Americans—see also individual nations 16–34, 44, 48, 74–75, 100, 148–49, 151, 153, 307–8, 359
Nauvoo, IL 36, 39, 44–47, 96
Nazarenes 11, 143–47, 283, 327
Natchez, MS 130
Nebraska 33, 62, 144, 186, 324, 366
Nephites 20
Nennig, Charles 225
Neuendettelsau, Bavaria 80
New Age 313, 335, 355, 364, 365
New Buda 58
New Hartford 293
New Jerusalem COGIC, Cedar Rapids 338
New London 93, 126
New Melleray 78
New Mexico 162, 277
New Orleans Mardi Gras 32
New Providence 17, 141–42, 159
New Sweden 102
New Thought 28, 241, 292, 302–6, 313
New Vienna 78
New York, NY 52, 57, 63, 77, 130–31, 142, 161, 208, 246, 256, 275, 279, 302, 308, 322, 348–49, 364, 376
New York *Times* 3, 250, 311
Newland, Vernon 339
Newton 14, 71, 113, 160, 172

Newton, Joseph Fort 13
Ng, William 249
Nichols, Sam 143, 319, 323, 334
Niemoller, Martin 340
Nisei 324
Nixon, RIchard 285
Nobel Prize 375
Non-Partisan Women's Christian Temperance Union 205–6
Norris, Frank 289–90
North Carolina 71, 121, 350
North English 71, 188
North High School, Des Moines 326
Norwalk 172
Norway 71
Northwestern College 40
Norwegians 1, 44, 50–51, 100–101, 103, 124–25, 258, 334, 336
Nudist Christian Church of the Blessed Virgin Jesus 11
Nuclear weapons 328, 332, 348, 353, 356, 369, 370, 373
Nuers 161
Nugen, William 126
Nugent, Joseph 169
Nuhn, Ferner 316

O'Brien County 10
O'Connor, William 279, 280
Odebolt 201
Oelwein 347
Oewig, Maria 219
Ojibwes 80
Oklahoma 153
Old Order River Brethren 69
"Old Rugged Cross" (hymn) 234
Old Zion Methodist Church, Burlington 110
Olmitz 144
Omaha Baptist Bible Institute 339
Omaha Presbyterian Theological Seminary 186
Omaha, NE 46, 190
Omahas 22
O'Meara, Thomas 266
Omrcanin, Margaret 230
Oneness Pentecostalism 364
Oneota Culture 21

468

Index

Oom the Omnipotent—see Pierre Bernard
Open Bible Standard Church 11, 147, 283, 338, 366
Orange City 40, 252
Order of Enoch 49
Orr Focus 21
Ortega y Gasset, Jose 12
Osage 153, 217
Osages 61
Oskaloosa 106, 107, 109, 113, 144, 146, 172, 212, 255, 328, 354
Oskaloosa College—see Drake University
Otoes 22, 33
Ott, Edward Amherst 169
Ottumwa 11, 14, 46, 113, 147, 148, 186, 188, 202, 244, 246, 272, 283, 292

Pacem in Terris Award 351, 356
Page, Kirby 305, 319, 328
Page County 161
Palmer College of Chiropractic 302
Palmer, B. J. 302–3
Palmer, D. D. 302–3
Palmer, Gregory 341
Palmer, Phoebe 145
Pantheists 6, 37, 42–43, 308, 310, 321, 323
Papua New Guinea 151
Parham, Charles 145
Parker, H. J. 338
Parker, Theodore 42
Parkersburg 64, 65, 251
Parkfair Mall, Des Moines 312
Parnell 14
Parsons College 157, 324
Paulina 71
Pawley, Christine 217
P. E. O. 174
Pearl Harbor, HI 318–20
Pearre, Caroline Neville 154
Pearson, James 237
Pearson, Maria 359
Pegler, Westbrook 308
Pella 10, 39, 65, 143, 237, 244, 288
Pella Christian Church 39

Pentecostal Church of God 147
Pentecostal Fellowship of North America 338
Pentecostal Holiness Church 141
Pentecostals 11, 47, 144, 149, 234, 283, 294, 296, 335, 338, 339, 364
Pennsylvania 56, 65, 66, 68, 197, 205, 209
People's Church, Sioux City 196, 198
People's Party 168–70
Peoria 259
Peorias 74
Perfectionism 195
Perry 249, 269
Perry, William Stevens 150
Peterson, Suzanne 370
Philippines 159, 183, 339
Phillips, C. W. 333
Phillips, Pauline Esther—see Abigail Van Buren
Pickett, Nina 299
Pietism 56, 57, 62, 69, 72, 80, 87, 91–92, 100–102, 123, 137, 139, 169, 199, 210, 288
Pietsch, W. E. 353
Pilgrims of Iowa (Douglass) 235
Piney Woods School, MS 154
Pins, Kenneth 346
Pisgah 46
Pitts, William S. 233
Plan of Union 82, 96
Plano, IL 491
Playboy Magazine 355
Pleasant Hill Christian Church, Washington 121
Plumbe, Joseph, Jr. 197
Plymouth Brethren 11
Plymouth Congregational Church, Des Moines 319, 332
Pocahontas 242
Polk City 71
Pollard, Adelaide Addison 234
Pomeroy 258
Pontifical Commission on Justice and Peace 353
Postville 66, 262, 373, 376
Potawatomis 29
Power to Become (Dunnington) 301
Poweshiek 31

Index

Poweshiek County 163, 217
Prairie City *Gleaner and Herald* 297
Prairie Club, Des Moines 300
Prairie du Chien, WI 74
Pratt, H. O. 205
Premillennialism
Preparation 48
Prescott, J. 109
Presbyterians ix, 14, 32–33, 36, 55, 58–60, 62–63, 65–66, 75, 82–84, 86, 89–90, 92–98, 112–18, 120, 126, 134, 144, 149, 152–53, 157, 159–62, 186, 188, 191, 205, 208, 216–17, 219, 223, 225, 229–30, 234–35, 237–39, 247, 249, 251, 259–60, 265, 270–71, 277, 284, 287–88, 293, 301, 305, 307–8, 313, 317, 332, 336, 338, 341, 343, 347–48, 352, 355, 370, 372–73, 376
    Colored Cumberland Presbyterians 93
    Covenanters 93
    Cumberland Presbyterians 32, 92, 285
    Free Presbyterians 96, 123
    New School Presbyterians 95–96, 133, 134
    Old School Presbyterians 95–96, 133–34, 139
    Orthodox Presbyterians 288, 293
    Reformed Presbyterians 95, 97
    Seceders 93
    Welsh Calvinist Methodists 93
Preuss, A. O. 340
Price, Hiram 197, 209, 211
Primghar 71
Princeton, NJ 162
Prisons and Prayer (Wheaton) 192
Private Thoughts on Theology (Kirkpatrick) 2, 3
Progressive Party 186
Prohibition Party 192, 205, 206, 209, 211
Prophetic sisterhood 173, 220, 304
Prospect Hill, Sioux CIty 152, 223
Protocols of the Elders of Zion 291
Pruitt, Edward 169
Puerto Rico 155

Pumpf, C. C. 223
Punjab 160

Quakers 3, 10–11, 17, 36, 51–52, 56, 89, 95, 98, 111–12, 122–23, 131–32, 138, 140–42, 145, 149, 152–53, 163, 170, 172, 189, 212, 215, 255, 261, 291, 305, 319–20, 324–25, 328, 332, 352, 354, 364
Quick, Herbert 274
Quincy, IL 46, 98

Radio Chapel, Mason City 291
Rand, Caroline 180
Rand, Carrie 180
Rauschenbusch, Walter 160
Ray, Robert E. 8, 359, 361, 379
Reasoner, Harry 51
Rebman, Edith 290
Red Oak 322
Redding 188
Reed, Julius 84
Reid, Isaiah 144
Reformed—see Dutch Reformed, German Reformed, and Czech Reformed
Regier, Gustav 71
Reno, Milo 12, 239
Reorganized Church of the Latter-Day Saints—see Community of Christ
Re-thinking Missions report 162
Revised Standard Version 339
R. F. D. (magazine) 359
Rhineland 54
Rhodes v. Iowa 208
Richland 71
Riceville 6
Rieger, Joseph 61
Rigdon, Sidney 45, 47
Righter, Walter 372
Riley, William Bell 289–91,
Riverview Park, Cedar Falls 292
Roadside Settlement, Des Moines 192
Roberts, Millard 355
Robertson, Pat 367
Robinson, Jackie 347
Robinson, John A. 253–54

Index

Robinson, Marilynne 25, 85. 99, 123,
Rock Island, IL 31, 108, 220
Rock Rapids 64, 65
Rockford 129
Roe v. Wade 366
Roerich, Nicholas 306
Rohme, Magnus 124
Rolla, MO 127
Rolvaag, Ole 101, 274
Roma 267
Roman Catholics ix, x, 2, 3, 6, 8, 10, 12–13, 29, 33, 36, 51, 54–56, 71, 75–79, 87, 91, 114–17, 130–35, 158–59, 163, 168–69, 186, 199, 210–11, 219–22, 226–27, 229–32, 238–40, 243, 246–47. 256, 264, 266–81, 297–98, 305, 314, 316–19, 321, 326–27, 337, 344–47, 351, 353, 356–58, 363, 369–71, 376–77, 379–80
Romance of African Methodism (Singleton) 338
Round Prairie Presbyterian Church, Kossuth 123
Roos, Charles 308
Roosevelt, Theodore 234, 250
Rorabaugh, William 195
Rubashkin family 123
Running Moccasin—see Pearson, Maria
Ruppel, Leona 160
Rum and Its Remedy (Dungan) 206
Russell, Howard 209
Russians 50, 55, 68, 189, 244, 308, 333, 376
Ruston, William O. 251
Ryan Thomas 210

Sac and Fox—see Meskwakis, Sauks
Saginaw, MI 80–81
St. Ambrose University 238, 280
St. Ansgar 50, 100, 127
St. Boniface 115
St. Bridget's Catholic Church, Postville 370
St. Gabriel's Monastery, Des Moines 264
St. George's Greek Orthodox Church, Des Moines 244

St. Joseph's Catholic Church, Ft. Madison 36
St. Joseph's Catholic Church, Sioux CIty 243
St. Louis, MO 8, 31, 63, 67, 70–71, 75, 77–78, 275
St. Mary's Catholic Church, Dubuque 275
St. Mary's Catholic Church, Iowa CIty 114, 318
St. Mary's Catholic Church, Marshalltown 320
St. Mary's Catholic Church, Waterloo 243, 321
St. Patrick 115
St. Paul, MN 73, 285, 315
St. Paul A. M. E. Church, Des Moines 338
St. Paul Methodist Church, Cedar Rapids 350–51
St. Peter Vietnamese Catholic Community, Des Moines 379
St. Raphael Cathedral, Dubuque 86
St. Siebald Lutheran Church, Strawberry Point 81–82
St. Vincent Catholic Church, Riverside 76
Salem 1, 21, 22
Salem Church of Lincoln 229, 265
Salem Evangelical Association Church, Des Moines 222
Salter, William 1, 35. 46, 77. 84, 85, 90, 117, 125, 128, 179–80.
Salter, William McKenzie 180
Saltzman, Eleanor 228
Salubria 41–42, 59
Salvaterra, David 266
Salvation Army 146
Sampson, Francis 321
San Francisco, CA 278, 304, 324, 349
Sanford, Nettie 166
Saukenauk 25, 31
Sauks 22, 25, 26, 30, 31, 33
Saturday Evening Post 322
Sawyers, Mott 271
Scattergood School, West Branch 324
Schindler, Oskar 326
Schleswig-Holstein 5, 58

Index

Schmitt, Aloysius 321
Schneider, Paul 19
Scholte, Hendrik 37–41, 59, 65, 380
School of Religion—see University of Iowa
Schroder, Joseph 71
Schuller, Robert 13, 252, 287, 305–6
Schumann, Wilhelm 258
Schwarz, Frederick 253
Scopes trial 287
Scot, Barbara J. 90, 93, 282
Scotch Grove Presbyterian Church 89
Scots 92, 94, 135, 235, 306
Scott v. Thompson 48
Scott, Martha 334
Scott, William 188
Second Baptist Church, Centerville 271
Second Baptist Church, Davenport 120
Second Baptist Church, Mt. Pleasant 108
Selma, AB 350
Session, Perrrigrene 35
Seven Years War 30
Seventh-Day Adventists 51, 132, 240, 319, 333
Sexual abuse scandal 371
Shambaugh 188
Shawnees 25, 30
Sheldahl 100
Sheldon 236
Sheldon, Charles 314
Shenandoah 237, 244, 358,
Sheridan, Frank J. 222
Sherlock, Wallace E. 234
Sherrill 62, 67
Sherwood, A. P. 260
Shideler, Mary McDermott 340–41
Shields, T. T. 285–90, 353
Shinar Cumberland Presbyterian Church, New London 93
Short, Wallace 191, 198, 380
Shueyville 66
Sibley 65
Sibley, Mulford Q. 316
Sigourney 61
Sikhs 379
Silver Lake, IL—see Baileyville, IL
Simpson College 324
Singleton, George 338

Siouan language group 22
Sioux (Lakota) 22, 25, 33, 359
Sioux Center 11, 41, 260, 339, 340
Sioux City 67, 115, 148, 152, 172, 191, 194, 198, 223, 226, 232, 243–47, 259, 272, 274, 278, 292, 342, 356, 359, 370, 380
Sioux County 35, 115, 274, 305
Sisters of Charity of the Blessed Virgin Mary 111
Sisters of Perpetual Adoration 159
Sivas, Turkey 155–56, 184
Skahill, Msgr. 266–67
Skunk River 110, 131, 259
Slater, Duke 186
Slater, George W. 178, 185–86
Slater Hall 186
Slavery 50, 79, 82, 83, 92, 98, 104, 107, 110, 111, 113, 114, 116, 121–24, 126, 133–37, 168, 172, 175–76
Slovaks 249
Smiley, Jane 148, 294
Smith, Al 270
Smith, Emma 47
Smith, Frank 339
Smith, Ida Belle 211
Smith, Joseph [Jr.} 20, 36, 44–48
Smith, Joseph III 49
Smith, Maynard 332
Smyth, Clement 78
Snethen, Nicholas 111
Social Gospel 160, 179, 181–91, 199, 213, 217, 235, 250, 283, 310, 341
Socialist Party 181, 187–88
Social Task of Christianity (Batten) 191–92
Society for the Propagation of the Faith 75
Society of the Temple of the People 307–8
Solon 85
Somalis 377
Some Luck (Smiley) 148
Sons of Temperance 197
The Soul's Sincere Desire (Clark) 305
S. O. S. Signal 237
South Dakota 12, 33, 62, 240
South English 130–31

Index

South Waterloo Church of the Brethren 70
Southern Christian Leadership Conference 351
Soviet Union 245, 321, 369
Spaulding, Benjamin 59
Speaking of Faith radio program 213
Speer, Robert 262
Spence, Hartzell 334
Spencer 165, 171
Spillville 115
Spirit Lake 33, 100
Spiritual Midwifery (Gaskin) 355
Spiritualists 96, 117, 303
Springdale 132
Springfield, MO 153
Srinivas, Megan 379
Stanton 102–103
Stanton, ELizabeth Cady 196, 203
Starbuck, Edwin 3
State University of Iowa—see University of Iowa
Statesmanship and Religion (Wallace) 295, 310
Stavanger 51
Steiner, Edward 242, 249–50, 253, 256, 317
Stephens State Forest 11
Stevens, James 267
Stirlen, Edythe 237
Stone, Barton 105
Stone, J. C. 260
Storm Lake 366
Story County 100, 218
Stout 65
Strangers and Guests (pastoral letter) 356
STRATCOM 369
Strawberry Point 81
Strilson 66
Strong, Josiah 156, 224
Student Volunteer Movement 161, 261–62
Stumme, Larry 350
Suburbanization 331–32, 363
Supralapsarianism 2
Suckow, Ruth 172, 230–31, 236, 253, 342

Sudan 161, 377
Sullivan Brothers 321
Sumner 66
The Sunbeam 197
Sunday, Billy 216–17, 234, 260, 281–82, 284–86
Sunday School 216–17, 234, 260, 283, 305, 309
Susquehanna River 8
Swander, Mary 269–70
Swedenborgians 6, 55, 70–71, 96, 305
Swedes 102–3
Syria 162, 243–44, 247, 377

Tabor 99, 123, 146, 192,
Taft, Stephen 51, 192
Tai Dam 4, 6, 379
Tally, Si 130–31
Tama 66, 226, 343, 377
Tama County 22, 27, 58, 66, 69, 88, 91, 97, 160, 213, 229, 265, 298, 343, 359
Tatum, Lawrie 153
Tax, Sol 27
Taylor, A. A. E. 120
Taylor County 173
Tecumseh 25
Temple B'nai Jeshurun, Des Moines 326
Templeton 211
Tenskwatawa 25
Theosophists 6, 171, 224, 283, 296, 297, 299, 303, 306–8, 313
Theravada Dhamma Society of Iowa 378
The Thief in the Night movie 365
Think Method 296
This Dark World (Briggs) 365
This Is Your Life (television program) 154
Thomason, Frazer 350
Thomason, Loris 350
Thompson, Charles 47
Thompson, Donald 165
Tibet 339
Tinker, Leonard 163, 352
Tipton 85
Titonka 65
Todd, John 99
Toledo 66

473

Index

Topeka, KS 145, 325
Toronto, Canada 289
Tory, Jenny 298
Townsend, Marquis 129
Transcendental Meditation 4. 5, 297, 313–14
Transcendentalists 42, 82, 215, 224, 303
Trappists 29, 78,
Trecy, Jeremiah 132
Trousers of Taffeta (Wilson) 160
Troyer, Noah 142–43
Turkey River 33
Turner, Asa 83–84, 86, 98–99
Tuttle [civil war general] 130
True Christianity (Cabet) 43
Trueblood, Benjamin 255
Twain, Mark 32, 60, 113
Tyrone 267
Tyrell, Ian 200

UCYM 358
Ukranians 376
Under Marching Orders (Hubbard) 158
Under Marching Orders in North China (Lane) 158
Underground Railroad 99, 114, 121–23
Union County 46
Union of Nazarene Yisraelite Congregations 11
Unitarians 13, 37 42, 51, 82, 90, 172–73, 192, 218, 220, 225, 256, 258, 283–84, 288, 301, 304, 333, 372
United Brethren 55, 65–66, 223, 232
United Christian Party 188–89
United Church of Christ 10, 61, 341, 352, 370, 372,
United Farm Workers 358
US Christian Commission 128
US Conference of Bishops 13, 356–57
United States State Department 348
Universalists 37, 41–43, 106
University Christian Church, Des Moines 332, 351
University of Chicago 186, 283, 343
University of Christiana 124
University of Iowa 3, 105, 111, 159, 163, 186, 220, 318, 325, 350, 366

School of Religion 279, 319, 334, 335–36
University of Nebraska 250, 323–24
University Park 144, 146
University Place 107
Upper Iowa University 154, 158, 160, 214, 262
Urban Religious Council, Des Moines 354
Urbany, Mary Dominica 159

Van Buren, Abigail 342
Van Buren County 42, 46, 71, 111
Van Vliet, Adrien 63
Vanderplaats, Bob 367
Varieties of Religious Experience (James) 308
Varnof, Peter 333
Vatican II 346, 351, 356–59, 361, 363
Vedanta Society 297
Vedic City—see Maharishi Vedic City
Vennard, Ivy Dunham 144
Vennard College 144, 146
Versaille, MO 261
Victor 71
Vienna, Austria 76, 78
Vietnam War—see Indochina War
Vietnamese 4, 5, 354, 361, 379
Villisca 188, 201
Vinton 201, 211
Viola 153
Virginia 50, 131
Visitation Catholic Church, Des Moines 169
Vivekananda 299–301
Von Rohr, John 85
Von Schwartz, Auguste 81
Vonnegut, Kurt 7

Wade, Martin 220–22, 250–51, 257, 273
Wakonda Christian Church, Des Moines 350
Walsh, Robert 278
Wallace, Henry 93, 95, 120, 126, 133, 136, 228, 234–35
Wallace, Henry A. 2, 12, 229, 295–96, 306–10, 314
Wallace, Henry C. 307

Index

Wallace's Farmer 93, 234
Walnut Street Baptist Church, Waterloo 293
Wapello 163, 229
Wapello County 111, 131, 239
Wapsie Valley School District 360
War of 1898 183
Ward, Leo 229
Ward, Myrle Olive 155
Warner, Kurt 380
Warren County 140, 326
Wartburg College 81
Wartburg Seminary 81, 86, 151, 349
Waseskuk, Brenda 27
Washington 95, 161, 187, 237, 261, 377
Washington County 10, 68, 71, 131, 261
Washington Prairie Lutheran Church, Decorah 100, 334
Washta 304
Waterloo 66, 70, 145, 148, 175, 186, 208, 243–44, 246, 267, 277, 288, 293, 321, 347, 351, 353, 379
Waterloo Human Rights Commission 353
Waukesha, WI 145
Wayland 260
Wayne, John 367
Wayne County 372
Weaver, James B. 12, 106, 166–70, 177, 180, 205
Webster City 66, 160, 187
Weinbrennerians (Church of God) 51
Weingart, Irving 352
Weitling, William 58
Welch, Dale 316
Wellsburg 65
Wesley, John 139, 158
West Bend 277
West Branch 141, 324
West Des Moines 11, 237, 350, 358, 359
West Liberty 128
West Point 68
West Union 66
Western Academy 64
Western College 66
Western Evangelist 106
Western Homes 67

Western Union College 67
Westmar College 67
Westminster United Presbyterian Church, Des Moines 308, 332
Westphalia 239
Wexford 78
Wexford, Ireland 77
What Cheer 210
What They Ask About... book series (Conway) 279
Wheaton, Eliza Ryder 192
White, Ellen 132
White, Harold 128
White, Trumbull 128
Whitmore, William Elliott 375
Wilcox, S. E. 231
Wilkerson, David 354
Wilkie, William 116, 197, 252
"Will the Circle Be Unbroken" (hymn) 233
Willard, Frances 183, 201, 203, 205–6
William Penn College 141, 212, 255, 328
Willson, Meredith 296
Wilson, E. Raymond 99
Wilson, James 94, 234–35
Wilson, Jonathan 372
Wilson, Margaret 94, 134, 139–40
Wilson, Theodore 310
Wilson, Woodrow 220, 233, 255–56, 287
Wilton 62, 233
Winchester 111
Windsor, William 121, 133–34
Wings of Faith 292
Winnebagos—see Ho Chunks
Winneshiek County 1, 50, 66, 124
Winnipeg, Canada 42
Wisconsin 33, 50, 61, 63, 75, 101, 103, 127, 255, 358, 360
Wittenberg 96
Wittenmyer, Annie 13, 128, 200–205, 211
Wolnerman, David 326
Women's Christian Temperance Union (WCTU) 200–206
Women's Crusade 202–3
Wood, Helen W. 333

Index

Woodward 144
Woodworth-Etter, Maria 292
Woolson 211
Work, John M. 187
World Council of Churches 349, 353
World Parliament of Religions 223–25, 256, 299
World War I 252–65
World War II 316–30
Worldwide Church of God 242
Wright, J. Roy 271
Wright, Milton 66
Wright County 68
WSUI 335
Wyatt, Thomas 292
Wyrick, Loduska 157

Yale Band 84
Yates, Pearl 267
Yeates, C. T. B. 332
Yidl in the Middle: Growing Up Jewish in Iowa (Booth) 342
Yoder, Sanford 254, 261

Yoga 6, 274
Yoseloff, Thomas 245
Young, Brigham 36, 45–46, 47
Young and Fair Is Iowa (Hoffmann) 135, 273
Young Men's Christian Association 262
Youth for Christ 338–30

Zarahemla 44
Zionism 245, 250, 360
Zurbriggen, Helen 258
Zwart, David 233
Zwemer, Samuel 162
Zwingle 61, 77

2nd Iowa 125
4th Iowa 127
5th Iowa 126
13th Iowa 129
15th Iowa 128
19th Iowa 127
24th Iowa ("Methodist Regiment") 129
15th Wisconsin 127

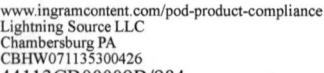